getaways»

BEACH HOLIDAYS

IN INDIA

First Edition 2008

Price: Rs 295
ISBN 81-89449-11-7

DISCLAIMER

As every effort is made to provide accurate and up-to-date information in this publication as far as possible, we would appreciate if readers would call our attention to any errors that may occur. Some details, however, such as telephone and fax numbers or email ids, room tariffs and addresses and other travel related information are liable to change. The publishers cannot accept responsibility for any consequences arising from the use of information provided in this book. However, we would be happy to receive suggestions and corrections for inclusion in the next edition. Please write to: The Editor, Outlook Traveller Getaways, AB-10, Safdarjung Enclave, New Delhi-110029

outlooktraveller.com
For updates, packages, news and new destinations, log on to our website
www.outlooktraveller.com

www.outlooktraveller.com

Editorial
EDITOR-IN-CHIEF Vinod Mehta
PRESIDENT & PUBLISHER
Maheshwer Peri
EDITOR Manju Rastogi
DEPUTY EDITOR Lesley A. Esteves
ASSOCIATE EDITOR Deepa A
CONSULTING EDITORS Ranee Sahaney, Nagraj Adve

Research
INFO AND RESEARCH COORDINATORS
Mridula Bhalla, Rani G. Kalra, Sophia L. Murphy, A. Prabhavati, Rajini Vasanth, Geeta Tuteja
RESEARCHER-WRITER Prerna Singh

Design
CONSULTING ART DIRECTOR
Runu Saxena
SENIOR DESIGNER Deepak Suri
DESIGNERS Rahul Sharma, Ashish Rozario, Ronald Joseph, Deepika Agrawal
GRAPHIC DESIGNER Rajesh K.G.
DTP COORDINATOR Ganesh Shah

Photography
PHOTO EDITOR Asmita Rangari
PHOTOGRAPHER Bharat Aggarwal
PHOTO COORDINATORS Priyali Saxena, Simrita Takhtar, Kuldeep Kalia

Production
GENERAL MANAGER Anup Dwivedi
REGIONAL MANAGER Rakesh Mishra
ASSOCIATE MANAGERS Shashank Dixit, Shekhar Pandey

Business Office
NATIONAL MANAGER Anand Dutt
NORTH Nazda Khan, Arti Marwah, Niraj Dubey
CIRCULATION Sudipto Mookherjee

Printed and published by
MAHESHWER PERI
on behalf of Outlook Publishing (India) Private Limited from AB-10, Safdarjung Enclave, New Delhi-110029

Printed at Infomedia India Ltd
A Wing, Ruby House, JK Sawant Marg
Dadar (West) Mumbai-400028

Dear Reader,

India's beaches make for some of its finest tourist attractions but the country's 7,500-odd kilometre long coastline seldom gets the attention it deserves. This is a pity, for, as we discovered in the course of putting this book together, a beach in India is much more than a strip of sand where surf and merry-making are guaranteed. Almost every beach presents a unique cocktail that mixes such unlikely ingredients as history and culture with the more ubiquitous doses of fun and adventure. *Beach Holidays in India*, the latest guidebook from *Outlook Traveller Getaways*, attempts to showcase these varied and remarkable aspects of India's beaches.

Much like the explorers who landed on India's shores in ancient times, the writers in this book were guided mostly by a sense of adventure and discovery. As you will see in the pages of this book, they approached each beach not just as another holiday destination but as a sum of many equally enticing and exciting parts. They capture the beach in its many forms: as an entertainment arena, where locals gather to watch the setting sun; as a source of nostalgia, where one is swept away by memories of childhood picnics or the flavours of mirchi bhaji and bhelpuri from another time; or as a symbol of the past, as glimpsed in the ruins of forts and ports that line our coast. At the same time, the book gives you all the information you need for a beach holiday. We tell you which hotels have the best views, whether the sea is safe for swimming, what water sports are on offer, and which beach shacks sell hummus and chilli chicken and everything in between. But we also remind you to pause to see the sea for what it's for many: a source of livelihood, a fact that the number of photos of fishing boats in this book testifies to, brimming with tales of intrepid voyagers who sometimes blundered their way onto our shores.

VINOD MEHTA
Editor-in-Chief

contents

MOVE

Discover the
PONDICHERRY
Shopping Experience
at CASABLANCA
Casablanca
The world is yours
Casablanca
The world is yours
165, MISSION STREET, PONDICHERRY - 605001 T: 2336495, 2226495
ISPAHANI CENTER 123/124, NUNGAMBAKKAM HIGH RD, CHENNAI. T: 28332111
Fashion Footwear Clothes Leather Goods Jewellery Perfume
Sportswear Watches Pizza Bric-a-brac

HOW TO USE THIS BOOK

How the book is organised

The book *Beach Holidays in India* opens with a section offering tips on what to pack, safety precautions to follow during a beach holiday, and a preview of water sports in India. The destinations in the book are arranged geographically, beginning with West Bengal on the East Coast, on to Orissa, Andhra Pradesh and Tamil Nadu, and down to the Andaman and Nicobar Islands. India's western coastline is covered all the way to Gujarat from Kerala in the south, with beaches in Lakshadweep, Karnataka, Maharashtra and Goa also being featured

Info Box

Each destination opens with this box, which has useful information about the place's geographical location. It also highlights the distances, journey time and routes from the closest metros

Fast Facts

Indicates the best time to visit a destination, with reference to the climate/ season. Also lists the tourist offices at the destination or at the nearest town, with icons indicating if only information is available there or if booking is also possible. The STD code is also appended

Beach Watch

Provides information on whether the sea is safe for swimming, if the beach has lifeguards and if sporting swimwear is advisable

The Information

This section, which appears in some destinations such as Mumbai and Chennai, offers info essential to planning your trip, such as how to get there and where to stay and eat. In some cases such as Lakshadweep, it also lists packages and agents

GETTING THERE

Air Nearest airport: Karipur International Airport, Kozhikode (90 km/ 2 hrs). A prepaid taxi to Thalassery costs

Rail Thalassery Station, served by all the trains that stop at Kannur (*also see Getting There in Kannur on page 202*)

Road Thalassery is connected to Kannur, Kozhikode, Kasargode, Mangalore, Panaji and Mumbai by NH17.

Getting There

Provides details on air, rail and road connections, nearest airports and railheads, and taxi fares to the destination. Info on convenient train and bus connections, road conditions and contacts of taxi and bus operators are also given

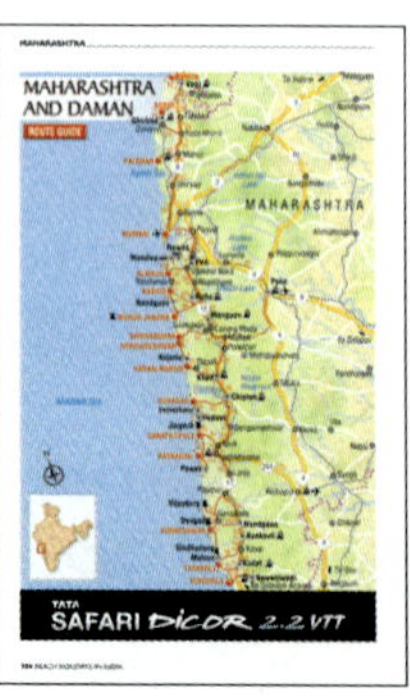

Route Guide

Each section in this book opens with a route guide showing the recommended routes, with distances, from the closest metros. Also highlights national and state highways, airports and railheads

Where to Stay

This is a representative listing of the accommodation options in each destination, with details such as phone numbers, facilities and tariffs (only the lowest and the highest rates are given). The writer's comments on the pros and cons of each stay option are also included

KARNATAKA

the 6-foot tall *atmalinga*, thought to convey the power of invincibility to the person who possesses it, is worth a visit. The devout take a dip in the sea before heading to the temple to offer prayers.
•**Temple timings** 6 am-12.30 pm and 5-8 pm **Note** Non-Hindus not allowed

The **Maha Ganapathy Temple** is just around the corner. A narrow lane from the Main Road-Car Street junction takes you to a huge tank called **Koti Theerta**. There are many Brahmin dwellings around the tank. Some of these tiled residences, with teak pillars and spacious verandahs, are over a hundred years old and belong to joint families whose members can number up to 40!
•**Maha Ganapathy Temple timings** 5 am-1 pm and 4.30-9 pm **Note** Non-Hindus not allowed

WHERE TO STAY

If you are in Gokarna only for the sun and sand, it makes sense to spend the night on the beaches. The accommodation options, which are simple thatched shelters, are cheap (tariffs start from Rs 50) and basic. It s advisable to carry your own sleeping bag although shacks do offer cots with mattresses. Toilets and bathrooms are often shared. The shacks on the isolated beaches of Half Moon and Paradise are usually full during the November-March peak season.

On Kudle Beach
Kudle has plenty of options if one is happy with shack-like accommodation. Most caf s, with exotic names such as Dragon Caf , Dancing Waves and Sunset Caf , offer accommodation besides food for as little as Rs 80 per head per night. If you don t want to rough it out in the shacks but would still like to spend the night on the beach, head to **Hotel Gokarna International Beach Resort** (Tel: 08386-257843; Tariff: Rs 500-900). They offer clean rooms with spacious balconies facing the sea.

On Half Moon and Paradise
The once temporary shacks on Half Moon and Paradise beaches, usually dismantled after peak season, are now to be found almost the year around (except during the rains). Now, a couple of them even provide Internet access to tourists who find it hard to move out of these beaches. **Om Shanthi Caf** and **Paradise Caf** on the southernmost stretch of Paradise Beach should keep one happy. The former (tariffs starting from Rs 50) has a relaxed ambience with shady palms and hammocks.

In the town
There are plenty of hotels in Gokarna Town if you prefer to stay close to the temples. **Hotel Shivaprasad** (Tel: 257032; Tariff: Rs 300-900), on Main Road, has spacious and well-kept rooms but is not as close to the centre of the town as the other hotels are. **Hotel Gokarna International** (Tel: 256622; Tariff: Rs 200-700), on Main Road, has neat rooms and a few with balconies overlooking a garden with palms. The baths are a little cramped though. **Hotel Shri Sai Ram** (Tel: 257755; Tariff: Rs 350-800) is a nice option that s close to the main hub. All the hotels arrange autos and taxis to take you around Gokarna.

For more hotels and details, see Gokarna Accommodation Listings on pages 538-539

WHERE TO EAT

From authentic traditional meals to Italian pastas, a range of dishes can be found in Gokarna. In the town, try the popular **Pai restaurants** (one on Main Road and the other on Car Street) for crispy dosas in the mornings. Hotel Gokarna International s **Purohit Restau-**

Moonlighting: Beach trekking at night

One of the most memorable moments to be experienced on the beaches of Gokarna is not when the sun is shining but when the moon is out in its full glory. A trek **from Gokarna Beach to Paradise Beach** on a full moon night, past the silvery sands of Kudle and Om, is an exciting, if romantic, option. The reflection of the moon in the sea, seen from the rocky cliffs along the way, is stunning. Do take a few precautions before the trek: always go in a group of six or more, carry torches and go with someone who has done this trek before. Also carry snacks and plenty of water.

Besides the night trek, you can also go on a longer trek along the coast lasting 3-4 days. One such route starts from the port-village of **Belikeri** near Ankola and goes all the way to Honavar, passing through the beaches of Gokarna. Part of the trek involves crossing the mouth of the **Gangavali River** by boat to continue the trek towards Gokarna. At the village of **Belekan** after the Paradise Beach, one needs to cross the mouth of the **River Agnashini** in a similar fashion. Apart from these rivers, there are numerous streams that open out into the sea along the way. While a few of them are shallow enough to wade across at low tide, for others, trekkers will need to take the help of local fishermen to get across.

The real treat is the expanses of completely deserted and pristine beaches on the way. This kind of adventure requires quite a bit of preparation: tents, sleeping bags and provisions need to be carried. But one is never really far from a friendly home in the villages that are dotted along the way. Hotels at Gokarna should be able to arrange for a guide to lead you on the trek.

Bronze images of elephants and gods for sale in Gokarna s shops

290 BEACH HOLIDAYS IN INDIA

GOKARNA

BEACH HOLIDAYS IN INDIA 291

Accommodation Listings

A listing of the stay options in each destination, for all budgets, with info on facilities, contact details and tariffs (the lowest and the highest). The listings should not be construed as recommendations either by the author or the publisher

USP Box

A short feature on a unique attraction at the destination, such as trekking from one beach to another at night at Gokarna, or the sand sculptures at Puri

Where to Eat

This section highlights the culinary experience that each destination offers. It mentions restaurants and the must-try dishes there, and even places to pick up savouries

Feedback

We hope you found this book useful. We welcome your comments and suggestions as to how we can make it even more so. Please do fill in the Feedback Form at the back of the book so that we can incorporate the best suggestions in the next edition. You will also receive email updates on special offers, travel features and news from our website www.outlooktraveller.com

Tourist Offices

Lists contact details of tourist offices across the country, with icons indicating if only information is provided or if bookings can also be done

Route Guide Legends

Distance in km	State Boundary	Boat Jetty	Bird Sanctuary
65 NH Number	Destination	Peak Height	National Park/ WLS
National Highway	Main Place/ Arounds	Water Body	National Park/ WLS
Road	Other Place	Fort	Volcano
Train Route	Airport	Temple	Marine Park
Route	Railway Station	Church	Waterfall
International Boundary	Bus Station		

PACK A PUNCH

A few tips on what to carry while on a beach holiday

In many popular Western soaps, the characters head to the beaches in designer swimsuits, fluffy beach towels or swanky surfboards in hand, and when not showing off their swimming prowess, stylishly prop themselves on the sand under equally stylish beach umbrellas. In India, a beach, especially if located close to a city or a town, is full of people who carry nothing more than smiles and occasionally, snacks. Here, the beach experience is cherished not because of the props but for what's offered in abundance free of cost: the breeze, the openness of the sea, and the company of dear ones.

Even then, you are sure to enjoy your holiday more if you pack some beach essentials. Given below are a few tips on what to throw into your suitcase:

- Carry Frisbees, kites and volleyballs or footballs if you are travelling in a group, especially if there are children
- If there's space, then you may want to take a few small spades or shovels, or a small bucket, for children to play in the sand and make sand castles
- Always pack gear to protect yourself from the sun: sunscreen, sunglasses, and even hats or anything else that can stop you from getting sunburn. Remember to apply sunscreen at least 20 mins before stepping out in the sun; reapply after a swim
- Essentials on the beach include swimwear (do check if it's alright to don swimwear in a particular destination; in each piece, the subhead 'Beach Watch' advises readers on the suitability of swimwear in that place) and swimming goggles. It may not always be possible to buy swimwear at the destination. Take towels even if not planning to swim; you can use them as rugs to spread on the sand
- While going to the beach, it might help to carry drinking water, though most beaches will have coconut vendors. Do remember not to leave behind bottles or wrappers on the beach as these will contribute towards degrading the environment
- Always pack a good pair of sandals, slippers or shoes for the beach. And do make sure these are waterproof
- If you're a water sports enthusiast, and have considerable experience in say, snorkelling, you may want to carry your own equipment. However, this is advisable only if you're an expert; almost all agencies offering water sports have their own gear

OTG Desk

VIVEK R NAIR

AMIT PASRICHA/ INDIAPICTURE

SAFETY IN THE SEA

A few tips to follow for a fun-filled and safe beach holiday

BY ASHWIN TOMBAT

It's with alarming regularity that reports of deaths by drowning in the sea garner reams of space in newspapers. While it's usually stated that the deaths are because of "strong currents", the truth is that you can be more or less sure of your safety if you follow a few basic precautions.

In each of the pieces in this book, there's a sub-head called 'Beach Watch' under which we have given broad advice on whether the beach/es at the destination are safe for swimming. We urge you to pay close attention to this section before planning a swim. In some cases, swimming is completely out of bounds; even if the sea is safe for swimming, avoid it at low tide. And never go swimming in the monsoons. Other tips to keep in mind are given below:

- Swim 300m away from any river along a beach. Currents come up mostly where a river or stream joins the sea. As the tide rises, water slowly fills the low-lying areas along riverbanks. When the tide starts to fall (usually every six hours; from low to high and then vice versa), the water rushes out through the river mouth, setting off a strong current that can sweep anybody out to sea
- Unless you are a strong swimmer, don't go in deeper than your waist. It's quite common to hear of tourists drowning in water that's only an inch higher than they are
- Don't panic. Use the power of the waves to get back to shore. If you do get swept off your feet, don't thrash your hands and feet about. That leads to exhaustion. Swim towards the shore with every wave, until you can put your feet down. Between waves, focus on floating
- Can you swim at least two lengths of a 50m swimming pool non-stop? If you can't, you are not a strong swimmer. It's best then to take a flotation device with you
- Never drink alcohol before going into the sea. Being drunk can drastically reduce your survival chances in case of a mishap. Carbonated drinks and alcohol can also dehydrate you. Second, listen to the lifeguard. He's been trained to recognise signs of danger. Lastly, swim only in the designated swimming area, where lifeguards are keeping watch. Steer clear of mechanised watercraft such as speedboats
- Rip currents run parallel to shore and are found a little distance away from the surf area. If you get caught in one, you could be carried along the coast well away from your entry point to the sea. Try to swim out of the current by swimming perpendicular to it towards the shore.

Inputs by Venkatesh Charloo

Courtesy BANGARAM BEACH RESORT

SPORTING ENCOUNTERS

Venkatesh Charloo offers us a preview of water sports in India

There's little else to match the sheer wonder of having a school of colourful fish for company while scuba diving, or the adrenaline rush you experience as you sail in a deep blue sea on a sunny day. India, with its over 7,500-km long coastline, offers a host of similarly astonishing experiences, ranging from exciting dolphin-spotting or crocodile-spotting boat rides to the more adventurous jet-skiing and parasailing.

It's true that water sports is as yet under-developed in India, perhaps because Indians don't quite take to water and water sports as easily as Europeans or North Americans do. But things are changing now.

Sports such as parasailing, speedboat, banana and bump tube rides are becoming popular, among other reasons because they offer instant gratification to people without them having to spend hours dedicated to learning the sport (this training, however, is quite essential in the case of scuba diving, water skiing, wake boarding or kite surfing, among others).

Water sports in India started in Goa in the early seventies, with a few diehard sports fans from Goa and Mumbai venturing into windsurfing and water skiing — as a hobby, that is. It did not become a commercial activity till the late seventies when the Commonwealth Heads of Government Meeting (CHOGM) was held at the Taj Holiday Village and Fort Aguada resorts at Candolim. Now the entire Baga-Calangute-Candolim stretch of beaches has a number of operators offering many water sports.

The new generation is changing the water sports scenario in India rapidly. The Internet has also played a role in this: it's easy now to get all the information on water sports facilities sitting at home and surfing the Internet. Today it's estimated that there are no less than 3,000 certified scuba divers and at least thousands more who have tried diving in India.

Apart from Goa, there are several other destinations that offer water sports facilities, such as the Andamans, Lakshadweep

Islands and Karnataka. Only a handful of operators such as Barracuda Diving India, Goa Diving and Goa Diving Center in Goa, Lacadives in Lakshadweep, and Barefoot Scuba and Dive India in Andamans offer diving. Though restricted to certain parts of the country where the water is clear and abundant in marine life, diving offers a wonderful opportunity to experience the underwater world of fish, coral and innumerable other marine animals.

The safety factor

Safety is a big issue as far as water sports is concerned, but unfortunately, operators as well as customers gloss over this important aspect. Operators try to cut costs by neglecting safety while customers try to get the cheapest deal possible. Obviously, this is not the right thing to do as the nature of the sport is such that accidents generally tend to be more serious than those in land-based activities.

Luckily, at least in tourist-friendly places like Goa, the government's Tourism Department has imposed quite a few restrictions. Lifeguards have been appointed on most popular beaches. Swimming areas are designated and are marked by floating buoys from which boats and jet skis are required to stay away. The operators are also required to cover all customer liabilities with a comprehensive Public Liability Insurance Policy. (This should not be confused with personal insurance cover for the customer.)

Before you undertake water sports in any part of the country, it will help to keep in mind the following tips:

- Ensure that the operators and their staff are qualified; their certifications should have been issued by a recognised organisation
- The equipment should be in good working order. Do your best to check if the operators service it regularly
- The water and weather conditions should be suitable for the sport you are opting for
- Your personal travel insurance should cover the activity you are opting for
- A first-aid kit should be readily available with the operator; make sure you, and the operator, know of the location and contact of the closest hospital
- The boats, or the crafts, should have life jackets and flotation devices, in the sizes of all the passengers on board the vessel, including children

In addition, when you are opting for an adventure sport like scuba diving, it's imperative that you keep the following in mind:

- Check out the credentials of the dive centre as well as the instructor who is accompanying or teaching you
- Ask the instructor to ensure the compressed air in the cylinders is of good quality
- See if the staff is trained in primary and secondary medical care, and that emergency medical oxygen is available on the boat as well as at the dive centre
- Ensure there is an emergency plan in place in case there is an accident
- A comprehensive medical kit should be available on the boat as well as at the dive centre. These should also have adequate communication facilities

Can you take up water sports?

That's an important question to ask before starting any activity. In the case of most water sports, the only pre-condition is that one should use one's common sense and be

Snorkelling in Lakshadweep

SAIBAL DAS

Tips for an eco-friendly holiday

Just as any form of manufacturing activity generates pollution and waste, mechanised sports too have a similar impact on the environment. Motor boats and jet-skis, in particular, burn up a lot of fuel and release exhaust fumes like the vehicles on land, thereby adding to pollution and global warming. Worse, the careless operation of vessels (especially if these run aground in corals) can destroy marine habitats.

Scuba diving and, to a lesser extent snorkelling, can affect marine life due to the carelessness of participants; if people step on corals or sponges, these could be killed. It has also been scientifically proved that noises generated by engines severely affect marine life. The sounds are amplified considerably underwater and also travel a long distance, affecting areas well beyond the immediate environs of beaches.

If you care about the environment and would like to enjoy water sports at the same time, we recommend that you follow these guidelines:

- Participate in environment-friendly sports such as sailing, surfing, wakeboarding, scuba diving and snorkelling, wherein no pollution is emitted. It also helps to be aware of what marine life is present in the area and how to avoid disturbing it; in particular, be conscious of actions that might affect the fragile environment
- Never leave behind trash and make sure it's disposed off properly
- A simple act such as taking live coral or live shells affects the local ecosystem's balance much more than you can imagine.

Therefore, collect dead specimens (if at all) on the beach and not in the water
- Avoid purchasing items made of shells or any threatened or endangered species
- Avoid ordering seafood caught using destructive methods such as fish bombing, drift net fishing and cyanide poisoning
- Do not feed marine animals as long-term studies on food that's safe for them have not yet been conducted. What is good for us may not (and generally is not) be good for them
- Do not attempt to touch, pick up or play with marine animals. Always interact with them passively

Following these simple steps will ensure that your beach holiday is an eco-friendly one as well.

in good health. As the sea is an unforgiving environment, one needs to be fairly good at swimming before venturing out far from the beach. Children should be supervised at all times, even if they are good swimmers.

Adventure sports such as scuba diving require that participants be a minimum age of 10 years. There's no upper age limit provided one is in good health and in reasonably good shape. Coronary, respiratory and sinus problems, blood pressure (high as well as low), and epilepsy are all contra-indications; participants with these conditions need to get the approval of a medical doctor knowledgeable about diving prior to trying the activity. This is obviously in the

PRASHANT PANJIAR

Anglers keep their fingers crossed during a boat ride in Goa

interest of the participant's own safety and hence should not be taken lightly.

Snorkelling can be undertaken by those of all ages and, if the conditions – such as clarity and depth – are right, can be almost as rewarding as scuba diving. You can wear a life jacket and try it even if you aren't a strong swimmer.

Activities such as windsurfing, wake boarding, surfing, sailing and water-skiing need training and practice, just like scuba diving. One needs to devote sufficient time to learn these properly. There's no age limit for these sports but it's something that's best left to the discretion of the instructor.

Jet-skiing, motor boating and parasailing do not require much skill. However, one has to ensure that these are not attempted in areas designated as swimming zones as the risk of accidents is quite high then. Age limits do not apply but to be able to operate a jet-ski or a motorboat, one should have sufficient experience and hold a licence to operate these.

The to-do list

Though a number of options are coming up, India still lags behind other countries as far as water sports is concerned. The development of water sports is hampered largely due to the following reasons: lack of proper facilities on beaches; inadequate number of lifeguards; insufficient berthing and anchoring facilities for boats; poor infrastructure for tourism-related activities; and disregard for safety on the part of operators, government departments as well as participants, resulting in many unnecessary accidents.

To promote water sports in India, there has to be more synergy between the government and the operators. First of all, the government should come out with more incentives to encourage operators. Secondly, the industry should organise itself (there's a dire need for regulation too). Operators themselves should ensure that all safety precautions are taken and pitch in with the necessary investment without cutting corners. The participants too should avail of the services of only qualified operators; they should cooperate by following the operators' guidelines and not drink alcohol or take banned substances before attempting any of the water sports.

Perhaps most important of all, everyone engaging in water sports activities must respect nature (*also see 'Tips for an eco-friendly holiday' on page 18*). It's incumbent on each and every one of us to act responsibly, in an environmentally friendly manner, to make these activities not only safe but also sustainable in the long run. ■

WEST BENGAL

Photographs by KUMAR ROY

BAKKHALI

TROPICAL COCKTAIL

State West Bengal
Location Bakkhali lies by the Bay of Bengal, on the southern tip of South 24 Parganas District, and is the country's easternmost beach
Distance 137 km S of Kolkata
Journey time ***By road*** $4^1/_2$ hrs from Kolkata
Route from Kolkata NH117 to Bakkhali via Shirakol, Diamond Harbour, Kulpi, Kakdip and Namkhana (*see route guide on facing page*)

BY RAJASHRI DASGUPTA

At Bakkhali, a pristine white beach snuggles against the fringes of a forest delta, offering a unique and astonishing tropical combination. The beach rests on the south-western tip of the mystical and exalted Sunderbans, famous as the habitat of the Royal Bengal tiger. Bakkhali is also one of the 54 alluvial island clusters formed by a network of meandering estuaries, tidal rivers and creeks, located where the Bay of Bengal caresses the land. Such illustrious legacy aside, the beach is a favourite haunt with tourists for reasons that are more down-to-earth. Mothers sigh with relief as their children can wade safely in the shallow, calm waters, and chase baby crabs that disappear into the fine, polished white sands stretching out next to the sea for more than a kilometre. The sands are firm, thanks to the silt of numerous rivers that has accumulated here, and hence a delight for walkers and older children looking to play a game of cricket.

Interestingly, the beach derives its name from the *bak*, or red-beaked seagull, which I could not unfortunately spot on my visit. There's yet another legend about the beach's name, which is just as appealing: apparently, the place's original name was Bagkhali, for tiger.

You can spend hours at Bakkhali, sitting at one of the makeshift tea stalls on the beach, sipping fresh coconut water or hot tea from earthen pots. Nearby, beckoning tantalisingly, is an island spread across 200 hectares of land with a beautiful beach. More rustic is the fishermen's village at nearby Frazergunj. All these montages marvellously come together to form the wonder that is Bakkhali.

BEACH WATCH

Though very safe, the 6-km long Bakkhali Beach is not great for swimming as its waters are too shallow. It's much more fun to wade and splash in the surf. One of the best parts about the beach is that it's lit up well up to 10 pm, thereby creating a space where tourists can linger and enjoy the sea breeze for long. There are no lifeguards here. Dress conservatively here — no one wears swimsuits.

ORIENTATION

The part of NH117 known as the **Frazergunj-Bakkhali Road** tapers off at the **bus stand**, located about 50 yards from the state-run **Tourist Lodge**, 100 yards from the beach. For **Henry's Island** (8 km north-west of Bakkhali), one has to leave the main road and turn left on a brick road. Going further down the busy main road and turning right gets you to **Frazergunj** (3 km north-east of Bakkhali). On either side of the road leading to the beach are numerous lodges and hotels, all falling within a $1^1/_2$-km long stretch.

Rickshaw vans (consisting of open wooden platforms set on three wheels) are the popular mode of transport; the drivers double as guides when they are not carting goods, and ferry passengers to hotels from the bus stand and take them

Evening blues: A fisherman heads home on the beach at Bakkhali

sightseeing up to Henry's Island. You can hire the entire rickshaw, which can seat at least six people, for Rs 100. For this price, you can visit Henry's Island and Frazergunj. In peak season, the fare can go up to Rs 150-200. There's no tourist office in Bakkhali, so contact the West Bengal tourist office in Kolkata for info and bookings (*see Fast Facts alongside*).

→ FAST FACTS

When to go Bakkhali is best in winter, from November to January; this is also when the beach is most crowded

Tourist office

● WBTDC
3/2 BBD Bag (East)
Kolkata-700001
Tel: 033-22485168, 22437260
Website: wbtourism.com

STD codes Bakkhali 03210, Kolkata 033

THINGS TO SEE AND DO

Bakkhali doesn't offer much by way of luxury and is more suited for the unfussy tourist looking for a dream beach set in natural surroundings.

Bakkhali Beach

At Bakkhali, most tourists walk on the sands and shoot the sea breeze. There isn't much else on offer here. You can also snack at the stalls on the beach; these offer basic food like bread and omelettes or onion pakodas. During peak season, stall owners fry fish for tourists, who can buy them fresh at the shore as the boats come in with the catch.

The friendly locals will not let you leave Bakkhali without seeing the **palm tree** with 16 'faces', a freak of nature. The tree trunk branches into 16 boughs with clusters of dates, instead of one. It's located on a brick-paved lane that falls to your left as you head to the bus stand.

GETTING THERE

Air Nearest airport: Netaji Subhas Chandra Bose International Airport, Kolkata (157 km/ $5^1/_2$ hrs), connected by flights to all metros by most airlines. There are pre-paid taxis at the airport but these don't go to Bakkhali. For that you'll have to make arrangements with private taxi operators (*see Road below*)

Rail Nearest railhead: Kakdip (27 km/ 30 mins), connected to trains running via the South Sealdah route. From Kakdip, tourists can take buses via Namkhana to Bakkhali. No autos or taxis are available. The train tracks are being extended to Namkhana (13 km), the town closest to Bakkhali, from where tourists can avail of the frequent bus service (Route No. 94) to the beach town

Road Direct buses to Bakkhali leave from the L 20 Bus Stand in Dharamtalla, adjacent to the Bidhan Nagar Market in Kolkata, daily at 7 and 8 am. The West Bengal Surface Transport Corporation runs non-AC buses (4 hrs/ Rs 70), which start from the same place. Book tickets at least seven days in advance. Taxi services are provided by agencies such as Travel House (Tel: 033-22882623), Peerless Travels (Tel: 22909974/ 269), Ruia Travels (Mobile: 09830162766, 09830260294) and Guide Travels (Tel: 24649529). The fare is Rs 2,466 (return). At Namkhana, there's no bridge across the Hatania-Doania River and hence a barge ferries vehicles to the other side. The service is run from 7 am to 10 pm. The cost of ferrying an Ambassador is Rs 160 and it's higher for heavier vehicles. If travelling by bus, you can hop on to one of the boats in the adjoining ghat, which ferry villagers across the river every few minutes for 25 paise

Henry's Island

A day-trip to Henry's Island, artificially created by the State Fisheries Department, will provide you a whiff of the Sunderban way of life. Though called an island, it's actually a project area where ponds have been dug to encourage fishing in the region. Half of the 200 hectares here consists of water bodies and brackish water ponds; there are also stretches of forests with 40 different kinds of species of shrubs and trees unique to the Sunderbans. Wild animals such as the *bagrol*, the small tiger of the wild cat family, roam around freely here.

You can also climb the 40-foot high tower here to get a spectacular view of the sea receding into the horizon. On the other side is an endless canopy of treetops and patches of fish ponds. Spend a morning observing the sunrise on the private beach here (don't try swimming as it's unsafe). If you wish to spend a few nights in the wilderness, book a room at the Mangrove and Sundari Tourist Complex (*see Where to Stay on page 28*).

Frazergunj

This is a thriving fishing harbour where one can see colourful boats in blue and yellow docked in the creek for repair and rest. Groups of fishermen sit and mend their fine nets and can regale you with stories of how they dodged river pirates.

SHOPPING

There is little by way of shopping in Bakkhali. Hyderabadi pearls and sea shells are sold at small shops by the road. Key-rings (each Rs 10) made of shells picked from the seashore are also available.

WHERE TO STAY

The government-run **Bakkhali Tourist Lodge** (Tel: 03210-225260; Tariff: Rs 400-800) is close to the beach and has a restaurant. The service is friendly but the hotel requires sprucing up and maintenance.

The other hassle is that you have to book in advance and pay 60 per cent of the room charges at the WBTDC booking office in Kolkata (Tel: 033-22437260). There's no online booking facility.

The attractive-looking **Dolphin** (Tel: 225296; Tariff: Rs 500-1,200), near the beach, has AC rooms and an attached restaurant. The hotel has a pretty garden and offers rooms facing the sea. The other hotel that's just a short walk from the beach is **Hotel Sea View** (Tel: 225282; Mobile: 09732828266; Tariff: Rs 350), located on Bakkhali-Frazergunj Road. Insist they change linen in front of you. In both the hotels, the rooms are sea-facing and fairly decent, though cramped. The bathrooms have leaky taps and could do with more scrubbing.

Hotel Ambrabati (Tel: 225248-49; Mobile: 09732619340; Tariff: Rs 200-500), on Bakkhali-Frazergunj Road, has cottages in two opposite rows, fringed by shrubs. The rooms, with big double beds, appear crowded and the bathrooms require supervised cleaning. The cheapest option at Bakkhali, located close to the bus stand, is **Balaka Lodge** (Tel: 225207; Tariff: Rs 250-550). The rooms are spartan and functional but well-ventilated.

At a souvenir shop at Bakkhali

On Henry's Island

The State Fisheries Dept (Kolkata Reservations Tel: 033-23376470; 23586832; 23572979) runs the **Mangrove and Sundari Tourist Complex** (Tel: 03210-225511) here. The lodge is close to the beach yet set deep in the island's forest. At night, you can hear the sound of waves crashing against the shores along with the screeches of jungle cats. The Mangrove Lodge that's part of the complex has 10 rooms in the Rs 300-1,000 range while Sundari Lodge has eight rooms for Rs 500, each named after a local wild animal or tree. At Sundari, the rooms are airy and functional with TVs; the bathrooms are clean; and there's a restaurant. At Mangrove, the rooms are cramped and unattractive.

Day visitors are encouraged to eat lunch at the **Sundari Restaurant** (Tel: 225511) here, provided they order ahead to avoid disappointment. Lodgers are treated to a variety of fish on order.

For more hotels and details, see Bakkhali Accommodation Listings on page 568

WHERE TO EAT

It's best to eat at the hotels themselves. It's advisable to book your table in advance and place orders for the food because they are not equipped to take on a large number of unexpected guests. Also do not expect varied cuisine, and stick to standard Bengali fare. If you love fish, opt for the fresh catch of prawns or the local variety of small sea fish that comes at an average price of Rs 40-80 in all the restaurants. Vegetables are best when you choose the seasonal fare at Rs 30 or so a plate. Unfortunately, you won't find any of the famous Bengali sweets here. ■

DIGHA

DOWN MEMORY LANE

State West Bengal
Location By the Bay of Bengal, in East Medinipur (Midnapore) District, close to the West Bengal-Orissa border
Distance 185 km SW of Kolkata
Journey time ***By road*** 4 hrs
Route from Kolkata NH6 to Kolaghat via Howrah; NH41 to Nandakumar Junction via Tamluk; SH to Digha via Kanthi (Contai) and 14 Mile Crossing (*see route guide on page 23*)

BY ABHIJIT GUPTA

Once upon a time, Digha was called the 'Brighton of the East'. Some websites still flaunt the tag, but it now sounds somewhat remote from reality. There was a time when the hard, flat beach at Digha stretched for miles, and the salt wind soughed among the romantic casuarinas. On the long walk to the *mohona*, one would come across beached boats, fishing nets, and an occasional giant turtle. Starfish-shaped outlines glittered in the sand till the tide came in and

DHRITIMAN MUKHERJEE

wiped them out. I remember all this from my first trips to Digha, as a child, in the early seventies.

Recently, I returned there after over three decades, and was disappointed, but not surprised, to see the changes that had taken place. Over 200 yards of the waterfront was now encased in concrete and stone, to prevent further erosion by the sea. Lining the stone embankments were rows of charmless foodstalls and shiny red plastic chairs. In a small bollard-marked break in the embankment, approximately a hundred bathers splashed in the shallow waters, as if taking a ceremonial holy dip.

I quickly walked past the shops and up a hillock to what remained of the casuarinas. Once upon a time, it was *de rigueur* to shoot almost all romantic Bengali films in this grove. Now, with a couple of stray dogs for company, I went over the crest and drew my breath in wonder. Stretching to my left for as far as the eye could see was the beach of my childhood, clean and glittering, uncontaminated by any human presence except a group of local boys playing beach cricket. As the sun set over the Bay of Bengal, I stood barefoot in the water and felt thankful for small mercies.

→ FAST FACTS

When to go You can visit any time of the year, but bathing is not possible during the rainy season. The best times are from October to March

Tourist office

- WBTDC

3/2, BBD Bag (East)
Kolkata-700001
Tel: 033-22437260, 22485168
Website: wbtourism.com

Info & Bookings

- Digha Development Scheme, Digha

Tel: 03220-266234

STD code 03220

ORIENTATION

There are now two beaches at Digha: the older one, and another one a kilometre to the west, known as **New Digha**. The waters at New Digha are supposed to be less turbulent for bathing, though two tourists drowned at New Digha the day I reached the seaside. This did not seem to have deterred anyone, for the very next day, the waterfront at New Digha pullulated with bathers. At the same time, however, the beach at Digha was out of bounds, with arpeggios of huge white waves crashing into the embankment.

The road connecting Digha with New Digha runs parallel to the sea, separated only by the beach and strips of casuarina. It runs past the **post office**, the **bus station**, a **marine aquarium**, a **science park**, and the **Digha train station** on the other side of the road, roughly halfway between the old and the new beach. Every second house is a hotel or lodge of some description. The older ones are within a stone's throw of the beach, while the newer ones have come up along the connecting road. It's a pleasant walk from old to new Digha if it's not too hot, but most tourists prefer to avail of a pedalled vehicle which is a cross between a rickshaw and a cart, seating about six.

BEACH WATCH

The waters at Digha can be pretty choppy, especially during the rainy season. The sea often looks deceptively calm, and it's not a very good idea to swim too far out. Swimming after sunset is an absolute no-no as the tide begins to come in. There are no lifeguards other than the purveyors of kiddy floats who might gesticulate and holler at you when you are too far out. At the New Digha Beach, a

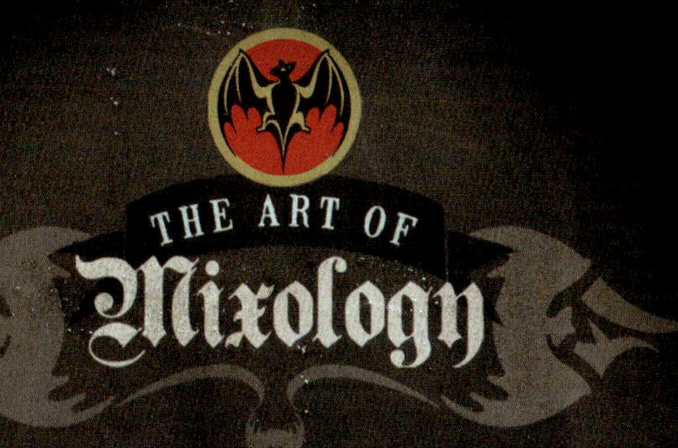
THE ART OF
Mixology

solitary lathi-wielding policeman patrolled the waterfront while hundreds made merry. Beach etiquette at Digha is pretty much Victorian, especially if you are a woman. Swimsuits are rarely seen but that does not mean you cannot wear one.

THINGS TO SEE AND DO

In recent years, a few offshore attractions have come up between Digha and New Digha, offering the visitor something more than the beach, but they should not occupy you more than a morning or an afternoon. A couple of days at Digha is pretty much what most tourists prefer; however keep another day in hand if you want to visit nearby beaches such as Mandarmani and Shankarpur (*see page 35*).

GETTING THERE

Air Nearest airport: Netaji Subhas Chandra Bose Airport, Kolkata (185 km/ 4 hrs). Prepaid taxis are available at the airport but they will not go as far as Digha. Car hire from Kolkata to Digha and back can cost you between Rs 2,500-3,500 for a two-day trip. The road trip can take up to 5 hrs depending on the state of traffic at the Kolaghat Bridge, which is currently one-lane
Rail Digha is now connected by rail to Kolkata (Shalimar Station). The 7.55 am Shalimar Digha Express is the best option for those leaving from Kolkata. From the station, the only mode of transport available is the rickshaw-van. The average fare should be about Rs 10-15
Road Buses leave all through the day to Digha from the bus station at Dharmatala and Howrah Station, as well as from other locations in Kolkata. The North Bengal State Transport Corporation runs two services at 1.15 and 2.50 pm while the South Bengal State Transport Corporation runs a rocket bus at 8 every morning. For luxury buses, it's best to contact the WBTDC (*see Fast Facts on page 30*)

The beach

At Digha, kids can opt for tyre floats and pony rides on the beach. Beach cricket or football is, of course, an option. Roving photographers will try to persuade you to pose with your near and dear ones. You can also shoot at balloons with a gun if you are bored! What is highly recommended though is a long, long walk — either at sunrise or sunset — along the deserted beach to tiny fishing villages, where you might see fish drying or trawlers putting out to sea. Or just occupy one of the stone steps on the embankment and look out at the moonlit sea. I spent hours looking at the stallions of the night, tossing their white manes and galloping into the shore.

By the beach

One of the main attractions that have come up in recent times is the **Digha Science Centre and the National Science Camp**, which is quite a mouthful so it's more conveniently known as the **Jurassic Park**. There is a garden full of model dinosaurs in the complex but I didn't get to see it since that portion of the camp was closed during my visit. The rest of the camp features fairground attractions based on simple scientific principles, such as elliptical carrom boards, crazy mirrors, magic magnets, and pulleys with which you can hoist yourself up. Unfortunately, the place suffers from lack of maintenance and many mechanisms don't work any more. Nevertheless, it's well worth checking out, especially for children.
◆**Location** Foreshore Road, Digha New Township **Entry fee** Rs 7 **Timings** 9 am-7 pm daily (tickets sold till 6.30 pm)

Within walking distance of the park is the **Marine Aquarium and Research**

Make India your playground.
Explore the offside. Explore the onside. Go for a straight drive.
Just hit the road with Speed, the high performance petrol and soak in the cricket frenzy gripping the nation.
Speed™
High Performance Petrol
INDIA
3.38 million Kms
Road Network
Bharat
Petroleum
Take the first
Road out.
To go places log on to www.speedfuels.com
SAATCHI & SAATCHI 122/2007 M

Centre, which was set up at great expense in 2003 with 24 display tanks. These were intended to exhibit sharks, octopus, sea snakes and crabs, but currently, most of these species are conspicuous by their absence. More than half the tanks are empty, while the others are not exactly bursting with bio-diversity either. There are some fierce-looking crabs and one particularly unpleasant eel.
◆**Entry** Free **Timings** 10 am-6 pm on all days except Tuesdays

SHOPPING

You will not exactly be spoilt for choice as far as shopping is concerned. There are rows of crafts shops close to the beach and these sell the usual shell artefacts and jewellery. I picked up a *madur* or a hand-woven mat, whose manufacture is a major Midnapore cottage industry. Also on display are a wide range of jute bags and suchlike. The district is known for its cashew cultivation, and cashew here is cheaper than anywhere else in the state.

Fried fish in many flavours at Digha

KUMAR ROY

WHERE TO STAY

Every second house in Digha is a hotel or a lodge of some kind, but even then it's hard to find a place during the tourist season, which is pretty much most of the year. So it's advisable to book ahead. One of the oldest and most reliable of Digha's hotels is **Sea Hawk** (Tel: 03220-266235/46; Tariff: Rs 200-1,900), less than 50m from the sea and having a large assortment of clean and airy rooms. Next to Sea Hawk is the somewhat more homespun **Saikatabas** (Tel: 266254; Tariff: Rs 170-340), also very close to the beach but with rather forbidding curfew hours and code of conduct. On the higher end, check out **Palm Resort** (Tel: 266489; Tariff: Rs 1,500-3,000), reportedly the only hotel in Digha to have a swimming pool!

For more hotels and details, see Digha Accommodation Listings on pages 568-569

WHERE TO EAT

Food in Digha is dull. There is some good fish to be had, but this is limited to the inevitable hilsa, pomfret, betki and prawn. This could be a faithful reflection of the average Bengali's unadventurous eating habits. Where, oh where, are the eels, mussels, squids, snappers, mackerels, clams and cuttlefish? The circular **Day-View** restaurant overlooking the beach does decent fish fries, but the best places to eat are usually the hotel restaurants, of which **Sea Hawk**'s is the best. On the beach, green coconuts are available in abundance while the beachside shanties will surreptitiously offer to sell you beer.

AROUND DIGHA

Shankarpur (16 km)
See page 35 ■

DHRITIMAN MUKHERJEE

SHANKARPUR

THE SECRETS OF THE SEA

State West Bengal
Location Shankarpur is by the Bay of Bengal, in East Medinipur (Midnapore) District, 16 km east of the more famous Digha Beach
Distance 183 km SW of Kolkata
Journey time ***By road*** $4^1/_2$ hrs from Kolkata
Route from Kolkata NH6 to Kolaghat; NH41 to Nandakumar Junction; SH to Shankarpur via Kanthi (Contai) and 14 Mile Crossing (*see route guide on page 23*)

BY RAJASHRI DASGUPTA

Travelling to Shankarpur is like revisiting your childhood. There is something about the silence of the secluded shore that revives memories of innocence lost, or of a secret that one was privileged to learn and cherish as a giggly child. Perhaps it's because Shankarpur itself is something of a surprise package, known to locals but largely hidden from the world. A secluded beach, it's fringed by casuarinas and eucalyptus trees.

As I take in the view of the rolling blue waves, I realise with shock that the waters have been gobbling up the land. A few metres of the road leading to the beach and some shops made of bamboo have fallen prey to a hungry tide. A wall of sandbags is being erected to prevent the onslaught of the sea. It's not clear what has caused the destruction — some erroneously blame the tsunami of December 2004 but a fisheries project nearby could just as well be the culprit — but Shankarpur does not let you dwell on it for long.

The beach here does not draw the madding crowds like nearby Digha. You can walk on the beach chasing the sunset, up to a point where the delta of two small rivers stops you from going ahead. Friendly villagers sell you beautiful shells of varied shapes and hues, each coming at a princely sum of two rupees. A few tourists run into the sea for a last dip before the onset of darkness even as mothers cajole their reluctant children to leave their games or their splashing about in the sea. As the sun sets, the sea turns an inky dark blue, and reluctantly, one steps away from the beach.

At the break of dawn, I visit pristine Mandarmani, a serene beach reached via a route past paddy fields and ponds. The sky is heavy and grey and yet the world around me is calm and quiet. I feel one with nature — perhaps it's the rustic quality of Shankarpur, where even electricity hasn't made its presence felt yet (all the hotels run on generators). I pick up a few shells thrown up by the high tide at night and stuff these into my pocket, the child in me surfacing once again. Only the tall, swaying trees by the sea share this moment of serenity with me.

→ FAST FACTS

When to go October to February
Tourist office
● WBTDC
3/2 BBD Bag (East)
Kolkata-700001
Tel: 033-22437260, 22485168
Website: wbtourism.com
STD code 03220

BEACH WATCH

Locals claim the beach is safe and vouch that there have been no mishaps or the phenomenon of shifting sands seen in some parts of Digha. But it wouldn't hurt to keep close to the shore, especially because there are no lifeguards here. Most people dress modestly on the beach.

ORIENTATION

The drive from **14 Mile Junction** off the main road to Shankarpur Beach, with the **Haldi River** to the right, is beautiful. On both sides of the road are trees in full bloom and you can see villagers on small wooden floats catching fish in a river that looks more like a canal. As you near your destination, the first imposing building is of **Hotel Nest** that spills into the road to your left. A few yards ahead, the road forks and the right turn leads to an enclave where the State Fisheries Department runs **three guest houses**, Matsyagandha, Kinara and Jowar. The enclave is pleasantly wooded, with many local trees, and boasts of a beautiful beach just 1 km from the gate. Unless you are a guest at Hotel Nest or at the government-run guest houses, you have to buy an entry ticket for Rs 5 to swim in this 'private' part of the beach. On either side of the road leading to this enclave are shops selling knick-knacks.

The closest town is **Ramnagar**, 1 km from 14 Mile, and also the largest **bus junction** in the vicinity. Travellers can disembark at Ramnagar as most buses don't stop at 14 Mile, and then take a trekker (an open jeep that carts as many as 15 people, if not more; fare Rs 4 per passenger) or hire a rickshaw-van for Rs 40 to Shankarpur. A few hotels like Hotel Nest send their own vehicles to pick up guests. Within Shankarpur, walking is the best way to get around though one

Photographs by KUMAR ROY

The lovely Mandarmani Beach offers serenity and solitude

can also avail of local rickshaw-vans, which are three-wheelers with open wooden platforms that can seat six. The fare is about Rs 10 from Ramnagar to Shankarpur. There's no tourist office in Shankarpur, so all the information has to be obtained from the West Bengal Tourism's Kolkata office (*see Fast Facts on facing page*).

THINGS TO SEE AND DO

Without electricity, Shankarpur has struggled to come into its own as a tourist destination. Hotels, however, run on generators but evenings are too dark to wander about. On the other hand, it also means that Shankarpur is largely peaceful and is perfect for someone looking for something that's off the tourist trail.

Shankarpur Beach

The beach is most lovely in the early mornings when fishermen cast their nets into the sea and young boys sit patiently separating prawn seedlings from the catch. Small shops sell tea and snacks such as bread and eggs and chips here; coconut water is also sold and makes for a refreshing drink.

Mandarmani Beach

You cannot leave Shankarpur without spending at least one day in Mandarmani. Those who have been to this beach cannot stop raving about its serenity and beauty. The journey to Mandarmani itself is an unforgettable, lovely drive. There's no electricity in this place either and all the hotels run on generators.

The glistening white beach is clean and unspoilt. There are no shops or vendors here and the utter solitude it guarantees is the beach's main charm. Though Mandarmani is new to the tourist circuit, hotels have already started coming up here, many of them in a haphazard fashion, blatantly encroaching upon the beach. Some have been pulled up by the judiciary for violating building rules.

◆**Location** 32 km east of Shankarpur **Connection** Drive from 14 Mile towards Kolkata (but away from Digha) for 10 km up to Chaulkhola; turn right and drive for another 15 km to the beach. From Chaulkhola, you can hire a rickshaw-van to the beach for Rs 100; cars can be hired one way for Rs 200-250. Taxis are to be found at Chaulkhola Junction; your hotel can also arrange your trip. To reach Chaulkhola, you can take a trekker from Shankarpur (Rs 10) or a bus from 14 Mile

WHERE TO STAY

Despite the lack of electricity, Shankarpur and Mandarmani offer a fairly good range of hotels.

→ GETTING THERE

Air Nearest airport: Kolkata's Netaji Subhas Chandra Bose International Airport (183 km/ 4½ hrs), connected by flights to all metros by most airlines. There are no pre-paid taxis to Shankarpur and you'll have to hire one through a private operator. The charges are Rs 8 per km for non-AC and Rs 12 per km for AC cars (these rates are inclusive of return fare)

Rail Nearest railhead: Digha (16 km/ ½ hr). There are frequent bus and trekker services between Digha and Ramnagar. From Ramnagar, visitors can cover the 7-km long road trip to Shankarpur in a rickshaw (Rs 10) or trekker (Rs 4)

Road From Kolkata, private and state buses leave from various important bus stations in the city for Digha almost every 30 mins. All buses stop at Ramnagar and the fare is between Rs 80 and Rs 120 for luxury coaches. The West Bengal Surface Transport Corporation (Mobile: 09932792858) has started buses on this route. Whiteliner (Tel: 033-30587788/ 99; Mobile: 09331268688; AC fare Rs 160) buses leave the city at 7 am daily from the city centre Esplanade for Ramnagar; the trip takes 4 hrs

At Shankarpur

The unimaginative and imposing **Hotel Nest** (Tel: 03220-264074/ 164; Tariff: Rs 750-1,800; dormitory bed Rs 150) stands out for its incongruous exterior but has an attached restaurant and bar. It provides vehicles for free to take guests to the beach. Though it offers the only roof garden in Shankarpur and organises boating for its guests, its impersonal service can put visitors off. **Sandy Bay** (Tel: 264693; Tariff: Rs 700-1,100) is a hot favourite because of its friendly service and restaurant. It has a few good sea-facing rooms. The rooms themselves are cramped and could do with some sprucing up and more comfortable furnishing.

For reasonable room rates and atmosphere, head to the Fisheries Department guest houses. The department has tied up with a private operator, **Global Tour and Travels** (Tel: 033-22133759) in Kolkata, to run Jowar and Matsyagandha guest houses. **Matsyagandha** (Tel: 265059; Tariff: Rs 350-825; dormitory Rs 60 per bed) has an old-world charm, which also means that the rooms could do with a change of linen and the leaky taps with some mending. **Jowar** (same telephone number and tariffs as Matsyagandha), with a beautiful garden and children's playground, is the place to be; the rooms are brightly ventilated with clean bathrooms. Book at Global Tour and Travels at least 15 days in advance for Jowar and Matsyagandha, if planning to visit on a weekend. Though the beach is about 1 km from the guest houses, tourists seldom complain; the walk through the beautiful wooded enclave to the beach is an incentive in itself. The department's **Kinara** guest house (Tel: 264577; Mobile: 09831033181; Tariff: Rs 300-700), located in the enclave, is drab and musty.

Those who want to be even closer to the sea can stay at **Sweet Home** (Tel: 265088; Mobile: 09831003490; Tariff: Rs 500-1,000), located at the furthest corner of the beach. It's clean and provides privacy and serenity. They also serve a fixed

thali (four times a day) for a total charge of Rs 150-175. **Ashoka Lodge** (Tel: 264275; Tariff: Rs 250-700) has a great view of the sea, but is tacky and the bathrooms could do with more cleaning. They offer a fixed thali for four meals for a total of Rs 150-175. For breakfast you get puri and vegetables, while for lunch and dinner, it's rice, vegetables and fish.

At Mandarmani

One ugly monstrosity jutting into the beach here is the **Rose Valley Hotel** (Tel: 033-25006470; Tariff: Rs 1,500-3000), painted in a shocking pink colour. Locals aptly call it the 'Titanic' because during high tide the seawater reaches the walls of the hotel and it's impossible to go out during those hours. But the rooms are well furnished and the view is amazingly beautiful as you almost hover over the sea. The hotel provides a free pick-up from Chaulkhola road junction. The restaurant is enclosed in glass to provide a panoramic view of the surroundings. Try the fish fingers and chicken momos.

The day's catch: Pomfret and crab

The neat thatched cottages of **Samudra Sakshi** (Mobile: 09332024328; 09830381880; Tariff: Rs 400-600) are inviting. The rooms are simple yet functional and comfortable, with attached bathrooms and small verandahs. A package meal (comprising four meals served through the day) is priced at Rs 170 per head. It has an attractive restaurant (offering a fixed thali, with *luchi* or puris and potato curry for breakfast, rice, dal, vegetables, fish or chicken, chutney and a sweet for lunch and dinner, and tea and pakoras in the evening) and is a pleasant place to spend hours reading a book. It's just 2 mins walking distance from the sea.

In the vicinity is **Garden Retreat** (Mobile: 09732995188, 09332355586, 09831167537; Tariff: Rs 450), with colourful bamboo walls and thatched roofs. It has a busy kitchen going. While the package meal is for Rs 150, you can order Chinese and Continental dishes off the menu card.

For more hotels and details, see Shankarpur Accommodation Listings on page 569

WHERE TO EAT

Most hotels have restaurants that serve simple but tasty Bengali cuisine. Though **Sandy Bay** came highly recommended, the food wasn't extraordinary. Price-wise too, it's more expensive than many other options. Each meal at the government guest houses and other lodges comes at an average price of Rs 30-35. Sandy Bay's and **Hotel Nest** claim to serve Continental, Chinese and Goan cuisine, but it's best to stick to Bengali cuisine. The fried pomfret at Rs 500 a plate and prawn for Rs 100 in Crab Hole is steep compared to the rates at other places but worth the price. On the other hand, the sumptuous breakfast of hot puris and potato curry topped with light black tea comes for a mere Rs 12 at **Jowar**. If you are not staying at Jowar and want to eat at the restaurant, order in advance. ■

ORISSA

Courtesy ORISSA TOURISM

CHANDIPUR

A SEA TO WALK ON

State Orissa
Location In north-east Orissa, by the Bay of Bengal, Chandipur Beach curves inwards like the letter C
Distances 16 km E of Balasore, 212 km NE of Bhubaneswar
Journey time ***By road*** 30 mins from Balasore, $4^{1}/_{2}$ hrs from Bhubaneswar
Route from Bhubaneswar NH5 to Balasore via Cuttack and Bhadrak; district road to Chandipur via Gadagadia Chhak and Jhampuda (*see route guide on facing page*)

BY SAROJINI NAYAK

It's true that Chandipur Beach doesn't make a good first impression. The sands aren't golden and the sea isn't even blue. Why would you come here then? Perhaps for that magical experience of watching the waves play hide-and-seek with the shore. Twice everyday, the waters touch the beach only to move far back, leaving behind a brown, sandy seabed that appears to stretch endlessly. At low tide, the sea recedes by as much as an unbelievable 5 km.

Walking on the empty seabed is a fascinating experience. There are small puddles of water with tiny fish, seashells scattered here and there, and red crabs that quickly disappear into the sand at the sound of an approaching footstep. As the tide rises, the waters start trickling towards the shore. This is a signal for you to walk back to the shore, perhaps along with the water. In a few hours, the water reaches the shore and at high tide, the waves start to gently lap on the shore.

→ FAST FACTS

When to go October to April
Tourist office
• Orissa Tourism
Panthanivas Building, Police Line
Balasore
Tel: 06782-262048
STD code 06782

The water is brown and muddy, but it's absolutely safe for swimming — there are no undercurrents or quicksand. As a local remarked, tongue firmly in cheek, "The sea is so safe here that even if you try, you cannot commit suicide."

ORIENTATION

Chandipur is a small seaside retreat, with a few hotels and shops, and a sprinkling

of houses. The **Main Road** leads to the beach and most hotels are located here. The bazaar area is called **Sunarpur Chhak**, and it is about 1 km from the beach. There is no beachfront as such, and the main access to the beach opens from the **Panthanivas garden** (*see Where to Stay below*).

All the places in Chandipur are within walking distance. Autos are also available and fares are negotiable; usually the rate from one place to another is between Rs 15 and 25. Tourist assistance is also available at Panthanivas.

GETTING THERE

Air Nearest airport: Bhubaneswar (212 km/ 4½ hrs). Taxis charge Rs 1,500 to Balasore, from where you can hire a taxi or auto (*see below*)

Rail Balasore (16 km/ 30 mins), the nearest town, a station on the East Coast Railway. Taxis charge Rs 250 and autorickshaws Rs 120 from Balasore to Chandipur. Local buses are also available and run once every 2 hrs; the bus journey takes at least 45 mins

Road From Bhubaneswar, take NH5 via Cuttack, Chandikhol, Bhadrak and Soro till Balasore. From here, take the road to Gadagadia Chhak and from there, go on the Defence Route (Chandipur Missile Testing Range) towards Jhampuda Bypass. On reaching the bypass, take a left turn that leads to Chandipur Beach. The road conditions are good. Private and government-run buses ply between Bhubaneswar and Balasore (one-way fare Rs 90). In Balasore, there are travel agents from whom taxis can be hired for local sightseeing, including Sanjita Travels (Tel: 06782-266016) and Shree Ganesh Travels (Mobile: 09861038291)

THINGS TO SEE AND DO

Spend at least 12 hrs on this beach to watch the sea at high and low tides. The tall, swaying casuarinas nearby add to the atmosphere.

On the beach

Although the time of the tide changes every day, evening is when most visitors come to the beach. Depending on the position of the water, people either sit on the beach or walk into the sea. A few vendors sell tea and snacks, and a couple of shops stock shell items. You can go on long walks or just laze around.

One can also visit the fisherfolk's village, **Balaramgadi** (2 km), where the River Budhabalanga flows into the sea. Here fishermen can take you on a boat ride at Rs 200-300 per hour. Take a cruise towards the mouth of the river and enjoy the lovely views of the green countryside and cattle grazing in the fields.

WHERE TO STAY AND EAT

Panthanivas (Tel: 06782-270051; Tariff: Rs 400-1,200), run by Orissa Tourism, is located right on the beachfront and is one of the best staying options in Chandipur. However, that isn't much of a compliment, as you'll realise once you enter. The rooms and bathrooms are just about average. What makes up for all that is the restaurant, which offers delicious grilled pomfret and golden fried prawns.

Several budget hotels are located at walking distance from the beach. These are not luxurious, but decent and clean. They have dining halls that mostly specialise in seafood and tandoor items. Some of these include: **Hotel Chandipur** (Tel: 270030; Tariff: Rs 225-650), **Hotel Subham** (Tel: 270025; Tariff: Rs 400-1,000) and **Hotel Anandamayee** (Tel: 270012; Tariff: Rs 250-1,150).

For more hotels and details, see Chandipur Accommodation Listings on page 562 ■

BACARDI®
made to mix
Enjoy responsibly
BACARDI and the Bat device are registered trademarks of Bacardi and Company Limited.

LOKESH ABROL

PURI

THE MYSTIC SEA

State Orissa
Location On the eastern coast of Orissa, by the Bay of Bengal, in Puri District
Distances 56 km S of Bhubaneswar, 478 km SW of Kolkata
Journey time ***By road*** $1\frac{1}{2}$ hrs from Bhubaneswar, 13 hrs from Kolkata
Route from Bhubaneswar NH203 to Puri via Pipli, Sakshigopal and Chandanpur
(*see route guide on page 43*)

BY SAROJINI NAYAK

Waking up at dawn to the sound of waves, I decide to take a walk along a narrow stretch to the sea. Street lamps illuminate my path. As darkness disappears, I see black specks far away, and realise that those are catamarans riding the voluminous waves. The roar of the sea seems louder at this hour, quiet as it is all around. The chimes of temple bells in the distance complete the mystic morning scene on the Puri beach.

Like the ancient town that is its home, the beach, known as Mahodadhi, is held to be sacred. It's impossible to separate the beach from the mythological legends attached to it — it's believed that Lord Jagannath was found floating as a log of wood on these shores. One often comes across devotees who pay obeisance to the ocean, taking a handful of saline water and sprinkling it on their head as if to cleanse themselves. Other visitors choose to relax on the beach, and some, like me, go searching for tea and food, both of which are sold by vendors. Like other eager customers, I sip tea and snack on hot samosas and rasgullas. It's refreshing food, one that makes me take a stroll towards the far end of the beach, where I find an entirely different setting. A few catamarans, those specks I had spotted at dawn, have come ashore and there is a flurry of activity around them. Waiting fisherwomen sort the catch, quickly fill their cane baskets with fish and then head towards the bazaar. Their work for the day done, fishermen roll their nets and head home to rest. And thus begins another day at the beach.

ORIENTATION

Besides the famed **Sri Jagannath Temple**, many smaller temples, mutts and religious institutions are located in Puri. The main beachfront stretches for about 5 km and most hotels face the sea. **Swargdwar** (Gateway to Heaven), near the beach, is considered a sacred spot.

The **Beach Road** is the stretch from the **Marine Drive Road**, past the Sri Chaitanya statue, towards the Mahatma Gandhi statue and the Governor's House, upto the **Chakra Tirtha Road** (CT Road). A half-kilometre stretch of this road is popular with foreigners and looks different from the rest of the town. It's full of cafés, curio shops, pizzerias and restaurants.

Taxis, autos and cycle rickshaws are the main mode of transport in Puri. Bargain hard before you hire one. Cycle rickshaws charge Rs 15 from the Jagannath Temple to the beach and autos Rs 25.

If you want to stay near the busy seafront, choose a hotel on the Beach Road, between Chaitanya and Gandhi statues. For quieter options, go in for those located on CT Road or Marine Drive. Most hotels arrange taxis for sightseeing; you can also go to the Orissa Tourism kiosk on Beach Road for help. Orissa Tourism organises a one-day tour of Konark, Puri and Pipli for Rs 150 per head.

BEACH WATCH

Said to be one of the finest beaches in the country, the flat, sandy beach in Puri is bound to delight any beach lover. However, the shimmering blue waters can at times be deceptive as strong undercurrents have been reported. If you intend to swim and aren't a strong swimmer, do take the assistance of *nolias* (fishermen), who will hold your hands and help you duck the giant waves. However, it's quite safe to splash in knee-deep water. It's inadvisable to sport beachwear in Puri.

THINGS TO SEE AND DO

The main beachfront, near Puri Hotel, is full of tourists and vendors. While mornings are relatively less crowded, the beach comes alive in the evenings.

On the beach

The beach resounds with shouts of vendors selling puffed rice (*jhal murhi*), samosas, tea and coffee. Also on sale are shells and semi-precious stones; do bargain — start from one third of the price quoted. Walk around and admire the structures made by sand artists (*also see 'Stories in sand' on page 49*). Children can opt for horse and camel rides (Rs 15 per ride).

Cultural programmes, exhibitions and festivals create a vibrant atmosphere

→ FAST FACTS

When to go Between October and April

Tourist offices

- Orissa Tourism
Paryatan Bhavan, Bhubaneswar
Tel: 0674-2432177
Email: ortour@orissatourism.gov.in
Websites: orissatourism.gov.in, otdc.in
- Government of Orissa Tourist Office
CT Road, near Banki Muhan
Puri-752002
Tel: 06752-222664

STD code 06752

throughout the year in Puri. The beach near the Mahatma Gandhi statue is the venue for the annual three-day **Beach Festival** in November, when dance and music performances are organised. The beach behind Hotel Pink House (CT Road) is the venue for **BYOFF**, or **Bring Your Own Film Festival**, held every February, when filmmakers from across the country gather to screen their documentaries.

Jagannath Temple Complex

The Sri Jagannath Temple's lofty spire, with its flag, can be seen as far as 7 km away. Ahead of the main gate is a 35-foot high pillar called **Arunastambh** (Arun is the bird considered the charioteer of the Sun God). The temple is said to have been built by Yayati Keshari (10th century CE). The annual Rath Festival at the temple, held in July, attracts millions of devotees. ♦**Timings** 6 am-10 pm **Note** Only Hindus are allowed in the temple. Cell phones, cameras and leather items such as purses and belts are not allowed inside

→ GETTING THERE

Air Nearest airport: Biju Patnaik Airport, Bhubaneswar (56 km/ $1^1/_2$ hrs). Buses and taxis connect Bhubaneswar to Puri. Taxi costs about Rs 650 and Rs 1,050 if taking a detour through Konark, which is 34 km from Puri via the East Coast Road known as Marine Drive

Rail The Puri Railway Station on the East Coast Railway is connected by direct trains to New Delhi, Kolkata, Ahmedabad, Guwahati, Jodhpur and Haridwar. Those travelling from the South will find it easier to get down at Bhubaneswar and proceed to Puri by road

Road NH203 from Bhubaneswar to Puri. If going via Konark, the distance between Konark and Bhubaneswar is 65 km and between Konark and Puri is 34 km. The roads are good. Private deluxe buses and government buses connect Bhubaneswar and Puri. There are many travel agencies from whom taxis can be hired, including Discover Tours (Tel: 0674-2435731) and Sand Pebbles Tours (Tel: 6532550)

SHOPPING

The **Grand Road** is a must-visit shopping destination. Apart from all kinds of puja paraphernalia, one can buy handlooms and exquisite handicrafts from the shops here. The **Grand Shopping Arcade, Padma Complex** and **Nayak Plaza** are good places to shop. **Utkalika, Boyanika** and **Amlan** in the Grand Shopping Complex on Bada Danda are reliable shops for handloom items. Another place for handlooms are the shops near **Swargdwar**; be careful, as many of them palm off duplicates as Orissa handlooms. For the discerning buyer, **Priyadarshini Handlooms** on VIP Road is the best place.

Puri is famed for its wood and stone carvings and to pick up a few, head to **Sudarshan Crafts** at Station Bazaar or **Sun Crafts** at Police Lines.

WHERE TO STAY

Accommodation options in Puri range from cheap hotels to posh resorts. **Toshali Sands** (Tel: 06752-227800; Tariff: Rs 3,200-7,700), on Marine Drive, is a luxurious resort set amidst lush gardens and manicured lawns. About 8 km from Puri, it has villas and cottages and is located about $1^1/_2$ km from the beach. The resort offers conveyance to the beach, through the day, for guests. **Mayfair** (Tel: 227800; Tariff: Rs 5,000-7,500) is a top-end hotel located on the beach, and is known for its aesthetic appeal. **Hotel Holiday Resort** (Tel: 222440; Tariff: Rs 1,350-4,800) is yet another well-known hotel on the beach. **Coco Palms** (Tel: 230038; Tariff: Rs 3,600-6,000) is located close to the beach.

Stories in sand

SANJIB MUKHERJEE

It's possible to find images of famous persons, gods and goddesses, or national and international events etched out on the golden sands of Puri Beach. You may come across a fallen world leader or an astonishing musician, or find sandy portrayals of the World Trade Center bombings, the tsunami that struck Asia in December 2004 or even World Cup cricket matches, complete with stadiums. All these comprise the sand art installations made by Sudarsan Pattnaik, a leading sand sculptor of Orissa. Pattnaik also runs a sand art school on Puri Beach, behind the Mayfair hotel. The most endearing aspect of this work is that although a sand sculpture is transient in nature — lasting one or two days at the most — artists take utmost care to do it well.

For a feel of the bygone British era, stay at the heritage **BNR Hotel** (Tel: 222063; Tariff: Rs 650-1,700), which has wide verandahs offering spectacular sea views. **Vijoya International** (Tel: 223705; Tariff: Rs 800-2,450) on CT Road has all modern amenities. **OTDC Panthanivas** (Tel: 222562; Tariff: Rs 690-1,500) on CT Road, overlooking the beach, seems run-down and offers a no-frills service. But the rooms are clean and airy.

Puri Hotel (Tel: 222114; Tariff: Rs 330-1,200) on Beach Road offers good service. Newer hotels like **Shreehari** (Tel: 231644; Tariff: Rs 1,800-2,200) and **Puri Beach Resort** (Tel: 231788; Tariff: Rs 950-2,200) on Marine Drive are sea-facing, and just right for a relaxed stay. **Hotel Sapphire International** (Tel: 226488; Tariff: Rs 400-1,850) on CT Road, with its blue façade, is a convenient place for budget travellers. The rooms are reasonably clean and food is provided on request. **Hotel Lee Garden** (Tel: 223647; Tariff: Rs 500-1,700) on VIP Road is another option, but it's slightly away from the beach.

If you want to stay in a tent on the beach, contact **Rangers** (Tel: 211057; Tariff: Rs 300-2,000) on the Puri-Konark Marine Drive, about 16 km from Puri. Their campsite, with a small restaurant, is also a lovely place to stop by for a snack.

For more hotels and details, see Puri Accommodation Listings on pages 563-564

WHERE TO EAT

In Puri, one can find culinary delights at both wayside foodstalls and posh restaurants. The local delicacy **kheera** (similar to *rabdi*) is available in most sweet shops. For vegetarian food, try the restaurant in the **Grand Complex** in front of the Jagannath Temple. **Annapurna Restaurant** near Janata cinema and the Marwari bhojanalayas on Grand Road offer wholesome vegetarian thalis.

If you are looking for a four-course Continental meal, place your order at **BNR Hotel**. For Chinese, **Chung Wah** on VIP Road is very good, and the prawn delicacies here are recommended. **Wild Grass** on VIP Road offers good food at pocket-friendly rates. The restaurant in **Puri Hotel** caters to Bengali tourists and the small cafés on CT Road are popular with budget travellers.

Try the fish, prawn and crab dishes sold on carts on the beachfront. The items are delicious but hygiene is, well, a bit fishy. At the other end are the multi-cuisine restaurants of high-end hotels like Mayfair, which serve quality food in an air-conditioned ambience. ■

SWAPAN NAYAK

KONARK

SERENDIPITY ON A SACRED SHORE

BY SAROJINI NAYAK

Famous for the exquisite Sun Temple, the sleepy town of Konark is a far cry from vibrant Puri. On most days it's quiet, and thus an ideal destination for someone looking for a laid-back holiday. The Chandrabhaga Beach here is known for the glorious sunrise views it offers, but it's more popular as a sacred spot where the devout congregate for a holy dip during the local festival of Maghamela, usually held in January. Whether you are here for religious reasons or not, the first glimpse of the beach will take your breath away. Emerald waters, long stretches of virgin beaches and casuarina groves transport one to an ethereal world. The best part is that the beach is mostly empty except in the evenings and early mornings, and the solitude it guarantees is certainly part of its charm.

ORIENTATION

The main beachfront is small, with a few stalls that sell shell crafts and a couple of tea vendors. On the southern side is the **Marine Drive** that goes towards Puri. The only mode of transport in Konark is the auto, and in the absence of meters, the drivers tend to overcharge. Ask around and bargain. The return fare from the **Konark Temple** to the beach is Rs 60. Taxis are available and the average rates for half-day sightseeing is about Rs 300.

BEACH WATCH

The choppy waters off the Chandrabhaga Beach are not safe and a signboard cautions that undercurrents are dangerous.

THINGS TO SEE AND DO

Konark is known for its temple but most people visit on a day-trip as stay options are limited.

Chandrabhaga Beach

The beach is 3 km from the town and sees crowds only in the evenings. One of the main attractions here is the **Konark Lighthouse**, which you can climb to get a spectacular view of the sea and the surrounding areas. The light-house is located amidst lovely casuarina

groves on the road leading to the beach, and is just about 3 mins walking distance from the main beachfront.
◆**Lighthouse entry fee** Adults Rs 5, children Rs 3 **Timings** 4-5 pm

Konark Sun Temple

This Sun Temple, with its exquisite stone sculptures, is a World Heritage Site that represents the magnificence of Oriya architecture. Shaped like a grand chariot drawn by seven horses, with 12 decorated wheels on either side, the temple is dedicated to the Sun God. Today, the monument is partly in ruins, but the intricate stone work and its colossal size are still awe-inspiring. The temple was built in the 13th century by the Ganga dynasty ruler Narasimhadev I (1258-64). Legend has it that it took 1,200 masons 12 years to complete the edifice. At the base of the temple, you'll find sculptures of scenes such as that of a king holding a conference or animals and birds. Floodlights are switched on after sunset, and the monument then looks surreal. The **Konark Dance Festival** is held here in December every year.

At the Sun Temple at Konark

BPS WALIA/ INDIAPICTURE

◆**Entry fee** Indians Rs 10, foreigners Rs 250 (free for children below 15) **Timings** 6 am-8 pm, open all days **Cameras** Still free, video Rs 25 **Note** Registered tourist guides can be hired; insist on checking approved fares before hiring a guide. Guide fees vary from Rs 60 to Rs 200, depending on the number of people in a group

Archaeological Museum

The museum has exhibits from the ruins of the Sun Temple, including colossal sandstone images of Surya, a reconstructed chariot wheel and sculptures of Varaha, Tribikrama and Narasimha. Also look for the stone panels depicting animal and plant motifs and celestial musicians.
◆**Location** Adjacent to the Yatri Nivas, and a 5-min walk from the Konark Temple **Entry fee** Adults Rs 5, children (below 15) free **Timings** 10 am-5 pm, closed on Fridays

WHERE TO STAY AND EAT

The Orissa Tourism Development Corporation-run **Yatri Nivas** (Tel: 06758-236820; Tariff: Rs 350-1,500; *more details on page 563*), close to the temple, is the only decent play to stay. The complex is clean and comfortable though service tends to be a little slack. The restaurant serves Indian and Chinese meals and the dishes just about pass muster. There are many inexpensive dhabas and Marwari bhojanalayas near the Sun Temple where simple food is available. The standard of hygiene is low. The **Sun Temple Hotel** in the main market area serves tasty food, and the fish fry is recommended.

FAST FACTS

When to go While winter is the best time, one can visit Konark throughout the year **Tourist office** Yatri Nivas, Konark **Tel** 06758-236821 **STD code** 06758

GETTING THERE

The nearest airport is Bhubaneswar (65 km/ 1½ hrs), connected by good roads to Konark. There is no railhead at Konark and the nearest railway station is at Puri (34 km). From Bhubaneswar, take NH203 towards Puri and take a left for Konark from Pipli (25 km from Bhubaneswar). If going from Puri, take the Marine Drive towards Konark ■

KALYAN PATRA

GOPALPUR-ON-SEA

FAR FROM THE MADDING CROWD

State Orissa
Location Gopalpur is by the Bay of Bengal, 16 km east of the bustling commercial town of Berhampur in Ganjam District, in South Orissa
Distances 166 km SW of Bhubaneswar, 286 km NE of Visakhapatnam
Journey time ***By road*** 4 hrs from Bhubaneswar, 5½ hrs from Visakhapatnam
Route from Bhubaneswar NH5 to Gopalpur-on-Sea via Khurdha, Balugaon, Rambha, Chhatrapur and Dura (*see route guide on page 43*)

■ BY SAROJINI NAYAK

Gopalpur-on-Sea is a sleepy hamlet that betrays no traces of its glorious past. Once a port around which maritime activities were centred, it's today a retreat for those looking for a quiet holiday. Only the ruins of an old port speak of a time that won Gopalpur its prominent place in Oriyan history. While kings may have sworn by trade and commerce, Gopalpur curried royal favour for other reasons as well. Its lovely atmosphere had the wealthy scurrying to this part of the Oriyan coastline to build their holiday homes.

One can understand why that would have been the case after a visit to Gopalpur. In the mornings, the beach is completely tranquil, except for the roar of waves. A strong breeze comes your way as the azure waters take on a silvery sheen in the midday sun. The kings have long left and the beach is almost empty. Yet, as you stand on the shore, you feel a bit like royalty yourself. The shore is yours as is the sea. And in your imagination, you can even summon a thousand boats to stop at this port of yesteryear.

ORIENTATION

The story behind the place's name has it that as many villages went by the name Gopalpur, the unique moniker Gopalpur-on-Sea was coined to distinguish it from others. A small temple to Gopalaswamy, located on the road to Gopalpur-on-Sea, is also believed to have given the place its name. The main beachfront at Gopalpur stretches for less than a kilometre and has a children's corner with slides, swings and the works. A few hotels are located on the beach, the base of their buildings almost touching the waves. The rest of the buildings are a little away from the sea, across the road, along the beachfront.

Gopalpur has a hilly topography and a sturdy pair of legs is enough to cover it. Autos are available; these don't run on meter but charge about Rs 20 for short rides. Bicycles are available for hire through the recommendation of hotels at Rs 5 per hr. There's no tourist office at Gopalpur but information may be available at the government-run Panthanivas (*see Where to Stay on page 58*).

BEACH WATCH

Swimming is not advisable because of the rough sea. Some *nolias* (fishermen) have certifications from the beach police and act as beach guards. They have been given identity cards to this effect. Beachwear is not recommended.

THINGS TO SEE AND DO

There is very little to do in Gopalpur except to laze around. Evening is the only time when the beach gets crowded.

On and around the beach

The Main Road leading to the beach has a **lighthouse** with a small but well-kept garden. It offers a spectacular view of the sea and the surrounding areas.
◆**Entry fee** Adults Rs 5, children Rs 3 **Timings** 3.30-5.50 pm

On Sunday evenings, the local community organises a cultural programme

→ FAST FACTS

When to go Winter is the best time
Tourist office
● Orissa Tourism
Dainik Asa Old Building, Hill Patna
Near Railway Station, Berhampur
Ganjam District
Tel: 0680-2210980
Mobile: 09437270005
STD code 0680

on the beachfront wherein artistes perform. The state Tourism Department holds a three-day **beach festival** in December, when the beach comes alive with dance and music programmes.

A small stretch of backwater near the beach is ideal for a boat ride, and people living in the fishing villages nearby often use the waterway. Organised boating facilities are not available here, but in winter, or when the sea is not rough, you can request the fishermen to take you on a ride in their catamarans. A fee of Rs 30-40 should suffice.

→ GETTING THERE

Air Nearest airport: Bhubaneswar (166 km/ 4 hrs), well-connected by flights from Mumbai, Kolkata, Chennai, New Delhi, Bangalore and Hyderabad. Taxi to Gopalpur costs Rs 1,600 one-way

Rail Nearest railhead: Berhampur (Brahmapur) Station (16 km/ 25 mins), on the East Coast Railway. Connected by trains from Chennai, Bangalore, Hyderabad, Kolkata, Guwahati and Patna. Taxi fare from Berhampur to Gopalpur is Rs 250; autos charge about Rs 150. There's no regular bus service between both places but jeeps ply on the route and charge about Rs 10 per person

Road From Bhubaneswar, take NH5 via Khurdha, Balugaon and Chhatrapur. Take a left turn towards Gopalpur-on-Sea at Dura, on the National Highway, 6 km before Berhampur. If you're travelling by bus, get down at the Berhampur Bus Stand and then take a taxi or auto from there. The road conditions are good. Private and state government buses ply between Bhubaneswar and Berhampur. Taxis can be hired from travel agents and tour operators in Bhubaneswar. These include Geo Travels (Tel: 0674-2544685/ 358), Lipsha Travels (Tel: 2595108), Trade Wings (Tel: 2531807) and Discover Tours (Tel: 2435731). If travelling by taxi from Bhubaneswar, factor in a stop at Barkul or Rambha, which fall on the way, and see the Chilika Lake

SHOPPING

Except for a couple of small shops selling shell items and trinkets, there is very little on sale at this destination. At the cashew processing units here, one can buy cashewnuts. There is one hand-processed cashew unit in Narayanpur, which is about 2 km from Gopalpur-on-Sea.

The nearby town of Berhampur is where compulsive shoppers can head to. Known as the 'Silk City' of the state, the town is well-known for its handwoven silk saris and dhotis. To pick one up, visit the shops and cooperatives located in the **Annapurna Market** and the **Burra Bazaar** area. If you fancy ornaments with stone settings (in gold and silver), check out the jewellery shops that line the main road at Burra Bazaar. The town is also famous for papad, pickles, namkeens and masala powders, found in grocery stores.

WHERE TO STAY

The only luxury hotel here is the **Swosti Palm Resort** (Tel: 0680-2242455; Tariff: Rs 1,980-4,950), about 200m from the Main Road. Aesthetically designed with well-furnished rooms and a neat garden, this is the best place to stay in Gopalpur. However, its only drawback is that it's slightly away from the beach and there is no sea view from the rooms.

The rest of the hotels are mostly in the budget and mid-range categories. But be warned that maintenance is lacking in most of these hotels. **Song of the Sea** (Tel: 2242347; Tariff: Rs 750-1,200) is a large, sprawling hotel, which is about 100m away from the beach, with sea-facing rooms. A family-run, well-furnished

SAROJINI NAYAK

The roadside stalls at Gopalpur-on-Sea serve up a platter for fish lovers

hotel, it's a quiet place with a homely ambience. The government-run **Panthanivas** (Tel: 2243931; Tariff: Rs 400-650), about 1 km from the Main Road on Arya Marg, has clean, large rooms with no frills and decent bathrooms. The rooms are sea-facing and the property opens out onto the beach. But its main disadvantage is that it's located almost $1^1/_2$ km away from the main beachfront. If you don't have a private or hired vehicle, you will have to walk back to the hotel.

If you want to stay right on the beach, then your options include **Hotel Sea Pearl** (Tel: 2242556; Tariff: Rs 660-1,000), which has an ideal location on the main beachfront. However, the rooms are average and the service is poor. **Hotel Kalinga** (Tel: 2242067/ 69; Tariff: Rs 500-800), located next to Hotel Sea Pearl, is another alternative, but it's slightly run-down. **Hotel Seaside Breeze** (Tel: 2242075; Tariff: Rs 400-500) is on the beach and the rooms have three or four beds. It's cheap but has basic facilities. **Hotel Green Park** (Tel: 2242016; Tariff: Rs 350-600) is one of the larger hotels with clean rooms. It's about 300m away from the main road, on the road to the beach, and the rooms on the top floor offer a view of the sea.

For more hotels and details, see Gopalpur-on-Sea Accommodation Listings on page 563

WHERE TO EAT

Like all seaside destinations, Gopalpur-on-Sea serves up a platter for fish lovers. In the evenings, roadside stalls serve delicious fish fry. A couple of vendors sell grilled fish and meat in the evenings. On the beach, snacks such as *jhal murhi* and channa chaat are available. The restaurant at **Panthanivas** serves a decent meal, and the popular dishes include mustard fish (cooked in the Bengali style) and fried fish. While most hotels serve common seafood items like fish, crabs and prawns, for a special dining experience, try the **Chilika Restaurant** at Swosti Palm Resort; their pomfret, prawns and Continental dishes are good. ■

ANDHRA PRADESH

Photographs by JOYDEEP MUKHERJEE/ SOUTHINDIAPICTURE

VISAKHAPATNAM

LIFE IS A BEACH

State Andhra Pradesh
Location Visakhapatnam, or Vizag as the locals call it, is a prominent port city on the East Coast, halfway up Andhra Pradesh's outstretched arm
Distances 625 km E of Hyderabad, 375 km NE Vijayawada
Journey time *By road* 12 hrs from Hyderabad, 7 hrs from Vijayawada
Route from Hyderabad NH9 to Vijayawada via Suriapet; NH5 to Visakhapatnam via Eluru, Rajahmundry and Anakapalle (*see route guide on facing page*)

BY SHEETAL VYAS

From your perch on the golden sand, you can see the sea shining like a million diamonds all at once as the waves catch the sun's rays. It hurts to gaze at this play of lights but you find that you simply cannot look away. Ships ply to the harbour, stop and leave, hinting at busyness while you, like the spoilt holidaymaker that you actually are, merely laze around. Here at Visakhapatnam, the horizon is never empty.

Once a fishing village, Vizag, with its natural harbour, became a popular port after it was colonised by the Dutch and later the British. Today, it's known for its industrial units but the beaches have carved out their own space in the tourist itinerary. And with good reason too. The sheer number of beaches in and around Vizag means that you can pick one according to your mood or the kind of holiday you are looking for.

Ramakrishna Beach, almost in the heart of Vizag, is the busier beach, and is a favourite roosting spot for locals. Rushikonda Beach, a bit away from the city, is more rustic. Bheemli or Bheemunipatnam, 28 kilometres from Vizag, offers little by way of facilities, but more than makes up with its stunning beauty. It's the only space where you are guaranteed solitude and a chance to enjoy some of the loveliest views of the Bay of Bengal.

ORIENTATION

Tucked into the Eastern Ghats like a basin, Visakhapatnam overlooks the Bay of Bengal to the east, and is bounded by three hill ranges in the north, south and west. The **Beach Road** helps the tourist get acquainted with all the beaches at once. A scenic 28-km long stretch from **Ramakrishna Beach** (aka RK Beach) to **Bheemunipatnam**, this road hugs the eastern coast and offers a delightful seaside drive. The **harbour**, the **fisheries** and the **port** are to the south of the road and the beaches to the north. By the road are hotels and restaurants, making it a self-contained space.

Vizag is a rather compact city, and many restaurants are to be found around the **Siripuram-Dutt Island** area, while the shopping is centred around **Jagdamba Junction, Dwaraka Nagar, Asilmetta** and **Daba Gardens**.

Within the city, autos are the most convenient way to get around; they don't run on meters and the fare is best negotiated before the journey and will be upwards from a minimum of Rs 10. For

longer trips, cabs are your best bet; you can try **Sri Uma Travels** (Mobile: 09290768877, 09393664448) or **Samudrika Travels** (Tel: 0891-2569644; Mobile: 09866323975). The charges are between Rs 70 and 150 per hour, depending on the vehicle and if its AC or non-AC.

The **Andhra Pradesh Tourism Development Corporation** (APTDC) has several tours in and around Vizag. Their **Heritage Tour** (Tel: 2788820; timings: 9 am-5 pm; tour fee: Rs 245 for adults, Rs 195 for children, inclusive of lunch charges and entry ticket, exclusive of boating fees and the Simachalam Temple) is organised daily.

TIP Mani Bhushan runs a 24-hr tourist helpline; call him on 09848418582. This is a free private service that provides information and guidance

BEACH WATCH

Vizag's beaches are not safe for swimming. Undercurrents are strong and the rocks make it inadvisable to venture out. There are no lifeguards on RK Beach but Rushikonda has two marine police staffers who have saved over a 100 lives in just the past couple of years, a number that should tell you that it's best to stick to the shore. Beachwear will make you conspicuous, so we recommend that you dress conservatively.

FAST FACTS

When to go November to February

Tourist offices

- Andhra Pradesh Tourism Development Corporation
Central Reservation Office
RTC Complex, Visakhapatnam
Tel: 0891-2788820, 09848813584
Email: info@tourisminap.com
Website: tourisminap.com
- APTDC Tourist Information and Reservation Centre
Main Entrance, Railway Station
Visakhapatnam
Tel: 2788821, 09848843583

STD code 0891

THINGS TO SEE AND DO

Vizag has much to offer the tourist by way of its beaches and other attractions. Plan your itinerary according to your mood for the day — it's a luxury one can't enjoy in other destinations.

Ramakrishna Beach

This beach gets its name from the Ramakrishna Mission Ashram that's nearby. It's a busy place with snack shacks, hawkers and balloon sellers. Museums, temples and several small eateries are located near the beach, making it possible for you to enjoy the surf and the sand in the cooler hours and explore the other attractions during the day.

APTDC offers half-hour Visakha **boat rides** from the fishing harbour here (timings: 10 am-5 pm; fee: adults Rs 50, children Rs 40). There is a boat ride every hour, and the free pick-up (starting from 9.45 am and continuing at hourly intervals) and drop to the Sukh Sagar Restaurant at RK Beach offered along with it makes it a convenient option.

Museums

Matysadarshini on RK Beach is a fish aquarium that holds fascinating sea creatures from all over the world, including moray eels, puffer fish and piranha.

◆**Entry fee** Rs 20 **Timings** 9 am-9 pm

Down the road, on the beach, you'll come across a gigantic black structure, which is Asia's only **Submarine Museum**. This is actually the INS Kursura, turned into a museum so that tourists can get a rare glimpse of what a submarine looks like from inside.

Catch me if you can: A child teases the waves on Ramakrishna Beach

◆**Entry fee** Adults Rs 25, children Rs 15 **Timings** Mon-Sat 2-8.30 pm, Sun 10.30 am-12.30 pm **Cameras** Still Rs 20, video Rs 100

Still further down the road is the **Visakha Museum**, which has an eclectic collection of artefacts. A **Maritime Museum** is also located on the same premises, and provides a comprehensive view of India's naval history and defence.

◆**Entry fee** Adults Rs 5, children Rs 2 **Timings** 11 am-7 pm on weekdays, noon-8 pm on weekends, closed on Mondays

Parks and gardens

Further north on Beach Road is **VUDA Park** (entry fee Rs 3; timings: 7-9 pm), a nice place to relax during the day. Adjoining this is a good amusement park to take kids to: the **MGM Selvee World** (main gate entry fee, inclusive of free rides: adults Rs 125, children Rs 80; VUDA Park gate entry fee, inclusive of four free rides: adults Rs 50, children Rs 65).

Rushikonda Beach

Rushikonda is a much quieter and cleaner beach than RK. Pony rides are offered in the mornings and evenings, and there are usually hawkers selling coconut water, corn, cucumber and other edible delights. On the beach itself is the 14th century **Sapta Rusheswara Temple** (timings: 6 am-noon and 2-7 pm). It has seven freshwater wells that are no longer open.

Water world

APTDC offers **boat rides** in Rushikonda (timings: 9 am-5 pm; Rs 150 per ride for four persons). A lifeguard is also there on the boat. Even more exciting is a recent introduction: **sailing** (timings: 9 am-5 pm; Rs 250 per person for 30 mins), conducted by the **Yachting Association of Vizag** (Mobile: 09848235793).

As part of these sailing expeditions, experienced sailors take enthusiasts out into the sea in Hobies, small fibreglass catamarans that can carry four people,

and teach them the finer points of the sport. The association also conducts week-long camps to teach sailing. Do remember that boating and sailing facilities are available subject to local weather and wind conditions.

SHOPPING

Vizag has good quality cashew nuts that visitors like to take home. Stop at **Nuts and Fruits** on Tycoon Junction and pick up a kilo for Rs 250-350. Also popular are the products of the **Girijan Cooperative Society**, located opposite VUDA Park. They have organic produce, amla and soapnut powder and their honey is particularly good (Rs 189 per kilo). It will be worth your time to check out shops such as **Kalaniketan** in Dwaraka Nagar and **Kankatala Silk Palace** and **Chandana Bros** at Jagdamba Junction. All these have good sari collections. **CMR Shopping Mall** at Jagdamba Centre is a six-floor complex where you will find articles you didn't know you needed.

For handicrafts, there is the government-run **Lepakshi Emporium** at Jagdamba Junction, which showcases all the crafts of Andhra Pradesh. **Kalasrusti** on Beach Road, near Matsyadarshini, also sells handicrafts.

→ GETTING THERE

Air Visakhapatnam Airport (15 km/ 30 mins) has flights from Mumbai, Kolkata, Chennai and Hyderabad. There are no pre-paid cabs at the airport but private taxis are plentiful. Fares are about Rs 250-400 into town

Rail Visakhapatnam Central Railway Station has daily connections from Hyderabad and Howrah. It's served by Dakshin Express from Delhi, Konark Express from Mumbai and the Mail and Coramandel Express from Chennai

Road Vizag is located on NH5 and is linked directly to Vijayawada, Chennai, Bhubaneswar and Kolkata. It's also well-connected to Hyderabad. APSRTC (Tel: 040-64528352, 64504352; Mobile: 09246534352, 09290150111) runs buses daily from Hyderabad. Private operators such as Kesineni Tours and Travels (Tel: 040-23232459/ 23420230) and Sri Kaleswari Travels (Tel: 23244799/ 23279380; Mobile: 09848497681) also run Volvo buses on this route

WHERE TO STAY

The tourist has two options in Vizag. One is to stay in the city, which ensures easy access to hotels, restaurants and shopping areas, and the other is to be near Rushikonda, where there are interesting stay options with good sea views.

On RK Beach

Heading the list of luxury accommodation is **The Park** (Tel: 0891-2754488; Tariff: Rs 3,800-7,000), a charming hotel on the beach. With 61 attractive sea-facing rooms, it's elegant and quiet. Nearer RK Beach centre is **Taj Residency** (Tel: 2567756; Tariff: Rs 3,800-9,000), tailored to suit the business traveller. Across the road is **Grand Bay** (Tel: 2560101; Tariff: Rs 3,800-9,000), which too faces the sea. This is quite an opulent, bustling hotel with three restaurants.

Among the mid-range stay options is **Palm Beach** (Tel: 2754026; Tariff: Rs 2,650-3,550), located on the beach but appearing somewhat run-down. The rooms, however, are a pleasant surprise, as they are squeaky clean and quite attractively done up.

Among the budget options, easily the best option on Beach Road is **Hotel Supreme** (Tel: 2782472; Tariff: Rs 700-2,000). A little beyond the 'up-market' part of RK Beach, this is a new hotel,

When I grow up, I'll become a mermaid: A child on a beach at Bheemunipatnam

clean and offering good value for money. About 6 km from the main part of the RK Beach, along Beach Road, is APTDC's **Haritha Hotel** (Tel: 2788824; Tariff: Rs 800-1,600). Although the rooms are tolerably clean, the views aren't great.

On Rushikonda

Stay options near Rushikonda are all mid-range, but there are budget guest houses that dot the entire route. Located at Sagar Nagar is the **Senora Beach Club** (Tel: 2723666; Tariff: Rs 1,000-1,200). It has only five rooms that don't offer good views. Senora's particular advantage, however, is the Sagar Nagar Beach, with its pristine sands, just down a path.

Overlooking Rushikonda Beach is another APTDC property, the **Haritha Beach Resort** (Tel: 2788826; Tariff: Rs 1,500-2,500). Laid out in a long line along the hillside, this resort is worth it for the view alone. The rooms are fairly clean. On the beach is **Sai Priya Beach Resort** (Tel: 2790333; Tariff: Rs 605-6,600), a sprawling place with rooms and cottages spaced out well. The bathrooms are not clean, and the service is tardy. Again, the seaside location is what makes up for this; a tree house gives an up, close and personal view of the beach.

In and around Vizag

Opposite the Collector's Office, overlooking a busy street, is **Lodge Sagar** (Tel: 2526397; Tariff: Rs 200-600), a popular old-fashioned hostelry. It's acceptably clean, with brisk, efficient service.

In a narrow road off Beach Road near the Collectorate is **Jaabily Beach Inn** (Tel: 2706026; Tariff: Rs 400-995), popular with the Bengali traveller. This is, however, a dimly lit place. Not on the beach but close enough to count is **Hotel Daspalla** (Tel: 2564825; Tariff: Rs 1,350-3,000) in Suryabagh. It has several excellent restaurants and the rooms are fairly tidy, if rather unimaginatively laid out.

The Eagle Hill

DINESH SHUKLA

After Uttar Pradesh and Bihar, Andhra Pradesh has the most number of Buddhist monuments in India. As many as 140 Buddhist sites have been found in the state so far. Between the 3rd century BCE and 7th century CE, Mauryan, Satavahana and Ikshavaku rulers of the region offered patronage to Buddhists and the religion flourished. Visakhapatnam, being close to the Kalinga of yore, also came under the influence of Buddhism.

One of the most enduring marks of that time is to be seen in **Thottlakonda**, a hilltop 15 km from Visakhapatnam on the way to Bheemli (*see page 70*). It was from this now-sleepy village of **Bheemunipatnam** that Buddhism spread to Sri Lanka and parts of South-East Asia, through the maritime trade conducted from this port. Thottlakonda is a monastery complex with several rock-cut troughs, called *thotti* in Telugu, which have given the hill its present name. The Buddhists, however, called it **Syenagiri**, or the Eagle Hill. You realise why they called it thus only from a few kilometres away, when you look back and see the hill. With two flat planes sloping away, it appears like an eagle.

For more hotels and details, see Visakhapatnam Accommodation Listings on pages 524-525

WHERE TO EAT

The luxury hotels on Beach Road all have restaurants that are popular with locals as well as tourists, and all are good for a fancy meal. The Park's **Vista**, a 70-seater glass affair, serves everything from Indian to Italian while Grand Bay's **Dakshin** offers authentic South Indian cuisine. The Taj Residency's **Ming Garden**, with its fine Schezwan fare, as well as its coffee shop **Stir**, have excellent ambience and good food.

Among the relatively cheaper options, the four restaurants at **Hotel Daspalla** at Suryabagh are the most popular. They are known for their South Indian meals and spicy Andhra non-vegetarian specialities. Also popular are **Hotel Tycoon** for Chinese food and **Heritage** for South Indian fare. Both are in Siripuram.

Fusion Foods, opposite VUDA complex in Siripuram, has a coffee shop and a multi-cuisine restaurant, which is just a touch shabby but the biryanis are justly famous.

At Dutt Island is a clutch of eateries that are extremely good. **Dhaba Express** with its all-Punjabi menu is superb; do try their ginger-mint appetisers. Down the stairs from there are **Kebabri** with a decent kebab menu and **Pastries, Coffee & Conversation**, known for its brownies. **Southern Spice**, attached to Hotel Green Park on Waltair Main Road, has interesting buffets and thalis.

For South Indian tiffins and local specialities, you couldn't do better than go to the inexpensive **Sri Sairam Parlour** at Dwaraka Nagar. They serve a range of breakfast tiffins — piping hot uthappams, tomato *baath* and dosas.

On Beach Road, the roadside eatery **Windy's** is good for snacks and refreshments. Next to that is **Spudds**, with its kebabs and non-vegetarian fare, open for dinner. For street food, head to the **Rajasthani Brothers** at the Pandurangapuram entrance; they serve utterly divine pav bhaji.

Explore a new highway. Search for a forgotten town. Find a new destination. Just hit the road with Speed, the high performance petrol and you will experience greater pick up, smoother drive and superior performance. Speed gives you the confidence to take on the road. Tank up, and head out. The whole of India is waiting for you.
Speed
High Performance Petrol
INDIA
3.38 million Kms Road Network
Bharat Petroleum
Take the first Road out.
To go places log on to www.speedfuels.com
SAATCHI & SAATCHI-147B/2007 M

SURAJ SHARMA/ DINODIA PHOTO LIBRARY

Golden glow: As the sun sets, fishermen head home at Visakhapatnam

AROUND VISAKHAPATNAM

Bheemunipatnam (27 km)
Situated at the mouth of the Gosthani River, Bheemunipatnam or Bheemli is a sleepy fishing village to the north-east of Vizag. It was once a Dutch settlement and still retains marks of that occupation. Next to the beach is a small 17th century Dutch cemetery. Also seen here is a lighthouse built by the Dutch. It's one of the eight **lighthouses** located along the Andhra coast between Kakinada and Srikakulam.

Bheemli has two other places of archaeological and religious interest: one is the **Narasimha Swami Temple**, a 12th century structure located almost at the village entrance. The other is **Bheemeswaralayam**, a cluster of 13 temples, each of which were constructed by different rulers and as a result, bear their distinctive styles. This temple compound is in the heart of the village. On the Vizag-Bheemli route, just about a couple of kilometres short of the village, you will find what the locals call the **Erramatti Dibbalu**. This geological curiosity comprises of vast and imposing hillocks made of red mud, and a walk here can be a fascinating experience.

Bheemli's untouched golden beaches are a revelation. These are generous expanses of sand, dotted with swaying palms. If the beaches haven't been 'discovered' as yet, it's because there is no place to stay in Bheemli. There are no restaurants or public toilets either.

You can grab a meal at the several tiffin centres near the town centre, but if you are picky, it's best to pack a meal from Vizag.

Cabs are a convenient mode of transport to reach Bheemli (Rs 500-800 inclusive of an hour's waiting charges, or Rs 70-150 per hour), and particularly worth it if you're planning to move around a bit. Autos charge about Rs 120-150 and share-autos are also available from Appu Ghar in Vizag for Rs 10-15 per person. ■

TAMIL NADU

P RAVI KUMAR

CHENNAI

COME HERE FOR THE SEA

■ BY TISHANI DOSHI

For as long as I can remember, Sundays have always been 'Beach Days', involving long drives, sun, salt, sand and copious amounts of food. Growing up in the early '80s in Madras, there were few diversions for children — no videogame parlours or bouncing castles or cartoon channels. We had our imaginations, sure, but when they lapsed or wilted from the humidity of the midsummer sun, there was always the sea — the vast, open-armed Bay of Bengal.

On Sunday evenings, after a day of running about with my cousins, my family would gear up in our Sunday best and head for **Marina Beach**. There, we'd ride Ferris wheels and painted wooden horses; feed our faces with neon pink candyfloss, corn on the cob and chilli groundnuts; stand by the shore in our frilly birthday cake frocks and gingerly dip our toes into the warm, dark water. We'd count the ships lined up for the harbour, look for phosphorescence and shooting stars, and try to see all the way to Sri Lanka.

Those were magical nights. But the beach in Madras (now Chennai) was only ever real for me when I was allowed to swim. Some Sundays, my family would decide to go further down the coast to spend the entire day at the beach. We'd pack the car with a picnic and drive to **Elliot's Beach** (which was deserted in those days), or **Fisherman's Cove** (*see page 83*), or **Silver Sands**. It used to feel like we were driving to the end of the universe for my sister and I, who had to suffer each other's presence in the backseat, squabbling like rats in a cage, dying to be let out in our bathing suits so we could jump into the waves.

I remember once being carried out very far into the ocean. I felt like a leaf bobbing around in a gale. My parents were standing like two matchsticks on the shore, screaming at me to swim back to shore. It was the first time I experienced real fear in my life.

When the tsunami hit our coast in December 2004, I heard this very same fear echo in every story of loss that I listened to. In some strange way, as residents of this city, the sea had bound us all together. So, the shock of listening to stories of people who had lost family members or their homes or their means of livelihood, while it was overwhelming and heartbreaking, was not quite the same shock that the sea had given us. The sea, who had always been our friend, had now turned on us, incomprehensibly.

People who spend their lives by the sea allow it to mark them in stages. Most of my memories begin and end with the sea. I have walked down the entire length of Marina Beach with my first love, hand in hand, past the many statues, memorials and parks that dot the way. I have sat on my terrace as a moody adolescent, watching the sea float like a teardrop between apartment buildings. I have scattered the remains of my young dead uncle into the sea on a grey November day. I have sat on the parapet of Elliot's Beach with my mentor and friend, the late Chandralekha, watching the moonrise, buying jasmine, talking of love.

At the heart of it, a city with a sea is built for romance in a way that no landlocked city can be. It's filled with countless possibilities: comings and goings, beginnings and endings. It allows you to reinvent yourself whenever you like, to pick up and go, and most importantly, to return whenever you need to. It's filled with transformations. Don't believe me? Go park yourself at Marina Beach for a day and see how it changes every hour. See how the early mornings belong to the walkers and the laughing clubs, the fishermen and body-builders. See how in the early afternoon it will appear as vast as a desert, isolated and bereft — the sea lies like a forlorn metal sheet in the horizon. By evening, when the sea breeze begins to set in, watch how it comes alive with fairground bustle: Romeos and Juliets, families and frilly frocks, geriatrics and gents — all packing the promenade, all coming here to reaffirm this idea of possibility.

And so I tell anyone who complains about Madras for its conservatism or slowness or lack of architectural prowess, I say to them, don't come here for any of these things. Come here for the sea. Sunday or not, if you allow yourself to swim until your skin prunes and browns, and your body and hair are filled with salt, you will sleep the sweetest sleep in the world. And what could be more precious than that?

THE INFORMATION

State Tamil Nadu
Location Chennai stretches 19 km along the Coromandel Coast, divided by the two east-flowing rivers of Cooum and Adyar
Distances 162 km NE of Pondicherry, 331 km E of Bangalore
Journey time *By road* 3 hrs from Pondicherry, 7 hrs from Bangalore
Route from Bangalore NH4 to Chennai via Kolar, Chittoor, Ranipettai, Sriperumbudur and Poonamallee **Route from Pondicherry** East Coast Road Expressway to Chennai via Mammallapuram and Covelong (*see route guide on facing page*)

ORIENTATION

Chennai extends north to south along the Bay of Bengal. **Anna Salai** or Mount Road is the arterial road. To the north are the **Central** and **Egmore railway stations**, from where trains depart for destinations within Tamil Nadu and outside. Chennai has excellent city buses. Express buses (these have yellow boards) are slightly costlier but emptier and faster. Autorickshaws don't ply to meters and drivers overcharge outrageously. Do not pay more than Rs 9-10 per km. A pleasanter option is the costlier but meter-compliant call taxi (Rs 50 for the first 3 km, Rs 10 per km thereafter). **Bharati Call Taxi** (Tel: 044-2814 2233), **Chennai Call Taxi** (Tel: 25384455) and **Fast Track** (Tel: 24732020) are among the most prominent services. The beaches fall to the south of Chennai.

BEACH WATCH

There are no lifeguards at Marina and Elliot beaches. There are, however, "beach policemen", who ride horses and keep an eye on people at both the beaches.

WHERE TO STAY

None of the main hotels in Chennai offers a sea view. However, several are located only a kilometre or two from the beach. The 5-star hotels, with tariffs starting at Rs 5,000 plus tax, include: **Taj Coromandel** (Tel: 044-66002827; Tariff: Rs 9,500-40,000), about 7 km from

THE INFORMATION

SRIKANTH KOLARI

V MUTHURAMAN

A girl walks the tightrope on Marina Beach (left); **the Egmore Railway Station**

Marina Beach, on Mahatma Gandhi Road, Nungambakkam; **Taj Connemara** (Tel: 66000000; Tariff: Rs 10,500-30,000) on Binny Road, 4 km from Marina Beach; **Sheraton Chola** (Tel: 28110101; Tariff: Rs 9,000-12,000) on Cathedral Road, 2 km from Marina Beach; **Le Royal Meridien** (Tel: 22314343; Tariff: Rs 12,500-40,000) on GST Road, St Thomas Mount, about 9 km from Elliot Beach; **Park Sheraton & Towers**, also known as Adyar Gate Hotel (Tel: 24994101; Tariff: Rs 11,000-35,000), 4 km from Marina and Elliot on TTK Road; and **The Raintree Ecotel Hotel** (Tel: 42252525; Tariff: Rs 6,000-13,000) on St Mary's Road, Alwarpet, 4 km from Elliot Beach.

Close to Marina Beach and Mylapore and around 5 km from Central Station is Radhakrishnan Salai, with a string of middle-range hotels. **New Woodlands Hotel** (Tel: 28113111; Tariff: Rs 750-5,760) is clean and comfortable, though the rooms are not as luxurious as you would expect in a 3-star hotel. It's 2 km from Marina Beach.

Hotel President (Tel: 28472211; Tariff: Rs 1,200-3,500), about 1 km from Marina Beach, is yet another old hotel with clean rooms and a good location. But you will have to arm yourself with mosquito repellents. **Hotel Nilgiri's Nest** (Tel: 28115111; Tariff: Rs 1,700-2,950), right opposite Woodlands, has clean and comfortable but dimly lit rooms.

Further down, on Kodambakkam High Road, is **Hotel Palmgrove** (Tel: 28271881; Tariff: Rs 900-2,600), about 6 km from Marina Beach. The rooms are clean but the hotel rents out its premises to noisy wedding parties, which may not suit a guest who wants quiet, and easy parking. **Quality Inn Sabari** (Tel: 28343030; Tariff: Rs 3,200-4,500) in T Nagar, about 6 km from Marina Beach, offers luxurious, tasteful and comfortable rooms. **The Residency** (Tel: 28253434; Tariff: Rs 2,700-5,000) in T Nagar is popular, with pleasing rooms, a Chinese restaurant, a multi-cuisine restaurant and a 24-hr coffee shop. **The Chariot** (Tel: 28341212; Tariff: Rs 1,800-3,200) has spotless rooms. The hotel is centrally located; it's 10 km from Elliot Beach.

For more hotels and details, see Chennai Accommodation Listings on pages 565-566

WHERE TO EAT

From functional and easy-on-the-pocket eateries to luxury options, Chennai has many places where you can enjoy South Indian food. There are also restaurants that serve Lebanese, Korean, Japanese, Mexican, Italian, Continental and Thai fare.

Karaikudi on Radhakrishnan Salai (branch at Second Avenue, Besant Nagar) is a good option for Chettinad cuisine. So is the **Banana Leaf**, near Vannandurai in Besant Nagar. Also check out the plump *medu vadai* (spiced black gram dal dough deep fried) and sublime sambhar at **Vishranthi**, a roadside

THE INFORMATION

eatery on Second Avenue. **Annalakshmi** on Mount Road (near Higginbothams) has a divine Tamil vegetarian thali that is served by volunteers of the charitable organisation that runs the place. For more of authentic Tamil fare, there's **Dakshin** restaurant at the Park Sheraton. For the Tamil eating-out experience, there is the **Saravana Bhavan** chain of 'high quality vegetarian food' restaurants spread all over the town. Try the multi-course meal styled buffet at **Swayam**, part of the Saravana outlet on Peters Road — excellent variety at a reasonable price (Rs 100 per head). **Vasantha Bhavan** and **Sangeetha's** are the competitors. The die-hard Madrasi street eateries are the **Military Hotels**, often grubby, but said to serve authentic non-vegetarian Madras curry.

Amethyst is a shop, a gallery and a cafeteria set in the charming 100-year-old Sundara Mahal, a former palace of the Jeypore princes located at Gopalapuram.

The **Grand Sweets and Snacks** in Gandhi Nagar, Adayar, is a must-visit for superlative sweets and savouries. **Sri Krishna Sweets'** *mysorpak* (gram flour sweet) is scrumptious. SKS has branches all over the city, in Gandhi Nagar, Cathedral Road, T Nagar, and one at the airport. Its best setting is at Purasawalkam, a renovated 120-year-old house. The **Adayar Ananda Bhavan** is another place to head for South Indian goodies. **Suswaad**, near Eloor Library in T Nagar, serves the best *jaangri* (black gram dal sweetmeat), besides a crunchy *manoharam* (gram flour crackers dipped in jaggery) and a highly recommended low-fat savoury 'mixture'.

Enjoying a meal at a restaurant

G SIVAPERUMAL

AROUND CHENNAI

At **Muttukadu**, backwaters merge with the blue-grey waters of the Bay of Bengal, a scenic setting that plays host to several boating opportunities. The Tamil Nadu Tourism Development Corporation (TTDC) organises boating trips on these backwaters. The motorboat fare is between Rs 220 and 275 for a 20-min ride. The charge is Rs 400 for a 10-seater deluxe motorboat. For rowboats, the charge is about Rs 80 for a 30-min spin and for pedal boats, between Rs 60 and 100.

◆**Timings** 9 am-6 pm **Cameras** Still Rs 5, video Rs 25 **Connection** Muttukadu falls on the East Coast Road from Chennai and can be visited while travelling to Mammallapuram (*see page 79*) as well. The most convenient mode of transport is taxi or bus. A cab costs about Rs 500 for a return trip from Chennai

FAST FACTS

When to go October to January is pleasant **Tourist office** Dept of Tourism, Govt of Tamil Nadu, Tourism Complex, 2, Wallajah Road, Chennai **Tel** 044-25368358, 25360294 **Website** tamilnadutourism.org **STD code** 044

GETTING THERE

Air Kamaraj (domestic) and Anna (international) airports, both at Meenambakkam (16 km), are connected to all major destinations in India and abroad. Pre-paid taxi costs about Rs 200-250 into town

Rail Chennai is well-connected to the rest of the country and has three major railway stations, Chennai Central, Chennai Egmore and Tambaram Station

Road Chennai has excellent highway connections to Kolkata, Bangalore, Trichy, Hyderabad and Pondicherry, the last by the scenic East Coast Road Expressway ■

Inputs by
Jaya Madhavan and Vinita Nayar

WRIJU/ PHOTOINDIA

MAMMALLAPURAM

FLOATING ON WATER

State Tamil Nadu
Location On the Coromandel Coast in Kanchipuram District, in north-east Tamil Nadu
Distance 58 km S of Chennai
Journey time ***By road*** $1^1/_2$ hrs from Chennai
Route from Chennai East Coast Road to Mammallapuram via Thiruvanmiyur, Uthandi and Covelong (*see route guide on page 74*)

BY VAISHNA ROY

I am aimlessly floating on water, some 5 km from the shore. The water is deliciously cold, the sun's rays are just beginning to turn golden, the waves lift me up and set me down gently, and fishes swim curiously by... I can do this forever. I am in a life jacket, a catamaran is anchored close at hand, there's no sound except that of the crashing waves, and in the distance I can see the faint familiar silhouette of the Shore Temple emerging from the hazy morning mist. This is Mahabalipuram, or Mammallapuram as it's officially known, at its very best.

Although most famous for its Pallava period rock sculptures, the World Heritage Site of Mammallapuram is also a great destination for a beach holiday, and has all the essential ingredients — sea, sand, sun, souvenirs and seafood. It's easy to reach — drive just over 50 km from Chennai and you are in this outpost of peace. There are many cheap lodges and hotels, but if your aim is to spoil yourself, then there are plenty of luxurious beach resorts here that you can check into.

There are some dangerous currents in the sea here, so swim close to the shore or paddle in the shallow parts. You can indulge in the sand all you wish — pick shells, build castles in the sand or in the air as you soak in the sun. It's too hot to be outdoors in the day, but there's plenty to do in and around Mammallapuram. The shops here are fun to browse in; there are clothes, footwear, stone and bead jewellery plus some fabulous stoneware on sale. Many of the resorts offer luxurious massages and beauty treatments, and it's a great way to unwind, especially when you can top it off with a snooze on the beach. For action-lovers, there's fishing or catamaran rides in the sea; for the rest, it's a lazy holiday.

ORIENTATION

Stretching for over 20 km along the Bay of Bengal, the Mammallapuram Coast is considered among the most pristine of Tamil Nadu's beaches and a dramatically picturesque one at that. The town itself is small and chaotic, with several lodges, restaurants and souvenir shops. Most monuments, shops, hotels and restaurants are within a 5-km radius, and autorickshaws (minimum fare Rs 20) are a convenient mode of transport, but bargaining is a must. It's easier and cheaper to hire a bicycle (Rs 50 per day) or a motorbike (Rs 200 per day) from the numerous rental places all around town. Most of the resorts have their own private beaches, but backpackers will have to find their own secluded patches of sand with the help of local guides.

The **bus stop** is in the middle of town, on **East Raja Street**, and there are frequent buses to Chennai, Pondicherry and other major towns. Resorts, restaurants, guest houses and curio shops are all north of the bus stand, on lanes leading east to the beach, off East Raja Street.

→ FAST FACTS

When to go November to February

Tourist office

- Department of Tourism

District Tourism Development Officer
Mammallapuram, Kanchipuram District
Tel: 044-27442232

STD code 044

BEACH WATCH

The waters on this stretch are fairly treacherous, so be very careful if you are not a strong swimmer. At the time of writing, there were no lifeguards on this stretch of beach but that could soon be rectified, as the **Rashtriya Life Saving Society** is in the process of setting up 'safe havens' here. As long as you are within the premises of a resort, the employees will warn you of currents and tides. Also, within the resorts you can get away with the skimpiest of swimwear.

THINGS TO SEE AND DO

Your time at the beach will have to be restricted to early mornings and evenings because the sun gets blazing hot from about 9 am onwards. In fact, even sightseeing in Mammallapuram is best kept for evenings and early mornings.

On the beach

Mammallapuram doesn't exactly seem at first glance to be a town by the sea. Except for the Shore Temple dramatically perched on the sands, the other monuments here are set more inland. Not until you clamber up the rocks do you get a great view of the coastline. The beach next to the Shore Temple is colourful, with picnickers and stalls.

Note There's a Rs 20 vehicle entry fee into the town, and a parking fee of Rs 5,

S SATISH KUMAR

The World Heritage site of Shore Temple, Mammallapuram's most famous landmark

for the parking lots at the Shore Temple and the Five Rathas

The heritage trail

The big attractions in Mammallapuram are its temples. This town was once one of the most important ports of the Pallava kings, who ruled between the 6th and 8th centuries. The temples were built largely during the reigns of Narasimhavarman Pallava (600 CE) and his successor Raja Simhavarman (780 CE), and it was in their time that the art of monolithic sculpture reached its pinnacle. Broadly, the sculptures of Mammallapuram can be classified as rock-cut caves, monoliths, structural temples, and bas reliefs, and there are superb examples of each here.

The **Shore Temple** is Mammallapuram's most famous landmark. Many of the carvings on its outer walls have been eaten away by wind and water in the 1,000 years that it has stood here, but what remains is still stunning.

One of the most beautiful works, though, is the bas relief of **The Descent of Ganga**, also popularly called **Arjuna's Penance**, located in the middle of the town. Measuring 27m by 9m, it's the largest bas relief in the world, and a wonderful example of rock art.

The next landmark is the **Pancha Ratham** or the Five Chariots, a cluster of mandapas built in five different styles of temple architecture, a kilometre south of Arjuna's Penance. Popular legend associates these temples with the Pandavas, but historians say these monolithic structures could have been intended as blueprints of temple art across the country.

There are also several **cave temples** to various gods and goddesses. The most prominent among them is the cave with a carving of Lord Krishna holding up the Govardhan Mountain and the Mandapa to Vishnu in the Varaha avatar.

◆**Entry fee** Indians Rs 10, foreigners Rs 250, ticket valid for Shore Temple and Rathas; entry elsewhere is free **Timings** 6.30 am-5.45 pm, open daily **Cameras** Still free, video Rs 25 **Illumination timings** Sunset-8 pm

The **Mahabalipuram Dance Festival** (December 25 to January 31), performed each year against the dramatic backdrop of Arjuna's Penance, showcases dances from across India. For schedules and tickets, contact the Tourism Department (*see Fast Facts on page 80*).

SHOPPING

The best thing to buy in Mammallapuram is stoneware. You can pick up beautiful statues here. Ganesha, Nataraja and Nandi icons are popular, as are temple dancers, tortoises, elephants and deer. The material used ranges from soft soapstone to cuddapah, granite and marble.

→ GETTING THERE

Air Nearest airport: Chennai (58 km/ 1½ hrs), connected by flights from all over the country. Taxi to Mammallapuram costs approx Rs 500

Rail Nearest railhead: Chennai; technically, the nearest railway station is Chengalpattu, which is about 25 km from Mammallapuram, but it's not a good option for tourists. Only local trains from Chennai stop here. Besides, the road journey from the state capital is far quicker. At Chennai, buses to Mammallapuram start from the bus stand close to the railway station; taxis are also available at the station

Road It's a smooth, lovely drive on the East Coast Road from Chennai to Mammallapuram via Thiruvanmiyur, Uthandi and Covelong. From Thiruvanmiyur, you can also head to Mamamallapuram via Padur, Kelambakkam, Tirupporur and Punjeri. Buses leave every 30 mins between 5.30 am and 10.30 pm for Mammallapuram from Chennai's Mofussil Bus Terminus at Koyambedu. Tickets start at Rs 30

You can also order customised images, which you can pick up or have delivered to your home address. Prices range from Rs 60 for the small ones to Rs 300-500 for statues about a foot high to Rs 1,500-2,500 for 3 to 4 ft tall ones, to several thousands for the large ones. You also get pretty stone lockets with carved faces for as little as Rs 10, not to forget incense holders, ashtrays, bowls, lampshades and pen-stands, all exquisitely carved.

Cheap leather footwear is available all over the place, but beware of cardboard soles. A safer bet is to buy straw flip-flops with colourful straps for Rs 100. And, of course, Mammallapuram is famous for its shell ornaments — from shell curtains and jewellery to table lamps and mirrors. Don't miss the gypsy women who sell really lovely beads and baubles. Bargain like fun everywhere.

WHERE TO STAY

A row of luxury resorts starts just before you reach Mammallapuram and extends all the way into the town. There are also many cheaper lodges and hotels in the town itself.

Off East Coast Road (ECR)

Located on the East Coast Road, in Devaneri, **Golden Sun** (Tel: 044-27442245-46; Tariff: Rs 1,450-2,800) has a pool, shopping arcades and a health club. **Ideal Beach Resort** (Tel: 27442240; Tariff: Rs 1,850-6,000) is slightly more luxurious, with beauty parlours and home theatres. They also provide beach-side services such as sunscreen, towels, snacks and drinks.

The **Mamalla Beach Resort** (Tel: 27442375/ 475; Tariff: Rs 1,300-1,750), also on ECR, is possibly the best value-for-money resort in this stretch, with its spacious, air-conditioned rooms, courteous service, swimming pool and several other amenities. Next door is **Hotel Tamil Nadu** (Tel: 27442361-63; Tariff: Rs 500-2,500), the TTDC beach resort, which has a swimming pool and bar.

Courtesy FISHERMAN'S COVE

Courtesy FISHERMAN'S COVE

FISHERMAN'S COVE: Luxury by the sea

BY VAISHNA ROY

Located 22 km north of Mammallapuram, Fisherman's Cove is a Taj resort on a stretch of pristine, private beach called Covelong, once the site of a Dutch trading settlement. In fact, the resort itself is built on the remains of a Dutch fort, although little is left of this except an armoury. One of the older establishments on this stretch, Fisherman's Cove looks ordinary from the outside, and there's little to suggest that it boasts of a fabulous stretch of sea and sand. That is until you get to the cottages, which are dramatically located on the seaside, with gardens leading to the beach. The rooms that offer sea views are good, of course, but pale beside these.

Once you check in, you can opt to spend the entire day at the beach — if you don't find the heat overwhelming, that is. For, there's plenty to do, from beach volleyball to beach cricket, football and kite-flying. Or else, you can go horse-riding or cycling on the sands (Rs 100 and Rs 500 per hour respectively), or take a boat trip on the backwaters (Rs 200 per head). For the more adventurous, there is deep-sea fishing, an experience that was an unqualified disaster in my case because I realised rather late that I could not handle the sight of dying fish. I had to head back to the shore, much to the disgust of the fishermen who took me out in their boat.

What I did love most was the absolutely amazing catamaran ride, a freaky but fun experience that's easily the nicest thing to do in the Bay of Bengal. A catamaran is a flimsy looking affair created by tying a few logs together. You get in, with a life jacket on, and hold on to a long rope for dear life. After the first oh-my-god moments, it's pure bliss, especially when they dump you into the water somewhere in the middle of the sea and you can float forever.

Indoors, the resort's reception lounge is rather interesting — it has been created as a pleasant informal space, with a pool table bang in the middle and a glass library leading off it, and you always find guests wandering in and out. The atmosphere here, as a result, is friendly and light.

The resort has done a nice job with **Upper Deck**, the newest restaurant on the beach. Tables are laid out in the open, the cuisine is Mediterranean with some excellent wine, and a sharp sea breeze adds an edge to your hunger. Then, there's **Seagull**, a coffee shop-cum-multi-cuisine restaurant that lays out an excellent breakfast buffet. There's also **Sunken Bar**, a poolside place with great cocktails and views.

♦**Tel** 044-67413333 **Tariff** Rs 10,000-16,000 (*for details, see page 568*) **Note** Boating and other activities are available for non-guests only on advance notice, but the restaurants are open to all **Connection** From Chennai, it's a 40 km/ 1 hr drive on the ECR; non-AC taxis charge about Rs 600. From Mammallapuram, taxis charge Rs 250-300 for the 30-min drive ■

GRT Temple Bay (Tel: 27443636; Tariff: Rs 7,000-14,000) is a superb luxury resort at the entrance to the town, on Covalam Road. Its chalets and rooms offer breathtaking sea views, and the kitchen is excellent. The resort arranges fishing trips and boat rides.

In Mammallapuram

Sterling Mahabalipuram (Tel: 044-24984114; Tariff: Rs 2,200-5,000) has a charming restaurant and lovely antiques in its lobby, all of which make this resort, located close to the Shore Temple, quite unique. **Mamalla Heritage Hotel** (Tel: 27442260; Tariff: Rs 1,250-1,500) has two restaurants, a pool and AC rooms and is located on South Mada Street. **Mahabs Inn** (Tel: 27442643-45; Tariff: Rs 1,200-1,500) has two entrances, one close to the bus stand and another near the Shore Temple, and a restaurant.

Of the many budget options clustered along Othavadai Street, **Tina Blue View Lodge** (Tel: 27442319; Tariff: Rs 200-500) is popular. Also on Othavadai Street is **Uma Guesthouse** (Tel: 27442697; Rs 200-900), which has both AC and non-AC rooms.

One for the camera at Mammallapuram

RAKESH SAHAI/ AGP PHOTOBANK

For more hotels and details, see Mammallapuram Accommodation Listings on pages 567-568

WHERE TO EAT

The restaurants here are rightly famous for their seafood. Try the fish fry, the prawn and crab curries, and the *calamari* or squid dishes. There are also places that serve South Indian staples such as idli, dosa and pongal. Most places in the tourist quarter are geared up to serve Continental dishes, and main courses are accompanied by potato and vegetables, or rice. Most places serve beer, although only the resort restaurants have full-fledged bars. All places close by 11 pm.

The Wharf is part of the upmarket Temple Bay resort, stunningly located on the beachside, and specialises in seafood. There's a limited vegetarian menu. All dishes come with a complimentary basket of breads, both Indian and Western, vegetable pulao and dal. There's an open kitchen where you can watch your prawn being grilled or marinate your seer fish yourself before putting it into the tandoor. **Pongamiya** is part of the Sterling Resort; try the garlic fish fry with *kal* dosa (a soft, thick, white dosa) in this airy restaurant built around a tree.

Blue Elephant on Othavadai Street is a favourite with foreigners. It serves a mean masala fish fry and tiger prawns. **Moonraker**, located right opposite and run by the same family, has almost the same menu but is roomier and has an AC section. Both places serve fruit juices and lassi.

New Café is a cosy balcony restaurant on the first floor of Lakshmi Lodge, also on Othavadai Street. They serve a limited but well-cooked menu. Try the banana fritters here — they are yummy.

Luna Magica and **Seashore** are both beach shacks famous for their seafood. The former has a fish tank with live lobsters and prawns. **Ananda Bhavan** serves a good South Indian thali. ■

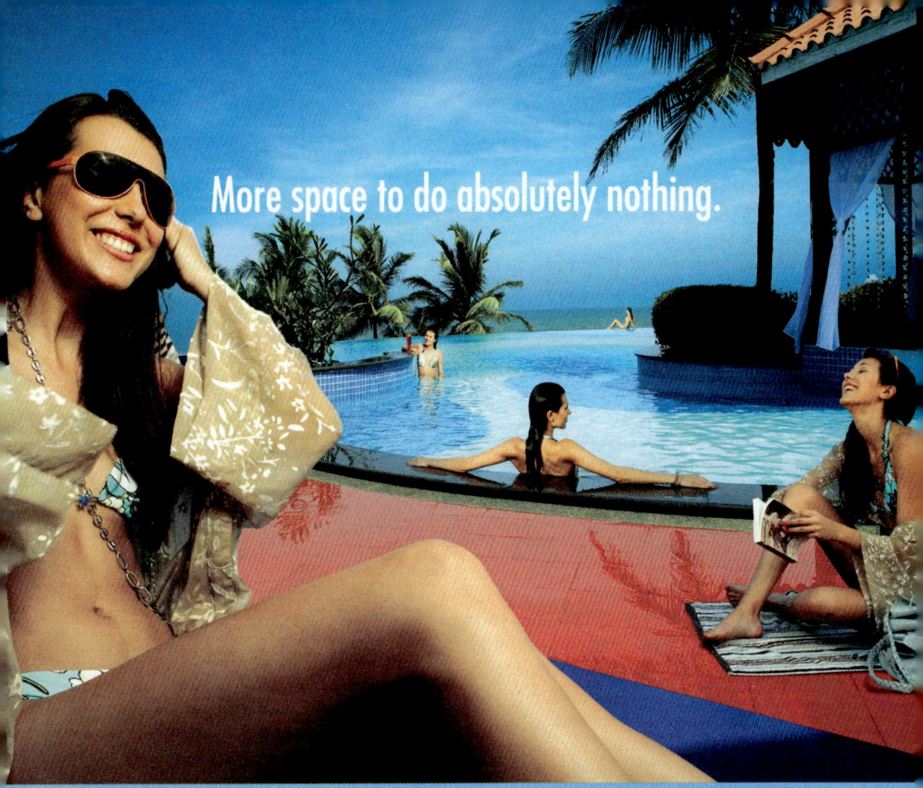
More space to do absolutely nothing.

KANYAKUMARI

TIP OF THE WORLD

State Tamil Nadu
Location The southernmost tip of India, Kanyakumari is a seaside town that sits at the very edge of the Indian peninsula, where the three oceans, the Indian Ocean, the Arabian Sea and the Bay of Bengal meet
Distances 87 km SE of Thiruvananthapuram, 359 km SW of Trichy, 691 km SW of Chennai
Journey time *By road* 2 hrs from Thiruvananthapuram, 8 hrs from Trichy, 14 hrs from Chennai
Route from Chennai NH45 to Trichy via Chengalpattu, Tindivanam and Viluppuram; NH45B to Madurai via Melur; NH7 to Kanyakumari via Virudunagar, Kovilpatti and Thirunelveli **Route from Thiruvananthapuram** NH47 to Kanyakumari via Padmanabhapuram and Nagercoil (*see route guide on page 74*)

■ **BY VAISHNA ROY**

If you are going to pack snorkel and spade and get all excited about going to the beach, then you are in for a letdown because that's not what Kanyakumari is about. If, on the other hand, you decide to travel to the southernmost tip of the country because, well, it's famous, and then you find you can do a spot of paddling too, bingo, you have the makings of a holiday.

Kanyakumari is in this book because technically yes, it's a seaside town. But its seafront is rocky and its claim to fame is as a religious destination. Tourists come here in droves to genuflect before the Maiden Goddess and the two men

V MUTHURAMAN

immortalised in stone. All three — Devi Kumari after whom the place is named, Swami Vivekananda who meditated here, and Thiruvalluvar the pithy Tamil poet — have their addresses on the seafront, and this is where the action is centred.

Once in Kanyakumari, you have two options. One, you can head straight for the tourist track. This involves standing in line patiently — only government launches ply to the two famous rocks — for the vessel across. On the rocks, you get great views and the statues of Vivekananda and Thiruvalluvar, the latter 133 foot tall. This is naff enough, but nothing that I recommend because it comes with mad crowds and endless queues. It's a lot more fun scrambling down the long pier made of rocks that stretches way out to the sea. The wind is strong enough to blow you off balance, the spray is in your hair and the sea is fabulous.

The second option is to catch the spectacular sunrises and sunsets in Kanyakumari. In between, hire a car and take off to Suchindram, a charming temple where a pujari will give you a guided tour and then leave you alone to wander at will. Or pack a picnic and head for the Dutch fort at Vattakottai, with its natural beach where you can swim. There are a couple of other beaches nearby and though they have little or no infrastructure, the drive down to these places is likely to be the nicest part of your holiday. Interior Kanyakumari is very reminiscent of Kerala and hilly Goa, all paddy and backwaters and vast banana groves. Octavio Paz wrote in *Near Cape Comorin* of "...herons and egrets, stainless amid such dramatic green," and indeed this is where Kanyakumari's real charm lies.

→ FAST FACTS

When to go November to March. It's crowded in summer and Puja holidays

Tourist office

● Tamil Nadu Tourist Office
Beach Road, Kanyakumari
Tel: 04652-246276

STD code 04652

ORIENTATION

Kanyakumari is tiny — everything lies within a radius of about 5 km. But this space is jam-packed with monstrous hotels, tawdry restaurants and souvenir shops. Everything is within walking distance, with the few hotels on **Main Road** and **Hotel Tamil Nadu** on **Beach Road** only a short auto drive away. There are plenty of autos (Rs 20 minimum fare) and tourist taxis (Rs 500 for half a day) available for the longer drives to the outlying beaches. The fares are more or less standard but there is room for some bargaining. Information and tourist maps are available at the **Tamil Nadu Tourism Development Corporation** office on Beach Road (*see Fast Facts above*), plus from local street vendors. The office is open from 10 am to 5.45 pm.

Other beaches that you can visit in Kanyakumari include **Sothavillai Beach** (18 km), **Sanguthurai Beach** (21 km), **Thekkuruchi** and **Muttom Beach** (35 km) and **Thengapattinam Beach** (54 km). All these beaches are to the northwest of Kanyakumari. Autos charge Rs 300 (return fare) to Sothuvillai, Rs 500-600 to Thekurruchi/ Muttom, and Rs 750 to Thengapattinam. To travel to the places around Kanyakumari, hire a taxi for half a day for Rs 500 and you can take it to Vattakottai and Suchindram. For Rs 1,000, you can visit Padmanabhapuram Palace and Udayagiri.

BEACH WATCH

The sea is mostly placid, but there are no lifeguards and in fact few signs of life. If you are a weak swimmer, it's safest to paddle. Also, swimsuits are rare enough to attract gawking, so be prepared. If you are driving out to the beaches nearby, then take umbrella, rug, food and water. You could spend the day there, but you might be stared at.

THINGS TO SEE AND DO

The beaches here are not yet developed. In fact, it's thanks to the ingenuity of local taxi and auto operators that these places have come into the limelight at all. While this means you get all the solitude you want to enjoy the sea in peace, you also need to carry all the beach paraphernalia yourself.

On the beach

On the rocky seafront at Kanyakumari, a boundary wall of sorts has been constructed above the shoreline. There is a walkway here that's frequented by bead sellers, ice-cream vendors and hawkers with seashells, starfish and conches. There are also shops that sell chips, coffee and knick-knacks.

→ GETTING THERE

Air Nearest airport: Thiruvananthapuram International Airport (87 km/ 2 hrs), connected by flights from Chennai, Bangalore and Mumbai. Taxi fare to Kanyakumari approx Rs 1,300-1,500
Rail Kanyakumari is connected to all major cities of India. The overnight Kanyakumari Express is a convenient train from Chennai
Road Private and government buses ply from Chennai (16 hrs/ Rs 350-525), Thiruvananthapuram ($2^1/_2$ hrs/ Rs 40-100) and Madurai (3 hrs/ Rs 80-100)

Devi Kumari Temple

Right on the beach, this ancient temple that lends its name to Kanyakumari houses the virgin goddess Devi Kanyakumari, made of blue stone. Locals believe that the temple once stood on the Vivekananda Rock, and the natural footprint-shaped indent found there is believed to be that of the Devi herself.
♦**Location** Beach Road **Timings** 4.30-11.45 am and 4-8 pm

Baywatch Water Park

This popular water park, which is 2 km from Kanyakumari on Kovalam Road, has all kinds of land- and water-based rides such as slides, roller coasters, artificial waterfalls and wave pools. There are two restaurants inside.
♦**Entry fee** Adults Rs 200, children Rs 150 **Timings** 10 am-7.30 pm

Vivekananda Rock

In 1892, Swami Vivekananda is said to have meditated on this rocky outcrop before he started his philosophical journey. In 1970, a memorial was built on the spot, consisting of a temple with his statue and a meditation chamber. It can be reached by a ferry run by the government (Rs 20).
♦**Entry fee** Rs 10 **Timings** 8 am-4 pm

Valluvar Memorial

On a second rock nearby is a 133-foot tall statue of Saint Thiruvalluvar, the author of the *Thirukkural* couplets. The 38-foot tall pedestal represents the chapters of the Kural's first part, 'Virtue', while the 95-foot statue represents the other two parts 'Wealth' and 'Love'.
♦**Timings** 8 am-4 pm

Other beaches

Sothavillai Beach has some gazebos, a viewing tower and a small shop that sells tea, cold drinks and bhajjis. **Sanguthurai Beach** is down the road from Sothavillai and offers a little less of the same things. Along the same line, you also have

V MUTHURAMAN

Visitors stop to take in the tranquillity of the Vivekananda Rock Memorial

Thekkuruchi and **Muttom Beach**, and **Thengapattinam Beach**. The last has a 1,000-year-old mosque.

SHOPPING

Kanyakumari doesn't have great shopping options. There are shells and starfish and coral, but the majority of these look suspiciously like plastic. There are also the ubiquitous shops that sell Kashmiri shawls and clothes with Kutch mirror-work. Swami Vivekananda fans can pick up mementoes from the Ashram here.

WHERE TO STAY

Kanyakumari is littered with hotels and lodges, most built with more enthusiasm than sense. The hotels are mostly safe for women travellers, although a lone woman should take extra care.

The façade of **Hotel Sea View** (Tel: 04652-247841; Tariff: Rs 1,400-3,800) is about as charming as a block of flats, but it's the biggest hotel the town has to offer. The rooms are spacious, the linen clean, the views good and the ambience mildly luxurious. Room TVs, laundry and a bar on the premises are the other pluses. It's bang on the crowded East Car Street. **Hotel Singaar's** (Tel: 247992; Tariff: Rs 950-4,000) chief claim to fame is that it's the only one with a swimming pool. It also has clean linen, quick service, and some rooms with a view, plus TV, hot water and helpful staff. It boasts of a bar and a 24-hr coffee shop. It's just a hop from the railway station but is located on Main Road, about a 10-min walk to the main market.

In the middle of all the noise is **Hotel Maadhini** (Tel: 246787; Tariff: Rs 500-1,500), on East Car Street, and it boasts of a garden restaurant and bar. The AC rooms are clean, with attached baths and standard facilities, but the non-AC rooms are seedy. The best feature of **Melody Park** (Tel: 246667; Tariff: Rs 650-3,000), also on East Car Street, is that it's brand new. The rooms, however, have strange balconies, and sometimes the view is just a blue patch between two tall buildings. Here too the non-AC rooms look iffy.

Down the road from the Kumari Temple is **Hotel Samudra** (Tel: 246162; Tariff: Rs 370-1,350), whose posters greet you the moment you alight from the train. It has some excellent views (all rooms have a view), clean linen, attached baths and reasonable rates. It's on Sannathi Street.

Stunningly located, as all government property invariably is, TTDC's **Hotel Tamil Nadu** (Tel: 246257; Tariff: Rs 475-1,200) on Beach Road is by far the most attractive staying option as far as sheer aesthetics go. As bonus, the linen is clean, there are attached baths and an in-house restaurant. The cottages are seedy, so opt for the rooms. Being a little away from town, it's also quiet and non-crowded.

For more hotels and details, see Kanyakumari Accommodation Listings on pages 566-567

WHERE TO EAT

Strangely, there's no seafood at Kanyakumari and most multicuisine restaurants serve tandoori items in scarlet gravy and everything 'Chinese' in oily clumps. The closest authentic fare you get is South Indian and it's best to stick to idli-dosa.

At the Padmanabhapuram Palace

SAIBAL DAS

If you want to drown your gastronomic sorrows in wine, there are a couple of licensed bars around. Hotel Maadhini's **Nisha Bar** is tucked away behind its restaurant, but it looks sleazy. Sea View's bar, **The Wave**, is far more forthcoming, with flashy lights and red decor, right next to its restaurant. However, I fear women travellers might just have to swallow the bad food and go to bed rather than gate-crash these male dens.

Annapoorna Restaurant, on Sannathi Street, serves vegetarian thalis, dosas, idlis, ice-creams and fruit juices (especially great mango juices), all in reasonably clean surroundings. Thalis are for Rs 35-45; otherwise a meal for two should be about Rs 150. **Saravana Restaurant**, also on Sannathi Street, has an identical menu, including the fact that the two restaurants advertise Gujarati thalis but don't serve them.

Sea View Restaurant, of the eponymous hotel, serves bad food in AC surroundings with bowing waiters who hover while you eat. It also boasts a couple of desserts like fruit salad, crème caramel and honey custard, which are not great but comforting in the culinary desert of Kanyakumari. Your best bet here would be the breakfast. Meal for two comes for Rs 450-500. **Srikrishna Restaurant** on Sannathi Street is evidently the local Big Mac surrogate, with pizzas, burgers and French fries, plus pav bhajis, cold coffees and milk shakes.

Bishwabharati on East Car Street is one among a couple of Bengali restaurants that cater to the huge number of their brethren who flock here in season. Unless you are among those who get withdrawal symptoms if they miss their daily fish curry, it's strongly recommended that you stay away. The restaurant is unclean and smells nasty.

Annapoorna Rajasthani, on a lane off Sannathi Street, is the cleanest Rajasthani eatery around. The thali has chappatis, two subzis, dal or kadi, rice and curd. The food is a bit too spicy but it's

tasty and filling for just Rs 35. And the thalis are available at night as well, till 10 pm. **Archana** on East Car Street is Hotel Maadhini's garden restaurant, with Formica tables and plastic chairs on a cement courtyard. Their claim to fame is their fish fry.

AROUND KANYAKUMARI

Vattakottai (7 km)
A short drive from Kanyakumari, this place is perfect for a lazy picnic, especially if the weather is good. There is an **18th century circular fort** here, built by a Dutchman called De Lannoy for the Travancore King Marthanda Varma, who had made Lannoy his army commander. It's now being preserved as a garden. There are some terrific views from the top — all sea and sky and palm trees — and the fort garden itself is pleasant and quiet, with a couple of lovely trees under which you should spread a rug and food and settle down with a book. The stretch of sand around the fort makes for a good natural beach if you are keen on swimming, but you'll have to carry everything from umbrella to cold drinks yourself, as the place is just wilderness.

Suchindram (13 km)
The temple at Suchindram is extraordinarily beautiful. Once a part of the Travancore province, the Kerala influence is clearly seen in the temple and the town. In fact, the temple was given its finishing touches by the Travancore kings. Parts of the temple date back to the 9th and 10th centuries. Various dynasties have built upon the original, adding shrines and carvings, creating a mélange that's strikingly beautiful.

It's a vast complex, with corridors and passages leading to more and more shrines tucked away inside, each with a beautiful story. The lingam here represents Brahma, Vishnu and Shiva, unique in itself, giving it the name of **Sthanumaalayan Temple** (*sthanu* means Shiva, *maal* is Vishnu, and *ayan* Brahma). There is a 22-foot high granite monolithic Hanuman statue and a huge Nandi made of mortar and seashell lime.

The temple is an architectural delight, with its rich carvings, its stunning assembly hall, and the monolithic musical pillars, 18 ft high, each of which strikes a different musical note. I also loved the fact that when you reach the navagraha shrine, it's empty... till you look up and see that the nine heavenly bodies and the corresponding zodiacal signs are all carved into the ceiling to represent them in the sky!

♦**Location** North-west of Kanyakumari on the road to Nagercoil **Timings** 7 am-12 noon and 4-8 pm **Note** Cameras not allowed. Men have to remove shirts and vests before entry; the temple is open to people of all faiths

Padmanabhapuram Palace (35 km)
The famous Travancore dynasty, under Maharaja Marthanda Varma, repulsed even the Dutch who were trying to establish a footing here, notably in the Battle of Colachel in 1741, one of the few telling reverses the Europeans suffered. Padmanabhapuram, located to the north-west of Kanyakumari, was once the capital of Travancore, and the **fort** here stands witness to that. The beautiful **palace complex** has 14 palaces spread around six acres, all built in wood, in the Kerala style of architecture, with shining black floors made of granite polished with a secret recipe. There is a museum as well, with sculptures, weapons and royal edicts on display.

♦**Entry fee** Adults Rs 10, children Rs 5 **Timings** 9 am-1 pm and 2-4.30 pm

Udayagiri Fort (30 km)
Built by King Marthanda Varma in the 18th century, the fort, to the north-west of Kanyakumari, has the tomb of his faithful Dutch general De Lannoy, who is credited to have built the Travancore kingdom's line of coastal defence. ■

THE NEW AIR INDIA FLIES ACROSS 5 CONTINENTS
AND 85 COUNTRIES TO BRING THE WORLD CLOSER
TO OVER 57 DESTINATIONS IN INDIA
WELCOME TO THE NEW AIR INDIA
एअर इंडिया
AIR INDIA
www.airindia.in

AMIT PASRICHA

PONDICHERRY

QUIET IS THE NIGHT

Union Territory of Pondicherry
Location Just north of the mouth of the Gingee River on the Coromandel Coast, 20 km north of Cuddalore
Distances 162 km S of Chennai, 304 km SE of Bangalore
Journey time *By road* 3 hrs from Chennai, 7 hrs from Bangalore
Route from Chennai East Coast Road to Pondicherry via Kelambakkam, Tirupporur, Mammallapuram, Sadras, Kuvuttur, Marakkanam and Kalapettai **Route from Bangalore** NH7 to Krishnagiri via Hosur; NH66 to Pondicherry via Thiruvannamalai, Gingee, Tindivanam and Kiliyanur (*see route guide on page 74*)

BY VAISHNA ROY

If you want a beach holiday in Pondicherry, don't go there — stop just outside the city. Pondicherry itself doesn't offer a sandy beach as it lies along a rocky seafront. What it does promise is a fabulous view from the seaside promenade, and of course, a city full of history and culture. If you're looking for a laid-back beach holiday, it's best to head to the various beach resorts outside Pondicherry. There, you can unwind by the sea and make short forays to nearby towns.

About 15 km north of Pondicherry is The Dune, where I am docked for a beach experience. Very appropriate too, these 25 acres of pleasingly designed resort. It's hot as the blazes when I arrive and I spend most time vegetating indoors. The terrace room is one excellent reason to come to The Dune in the first place. It's on the first floor, with French windows opening out to a private terrace garden from where there is a lovely view of the boundless sea. You can lie in bed all day, watching the water turn from blinding blue to shimmering grey. Have tea on the terrace, and at night lie on the grass picking out constellations to the background hum of waves. There's a long stretch of beach, where you can swim, pick shells, or lounge on deckchairs. There's a quirky door from the resort to the sands, straight out of Alice's Wonderland, through which you walk down to the water. The other side of the door is the swimming pool and a seafood restaurant.

Early next morning, I walk down to the village to watch fishermen haul their catch in; then hitch a ride in a fishing boat. It looks smooth as silk, but when they push the boat out and it hits the first wave, you end up with a sore backside! Back at the resort, I get to choose between a walk in a farm, flying a kite on the sands or lolling with a drink. The Pondicherry air tells me the last is the best.

ORIENTATION

The best beaches in Pondicherry lie to its south and north. These include **Serenity**, **Paradise** and **Quiet** beaches. There aren't many resorts, so the beaches are clean and quiet but, equally, without many facilities or attractions. Although there are several excellent hotels to stay in at Pondicherry, you'll be cut off from the beaches, so it's best to stay at a beachside resort itself. The town itself is small, and you won't have problems getting around. Cycles (available for hire) and autos (minimum fare Rs 20) are quick ways of getting around. There is an excellent bus service to all neighbouring towns.

Pondicherry is basically a squarish town intersected by canals. The section facing the sea is the **French Quarter**, and the interiors the **Tamil** one, and the architecture distinctly divides the two. **Goubert Avenue**, running parallel to the sea, is the main road in the French section. Inside the town is **Auroville Ashram**, but to get to the Auroville commune, you have to turn west off the highway 8 km north of Pondicherry (approx Rs 200 by auto and Rs 350 by taxi).

BEACH WATCH

The currents at the beaches can be treacherous, so stay close to the shore while swimming or just paddle if you are a novice. Don't take a boat or catamaran ride if they don't provide a life jacket.

THINGS TO SEE AND DO

There are no water sports in Pondicherry, so it's essentially a take-it-easy break with plenty of walks, some shopping, history and culture thrown in.

Chunnambar

About 8 km south of Pondicherry is **Chunnambar**, a park developed by

→ FAST FACTS

When to go Between July and March

Tourist offices

- Pondicherry Tourism Development Corporation
40, Goubert Avenue, Beach Road
Pondicherry
Tel: 0413-2339497
Email: tourism@pon.nic.in
Website: tourism.pon.nic.in
- Department of Tourism
Govt of Pondicherry, 40, Goubert Avenue, Beach Road, Pondicherry
Tel: 2333590

TIP The staff is helpful and will supply you with a map (free) and directions

STD code 0413

NAMIT ARORA/ PHOTOINDIA

The beach at Pondicherry doubles as a venue for games

Pondicherry Tourism with tree houses, cottages and eateries. Its chief attraction is the boating down the charming **Chunnambar River** up to **Paradise Beach**, which is actually a giant sandbar between the river and the sea. The place has gazebos, swings and viewpoints but be warned that the park is usually noisy and crowded. A regular ferry deposits visitors here for a few hours, and later ferries them back to the mainland. A restaurant serves a minimalist menu, rather greasy, plus cold drinks and water. The beach is gorgeous, and you can swim in the sea for hours. There are toilets and changing rooms. Chunnambar also has a large pontoon that you can hire for floating parties at Rs 2,500 per hour. It carries about 30 people, and Pondicherry Tourism organises food and liquor for a fee.

◆**Entry fee** Adults Rs 3, children Rs 2 **Park timings** 9 am-6 pm **Paradise Beach timings** 9 am-4 pm **Boating fee** Rs 60 per hr

Other beaches

Serenity and **Quiet** are the two beaches here, the former close to the Auroville turn and the latter further down. Both are popular with Aurovillians and foreigners, but have few facilities. Quiet Beach has the **Quiet Healing Center** (Tel: 0413-2622646) for Ayurvedic massages and nature cures. Both the beaches are beautiful and perfect for swimming. The other stretches of beach are those found alongside the chief resorts such as Kailash, Dune and Hotel Ashoka.

Heritage walk

INTACH, which has done some great restoration work in Pondicherry, organises a 2-hr heritage walk, as part of which you will be shown old photographs, taken to both the French and Tamil quarters, and inside old historical buildings such as the **Pondicherry Police Headquarters**, the **Romain Roland Bibliothéque, Maison Colombani,** and **Hotel de l'Orient**, which once housed the French Education Department. INTACH's new office, where the walk starts, is itself being done up as a heritage centre and should be soon ready for visitors.

◆**Walk fee** Rs 500 per head or per couple (any additional member Rs 100) **Contact** INTACH (Tel: 0413-2225991, 2227324), 62 Aurobindo Street **Note** One-day notice compulsory

Discover a new Pondicherry
Luxury on the Beach
The
PROMENADE
A HIDESIGN HOTEL

Aurobindo Ashram and Auroville

At the unassuming building of the **Aurobindo Ashram** on Rue de la Marine, you can visit the samadhis of Aurobindo and The Mother, whose creation of Auroville, the one-nation commune, is responsible for giving Pondicherry much of the international character it now enjoys.

◆**Timings** 8 am-12 noon and 2-5 pm

Auroville is 14 km from Pondicherry and was set up in 1968 by The Mother, Aurobindo's most famous disciple. **Matrimandir** is a golden dome-like structure that is "dedicated to the universal mother". You can view it only from outside, from 10 am to 4 pm.

SHOPPING

You can't miss the glazed stoneware pottery in Pondicherry, pioneered by American Ray Meeker. Pick up beer mugs, coffee cups, tea or dinner sets in lovely colours and textures. Check out **Boutique Auroshree** (18, Nehru St), **Little Shop** (21, Rue de la Compagnie), **Kalki** (134, Mission St) and **Nirvana** (53, Suffren St). Also look for leather goods, handmade paper and clothing, which most showrooms and Auroville shops stock. The shops on the approach road to the Auroville Info Centre have some lovely paper lampshades and wooden birds. The fresh bread and croissants (including chocolate ones) at the Auroville bakery are pretty good. **Anglo French Textiles** on Mission Street has been making cotton textiles since 1898, and is a good place for bed linen and furnishings.

→ GETTING THERE

Air Nearest airport: Chennai (162 km/ 2½ hrs), connected to all major cities. Taxi to Pondicherry costs Rs 1,500

Rail Pondicherry has a metre gauge station connected to Viluppuram on broad gauge, which is a better railhead (38 km/ 45 mins). Pondicherry Station is connected by local trains to Chennai's Egmore Station (2-4 hrs). If travelling from outside the state, the nearest option is Chennai, connected to all metros

Road State transport buses leave every 30 mins from Chennai's Mofussil Bus Stand at Koyambedu. Praveen Travels' (Chennai Tel: 044-28193538) bus services leave at 4.30 and 6 pm (Rs 150-200)

WHERE TO STAY

There are plenty of stay options in Pondicherry itself, although these are not near the beaches. You could stay here and make occasional forays to the nearby beaches, while enjoying Pondicherry's other delights. Or else you can stay at one of the beach resorts outside Pondicherry, in which case you also get to enjoy your own stretch of beach.

Outside Pondicherry

The Dune (Tel: 0413-2655751; Tariff: Rs 3,300-14,500) takes its eco-resort appellation seriously, with a health-friendly diet on its menu, organic vegetables from its own gardens, and battery vehicles and cycles to go around the premises. Plus, there's seaside pool and a pottery wheel, fishing trips and boat rides. It's located 15 km north of Pondicherry, in Pudhukuppam, Keelputhupet.

Kailash Beach Resort (Tel: 2619700-03; Tariff: Rs 2,700-4,500) is 8 km south of the city, on a turn-off from Cuddalore Road, well hidden inside Purnankuppam Village. The rooms are spacious, with all modern conveniences. It has a long stretch of beach, plus two restaurants serving French and Indian cuisine.

Hotel Pondicherry Ashok (Tel: 2655160-63; Tariff: Rs 2,500-3,500) is an ITDC-owned resort that is fabulously located but not so fabulously managed. It

Courtesy NEEMRANA RESORTS

TRANQUEBAR

BY VAISHNA ROY

A great idea is to use Pondicherry as a base and drive down the East Coast Road to Tranquebar, where the remains of a 17th century Danish fort by the sea make for an unusual beach break. Neemrana Resorts has restored the Collector's residence here as a resort that it calls, simply, **Bungalow on the Beach**. And it is perched stunningly right on the beach, with the sea just a stone's throw away. From the fabulous first-floor balcony you get uninterrupted views of the sea and the sky and the imposing fort across the road. And total peace and quiet.

The 17th century bungalow, once the residence of the Danish Governor's ADC and later the British Collector's, is a typical colonial house and has been lovingly restored, with gleaming bannisters and shining floors. The reception area has old prints on the walls, comprising maps, prints of the original house, and drawings of the fort. The rooms are all named after the Danish ships that docked here. I am in Queen Anna Sophia, which came to Tranquebar in 1721. The French window with its long billowing blue curtains opens out to the balcony where I sip coffee and watch a fishing boat far out in the sea. Just below and perched precariously on the rocks is a ruined **Pandya temple** that dates back to 1305. Each year, it seems to lose more of itself to the sea. On Sundays, it's frequented by picnic-makers and couples, who take refuge under its remaining porticos. In fact, with the ice-cream seller and peanut man, there is quite a mela-like air to the place. Near the fort, the shoreline is rocky, but with stretches of clear sandy beach. However, it's still a fishing village and the sands belong to the fishermen with their boats and nets.

The **fort** expectedly dominates the landscape, a solid square structure in a dull shade of mustard. The air of total isolation it wears and the desolate sweep of sand it stands in make it difficult to believe that this could once have been the headquarters of the Danish trading company. The road just below the resort leads past the temple to a fishing village, where on **Goldsmith Street** a Danish trust has bought five old Tamil houses and restored them for letting to institutions or offices. They look mouth-wateringly gorgeous — dazzling white walls, gleaming wooden pillars and beams, open courtyards and dark, cool rooms. From the village, I walk back to the walled 'white' city, which you enter through an **archway** built in 1792, bearing a Danish coat of arms. On the way, I stop by to look at the gravestones in the New Street Churchyard and admire the **New Jerusalem Church**. And walk slowly past the row of charming old houses that make up Kongensgade or **King Street**, once the main street of this Danish outpost.

Tranquebar is a tranquil place, and now the Neemrana Resort gives you a great staying option here, making for a perfect weekend break. Neemrana also runs the government-owned **Tamil Nadu Hotels** next door. While the former has a small menu with Indian and European dishes, slightly bland, the latter offers good, reasonably priced South Indian fare like rice, chicken and fish curry.

◆ **Bungalow on the Beach Tel** 04364-288065, 289034 **Tariff** Rs 4,000-5,000 **Tamil Nadu Hotel Tariff** Rs 600 (room), Rs 150 (dorm bed) **Connection** Tranquebar is 120 km/ 3 hrs from Pondicherry; non-AC taxi costs Rs 1,500 (return)

For details, see Tranquebar Accommodation Listings on page 565 ■

has a wonderful stretch of beach and great views but lacks zing.

In Pondicherry

Le Dupleix (Tel: 2226999; Tariff: Rs 3,250-6,500) is a beautiful heritage hotel housed in the former house of the French governor. **Hotel de l'Orient** (Tel: 2343067; Tariff: Rs 2,000-5,000) is a Neemrana property housed in a gorgeous 18th-century heritage building. On Rue Romain Rolland, in the heart of the French Quarter, with an in-house restaurant called Carté Blanche, it's comfortable and gracious. **Hotel de Pondicherry** (Tel: 2227409; Tariff: Rs 1,500-2,800) is also housed in an old French colonial mansion, and has just 10 comfortable rooms with an old-world air, plus an in-house Ayurveda centre.

Continental Guest House (Tel: 2225828; Tariff: Rs 300-550) on Rue Labourdonnais is a budget option, as is **Dumas Guest House** (Tel: 2225726; Tariff: Rs 600-1,500) on Rue Dumas. **Hotel Mass** (Tel: 2204001; Rs 1,500-5,000) on Maraimalai Adigal Salai has comfortable and clean rooms but is located on a noisy main street. **Hotel Surguru** (Tel: 2339022, Tariff: Rs 860-1,350) on Sardar Patel Road is the other option in this category.

The French connection in Pondicherry

NAMIT ARORA/ PHOTOINDIA

For more hotels and details, see Pondicherry Accommodation Listings on pages 564-565

WHERE TO EAT

Tourism brochures will go on about how you can find French cuisine and coffee at every Pondicherry restaurant. Actually, the coffee is mostly indifferent and most places offer pasta and pizza, which is as French as I am. Happily, they are mostly pretty well made, and the pizza especially is thin and crisp and not drowned in cheese. However, some places do have a few good French dishes, like a *coq au vin*, confits, salad Niçoise or French onion soup, but it's a bit hit-and-miss. Almost all restaurants serve liquor, or at least beer.

The rooftop **Rendezvous** on Suffren Street is one of Pondicherry's landmarks, with an extensive menu and cool terrace tables, but the service is often poor, especially if the place is crowded. Meal for two comes for Rs 800. **Satsanga** on Labourdonnais Street is another popular joint, with tasty pasta, a relaxed ambience and good service. Meal for two is for Rs 600.

La Térrasse on Subbiah Salai is a thatch-top café with good food at great rates but no liquor.

The Auroville turn-off has some small restaurants and cafés that are worth a dekko. I went to a dingy-looking roof-top restaurant called **Pizza Roof** and was taken aback when I got an excellent pasta and crisp pizza with fresh herbs. South Indian fare is available at **Adyar Ananda Bhavan** (Nehru Street), **Surguru** (Sardar Patel Road) and **Indian Coffee House** (Nehru Street), good quality and great rates. ■

THE ANDAMANS

ANDAMAN ISLANDS
TOURIST GUIDE
Coco Channel
Landfall Island
Cape Price
Narcondam Island
North Andaman
Port Cornwallis
Saddle Peak WLS
Madhupur
DIGLIPUR
West Coral Reef
North Reef WLS
Austen Harbour
Andaman Trunk Road
Mohantapur
MAYABUNDER
Interview WLS
Port Andaman
Middle Andaman
Rangat
Padmanabhapuram
Port Blair - Kolkata (678 nautical miles)
Port Blair - Rangoon
Middle Coral Reef
223
Long Island
Middle Button WLS
Barren Island
BARATANG
North Button WLS
Udaygarh
South Button WLS
Nilanbur
Hajataurh
South Andaman
Visakhapatnam - Port Blair
Port Campbell
HAVELOCK
NEIL ISLAND
Ross Island
Ferrarganj
PORT BLAIR
Wandoor
Corbyn's Cove
Chennai - Port Blair (643 nautical miles)
Mahatma Gandhi NP
Chidiya Tapu
ANDAMAN SEA
Rutland Island
Portman Bay
Manners Strait
Invisible Bank
Duncan Passage
Cinque Islands
Port Blair - Penang
North Brother Island
Port Blair - Car Nicobar
South Sentinel WLS
Ektte Bay
South Brother Island
Palalankwe
Nachugeo
Titaije
LITTLE ANDAMAN
Chetamals
Hut Bay
Toibuebe
Toibalewe

ATUL LOKE

20,000 leagues above the sea

BY AMIT MAHAJAN

My first sight of the Andaman and Nicobar Islands fundamentally changed my world-view. Flying from Chennai to Port Blair, from 20,000-odd ft above the sea, island after island looked like the top of a submerged hill coming out of the sea, rising to a certain height, looking around, surveying its surroundings, and then receding into unknown depths. We humans think of the earth as large masses of land interspersed by seas, our imagination predominantly determined by our circumstance of being land animals. As I began to see the Andaman and Nicobar Islands from above, I was suddenly and radically liberated from this conception. From above, the archipelago offered an alternative vision of earth — vast expanses of bluish-silver water occasionally interrupted by bits and pieces of land.

It's in traversing this world of water — in ferries, boats, small ships and *doongis* (motorboats) — that the pleasure of visiting the Andamans lies. Going up a creek, swimming in a cove and snorkelling in a bay become daily episodes of a life lived on beaches and shores.

Andamans is part of the 'Indian' imagination as Kaalapani — the infamous penal colony symbolising British colonial oppression. As the 'land of aboriginals'. As — and we owe this to the tourism industry — a repository of 'picture-postcard beauty', 'emerald islands', 'turquoise waters' and 'white-sand beaches'. While none of this turns out to be untrue, this description portrays more an imagined place than the real — the actual experience in these islands is much more varied than these catch-phrases can convey.

The dominant reality in Andamans is of a multitude of farming and fishing villages, settled here from the Indian sub-continent (mainly from Bengal, Bangladesh, Tamil Nadu, Jharkhand and Myanmar) over the past century or more, by various governments, causing a retreat of the forests and forest-dwelling communities. The world one comes across in towns and villages here is built around the lives of these peasants and fisherfolk. It's in the interstices of this existence that one finds golden beaches, multi-hued corals and green mangroves.

The forests of the picturesque Andaman and Nicobar Islands are home to six tribal communities who have lived here, by some estimates, for as long as 20,000 years. For some reason, the shipping lines of the Indian Ocean gave a miss to this archipelago, allowing these tribes to live undisturbed till 150 years ago. After the beginning of the penal colony, with timber logging and settling of people from the mainland, the tribes rapidly diminished. The Andaman group of islands have four tribes of Negrito origin: the Great Andamanese, the Onge, the Jarawas and the Sentinelese; their combined population is less than 500 now. The Nicobar Islands are home to two tribes of Mongoloid origin: the Shompen and the Nicobarese. Shompens number 200, and Nicobarese number 20,000, the latter being the only tribe that has withstood the onslaught of civilisation.

A tourist takes in the beauty of the sea

MANDIP SINGH SOIN

The Andaman and Nicobar Islands are the largest group of islands in the Bay of Bengal. Islands, islets and rocky outcrops (people who keep count of such things say 572 in all) are spread over 8,200 square kilometres in a narrow arc that begins south of Myanmar and runs over a distance of 800 km south and southwest to end up just short of Sumatra in Indonesia. The islands are considered to be the submerged extension of the Arakan Yoma mountain range of Myanmar.

For administrative and conceptual reasons, the islands are divided into many groups. The Andaman Islands and Nicobar Islands are the two main sub-groups, separated by a 10-degree latitude. The Andaman Islands are located to the north of the 10° N parallel and the Nicobar Islands are to its south. The Andamans consist of North, Middle and South Andamans, and Baratang, Ritchie's Archipelago and the Labyrinth group of islands. Nicobar Islands are made up of the Northern group (Car Nicobar and Batti Malv), the Central or Nancowry Islands and the Southern group (consisting of Little and Great Nicobar, and others).

Only some islands are inhabited, and their number varies between 34 and 38. About one-third of the area of the Andamans and the entire Nicobar has been declared a tribal reserve. Thus, only the non-reserved areas of Andaman Islands are open to tourists, and only a few destinations have the wherewithal to support any tourism. Port Blair, Havelock and Neil have some hotels; otherwise tourists have to make do with Andaman Public Works Department guest houses, forest rest houses and camping if and

DHRITIMAN MUKHERJEE

A view of Havelock, one of the most beautiful islands in this part of the world

where allowed. Ferries are the main means of transport between islands. The Directorate of Shipping Services operates inter-island ferries. From Port Blair, there are services for Havelock, Neil, Rangat, Diglipur, Bamboo Flat and Little Andaman. Enquire at Phoenix Bay for detailed schedules and reservations. There are buses to Middle and North Andaman on the Andaman Trunk Road from the Main Bus Stand near Aberdeen Bazaar in Port Blair.

FAST FACTS

When to go October to early May
Tourist office Directorate of Information, Publicity and Tourism, Andaman and Nicobar Administration, Port Blair **Tel** 03192-232694, 232747, 230933, 230234 (Director) **Email** ipt@and.nic.in **Website** tourism.andaman.nic.in **Timings** 9 am-4.30 pm, closed on Sundays
TIP The information desk is helpful, though a bit bureaucratic. Brochures and information are readily available. Some tour packages are offered, and bookings for the hotels run by the Directorate of Tourism are made here
Permits All foreign nationals require permits to visit the Andaman and Nicobar Islands. Those arriving by air are granted permits on arrival at Port Blair. Indian tourists do not require a permit to visit the Andaman Islands, but for Nicobar Islands and the areas reserved for tribals, they need special permits from the Deputy Commissioner, Port Blair (Tel: 233089)
STD code 03192

GETTING THERE

The Andaman and Nicobar Islands are accessible only from mainland India, and Port Blair, the capital, is the only point of entry and exit to the islands
Air There are daily flights both to and from Chennai and Kolkata operated by Indian, Jet Airways, Air Deccan and Sahara. All flights are 2 hrs long. Taxis are available; these cost Rs 200 to the town centre
Sea The Shipping Corporation of India (SCI) runs services from Chennai, Kolkata and Visakhapatnam. The trips take 56 to 64 hrs depending on the sea conditions. The services operate in all seasons. The fare varies between Rs 1,500 and 6,000 **SCI Chennai Tel** 044-25220841 **Kolkata Tel** 033-22482354 **Port Blair Tel** 03192-233590 ■

V MUTHURAMAN

PORT BLAIR

OF PIERS, JETTIES AND WHARFS

Union Territory of Andaman and Nicobar Islands
Location On the east coast of the main island, the South Andamans
Distances 643 nautical miles E of Chennai, 678 nautical miles SE of Kolkata
Journey time ***By air*** 2 hrs from Chennai and Kolkata (*see tourist guide on page 104*)

BY AMIT MAHAJAN

Like most others, I reached Port Blair with a baggage of hype about the Andamans offering 'sylvan sands' and 'idyllic islands'. The view from the airplane only reinforced the build-up. However, the first impression after landing was of a small town not very different from many others I have seen — similar houses, similar roads, similar shops. The landscape was somewhat undulating, and in fact, that was enough to cause a flutter in my heart that had endured and grown up on a diet of the flat featureless plains of the north of mainland India. Here, gradually, the bays and coves began to reveal themselves like the secret alleyways of a town. I discovered that newspapers carried the time of high tide and low tide, buses went to wharfs or jetties, roads ran the length of seashores and the reservation counter sold tickets for the berthing of an overnight boat. Water and its pleasures engulfed everything, and an entire maritime life and economy unfolded, ready to enchant me. And oceans and islands and beaches beckoned.

One cool afternoon I walked the road skirting the north-east edge of the island, running above a cemented wall next to the sea. The water, 20 ft below, was crystal clear. The tiny waves moved slowly and I could see each and every stone and pebble, their greys and browns magnified under the now-concave, now-convex surface of the water. Something caught my eye and made me stop. Something green and red and blue, all the colours flashily fluorescent — it was a fish more than two feet long near the surface. As I concentrated on the water around it, a dozen of these colourful fish appeared, and half-a-dozen kinds more. And then the water seemed to change, its colour and texture became ever so slightly different, and I could perceive some movement. A school of smaller fish was out for an evening ramble. A blackish snake also joined the action, as did a long and slender eel-fish. In the steady and moist sea breeze this entire experience became exhilarating — it was like enjoying a particularly colourful aquarium without the guilt of seeing captive animals.

For most people Port Blair is primarily an erstwhile penal colony, while for some it's the gateway to the 'pristine' islands and beaches of Andaman and Nicobar. Port Blair is both this but also an island town offering small cruises in the sea, water-based activities like snorkelling and scuba diving, and a glimpse of the history and culture of this region.

ORIENTATION

Port Blair is the capital of the Union Territory of Andaman and Nicobar Islands. It's located on the east coast of an island in the South Andaman group. The **Aberdeen Bazaar** forms the centre of the town. Most restaurants and hotels are around this area. The main **bus station** is just west of the bazaar. The airport is 5 km to the south-west. The main passenger dock for ferries, the **Phoenix Jetty**, is 1 km to the north-west.

The Aberdeen Jetty, the **Andaman Water Sports Complex**, and the **Cellular Jail** are close to each other, half a kilometre north-east of Aberdeen Bazaar. **Corbyn's Cove**, the beach nearest to Port Blair, is 7 km to the south. **Chidiya Tapu** and the **Mahatma Gandhi Marine National Park** in Wandoor are 30 km from the town centre, to the south and south-west respectively.

Walking is an option in the centre of the town. Otherwise, autorickshaws are the most convenient transport within Port Blair. The vehicles are not metered, but the drivers are friendly and fair; Rs 20-60 will cover most destinations. Taxis are available near the main bus stand;

The abandoned jail on Viper Island

ATUL LOKE

expect to pay Rs 1,200-1,500 for a full day. The State Transport Service and private operators run plenty of local buses between 6 am and 10 pm; the buses are not crowded except during office hours.

The Directorate of Information, Publicity and Tourism, half a kilometre southwest of Aberdeen Bazaar, has helpful staff and gives information, brochures and organises some tours. **Island Travels** (Tel: 03192-233358) and **Shompen Travels** (Tel: 232622/ 44) organise package tours, diving, snorkelling, vehicles for hire and air tickets.

BEACH WATCH

Corbyn's Cove is a small, sheltered concave stretch of the coast; by the beach, the sea is safe for swimming. There are no lifeguards, so don't venture deep into the ocean. Beachwear is acceptable here but there are no shops selling it. If you plan to snorkel at North Bay, Jolly Buoy, Red Skin and Chidiya Tapu, do not do it unaccompanied unless you are an expert.

Corbyn's Cove has a shapely beach

DHRITIMAN MUKHERJEE

THINGS TO SEE AND DO

There are two types of tourists who visit Port Blair. Some come to Port Blair and spend a few days in the capital trying to make sense of the infamous Kalapani. Others want to escape to a lonely beach, or even an idyllic island, but the logistics of travel in the Andamans force a stay in Port Blair of at least a day after arrival and a day before departure. Most ferries to various islands and the buses to Middle and North Andamans leave early in the morning before the flights come in. Again, on the way back, tourists need to reach Port Blair at least a day before their departure because the ferries between islands can be erratic as their schedules and speeds can change depending on weather conditions.

There is enough in and around Port Blair to justify a stay of three or four days. The Harbour Cruise and trips to Ross Island, North Bay, Cellular Jail and museums can be done during the day. Late afternoons and evenings are best spent at Corbyn's Cove and Chidiya Tapu. A trip to Mahatma Gandhi Marine Park in Wandoor requires most of a day.

Corbyn's Cove

Corbyn's Cove is situated outside the main Port Blair habitation (7 km south) and gives a sense of being away from the town. Yet it's close enough to hop over to for an unplanned spontaneous getaway. It's famous for its shapely beach that has just the right curve to ensure a calm sea for endless swimming. Clean loos and showers are provided for swimmers on the beach. Just across the road from the beach is the **Peerless Resort** with a restaurant and a bar set in a large garden. **Waves**, located right next door, is another restaurant and bar. An auto will charge Rs 250 or more for a return trip depending on the waiting time.

LOKESH ABROL

Overgrown vines and roots have taken over the ruins on Ross Island

North Bay

North Bay is a beach on an island, which as the name indicates, is just north of Port Blair. The beach and the **snorkelling** opportunities in its fringing coral reef are the closest ones you will find to Port Blair, and therefore, it gets quite crowded. A ferry (Rs 125; 9 am and 2 pm; 30 mins) will take you across from the Aberdeen Jetty and bring you back after a 3-hr stay. The corals at North Bay are rather good and spread over a large area. You're very likely to spot many fish, a lobster or two, and even clams on the coral reef. Snorkelling will cost Rs 50-500 for 10 mins to an hour. Snacks and basic meals are available in some shacks on the beach.

Ross Island

A small, 0.6 sq km of land that's a short ferry ride across from Port Blair encompasses in a way the entire life of the Andamans. It was the home of the indigenous Great Andamanese whose numbers dwindled from 5,000 to just 28 within 20 years of the initial British occupation. The island served as the capital from 1858 till 1941, when the Japanese occupied it and converted it into a PoW site. The ruins of the church and the Chief Commissioner's house among overgrowing vines and aerial roots are the most evocative of the remains. Ferries (Rs 60; 8.30 am, 10.30 am, 12.30 pm and 2 pm; 15 mins; not available on Wednesdays) will take you across from the Aberdeen Jetty and bring you back after an hour's stay.

◆**Entry ticket** Rs 20 **Camera** Rs 25

Viper Island/ Harbour Cruise

The Harbour Cruise begins at the Phoenix Jetty, takes you leisurely around the Port Blair Harbour, winding its way past the ships anchored there; it also includes a stop at the Viper Island. The tiny island situated inside the Port Blair Harbour gets its name from the vessel, *The Viper*, on which Lt Archibald Blair of the British East India Company came here in 1789 in an unsuccessful attempt to create a colony. It was after him that Port Blair was later named. Most visitors come here

AFP

Coral: Which colour do you want?

A blue streak leads to a violet blur with a pink and lilac border. You can also discern some red patches. Underwater coral-viewing is one of the most colourful experiences you can have.

Corals are one of the main reasons for diving and snorkelling. The multi-coloured hues below the water, and the sight of a variety of fish zigzagging their way through coral colonies, are one of nature's true delights. So what is coral?

Corals are tiny aquatic animals that have an outer stony protective skeleton and live in colonies in the sea. Each coral animal is called a polyp and lives inside a cup of limestone. A coral polyp has a mouth at the top surrounded by tentacles, which help capture food. Sensing danger, the polyp can withdraw into its cup (like a turtle withdraws into its shell). A coral polyp's cup is permanently attached to the surface below.

Many thousands of coral polyps are connected to form a coral colony. A coral colony keeps growing with more and more addition of coral polyps. A solid mass is formed with each animal cemented to the other. New colonies grow over dead ones, and eventually, over thousands of years, the huge limestone mass and living coral form a reef.

Coral colonies are of many shapes and colours. The colours are not the corals' own. There are many types of algae living in the coral and they provide the colour, for which corals are so often famous. Coral reefs provide a habitat to not only these algae but also many other sea creatures — anemones, sponges, a variety of fish, crabs, shrimps, sea urchins and the giant clam.

Corals are part of the same group of animals as sea anemones and jelly fish. Corals are very sensitive and specialised animals. They grow in warm, clear and shallow tropical waters where sunlight penetrates to the bottom. They flourish in a very narrow temperature range — 23°C to 25°C. In India there are only four major regions where coral reefs are found — the Gulf of Mannar, Gulf of Kutch, Lakshadweep and Andaman and Nicobar. Across the globe, the Caribbean and South Pacific Seas, Indonesia, Malaysia and Australia are famous for their coral reefs.

LOKESH ABROL

Stories of freedom fighters and British brutality echo across the Cellular Jail

to see the abandoned jail and gallows. The trip to Viper Island (Rs 60; 3 pm) begins at Aberdeen Jetty, goes through the Port Blair Harbour and takes 2 hrs.

Cellular Jail

The most prominent landmark in Port Blair, the Cellular Jail is unusual because, unlike most other late 19th-century and early 20th-century institutions in India, it was discontinued as a functioning establishment after the changes in governance in India in 1947, was declared a national monument and became a symbol of colonial oppression. Hundreds of visitors here daily relive the stories of British brutalities and the heroism of the national liberation struggle.

♦**Entry ticket** Rs 5 **Timings** 9 am-12 noon, 2-5 pm, Mondays closed **Cameras** Still Rs 10, video Rs 50

Andaman Water Sports Complex

Located at the Aberdeen Jetty, the club offered a host of water sports till the tsunami hit it and caused major damage in December 2004 (*also see 'Tsunami: Killer spree' on page 118*). The club was under repair at the time of writing. When it reopens, it will again offer water-skiing, wake board, sail boat, wind surfing and much more.

SHOPPING

If it's a shopping trip that you're looking for, don't go to the Andamans. Not that there is nothing on offer for tourists. But one needs to be careful about not picking up stuff sold illegally, and thereby promoting the destruction of the islands. There are many shops in the **Aberdeen Bazaar** selling shells and corals. However, most of this trade is illegal, and more importantly, it's harmful to the ecology of the islands. Photographs of the indigenous tribes are also peddled — these too vitiate the already fragile cultural environment in the Andamans.

Sagarika, which is a small-scale industries emporium (9 am-7 pm) at Middle Point, has a wide array of souvenirs on offer, including jute bags (Rs 50-100), bamboo trays (Rs 30-100), table mats (Rs 60), baskets (Rs 100) and decoration pieces made of shells (Rs 30-2,000).

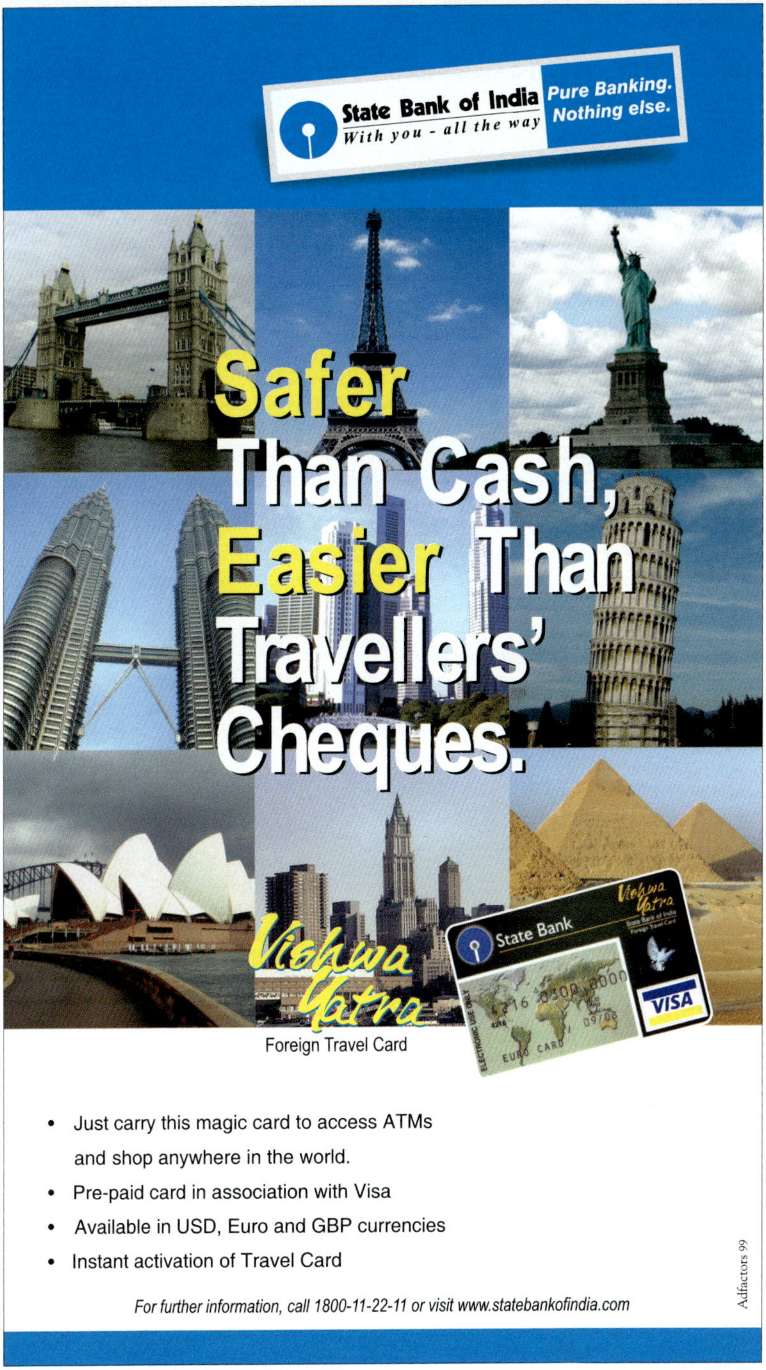
State Bank of India
With you - all the way
Pure Banking. Nothing else.
Safer Than Cash, Easier Than Travellers' Cheques.
Vishwa Yatra
Foreign Travel Card
State Bank
VISA
• Just carry this magic card to access ATMs and shop anywhere in the world.
• Pre-paid card in association with Visa
• Available in USD, Euro and GBP currencies
• Instant activation of Travel Card
For further information, call 1800-11-22-11 or visit www.statebankofindia.com
Adfactors 99

Another option is a small **souvenir shop on Ross Island**, which sells lovely wooden and jute items. Bangles come for Rs 35, bracelets for Rs 50-100, trays for Rs 100, baskets for Rs 50-200, and decoration pieces for Rs 20-300.

WHERE TO STAY

Fortune Resort-Bay Island (Tel: 03192-234101; Tariff: Rs 2,950-8,559) has an excellent location on the sea at Marine Hill to the north of Port Blair. The woodwork and the aesthetics of the lobby are lovely, though the size of the rooms does not match up to the prices.

Hotel Sinclairs Bayview (Tel: 227824; Tariff: Rs 2,550-3,900) is on the eastern edge of the island at South Point, quite away from the bustle of the town; all rooms have balconies offering spectacular views of the sea. **Peerless Beach Resort** (Tel: 229311/ 13; Tariff: Rs 3,000-5,500) is designed around a big garden next to the beach at Corbyn's Cove. As often in Port Blair, the rooms are small.

North Bay is a vision in green and blue

DHRITIMAN MUKHERJEE

Andaman Teal House (Tel: 232642, 234061; Tariff: Rs 400-800) in Delanipur is run by the Tourism Department. The rooms are clean and spacious but bare. **Hornbill Nest Resort** (Tel: 229130; Tariff: Rs 400-800) near Corbyn's Cove has decent views and plain rooms.

Hotel Shompen (Tel: 232360; Tariff: Rs 800-2,000) at Middle Point, **Holiday Resort** (Tel: 230516; Tariff: Rs 500-800) at Prem Nagar and **Hotel Dhanalakshmi** (Tel: 233952-53; Tariff: Rs 400-1,500) in Aberdeen Bazaar are quite clean and as bonus, centrally located.

For more hotels and details, see Port Blair Accommodation Listings on pages 523-524

WHERE TO EAT

In the Andamans, various settlers have mostly given up their original culture and food to create something that has a bit of everything. In this 'pot luck' cuisine, seafood stands out for its variety and easy availability. The Andaman Sea abounds with varieties of fish, crabs, lobsters and prawns, and they routinely end up on the dining tables. North Indian, South Indian, Continental and Chinese dishes are also common.

Mandalay Restaurant in Fortune Resort may well be the best place in Port Blair to have a meal, though this privilege doesn't come cheap. They serve South Indian, North Indian, Chinese and Continental cuisine and some options include club sandwiches for Rs 150, jhinga malai curry for Rs 340, *meen moilee* for Rs 200 and chilli crabs for Rs 400.

The Palm at Hotel Sinclairs serves Continental, Chinese and Indian cuisine. **Corbyn's Delight** at Peerless Resort serves Continental at reasonable prices — grilled prawns are for Rs 175, and baked fish for Rs 130. **Waves** at Corbyn's Cove

एअर इंडिया
AIR INDIA

has good Indian and Chinese food — dum aloo, chicken curry and Chinese prawns are some options.

The **New Lighthouse** restaurant, located ahead of the Aberdeen Jetty, is a breezy place to have beer in the evening as also fresh seafood: fish (Rs 150-400), lobster (Rs 200 and more), and crabs (Rs 150 and more).

AROUND PORT BLAIR

Mahatma Gandhi Marine National Park, Wandoor (29 km)
Creeks lined with mangroves, islands occupied by rainforests, and lagoons, coves, coral reefs and beaches teeming with marine life. The MG Marine National Park, which encompasses 281 sq km comprising 15 uninhabited islands and the surrounding sea, holds all this and more. It was created in 1983 to preserve the tropical ecosystem, which is under threat all over the globe. Only two islands, **Jolly Buoy** and **Red Skin**, are open to visitors, alternately for six months each. The tour begins at **Wandoor Village**, the base to visit these islands, with a ferry ride weaving its way through islands from Wandoor to Jolly Buoy or Red Skin past some particularly lush mangroves. Near the island, people are shifted to smaller glass bottom boats and after a 10-min tour of the coral reef, dropped at the beach. For the next 3 hrs, tourists swim, snorkel (15 mins, included in the package) and picnic (all food and water to be brought with you).

Jolly Buoy and Red Skin islands have silvery sand beaches and the waters around them offer a breathtaking view of underwater coral and marine life. You can view coral colonies and reefs, which are nurseries for fish, and many other

Tsunami: Killer spree

The plaster had dried but big yellow patches of the sea were left on the wall. The wooden beam was tilted at an awkward angle. The damage to the forest rest house at Wandoor was visible, even two years and more after the devastating tsunami in December 2004. This hardly surprised me. However, the fact that the rest house was on top of a hill (howsoever small and howsoever close to the sea) again shook me as it pointed to the enormity of the tsunami.

The tsunami, variously known as the Asian Tsunami, the Boxing-day Tsunami and the 2004 Indian Ocean Earthquake, was one of the deadliest disasters in modern history. It was the biggest ever recorded tsunami, and the earthquake that triggered it (estimated to be between 9.1 and 9.3 on the Richter scale) was the second largest earthquake ever recorded. The earthquake originated in the Indian Ocean just north of Simeulue Island, off the western coast of northern Sumatra. The farthest recorded death due to the tsunami

AFP

occurred 8,000 km away in South Africa. The worldwide toll exceeds 200,000 people.

The centre of the tsunami was very close to the Nicobar Islands and these suffered much more damage than the Andamans. Many earthquakes rocked the islands during and after the tsunami. Fishing and tribal communities were the most affected and there was extensive damage to buildings and facilities in many islands. Rebuilding and prevention activities are still going on, but unfortunately, not all of them appear to be ecologically sound.

DHRITIMAN MUKHERJEE

Tree trunks play a symphony on the waves at gorgeous Chidiya Tapu

organisms such as starfish, sea anemone, plankton and sea cucumber. No plastic (or plastic bags) are allowed here; returnable jute bags are available at the ticket counter to carry things, for a security of Rs 100. Plastic water bottles are allowed with a security deposit of Rs 100 for up to four bottles. The deposit is refunded on return once you show the authorities the bottles you have carried back.

◆**Location** South-west of Port Blair **Entry fee** Rs 300, includes boat transfer and snorkelling **Camera** Rs 25 **Timings** Trip begins at 10 am, returns by 3 pm; closed on Mondays **Connection** Taxis charge Rs 1,000-1,200 for a round trip

Chidiya Tapu (30 km)

Even half an hour before the sunset, there are crowds at Chidiya Tapu, waiting for the sun to set. And there's a crowd because Chidiya Tapu has become famous for the 'sunset experience' it offers, an idea that you initially scoff at. But as the sun changes its colour, becomes mellow enough so that you can hold it in your gaze, everything changes. Life takes on an aspect of an indefinable softness, birds start twittering in the trees above and the reds and browns and blacks play a symphony on the waves... you desperately want to be with the descending ochre ball, like the actors in Hindi films who run to the end of the platforms as the trains move away carrying their beloveds.

Before the sunset, enjoy a swim at **Munde Pahar Beach**, which is 1 km further ahead of the bus stand. Next to the bus stand, there are a couple of shops selling tea and snacks. **Coral Travels** (Tel: 03192-281025) has a desk in front of these shops and offers snorkelling (Rs 400 for an hour) and glass boat rides to see the coral near the beach. **Bhumi Divers** (located at Ananda Hotel, Port Blair; Mobile: 09434277834) offers diving at **Rutland Island**, which is approached by boat from Chidiya Tapu.

◆**Location** South of Port Blair **Connection** Taxis from Port Blair cost Rs 800 for a half-day trip

Collinpur (35 km)

See page 142 ■

DHRITIMAN MUKHERJEE

HAVELOCK ISLAND

ODE TO PERFECTION

Union Territory of Andaman and Nicobar Islands
Location The biggest island in Ritchie's Archipelago, it lies to the north-east of Port Blair
Distance ***By sea*** 21 nautical miles NE of Port Blair
Journey time ***By sea*** 2½-4 hrs from Port Blair, depending on the sea conditions (*see tourist guide on page 104*)

BY AMIT MAHAJAN

Perfection is when the sand slopes at just the right angles to ensure a gradually deepening pool of water — water that's appropriately deep. Perfection is when that water is deep enough to be exciting but, at the same time, shallow enough to be safe. Perfection is when the beach curves in a lovely smooth arc usually referred to as the shape of the crescent moon, such that a bay is formed where the waves come ashore relentlessly, but not treacherously. Perfection is when it's perfect but it still gets better.

Perfection was Radhanagar Beach. And it became better when the elephant came. She came not from the forest behind us, but emerged right in front from the sea. A mahout was beside her, occasionally prodding and stroking her, while she played in the water. Must have gone for a swim, we reasoned. Nevertheless, we were stunned, and mesmerised.

For a while everyone gaped at the big creature with sad eyes, then the trance broke and all rushed to their cameras.

Radhanagar Beach may well be the most sought after place in the Andamans. And the pride of Havelock Island. But Havelock has umpteen other charms. There's the other gorgeous beach — Vijaynagar. That can be a bit craggy in places but if you can find a nice sandy nook with a sea *mahua* tree that's not sure whether it wants to grow horizontally or vertically, then you would not move from there for ages. Then there are the long walks you can have on cool dark breezy evenings on black serpentine roads flowing past paddy fields and coconut plantations. To top it all, there are the diving and snorkelling opportunities. Havelock has the biggest concentration of the most marvellous diving sites in all of Andaman, a variety of coral and fish life, and a choice of good diving schools. In addition to the touristy stuff, Havelock also gives you a chance to interact with the farming communities of these islands, settled here from the mainland, and living their uncertain peasant lives.

ORIENTATION

Havelock is a longish piece of land, lying on a north-west to south-east axis in the group of islands collectively called the **Ritchie's Archipelago**, located north-east of Port Blair. People have been settled only on the northern, one-third part of the island, and each village and the adjoining beach are referred to both by a number and a name. The **jetty** is in the north at **Village No. 1** and is the conceptual centre of the island. **Radhanagar Beach** (No. 7) is 12 km to the south-west. **Vijaynagar** (No. 5) is 4 km south-east of the jetty. The main bazaar is at **No. 3.** Most of the accommodation is located in No. 5 (Vijaynagar). There are some hotels in No. 3, No. 1 and No. 7. Autorickshaws are the main mode of transport; fare varies from Rs 20 to 150; full-day hire costs Rs 800-1,000. Taxis are available near the jetty (Rs 1,200-1,500 for a day) or your hotel can arrange them.

All hotels, taxi drivers, auto drivers and anybody on the street in Havelock will offer boat rides, snorkelling and scuba diving. For diving, there are two diving schools in Andaman: **Barefoot Scuba** (Tel: 03192-282181) and **Dive India** (Tel: 282187) and everybody will take you to one of these. Snorkelling and boat rides are offered by many; ask your hotel or talk to the boatmen near the jetty at No. 1 if you need help deciding.

For a more professional operation, approach **Havelock Tourist Services** (Tel: 282439) opposite the jetty, fast turning into Havelock's only travel agent.

BEACH WATCH

At Radhanagar Beach, be careful at high tide as water can rush in. Otherwise the beach is safe and sandy. Vijaynagar Beach is rocky, and take care not to hurt yourself on the stones. Beachwear is acceptable, even preferable to any other clothing. You can buy it in a few shops near the jetty too.

THINGS TO SEE AND DO

The doing and seeing option in Havelock are centred around its beaches and

→ GETTING THERE

Sea Boats from Phoenix Bay Jetty in Port Blair go twice daily (6.15 am and 2 pm) to Havelock and return. Travel time: $2^{1}/_{2}$-4 hrs. Tickets from Port Blair should be booked in advance, especially for the morning boat. There is no advance booking from Havelock

the diving and snorkelling sites. Besides that, you can while away time in restaurants with unhurried service, and take long leisurely walks amidst paddy fields and coconut and banana plantations.

Radhanagar Beach (Beach No. 7)

Enjoying the Radhanagar Beach is the most do-able activity in Havelock. Some people on package tours come by the morning boat, spend the afternoon on the beach and move on by the evening boat. This is a 'fast-forward' way of 'doing' Radhanagar, but the recommended way is, of course, to spend a couple of days on the beach even though there is no shop or 'activity' at the beach. The white sand, the tall trees behind you and the wave after wave of water to your front are all that you'll need. Get your swimwear, some food and water (remember to not litter and to carry all rubbish back), a book and a towel, and you are all set. You can then swim, take long walks along the shore, read, make friends, play and be merry. An auto from the jetty will charge Rs 150 for a drop. Get them to wait or arrange for a pick-up, as there are no autos or taxis available on the beach.

Fun and frolic on Havelock Island

V MUTHURAMAN

Vijaynagar Beach (Beach No. 5)

Vijaynagar is a long stretch of sand on the east coast of the island, punctuated occasionally by rocky sections. Most of the beach is lined by sea *mahua* trees, large trees whose trunks grow along the ground for many feet before they begin to climb vertically. These trees have lent a distinct character to the seafront, and provide shade close to the water. Vijaynagar Beach is perfect for long walks along the sea. Hotel Dolphin, Wild Orchids, Sunrise and many smaller hotels (*for details, see Where to Stay on page 123*) are located on this beach and their restaurants ensure easy availability of beer and seafood. Autos from the jetty charge Rs 50 for Vijaynagar.

Diving

The sea along the coast of Havelock has an abundance of marine life and provides a rich variety of diving possibilities. It has many diving sites. **Seduction Point** is a huge submerged rock with stag horn coral and different kinds of aquatic life, including Napoleon fish. **Aquarium** has a hard, fringing coral (a coral formation directly attached to the shore) with lots of fish. **Lighthouse** has both hard and soft coral. The site is suitable even for dives in the night, when day-time creatures rest and night-time creatures such as lobsters, squid and stingray come out. **Pilot Reef, Mac Point, Minerva Ledge** and **Turtle Bay** are other promising areas for diving.

There are two licensed diving clubs in Havelock. They charge Rs 3,000-4,500 for a 'Discover Scuba Diving' package — a half-day course to introduce diving to beginners; the tariff includes one dive. The clubs are: **Dive India** (Tel: 282187) at Island Vinnie's Tropical Beach Cabanas Resort on Beach No. 3 and **Barefoot Scuba** (Tel: 282181) at Café Del Mar, also on Beach No. 3.

DHRITIMAN MUKHERJEE

In seventh heaven: Beach No. 7, or Radhanagar Beach, is the pride of Havelock

I tried out the **Discover Scuba Diving package**. First, I was given an introduction to diving, as part of which I learnt the ropes about the equipment and the sign language, among other things (*also see 'Scuba diving tips' on page 124*). Afterwards, the trainer took me into a shallow pool of water near a mangrove-forested beach. Here I was initiated into the art of going underwater with the scuba equipment. We practised this for half an hour or so, and I was declared ready to dive. A boat took us out to the Lighthouse dive site, and we went under.

Inside the water, we glided along a coral shelf. The water got cold and the coral formations became strange and striking. It was an entirely new world, difficult to imagine from outside. Fish swam with us, nibbling at colourful algae. Sea anemones and planktons added to the beauty. We drifted around for 45 mins and then it was time to come up. As we surfaced, the waves made the ocean seem more turbulent but there was little indication of the lives being lived under the surface, a glimpse of which we had caught just a while ago.

Snorkelling

Snorkelling is offered in the shallow areas of the coral eco-systems. **Aquarium** and **Elephant Beach** are the most frequented ones for this. Both these sites have to be reached by boats. Most hotels and Havelock Tourist Services (Tel: 03192-282439) organise snorkelling for Rs 1,000-2,000.

WHERE TO STAY

Havelock's staying options range from chic resorts to camping sites on the beaches. **Barefoot at Havelock** (Tel: 03192-282151; Tariff: Rs 3,200-7,800) is located in a jungle next to Radhanagar Beach. The resort is a group of neat and spacious bamboo cottages and offers all kinds of nature activities: snorkelling, scuba diving, nature walks and yoga, among other things.

Silversand (Tel: 233767, 329499; Tariff: Rs 4,999-7,999) on Vijaynagar Beach is over-priced even for its meticulously laid-out and well-maintained bamboo cottages. **Dolphin Resort** (Tel: 282235/411; Tariff: Rs 1,000-2,000; reservations to be made from the tourist office at Port

Simply smooth: Scuba diving tips

To put it very simply, the process of diving involves going underwater, being able to swim like a fish, breathing normally and seeing clearly. This surely is a drastic change and very precise equipment is needed to achieve it. The diving apparatus consists of a mask that seals off the eyes and the nose from water.

Underwater, you do not breathe through your nose and it has to be ensured that water does not enter the nose. This is achieved through a gas tank that has air (not only oxygen) in it at atmospheric pressure, and a device called the snorkel that connects the gas tank to the mouth via a tube — it's through the snorkel that you breathe. Body suit and flippers on the feet help you move in the water with ease.

There is an inherent risk in going underwater, as any snag in the equipment can be life threatening. To reduce this risk to practically zero, diving has been made into a formalised routine and involves strict precautions. For example, nobody, no matter how experienced, dives alone. In case of any emergency, the partner simply brings you to the surface. Preparation for the first dive takes a few hours in which you learn to use the equipment and some basic signals like 'ok', 'not ok' and 'take me up'.

The most important lesson to be learnt, however, is to not panic, to gain the confidence that whatever happens, your instructor will bail you out, not because they are superhuman but because there are a series of simple premises by which they can do it. It's imperative that you dive only with an instructor licensed by one of the professional diving organisations such as PADI, CMAS, BSAC, SSI and NAVI.

If you can learn this lesson (to not panic), you can dive. There are very few other constraints: you should be more than 10 years old, not have a respiratory problem, be able to learn a few basic visual signals and be able to afford it (it's not too expensive).

Besides this excitement, the purpose of recreational diving is to see life underwater and the best places where you can do that without going too deep — initial dives take you 8-12m down — are coral reefs that (if not damaged) are full of marine life, including coral themselves, algae, fish, planktons and much else.

Blair), run by the Tourism Department, occupies a divine location on the sea on the same beach but offers soulless concrete cottages. The **Wild Orchid Resort** (Tel: 282472; Tariff: Rs 1,500-3,500) next door has wood cottages beautifully laid out among trees. Budget options include **Orient Legend** (Tel: 282389; Tariff: Rs 200-800) and **Sunrise** (Tel: 282408; Tariff: Rs 300-1,000). Both offer basic, stand-alone cottages, and the cheaper ones come without attached baths.

For more hotels and details, see Havelock Accommodation Listings on page 522

WHERE TO EAT

Havelock doesn't have many stand-alone restaurants, but most hotels have their own restaurants, open to everybody. The restaurant at **Wild Orchids** is an attractive construction in understated bamboo. They serve Indian and Chinese cuisine, among others (fish and chips Rs 200, fish curry Rs 150, mixed vegetables Rs 65, vegetarian cheese sandwich Rs 125). The food at **Silversand** (Indian and Continental) is overpriced for its quality: Russian salad costs Rs 125, prawn cocktail Rs 175, crab au gratin Rs 350, chicken biryani Rs 150, and dum aloo Rs 60. Their buffet (Rs 350) is best avoided. **Dolphin Resort** serves Indian cuisine; the dishes are basic (thali Rs 50).

Barefoot is the way to be on Havelock

SWAPAN NAYAK

AROUND HAVELOCK

Long Island (25 nautical miles)
If turtles were to write a travel book, **Lalaji Bay** (nobody knows which Lalaji it refers to) on Long Island, north of Havelock, would feature as a nesting ground of humans, mainly of the Israeli stock. Twice a week, the ferry from Port Blair stops at Long Island and deposits 20 to 50 above-mentioned specimens (and their camping gear), who then trek an hour through the forest to reach the sandy beach at Lalaji Bay on the other side of the island from the jetty. Here they camp, cook, play and swim to their heart's content and go back after a few days.

For those not able to camp, the **Forest Guest House** (Tariff: Rs 400; for bookings call the Chief Wildlife Warden in Port Blair on 03192-233549), if vacant, is a possibility. It has two double bedrooms with bath. In the small market here, there are a couple of dhabas.

◆**Connection** It's best to take the boat from Port Blair (leaves at 6.15 am) via Havelock (the service is available between 10.30 am and 12 noon, only on Wednesdays and Saturdays). The fare is Rs 41 (the journey takes 6 hrs) from Port Blair and Rs 25 ($3^1/_2$ hrs) from Havelock. No prior reservation is needed at Havelock; at Port Blair, reservations can be made at Phoenix Bay. The boat doesn't stay at Long Island for long ■

DIGLIPUR

FARAWAY FIELDS

Union Territory of Andaman and Nicobar Islands
Location Amidst the paddy fields of North Andaman, next to Saddle Peak Wildlife Sanctuary
Distances ***By road*** 310 km N of Port Blair ***By sea*** 100 nautical miles
Journey time from Port Blair ***By road*** 12 hrs ***By sea*** 13 hrs
Route from Port Blair Andaman Trunk Road to Diglipur via Baratang, Rangat and Mayabunder (*see tourist guide on page 104*)

BY AMIT MAHAJAN

Though the Andaman Islands spread much further north off Diglipur, it's the northernmost region in Andamans even for the most adventurous of tourists. Here I was, much removed from my world, and as I sat thinking about my journey, it seemed very unreal. I first took a flight to the East Coast at Chennai, then travelled a thousand kilometres over the sea to Port Blair, and island-hopping from there on ferries and buses, reached Diglipur. Again I was on a motorboat, going to the Ross and Smith Islands. Delhi, where I live, seemed far, far away.

Photographs by NONI CHAWLA

Hari was driving the motorboat, I was the only passenger and I was trying to understand Diglipur through his life. His family came to the Andaman Islands from near Ranchi in Jharkhand and settled in a village near Diglipur. They were members of a community of traditional forest-dwellers who had found sustenance difficult and had looked at farming as a promising alternative. They came here when land for farming was promised to them. Forests were cleared and fields laid out, and his parents learnt to tend paddy fields and coconut palms.

Just 30 years later, their existence has become precarious. Now, Hari looks for odd jobs — like driving motorboats — whenever possible in Diglipur. He has also endured the tortuous route to Delhi, that I took in the other direction, and has spent the previous tourist off-season working in a factory in Noida but came back after two months of too little money for too much work in a place too far.

The faraway fields of Diglipur abound with these stories. It's among such stories that the beaches and islands and forests of Diglipur are situated, waiting to enchant the traveller.

ORIENTATION

Diglipur is a small town; the **bus stand** and the half-a-kilometre long **bazaar** around it constitute most of the town. The **APWD Guesthouse** is on a hill at the north-east edge of the market. **Aerial Bay** is 9 km south-east of the town; **Ross and Smith Islands** are 3 km into the sea from there. The same road goes further south to **Turtle Resort** and **Kalipur Beach**. Autos (minimum fare Rs 20, Rs 500 for the day) can be hired at the bazaar. Taxis can be rented from **A2Z Travels** (Tel: 03192-271666) for Rs 1,200-1,500 per day.

BEACH WATCH

Waves can be rough at Kalipur, so don't go deep into the sea. It's safe to swim near the beach. You can wear swimsuits but you won't be able to buy any here.

THINGS TO SEE AND DO

Blue water, rainy days and starry nights define Diglipur. A green shawl spreads over it in the rains. Till a few decades ago, this green shawl was a rainforest. Now, it's made up of paddy fields. After settlements were established here in the 1950s, Diglipur came to be known as the 'Rice Bowl of Andamans'. This small town serves the needs of the villages around it and the few tourists who land up this far in the Andamans. The Kalipur Beach and Ross and Smith Islands are day-long excursions from Diglipur.

Ross and Smith Islands

Do Ross and Smith comprise one island or two? There's a valid reason for this confusion. Ross and Smith are two

→ GETTING THERE

Sea Boats from Phoenix Bay Jetty in Port Blair go five days a week to Aerial Bay Jetty in Diglipur. The travel time is 13 hrs and the fare is Rs 200

Road Diglipur is connected to Port Blair by the Andaman Trunk Road (ATR) via Baratang, Rangat and Mayabunder. At Kadamtala and again at Baratang, vehicles cross a creek on ferries. While the tourism industry promotes the ATR (NH223 upto Mayabunder), especially the 'attraction' of going through tribal areas, sea travel is a more eco-friendly way of travelling in the islands. The travel time is 12 hrs. Buses run early in the morning both ways: 6.30 am from Port Blair, and 5 am from Diglipur. The fare is Rs 250 for deluxe buses, and Rs 150 for ordinary

Tropical rainforests: Tall, dark and handsome

Only an aerial shot can do it justice: three-fourths of the frame covered by an island, a green jewel floating in deep blue waters, confident of its captivating beauty. It's one of the enduring, even clichéd, images of the Andaman and Nicobar Islands. This thick green cover one sees on the islands is courtesy a tropical rainforest. And the impression this image conveys is that no one has ever penetrated this covering and nothing can ever be known of what goes on underneath. Some things, however, are known about such forests — enough to make us realise that they are something special.

The tall, dark and majestic tropical forest is full of tall trees. These forests are found in wet regions, mainly in the tropics in the American, African and Asian continents. The temperature in a rainforest rarely exceeds 34°C or drops below 20°C. Tropical forests cover less than one-twentieth of the earth's surface, but contain maybe half of the world's plant and animal species. They also produce 40 per cent of the earth's oxygen. One-fourth of all the medicines we use come from tropical rainforests. The vegetation in a rainforest exists in four layers: giant trees (60m and more) hovering above all else, then a canopy (about 30m), followed by an understorey and a forest floor. Various animals live in these layers, but rainforests do not have large predators such as tigers or leopards. These ecosystems are important for attracting rain clouds, for protecting the coasts from erosion, for maintaining bio-diversity and much more.

But they are depleting very fast. In the past 150 years, the undisturbed forest cover of Andaman and Nicobar Islands has gone down from 96 per cent of the total land area to 21 per cent. And the regrown forests, leave alone plantations, just do not measure up.

islands at high tide, but as the waters ebb, a sand bar connecting the two emerges out of the ocean and forms a glowing white passage connecting the two. The connecting limb also becomes a fantastic beach — there's clear, undisturbed sand with shallow coves and ideal swimming pools on its two sides.

In contrast, the bulk of the two islands is covered with evergreen tropical forests. Together, the two islands form a dumbbell-like shape — two circular pieces of land covered with tall trees and connected by a low lying stretch of sand. Thus, twice in a day, Ross and Smith are two separate islands and the rest of the time they are one island. The region also had some splendid fringing corals, but most got destroyed in the tsunami of December 2004.

◆**Location** Near Aerial Bay Jetty **Permit fee** Indians Rs 50, foreigners Rs 500; permission to visit has to be secured from the Range Office at Aerial Bay Jetty, located across the road **Connection** The islands are 30 mins away by motorboat (Rs 600 or

Evergreen tropical forests cover most of the Ross and Smith islands

more, ask at the Aerial Bay Jetty) from Aerial Bay (9 km from Diglipur)

Kalipur Beach (22 km)

A beautiful and idyllic beach lined with palm trees, Kalipur offers great views of Ross Island. This beach is perfect for swimming, sunbathing and walks. Kalipur is further south from Aerial Bay and located among fishing and farming villages far away from town. The road winds along the coast, sometimes hugging it. Turtle Resort (*see below*), run by the Tourism Department, is located atop a hill nearby, and can provide food if given prior notice.

WHERE TO STAY

There are only two options here. **Turtle Resort** (Tel: 03192-220603; Tariff: Rs 400-800; reservations to be made at the tourist office in Port Blair) is 18 km from the town centre, and is a guest house run by the Tourism Department. It occupies a great location atop a hill only a short distance from Kalipur Beach. The **APWD Guesthouse** (Tel: 272206; Tariff: Rs 400-800; permission to be secured from the executive engineer next door) is perched atop a hill in the middle of the town.

For more details, see Diglipur Accommodation Listings on page 522

WHERE TO EAT

Turtle Resort has a restaurant that can give you a meal of dal, rice and vegetable (Rs 20) and an omelette (Rs 12) and toast for breakfast. The kitchen in the **APWD Guesthouse** will dish out similarly simple fare. The main bazaar next to the bus stand has a couple of dhabas for tea, snacks (samosa, namkeen) and food (dal-rice-noodles). ■

RAKESH SAHAI/ AGP PHOTOBANK

MAYABUNDER

THE SOLITARY REAPER

Union Territory of Andaman and Nicobar Islands
Location In the northern part of Middle Andaman Island
Distances ***By road*** 242 km N of Port Blair ***By sea*** 73 nautical miles
Journey time from Port Blair ***By road*** 9 hrs ***By sea*** 11 hrs
Route from Port Blair Andaman Trunk Road (NH223) to Mayabunder via Nilanbur, Udaygarh and Rangat (*see tourist guide on page 104*)

BY AMIT MAHAJAN

I had a feeling I was the only tourist in town. The only other guest in the APWD Guesthouse, where I was staying, was a business executive. The day before, I had heard of three foreigners who had been to Avis Island before me, but my boatman was sure that their plan had been to return to Rangat the same day. In my two hours at Karmatang Beach, I had been in the water thrice. In between I had been lying with my book under a palm tree, munching on the cashews I had brought along. And all this while there had been nobody on the beach. Then I saw a few specks far to the north-west along the coast slowly shaping into human forms. Fifteen minutes later this became a group of men, saddled with rucksacks, seemingly out for a hike or a trek and out to prove my 'only-tourist' hypothesis wrong. They were trekkers who were planning to walk the coast of the Andamans, from near Diglipur to Rangat, camping on beaches or near villages on the way. Now they were looking for some fresh water to cook a meal. I directed them to a house in the farmland behind the beach and dug out my map of the islands to see what route they would be travelling along. Looked like a cool way to discover the islands.

You'll rarely see any other tourists in Mayabunder. What you'll encounter instead is a market town with a bit of bustle about it, a large fishing community cooped next to the sea, and a few villages scattered around.

If you come for a holiday here, you'll not be offered a menu of touristy things that you can choose from, rather you'll have to conjure up your own recipe using the sea, the beaches and the islands as the chief ingredients.

ORIENTATION

Mayabunder is located on the northernmost edge of Middle Andaman Island. The town juts out as a peninsula into the sea northwards between Middle Andaman and North Andaman Island. The main **bus stand** is at the north-western end of the town. Half a kilometre to the east is the **APWD Guesthouse**. The main **market**, which is also the town centre, is half a kilometre south of the APWD Guesthouse. **Avis Island** is 2 km north-east of the main market. The two main beaches **Rampur Beach** and **Karmatang Beach** are to the south-east of the town, 4 km and 12 km respectively from the town centre. There are no travel agents in Mayabunder. Taxis (Rs 1,200-1,500 per day) and autorickshaws (Rs 10 per km approx, min Rs 20) are available in the town centre.

FAST FACTS

Road Mayabunder is connected to Port Blair by Andaman Trunk Road (ATR) via Baratang and Rangat. There are daily State Transport buses from the main bus stand near Aberdeen Bazaar (6 am). The travel time is 9 hrs and the fare is Rs 190 (deluxe), and Rs 100 (ordinary)

BEACH WATCH

Be careful at the beaches; not only are there no lifeguards, but there might also not be anybody besides you at the beaches. Before going to the beaches, enquire about the high and low tide timings from the locals. Beachwear is fine as nobody is going to be looking anyway, but of course, you can't buy it here.

THINGS TO SEE AND DO

Go to Mayabunder only if you're comfortable with the idea of doing nothing for most of the day. A tourist's itinerary in Mayabunder primarily involves sitting outside the APWD Guesthouse and gazing at the sea below, doing nothing. Or spending a day on Avis Island, doing nothing. Or going to a beach for some hours, again doing nothing.

You can go to the beaches any time but do remember that when the sun is high, there's not too much shade. It's better to go to Avis Island in the morning because the boats that will take you there are used for fishing in the afternoon.

Avis

If you have contemplated Avis Island from the APWD Guesthouse, and formulated a plan to go to the island, change into your swimwear and get wet, you need to rework it. For, you'll be not just wet but soaked before you reach the island. You'll have to wade through knee-deep water to reach the *doongi* (motor boat) that will transport you. And then

SETH LAZER

The family tree: Tracing roots in the Andamans

Stretching along large parts of Andaman and Nicobar Islands' coastlines, where the land meets the sea, are green ribbons of life. These are the mangrove swamps that are full of plants and animals that can live in inter-tidal zones. Mangrove swamps are formed around mangroves, which are special types of trees that can grow in the near impossible conditions of the inter-tidal zone. Here there's seawater, unstable, salty soil and regular, twice-daily flooding when the tide comes in. The mud is very sticky, closely packed and does not have much oxygen. It's a tough habitat for any tree. But mangroves have adapted well and they not only survive themselves but also provide food and shelter to a variety of marine animals and birds.

There are many species of mangroves and about 110 have been identified. They have all evolved in various ways to be compatible with the conditions. To anchor themselves firmly in the soil, some mangroves develop **prop roots** — long roots that grow down from the trunks and branches of the trees and get anchored in the mud. These stilt-like roots trap leaves, detritus and other floating debris, making the trees' footing firmer. Prop roots have tiny pores called **lenticles**. These help the mangrove trees breathe since the soil has a low level of oxygen. There are other trees that send up stick-like "breathing roots" from the mud called **pneumatophores**.

To handle the problem of salinity, the roots of mangroves develop filters that keep the salt out; some plants have **salt glands** on the leaves through which extra salt exits; or the leaves themselves store salt and become fleshy.

Mangroves play an indispensable role in the protection of the coasts and in maintaining their bio-diversity. Mangroves are home to a variety of creatures: periwinkle, prawn, eel, fiddler crab, oyster, frogs, herons, kingfishers, sandpipers and others.

Mangroves slow down the tidal waters and help dissipate the tidal energy, thus acting as storm breakers. The rainwater that flows from land to sea contains fine mud called silt and leaves. Mangroves trap these and they are used as nutrients by plants and animals. They also create more land area by slowly inching their way towards the sea, colonising a tiny bit of sea each year.

Unfortunately, mangrove forests across the world have been degraded and devastated and the habitats of many plants and animals are threatened. The Andamans have lost many mangroves to development and building activities, but their usefulness against the destructiveness of the sea was underscored during the tsunami, when the trees managed to lessen the impact of the waves. This has spurred efforts to save mangroves in these islands.

Courtesy IP & T DEPARTMENT

Looking out at the sea: At a government guest house in Mayabunder

chances are that as the boat cuts through the wavy waters, a constant spray will be directed at your person. Therefore, do remember to change into your swimwear before you start.

My advice to the weak of heart is to skip this trip. Time after time, it'll seem that the boat is going to turn turtle. Besides, there are enough beaches in the Andamans that can be accessed without going through this rather demanding experience. However, if truth be told, Avis is different from other islands. For one, it's a convex beach; unlike most others, the beach protrudes into the sea. And then there is the island — a small, beautiful piece of land with a coconut plantation in the middle and a gorgeous white ring along most of the periphery.

Permission (Rs 50) is to be taken from the current head (she was an elderly lady when I visited) of the cooperative that manages the coconut plantation on the island. Auto drivers and boat-wallahs will guide you about getting this done. A boat will cost Rs 600 for the return trip, including a couple of hours at the island.

Karmatang and Rampur beaches

Rampur Beach is on the outskirts of the town and Karmatang further afield. Karmatang Beach is hidden from the road going past it by a rocky outcrop and coconut plantations. The approach to the beach is also an unmarked, inconspicuous footpath. It, therefore, gives the impression of a secret hideout that's facing vast open seas. The place is quite enchanting. The water is clean, the waves not too rough and the sand soft under the feet. Autos will charge Rs 400 for half a day, a taxi Rs 700-800.

Rampur Beach is smaller of the two and with less shade. It's right next to the road and the children at the village will usually give you company and, may be, a chance to play with them. Close to the beach you can also see a portion of a mangrove forest. Autos will charge Rs 60 for a drop.

WHERE TO STAY

The **APWD Guesthouse** (Tel: 03192-273211; Tariff: Rs 400-800; permission has

to be taken from the assistant commissioner's office next door; Tel: 273208) is the only real choice among places to stay. The rooms are spacious and clean, and the view from the lawns is simply breathtaking. The guest house is located atop a cliff right on the sea and you can see far into water from here. **Anmol Guesthouse** (Tel: 262695; Tariff: Rs 100-400) near the main market is a basic place to stay with small, tidy rooms, some with attached baths.

For more details, see Mayabunder Accommodation Listings on pages 522-523

WHERE TO EAT

The **APWD Guesthouse** has a restaurant for residents and serves simple fare: egg (Rs 10-15), toast (Rs 12), parantha (Rs 10), tea, coffee for breakfast; dal, subzi, roti and rice for lunch and dinner (Rs 40). There are a few dhabas and tea and snack shops in the main market.

Another quiet day at Mayabunder

DHRITIMAN MUKHERJEE

AROUND MAYABUNDER

Cutbert Bay, Rangat (54 km)
Cutbert Bay is a different thing for different people. For the motorist travelling on the Andaman Trunk Road, it's a minor halt marked by the Tourism Department's guest house and a couple of teashops. For the fishing village (oddly called RRO) close by, it's a good source of sea fish. For the traveller, it's a long beach with even sand that's ideal for long walks on wet sand and occasional dips in the water.

The bay is also a traditional nesting site for turtles. Between November and January, especially on moonless dark nights, mother turtles come to the beach for anything from 30 to 45 mins, lay their eggs, bury them in the sand and toddle off to the sea. If you have patience and if luck is with you, you might be able to witness this.

The eggs are under grave threat from dogs and humans, and therefore people from the turtle hatchery (run by the Forest Department) located on the beach are quick to collect any such eggs.

Hawksbill Nest (Tel: 03192-279159; Tariff: Rs 200-800; reservations to be made from the tourist office), the only place to stay here, is a plain structure by the roadside, run by the Tourism Department, but sometimes closed due to water shortage. They have a restaurant that can dish out a simple dal, rice, a seasonal vegetable, fish and a thali (vegetarian Rs 55 and non-vegetarian Rs 120).

◆**Location** Rangat lies south of Mayabunder, on the Andaman Trunk Road, in Middle Andaman **Connection** From Mayabunder, State Transport buses run to Rangat, which stop at Cutbert Bay, right outside Hawksbill Nest. There are five to six bus services from Mayabunder during the day; the bus fare is Rs 20 ■

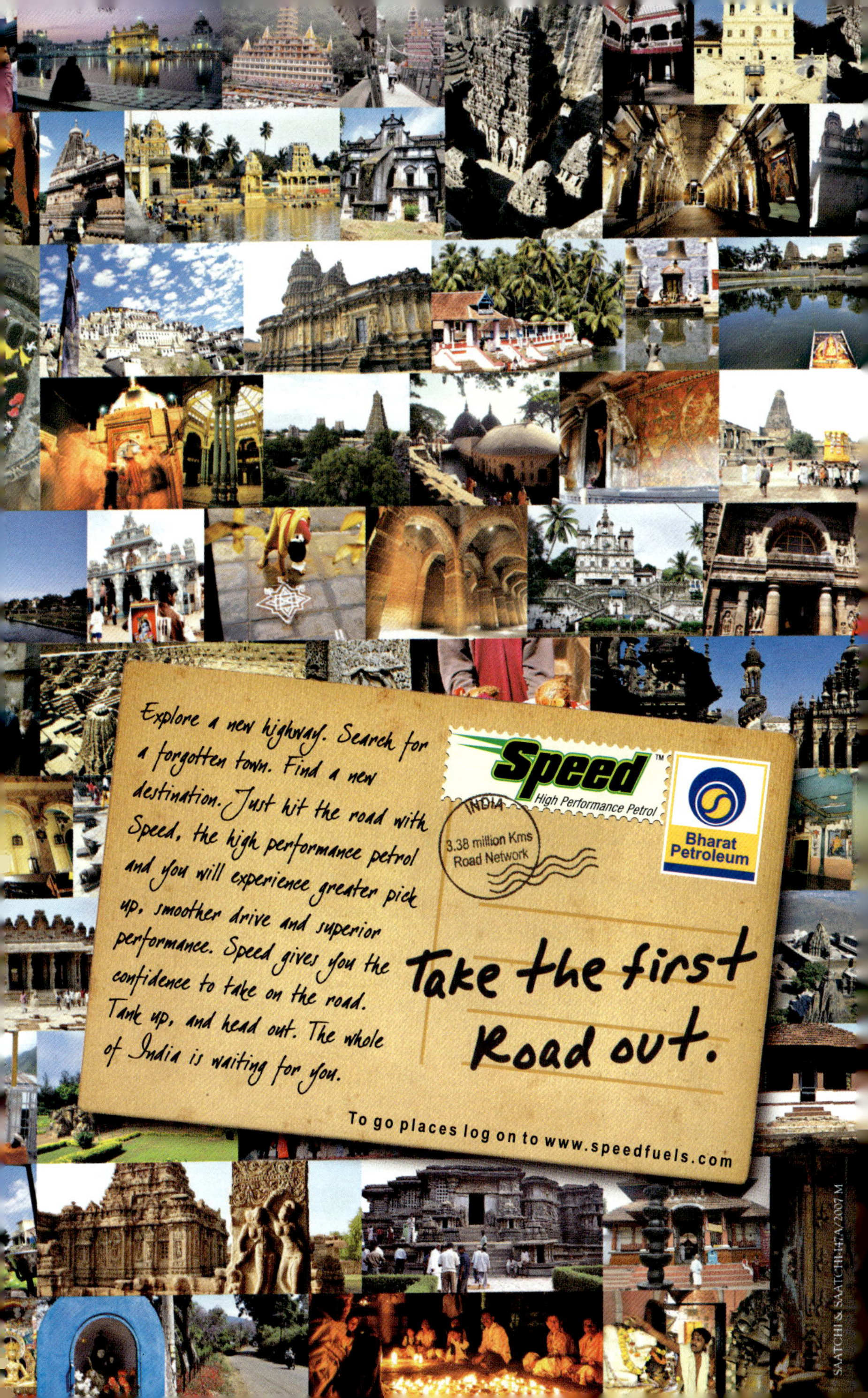

Explore a new highway. Search for a forgotten town. Find a new destination. Just hit the road with Speed, the high performance petrol and you will experience greater pick up, smoother drive and superior performance. Speed gives you the confidence to take on the road. Tank up, and head out. The whole of India is waiting for you.
Speed™
High Performance Petrol
Bharat Petroleum
INDIA
3.38 million Kms
Road Network
Take the first Road out.
To go places log on to www.speedfuels.com

RAKESH SAHAI/ AGP PHOTOBANK

WHERE TO GO NEXT

■ **BY AMIT MAHAJAN**

Apart from the destinations in the Andamans that we have covered earlier in this section, there are many more options for the intrepid traveller looking to discover the path less explored. Given below are a few places that you might want to visit.

NEIL ISLAND

A beautiful island called the 'Vegetable Bowl of the Andamans' — as most of the land here is under cultivation — Neil's main attractions include lush forests and sandy beaches such as **Lakshmanpur**, **Bharatpur** and **Sitapur**. **Hawabill Nest** (Tel: 03192-282630; Tariff: Rs 600-800) is the tourism guest house here. It has four AC rooms and two four-bedded non-AC rooms; it also has a restaurant.

◆**Location** 19 nautical miles by sea, north-east of Port Blair **Connection** By ferry from Port Blair, four days a week

TIP Bookings for all the Tourism Department-run guest houses and hotels have to be made at the Andaman and Nicobar Islands Tourism Department office at Port Blair (*for contact details, see page 107*)

BARATANG

An island that lies between the South and Middle Andaman Islands, Baratang is famous for its mud volcanoes, which

RAKESH SAHAI/ AGP PHOTOBANK

PANKAJ SEKHSARIA

The undiscovered gems of Andamans: Solitude for the asking at Little Andaman (facing page); **Baratang has beautiful beaches** (above left) **and Neil Island** (above right)

spew mud and gas. It also has its share of beautiful attractions, such as limestone caves and beaches, including the **Baludera Beach**. Also located here is **Tota Tekri**, an islet surrounded by mangroves that host hundreds of parrots at sunset daily. The **APWD Guesthouse** (Tel: 279526; Tariff: Rs 400-800) is the only option here. It has five rooms, two of which are air-conditioned. Food is available at the restaurant here.

◆**Location** 100 km north of Port Blair by road **Connection** As the road to Baratang passes through tribal areas, vehicles travelling through the region need to have a permit (not the passenger); a few travel agencies such as Allan Travels (Tel: 233358, 233034) offer tours to Baratang (Rs 5,500 by car, exclusive of accommodation costs; Rs 600 per person by bus for a one-day trip). Two state transport buses run to Baratang from Port Blair; the journey takes 4 hrs one-way. If you're opting for the bus, you don't need a permit to travel here

LITTLE ANDAMAN

This island is further south of the South Andaman Island. **Hut Bay** is the entry and exit point, and has a diving site nearby. **Butler Bay** is a popular beach here. There are two waterfalls too.

◆**Location** 65 nautical miles from Port Blair by sea **Connection** Daily ferry from Port Blair's Phoenix Jetty ■

PANKAJ SEKHSARIA

COLLINPUR: Picnic on the beach

BY SAROJINI NAYAK

Hidden amidst swaying palms, arecanut plantations and tall gigantic trees is the tiny, U-shaped Collinpur Beach. While every beach in the Andamans has its own charm, what sets apart this slightly off-beat destination is its tranquility and the amazing rock formations that adorn the beach. A fascinating combination of gnarled trunks of ancient trees, huge boulders and driftwood is strewn carelessly on the shoreline, and the lush green tropical forests provide a unique backdrop to the blue waters that gently lap the shore.

The beach, about one and half kilometres in length, is narrow; at some places, trees stand right on the shoreline, almost touching the waves. Huge rocks of various shapes and sizes, with overgrown trees perched on them, can also be seen. A small concrete structure lies half submerged on the beach – a Japanese bunker that was washed ashore long ago.

Although Collinpur doesn't offer any water sports, it's today a popular picnic spot. One can explore the forest on the seashore and climb the rocks. Swimming, snorkelling, camping and fishing can be done, but you need to have your own gear. You can request a local fisherman to give you a ride on his boat for Rs 200-300. Like most beaches in the Andamans, corals, shells and other fascinating objects from the ocean can be seen scattered on the shore. Apart from Corbyn's Cove (*see page 110*), Collinpur is the beach nearest to Port Blair where you can swim and bathe. And unlike Corbyn's Cove, it's not crowded, and in my opinion, much prettier.

GETTING THERE

Collinpur is 35 km south of Port Blair and it takes about an hour to reach here by road. Take the Andaman Trunk Road (ATR) that goes from Port Blair to Diglipur. Head past Gharacharma and Chouldharui, and at Tusnabad, branch off from the ATR and take the bypass to Collinpur Junction. Collinpur Village is about 3 km from Collinpur Junction. Vehicles have to be parked at Collinpur Village, and one has to walk about 5 mins to the beach. Taxis can be hired from Port Blair and they usually charge a full day's rental of about Rs 800. Alternatively, one can take a State Transport bus from Port Blair to Collinpur Junction (one-way fare Rs 12) and from there, hire a jeep to reach Collinpur Village (jeeps generally charge about Rs 100 as return fare). The jeep driver will drop you off and then return to pick you up at the given time. ■

KERALA

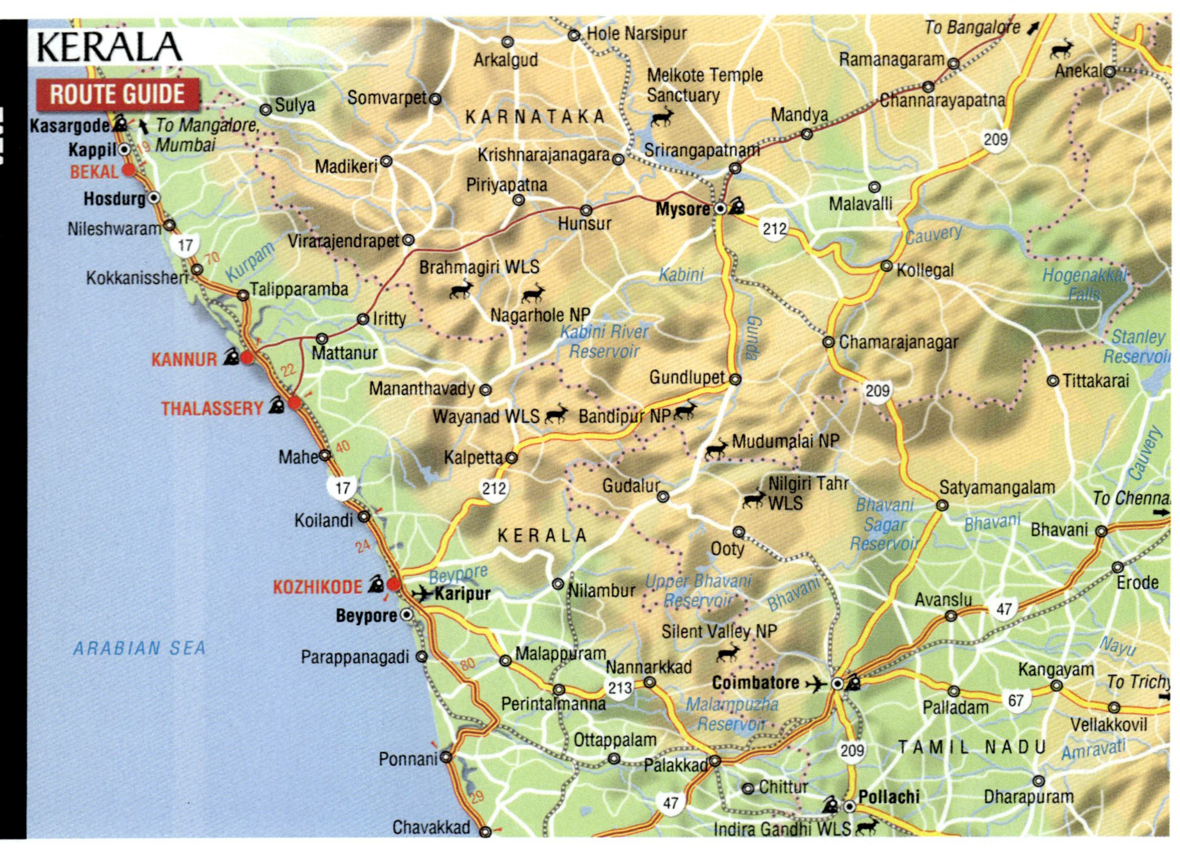
KERALA
ROUTE GUIDE
TATA
SAFARI DICOR 2.2 VTT
ARABIAN SEA
KARNATAKA
KERALA
TAMIL NADU
To Mangalore, Mumbai
To Bangalore
To Chennai
To Trichy
Kasargode
Kappil
BEKAL
Hosdurg
Nileshwaram
Kokkanissheri
KANNUR
THALASSERY
Mahe
Koilandi
KOZHIKODE
Beypore
Parappanagadi
Ponnani
Chavakkad
Sulya
Somvarpet
Madikeri
Virarajendrapet
Talipparamba
Kurpam
Iritty
Mattanur
Brahmagiri WLS
Mananthavady
Wayanad WLS
Kalpetta
Nagarhole NP
Kabini River Reservoir
Kabini
Arkalgud
Piriyapatna
Krishnarajanagara
Hunsur
Hole Narsipur
Melkote Temple Sanctuary
Srirangapatnam
Mysore
Mandya
Ramanagaram
Channarayapatna
Malavalli
Kollegal
Cauvery
Hogenakkal Falls
Stanley Reservoir
Anekal
Tittakarai
Chamarajanagar
Gundlupet
Gunda
Bandipur NP
Mudumalai NP
Nilgiri Tahr WLS
Gudalur
Ooty
Satyamangalam
Bhavani Sagar Reservoir
Bhavani
Erode
Nilambur
Karipur
Upper Bhavani Reservoir
Silent Valley NP
Malappuram
Perintalmanna
Nannarkkad
Ottappalam
Palakkad
Malampuzha Reservoir
Coimbatore
Chittur
Pollachi
Indira Gandhi WLS
Avanslu
Palladam
Kangayam
Vellakkovil
Dharapuram
Nayu
Amravati
209
212
17
47
67
213
22
24
29
40
70
80

To Dindigul
Trichy, Madurai
To Thirumangalam
Madurai
To Madurai,
Hyderabad
Kovilpatti
Palani
Kodaikanal
Periyakulam
Usilampatti
Theni
Anamalai WLS
Eravikulam NP
Devikulam
Munnar
Painavu
Idukki
Thekkady
Periyar WLS
Periyar Lake
Srivilliputtur
Kadiyanallur
Tenkasi
Tirunelveli
Kalakad WLS
Nanguneri
Kodyar Lake
To Kanyakumari
Peppara WLS
Nedumangad
Thattekkad WLS
Kakki Reservoir
Pathanamthita
Punalur
Kanjirapally
Pala
Changanassery
Thiruvalla
Adur
Kottarakara
Ashtamudi Lake
Attingal
Attingok
Mangalapuram
Anjengo
THIRUVANANTHAPURAM
KOVALAM
POOVAR
VARKALA
KOLLAM
Thangassery
Chavara
Karunagapally
Haripad
Ambalapuzha
ALAPPUZHA
Vembanad Lake
Cherthala
Vaikom
Kottayam
Muvattupuzha
Ernakulam
Nedumbassery
Aluva
KOCHI
Vypeen
CHERAI
Kodungalloor
Irinjalakuda
Trichur
Peechi Vazhani WLS
Parambikulam WLS
Parambikulam Reservoir
Periyar
Lakshadweep Sea
ARABIAN SEA
N
TATA
SAFARI Dicor 2.2 VTT

KOVALAM

THE GOLDEN MILE

State Kerala
Location Close to state capital Thiruvananthapuram, at the southern end of the Kerala Coast
Distance 13 km S of Thiruvananthapuram
Journey time ***By road*** 1/2 hr from Thiruvananthapuram
Route from Thiruvananthapuram NH47 Bypass to Kovalam (*see route guide on pages 144-145*)

BY NILANJANA BISWAS

In Kovalam, you can spend blissful hours doing absolutely nothing in a deck chair by the sea. The urban life you led no more than a few days ago recedes from memory. In the morning, as the sun climbs up the sky, local fishermen bring their wooden boats back from the sea, dragging nets and skeins with thick coir ropes. Soon the beach starts to fill up with tourists and sunbathers. By the time the sun is overhead, the beach is deserted except for the stray mongrel, crow or eagle. It's in the evening that Kovalam wakes up. Restaurants put out seafood on slabs of ice and owners tempt passing crowds with promises of delicious meals. Touts and hawkers run after tourists calling out greetings in a mind-boggling variety of languages. From Pink Floyd to the Beatles, from FM radio to soul, there is music playing in every shack. Sunsets are glorious and best watched with a drink in hand from one of the wayside restaurants. Only the circling beam of light from a nearby lighthouse signals the end of yet another day.

Kovalam's golden sands, cerulean blue waters and high surf enchant even its most vocal detractors. No doubt tourism has boomed in this once-sleepy village.

PRASHANT PANJIAR

However, if you're willing to ignore the problems of overcrowding, the atmosphere is resort-like, festive and exuberant. Once you're there, you can't remain unmoved by the magic that is Kovalam.

ORIENTATION

Kovalam is spread along three crescent beaches separated by rocky promontories. From north to south, these are the **Samudra Beach**, the **Hawah** (or **Eve's**) **Beach** and the **Lighthouse Beach**, connected through well-laid out roads to the main road towards Kovalam Junction and Thiruvananthapuram. Not far from Kovalam are the **Vizhinzam Harbour** and **Chowara Beach**. Further south, 18 km from Kovalam, is **Poovar**. While the Hawah Beach leads to the Lighthouse Beach in a single stretch, a 15-min walk from these twin beaches, or an auto (fare Rs 25) will take you to Samudra Beach. Hire an auto to reach **Vizhinzam** (Rs 50) and **Chowara** (Rs 100). Poovar is a 20-min ride from Kovalam by taxi (Rs 450) or by auto (Rs 200). Both taxis and autos are available at the taxi stand at the entrance to Hawah Beach.

BEACH WATCH

Except during the monsoon, Kovalam's beaches are excellent for swimming and are patrolled by lifeguards. Surfing and boating opportunities are plentiful. It must also be mentioned that there seems to be some kind of unwritten cultural code regarding beachwear and Indian women across Kerala, one followed in Kovalam as well. Among foreigners, women dress in beachwear but this writer did not see a single Indian woman in beachwear. Indian men, on the other hand, don all kinds of swimwear.

THINGS TO SEE AND DO

There are many tourist attractions in and around Kovalam. A stay at the enchanting island of Poovar (*see page 152*) can be rejuvenating.

FAST FACTS

When to go October to March
Tourist offices
- Tourist Facilitation Centre
Dept of Tourism, Govt of Kerala
Near The Leela Kempinski, Kovalam
Tel: 0471-2480085
- KTDC
Central Reservations, Hotel Mascot
Thiruvananthapuram
Tel: 0471-2316736, 2318990
Email: centralreservations@ktdc.com
Website: ktdc.com
- District Tourism Promotion Council
Opp Raj Bhavan, Kowdiar PO
Vellayambalam, Thiruvananthapuram
Tel: 0471-2315397
Website: keralatourism.org

STD code 0471

Kovalam's beaches

During the season, Kovalam's beaches, though ideal for swimming, sunbathing and surfing, tend to get overcrowded. The crowds thin out as the day gets hotter. Evenings are ideal to hang out in the many open-air cafés and pizzerias overlooking the sea and enjoy Kovalam's resort-like ambience. Deck chairs and surfing boards can be hired at Rs 50-75 per day. Local fishermen offer boat rides on simple country boats at Rs 300 per hour but be warned that recent accidents have made the administration strict about licences. To be safe, take a licensed boat from Vizhinzam Harbour.

Samudra is the quietest of Kovalam's three beaches. With the arrival of upscale hotels, it's however going through a rapid transformation from a laidback, fishing

village to a posh tourist spot. The bustling **Hawah** and **Lighthouse** beaches are more or less a continuous stretch lined with eateries, hotels and shops. The Lighthouse Beach has a lighthouse, perched atop the Kurumkkal rock on the southern tip of the beach. It offers a spectacular view of the sea and the Vizhinzam Harbour. The beach also offers surfing opportunities. There are a number of private operators on Hawah Beach who rent out surfboards and deck chairs at Rs 50 per piece for the day. However, many hotels provide these on a complimentary basis to their guests; check with the hotel you are staying for free equipment.
♦**Lighthouse entry fee** Rs 5

GETTING THERE

Air Nearest airport: Thiruvananthapuram International Airport (19 km/ 1/2 hr). Taxi fare to Kovalam Rs 350-500
Rail Nearest railhead: Thiruvananthapuram Central (13 km/ 20 mins), connected to Delhi by the Kerala Express; to Chennai by the Trivandrum Mail, Trivandrum Express, Anantapuri Express and MS Guruvayur Express; to Mumbai by the Kanyakumari Express and Netravati Express; to Bangalore by the Kanyakumari Express; to Kolkata by the Howrah-Trivandrum Express and the Gurudev Express
Road Kovalam is on the NH47 Bypass, 13 km off NH47, which links Salem to Kanyakumari via Palakkad, Thrissur, Ernakulam, Alappuzha, Kollam and Thiruvananthapuram. Kovalam's KSRTC Bus Stand is in Vizhinzam on the Vizhinzam-Poovar Road. Buses ply every 15 mins to Thiruvananthapuram. The road from the state capital to Kovalam is broad and excellently laid out though busy

Ayurveda on the beach

Ayurveda is ubiquitous in Kovalam with every hotel and resort offering a variety of Ayurveda packages as an added attraction. Everywhere, signboards advertise Panchakarma and other treatments, which are in reality no more than quack massages. In an effort to regulate the mushrooming of Ayurveda services, the government has recently introduced special certification — Green Leaf and Olive Leaf — based on the adequacy of space, trained personnel and medical infrastructure at the centre. A Green Leaf-certified centre is one that is most compliant with regulation criteria while an Olive Leaf-certified centre complies with some criteria but not all.

Vizhinzam

A tiny and visibly poor fishing village, Vizhinzam offers a picturesque view of a bay with dozens of colourful fishing boats bobbing about in its blue waters.
♦**Location** Close to Kovalam Junction, down Temple Road

Thiruvallom

At Thiruvallom, the Killi River and Karamana River join the Arabian Sea in an idyllic confluence of backwater, estuary and sea. Boat rides are organised by the **Thiruvallom Boat Club** (Rs 300 per hour) through the backwaters. **Pozhikkara Beach** is a unique spot close to Thiruvallom where the Karamana River and Parvathy Puthanaar River join the Arabian Sea.
♦**Location** 8 km from Kovalam **Temple timings** 3.45-11 am and 5-8 pm

Chowara Beach

Located at the foot of the **Chowara Ayyappa Temple**, the beach offers a delightful expanse of golden sand and clear waters. The serene ambience has encouraged the development of several upscale heritage resorts and Ayurveda centres in the area.
♦**Location** 8 km south of Kovalam

V MUTHURAMAN

Catching them early: Tiny tots out on a walk by the sea

SHOPPING

Shops selling artifacts and jewellery have mushroomed in Kovalam. The cemented path that runs along Lighthouse Beach and much of Eve's Beach has several shops, cafés and restaurants. Some of the shops sell paintings, carpets, metalwork and woodwork articles. Tibetan shawls and woodwork are to be found in **Yak Boutique** and **Heaven Handicrafts**, which also sell Indian crafts.

If you're looking for something Keralite, try **Surabhi Handicrafts**, a state-run co-operative located outside the car park at Kovalam Junction, for bric-a-brac fashioned out of bamboo, banana fibre, coir and coconut. At the **Kashmir Cottage Crafts Industries**, opposite Kovalam Bus Stand, you can buy jewellery, Kashmiri shawls and carpets, Kashmiri papiér maché items and brass statues.

WHERE TO STAY

Kovalam has something to suit almost everyone's budget though good-value, inexpensive accommodation is hard to find. The beaches are full of touts and chances are that your auto driver will be a hotel's commissioned agent.

On Samudra Beach

The **Leela Kempinski Kovalam Beach Resort** (Tel: 0471-2480101; Tariff: Rs 7,500-55,000) is the premium luxury option near Samudra Beach, spread over an entire hillside, with its own private beach, a pool and an Ayurvedic wellness spa. In the same league is the **Taj Green Cove Resort** (Tel: 2487733; Tariff: Rs 7,500-23,600), situated over 10 acres of garden. The best mid-range option is KTDC's superbly located and beautifully landscaped **Hotel Samudra** (Tel: 2480089; Tariff: Rs 3,369-9,218) on Samudra Beach. The rooms are modern, well-appointed and offer a brilliant sea view. The **Puja Mahal** (Tel: 2481245; Tariff: Rs 1,500-3,500), also on Samudra Beach, offers a sea view from several rooms.

On Eve's Beach

Close to Hawah or Eve's Beach, the **Best Western Swagath Holiday Resort** (Tel: 2481148-49; Tariff: Rs 1,700-6,500) is a

Courtesy POOVAR ISLAND RESORT

POOVAR

THE STREAM OF FLOWERS

BY NILANJANA BISWAS

The taxi drops me off at a beautiful stone-and-tile jetty, the pick-up point, I am told, for hotel guests. A uniformed guard uses a tiny receiver, crackling with static, to inform the hotel about my arrival. Fifteen minutes later, our conversation is broken by the roar of an approaching speedboat. Full of anticipation, I step into the boat and soon enough discover that the ride could be straight out of a thriller. On either side of the winding Neyyar River is dense vegetation. Birds swoop and soar out of creepers and vines. Amidst the call of birds and the chatter of monkeys, the motorboat engine is an alien sound. The backwaters of the Neyyar that we are slicing through are so tranquil and still that to take a photograph seems like an intrusive act. The boat navigates a sharp curve and suddenly looming in front of me, separated from the backwaters by a golden sandbar, is the frothing Arabian Sea. The sight is so enthralling that it takes me a while to notice that the engine is now quiet. The boat is being moored at the hotel jetty. We have arrived at the enchanting little island of Poovar. The extraordinary confluence of river, lake, beach and sea is Poovar's unique offering. This tiny island is surrounded by the backwaters of the River Neyyar, which swell into a serene lake separated from the restless Arabian Sea by a stretch of golden sand beach.

Here I learn that the island's name has a historical association with Raja Marthanda Ravi Varma (1706-1761), Travancore's legendary king. Challenged by a succession struggle, the king is said to have found asylum in Poovar from where he reconsolidated his kingdom with local patronage. Flowers that had fallen from overhanging Kovala trees covered the River Neyyar with a carpet of red, a scene the king described as 'Poo-Aar' or the 'Stream of Flowers', an apt description that even today succinctly defines this island of great beauty.

ON THE ISLAND

Poovar is an ideal choice for a relaxed getaway. The three hotels on this little island (*see Where to Stay and Eat on facing page*) provide a range of activities to occupy guests. Each has a swimming pool and deck chairs as well as hammocks strung on coconut trees where you can laze all day with a book. In addition, each of the hotels can arrange a country boat to take you on a meandering backwaters ride at a cost of Rs 300 per hour. In the evenings, the hotels typically organise live music recitals, Kathakali performances and fireworks displays.

For those looking for stress management, rejuvenation therapy or any other kind of specialised treatment, the Isola di Cocco (*see Where to Stay below*) has Green Leaf-certified Ayurvedic and Yoga services (*also see below*).

AYURVEDA AT POOVAR

In Kovalam, I had tried out rejuvenation therapy at a randomly selected hotel that advertised Ayurveda as one of its attractions. A visit to Isola di Cocco's Green Leaf-certified Ayurvedic centre, Bela, helped explain why a certification makes a vast difference. The centre here is equipped with spacious rooms, has high standards of cleanliness, proper infrastructure, trained personnel, and a registered Ayurvedic practitioner prescribing and supervising the entire treatment.

As opposed to the herb oil massage that lasted under 30 mins in Kovalam, my treatment session in Poovar, called the **Rasayana Chikitsa** or rejuvenation therapy, was unhurried and carefully administered. The masseuse held a rope attached to the ceiling and used her feet to administer the massage. Her years of training were evident from the skill with which she controlled the pressure to find and dissolve knots of tension in the neck, shoulders and back. After the oil massage, I was covered in a sandalwood pack that was both aromatic and refreshing. I was instructed to rest for an hour after the treatment before a hot steam bath. It was truly a rejuvenating experience.

Although I opted for a day-long treatment session, Rasayana Chikitsa is normally offered as a 7- to 14-day treatment package to counter degenerative processes hastened particularly by a stressful urban life. It includes a variety of massages and treatments like **Shirodhara** (where medicated oil is poured rhythmically on the forehead) and **Navarakizhi** (where special hot boluses are applied to the body). Each session lasts from 90 to 120 mins per day and is combined with meditation and relaxation techniques. It costs about US$ 1,100 per person for seven days. The treatment package includes consultation, accommodation, a vegetarian diet and a minimum of three treatment sessions per day along with yoga. Other treatment packages offered are **Vyadhi-kshamathwa** or body immunisation therapy (US$ 2,600 for 7 days), **Panchakarma** or body purification therapy (US$ 2,600 for 7 days), **Manasika Chikitsa** or de-stress therapy (US$ 1,300 for 7 days), **Soundarya Sanarakshana** or beautification therapy (US$ 1,250 for 7 days), the **Sthoola** or slimming programme (US$ 4,050 for 21 days), and a spine-and-neck care programme (US$ 1,300 for 7 days).

The other resorts in Poovar also offer Ayurvedic services but only Isola di Cocco's centre has a Green-Leaf certification.

WHERE TO STAY AND EAT

This tiny island offers three expensive resorts to choose from. By far the best is **Isola di Cocco** (Tel: 0471-2210008/ 800; Tariff: Rs 2,500-9,000), with heritage cottages, a fine swimming pool, complimentary yoga and excellent cuisine. The meals, available only for hotel guests, are buffet style and combine the flavours of traditional Kerala cooking (*meen pollichathu*, *karimeen* fry, grilled prawns), with superb Continental fare.

The **Estuary Island Resort** (Tel: 2214355/ 66; Tariff: Rs 3,000-8,000) has a choice location, modern, well-appointed, sea-facing rooms and though the cuisine is excellent, hospitality standards can be erratic. This writer had to change rooms thrice because in each there was a problem with the air-conditioning. The room service too was quite bad.

The **Poovar Island Resort** (Tel: 2212068-69; Tariff: Rs 4,000-12,000) has a row of lovely cottages moored on the estuarine lake overlooking the sea and a great swimming pool. The hotel caters only to those staying there and serves a variety of buffet and à la carte options, mainly Keralite and Continental dishes.

For more details, see Poovar Accommodation Listings on page 548

◆**Getting There** Poovar, 18 km south-east of Kovalam, is a straight drive along the coast from Thiruvananthapuram via Kovalam ■

good, mid-range option. **Seaface** (Tel: 2481835-36; Tariff: Rs 3,000-7,000) is the more expensive of the mid-range hotels but is superbly located right on the beach. **Hotel Neelakanta** (Tel: 2480321; Tariff: Rs 1,800-4,000) opens out on the beach, has a lovely café, a good restaurant and sea-facing rooms.

On Lighthouse Beach

The **Hawah Beach Resort** (Tel: 2481951; Tariff: Rs 1,400-5,500) has standard facilities and comfortable rooms with some offering a good sea view. For the budget traveller, there are several options near the Lighthouse. A very good choice would be the **Pappukutty Beach Resort** (Tel: 2480235; Tariff: Rs 500-1,400) located on Lighthouse Beach. Every room has a sea view and a small balcony. Other options include **Hotel Seaweed** (Tel: 2480391; Tariff: Rs 600-1,400) and the **Marine Palace** (Tel: 2485428; Tariff: Rs 1,750-3,600) on Lighthouse Beach. Both are clean and efficiently run and have well-appointed, comfortable rooms.

A private beach resort near Kovalam

RYAN LOBO

On Chowara Beach

Somatheeram Ayurvedic Beach Resort (Tel: 2268101; Tariff: Rs 3,000-12,000) at Chowara is an Ayurvedic resort with a private beach. They organise boat rides and cultural programmes and the kitchen at the resort offers 285 vegetarian dishes. **Manaltheeram Ayurvedic Beach Village** (Tel: 2268610; Tariff: Rs 3,000-12,000) is Somatheeram's sister concern offering similar facilities. **Nikki's Nest** (Tel: 2268821; Tariff: Rs 4,750-9,500), a seaside resort on Temple Road, Chowara, is actually located on a hilltop that slopes down to a private beach that this hotel shares with another resort. An Ayurvedic clinic, cultural programmes and beach barbecues are offered here.

For more hotels and details, see Kovalam Accommodation Listings on pages 546-548

WHERE TO EAT

Kovalam is where you get fine European food — seriously! Its bakeries offer mouth-watering cakes and lovely coffee. The pizzerias do great pastas and pizzas. Try **Café De La Mer** or the rooftop **German Bakery, The Fusion Café** or **The Pizzeria** on Lighthouse Beach. The seafood is excellent. Every evening fresh catch is spread outside each seafood restaurant and the brave can point out what they'd like to try, which is then weighed and cooked. Try the **Sea View Restaurant** on Hawah Beach for excellent seafood dishes. For wholesome vegetarian meals, try **Lonely Planet** behind Lighthouse Beach. There are many cheap wayside eateries serving cheap idli-vada meals. The German Bakery serves a great vegan breakfast, and also excellent bakery products such as cinnamon rolls, apple strudels and apple pies.

AROUND KOVALAM

Poovar (18 km)
See page 152 ■

Photographs by VIVEK R NAIR

VARKALA

DIAMONDS ARE FOREVER

State Kerala
Location Varkala stretches along a set of laterite cliffs in the north of Thiruvananthapuram District, by the Lakshadweep Sea
Distance 46 km N of Thiruvananthapuram
Journey time ***By road*** 1 hr from Thiruvananthapuram
Route from Thiruvananthapuram NH47 to Kallambalam Junction via Mangalapuram and Attingal; state road to Varkala (*see route guide on pages 144-145*)

■ BY NILANJANA BISWAS

The candle, stuck in a sand-filled earthen bowl and shielded from the wind by a glass cover, begins to flicker and then dies. I look around for a waiter but in this tiny shack-restaurant, the service is as laidback as the ambience is meditative.

The moon is a huge yellow orb and the sea, an infinite black mass that heaves and roars and flings itself upon the shore. Suddenly, the moon is hidden by passing clouds. The yellow grey darkness sharpens every sound — a lapwing's cry; a shout from the cliff top; the rhythmic crash of the waves. In the distance, I see men and women praying knee-deep in the waters of Papanasham Beach. Thousands come here every year in the belief that their sins will be washed away by Papanasham's holy waters. Their prayers are a coda to the medley of nocturnal sounds.

This is my third evening in this shack and already I recognise the regulars. An old Spanish woman who sits alone at the same table every night, clearly loved by the waiters who often stop by for a chat; a British couple who share a beer in companionable silence; a man with a powerful Nikon camera, who speaks so little that I can't tell where he's from. You can spend hours here observing people. There's no one eyeing your table, no one hurrying you out.

Varkala is like a magnet for the international beach-buff; the scenic, quiet and affordable alternative to upscale Kovalam. Is it the town's ancient temple tradition that suffuses it with such a sense of peace? Or it is the sheer, breathtaking beauty of palm-fringed cliffs overhanging the rolling Arabian Sea that humbles and pacifies the spirit?

Candle in hand, a waiter is hurrying towards my table. No, not necessary, I gesture to him. The clouds have moved on. When it reappears, the moon is high up in the sky, no longer yellow but a brilliant silver. And suddenly, the sea is a vast stretch of sparkling diamonds.

ORIENTATION

Varkala is a small town spread over laterite cliffs that drop rather dramatically to two main beaches. One is the **Papanasham Beach**, a golden sand beach lying in a cove between the North Cliff and the South Cliff. The other is the **Thiruvambadi Beach**, a black sand beach at Varkala's northern end. The shop-lined plateau atop **North Cliff** offers a brilliant view of the sea and a rather more up-market ambience than the laidback **South Cliff**. The plateau hosts a helipad from where Cliff Road takes you to the heart of Varkala Town.

About 9 km from Varkala is another idyllic beach spot: the **Kappil Beach**. Autos are the best transport option but don't run on meter and quote a flat rate starting from Rs 50. Bike lovers can hire motorbikes on a per day basis here. Contact Anbu (Mobile: 09847080412, 0387974698) at the Wheel of South India, North Cliff, Varkala. Bikes without gear cost Rs 250; bikes with gear start

→ FAST FACTS

When to go November to March

Tourist offices

● District Tourism Promotion Council
Kowdiar PO, Vellayambalam
Thiruvananthapuram
Tel: 0471-2315397

● Tourism Information Counter
Park View
Thiruvananthapuram
Tel: 0471-2321132
Website: keralatourism.org

STD code 0470

with Pulsars for Rs 350, Thunderbirds for Rs 450 and Bullet-Enfields for Rs 500. All the rates mentioned are for a 24-hr hire.

BEACH WATCH

Varkala's main beaches are excellent for swimming for about five months in the year between October and February. From March right through the monsoon period the sea is turbulent and unsuitable for swimming.

THINGS TO SEE AND DO

Depending on your orientation, Varkala can either be a place for a relaxed beach holiday or a site of religious and historical interest. You could of course aim for a combination of both: visit the beaches in the mornings or evenings and reserve the day to see the lovely shrines of this temple town. If you have the time, do try out an Ayurvedic massage at any Green or Olive Leaf-certified centre found in the hotels by the beach. These certifications, awarded by the Kerala Government, bring in a measure of accountability in the generally unregulated Ayurveda sector. Green Leaf and Olive Leaf are the two types of classification available. Ayurveda centres that maintain certain standards in facilities, equipment, personnel, medicines and health programmes can apply for either of the classifications, with green signifying utmost compliance.

Two young tourists on Varkala's sands

Papanasham Beach

The last bend of the hotel- and shop-lined Beach Road brings you to the southern tip of Papanasham Beach. It takes no more than 10 mins to walk the stretch of golden sand from south to north. Steps carved out of the cliff-face make for a steep but spectacular climb from Papanasham to the cliff-top plateau. In the safe months — October to February — the sea is ideal for swimming. Deck chairs and sun umbrellas are easy to hire at about Rs 50 for the day. A few lifeguards patrol the beaches intermittently. A Tourism Police outpost provides a variety of assistance. An auto from the railway station would charge about Rs 50 to bring you here.

◆**Location** 5 km from the railway station down the Beach Road

Janardhana Swamy Temple

This beautiful 2,000-year-old Vaishnavite shrine is situated at the entrance of the Beach Road. A flight of steps leads to the temple precincts where statues of Shiva and Hanuman are illuminated by the soft glow of oil lamps. Ancient brass bells hang from the ceiling.

A perennial spring feeds the sunken temple tank across the road where hundreds come to bathe. Cameras are not allowed inside the sanctum sanctorum and a strict dress code is observed: saris for women and *mundus* for men. The main annual temple festival is held in March over 10 days.

PRASHANT PANJIAR

Dances with waves: Kathakali and the Kerala Coast is an irresistible combination

♦**Location** At the entrance of Beach Road, close to Papanasham Beach **Timings** 4 am-noon and 5-8 pm

Thiruvambadi Beach

A relatively small but clean and beautiful expanse of black sand, Thiruvambadi Beach offers excellent swimming opportunities and several mid-range hotels (*see page 162*). The beach is lined by a frond of coconut trees that offer welcome respite from the sun and suggest many possibilities for an afternoon spent in a hammock. An auto from the railway station to the beach would cost about Rs 60. You can also walk down the North Cliff on the Thiruvambadi side to reach the beach.

♦**Location** 4 km from the railway station down Thiruvambadi Road

Kappil Beach

The bus route from Varkala to Kollam takes you through the enchanting estuary of Kappil where the backwaters of the Kappil River meet the sea. Incredibly picturesque, here you have a golden sand beach on one side of the road, and on the other, the tranquil estuary and backwaters against a palm-fringed skyline dotted with water birds in flight. A solitary lodge and a boat club are the only tourist attractions and explain the seclusion of this idyllic beach.

The only resort here, called Lake Sagar Beach Resort and Water Park, organises **water sports** (*also see Where to Stay on page 164*). **Rides** are on offer on **speedboats** (Rs 600 per hour), canoes (Rs 50 per hour), coracles (Rs 60 per hour), row-boats (Rs 60 per hour) and country boats (Rs 500 per day). The timings are from 10 am to 5 pm. The resort also organises swimming in clean backwaters with a lifeguard or coast guard support. They are also planning to set up a **children's park**.

For estuary boating, contact Kappil's Priyadarshini Boat Club (Tel: 0470-2662 323). The rates are Rs 60 per hour for a four-seater rowboat or a two-seater pedal boat and Rs 500 per hour for a 10-seater safari boat. Boat rides are on offer from 10 am to 6.30 pm.

♦**Location** 9 km from the railway station down the road to Kollam

Sivagiri Mutt

The terraced Sivagiri Mutt holds the remains of the great social reformer and saint, Sri Narayana Guru, renowned for his simple philosophy, "One caste, one religion, one god".

In the grounds below the Mahasamadhi is his old residence where some of his possessions are displayed. A Sharada Temple is nearby and also a bookstall where you can pick up works in Malayalam and English on Sri Narayana Guru's life and teachings. The mutt premises spread across 200 acres.

♦**Location** 4 km east of the town centre
Timings 5.30 am-noon and 4.30-7 pm

Kathakali performances

The **Varkala Cultural Centre** (Tel: 0470-2608793), close to North Cliff, organises Kathakali performances every evening during the peak tourist season. Tickets cost Rs 150 and the performances are held between 6.30 and 8 pm. The **Kuttikkad Temple**, also close to North Cliff, often holds its own Kathakali performances which start in the evening and continue through the night. These are open to the public and free of cost. Visit the temple to enquire about any performances scheduled during your stay.

→ GETTING THERE

Air Nearest airport: Thiruvananthapuram (52 km/ $1\frac{1}{4}$ hrs). Taxi fare to Varkala is about Rs 1,500; pre-paid taxis available
Rail Varkala Railway Station, connected to Delhi by the Kerala Express, to Chennai by the Trivandrum Mail and the MS Guruvayur Express, to Mumbai by the Kanyakumari Express and the Netravati Express, to Bangalore by the Kanyakumari Express and to Kolkata by the Gurudev Express
Road Varkala is 11 km off NH47, which runs from Salem to Kanyakumari via Palakkad, Thrissur, Ernakulam, Kollam and Thiruvananthapuram. Get off at Kallamballam Junction (9 km) and take a local bus or auto to Varkala

SHOPPING

The row of shops lining the **North Cliff** sell more or less the same items: silver jewellery, semi-precious stones, silver and brass statuettes and mementos, small Kashmiri silk carpets, as well as Tibetan and Rajasthani handicrafts, all at extortionate rates. A cloth bag that you may be able to pick up for Rs 75 at Janpath in Delhi will come for Rs 350 (if you're Indian) or Rs 800 (if you're a foreigner). Haggling is the norm. You'll find the same kind of shops, fewer in number, on **Beach Road** as well.

WHERE TO STAY

One of Varkala's star attractions is the immense number of stay options the destination offers, spread across all budgets and with excellent sea views.

On South Cliff

The **Taj Garden Retreat** (Tel: 0470-2603000; Tariff: Rs 4,000-6,000), on the way to the cliff, is an upscale but great-value stay option. The view is superb and they have a lovely swimming pool as well as an excellent poolside restaurant and sunken bar. The **Hindustan Beach Retreat** (Tel: 2604255; Tariff: Rs 3,000-5,000) is located on the cliff but in a rather crowded area, just a stone's throw from Papanasham Beach. All the rooms here are air-conditioned, large, well-furnished and sea-facing. The **Sea Pearl Chalets** (Tel: 2660105; Tariff: Rs 850-1,500) at South Cliff offers a lovely view. It has several clean, modestly furnished but comfortable cottages overlooking the Papanasham Beach.

The soft glow of candles adds to the romantic ambience at a restaurant in Varkala

On North Cliff

The **Krishnatheeram** (Tel: 2601305, 2156444; Tariff: Rs 1,000-3,800) is a good option with a superb sea view, a private walkway to the beach, a good multi-cuisine restaurant as well as Green Leaf-certified Ayurvedic services. It has 12 rooms and 16 well-furnished cottages, both AC and non-AC, with modern, attached bathrooms and round-the-clock room service.

All the rooms in **Green Palace Seaside Hotel** (Tel: 2601962; Tariff: Rs 1,500-3,000) are sea-facing, with attached baths and private sit-outs. Both standard double and deluxe double rooms are available with an assorted range of guest services including Internet facilities.

The **Raja Park Beach Resort** (Tel: 2607060; Tariff: Rs 700-3,200) has a variety of clean and well-appointed rooms to choose from: AC heritage cottages, pool-facing deluxe rooms and garden-facing standard rooms. It also has a jacuzzi and a poolside restaurant serving both traditional Kerala fare as well as Chinese and Continental cuisine.

Preeth Beach Resort (Tel: 2600942; Tariff: Rs 560-2,800) offers clean and comfortable rooms: air-conditioned and non-air-conditioned cottages, deluxe and standard rooms as well as apartment-style eco-cottages. It also has a travel desk, a swimming pool, an outdoor restaurant and an Ayurvedic clinic.

The **Deshadan Cliff and Beach Resort** (Tel: 3204242; Mobile: 09846031005; Tariff: Rs 3,000) has well-appointed rooms, each one of which is styled to reflect a different Indian tradition. If one room displays Rajasthani decor, then another is done up in the Chettinad style. Also offered are excellent restaurant and swimming pool facilities.

On Thiruvambadi Beach

The **Seabreeze** (Tel: 2603257, 3292685; Tariff: Rs 500-2,800) is right on the beach and has clean, spacious, comfortably furnished sea-facing rooms and a variety of facilities such as Internet and an open-air restaurant.

The **Thiruvambadi Beach Retreat** (Tel: 2601028; Tariff: Rs 800-2,500),

located just off the beach, has both spacious and comfortable rooms as well as well-appointed cottages. Though not all rooms have a sea view, the sea is just a minute's walk away.

On Kappil Beach
The **Lake Sagar Beach Resort and Water Safari Park** (Tel: 0474-2514300; Tariff: Rs 400-1,350) is the only choice here but an excellent one in view of its ambient location, lake-facing restaurant, well-furnished rooms and exciting water sport facilities (*also see Kappil Beach on page 159*).

For more hotels and details, see Varkala Accommodation Listings on pages 549-550

WHERE TO EAT

On South Cliff, the **Varkala Marine Palace** restaurant serves exquisite seafood. Try out their delicious calamari crumb fry. The multi-cuisine restaurants on North Cliff are more up-market and offer a superb view and good seafood. Try the **Sea Rock Café** on North Cliff for excellent pasta and fish. A number of restaurants here offer delicious Tibetan fare — momos, thukpa and Tibetan tea, among others. The Taj Garden Retreat's **Cape Comorin** restaurant does superb Kerala cuisine, particularly fish preparations such as the leaf-wrapped and grilled *meen pollichathu*. Also, the lobster at the restaurant in **Raja Park Beach Resort** is a must-try.

A man dries coir in the sun

AROUND VARKALA

Ponnumthuruthu Island (20 km)
Located near the fishing villages of Anjengo and Nedunganda, the little island of Ponnumthuruthu (literally, Golden Island) houses a beautiful **100-year-old Shiva-Parvati temple**. A boat belonging to the temple regularly ferries people to and fro across Anjengo's backwaters, between Nedunganda and the temple. The charming ride is made all the more pleasurable by the calm ambience of this tiny island. The temple is open to people of all faiths; the ferry is free of cost and plies from the temple to Nedunganda and back every 15 mins. You can take an auto from the town to Anjengo (*see below*).
◆**Temple timings** 5.30 am-noon and 4-7 pm

Anjengo Fort and lighthouse
The fishing village of Anjuthengo, more popularly known by its shorter name Anjengo, is the site of a small fort built in 1695 by the Portuguese. There is also a 130-foot tall **lighthouse** nearby. The Anjengo Fort was used as a merchandise and munitions depot by its builders and later became a British bastion. Anjengo served as the first signalling station for ships arriving from Britain and functioned as a depot for the pepper and coir trade. Take an auto from Varkala to the fort; the fare will be around Rs 200.
◆**Lighthouse timings** 9 am-6 pm ■

PRASHANT PANJIAR

KOLLAM

THE RAIN SONG

State Kerala
Location A picturesque town on the banks of the Ashtamudi Lake and the Lakshadweep Sea, Kollam lies at the southern extremity of a network of backwaters in South Kerala
Distance 63 km N of Thiruvananthapuram
Journey time ***By road*** $1^1/_2$ hrs
Route from Thiruvananthapuram NH47 to Kollam via Mangalapuram, Attingal and Paripally (*see route guide on pages 144-145*)

■ **BY PN VENUGOPAL**

The rain is like a grey bedspread that's been pulled over the heaving sea. As if to match the sky's weightiness this morning, the waves are thundering against the shore, lashing the sands for hitherto forgotten sins. A howling wind is trying to snatch the umbrella away from my tight grip. It's a battle that's doomed to be lost — the wind wins, the rain has me cowering in seconds, and I am enjoying every moment of this unusual beach visit. One wouldn't associate a beach holiday with the monsoon, but as luck would have it, I am visiting Kollam in the beginning of the south-west monsoon, which rain aficionados chase, from the tip of Kerala all the way to the deserts of Rajasthan. I prefer the rains to the heat and dust of summer, and I feel the sea's ferociousness in the monsoon is more charming than her subtle moods in summer. The beach is usually empty then and it's just you and the sea and the rain.

Monsoon mystery

Every monsoon, the Kerala coast witnesses a unique natural phenomenon that fisherfolk eagerly await called Chakara. This is when mud banks form in the sea, resulting in the waters becoming very calm, in turn drawing fish of all varieties. This is a boon for the fisherfolk as they are then able to net fish in bulk. There is much debate around the causes of Chakara and the reasons for the formation of the mud banks. These banks, which occur within a week or so after the onset of the south-west monsoons, disappear with the rains in September or October. It's said that the banks are created by the clay from the backwaters that's pushed into the sea because of the strength of the rains; the clay's organic matter attracts the fish.

The earliest mention of Chakara was made by Pliny, the famous traveller of the 1st century CE. Chakara also has a prominent place in Malayalam literature, just as it does in the hearts of the fisherfolk.

→ FAST FACTS

When to go August-April, June-July if you like the monsoons and a raging sea

Tourist offices

- District Tourism Promotion Council
City Office, Tourist Reception Centre
KSRTC Bus Station, Kollam
Tel: 0474-2745625
Email: contact@dtpckollam.com
Website: dtpckollam.com

TIP Contact DTPC for booking houseboats and backwater cruises, or for watching martial arts and classical dance performances

- DTPC, Main Boat Jetty, Kollam
Tel: 2750170

STD code 0474

When the rain lets off, if only for a while, the sea transforms into her quiet self, and it seems to me as if this is the literal 'calm before the storm'. The waves take a break from their punishing schedule, the wind quietens down and off I go to find a raincoat before the next shower, infinitely wiser from experience.

ORIENTATION

A kilometre-and-a-half long, the beach is wide and packed with hundreds of families in the evenings. But one can find one's own solitary corner if so inclined. Just 2 km from the heart of the town, an autorickshaw is the most convenient way of getting here. The fare will be around Rs 15. Most tourist attractions are within a radius of 8-10 km of the town.

BEACH WATCH

The sea here is rough irrespective of the season. Therefore, swimming or even bathing is unsafe. A notice put up on the beach warns against swimming in the sea, pointing out that 18 lives have been lost in the past three years.

THINGS TO SEE AND DO

There are no water sports here, and not much by way of activities. Your best bet is to take a relaxing stroll on the sands.

On the beach

There's a lovely park bordering the beach, with seesaws and slides, where children can play around. The park is open from 3 to 7 pm. A beautiful statue of a nude woman is to be seen in the park.

Thangassery Beach

Five kilometres and a 15-min bus ride from Kollam town lies Thangassery. A historically important town, it houses the ruins of a **Portuguese fort** as well as an **18th century church**. The 3-km long beach has a **lighthouse** that is open to

visitors between 3.30 and 5.30 pm. Built in 1902, its light can be seen from 13 miles out at sea. A drive down the Lighthouse Road promises many stunning views of the sea.

Thirumullavaram Beach

Just 6 km north of the town and accessible by bus is this beautiful and quiet little beach, ideal for swimming or just soaking up the sun.

Neendakara

Located 10 km from Kollam, on NH47, Neendakara is a fishing harbour famous for a post-monsoon phenomenon called 'Chakara' (*see 'Monsoon mystery' on page 166*). From the Neendakara Bridge, you can see the Ashtamudi Lake joining the sea on one side and islands on the other.

In the town

A **houseboat trip** is a must in Kollam. DTPC Kollam (Tel: 0474-2745625) offers a number of rides along **Ashtamudi Lake** and its offshoot channels. There are many colonial relics to be seen in Kollam, including a **clock tower** built in 1944.

→ GETTING THERE

Air Nearest airport: Thiruvananthapuram International Airport (69 km/ $1^1/_2$ hrs). Taxi to Kollam costs Rs 1,000-1,200

Rail Kollam Junction, connected daily to Mumbai by the Kanyakumari and Quilon expresses, and to Delhi by the Kerala Express. All trains that go to Thiruvananthapuram Central serve Kollam

Road Kollam is served by three national highways. It's on NH47, which links Salem to Kanyakumari via Palakkad, Thrissur, Ernakulam and Alappuzha. NH220 to Theni and NH208 to Thirumangalam near Madurai originate here. There are frequent buses from Thiruvananthapuram, Ernakulam, Alappuzha and Kottayam to Kollam's KSRTC Bus Stand

WHERE TO STAY

There are no places close to the sea in Kollam, but there are plenty of stay options from where you can travel to the beach easily. The only seaside resort, **Ashtamudi Resort** (Tel: 0476-2882310/ 365; Tariff: Rs 5,000-10,000) is located outside the town at Chavara, just north of Neendakara Port. It's one of the best hotels in the district. **Hotel Sudarsan** (Tel: 0474-2744322; Tariff: Rs 450-1,650) is conveniently located in Parameswar Nagar, in the heart of Kollam Town. It has a multi-cuisine restaurant and a bar. **Hotel Sea Bee** (Tel: 2744696; Tariff: Rs 200-2,200), near the bus stand, is also a decent option. The **Shantigiri Ayurveda Centre** (Tel: 2763014; Tariff: Rs 300-750) has a lovely little lawn by the lake.

For more hotels and details, see Kollam Accommodation Listings on page 546

WHERE TO EAT

Kollam is cashew country. You can buy cashew nuts, delicately flavoured cashew biscuits and green pepper pickle at **Supreme Bakery** at Chinnakkada. They have two more branches in the town. If you are looking for an exotic experience, the place to visit is an old **tavern** on the beach at Thirumullavaram. Set amidst coconut trees, the toddy shop serves excellent seafood (the crab is a must-try) along with delicious toddy.

Many hotels and restaurants in the town serve typical Keralite fare, from the usual vegetarian meals to delectable seafood. At **Hotel Sudarsan**, try the prawns and beef *ulathiyathu*. Opt for the fish biryani at **Chillies** in Jerome Nagar. Also here is the **Coffee Bar**, which serves good appam and egg curry. ■

PRASHANT PANJIAR

ALAPPUZHA

THE SILENT SHORE

State Kerala
Location A strip of land sandwiched between the Lakshadweep Sea and the Punnamada backwaters, Alappuzha is dotted with lagoons, canals and rivers
Distances 71 km S of Kochi, 147 km NW of Thiruvananthapuram
Journey time $1^1/_2$ hrs from Kochi, 4 hrs from Thiruvananthapuram
Route from Kochi NH47A to Ernakulam; NH47 to Alappuzha via Arur and Cherthala
Route from Thiruvananthapuram NH47 to Alappuzha via Kollam, Karunagapally, Kayamkulam, Haripad and Ambalapuzha (*see route guide on pages 144-145*)

BY PN VENUGOPAL

The sand is ochre, not golden or white as glossy postcards would like it to be. But it doesn't detract from Alappuzha's beautiful beach, spreading across all of 2 km like a pretty painting that has come together in the oddest way. The beach is silent except for the melody of the undulating waves lapping at the shore, and often the only ones listening to this soothing score are the dilapidated godowns and the buildings dating back to the 19th century that dot the seashore. These are signs of Alappuzha's previous life as a flourishing harbour, when ships berthed at the sea and country dhows carried goods to the shore, signalling the beginning of festivities and the hustle and bustle that was typical of port towns.

A good three decades have passed since the last ship stopped at this port, but a few motor and country boats are to be seen now on the horizon, somewhat hazy, and bobbing, reminders of the glory of yesteryear. But the visitor will find it difficult to imagine that something is missing here. Birds flutter above the sea as a lone angler stands on the pier, waiting for the big catch. At sunset, the sun is a red ball of fire sneaking into the quiet depths of the ocean. And the silence makes the view of the sea, reflecting the colours of the dusk, just picture-perfect.

ORIENTATION

The beach in Alappuzha is located about 3 km west of **Mullackal**, which is the town centre. It takes 20 mins by bus and even lesser by auto (minimum fare Rs 10). The beach has an old and dilapidated **pier** and a **lighthouse**; a **port house** built in 1865 stands across the road from the beach. Close to the beach is the **Vijaya Park**, which has a children's play area and a lake. Several hotels are located close to the beach, to the east of the **Beach Road**. **Mararikulam** (*see 'One with nature' on page 174*) lies to the north of Alappuzha and is 17 km away.

→ FAST FACTS

When to go October to May

Tourist offices

- District Tourism Promotion Council
Opp Canara Bank, Boat Jetty Road
Alappuzha
Tel: 0477-2253308, 2251796
Website: alappuzhatourism.com

TIP For hotel reservations, daily backwater cruises, 'Round the Venice of the East on Foot' tours (min 10 pax), houseboat and car rental

- Tourist Information Office
Department of Tourism, Government of Kerala, Near Boat Jetty
Tel: 2260722

STD code 0477

It is also quite a good option for an unforgettable beach holiday.

BEACH WATCH

The sea is generally friendly here except during the monsoons, when it assumes monstrous proportions. Swimming is possible but it's not advisable to go far out; most swimmers stick close to the shore. The beach has lifeguards. People do wear swimsuits but you can't go wrong if you dress a bit conservatively.

THINGS TO SEE AND DO

You can swim in the sea, laze on the sands and watch the gentle waves. It would be a mistake not to go around Alappuzha as the town has many lovely tourist attractions. Keep aside at least a day for the beach; if interested in a houseboat package and also a visit to the Marari Beach, factor in another two days.

By the beach

First head to the **lighthouse** (timings 10 am-5 pm) on the beach; it offers a panoramic view of the sea and the town. You could also join a game of **beach volleyball**, which is a popular game with visitors. The beach also has a **children's park** run by the District Tourism Promotion Council (DTPC), which is quite nice if you discount the rather garish swings. **Boating** facilities are also on offer here. ♦**Park entry fee** Adults Rs 5, children Rs 3 **Timings** 3-8 pm

Cruising along

Alappuzha is known for its backwaters. You can go on a **backwater cruise** on the **Punnamada Kayal**, which will take you past scenic islands such as **R** and **QST Block islands**, while also offering views of coconut and paddy fields. Boats can be hired from the Tourist Boat Jetty near the bus stand. The Kerala State Water Transport Department (Alappuzha Boat Jetty Counter Tel: 0477-2252510; 10 am-5 pm)

offers cruises to R Block on the service boat for Rs 6-7. You can also ask DTPC (Tel: 0477-2253308) for a private cruise (Rs 250 per hour for a group of 10 and Rs 350 for a group of 20; 8 am-7 pm) at the jetty behind the DTPC office. The Punnamada Kayal here is the starting point of several boat races, including the famous **Nehru Boat Race**.

SHOPPING

Lovely coir mats and other coir products, as well as handicrafts made out of various parts of coconut trees, are souvenirs one can look out for here. Mullackal is the main shopping centre. Also found here are about 30 jewellery shops, clothes shops such as **Khadi Gandhi Store** and **Seemati**, and an excellent stationery shop in **PA George Company**.

GETTING THERE

Air Nearest airport: Kochi International Airport, Nedumbassery (90 km/ 2 hrs). Pre-paid taxi to Alappuzha will cost Rs 990-1,680

Rail Alappuzha Station, connected daily to Ernakulam and Thiruvananthapuram by the Jan Shatabdi, Ernakulam and Netravati expresses. The latter also serves Kozhikode and Mumbai. The overnight Alleppey Express is one of four daily services from Chennai

Road Alappuzha is on NH47, which connects Salem to Kanyakumari via Palakkad, Thrissur, Ernakulam, Kollam and Thiruvananthapuram. SH11 links Alappuzha to Changanassery and the eastern bank of Vembanad Lake in Kottayam District. Alappuzha's KSRTC Bus Stand, 5 km from the railway station on NH47, has frequent services to Ernakulam, Kottayam, Kollam, Thiruvalla and Thiruvananthapuram

WHERE TO STAY

There are a number of good stay options in Alappuzha, many of them on the beach. The **Beach Bungalow** (Tel: 0477-2263347; Tariff: Rs 2,500-5,000), on the Beach Road, is a heritage homestay. It's a lovely mansion dating back to 1865, with high ceilings, arched doorways and spacious rooms. Four of the rooms here have beach views.

Raheem Residency (Tel: 2230767; Tariff: Rs 5,178-14,384) is another heritage home that's on the beach. The 10 spacious rooms are furnished with traditional items made of teak, and there's a two-bedroom independent unit in a separate courtyard, refurbished from old outhouses once used to store coconuts. Yet another stay option is the aptly named **Alleppey Beach Resorts** (Tel: 2263408; Tariff: Rs 1,500-2,990), which has its own stretch of private beach and sea-facing rooms.

The **Lake Palace** (Tel: 2239701; Tariff: Rs 4,500-6,500), **Pagoda Resorts** (Tel: 2251697; Tariff: Rs 1,500-3,700) and **Hotel Arcadia** (Tel: 2251354; Tariff: Rs 200-1,100) are some of the options available in Alappuzha Town, just 3 km away from the beach. The hotels have all the modern amenities imaginable. Kerala Tourism Development Corporation's **Motel Yatri Nivas** (Tel: 2244460; Tariff: Rs 350-1,100), at Kalappura, is a cheap option. They also have a restaurant. The Coir Board's guest house **Padipura Residence** (Tel: 2244978, 2245001; Tariff: Rs 600-1,100), near the District Court, offers 32 rooms including three dorms, and meals on request.

Many people also choose to stay in houseboats, run by private operators and the DTPC (*see Fast Facts on page 170*).

For more hotels and details, see Alappuzha Accommodation Listings on pages 543-544

MARARIKULAM: One with nature

Courtesy MARARI BEACH RESORT

Courtesy MARARI BEACH RESORT

About 50 km from Kochi and 17 km from Alappuzha is the Mararikulam fishermen's village, practically untouched by modernity and looking exactly as it would have hundreds of years ago. Behind tall coconut trees stand little huts where fishermen live, and on the beach are country boats that take off to the sea in the early morning. Sometime around noon, the boats return with their catch, and the atmosphere at that time has to be experienced to be believed. Nets are hung out for drying in the afternoon, and walking on the beach then is akin to navigating around a maze.

The beach is perfect for those looking for a relaxed, undisturbed getaway. Backing that claim is the excellent CGH Earth resort, **Marari Beach Resort** (Tel: 0478-2863801-09; Tariff: Rs 8,500-24,500), which is spread across several acres, extending all the way to the beach. The resort has 62 cottages separated by swathes of green, and it reflects its pristine environs. Take the cottages themselves; these have thatched roofs, and even a little tap at the entrance where you can wash your feet before you enter. Inside, luxury finds a say in the elegant furniture and modern amenities.

At the resort, the emphasis is on relaxation, so you won't find water scooters and other such facilities here. For some of us, that will be part of Marari's charm. Guests can soak in the sun and the sea while lying on the hammocks tied between coconut trees; sit by the pools with a book; join a yoga and meditation class; swim in the sea; or sign up for the walks and bicycle tours around the village that the resort offers. There's plenty to chew on too: with the sea next door, the cuisine centres on seafood, cooked in the typical Keralite way. Prawns, lobsters, crayfish, appams and chicken curries feature on the excellent menu.

Another stay option at Mararikulam is the **Marari Beach Homes** (Tel: 0477-2243535; Tariff: € 125-150), which has four well-designed cottages located right on the beach. ■

WHERE TO EAT

Alappuzha's proximity to the sea, and the many canals that crisscross it, have ensured that the area is famous for seafood delicacies. Options on the beach include: the **Indian Coffee House**, where you can slouch at a table with a cup of coffee for hours; also try out their delicious dosa, mutton omelette and Bombay toast. The **Harbour Restaurant** is also on the beach, and serves Keralite, Chinese and North Indian cuisine. Must-trys include their appams and stew, and prawn chowmein. **Sealap Shimmers** has Jain food; try their snacks such as samosas and pav bhaji. The **Gujarathi Street** near the beach has good hotels specialising in North Indian food.

In the town, try the appam and stew at **Hotel Green Corner** in Pazhayangadi. **Hotel Aaryas**, near the medical college, serves good vegetarian food. The Mullackal area has good Udupi veg fare. ■

CHERAI

THE BEST OF TWO WORLDS

State Kerala
Location Cherai is a beach on the northern tip of Kochi's Vypeen Island, which separates the Lakshadweep Sea from the backwaters
Distances 26 km NW of Ernakulam, 170 km S of Kozhikode, 249 km N of Thiruvananthapuram, 551 km SW of Bangalore
Journey time ***By road*** $^1/_2$ hr from Kochi, 1 hr from Ernakulam, 5 hrs from Kozhikode, $5^1/_2$ hrs from Thiruvananthapuram, 10 hrs from Bangalore
Route from Ernakulam Goshree Overbridge to Cherai via Bolgatty and Vypeen
Route to Kochi from Thiruvananthapuram NH47 to Ernakulam via Kollam, Kayamkulam, Alappuzha and Cherthala; rest as above (*see route guide on pages 144-145*)

BY NILANJANA BISWAS

The sound of music from an elevated, thatch-covered bamboo platform draws me to it. Inside, a man and woman play a foot-tapping violin and rhythm duet. The baton the man uses to cheerfully invite me in seems no less than a magic wand. The platform creaks alarmingly as I climb up to join them. Before me there is only the sea, miles of azure blue waves that meet the stony embankment at the foot of our platform in a flouncing skirt of foam. Birds dip and soar as the music plays on, and time trips along andante.

Photographs by VIVEK R NAIR

In Cherai, you can't help but notice that the pulse and pace of life changes just as often as the sea changes its moods. In this narrow strip of land, a northern extension of Kochi's Vypeen Island cradled between the coast and backwaters, the tranquility of the estuary meets the rhythmic cadence of the sea. Along the backwaters are coconut groves and paddy fields where men and women work at an unhurried, unchanging pace. Mothers scrub down squealing babies by the river and men clean out their wooden *kettuvallams*, boats that are no different from the one you glide past the backwaters in. A streak of brilliant blue vanishes into the water and moments later, a kingfisher emerges in a spray of water, a fish twisting in its beak. On your left is the Cherai Island from in between whose thatched houses and coconut trees, flashes of a shimmering blue vastness appear.

With the beach at Fort Kochi considerably reduced by rising sea levels, the 15-km long island of Cherai is today rapidly being developed as Kochi's own beach destination, and with excellent reason. In the evening, as the sun sets, the waves throw up a bountiful feast of orange and purple crabs for a pair of eagles to swoop down upon; a few beach buffs sit in contemplative silence. As the curtains close upon yet another day, you find yourself hoping that when this magical beach opens up to the outside world, it does so gently, and when people come, they leave behind no more than footprints for the sea to quietly wash away.

FAST FACTS

When to go September to May

Tourist offices

- District Tourism Promotion Council
Old Collectorate Building
Park Avenue Road, Ernakulam
Tel: 0484-2367334
- Tourism Information Counters
Department of Tourism
Government of Kerala
Near Government Guest House
Shanmugham Road
Ernakulam
Tel: 0484-2360502
- Information Counter, Nedumbassery Airport
Tel: 0484-2610115
- KTDC Tourist Reception Centre
Opp Hotel Taj Residency
Shanmugham Road
Ernakulam, Kochi
Tel: 0484-2353234

STD code 0484

ORIENTATION

Cherai is situated 26 km from Ernakulam City at the northern end of Vypeen Island. At the time of writing, ferries were not plying but it was accessible from Ernakulam by road via the **Goshree Bridge**. This bridge connects the islands of **Bolgatty**, **Mulavukadu**, **Vallarpadam** and **Vypeen**. The journey is picturesque and you may want to hire a taxi (Rs 450 from the city) to be able to stop to take photographs.

The cheaper option is to board any bus to Paravur (there's one every 20 mins) from Ernakulam's High Court junction and get off at the Cherai Bus Stop. The journey time is about 45 mins and the fare is Rs 11. From the Cherai Bus Stop, the beach is a 10-min ride by auto (Rs 50). One can also reach Cherai directly from the Kochi International Airport via North Paravur, a distance of approximately 22 km. A narrow sandbar over a tranquil backwater lake connects the 15-km long village of Cherai to its beach.

The waters on the southern side where the **Cherai Beach Resorts** is located are clean, shallow and gentle. At the opposite end, the beach thins out and

CHARUKESI RAMADURAI

The sea is a palette of rich colours as fishermen set out on their boats

disappears into a stony embankment close to the road.

BEACH WATCH

Cherai Beach is generally free from undercurrents and perfect for swimming from October to March. Check with the hotel where you are staying for any safety regulations that may be in force at that particular time.

THINGS TO SEE AND DO

Cherai is the place for a quiet beach holiday with plenty of opportunities for swimming and sun bathing. You could use Cherai as your base to explore the many tourist attractions at hand in nearby Vypeen, Ernakulam, Fort Kochi, Bolgatty and Mattancherry (*see 'The queen of the sea' on page 182*).

Cherai Beach

A quiet, serene beach, Cherai is an excellent place to relax. Dolphins are often spotted here and the best time for dolphin watching is early morning. Hotels and resorts provide deck chairs and sun umbrellas, perfect props to enjoy Cherai's beauty. A leisurely walk south to north of the beach will take you about 45 mins; on the way, stop to savour a glorious view or a replenishing drink at a rooftop restaurant. The waters are calm and it's not uncommon to find children leaping into the waves and being washed back, squealing delightedly, to the shore.

Also nearby are Cherai's plentiful backwaters, fringed by palm trees and paddy fields. These provide idyllic opportunities for boating. A country boat will cost you Rs 300 for an hour's ride in the backwaters. At the local lake, pedal boating is offered at Rs 50 per hour. The hotels and restaurants at Cherai have tie-ups with local fishermen and routinely arrange boat rides for guests and visitors.

Pallipuram Fort

Built in 1503 by the Portuguese and captured by the Dutch two centuries

later, this beautiful hexagonal fort is situated at Pallipuram on the northern end of Vypeen Island. The fort is maintained by the Archaeological Survey of India. Frequent buses plying from Vypeen will take you there for a nominal cost. The 4-km long ride from Cherai costs about Rs 100 by auto.
◆**Location** 4 km north of Cherai **Entry** Free **Timings** 9 am-5.30 pm, open on all days

Lighthouse

The 46-m tall lighthouse at Ochanthuruth on Vypeen Island offers an absolutely breathtaking view of the Arabian Sea. The lighthouse was built in 1979. It takes about 20 mins by auto from Cherai Beach to the lighthouse (fare between Rs 100 and 150). Buses from Cherai Village regularly ply to the lighthouse, so you could take an auto to Cherai Village (fare Rs 50) and then take a bus from there.
◆**Entry fee** Adults Rs 5, children Rs 3 **Timings** 3-5 pm daily

GETTING THERE

Air Kochi International Airport, Nedumbassery (22 km/ 40 mins). Taxis cost about Rs 450; pre-paid taxis are available at the airport
Rail Nearest railhead: Ernakulam (26 km/ 40 mins), connected to Delhi by the Mangala Lakshadweep Express and Kerala Express; to Chennai by the Tata Alleppey Express, Trivandrum Mail, Trivandrum Express and Alleppey Express; to Mumbai by the Mangala-Lakshadweep Express, Kanyakumari Express and Netravati Express; and to Bangalore by the Kanyakumari Express and Ernakulam SF Express
Road Ernakulam is linked to Cherai by the Goshree Bridge and to Willingdon Island by two bridges. Ernakulam is on NH47 that links Salem to Kanyakumari via Palakkad, Thrissur, Ernakulam, Alappuzha, Kollam and Thiruvananthapuram. From Mumbai, NH17 leads up to Edappally, just north of Ernakulam, via Panaji, Mangalore, Kannur and Kozhikode. Ernakulam's KSRTC Bus Stand is connected by daily services to most major towns in the state

Gowreeshwara Temple

Built in 1912 and dedicated to Sri Subramanya Swamy, this lovely temple is most famous for its annual nine-day festival, which is held during February-March. Dozens of caparisoned elephants are then taken out in a spectacular march to the accompaniment of a fine fireworks display. The dates for the festival, which depend on the Malayalam calendar, vary every year. Contact the local tourism office for details.
◆**Location** Cherai main village, about 500m from the beach **Note** Only Hindus are allowed in the temple; there is a strict dress code of saris for women and *mundus* for men

Azheekkal Temple

Famous for its grand chariot, pulled by thousands of devotees during the bi-annual *rathothasava*, or chariot celebrations, the Azheekkal Sri Varaha Venkateshwara Temple is the only one where two deities — Sri Varaha and Sri Venkateshwara — installed next to each other are worshipped as one god.
◆**Location** Cherai main village, about 1 km from Cherai Beach **Note** The same dress restrictions as in the case of the Gowreeshwara Temple apply here

SHOPPING

There are no souvenir and handicraft shops in Cherai. A few shacks near the beach entrance sell locally made utility items such as hand umbrellas, caps and

scarves. For souvenirs typical to Kerala such as Kathakali masks, cotton weaves and handicrafts made out of coconut fibre and shell, banana fibre, coir, sandalwood and teakwood, visit the two state emporia located on Kochi's MG Road: the **Kerala State Handicraft Apex Society** and **Kairali** (Kerala State Handicrafts Development Corporation). *For more on shopping in Kochi, see page 184.*

WHERE TO STAY

The **Cherai Beach Resorts** (Tel: 0484-2416949/ 2481818; Tariff: Rs 1,000-4,500) is by far the most comfortable option and its proximity to both the beach and the backwaters ensures a uniquely picturesque ambience. It has a variety of clean, well-appointed cottages, both AC and non-AC, to choose from. Excellent buffet-style meals, both traditional Kerala and Continental fare, are provided as part of the tariff. The resort also offers good boating and Ayurveda services.

High comfort at Cherai Beach Resorts

Baywatch Beach Homes (Tel: 2480299; Tariff: Rs 2,000-2,500), located right on Cherai Beach, has clean cottages with basic but comfortable amenities, as well as modern rooms on offer. It also has a great rooftop restaurant, offering spectacular views and excellent food.

The **Sealine Beach Resort** (Tel: 2418055; Tariff: Rs 2,500-4,000) is a double-storeyed building on the beach and has a rooftop restaurant. It offers spacious, clean and comfortable AC and non-AC rooms.

Amravathy Resorts (Tel: 3243521, 2417110; Tariff: Rs 750-3,500) is a timber and brick house converted into a hotel. Though the rooms are small, they are clean and comfortable, and each room has a sit-out that offers a great view of either the sea or the backwaters.

If you would like to stay in Kochi, see Where to Stay in Kochi on page 184.

For more hotels and details, see Cherai Accommodation Listings on pages 544-545

WHERE TO EAT

Although there are very few eateries in Cherai, the ones that exist offer excellent local cuisine. The resorts normally serve only their lodgers but there are a few hotels and restaurants where anyone can stop by. The restaurant at **Baywatch Hotel** offers very good seafood. Try their lobster and crab preparations, particularly the king prawn fry.

The restaurant at **Sealine** serves great multi-cuisine food. However, the tastiest food is to be found in the wayside shacks. These line the coastal road that runs along Cherai. The *kallumakaya* (mussels) and prawn dishes here are a must-try. *For eating-out options in Kochi, see Where to Eat in Kochi on page 184.* ■

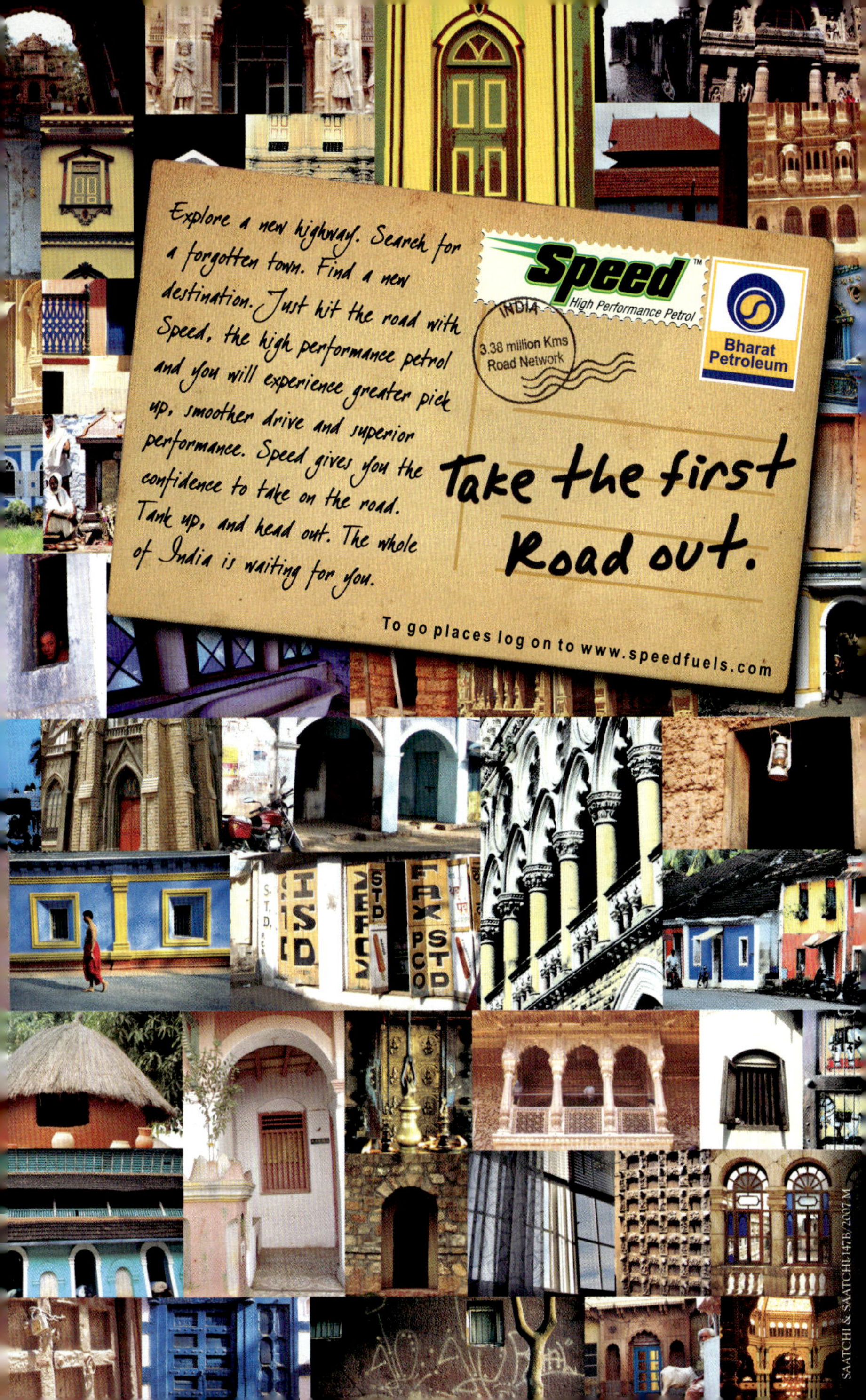
Explore a new highway. Search for a forgotten town. Find a new destination. Just hit the road with Speed, the high performance petrol and you will experience greater pick up, smoother drive and superior performance. Speed gives you the confidence to take on the road. Tank up, and head out. The whole of India is waiting for you.
Speed™
High Performance Petrol
INDIA
3.38 million Kms
Road Network
Bharat
Petroleum
Take the first
Road out.
To go places log on to www.speedfuels.com
SAATCHI & SAATCHI-147B/2007 M

V MUTHURAMAN

The road to the past: Antique shopping at a street in Kochi

KOCHI

THE QUEEN OF THE SEA

BY NILANJANA BISWAS

There is no beach in Kochi that's worth visiting anymore, but if you are in Cherai, then it makes sense to spend some time in this city, also one of the most beautiful destinations in Kerala. Kochi and its surrounding cluster of islands offer a rich and multi-cultural experience where mosques and temples, churches and synagogues coexist harmoniously and in a staggering diversity of architectural styles. You are after all in an ancient port town whose harbour, formed by a cataclysmic flood in 1341, opened the town to the influence of generations of European traders, each of whom left an indelible and unique imprint on the local culture. From glorious sunsets in the Kochi harbour foregrounded by slow moving cargo-laden ships and country boats to the aroma of spices in the Jewish heart of Mattancherry, Kochi captures one's senses like no other town.

There are many transport options for getting around Kochi; autos are the most useful for negotiating across Fort Kochi and Mattancherry. With two bridges linking Ernakulam to Willingdon Island and a new bridge connecting it to Vypeen, bus travel is convenient and cheap. However, the most picturesque way of getting around is the ferry. Kochi has two jetties — the **Main Jetty** from where ferries leave every 30 mins or so to Willingdon Island (2 km) and Vypeen Island (4 km), and the **High Court Jetty**, from where ferries leave again every 30 mins or so to Bolgatty Island (500m) and Vypeen Island (3.5 km). Ferry charges are nominal, approx Rs 2.50 per ride.

IN MATTANCHERRY

Mattancherry is accessible from Vypeen Island and Ernakulam by ferry, and it takes no more than a half-day walk to absorb the ambience of the Jewish past of this trading site.

Mattancherry Palace

Built by the Portuguese and gifted to Veera Keralavarma, a Kochi king, in 1555, the

Mattancherry Palace is also known as the Dutch Palace on account of the extensive additions made by the Dutch. It's a treasure house of friezes, paintings and old maps, and has rare regalia such as coronation robes and weapons.
♦**Entry fee** Rs 2 **Timings** 10 am-5 pm, closed on Fridays and national holidays **Note** Photography prohibited

Jewish Synagogue

Built in 1568 and rebuilt a century later, this is also known as the Pardesi Synagogue. It houses a collection of interesting historical items, including fourth century copperplate inscriptions, the Great Scrolls of the Old Testament and elaborate Chinese hand-painted tiles.
♦**Timings** 10 am-noon and 3-5 pm daily, except on Saturdays and Jewish holidays

IN FORT KOCHI

North-west of the Mattancherry Palace, across a canal, lies Fort Kochi, which is marked by its lively Anglo-Indian and Portuguese past. A row of **Chinese fishing nets** line Fort Kochi's seafront and are particularly glorious to view against the backdrop of the setting sun.

St Francis Church

A brisk 10-min walk from the Chinese fishing nets along Church Road in Fort Kochi brings you to this church built by the Portuguese in 1510. Three wooden arch-shaped windows dominate the white façade of the church, with a belfry and spire rising high over the middle window. The remains of the Portuguese explorer Vasco da Gama were interred here in 1524 and 14 years later moved to Portugal.
♦**Timings** 6 am-7 pm

Santa Cruz Basilica Church

Proclaimed a basilica by the Pope in 1984, this 14th-century blue-domed Roman Catholic Church is situated close to St Francis Church and has ornate interiors with beautiful paintings.
♦**Location** On Rampart Road **Timings** 9 am-1 pm, 3-5 pm

Maritime Museum

A tribute to India's maritime heritage, this museum, located off Beach Road, showcases shipbuilding activities down the ages from the period of the Indus Valley Civilisation.
♦**Location** Off Beach Road **Timings** 9.30 am-1 pm and 2-6 pm, closed on Sundays and national holidays

ON KOCHI'S ISLANDS

There are a number of islands around Ernakulam and Vypeen that are easily accessible by ferries, which ply frequently.

Bolgatty Island

This island is a long, finger-shaped island connected by the newly built Goshree Bridge to Ernakulam Town. The Bolgatty Palace dominates the seafront. Behind the palace precincts are villages where fisherfolk live. Built by the Dutch in 1744, the **Bolgatty Palace** served as a British Residency until 1947 and is today a heritage hotel run by the Kerala Tourism Development Corporation. The palace (Tel: 0484-2750003/ 500; Tariff: Rs 2,058-11,450) is superbly located on the seafront and you can choose a room with a view of Kochi's harbour, the backwaters or the sea. The hotel has a lovely swimming pool and a golf course.

Willingdon Island

This man-made island, built with dredging materials obtained when Fort Kochi was deepened in 1924 in operations overseen by the legendary Sir Robert Bristow, is separated from Ernakulam and Mattancherry by backwaters. An important naval base, it houses the Southern Naval Command Headquarters, the naval port and naval airport. The view on the island is splendid; the island itself, being entirely man-made, is an architectural marvel. Besides, some of the best hotels such as the **Taj Malabar** and the **Casino Hotel** (*see Where to Stay on page 184*) are located here.

IN ERNAKULAM

Cherai is connected by road to Ernakulam via the Goshree Bridge. A regular bus service operates from the Cherai Bus Stop to the town and the journey time is about an hour. The more picturesque route used to be the ferry ride from Vypeen Island but, at the time of writing, it was not operational.

Marine Drive

This stretch of paved seafront in the heart of Ernakulam offers a spectacular view of backwaters on one side and the trading ports of Mattancherry and Fort Kochi on the other where cargo ships and boats are anchored. The Marine Drive fronts **Broadway**, where buildings retain their sloping roofs and inverted V-elevations. There is nothing that a shopper can't get here. Ernakulam also has a number of museums that are worth visiting.

SHOPPING

Mattancherry and Jew Street in Fort Kochi, and Broadway and MG Road in Ernakulam, are the shopping hubs. In Mattancherry you can pick up quaint antique items, spices, coffee and tea besides the usual souvenir bric-a-brac. Try **RK Spices** in Mattancherry for black pepper, dry ginger, red chilli and galangal. Ask around for the **Jew Street spice market**. Try **Malabar Spices Shop** for fresh spices. **MG Road**, the main road running through the heart of Ernakulam, is where the branded shops are located. If shopping for gold, this is the place to be.

WHERE TO STAY

In Fort Kochi

Ranging from heritage homes to paying guest rooms, most of these options in the heart of Kochi's heritage zone offer atmosphere and character in large doses. The CGH Earth Group's **Brunton Boatyard** (Tel: 0484-2215461-65; Tariff: Rs 6,600-21,000) is built on a former boatyard, near the Chinese fishing nets. Its simple whitewashed walls, sloping tile roof, and terracotta floors with a giant raintree in front, blend with the old town's casual spirit. Kochi's culinary heritage is documented at the History Café in the hotel.

The **Ballard Bungalow** (Tel: 2215854; Tariff: Rs 1,200-2,800), set in a heritage Dutch colonial mansion near Port Boat Jetty on Ballard Road, is owned and run by the Cochin Diocese. The mansion has seven rooms, a restaurant and a travel desk. Set in another heritage Dutch mansion is **Fort Heritage** (Tel: 2215333/ 455; Tariff: Rs 2,401-2,837) on Napier Street, near the beach. Kochi's Portuguese heritage is also preserved in **The Old Courtyard** (Tel: 2216302; Tariff: Rs 2,250-4,600) on Princess Street, and in **Delight Tourist Resort** (Tel: 2217658; Tariff: Rs 800-1,400), at Parade Ground.

On Willingdon Island

The suites at the deluxe **Taj Malabar** (Tel: 2668292; Tariff: Rs 9,000-16,500), near the tip of the island, look out onto the lagoon. The CGH Earth Group's flagship **Casino Hotel** (Tel: 2668421; Tariff: Rs 4,100-10,000) is also on Willingdon Island. It offers unmatched views of the harbour, and fabulous dining and Ayurvedic treatments. The bar even has cocktails based on homegrown Kerala liquor and health drinks based on Ayurvedic concepts. **ATS Willingdon** (Tel: 2667643; Tariff: Rs 850-1,850) has 22 rooms and arranges sightseeing.

For more hotels and details, see Kochi Accommodation Listings on pages 544-545

WHERE TO EAT

Kochi is a gourmet's delight, and at all the quality hotels, the cuisine is as diverse as it is remarkable. There is huge variety in seafood, ranging from shrimp, crisp-fried mussels, grilled prawns, lobsters and squid done just right to soft-shelled crabs tossed Kerala-style. But the *meen pollichathu*, a delicious fish fillet coated with spice paste, wrapped in banana leaf and roasted, should be a priority. Try the one at the **Grand Hotel's restaurant**. Both **Nalukettu** on Chittoor Road and **Krishna Inn** on Warriam Road have traditional décor and specialise in Kerala cuisine. Try the appam-stew or appam-chicken curry at Nalukettu.

The biryani at **Kaikka's** in Mattancherry is legendary. The scented rice cooked in ghee and strewn with succulent mutton pieces is complemented with chutney made from plump dates marinated in lime juice. They serve the staple *kappa kari*, which is made with tapioca, and *puttu* (steamed flour cakes) with beef roast. You can also choose from the fresh catch — prawns, pomfret or cuttle fish. There are some exotic items there as well, like rabbit meat.

For Fast Facts and Getting There info on Kochi, see pages 176 and 178 ■

Inputs by Anil Nair

Photographs by PRASHANT PANJIAR

KOZHIKODE

SEASIDE DREAMS

State Kerala
Location Between the backwaters of Kallai and Beypore rivers in North Kerala, Kozhikode lies by the Lakshadweep Sea
Distances 199 km N of Kochi, 224 km S of Mangalore, 350 km SW of Bangalore
Journey time ***By road*** $5^1/_2$ hrs from Kochi, $5^1/_2$ hrs from Mangalore, 8 hrs from Bangalore
Route from Kochi NH47 to Edapally; NH17 to Kozhikode via Kodungalloor, Ponnani and Feroke (*see route guide on pages 144-145*)

BY PN VENUGOPAL

One June afternoon, the sun is hiding behind the monsoon clouds that have just turned up over the Malabar Coast. The sea is overcast and grey and the waves lash against the shore, somewhat furiously, as if venting out feelings that were submerged in its depths all summer. There is a slight drizzle, forever threatening to turn into pouring rain, the kind that would drive the hardiest monsoon lover indoors. But somehow, none of this has any effect on the people standing all along the long beach, said to be the third longest beach in the world. Some stand by the road, close to the waves, while others sit on the sands by a cluster of casuarinas, huddling under black umbrellas that aptly reflect the moodiness of the sea. There are no water sports here, no magical colours on the horizon at this hour, and certainly there's nothing to do except to stare at the rumbling sea that appears to be competing with the sky. Yet, all these people on the shore sit or stand facing the sea as if bewitched, welcoming the monsoon, and enjoying the paradox of a quiet afternoon and a stormy sea.

Kozhikode Beach isn't one of those Goan beaches. In fact, it isn't even Kovalam. But there is something about the sea here, the way the beach so seamlessly fits into the life of Kozhikode's residents, which makes it, for lack of a better word, adorable. On most days, the beach is alive long after sunset, with purdah-clad women and children thronging the sands till midnight. The ice-cream and snack vendors close shop around 10 pm, but the twinkling stars and the shining moon take over. The two dilapidated piers on the beach disappear in the dark as the beacon from the lighthouse flashes its beam across the horizon.

Kozhikode is also an ideal city to base yourself to visit beaches nearby: Kappad, famous for historical reasons, where the Portuguese explorer Vasco da Gama landed in 1498; Payyoli, on whose sands one of India's most noted women athletes PT Usha trained; and Beypore. The past and the present deftly come together in Kozhikode, offering a holiday by the sea like no other. Standing on Beach Road in the town, watching the waves crash against the shore on a rainy day, you realise why the sea can be so mesmerising. It's hypnotically rhythmic, and strangely soothing. Indeed, what better way can there be to spend an afternoon?

FAST FACTS

When to go September to February is the best time. Kozhikode is battered by the monsoon (June to August) but this is the time for Ayurveda treatments

Tourist offices

- District Tourism Promotion Council
Mananchira Square, Kozhikode
Tel: 0495-2720012
- Dept of Tourism, Govt of Kerala
Tourist Information Counters
Kozhikode Railway Station
Tel: 2702606
- Karipur Airport Counter
Tel: 0483-2712762

STD code 0495

ORIENTATION

The **Kozhikode Beach** is located just 1$\frac{1}{2}$ km from the railway station. Facing it are several government offices. The **Beach Road** has ice-cream parlours and small cafés, as well as temporary dhabas that keep sprouting up. A few hotels are to be found on this stretch. The town itself grew around the **Mananchira Square** and some of the main tourist attractions such as the **Mishkaal Mosque** and the **Thali Temple** are located near it. Autos are a convenient mode of transport; the average fare is Rs 15. From the town centre, the auto fare is Rs 15 to the beach.

Kappad Beach, to the north of Kozhikode, is 19 km from the town off NH17, and is accessible by bus. However, buses are few and far between. A better option is to hire a taxi from one of the taxi stands in the town. From Kozhikode, a taxi to Kappad costs around Rs 280. The beach has one stay option. **Payyoli** (42 km) is further north of Kappad and is also connected by bus from Kozhikode. A taxi to Payyoli costs Rs 300. **Beypore** (13 km), which is to the south of Kozhikode, is connected to the town by bus and taxi. Taxi fare to Beypore is about Rs 100.

BEACH WATCH

The sea is safe for swimming, except during the monsoons. However, people generally do not venture far out, and it's best to follow suit as there are no lifeguards. Dress conservatively.

THINGS TO SEE AND DO

The visitor to Kozhikode has to be warned that there are hardly any activities on

The beach is an integral part of the daily lives of Kozhikode's residents

the beaches here. What's offered here instead is peace and quiet, and plenty of time to stand and stare.

Kozhikode Beach

Early mornings or late evenings are the best times to visit the beach as the sun is otherwise too strong. Nearby is a **Lion's Park** for children offering seesaws and some simple rides. The beach also has a **Dolphin Point** at the tip of an old bridge, from where it's said one can spot dolphins. However, residents say they haven't spotted dolphins in quite a while. The park is open through the day; there is no entry fee.

In Kozhikode Town

Apart from the beach, there's much to see in Kozhikode. This includes the **Mananchira Square**, once the private bath of the royal Samuthiris. Today it's a complex with gardens, fountains, the Town Hall and a library. The square also has the **Lalitha Kala Academy Hall**, which hosts many exhibitions by artists from Kozhikode. The **CSI Church**, the renovated **Pattalam Mosque** and the 500-year-old **Commonwealth Spinning Mill** are some of the other landmarks that dot the square. **Kuttichera**, an old Muslim settlement where the **Mishkaal Mosque** is located, is nearby.

Kozhikode boasts of several mosques and temples that are worth visiting, as well as museums.

Kalaripayattu, Kerala's ancient martial art form, has close links with Kozhikode. Apart from the Kalari centres here, the brave hero of the *Vadakkan Veera Gatha* (Folktales of the North), Thacholi Othenan, is said to have been born in **Vadakara** (45 km from Kozhikode). **CVN Kalari Sangam** (Tel: 04950-2769114) is a famous training centre of Kalaripayattu. The Sangam's centre in Nadakkavu arranges demonstrations on request.
♦**Timings** 6-9 am and 5-7 pm

Kappad Beach

It was here that Vasco da Gama landed in 1498, triumphant at last in his quest for spices. The beach, however, doesn't show off its historical importance. A not-so spectacular, moss-covered monument-like structure is the only reminder of the famous landing. The beautiful beach is usually deserted and therefore peaceful. Also known as **Kappakadavu**, the beach has huge rocks protruding into the sea, caressed by the seemingly friendly waves.

North of Kappad Beach is **Elathur**, located where the **Korapuzha River** meets the Arabian Sea. You can hire a country boat for a ride across the river. No one organises these trips but you can see the boats and the boatmen around; bargain and agree on a price before you head out. A fare of about Rs 60 is alright for a ride across the river and back. Shellfish and *kallumakaya* (mussels) are abundant on the rocks jutting out into the sea.

Beypore Beach

This beach is located at the mouth of the River Chaliyar. There is a stone bridge that stretches out for about 2 km into the sea here and it's a pleasure to walk on it. The atmosphere is serene and the ambience perfect for a romantic evening. In the night, the white threads of the fishing nets, left on the beach to dry, evoke illusions of stepping inside a maze.

Beypore's fame, however, is more centred on another activity: for centuries now, the coastal town has been famous as a **shipbuilding centre**. The *uru*, or the country craft built here by traditional shipbuilders known as Khalasis, has a huge market even now and continues to attract buyers from across the Arabian Sea. At the mouth of the Chaliyar River, near the beach, under thatched roofs, are large boats (some 65-m long and 700 tonnes in weight) being worked on, often by wizened old Khalasis.

Amazingly, almost all the work, including rolling the huge beams into place, is done manually. It often takes 50 Khalasis over a year to carve and shape an *uru* out of teak and jackfruit logs. It's then towed to a West Asian port such as Dubai, where it's fitted with a diesel engine. There's not much activity during the monsoons or when the business is dull, so check at your hotel if boat building is happening before you set out for Beypore.

Kappad, where Vasco da Gama landed

Payyoli Beach

This beach was the 'synthetic track' of PT Usha, one of the most successful Indian athletes. Even today, you can see students from her sports school here practising on the Payyoli sands early in the morning. If you are lucky enough, you can catch the 'Payyoli Express' herself, as Usha was nicknamed, amidst her wards.

Payyoli Beach used to be a lively and small harbour, where boats would return from the sea with the catch, till a few years ago. But all the activities have currently shifted to a fishing harbour further north. Now the main reason for visiting Payyoli is to catch a glimpse of the **Velliyamkallu** (Silvery Rock), a huge rock formation that's 14 km out at sea. It covers 2 acres and its only inhabitants are a few rare birds. You can make a trip to Velliyamkallu in a fibreglass boat that

SAIBAL DAS

Message in a bottle: For centuries, Beypore has been a famous shipbuilding centre

fishermen here own; the journey takes about an hour and the minimum rate is about Rs 250.

SHOPPING

The Kozhikode Beach is close to the town; the latter offers several souvenirs, including traditional handicraft items. Kozhikode's most famous souvenir, however, is of the edible kind. The sweet Kozhikodan halwa, seasoned with dry fruits and prepared in pure coconut oil, is available in many shops across the town, near the bus stands and the railway station. But the best bet would be to buy it from one of the shops in **Mithai Theruvu**, literally Sweet Meat Street, which starts from Mananchira Square.

Kozhikode's banana chips are another sought-after item. There are many small units around the town where you can see bananas being peeled and sliced into circular pieces (with such speed that you realise it's an art in itself) and then fried in boiling oil. You can see the pieces taking on a golden hue and eat it straight from the pan, if you are brave. One decent stall is on **Kannur Road**, under the overbridge near the Head Post Office; yet another is at **Chakkorathukulam.**

Also visit the **spice market** at Valiyangadi. Go to **Chembotti Theruvu** to shop for bell metal artefacts. Models of *urus* can be bought at Beypore. Those made from teak can cost up to Rs 15,000 and those from coconut Rs 500. Kozhikode was once famous for its muslin and handloom cloth. Today, you can pick up, among other things, *mundus* priced between Rs 150 and 250 from any of the textile stalls in Mithai Theruvu.

WHERE TO STAY

Kozhikode has plenty of choices to suit every pocket. However, there are very few hotels on the beaches themselves. Advance booking is not necessary.

In Kozhikode

Seaqueen Hotel (Tel: 0495-2366604; Tariff: Rs 700-2,250) is on the Beach Road, with several sea-facing rooms and a roof garden restaurant. The rooms are clean and the place is well-maintained. **Hotel Beach Heritage Inn** (Tel: 2762057; Tariff: Rs 1,500-2,200) is another good hotel on the beach, but it has only 6 rooms.

The **Victorian Beach Heritage Inn** (Tel: 2762055-56; Tariff: Rs 1,200-1,400) on Beach Road is a heritage hotel. It was built in 1890 as a watering hole for the burra sahibs. Fifty years later, it was converted into a hotel, and has hosted Somerset Maugham and Jawaharlal Nehru, among others.

Slightly away from Kozhikode Beach is the **Taj Residency** (Tel: 2765354; Tariff: Rs 3,100-6,500), on PT Usha Road, with an Ayurvedic centre. **Malabar Palace** (Tel: 2721511-16; Tariff: Rs 1,550-4,050) on Manuelsons Junction, **Hyson Heritage** (Tel: 2766423; Tariff: Rs 650-3,500) on Bank Road, and Kerala Tourism's **Malabar Mansion** (Tel: 2722391; Tariff: Rs 250-650), at Mananchira in the centre of the city, are other high-end hotels providing excellent accommodation. **Fortune Hotel** (Tel: 2768888; Tariff: Rs 1,980-2,970) at Chakkorathukulam is another good hotel, with a restaurant serving authentic Keralite food.

Calicut Towers (Tel: 2723202; Tariff: Rs 410-1,500) on Mavoor Road, **Hotel Maharani Puthiyara** (Tel: 2723101; Tariff: Rs 400-1,700), on Taluk Road, and **Alakapuri Guest House** (Tel: 2723451; Tariff: Rs 175-1,000) on MM Ali Road are other options for clean accommodation.

A fine choice for a homestay where you can opt for Ayurvedic treatment is **Harivihar** (Mobile: 09847072203; Tariff: Rs 4,000-5,000), a hotel set in the 150-year-old ancestral home of the Kadanathu royal family, located in Bilathikulam, a quiet corner of town.

On and around Kappad Beach

Kappad Beach Resort (Tel: 0496-2688777; Tariff: Rs 2,000-3,000) is the only accommodation on Kappad Beach. The resort has 16 elegantly furnished rooms, most of them facing the sea. There is a swimming pool and an Ayurvedic centre here as well. The hotel provides umbrellas and other assistance on the beach.

Around Beypore Beach

Close to Beypore Beach is **Tasara Centre for Creative Weaving** (Tel: 2414233; Tariff: Rs 1,500-2,500), which offers weaving, dyeing and printing courses — all this apart from accommodation. Their

→ GETTING THERE

Air Nearest airport: Karipur Airport (26 km/ $^3/_4$ hr), connected to Coimbatore, Delhi, Kochi, Mumbai and Chennai. Prepaid taxi to Kozhikode costs Rs 405 from Karipur Airport, which is just across the border in Malappuram District

Rail Kozhikode Station, well-connected daily to Ernakulam and Thiruvananthapuram by the Cannanore, Netravati and Parashuram express trains and to Mumbai by the Netravati and Mangla Lakshadweep express trains. The latter begins at Delhi, to which Kozhikode is also connected by the bi-weekly Trivandrum Rajdhani. The Mangalore Mail is an excellent daily link from Chennai

Road Kozhikode is connected to Kannur, Kasargode, Mangalore, Panaji and Mumbai by NH17. Buses from Kochi, Thrissur, Palakkad, Kannur and Perinthalmanna stop at Kozhikode's KSRTC Bus Stand on Mavoor Road. Buses connect Bangalore, Mangalore and Madurai to Kozhikode. Apart from KSRTC (both Kerala and Karnataka Transport Corporations), Kallada Tours and Travels (Tel: 080-25523003) has AC and Volvo buses (fare Rs 520) from Bangalore to Kozhikode

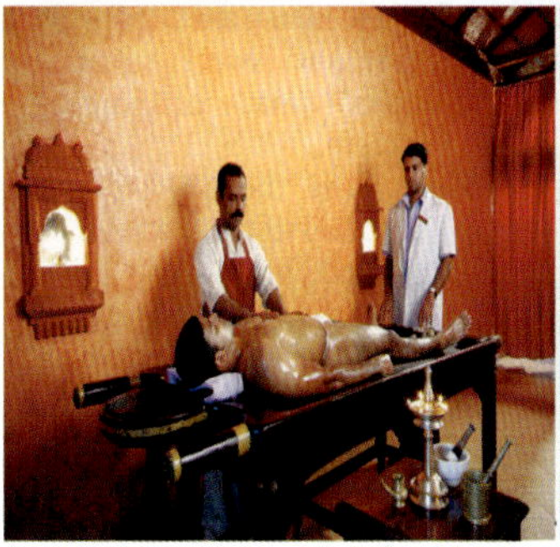

Weaver Bird Package for 3N/ 4D, inclusive of meals, costs Rs 11,000. You can learn weaving, printing and dyeing at the centre, set up by the Vadakkiniyedath family in 1979 to preserve this lesser-known craft heritage of Beypore.

About 8 km from Beypore is the **Kadavu Resorts** (Tel: 0483-2830570; Tariff: Rs 2,500-8,500), beautifully located by the green banks of the Chaliyar River.

For more hotels and details, see Kozhikode Accommodation Listings on pages 548-549

WHERE TO EAT

At the busy port of Calicut of yore, traders from across the seas left their indelible mark both on the land's history and cuisine. Before the visitors from the West landed at Kozhikode, the cuisine already showed a marked Arab influence. The Westerners also contributed their flavours to the dishes. Today's Kozhikode offers a wide variety of cuisines, from simple vegetarian to meat-heavy, spicy dishes. *Kallumakaya porichathu* (mussels fry, had with rice) and *pathal* (a ring-shaped rice *pathiri*) are must-trys while in Kozhikode.

The sweet Kozhikodan halwa

SAIBAL DAS

There are a number of small eating joints serving snacks and several ice-cream parlours dotting the Beach Road in Kozhikode. **Mummy & Daddy**, right on the beach, serves excellent non-vegetarian dishes at reasonable prices. *Muttamala*, an egg preparation, is one of their specialities. **Woodlands Restaurant** on the eastern side of the Beach Road serves vegetarian delicacies and dosas. The roof garden restaurant of **Hotel Seaqueen** and the restaurant of **Beach Hotel** serve delicious vegetarian and non-vegetarian dishes such as vegetable pulao, mussel roast and Malabar chicken.

A couple of hundred metres from the beach is the restaurant **Zains.** Here you will get *puttu* with local fish stew, or wheat *pathiri*, served with *kozhi nirthiporichathu*, a chicken fry with egg or *kada* (a small bird) fry. The ghee rice is also popular, and it's best had with a mellow beef stew prepared in coconut milk. *Kozhikodan pazham nirachathu* (banana fry with coconut) and sweet coconut samosa, or *bayakkada* (made of banana) are also available here.

Sagar Hotel, near the KSRTC Bus Stand, serves Malabar-style chicken or mutton biryani, and beef curry with Malabar porotta. **Bombay Hotel** near St Joseph's Boys High School and **Hotel Alakapuri** are old establishments known for their biryani and chicken fry.

Paragon Restaurant near the Head Post Office is the best choice for fish, especially fried prawns or prawn curry accompanied by *vellapam*. **Rahmath Hotel** on KP Kesava Menon Road is famous for its beef *varattiyathu* with porotta. For tiffin, try **Dakshin the Veg** on Indira Gandhi Road, near the KSRTC Bus Stand, and **Vasantha Bhavan** on Court Road. ■

Inputs by NP Hafiz Mohamad

PRASHANT PANJIAR

THALASSERY

COUNTRY ROADS, TAKE ME HOME

State Kerala
Location Thalassery is a port town in the North Malabar region, just 6 km north of Mahe
Distances 22 km SE of Kannur, 64 km NW of Kozhikode, 310 km SW of Bangalore
Journey time ***By road*** $^{3}/_{4}$ hr from Kannur, $1^{1}/_{4}$ hrs from Kozhikode, $8^{1}/_{2}$ hrs from Bangalore
Route from Kozhikode NH17 to Thalassery via Koilandi and Mahe **Route from Bangalore** SH17 to Mysore via Maddur, Mandya and Srirangapatna; SH88A to Periyambadi via Hunsur and Gonikoppal; SH88B to Wetecolly; Kerala SH30 to Thalassery via Iritty and Mattanur (*see route guide on pages 144-145*)

■ **BY NILANJANA BISWAS**

If you look out at the sea at Thalassery, you will easily lose track of time. The gently rolling waves transport you to a different historical period, for, it was on this part of the Malabar Coast that the British East India Company established its first regular settlement. It was also from this port town that the Company secured, in the 18th century, complete control of the pepper trade. Little wonder then that on the ramparts of the Thalassery Fort, you find it easy to conjure up a bloody battle scene. At the bay, you can imagine men carrying sacks of pepper, coffee and spice up the gangway of a large, magnificently carved ship, flying a foreign flag, getting ready to sail.

Today, Thalassery's serene Muzhippilangad Beach is famously known as India's only drive-in beach where the sand is so tightly packed that it's possible to drive along its entire length of 4 km. As I walk the stretch, small birds — sand plovers, terns and ibises — peck about in the sand. The sea, a calm pigeon-wing blue, laps gently at my feet. When I reach the little port of Dharmapattanam situated at the southern tip of Muzhippilangad, I try to imagine how different this bustling marketplace must have been two centuries ago. What battles, what bitter disputes had taken place here between imperial Britain and the local Kolathiri, Kottayam and Ali kings!

Thalassery's colonial past presents itself constantly, in the most unexpected ways. You find that the road you're walking along is named after William Logan, the man who authored one of the most readable regional administrative manuals ever written; at the curve of the road, barely visible through the hedge, is a charming bungalow, all trellis and woodwork, with geraniums nodding from its window boxes; the town's seaside promenades, which could well be part of any British coast, are thoughtfully fitted with wrought iron railings and curved seats. Past and present co-exist in this port town, creating a magical spell.

ORIENTATION

Thalassery Town has developed on a coastal stretch of land by the busy NH17, with Mahe in the south and Kannur in the north. The **Muzhippilangad Beach** is a beach-lover's delight. A park near the beach provides a stunning sea view. The historical sites in the heart of the city are bounded by **Logan Road** and **Gundert Road** (named after the German scholar Rev Dr Hermann Gundert). The town offers budget to mid-range accommodation and inexpensive transport facilities. Autos and taxis run on meter. The minimum auto fare is Rs 10; thereafter, Rs 10 is charged for every extra kilometre. Taxis charge Rs 30 per km.

FAST FACTS

When to go December to May

Tourist offices

- District Tourism Promotion Council (DTPC)
Near Collector's Office, DTPC Complex
Taluka Office Campus, Kannur
Tel: 0497-2706336
- DTPC
Kannur Railway Station
Tel: 0497-2703121

STD code Thalassery 0490, Kannur 0497

BEACH WATCH

Black rock formations along Muzhippilangad Beach protect the waters from deep currents and make it ideal for swimming. There are no lifeguards on patrol but the District Tourism Promotion Council (DTPC) is taking steps to deploy safety personnel. Make sure that you carry enough drinking water supplies as very few services exist on the beach. The beach is off-limits during the monsoon.

THINGS TO SEE AND DO

Enjoy yourself at the Muzhippilangad Beach. Dolphins are said to make their appearance in the early morning. Mornings (and evenings) are also the best time to visit as the day is usually very hot. Remember to tour colonial Thalassery and soak in the unique ambience of this small town's multi-cultural past.

Muzhippilangad Beach

As India's only drive-in beach, a must-do here is a slow drive along the beach, from Ezhikkad in the north to Dharmapattanam in the south. It is a unique experience, though the water birds that are intent on prying open the *kallumakaya* (mussels) on the beach scarcely take note of your passage. In the mornings you may be lucky enough to glimpse a school of dolphins playing in

PRASHANT PANJIAR

Where the sea and the sky converge: The view from Overbury's Folly

the waters while evenings offer glorious sunset views. You can swim up to 2 km into the sea except during the monsoon when the sea is rough. On the southern side near Dharmapattanam, stop to watch local fishermen return with their catch. Nearby, vendors sell the region's delicacy: mussels cooked in a variety of styles. From this point, you also have a clear view of the tiny and lush-green Dharmadam Island (*see below*).

In the low tide period between April and June, the **Adventure Academy**, located at Ezhikkad towards the north of Muzhippilangad, organises 'Adventure Carnivals' consisting of activities such as boating, parasailing, paragliding and swimming. It also organises night camping expeditions complete with tent and campfire on Dharmadam Island. Contact Sebastian on 09847315145 for details.

Dharmadam Island

This 5-acre wide island is locally called Pachha Turuth (literally, Green Island), so named because of the lushness of its vegetation. Inaccessible to tourists without special permission from the DTPC (*see Fast Facts on facing page*), this tiny island lies at a 100m distance from Dharmapattanam and is a site of religious significance, as ancient Buddhist images are believed to have been found here. A drive southwards from Ezhikkad along the Muzhippilangad Beach brings you to the confluence of the Anjanakandi and Thalassery rivers from where the island is clearly visible. In summer, the waters recede to such an extent that it is possible to wade through to the island. At other times, contact the Adventure Academy (Mobile: 09847315145) for boat trips to the island.

◆**Location** 4 km north of Thalassery

Thalassery Fort

Constructed by the British in 1708 on the seafront in Thalassery Town, the Thalassery Fort is an imposing monument with walls and turrets built out of solid laterite stone. Steps from the inner fort lead to secret tunnels, now blocked, that once opened into the sea, and vaults that held vast quantities of pepper

and spice. It houses a modest gallery where pictures of other ASI-protected monuments and sites are displayed. A small lighthouse near the fort lies in a state of disuse.
◆**Entry** Free **Timings** 10 am-5 pm

Odathil Palli
Half a kilometre from the Thalassery Fort stands the imposing Odathil Palli, a mosque built by a rich Arab trader following a syncretic Hindu-Muslim architectural style. Said to be 500 years old, the mosque has neither domes nor minarets and has a ceiling made of copper. Its walls have fine carvings. It is not open to non-Muslims.

Gundert's Bungalow
This colonial-style bungalow is where the famous German scholar and lexicographer Rev Dr Hermann Gundert, who compiled the first Malayalam dictionary, lived and worked for 20 years from 1839. Visit with permission from the principal of the Technical Training Institute (Tel: 0490-2351423) that's now housed here. The bungalow is a typical colonial-style building in timber and tile with wide verandahs and deep eaves.
◆**Location** Close to the town at Illikunnu on NH17 **Timings** 8 am-5 pm

GETTING THERE

Air Nearest airport: Karipur International Airport, Kozhikode (90 km/ 2 hrs). A prepaid taxi to Thalassery costs about Rs 1,300
Rail Thalassery Station, served by all the trains that stop at Kannur (*also see Getting There in Kannur on page 202*)
Road Thalassery is connected to Kannur, Kozhikode, Kasargode, Mangalore, Panaji and Mumbai by NH17. The 263-km drive north from Ernakulam leads to Thalassery via NH47 till Edappally and then via NH17. The nearest KSRTC Bus Stand is at Kannur. Buses from Mangalore and Kasargode, running to Kozhikode, Thrissur and Ernakulam along NH17, stop at Thalassery

Overbury's Folly
Overbury's Folly earned its name from the fact that its builder EN Overbury started but couldn't complete the construction of a recreation spot on a hilltop adjacent to the sub-collector's bungalow. Today renovated with an open-air coffee shop and park, Overbury's Folly offers a splendid view of the sea.

Dances with weapons
Visit the **CVN Kalari** located at Chellattom Veedu, Thiruvangad, about 1 km from Thalassery, to see students learning the Keralite martial art form of Kalaripayattu, said to be the forerunner of kung-fu. The kalari officials also do *marmachikitsa*, which is a treatment based on the training techniques of the martial art, used for curing fractures and improving circulation.
◆**Entry fee** Rs 100 **Timings** 4-10 am and 4-7 pm **Tel** 0490-2320030

Mahe
Part of the Union Territory of Pondicherry, Mahe is situated 6 km south of Thalassery along NH17. Once the bastion of the French who fought the Portuguese from here, the French legacy of this tiny port town lends it a charming and distinctive ambience. The waterfront provides a superb sea view and the beach is ideal for relaxation. The landscaping at the **Tagore Park** near the beach exhibits a strong French influence. Mahe's **St Teresa's Church**, built in 1736, is known to be one of the oldest churches in Malabar and draws pilgrims from all over Kerala during its annual October feast.

V MUTHURAMAN

Cricket came to Thalassery years before the game was played in Kolkata

Of cake, cricket and circus

Thalassery is popularly associated with the three Cs: cricket, cake and circus. Cricket was introduced to Thalassery in the 1790s by Colonel Arthur Wellesley, years before the game was played in Kolkata in 1860. The famous English Test cricketer, Sir Colin Cowdrey, the youngest player ever to appear in a match at Lord's when, at the age of 13 in July 1946, he represented Tonbridge against Clifton, played cricket at Thalassery. His father, a tea planter, was responsible for laying the town's cricket pitch in the beginning of the 19th century. This town also saw the establishment of Kerala's first bakery: the **Mamballa Bakery**. (It was shut at the time of writing and the family running it plans to reopen it at the Harbour City Complex near the Government Hospital.) And finally, Thalassery is considered to be the birthplace of the Indian circus with more than 90 per cent of circus artistes hailing from this region. The legendary Keeleri Kunhikannan is credited with having started Thalaserry's circus tradition. His mastery over Kalaripayattu, the ancient martial art of Kerala, and wrestling, helped him to study both gymnastics and sports practised by the English and eventually led him to develop Thalaserry's great circus tradition.

Malayala Kalagramam

This cultural and fine arts centre situated at New Mahe is dedicated to preserving Malabar's cultural heritage. It offers courses on a range of arts and disciplines such as yoga and meditation.
◆**Entry** Free **Timings** 10 am-6 pm

Anjarakandy Cinnamon Estate

A visit to the biggest cinnamon plantation in Asia, established by the British East India Company agent Murdoch Brown in 1798, is a must-do. It's 15 km south-east of Thalassery and is connected to the town by bus. But first, you have to get permission from the Prestige Educational Trust to visit. Call 0497-2851255.

SHOPPING

Thalassery offers limited shopping possibilities. The best bet is to pick up some of the black peppercorn that this town is famous for. Good quality cashew is cheap and easily available and is the other produce that you can take back with you. Visitors to these parts normally shop for cotton weaves at Kannur.

WHERE TO STAY

Thalassery has a handful of good value budget and mid-range accommodation options. An excellent option near the sea is the **Razeena Beach Resort** (Tel: 0490-2320672, 2323993; Tariff: US$ 150), which faces the sea on Holloway Road. It has a few premium rooms, well-appointed and clean, with a good sea view. It also has a good restaurant serving multi-cuisine food. **Saravanapriya Guest House** (Tel: 0497-2827333; Tariff: Rs 90-495) offers budget accommodation, clean and comfortable, near the Muzhippilangad Beach, with sea-facing rooms.

Away from the sea are a few options such as the **Pearlview Regency** (Tel: 2326702-03; Tariff: Rs 800-1,550), 2 km from the local railway station. The rooms are large and well-appointed and the hotel has a swimming pool, a bar, a multi-cuisine restaurant and an Ayurvedic centre. Internet services are also available. **Sharara Plaza** (Tel: 2341101-03; Tariff: Rs 500-1,800), on AVK Nair Road, is a new, mid-range hotel with a multi-cuisine restaurant with live 'mehfil' music on weekend nights. The rooms are large, lavishly decorated, well-fitted and comfortable.

Paris Presidency (Tel: 0490-2342 666-68; Tariff: Rs 360-780) is located in the heart of town on Logan Road; it has clean, comfortable rooms and a multi-cuisine restaurant.

For more hotels and details, see Thalassery Accommodation Listings on page 549

The art of making Malabar porottas

SAIBAL DAS

WHERE TO EAT

Thalassery is famous for its banana halwa. This is available in most of the sweet and condiment shops here and is quite delicious though rich in ghee. Crisp banana chips are a tasty snack. Mussels are another delicacy. Roadside shacks offer the most delicious mussel preparations: steamed with rice and shallow-fried (ask for *azhikkadaka*) or curried. *Pathiri* (a kind of Indian bread, in this case stuffed with meat or fish, and fried) is another local speciality. Biryani and seafood prepared in the traditional Malabar style are also must-trys. The **Paris Presidency's** restaurant is well-known for its Thalassery dum biryani while the **Shahara Plaza** offers good Malabar cuisine. Try the restaurant at **Razeena Beach Resort** for great Malabar fish curry and prawn fry served in a delightful ambience.

AROUND THALASSERY

Kozhikode (64 km)
See page 185 ■

Inputs by Maya Jayapal

PRASHANT PANJIAR

KANNUR

THE MAGIC OF MALABAR

State Kerala
Location Kannur, earlier known as Cannanore, is situated in North Malabar
Distances 86 km NW of Kozhikode, 307 km SW of Bangalore
Journey time ***By road*** 2 hrs from Kozhikode, 9 hrs from Bangalore
Route from Kozhikode NH17 to Kannur via Koilandi, Mahe and Thalassery **Route from Bangalore** SH17 to Mysore via Srirangapatna; SH88A to Periyambadi via Hunsur and Gonikoppal; SH88B to Wetecolly; Kerala SH30 to Mattanur via Kuttupuzha and Iritty; state road to Kannur (*see route guide on pages 144-145*)

BY NILANJANA BISWAS

The beaches of Kannur are probably Kerala's most well-kept secrets — long stretches of golden sand unvisited by crowds and though not far from the town, unaffected by urban life. Of these, only Payyambalam Beach, situated at a stone's throw from town, attracts tourists and day-trippers. When I arrive here, at least four games of beach football are underway and a fine tackle always draws a round of warm applause. Laughter rings in the air. Children take spirited dives into the Arabian Sea; couples stroll through ankle-deep surf; and sand castles catch the last rays of the sun.

Kannur's other beaches offer seclusion. In Meenkunnu Beach, I am alone in a long curve of sea, surf and golden sand. Sand plovers and ibises race along the beach in search of mussels and crabs. Just as I focus my camera on a plover against the perfect backdrop of foamy surf, it's gone! Only a delicate line of three-pronged footprints, washed away moments later by the rolling waves, remain as an image captured for posterity.

Moving on, nowhere does one experience the magic of a pristine coast more powerfully than at the twin beaches of Kizhunna Ezhara and Thottada in Kannur. Steep laterite cliffs plunge dramatically down to these quiet beaches, offering the most breathtaking views. Is that a school of dolphins in the distance? From the vantage point of the cliffs, I can see curved black surfaces playfully appear and disappear among the waves. Tense with excitement, I can scarcely breathe. Moments later I wonder if that isn't just a cluster of rocks surrounded by swirling waters. But I push the thought out of my mind. In this enchanted land, imagination finds idyllic release from its usual prosaic moorings. In my mind, why yes, I have seen the laughing dolphins!

ORIENTATION

The **railway station** lies at the heart of the town and a stone's throw away is the **District Tourism Promotion Council** (DTPC) office, opposite the **main bus terminus.** There are several clean beaches around Kannur. Towards the north, 12 km from Kannur, is **Meenkunnu Beach.** On the southern side, 2 km from Kannur Town, is the **Payyambalam Beach. Burnassery's Baby Beach** is a small extension of Payyambalam, 4 km from the city centre in the Cantonment area. About 11 km south of Kannur are the **Kizhunna Ezhara** and **Thottada** beaches.

Kannur has good hotels in the heart of town but only a few on the seaside. However, there are homestays near the beach.

Autos and taxis run by meter. The minimum auto fare is Rs 10. Taxis cost Rs 30 per km. A non-AC taxi for the day charges about Rs 1,300 for 150 km, with Rs 30 for every additional kilometre.

BEACH WATCH

Barring the monsoon time, the beaches around Kannur are free of undercurrents and are known to be safe for swimming. However, be warned that neither are tide lines marked nor coastguards deployed. Opting for beachwear would be unwise.

THINGS TO SEE AND DO

Beach tourism in North Malabar is in a stage of infancy and there are no water sports facilities. However, the beaches are ideal for leisurely walks or brisk jogs. Just as excitingly, this is dolphin country. Early morning walks along the beach often reward nature enthusiasts with the breathtaking sight of schools of dolphins splashing about in the Arabian Sea.

Payyambalam Beach

Just 2 km west of Kannur Town, the Payyambalam Beach comes to life every evening with people gathering to watch the sunset, build sandcastles and play football on the beach. A walk along the laterite cliffs jutting into the sea offers a splendid view.

Ezhara and Thottada beaches

Narrow paths from steep laterite cliffs drop down to the golden sands of the twin beaches of Kizhunna Ezhara and Thottada, approached via NH17. Safe from undercurrents, the waters here are

FAST FACTS

When to go December to May

Tourist offices

- District Tourism Promotion Council
  Near Collector's Office, DTPC Complex
  Taluka Office Campus, Kannur
  Tel: 0497-2706336
- DTPC
  Kannur Railway Station
  Tel: 0497-2703121

STD code 0497

ideal for swimming but the absence of lifeguards introduces an element of risk. These palm-fringed, golden sand beaches are for the most part deserted, except for a few local fishermen. The beaches are marked by the total absence of shops, restaurants and hotels.

Mappila Bay

A fishing harbour where country boats abound and fishermen are always hard at work untangling nets and harvesting their catch, Mappila Bay has a historical background. It was the seat of the Kolathiri kings, who by the 14th century had established an independent hold over North Malabar. They were the political rivals of the Zamorins of Kozhikode and were a power to reckon with at the time of the arrival of the Portuguese towards the end of the 15th century.

Boating here is an unforgettable experience. As you leave the jetty, the façade of Fort St Angelo (*see below*) comes into view. Gulls and ibises wheel in the air, swooping down into the waters with military precision and emerging moments later with small fish thrashing about their beaks. Although there is no organised boating here, fishermen will offer you a ride for Rs 150 for an hour.

♦**Location** 3 km from Kannur, after the Burnassery Cantonment

→ GETTING THERE

Air Nearest airport: Karipur Airport, Kozhikode (112 km/ $2^1/_2$ hrs). Taxi fare to Kannur is Rs 1,350. Pre-paid taxis are available at the airport

Rail Kannur is well-connected to all major cities in Kerala and most metros. From Delhi, there's the Mangala Lakshadweep Express; from Chennai, the Mangalore Mail, the MS Mangalore Express, the West Coast Express and the Mangalore Express; from Mumbai, there's the Netravati Express; and from Bangalore, the Yeshwanthpur-Cannanore Express

Road Kannur is connected to Kozhikode, Mangalore, Panaji and Mumbai by NH17. From Kochi, take the NH47 via Edapally and then the NH17 to Kannur via Kodungalloor, Ponnani, Kozhikode and Thalassery; it's a 6-hr journey. Kannur's KSRTC Bus Stand, opposite the Collector's Office near NH17, has regular services to Kozhikode, Ernakulam, Bangalore and Mangalore

Fort St Angelo

The first Portuguese Viceroy of India, Don Fransisco de Almeyda, started the building of the fort with the permission of a Kolathiri king in 1505.

Surrounded by the sea, with a wide moat at the entrance, the fort still holds a row of sea-facing cannons hewn out of its laterite walls — a silent reminder of the violent battles through which the control of the fort passed from Portuguese hands to the Dutch and finally to the British, who later developed Kannur as a cantonment town. Today, the Archaeological Survey of India protects the fort. Contact the Tourism Police outpost at the entrance of the fort for assistance.

♦**Location** Near Mappila Bay **Entry** Free **Timings** 8.30 am-6 pm

Arakkal Kettu

Formerly the residence of the Arakkal Ali Rajas, Kerala's royal Muslim family, today this is a museum protected by the Archaeological Survey of India.

The palace complex includes beautiful residential quarters in laterite and timber with exquisitely carved furniture, a mosque in the precincts, the *pandikasalas*, or the erstwhile royal storehouses, and a bell-tower at the entrance.

♦**Location** Close to Fort St Angelo **Entry fee** Rs 5 **Timings** 10 am-5 pm, closed on Mondays and national holidays

S VINAYAKUMAR/ SOUTHINDIAPICTURE

The Payyambalam Beach comes to life as people gather to watch the sunset

Meenkunnu Beach

Reached via NH17, Meenkunnu Beach offers a clear expanse of sea, surf and sand. This palm-fringed beach is ideal for swimming, walking about and watching water birds pick at crabs and shells.

Parassinikadavu Temple

Dedicated to Sri Muthappan, the nonconformist, dried-fish-and-toddy loving incarnation of Lord Shiva, the three-tiered temple at Parassinikadavu, located on the banks of the Valapattanam River 18 km north-east of Kannur, is probably the region's most important shrine. This is also the only temple where Theyyam, an extraordinary trance dance, is performed twice daily except on moonless nights. To be in time for the dawn Theyyam, arrange for an auto or taxi to pick you up from Kannur at about 5 am. The temple is open to people of all religions.

◆**Theyyam timings** 5-8 am and 4-8 pm

SHOPPING

The beaches in and around Kannur are as yet undeveloped and do not offer any shopping attractions. Kannur, however, is known for its cotton weaves. Pick up a range of handloom products including linen, saris and dhotis from the government-run **Hanveev** on Sri Narayanana Road, close to Payyambalam Beach.

WHERE TO STAY

Kannur has a number of hotels to choose from, but if you are looking for something close to the beach, then your stay options are limited to a few quiet homestays. The DTPC *(see Fast Facts on page 201)* has a network of classified homestays with standard facilities in a number of places including the beach sites of Burnassery, Payyambalam and Thottada; they can also help with bookings. Homestays are a hugely popular tourist option in Kannur. Some homestays are renovated heritage homes while others offer modern, well-appointed cottages.

All homestays typically combine the beach experience with a uniquely homely and personalised Malabar ambience. Kannur's homestays are on secluded beaches where you will not find a single shop or restaurant, ideal for those who want a quiet getaway.

On the beaches

Costa Malabari (Tel: 0497-2836174; Tariff: Rs 2,000-2,500) is in Thottada, 8 km north of Kannur Town, and offers a quiet getaway in palm-fringed surroundings close to the beach. Accommodation is arranged in a five-bedroom, cottage-style guest house, with well-appointed rooms and attached baths with hot water. It offers delectable Malabar cuisine. The travel desk is helpful and knowledgeable about local Theyyam performances.

KK Heritage (Tel: 2835240; Mobile: 09447486020; Tariff: Rs 1,200-1,500) is an excellent homestay in Thottada, located 100m from the beach. The tariff includes a choice of exquisite Malabar or Continental-style breakfast and dinner. Two cottages and three rooms make up this clean five-room guest house, styled in laterite and timber, totally free of concrete, with old-style furniture including easy chairs and double beds, as well as large Western-style attached baths.

Kannur Beach House (Tel: 2836530; Mobile: 09847186330; Tariff: Rs 900-1,100 per person per night) is another lovely heritage homestay option, more than 100 years old, with five clean and well-appointed cottages, minutes away from Thottada Beach. A small river runs along the house and shelters mangroves and 200 bird species. All meals, cooked in traditional Malabar style, are included in the tariff, with seafood dishes, particularly mussels and shrimp, being the specialities. For guests, complimentary river canoeing is an added attraction.

A curry made with fried prawns

SAIBAL DAS

Kala Holiday Home (Tel: 2742933; Tariff: Rs 1,500-2,500) is situated 3 km from Palliamoola Beach and offers one comfortable, modern cottage with two rooms and additional facilities like a common living room, kitchen and a large clean lawn. The tariff includes a traditional Kerala-style breakfast. For other meals, guests may either use the kitchen and fridge facilities or avail of the catered meals arranged by the homestay at a nominal cost. Also on offer is Ayurveda.

The only resort that's close to the beach is the **Mascot Beach Resort** (Tel: 2708445; Tariff: Rs 700-2,500), near Baby Beach, Burnassery; it's superbly located with an open-air restaurant overlooking the sea. **Sagar Heritage Home** (Mobile: 09447449171; Tel: 2701153; Tariff: Rs 2,500) is a clean, well-appointed private guest house on Kizhunna Beach with two double rooms, and a large living room surrounded on all sides by a beautiful verandah. The beach is a few minutes walk from the guest house.

In the town

If you wish to stay in the heart of Kannur Town, there are several options. **Malabar Residency** (Tel: 2701654-55; Tariff: Rs 600-2,500), next to the railway station, on Thavakkara Road, has Internet, two restaurants and a 24-hr coffee shop. KTDC's **Yatri Niwas** (Tel: 2700717; Tariff: Rs 200-800), located close to the railway station and the Police Club at Thavakkara, offers clean and good-value budget AC and non-AC rooms.

The **Royal Omars** (Tel: 2769091-96; Tariff: Rs 650-2,500) on Thavakkara Road is a mid-range, 3-star hotel with

PRASHANT PANJIAR

A Theyyam performance in progress at a temple in Kannur

clean, well-furnished rooms and a fine restaurant and bar. **Kamala International** (Tel: 2766910; Tariff: Rs 990-1,990) on SM Road is a large hotel with well-appointed double rooms and suites with clean and luxurious attached baths. It also has a good restaurant, a coffee shop and a helpful travel desk.

Less than 3 km from the city centre are a few options such as the **Palmgrove Heritage Hotel** (Tel: 2703182; Tariff: Rs 200-1,000), an Arakkal palace now converted into a budget hotel in the clean and ambient Cantonment area. **Cliff Exotel International** (Tel: 2712197; Tariff: Rs 800-1,500) at Payyambalam has good rooms, and also organises houseboat cruises on the Valapattanam River.

For more hotels and details, see Kannur Accommodation Listings on pages 545-546

WHERE TO EAT

Biryani and seafood cooked in Malabar style are Kannur's specialities. Try **Mascot Beach Resort**'s open-air restaurant for delectable Malabar cuisine. The Malabar-style prawn curry is a particularly good choice. Fine Kerala cuisine is also available at the Royal Omars **Paris** restaurant, famous for its biryani. At Malabar Residency's **Grand Plaza** restaurant, you can sample delicious fare ranging from the local Malabari to Chinese, Mughlai and Continental dishes. *Kadukka neruchathu* or stuffed mussels are a must-try as also the aromatic Kannur-style fish curry cooked in a *chatti* or clay pot. For good quality vegetarian food, like dosas and idlis, try **Chaithram Hotel, Bharat Restaurant and Lodge House** and **Indian Coffee House**. Kannur's many roadside restaurants offer a wide range of snacks and breakfast foods made from rice flour: the long, coconut-flavoured *puttu*, the spongy *vatayappam*, the lace-thin *palappam*, the fried sweet *uniappam* and the noodle-like *idiappam*.

AROUND KANNUR

Thalassery (22 km)
See page 193

PRASHANT PANJIAR

BEKAL

MAKING WAVES

State Kerala
Location In North Kerala's Kasargode District, the Bekal Beach spreads below a fort
Distances 64 km SE of Mangalore, 156 km NW of Kozhikode, 415 km SW of Bangalore
Journey time ***By road*** $1^1/_2$ hrs from Mangalore, $3^1/_2$ hrs from Kozhikode, 8 hrs from Bangalore
Route from Kozhikode NH17 to Kasargode via Koilandi, Payyoli, Vadakara, Mahe, Thalassery, Kannur, Payannur and Nileshwaram; SH to Bekal **Route from Bangalore** NH4 to Nelamangala; NH48 to Mangalore via Hassan and Sakleshpur; NH17 to Kasargode via Manjeshwar; SH to Bekal (*see route guide on pages 144-145*)

BY PN VENUGOPAL

The Bekal Beach curves around the imposing fort with which it shares its name, calm and composed in most seasons, its tranquillity belying much of the Tourism Department jargon about Bekal being the "Destination of the Future". On occasion one is thankful the future is not here yet, for how else can one enjoy this shallow beach, with its scurrying crabs and multitude of sea-shells, in solitary splendour? Though made famous by the movie *Bombay*, where the fort and the sea are lovingly captured at the height of the monsoon's fury, Bekal remains endearingly small-town-ish. There are no tourist trappings here, and the only thing you can take home is a memory of the sea's heart-aching beauty, as glimpsed from a moss-covered window at the fort. Truly, some of the best things in life are indeed free.

ORIENTATION

The 2-km long beach is located behind **Pallikere Railway Station**. Unlike other

beaches, the Bekal one is an enclosure, and you have to pay Rs 5 per person and Rs 10 per vehicle for entering. Unfortunately, the guards here force you to leave by 7 pm and allow you to enter only at 10 am, making you miss the beauty of the beach at both sunrise and sunset. To reach the beach from **Kanhangad**, the nearest town 11 km away, take an auto (Rs 30) or bus (Rs 5). The beach is 19 km south of the district headquarters **Kasargode**, and it costs Rs 45 by auto and Rs 7 by bus to get to Bekal from there.

BEACH WATCH

Swimmers are advised to avoid the curve of the beach and stick to the straight stretch. Always stay near the shore even though there are a couple of lifeguards. Beachwear is best avoided.

THINGS TO SEE AND DO

Bekal's beach and fort are likely to occupy much of your attention but do remember to make a detour to the Kappil Beach nearby.

→ FAST FACTS

When to go September to February
Tourist offices
- District Tourism Promotion Council
Kasargode
Tel: 04994-256450
- Bekal Resorts Development Corporation
Bekal Fort
Tel: 0467-2272900/ 07
Kasargode Tel: 04994-220445
Mobile: 09447010445

STD codes Bekal 0467, Kasargode 04994

Bekal Beach

The shallow beach has piles of granite stones on which you can sit and watch the changing colours of the sea. Nearby is the **Bekal Aqua Park**, a small pier with pedal boats and water cycles, the latter being the smaller version of pedal boats that can accommodate just one person. At the time of writing, however, the park was shut. The services are expected to be resumed soon; the beach timings will apply here as well. Recently, pathways were constructed on the beach. Horse cart and camel rides are also offered. It's, however, quite discomfiting to see camels, brought all the way from Rajasthan, on a beach in Kerala.

Bekal Fort

The 300-year-old fort made of laterite juts into the sea. The view from its ramparts, located 130 ft above sea level, is astonishing: waves crash against the fort's base in a cyclical, hypnotic rhythm. Important features of this fort include a tank with a flight of steps; broad and wide steps leading to an **Observation Tower** from where one can view everything around: an ancient **Anjaneya Temple**, a newly renovated **mosque**, and a sea bastion.
◆**Entry fee** Indians Rs 5, foreigners Rs 100 **Vehicle entry fee** Rs 10 **Timings** 10 am-5 pm

Kappil Beach

Located 6 km to the north of Bekal, Kappil is a secluded beach, long, wide and usually clean. You can swim in the sea and take a break on the 'Kodi Cliff', a huge rock on the beach that doubles as a resting place. However, be warned that there are no lifeguards here.

Hosdurg Beach

About 12 km south of Bekal is one of the many forts in Kasargode District, the **Hosdurg Fort** built by the Ikkeri Nayaks, who had fortified the Bekal Fort in the mid-16th century. However, the Hosdurg Fort is only a huddle of stones though the

Explore a new highway. Search for a forgotten town. Find a new destination. Just hit the road with Speed, the high performance petrol and you will experience greater pick up, smoother drive and superior performance. Speed gives you the confidence to take on the road. Tank up, and head out. The whole of India is waiting for you.
Speed™
High Performance Petrol
INDIA
3.38 million Kms
Road Network
Bharat
Petroleum
Take the first Road out.
To go places log on to www.speedfuels.com
SAATCHI & SAATCHI-147/2007 M

beach near it is worth a visit. It's a long strip of tawny sand fringed by casuarinas.

WHERE TO STAY

K-Tees Residency (Tel: 0467-2275633; Tariff: Rs 200-1,500) is the hotel nearest to the Bekal Beach, close to the Pallikere Railway Station, with rooms and cottages. The rooms are clean but the sound of passing trains can be a nuisance. **Gitanjali Heritage** (Tel: 2234159; Tariff: Rs 2,500-4,000), 5 km from Bekal at Panayal, is a *tharavad* (traditional Keralite house with two inner courtyards) that has been converted into a homestay. **Chandralayam Homestay** (Tel: 2236456; Tariff: Rs 500-5,000), 4 km from Bekal, has an Ayurvedic massage centre. **Hotel Bekal International** (Tel: 2202017; Tariff: Rs 200-1,300), located in Kanhangad, has AC rooms.

Bekal Boat Stay (Tel: 2282633 Tariff: Rs 8,000 per day for four, including food) is a unique option offered by the Bekal Resort Development Corporation, wherein you spend your night in a houseboat as it cruises the Valiaparamba backwaters, about 21 km from Bekal.

For more hotels and details, see Bekal Accommodation Listings on page 544

Delicious, irresistible fish moilee

SAIBAL DAS

GETTING THERE

Air Nearest airport: Bajpe Airport, Mangalore (64 km/ 1½ hrs), connected daily to Mumbai, Bangalore and Chennai. A pre-paid taxi from Bajpe Airport to Bekal costs Rs 1,300

Rail Nearest railhead: Kasargode (19 km/ ½ hr), well-connected to Kozhikode by the Mangalore Mail (also a daily link from Chennai) and Parashuram Express, among several daily trains. Netravati Express is an excellent option from Ernakulam, Thiruvananthapuram and Mumbai, as is the Mangala Lakshadweep Express from Delhi. You can get a bus or taxi to Bekal from the station

Road Bekal is connected to Mangalore, Kannur, Kozhikode and Mumbai by NH17. Kasargode's KSRTC Bus Stand has frequent daily services to Mangalore, Kannur, Thalassery, Kozhikode and Kochi, among other places

WHERE TO EAT

The seafood here is excellent as are the typical North Malabari mutton dishes such as the Malabari mutton biryani. But don't get your hopes high at the **Kerala Tourism Department Corporation** (KTDC) **restaurant** at Bekal Beach; it has unappetising tea, coffee, cold drinks and packed snacks. They do serve lunch (fish curry and fish fry are the specialities) if you order well in advance and are travelling in a group.

K-Tees International Restaurant, located quite close to the beach, serves only vegetarian food; their masala dosa comes highly recommended. **Oottupura Family Restaurant**, in Hotel Bekal International, Kanhangad Town, offers Keralite, North Indian and Continental dishes. **Hotel Malanadu** and **Elite Tourist Home** at Kanhangad are two other options for good Keralite food such as fish moilee. Both places are also quite clean. ■

LAKSHADWEEP

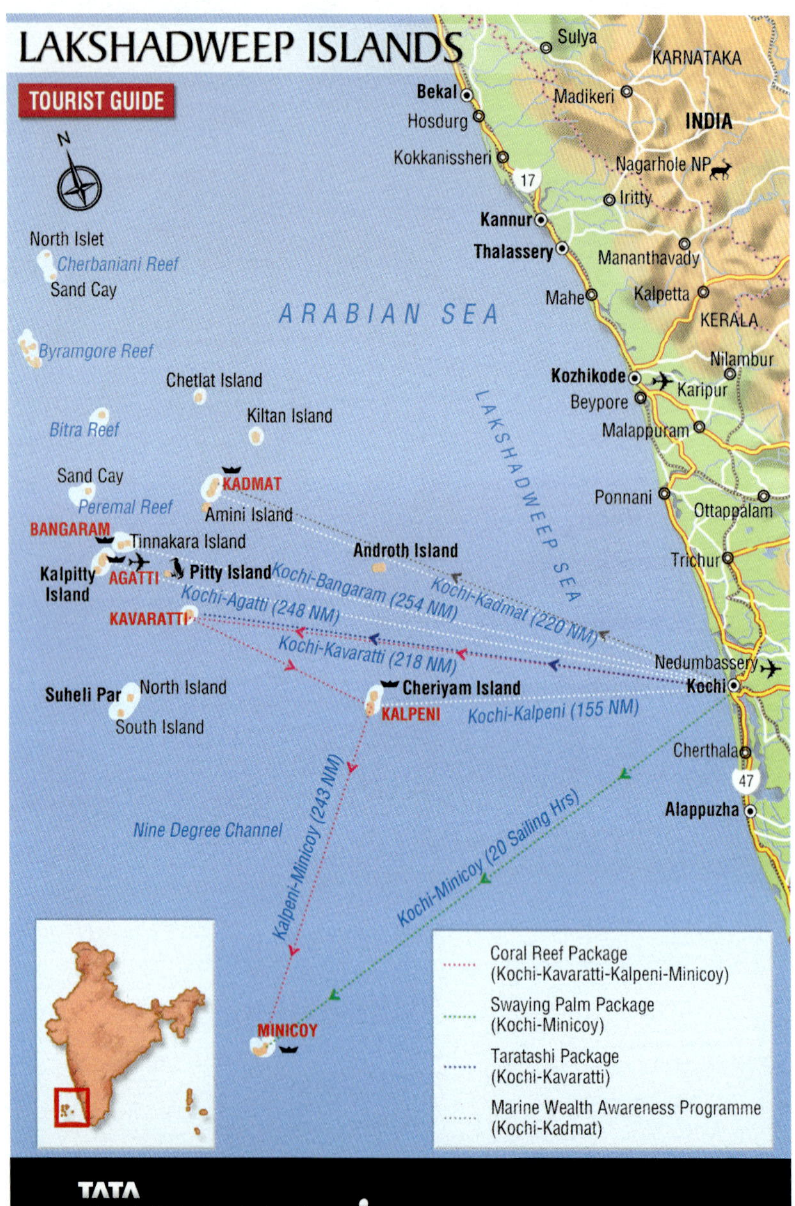
LAKSHADWEEP ISLANDS
TOURIST GUIDE
N
North Islet
Cherbaniani Reef
Sand Cay
Byramgore Reef
Chetlat Island
Kiltan Island
Bitra Reef
Sand Cay
KADMAT
Peremal Reef
Amini Island
BANGARAM
Tinnakara Island
Kalpitty Island
AGATTI
Pitty Island
Androth Island
KAVARATTI
Kochi-Bangaram (254 NM)
Kochi-Agatti (248 NM)
Kochi-Kadmat (220 NM)
Kochi-Kavaratti (218 NM)
Suheli Par
North Island
South Island
Cheriyam Island
KALPENI
Kochi-Kalpeni (155 NM)
Nine Degree Channel
Kalpeni-Minicoy (243 NM)
Kochi-Minicoy (20 Sailing Hrs)
MINICOY
ARABIAN SEA
LAKSHADWEEP SEA
Sulya
KARNATAKA
Bekal
Madikeri
Hosdurg
INDIA
Kokkanissheri
17
Nagarhole NP
Iritty
Kannur
Thalassery
Mananthavady
Mahe
Kalpetta
KERALA
Nilambur
Kozhikode
Karipur
Beypore
Malappuram
Ponnani
Ottappalam
Trichur
Nedumbassery
Kochi
Cherthala
47
Alappuzha
Coral Reef Package (Kochi-Kavaratti-Kalpeni-Minicoy)
Swaying Palm Package (Kochi-Minicoy)
Taratashi Package (Kochi-Kavaratti)
Marine Wealth Awareness Programme (Kochi-Kadmat)
TATA
SAFARI DICOR 2.2 VTT

Courtesy BANGARAM BEACH RESORT

Eternal sunshine of a spotless sea

BY PRAHLAD KAKAR

On my first-ever diving expedition, which was in the Mauritius, I found a Quran. It must have been a sign because a few years later, I started my own diving school in Lakshadweep, which has a 99.9 per cent Muslim population.

I was stunned by Lakshadweep's beauty on my first visit in 1990. The Union Territory looked like little emerald dots in an Adriatic blue sea that turned aquamarine upon nearing the shorelines of white sand. So clear and pristine were the waters that I could spot the anchor chain even when it was a 100 ft below, surrounded by fish in varying hues. In the beginning, I had such withdrawal symptoms for Mumbai that I actually stood near puttering scooters to inhale some carbon monoxide — I wasn't used to air that was so pure!

At that time, nobody knew where Lakshadweep — India's only group of coral reef islands — was located. People thought it was in the Andamans. This was mainly because government authorities preferred to hold onto it as a top secret, Lakshadweep being their private holiday destination. To date, no one can land there just like that. You still have to acquire a visa-like permit from government officials at Kochi, who can decide whom to allow on the islands. But to an extent this has helped in keeping this heaven unaffected by commercialisation and pollution.

Lakshadweep's locals constitute 55,000 proud and fiercely independent islanders, originally the Moplahs from Kerala. Their language is Malayalam, but they are familiar with Hindi and English. Coconut and tuna are all that the island provides, as even rice isn't cultivable here because of the sandy environs. Everything else has to be procured from mainland Kerala. Octopus is a delicacy here and the food at Ramzan is simply mouth-watering. Alcohol is banned on all the islands except Bangaram. But the sheer beauty of this paradise is intoxicating in itself.

Thirty-six islands form Lakshadweep, of which only 12 are inhabited. Tourists are allowed only on Agatti, Kalpeni, Kavaratti, Kadmat, Minicoy and Bangaram. It's just you and your fishing boat from here on if you wish to explore the rest. We did just that on my first visit where we managed to visit five of the islands in 12 days! That's when we realised how this untouched

Courtesy AGATTI BEACH RESORT

EASY ACCESS

terrain could be the locale for one of the world's best diving schools.

It took us five years of running around to get it started, for everyone was skeptical about granting us permission. At last, we were allowed to start at Kadmat and later at Bangaram in 2000. Our institute is called Lacadives, a name by which Lakshadweep was initially known. Initially it was difficult to get students, especially Indians, who are largely scared of water and who prefer holiday destinations where they can shop. So we began by roping in friends, family and even locals, some of who went on to become diving instructors trained to International CMAS (World Underwater Federation) standards. My wife, Mitali, is a qualified instructor and the founder of the Reef Watch Marine Conservation, a non-government organisation that works for marine and coral conservation. In fact, we even brought out *Secrets of Eternity*, a compilation of poetry by divers whose lives the ocean touched through Lacadives.

I believe diving helps you deal with your fear of the unknown, of not knowing — at least initially — what lies at the bottom of the usually dark seabed. Once you overcome it, it will feel as if you were going back to the womb, or as if you were becoming part of a planet that nobody has ever been on before. That's the experience that Lakshadweep provides and I am happy that I could involve all my three children in this activity, as a part of their growing up. Even now, we still keep stumbling upon new diving sites and we baptise these with names such as Stingray City and Manta Point. My favourite is Shark at Alley, which a fellow diver, Shaukat, discovered. We go there to spot sharks, but each dive has ensured encounters with different species such as the yellow fin tuna and the guitar shark. We also spotted a school of around 5,000 or more jacks, 20 stingrays, and a flight of 40 batfish, which is rare.

I have to add here that global warming, a myth at the time, is now a reality. I realised a catastrophe was on the cards in 1998, when the reefs — the thermometers of the ocean — were attacked by an epidemic of the crown of thorns starfish, which eat coral.

On its heels came the El Nino current that recurs every three years, but it was warmer than normal, resulting in long coral stretches dying, resembling a huge graveyard. After I saw that the sites we had named 'Garden of Eden' and 'North of Eden', for their stunning beauty, had died, I cried.

From here came the inspiration to make a film, to create awareness about the subject. Titled *Troubled Waters*, it ultimately won the best environmental film award at the Vatavaran Film Festival in 2003. But the best part is that many of those coral expanses are today coming back to life.

All you need to get with you while coming to Lakshadweep are two swimming trunks, three T-shirts, two *lungis* and a toothbrush. This way you won't leave behind any garbage but just the bubbles you form while diving. ■

As told to Ornella D'Souza

SAIBAL DAS

BANGARAM

ISLAND IN THE SUN

Location Bangaram and the isles of Tinakkara and Parali I, II and III (erosion has cut up Parali into three bits) lie 5 to 6 nautical miles north-east of Agatti
Distance 254 nautical miles west of Kochi, or 1 hr sailing time from Agatti

■ **BY LATHA ANANTHARAMAN**

At first it sounds like someone is trying to build my character. We have just been received at the Bangaram Island Resort by John, and along with the regulation tender coconut water, we are getting a lecture on what not to expect. No air conditioning, no telephones, no television, no room service, no newspapers, no running hot water. He is also telling us not to waste water or use too much soap, which pollutes the groundwater and soil. If we weren't sitting at a well-stocked bar at which guests are already plying their swizzle sticks, although it's only noon, this would remind me of summer camp.

The place is not cheap, and it takes quite an effort to get here. But for the past 16 years, a small, committed band makes it here to this tiny piece of Lakshadweep. They get their permits, wait out cancelled flights, keep their breakfast down on an aircraft smaller than a bus, then brave a stomach-churning boat ride from the island with the airport to the island they want to be on.

What draws them is not the luxury of jacuzzis and turbaned staff, but the thrill of discovery and access to a seascape well beyond the bounds of their imagination. Whether you see these islands from the air, with their frothy plumes at one end and swirling tails of peacock blue at the other, or from the sea, as the flattest conceivable accretions of sand and shell, they are a delicate habitat, on which we must tread lightly.

Nothing is dressed up. Apart from a few clay pots sunk in the sand there is little décor, and we inhabit an austere landscape under the shelter of bamboo and coconut thatch, designed to be comfortable rather than lavish. And yet there is a bar open all day, a multilingual library and cocktail lounge, an ample spread at mealtimes, tea and cookies whenever you like, and friendly faces all round. There's not a motor vehicle to be heard, and it's just us on the islands, guests and staff and a few visitors from the neighbouring island of Agatti who have come to harvest coconuts.

The resort is full, and yet there is unimaginable space for us all. For the early swimmers in the lagoon. For those who sit back with a cup of tea to just fill their lungs and watch the sun rise. And for the brisk walkers along the beach.

EXPLORING THE ISLAND

On and in the water

The extraordinary variety of underwater life along the coral reefs of Lakshadweep attracts divers from around the world. The resort at Bangaram offers diving instruction and certification, and teaching is one on one. Twice a day, groups of

Birds on Bangaram

Birds are essential to the sustenance of the islands. As sandbars form from the action of waves on coral, they trap chunks of dead coral and shell, and birds hunt the fish and other animals caught here. Their droppings make the sand fit to nourish the beginnings of plant life.

Ornithologist Chris Gent comes year after year for the birds as well as the diving. He has shared his list of birds spotted here (127 and still counting) with the resort for the benefit of all visitors. For birdwatching on these islands, he suggests the visitor carry an illustrated guide. On a morning walk around the island's 'lake' – a largish pond formed when two spits of sand met at the other end – he points out the most common waders to be seen: redshanks, greenshanks and the common sandpiper. A golden plover is just visible on the muddy edges of the water. An

CHARU SONI

abrupt 'tsk' from the shrubs on the opposite bank, he says, is that shy bittern that may come out in front of a lone watcher, but is put off by our voices.

Swallows swoop overhead, and high in the coconut fronds a grey heron and several egrets are drying out. Back by the seashore, Chris stops to show me turnstones, sanderlings and sand plovers by the water's edge.

Courtesy BANGARAM BEACH RESORT

Tread lightly: Tourists arrive by boat to Bangaram Island

intrepid divers set off in a boat with their minders and plunge into a world of sharks, manta rays, sea turtles, moray eels, squirrel fish, puffer fish, barracuda, parrot fish, groupers and sweetlips. Glass-bottom boats (Rs 600 for a couple/ 45 mins) are an option for those who don't dive but would like to see this teeming life.

Anglers head out in the morning and evening to fish in the deep sea (Rs 2,000/ 3 hrs, rate inclusive of boat ride and fishing equipment). Snorkellers explore the lagoons enclosing the small satellite islands for tiny blue cleaner wrasses, angelfish, butterfly fish, clown fish, surgeonfish, and uncounted striped and spotted beauties darting through the coral in the glassy water. The resort also takes guests to Bangaram's satellite islands of **Tinakkara, Parali 1** and **Parali 2** (Rs 450 per head/ 2 hrs). The trip from Bangaram to the **Tinakkara shipwreck** costs Rs 1,500 per couple.

During the rainy season, deep-sea fishing and scuba diving are not possible, but all other activities take place in the lagoon, where the waters are always calm. It's best to inform the staff about your water sports plan at least 24 hrs in advance. Boats go out and come in at various times depending on the tides, so it's not always possible to go diving or snorkelling at short notice.

On the beach

On the sandbars, crabs swarm out of tiny pinholes or larger hideouts with an alarming mound of sand heaped close by. Striped orange crabs hunch their bodies high. Most of the crabs are the same pale ivory colour as the sand, as we don't see them until they suddenly lift up their skirts and skitter away sideways.

A walk in the shallows at low tide gives us a more prickly experience of the lagoon. There is live coral here, branch coral tipped with fluorescent blue or lumps stained in patches of red, bread-like growths, brain coral and table coral.

The reef, pronounced dead a few years ago, is now coming back to life. Here I see a stranded blue starfish, surgeonfish, the velvet innards of curled clams in browns and strange purples. One of my fellow walkers turns over a sea cucumber with his stick and the thing squirts water out an end. And under a slab of table coral lurks a vicious-looking, unnamed, black ball of spines, which others say is poisonous.

WHERE YOU'LL STAY AND EAT

Walking through knee-high water all afternoon under a blinding sun can be quite a workout, and the next logical step is a massage. Like most good resorts in the region, the CGH Earth group of hotels' **Bangaram Island Resort** (Kochi Tel: 0484-2666821, 2668221; Tariff: Rs 14,500-28,000, inclusive of meals) has an Ayurvedic doctor on hand and a massage centre with separate facilities for men and women. Then there is my new sporting discovery for the trepid — hammocking. I get in the hammock, ensuring as little sway as possible, lie back, and put a cap over my eyes. I listen to the clicks and rustles of the gold-green coconut fronds overhead answering the deep murmurs of the waves. Chittering white-eyes swarm up out of the kanni bushes behind me. Time stands still.

A burst of colours in the sea's depths

Courtesy BANGARAM BEACH RESORT

Fade back in to the smell of firewood on which dinner is being cooked. I walk to the tables laid out on the beach, and the sky on this moonless night has exploded into shards of light. I know a handful of stars by name and have a nodding acquaintance with others. But it turns out there are stars between the stars, and even more between those. As I leave the island next morning, the boat circling the long way round, there are sprays of tiny silver fish flying out of the water. The sea always saves a surprise for the last.

For more details, see Lakshadweep Accommodation Listings on page 551

OTHER INFO

The resort supplies soap and shampoo, and its shop sells basic needs such as mosquito repellent, but there are absolutely no other shops on the island, so carry your own sunblock, conditioners, moisturisers and other requirements.

Bring along a pair of rubber slippers or canvas shoes for walking in the water. The coral and shell can cut bare feet, and you don't want to step on a poisonous stonefish. Carry a cap to protect yourself against the sun. Visitors are able to use their mobile phones, but otherwise there is only a radio phone for emergencies.

The resort offers many attractive off-season packages between May and September, including 7N/ 8D for Rs 54,000, 5N/ 6D for Rs 41,500 and 3N/ 4D for Rs 25,000. The rates are per person, on a twin-sharing basis, and are inclusive of all meals and taxes. Bookings have to be made at the **Casino Hotel** (Tel: 0484-2668221; Website: cghearth.com) on Willingdon Island in Kochi.

For details on getting to Bangaram Island, see The Information on page 247 ■

Nature holds forth the secret of life in her hands, knowing that only the wise will reach out.

Coconut Lagoon, beside the fertile banks of the breathtakingly beautiful Vembanad Lake in Kumarakom, celebrates the simple joys of life. Here,

in the midst of the backwaters and the never-ending lake, stands a tile-and-timber mansion, a typical traditional Kerala tharavad, painstakingly transplanted and restored. An architectural marvel, this homestead exudes the charm of the Kerala life of yore. And transports one back in time to a world of peace and contentment.

STARK.Tvm.3328

Central Reservations: Casino Building Cochin Kerala India Phone: +91-484-3011711 Fax: 2668001
Email: contact@cghearth.com **www.cghearth.com**

AGATTI

WALK THE SEA

Location Agatti is the most westerly of the Lakshadweep Islands, with two satellite atolls. Agatti's lagoons are linked to the isles of Bangaram, Tinakkara and Parali I & II
Distance 248 nautical miles, or 18-22 hrs sailing time, from Kochi

BY CHARU SONI

On the west side of Agatti Beach, stretching as far as the eye can see, a shimmering aquamarine lagoon fringed by a reef appears to merge with the bright blue horizon, as if it were swallowing the inky blue sea. The sheer range of blues is enough to stun the senses and provoke a not-so-unreasonable urge to swim the colours. And we haven't even gone into the dazzling white of the sand. Agatti is certainly one of the most beautiful isles in Lakshadweep.

PHOTOS COURTESY AGATTI BEACH RESORT

The island's charm lies in its composition: its beach has milky white sands, the translucent turquoise waters have multicoloured fish, there are coconut and palm groves surrounded by brushwood, and a magnificent reef that bewitches you the moment you lay your eyes on it. Then there are friendly fishermen, simple huts and mosques, and a museum where you can trace the history of the Lakshadweep Islands. To top it all, there's a comfortable resort where you can put your feet up. Agatti is a private paradise that offers an unforgettable adventure and every ingredient that goes into making a perfect holiday.

ORIENTATION

The island lies on a north-to-south axis with the **airstrip** at the southernmost tip. The quaint **airport**, with just small huts serving as its arrival and departure halls, must be among the tiniest in the world. Less than half-a-kilometre outside the airport grounds is the **Agatti Beach Resort**. **Agatti Beach** runs along both the western and eastern shores.

The southern and northern tips of the island are connected by a single road that meets at a crossing near **Agatti Village**. It's about a kilometre from the **Embarkation Jetty**, from where one can get an inter-island ferry.

EXPLORING THE ISLAND

Swim the colours

You get your first glimpse of Agatti from the plane and wonder what all the fuss is about. It's just a long, thin stretch of land with swaying palms and coconut trees and an airstrip at one end. Then you land and walk across to the beach. Enclosed between the island and the flat reef is the finest lagoon in all of Lakshadweep. That's when you want to abandon all thought and plunge into its warm, inviting waters. Bliss! A diagonal path across a patch of coconut and palm groves, from the west side of Agatti, gets you to the eastern beach. Come here at low tide to have more of the beach to explore, as the waters of the lagoon recede into the sea then. The treasures of the atolls, brilliant white coral of all shapes and sizes, litter the white sand. Coral pumice stone is often washed ashore on this side of the beach.

Tourists enjoy a boat ride near Agatti

In the shimmering waters there are schools of colourful fish, live coral, sea anemone, starfish and sea cucumbers. The easiest way to access this amazing world is to snorkel around the reefs or take a glass-bottomed boat ride. Of the two, snorkelling is infinitely more satisfying even though non-swimmers might find it daunting at first — take heart, the waters in the lagoon are quite shallow and it's possible to literally walk the sea.

Hire a bike

The road to **Agatti Village** meanders gently past coconut and palm groves, and

Down under: A whole new world

A face mask, a pipe and rhythmic breathing are what it takes to snorkel in the lagoons. Underwater, the wonderful world of fish and sea creatures invites you to become one among them. Have a chance to scuba dive? Do it. Age no bar.

For deep sea diving, steel your nerves first, not because the equipment is cumbersome but because you'd want to stay under the water forever even though your ears may be popping. So amazing are the creatures of the ocean floor. At 66 ft, you'll get to meet sea turtles, manta rays, sharks and anemones. Enchanting. But if any discomfort sets in, get out of the sea on the double. Those who are asthmatic need to be extra careful. So do heart patients. *(For more tips on precautions to be taken during scuba diving, see 'Simply smooth: Scuba diving tips' on page 124 and 'Sporting encounters' on page 16.)*

The **Agatti Resort** now collaborates with a German water sports company DiveLine to offer tourists packages; the rates are inclusive of diving fees and room tariffs.

tiny fishing settlements. The Malayalam-speaking inhabitants of Agatti are friendly, hospitable and willing to stretch themselves for the curious tourist. The fisherfolk here cast their nets in the waters between Agatti and Bangaram, hand-weave coir ropes, and dry tuna and coconut kernels. Cycling is an excellent way of getting around; it will also give you many glimpses of life on Agatti. The resort offers cycles on rent (Rs 60 for 4 hrs).

Two gold coins

At the northern end of the island, just a few houses away from the jetty, is the **Golden Jubilee Museum**, the only one of its kind in Lakshadweep. The two-storey museum is still in the process of getting its collection together. At present, it houses an intricate model of a traditional Minicoy *jagthoni* (sailboat), and a room full of jars, pots, platters and wooden chests recovered from various islands and a few shipwrecks. Ask to see the gold coins found in a graveyard near the Jama Masjid in Agatti, said to have been issued by Sultan Sulaiman in 1560. On the ground floor are two busts of the Buddha (dated variously between the 9th and 12th centuries CE), found on Androth Island, which point to the island's pre-Islamic past. It's a very simple museum,

It's surf-and-snack time at the Agatti Island Beach Resort for a tourist

but you must visit it as it's the only storehouse of Lakshadweep's artefacts.
♦**Timings** 10 am-5 pm

Mohiyudeen Mosque

Don't miss the oldest mosque on the island, the 16th century Mohiyudeen Mosque. Situated in a grove of palms and surrounded by intricately carved tombstones that date back several centuries, the mosque exudes calm. Built in the style of a Malabar temple, complete with red Mangalore tiles, the mosque has no minarets. A stone panel with Arabic lettering decorates its front cornice. The tombstones are strewn around on the grounds surrounding the mosque. A large tank and a well complete the picture.

Kalpitty Island

To the south of Agatti, separated by a narrow channel, is the small island of Kalpitty (meaning Stone Island) and further on and nearer to Bangaram, **Tinakkara** and **Parali I and II**. All these islands are uninhabited; the resorts in Bangaram and Agatti organise day-picnics in the islands or use these as a base for diving and snorkelling in the lagoons.

WHERE YOU'LL STAY AND EAT

Agatti Island Beach Resort (Kochi Reservations Tel: 0484-2362232; Tariff: Rs 3,600-31,200) sprawls across South Agatti, and is within walking distance of the airport. Spacious cottages come with attached baths and porches facing the lagoon. If you are here on a full moon night you may be privy to the amazing sight of baby turtle hatchlings at midnight. The resort offers many packages that include glass-bottomed boat rides, lagoon fishing and visits to uninhabited isles. Meals comprise tuna, sambhar, avial and rice.

For more details on stay, see Lakshadweep Accommodation Listings on page 550; and for details on getting to Agatti Island, see The Information on page 247 ■

KADMAT

EVE'S OWN ISLE

Location This club-shaped island, a mere 8 km long, is the northernmost island in Lakshadweep that tourists can visit
Distance 220 nautical miles from Kochi, or $^1/_2$-1 hr sailing time (high-speed boat) from Agatti

BY CHARU SONI

Some islands were meant to be left alone. Kadmat is clearly one of them. Unknown and unexplored till the 18th century, Kadmat served as a fishing outpost for the villagers of neighbouring Amini Island, who'd explore its waters during the monsoons, when fishing in the sea became dangerous.

Now, tourists flock here to enjoy Kadmat's beauty and the languid lifestyle it promises. It's a seductive combination, one that charmed Mumbai adman

ATUL LOKE

Prahlad Kakar as well. He first visited the islands some years back and stayed behind to set up a diving school.

Kadmat is ideal for swimming and spending lazy afternoons gazing away at the sea. And like Agatti, Kadmat exposes her eastern underbelly at low tide when the sea recedes, leaving in its wake soft sand. The distant coral ridge is within reach then, as is the sea, which splashes wildly against the corals. Elsewhere on the island, life goes on as usual. There are coconuts to be picked and dried, fish to be caught and coir to be soaked, dried and turned into ropes. With just over 5,000 people, it's a laidback life. But who's complaining?

ORIENTATION

Kadmat is 8 km long and 550m wide at its widest point, quite similar in its layout to Agatti. To its southern end lies a large bewitching lagoon and to its east, a rich coral outcrop.

A fisherman looks for his next meal

SAIBAL DAS

EXPLORING THE ISLAND

Take a walk

Kadmat Beach has one of the most exceptional stretches of white sand in Lakshadweep. It helps that the beach is surrounded by a turquoise lagoon. The sand is so fine and beautiful that one could be forgiven for digging into it to create some sort of imperfection. But the phenomenon is completely natural. The sand is thus because it's composed mostly of calcium carbonate with little or no silica.

Clumps of dark-green sea grass float on the lagoon, which encircles the southern tip of Kadmat. This must be among the most irresistible coastal stretches in Asia. Not far off on the horizon is Amini, softly swaying its palms in salutation. Its inhabitants were the first people in the Lakshadweep Islands to convert to Islam in 7th century CE.

It's not unusual here to come across beautiful red-tinged coral. You may be tempted to pocket some, but taking coral from the islands is illegal. Leave these for everyone to enjoy. According to geologists, the substratum of Kadmat contains fairly hard coral stone, which has been used extensively in the construction of both government and private houses on the island.

A morning and evening walk on the beach is ideal for spotting hermit crabs scurrying towards the sea or curled up in their shells. Try coaxing a hermit crab out of the shell and you'll be left wondering who's more shy, the crab or you. Mister Popular in Lakshadweep, the hermit crab likes his own company. There are some 500 different species of hermits in the world; most of these can be found living on the Indian Ocean floor. But some also live on land where they feed on worms, plankton and organic debris.

While the sun rises rather rapidly in Kadmat, the setting sun is particularly spectacular. Lasting a little over an hour, the sun's daily rendezvous with a dark and mysterious sea follows a red-tinged

MANU BAHUGUNA/ PHOTOINDIA

Tourists off Kadmat Beach, which has a strikingly white stretch of sand

trajectory, and its glory is reflected in the stark blue waters. At night, a million stars twinkle impishly at the island's residents, reminding everyone of the sea journeys undertaken to reach this paradise. It's a pity the Lakshadweep Tourism Resort doesn't offer a telescope that will allow visitors to comb the sky.

Watch the fish come in

You might come across a solitary fisherman walking around with his casting net, trying to catch a meal in the lagoon. This sort of fishing is largely done for self-consumption and is, as a result, done when the need arises. Body taut and eyes darting, the fisherman identifies his prey before throwing the net over his shoulders. Net cast, he rushes in to corner his prey. More often than not, the effort pays off with a handsome catch of four to five fish after an hour or so of hard work.

Diving with Lacadives

Near the Lakshadweep Tourism Complex and just next to the private jetty of the Tourism Resort, is Prahlad Kakar's **Lacadives Dive School** (E-20, Everest Building, Tardeo Road, Mumbai-400034. Tel: 022-66627380-82; Fax: 66669241; Website: lacadives.com), which has its main base on Kadmat. It's the first and only CMAS (Confédération Mondiale Des Activités Subaquatiques or World Underwater Federation) dive school in India. Lacadives offers several packages for diving holidays on Kadmat. The 8D/ 7N Rs 32,000 Kadmat packages include boarding and lodging on a twin-sharing basis, and are inclusive of equipment charges and dives (four lagoon dives and six open water dives). Agatti-Kadmat-Agatti transfers and ship fares are extra. Divers must carry a doctor's certificate stating that they are fit to dive. Certified divers must carry their certification/ licence and dive log book. Lacadives also offers non-diving packages, teaches snorkelling and offers an introduction to scuba diving.

TIP Lacadives also offers diving at Bangaram (*see page 215*); they also warn that seven nights could be a bit too long to spend on Kadmat, and divers — even inexperienced ones — might want to move to another island earlier

Going nuts

The road towards the island's embarkation jetty is palm-shaded and straight as an arrow. En route is the government-run **Coconut Desiccating Plant**, where one can watch the simple process of producing dry coconut powder. The husk is peeled and the fresh kernel scooped out of the nut. These are washed and ground into fine pieces (or desiccated) by a machine. Once desiccated, the shredded coconut is put through a drying press that turns it into fine coconut powder. Coconut oil units make use of the husk and the peels.

TIP Visits to the desiccating unit are organised by the Lakshadweep Tourism officials at the resort

A few village blocks ahead is the **Coir Factory**, where islanders make coir rope with the help of machines. At its entrance are open tanks in which coir is soaked to make it soft and usable. Rope-making continues to be an important occupation on the island, whether it's done by hand or machine. On the islands, the rope is used for stitching fishing boats, weaving roofs and tying ferries and boats to the jetty or other anchoring points.

The coir is exported to Kochi, Beypore and Mangalore. Be warned, however, that some may find the musky smell that permeates the air here nauseating.

A quiet vista on Kadmat

MANU BAHUGUNA/ PHOTOINDIA

Kadmat Jetty

The proximity of Amini Island, a few nautical kilometres off the southern coast, accounts for the busy traffic between the two islands and the rather crowded Embarkation Jetty. As on other islands, the lagoon jetty is only a take-off point for the sea, where large sea vessels are usually parked. Spend an evening watching the sun set here.

WHERE YOU'LL STAY AND EAT

The Lakshadweep Tourism's **Kadmat Beach Resort** (Kochi Reservations Tel: 0484-2668387; Tariff: Rs 3,000-4,000) sprawls over $1^1/_2$ km and includes AC and non-AC cottages with an attached bath, a foyer and a porch. Meals are served in a small complex that also houses the administrative office, a gymnasium, a conference room and bathing units for those who walk in straight from the sea.

The food here is limited to the resort where buffet-style meals are laid out. Kerala cuisine is *de riguer*, so sambhar, rice and curry with some dry vegetable dish is served. The speciality, as elsewhere on Lakshadweep, is tuna fish, fried, curried and pickled. Breakfast usually comprises idli, puri and potato curry.

Kadmat is visited as part of Lakshadweep Tourism's Marine Wealth and Scuba Diving Packages (*see The Information on page 247*).

For details on stay, see Lakshadweep Accommodation Listings on page 551 ■

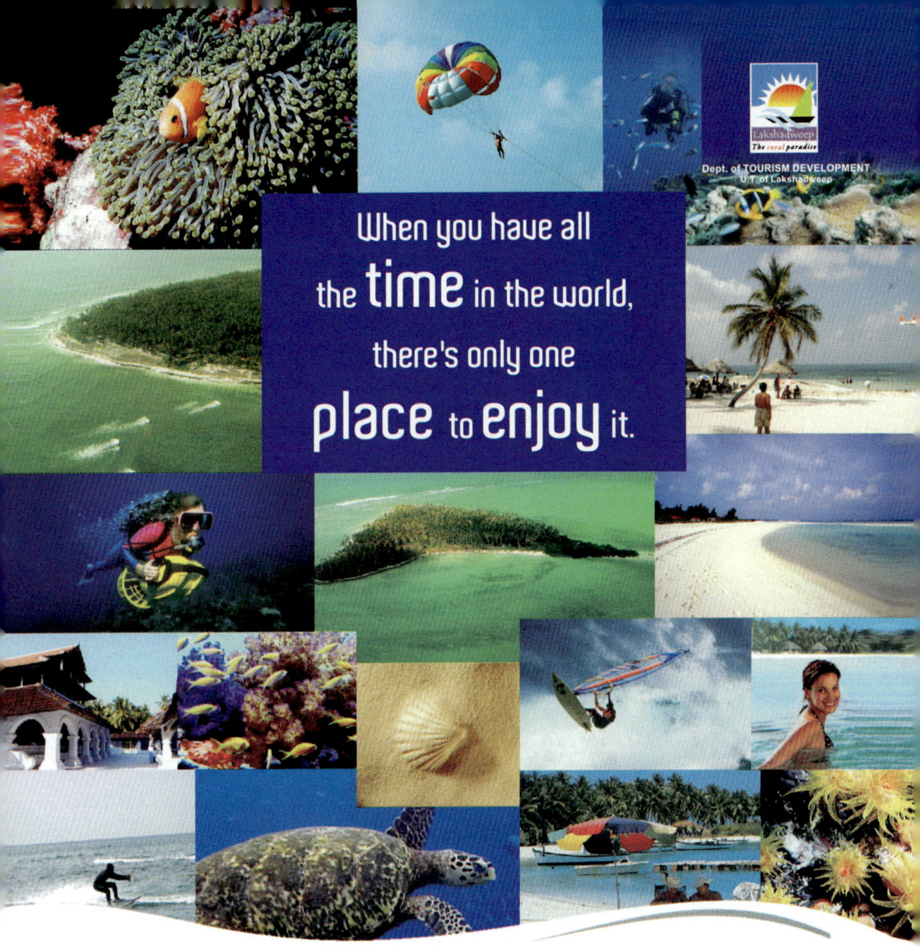

Photographs by SAIBAL DAS

KALPENI

SLEEPING BEAUTY

Location Kalpeni is closest to the mainland after Androth Island and lies to the south-east of Kavaratti, the administrative centre of Lakshadweep
Distance 155 nautical miles from Kochi, or 3 hrs sailing time (high-speed boat) from Agatti

BY CHARU SONI

Kalpeni, a short strip of land with three tiny satellite isles, shares her identity with the mainland. She learnt of Buddhism from Kerala, when the faith travelled here from Kodungalloor between the 3rd and 6th centuries CE. Later, the Hindu landlords, the Koyas, colonised her and other islands. Finally, when the Arabs discovered her in the 13th century, she turned Muslim and was called Koefaini. Fate was not too gracious thereafter.

As time passed and age-old social structures gradually began to collapse, Kalpeni started to lose its prominence. Like Androth, she began playing second fiddle to Kavaratti, the new power centre. Today, like a forlorn bride she waits to be re-discovered. Her ancient mosques may be crumbling, but her beautiful lagoon and shallow waters around the three isles wait for marine enthusiasts. Sadly, the administration does not care much and is surprised when travellers want to explore her. "Kalpeni, why do you want to go there?" they ask. Maybe it's because there is no proper resort here, or perhaps they simply don't care.

Once, turtle shells were collected here for markets in Kodungalloor. Today, it's cowries. Fishermen still cast their nets near Cheriyam Island, where a 2-km long coral debris ridge divides the lagoon from the sea. Their favourite catch? Octopus! Eaten pickled or fried, it's a delicacy here. Whether you want to try it or not, Kalpeni has much else to offer the curious tourist.

ORIENTATION

Kalpeni is strangely shaped — bulging in the south and narrowing to a ribbon in the north. The island is 2.8 km long and 1.2 km at its widest point. To its north is **Cheriyam Island**, and to its south-west, the small, uninhabited isles of Pitty II and Tilakkam I, II and III.

EXPLORING THE ISLAND

Beach, resort and lagoon

The tourist stop at Kalpeni is a tiny complex of a few bathrooms, toilets, a kitchen and an office, collectively called the **Koomel Beach Resort**, set at the south-west end of the island. The word 'resort' is a misnomer as there are no facilities to put up tourists on the island other than the Dak Bungalow, and this is only for government servants.

The narrow beach on which the resort is situated is littered with palm fronds and coral debris. But the surrounding lagoon overlooking the isles of Tilakkam I, II and III and Pitty II is rich in dark-green sea grass, making the seabed look as if it were coated in gold. The sight is mesmerising, particularly when a school of colourful fish swim by or a turtle floats in. From the 'resort', it's possible to take a small boat and visit the three islands, which at low tide would be within walking distance of about 100m to half a kilometre each. These tiny isles are covered with scrub and all open out to beautiful vistas of the lagoon and the sea beyond.

On Tilakkam II stands a signpost bearing India's three-lion emblem, declaring to all who land upon its shores that the island is Indian property. All the three islands abound in calcified corals and its favourite residents — crabs and snails. But they don't have beaches.

Why does Kalpeni have no beach?

The answer to this riddle probably lies in the devastating storm of 1847 that convulsed and reshaped the island. According to scientists, the storm redrew the map of Kalpeni, cutting off what is now the island of Cheriyam, once a part of the Kalpeni mainland. It also created a bank of sea coral debris that to this day

Snorkelling near Cheriyam Island

The wheel of life: A Kalpeni resident goes about her daily chores

litters the waters between the islands, having eaten up whatever beaches that might have existed here.

Ironically, this long stretch of coral debris arrayed like a bank along the east and south-east shore today acts as a barrier against any further natural disasters. Kalpeni, and Androth in particular, lie in the path of great storms across the Indian Ocean that periodically lash their shores (this happened in 1922, 1965 and most recently the El Nino in 1998). But these were spared the devastating tsunami of December 2004.

The sea around is rich in marine life and yields good catches of seer, skate and bummalo (Bombay Duck), all of which are eaten dried and salted. If you would only like a glimpse, **snorkelling** is an option. But it is not easy as the waters are shallow and full of pointed coral debris strewn on the lagoon bed. However, if you do go snorkelling, you might come across Picasso triggerfish, star coral and octopus. You can also take a kayak and explore the seabed and its waters here.

Tip top

The northernmost tip of the island is simply called **Kalpeni Tip Beach**, which houses a small café where tea and some snacks can be had. The islanders hang out here in the evening to gossip, after spending a few hours searching for cowries. These are collected to this day for markets in Kodungalloor, where they are used to decorate Kathakali costumes and as tools of divination by astrologers.

Cheriyam Island

If you start your expedition when the tide is low, it's possible to walk through the coral debris all the way to Cheriyam Island. You must first traverse the tiny isle of **Koditalla**, a kilometre from the café. The large boulders of coral strewn on the way are home to many of the sea creatures that live in the shallow waters, including a variety of crabs, eels, sea cucumber and tiny fish. But the walk is not easy. You have to jump from boulder to boulder, or walk ankle deep in water along the sandy side of the coral reef.

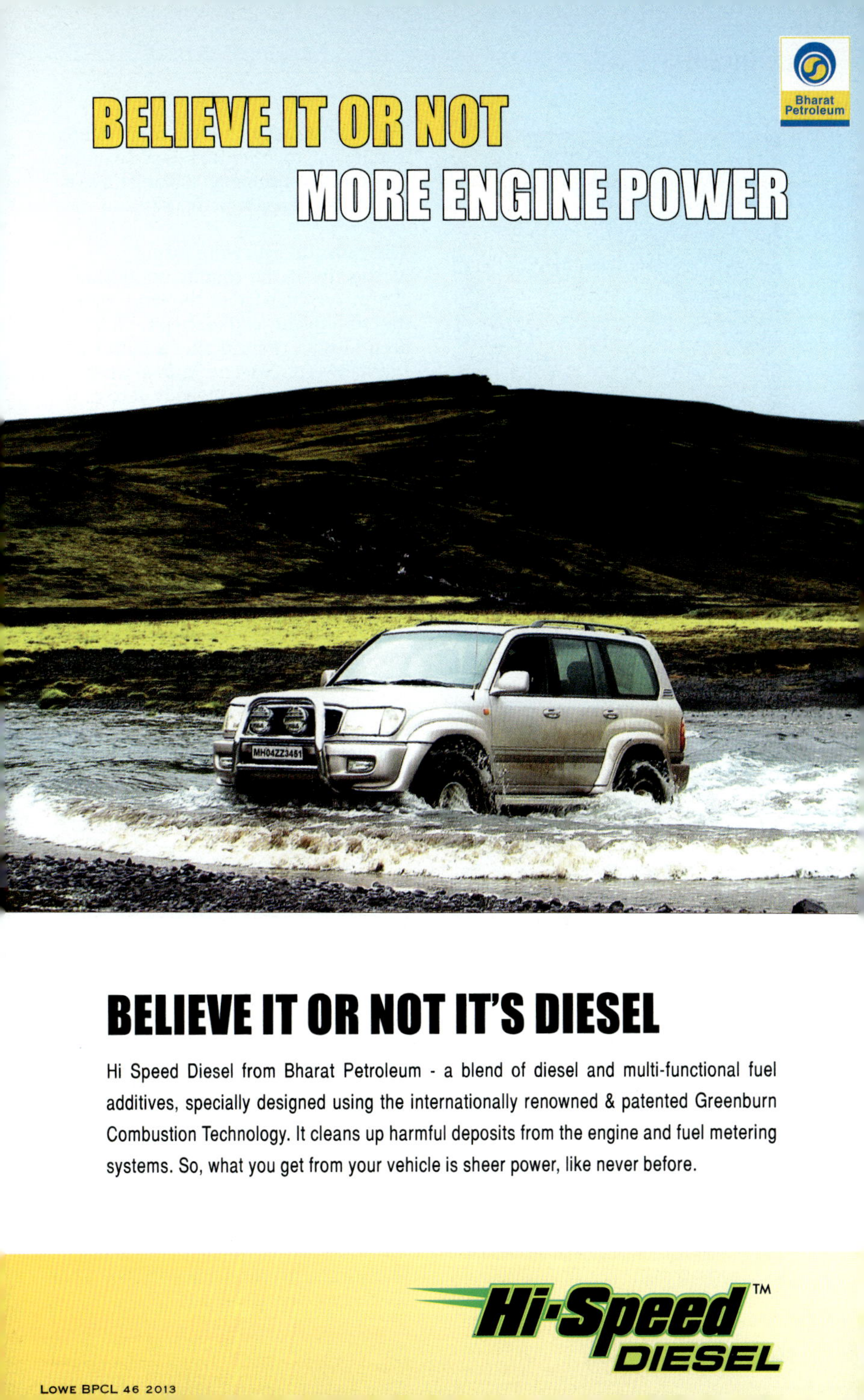
Bharat Petroleum
BELIEVE IT OR NOT
MORE ENGINE POWER
MH04ZZ3481
BELIEVE IT OR NOT IT'S DIESEL
Hi Speed Diesel from Bharat Petroleum - a blend of diesel and multi-functional fuel additives, specially designed using the internationally renowned & patented Greenburn Combustion Technology. It cleans up harmful deposits from the engine and fuel metering systems. So, what you get from your vehicle is sheer power, like never before.
Hi-Speed™ DIESEL
LOWE BPCL 46 2013

TASHI TOBGYAL

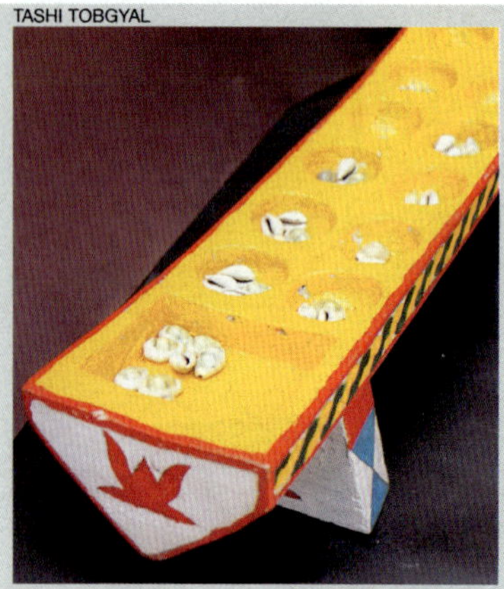

Every woman's game

On lazy afternoons, when most of the men are taking their siesta after fishing in the sea all morning, women stretch out their legs on the verandah of their homes to play kuyppter. Known to some and unknown to most, the game requires 56 tiny cowries, a board shaped like a boat or a fish, and two to play. The game board has 14 pockets, seven for each participant. It's a simple game really, almost childish but fun.

The game starts with four cowries placed in each of the pockets. Each player by turn picks up and drops a cowrie into the pockets. If your last cowrie completes a set of four in any of the pockets, you get to collect all four cowries and you're on your way towards winning the game. Keep on collecting till all cowries are removed from the game-board. The player with the maximum cowries wins the game.

Beautiful kuyppter sets engraved in teak can still be found in old aristocratic homes in Kerala, which raises doubts about whether the game originated from the islands or the other way round.

Either way, while the mainland has relegated it to forgotten family chests, the Lakshadweep Islands have very much kept it alive. Here, it's every woman's game, played to this day.

The haphazardly strewn coral debris leading up to Cheriyam is a favourite spot for local fishermen looking for seer, tuna fish and *appal* (octopuses).

The mosque everyone forgot

At the tip of the southernmost shore, almost on the edge of the land, stands the somnolent and decrepit Moinuddeen Mosque, named after a saint from Lakshadweep. No one knows when it was built, though everybody reveres it. Hence it exudes an air of mystery. Built in the Keralite style, the roof is still covered with old Mangalore tiles made by Coelho Brothers.

◆**Timings** Open during prayers

Souvenir shopping

At the back of the Koomel Resort is a local handicrafts workshop, where the island's craftsmen make models of boats out of coconut and shrub bark. Priced at Rs 200 upwards, these make for excellent souvenirs and gifts. Another interesting item on sale is the island game of kuyppter (*see 'Every woman's game' alongside*). You can also buy your Lakshadweep Tourism T-shirts (Rs 50-75) at the local hosiery unit located on the eastern side of Kalpeni.

WHERE YOU'LL STAY AND EAT

Lakshadweep Tourism at present offers only day stays at **Koomel Beach Resort**, which has a bath and changing rooms. Local delicacies for lunch could include *chura porichathu* (fried tuna), or a vegetarian dish of ladyfinger or carrot and yam with grated coconut. Consumption of alcohol is prohibited on the island. The only local drink that's available in plenty is the humble coconut water.

Do note that Lakshadweep Tourism organises shows of traditional dance forms such as Parichakkali and Kolkali here. Kalpeni is part of Lakshadweep Tourism's Coral Reef Package (*see The Information on page 247*). ■

Photographs by SAIBAL DAS

KAVARATTI

THE BLUE LAGOON

Location Kavaratti is the most centrally located island of the group, and hence the administrative centre of Lakshadweep. The island of Suheli Par is to the south-west and Pitty Bird Sanctuary to the north-west
Distance 218 nautical miles from Kochi, or $^1/_2$-1 hr sailing time (high-speed boat) from Agatti

■ **BY CHARU SONI**

The island of Kavaratti, the administrative centre of the Lakshadweep Union Territory, is a busy place. There are people everywhere. In the sea, on the land, in the boats, on the jetty... it all seems a bit crowded after the relative solitude of Kadmat, Agatti or Bangaram. Imagine 10,113 people (as per the 1991 census) crammed into 5 sq km and you get the picture.

Unlike other islands, Kavaratti's shore is an apology for a beach. Narrow, busy and littered with organic and human waste, it almost spoils the beauty of the magnificent lagoon here, which is home to enchanting starfish, anemones, sea cucumbers and schools of colourful fish. This amazing marine life is the reason why you must come to Kavaratti, and to explore it, you have to dive.

Apart from a short trip to the magnificent white Ujra Mosque and the museum-cum-aquarium, there's little else to see here. But at night, a sky studded with a million stars and the sound of waves lapping the shore will keep you awake, strumming dreams of distant lands. That's when you realise that you have to hand it to Kavaratti: crowded or not, the island manages to bewitch you.

Early morning at Kavaratti

ORIENTATION

Kavaratti has a bulbous north and narrow south. The narrow island is 5.6 km long and no more than a kilometre abreast, with most of the government and port offices, and the **Kavaratti Tourism Huts**, situated near the **jetty** on its eastern bank. It's probably the only island where there is a junction complete with traffic lights, connecting the intersection between the **MG** and **Lagoon roads**, the two roads that circumvent the island. There is no beach or lagoon on the western side.

EXPLORING THE ISLAND

On the beach

Though not as pristine as Kadmat or Agatti, Kavaratti's sandy stretch and its large saucer-like lagoon would have been pretty had the beach been broader, less crowded and cleaner. Nature's own litter — swathes of seaweed floating near the shore — does not help either, nor does the water pipeline that juts out like a long sore thumb in the lagoon.

Though considered ideal for swimming, the sheer activity in its waters — fishing boats anchored near the shore, fishermen walking around with casting nets, ducks and turkeys taking a stroll, men working by the jetty and the pipeline — are altogether too intrusive. The lagoon waters are deep and full of sea grass and weeds, which unfortunately mar underwater visibility, particularly near the shore. But further into the lagoon, the visibility improves dramatically. It's best to take off to the north towards the Dolphin Dive Centre, which is roughly 1 km away.

Dive like a dolphin

A turn away from the museum and round a school courtyard lies the government-run **Dolphin Dive Centre** (Tel: 04896-263649; SPORTS Office Tel: 262105; Shaukat Ali's Mobile: 09447822701), run by PADI-trained Dive Master Shaukat Ali, who currently conducts dives for both amateurs and professional divers. The centre offers a variety of PADI programmes. The Professional Association of Diving Instructors (PADI) is the largest leisure diving organisation in the world and has certified millions of divers worldwide. PADI Discover (Rs 500 per dive) for amateurs in the lagoon offers no certification, nor do Discover Scuba (Rs 500), Discover Scuba Diving (Rs 1,200) and Discover Local Diving (Rs 1,500). PADI Open Water Diver courses are week-long (Rs 15,000, which includes instruction charges, certification and equipment). Other longer courses include Advance Open Water Diver (Rs 11,500), Adventure Diver (Rs 16,200), Rescue Diver (Rs 13,500) and Dive Master (Rs 19,500). Daily dives cost Rs 1,100-1,300 and Adventure dives Rs 1,300-1,500.

TIP Diving bookings must be done through the SPORTS office in Kochi (*see The Information on page 247*)

White marvel

The whitewashed **Ujra Mosque** in the south-eastern part of the island is stunning. This 17th century structure is said to have been built by Sheikh Mohammad Kasim, known as Thangal, who introduced the practice of *ratheeb*, a religious performance conducted to invoke blessings of intermediaries between god and man. Sheikh Kasim was the first Thangal on the island. Many miracles are attributed to him, including the absence of crows on the island! His grave is within the mosque and is a place of pilgrimage for people from all across the Lakshadweep Islands.

The mosque is open to all, though women are not allowed inside the prayer hall. Built without minarets, it includes a beautifully carved ceiling and pillars believed to have been sculpted some hundred years ago. The entire ceiling of the mosque's verandah was carved out of a single piece of driftwood. At the back of the mosque are the graves of the Sheikh's family members. The tombstones are testimony to the dexterity of the stone carvers who chiselled the delicate Arabesque designs. It's a peaceful place, so stay awhile.

♦**Timings** 10 am-6 pm

Holy shark!

A short walk from the Tourist Huts along Lagoon Road, past a khadi outlet, petrol shack and a video lending library, is an unusually well-appointed **museum-cum-aquarium**. The small aquarium includes a year-old shark that glares at you from behind the large glass panel, and some anemones, sea cucumbers, octopuses and schools of small fish. In the museum wing, you'll find everything you wanted to know about the water world — the different varieties of shells, including the cowries that served as money across the

Waiting to exhale

Oxygen cylinder on my back and mask over my eyes, I moved slowly towards a colourful mound in the middle of the lagoon.

Just 5 ft under, a whole new world of purple anemones and pockmarked starfish opened its arms to me. I was apprehensively anticipating the big fish, but those swim in deeper waters, assured the diving instructor, Shaukat Ali. I had seen a year-old shark in the museum and believe me, I was quite relieved to be among the Lilliputians. It's safer, more colourful and so much fun.

Funnily enough, all that diving equipment proved superfluous since one could swim around the same mound with just a snorkelling mask clasping one's face!

TIP First-time divers are not taken to depths over 5m

The whitewashed Ujra Mosque, a 17th century structure, radiates serenity

Indian Ocean before minted currency came into the picture, amazing corals and many, many species of fish preserved in innumerable glass jars.
◆**Entry fee** Rs 5 **Timings** 10 am-5 pm **Camera fee** Rs 15

Suheli Par and Pitty Bird Sanctuary

The islands of Suheli Par and Pitty Bird Sanctuary are out of bounds for tourists. However, if you have opted for a diving package on the island, you might be taken for a dive in its waters.

Suheli Par, according to one version, was named after a shipwrecked Jewish seaman called Suheli. Its waters provide rich catches of fish and cowries. During the British rule, there was some attempt to colonise Suheli Par, but lack of potable water on the island made it impossible. Its lagoon is currently a watery abode to some WWII jeeps and trucks, thrown overboard after the steamer carrying them struck some rocks near the island.

Pitty, known for Indian sooty tern and Philippine noddy, which migrate here to breed, has earned the sobriquet of 'Shrieking Island'. It's a pity, but you can't go to Pitty.

WHERE YOU'LL STAY AND EAT

The **Kavaratti Tourism Huts** are situated near the jetty. These come complete with tiny bathrooms and a small verandah. The service is indifferent, and the rooms are not regularly swept. Most of the time, the property is used for government dinners. Boats and kayaks are parked right in front. Lakshadweep Tourism organises Kolkali and Parichakkali performances here. In Kolkali, the dancers form pairs and dance in a circle with sticks. In Parichakkali, they use a wooden sword and shield. Look out for the crescendo of agile movements towards the end of the dance. All meals are served buffet-style at an appointed time. These are mostly Malabar-style. Tuna fish, chicken and sweet potatoes are the staple. Kavaratti is visited as part of Lakshadweep Tourism's Coral Reef and Taratashi packages (*see The Information on page 247 and Lakshadweep Accommodation Listings on page 551*). ■

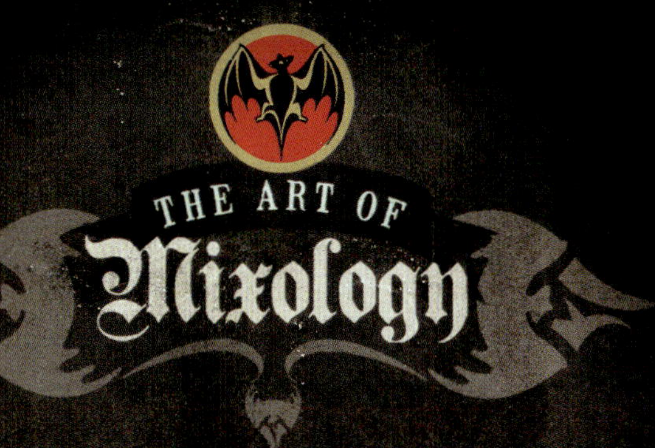
THE ART OF
Mixology

Photographs by SAIBAL DAS

MINICOY

SOUTHERN COMFORT

Location Minicoy is the southernmost Lakshadweep Island, and geographically part of the Maldives archipelago. It has a narrow sandy ridge to its north and an uninhabited island, Vringili, to its south

Distance 243 nautical miles from Kalpeni, the nearest Lakshadweep island, and 75 nautical miles from Addu, the northernmost island of the Maldives; 20 sailing hrs from Kochi

BY CHARU SONI

Enchanting Minicoy is like none other. She's beautiful and interesting. Colourful and challenging. And most of all, magical. Just like a child's storybook.

The southern belle of Lakshadweep has had a long affair with the sea. Her people have sailed its waters in search of new lands and fished in its womb for sustenance. She was annexed by the British in 1908 and became a part of the Indian Union in 1956, but she speaks a different language (Mahl), writes in a different script (Thana), looks and dresses (in long toga-like capes) like the Maldivians, but chews her betel like a true Malayalee.

Minicoy embraced Islam in the 7th century CE, yet has managed to retain her matrilineal and monogamous traditions. The island is organised into 10 villages, or *athiris* or *avahs*, each of which is headed by a unanimously elected *moopan* (a male village administrator).

Each *athiri* has an intriguing name and can be identified by colours or symbols — Falessery and Kendifatty (an offshoot of Falessery) like to colour themselves red, Kudehi blooms in peacocks while elephants add gravitas to Funhilol. Aloodi dazzles everyone with a profusion of yellow, Sedivalu covets the pineapple, Rammedu a key, Boduathiri a horse and Aomagu shocks with white and blue geometric patterns.

The British named this island Minicoy, a term she detests for its derisiveness, even though some insist it means 'majestic'. She'd like to be simply called Maliku, the good harbour, not mini and coy. "Just because our people are short and shy?" asks one islander sardonically.

In her lagoons and on her land you'll find her busy at work. Her people dry tuna and build sea vessels as they keep time with ancient sundials and offer namaz five times a day. She used to have clubs, which were the centre for gay life in olden days. Today, only one survives and is used for festivities on the island. Situated in Falessery, one can still trace some beautiful wood engraving on its walls, which speak of a different life.

Some of her men may be out, sailing the vast waters on international trade routes like they have been doing for centuries. Marco Polo, who passed by Minicoy's waters in the 13th century, found half her population missing and added another romantic sea myth to the sailor's bible — the myth of the "female island". Merrily, she laughs off the legend, all the while looking forward to the return of her men. In the meantime, she waits surrounded by god's own masterpiece — the magnificent, stunning Arabian Sea.

ORIENTATION

The beautiful crescent-shaped island of Minicoy is the southernmost island in the Arabian Sea. It covers an area of 4.8 sq km and is the second largest Lakshadweep island after Androth.

Minicoy has **two roads** (**Mae Magu**, or main road and **Lenu Magu**, or inner road), which merge into one in the south and north. Its northern tip is a sandy and rocky ridge. The southern tip has a **helipad** and the famed **lighthouse** constructed by the British. The **resort** is situated near the lighthouse, and **Minicoy Village** lies in the centre of the island, near the jetty.

It takes over 45 mins to reach **Minicoy Jetty** from the ship, as the boats have to manoeuvre their way through the treacherously shallow lagoon, which at certain points is no more than a few feet deep, and chances of getting stuck are quite high. Once on the island, the mode of transport is the humble tempo with

On a boat ride to Minicoy

plastic chairs arranged in its hold. It might not be the most comfortable thing on earth but this is the fastest vehicle next to a couple of government cars on the island.

EXPLORING THE ISLAND

Scuba diving

Lakshadweep Tourism has started offering scuba diving in Minicoy from October 2007. Some exciting diving spots have been mapped out for interested tourists, according to Shaukat Ali of Dolphin Dive Centre (*for contact details, see page 236 in Kavaratti*). A few of the major attractions here include **three ancient shipwrecks**; these lie at shallow depths ranging between 8 and 18m. There are several other diving points as well and you can spot turtles, Oriental sweetlips, manta rays, sharks and barracuda, among others. The visibility in these waters is over 30m and the best time to dive is from September to October, and January to February.

A folk dance performance at Minicoy

Matchless nature

The magnificent Minicoy lagoon includes a secluded beach complete with a lake surrounded by the only clump of mangroves on the Lakshadweep Islands. The shimmering lagoon is wonderful to swim and snorkel in, even though its rocky bottom discourages any sea-walking. The lake is home to many water crabs, turtles and tiny schools of fish, which can be seen from an overbridge. This side of Minicoy was hit by the tsunami of December 26, 2004, but escaped damage, save for the overbridge, which developed a crack.

The village

The traditional homes of the Maliku people are situated at the centre of the town, separated from the administrative centre by the **Embarkation Jetty** on the mid-western side of the island.

Minicoy Island is home to 10 villages, each of which in the past used to have one house for all the women (known as *verhange*) and men (known as *avazhoge*), a practice that was discontinued after the 1960s. Though Muslim, the Maliku follow the matriarchal system of social organisation. The community is divided into four strata — Manikfan (Bodun, or high born), Thakurufan (Niyamin, or administrators), Thakuru (Dathuruverin, or sailors) and Raaverin (toddy tappers).

A walk through the village dotted with well-appointed houses covered with Mangalore tiles is rewarding, particularly nearer the shore, where one can admire the colourfully painted houses. A typical Maliku house consists of two rooms and a separate building for the kitchen (known as *boduarifi*).

Each of the villages is headed by a *moopan* (headman) who is chosen for his administrative abilities. Enlist the help of Lakshadweep Tourism officials to visit the house of a *moopan*.

A boat is the best place to capture the blues of the sea and the sky at Minicoy

Look for an old **sundial** near Aloodi Village (which the locals still follow — their time being roughly 45 mins behind IST!) pointing to Maliku's ancient knowledge of astronomy.

Interestingly, each of the villages has a separate mosque that is identified with a specific community. There are also some private mosques.

Incidentally, the houses situated on narrow streets are built close to each other to prevent "bad spirits and ghosts from doing mischief", according to the local chronicler KG Mohammad.

Mapping the sea

Nothing exemplifies the fishing economy of Minicoy more than the quaint **wooden chests** that can be seen floating in the lagoon or on the shore. These chests are used for extra storage space during the long sessions of fishing in the lagoon and the deep sea. Bobbing up and down next to brightly coloured boats, they make quite a beautiful and unforgettable sight.

Walk like a crab

The southern sand and coral ridge stretches from what was once a colony of leprosy patients to the tip of the island (approx 2.5 km north of the villages), where one can come across several pieces of rusted iron floating in the lagoon (assorted portions of ships wrecked on its southern shore). There will also be, literally, a thousand-odd hermit crabs lumbering to and from the sea. This stretch is also rich in shells and red, white and greenish coral.

At the very tip, moss-covered brain corals dot the landscape. And then there's the lagoon and the deep sea. From here one can view the tiny uninhabited isle known as **Bose Point**, where people afflicted with small pox used to be isolated.

And then there was light...

The British may not have done much for the Lakshadweep Islands, but the few contributions they made survive to this day. Minicoy's famous **lighthouse** with

CHARU SONI

CHARU SONI

Ancient knowledge, modern voyages

If there are places where time stands still, Minicoy is surely one of them. Here the art of boat-building seems to be flecked with memories of past sea adventures that took energetic sailors across the globe.

It's a tradition so richly preserved in oral lore that to this day a Maliku sailor can construct a complicated sea vessel without consulting any written material. No one recognised their talent more than one of the greatest living explorers of our time, Tim Severin, who in 1994 retraced the journey of Sindbad the sailor in a sailing vessel (an *odi*) built by Maliku's sailors. Severin's successful journey attracted the attention of navigation historians and captured the imagination of the sailing fraternity across the globe.

The prohibitive costs of building sea vessels and the dependence on modern transport (introduced by the government) have had an impact on boat-building, particularly since the 1970s. As a result, big vessels are no longer built on the island, though smaller vessels like *jagthonis* (racing boats that are similar to Kerala snakeboats) are periodically constructed. These boats are still made by the traditional method of stitching wood planks with coir. What is most astonishing is that not a single nail is used to hold the boat together!

its strong white beam is one of them. Built in 1885, the lighthouse offers unparalleled views of the vast sea and Minicoy Island, with the largest lagoon in Lakshadweep stretching below. You can climb to the very top.

Canned!

Situated in the administrative centre of the island, next to the Naval Reserve on Mae Magu (Main Road), is Minicoy's pride, the **Tuna Canning Factory**, where foot-long tuna are processed, canned and pickled. Roughly 50,000 kg of tuna is processed from September, right until the onset of monsoon at the fag end of May. Currently, this canning unit exports tuna to North African countries such as Tunisia and Libya. In India, you can buy Minicoy tuna in Delhi, Mumbai and Kolkata.

No one knows tuna better than the Minicoy islanders, who perfected the art of preparing the delectable fish for self-consumption and export long before machine processing came into being. This is what they do: they de-bone the

fish and cut it into pieces, wash it in fresh water and boil it in equal parts of fresh and sea water. The boiled fish is then smoked with smouldering husks and spread out to dry in the sun till it no longer yields to touch. Try it either pickled or cooked.

Vringili

The uninhabited island of Vringili, just off the south coast of Minicoy, is mostly visited by fishermen in search of a large catch. Lakshadweep Tourism also organises picnics for tourists on the island. The island has a burial ground for people who die of unknown, sudden causes.

SHOPPING

Minicoy loves to craft wood and paint it in vibrant colours. One of its most attractive items is the bridal trousseau. There was a time when every Maliku bride got one of these from her groom — a woven straw betel pouch with a silver ornament and an arecanut cracker. The unusual ornament comes with a casket for storing *chunam* (calcium paste) and arecanut or tobacco, and a long silver chain with tiny silver implements for personal grooming. All three are engraved in teak and decorated with floral patterns. Though wood is fast being replaced with cheap plastic, it's still possible to view some of these items in the homes of two surviving craftsmen, Hussain Dommuthege in Funhilol Village and Hassan Dombadge in Falessery Village.

Faratta, a sweet dish from Lakshadweep

WHERE YOU'LL STAY AND EAT

The 20-bedded **Minicoy Resort** (Kochi Reservations Tel: 0484-2362232; Tariff: Rs 3,000-4,000), situated at the southern end of the island near the lighthouse, is the smartest government-run resort on the Lakshadweep Islands. Its one-room cottages are well appointed and include open-to-the-sky bathrooms with coral floors. The service is prompt and courteous. Food is served in a courtyard at the entrance of the resort. This is where Lakshadweep Tourism also organises traditional Minicoy Bandiya and Lava dances.

You can eat what you're served, but you must try Minicoy fare that can be arranged with advance notice. Like the delicious *rayereha* (red tuna curry), *sannath* (white coconut tuna curry made with potatoes and tender papaya), *khirupuli* (rice chappatis like Moplah pathiris), *faratta* (like the Malabar porotta) and Maliku vegetable *achar*.

Ask for *kadalakka*, sugar-coated savouries made of ground rice and pulses. Though there are a few shacks on the island offering Kerala sambhar, rice and tuna, these cater exclusively to local traders passing through.

Minicoy can only be visited as part of Lakshadweep Tourism's Swaying Palms and Coral Reef Packages (*see The Information on page 247 and Lakshadweep Accommodation Listings on page 551*). ■

THE INFORMATION

CHARU SONI

MV Tipu Sultan, which connects Kochi to some of the Lakshadweep Islands

WHEN TO GO

October to December is the best time to visit the Lakshadweep Islands. January and February are also good, though slightly hotter

TOURIST OFFICES

KOCHI SPORTS Lakshadweep Tourism, Indira Gandhi Road, Willingdon Island, Kochi **Tel** 0484-2668387, 2666789 **Fax** 2668647 **Website** lakshadweeptourism.com

- Kochi International Airport, Nedumbassery, Domestic Terminal **Tel** 0484-2610115
- New Delhi Liaison Officer, Union Territory of Lakshadweep, F-301, Curzon Road Hostel, Kasturba Gandhi Marg, New Delhi **Tel** 011-23386807 **Fax** 23782246
- Kavaratti Tourism Huts **Tel** 0489-6262289

Kochi Reservations 0484-2668387

TIP Tourist counters are also located at the Minicoy, Kadmat and Kalpeni resorts

AUTHORISED AGENTS

NEW DELHI Ashok Travels & Tours, ATT Garage, Janpath Hotel, Janpath, New Delhi **Tel** 011-23349067, Ext 2888 **Fax** 23349066 **Email** tours@attindiatourism.com

MUMBAI Ashok Travels & Tours, 9, Ground Floor, Sai Vihar, 22, Mint Road, Fort, Mumbai **Tel** 022-22668731, 22691421 **Fax** 22691508 **Email** attmumbai@vsnl.net

- Lakshadweep Travelling, Passport Studio Annexe, Jermahal Building, Dhobi Talao, Mumbai **Tel** 022-22054231, 09821182350 **Email** info@visitlakshadweep.com

KOLKATA Ashok Travels & Tours, 3-G, Everest Building, 46-C, Jawahar Lal Nehru Road, Kolkata **Tel** 033-22885254, 22880901 **Fax** 22880922 **Email** itdceast@gmail.com

TRAVEL RESTRICTIONS

Indians may travel to Agatti, Bangaram, Kadmat, Kavaratti, Kalpeni and Minicoy. Foreign nationals may travel only to Agatti, Bangaram and Kadmat. Only a limited number of tourists are permitted on the islands at a time. It's imperative to book in advance.

ENTRY PERMITS

All visitors, both Indian and foreign nationals, must have an entry permit to travel to the Lakshadweep Islands. There is no charge for obtaining the permit, which can be secured by providing information such as name, address, date and place of birth, and passport and visa details (in the case of foreign nationals) to the resort or to the Lakshadweep

THE INFORMATION

Tourism and SPORTS office in Kochi (*see page 247*).

GETTING THERE

BY AIR

Indian Airlines flight IC502 (dep 9.15 am, arr 10.50 am) flies from Kochi International Airport to Lakshadweep's Agatti Airport five days a week, Monday to Friday. These return to Kochi as flight IC501 (dep 11.15 am, arr 12.50 pm). Maximum baggage allowance per person is 10 kg (*see tourist guide on page 212*)

Private Chartered Flights

Bangalore-based **Taneja Aerospace** (Tel: 080-25574600/ 10-11; Fax: 080-25574617; Email: flightoperation@taal.co.in; Website: taal.co.in) runs 5-seater chartered flights for four people for Rs 3,10,000 (Bangalore-Kochi-Agatti-Kochi-Bangalore). The rates are calculated from Bangalore as the aircraft is located at Hosur near Bangalore. During season (December to March), **Bangaram Island Resort** (Kochi Tel: 0484-2668221; Mobile: 09846004772) offers its own charter flight (return fare Rs 14,000 approx) from Kochi to Agatti. Bangaram Resort does not have any flights of its own. There are supplements to airport transfer via helicopter for Rs 6,000 per head (up and down; only during the monsoon). At other times, connections are by boat, at the rate of Rs 900 per head

BY SEA

Shipping Corporation of India's MV Tipu Sultan, MV Bharat Seema, MV Minicoy and MV Amindivi link Kochi to Agatti (18-22 hrs; AC chair car Rs 1,500, first class cabin Rs 3,000 and second class cabin Rs 1,500). All ships depart from Kochi at 11.30 am. Services can be just one a week or four, depending on the traffic and the weather. Contact the SPORTS office in Kochi (*see page 247*) for bookings

TIP There are no ship services during the monsoon, May 15-September 15

ISLAND TRANSFERS

Boat transfers to Bangaram, Kalpeni and Minicoy from Agatti can be availed of only if visitors opt for package tours. Independent travellers to Kadmat and Kavaratti need to pre-book their boat transfers (Rs 1,270 return per person per island) at the SPORTS office (*see page 247*) in Kochi. If bookings are made locally, then visitors will have to bear the full fare of charting the entire boat even if travelling without company

SPORTS PACKAGES

Five-day Coral Reef Package

A cruise to Kavaratti, Kalpeni and Minicoy on MV Tipu Sultan. Days are spent on the island, with swimming, snorkelling and other water sports, lunch and refreshments ashore. Nights are spent on board.

■ **Tariff** Deluxe 2-berth cabin Rs 15,500, First Class 4-berth cabin Rs 13,260, Tourist Class Rs 9,040, students Rs 6,250

Swaying Palm Package to Minicoy

A 6-day tour to Minicoy Island. Stay is at Minicoy Resort.

■ **Accommodation** Rs 2,000-2,500 per night **Transportation** Deluxe Rs 7,000, First Class Rs 6,000, Tourist Class Rs 3,500

Four-day Taratashi Package to Kavaratti

Swimming, snorkelling, scuba diving, lagoon cruises and other water sports are on offer. Stay is in Tourist Huts.

■ **Accommodation** Rs 1,500 **Transportation** Deluxe Rs 7,000, First Class Rs 6,000, Tourist Class Rs 3,500

Six-day Marine Wealth Awareness Programme at Kadmat

Includes four days on the island, swimming, snorkelling, scuba diving as well as several other water sports.

■ **Accommodation** Rs 2,000-2,500 **Transportation** Deluxe Rs 7,000, First Class Rs 6,000, Tourist Class Rs 3,500

TIP Lakshadweep Tourism also offers special scuba diving packages. All ship tariffs indicate return fares ■

KARNATAKA

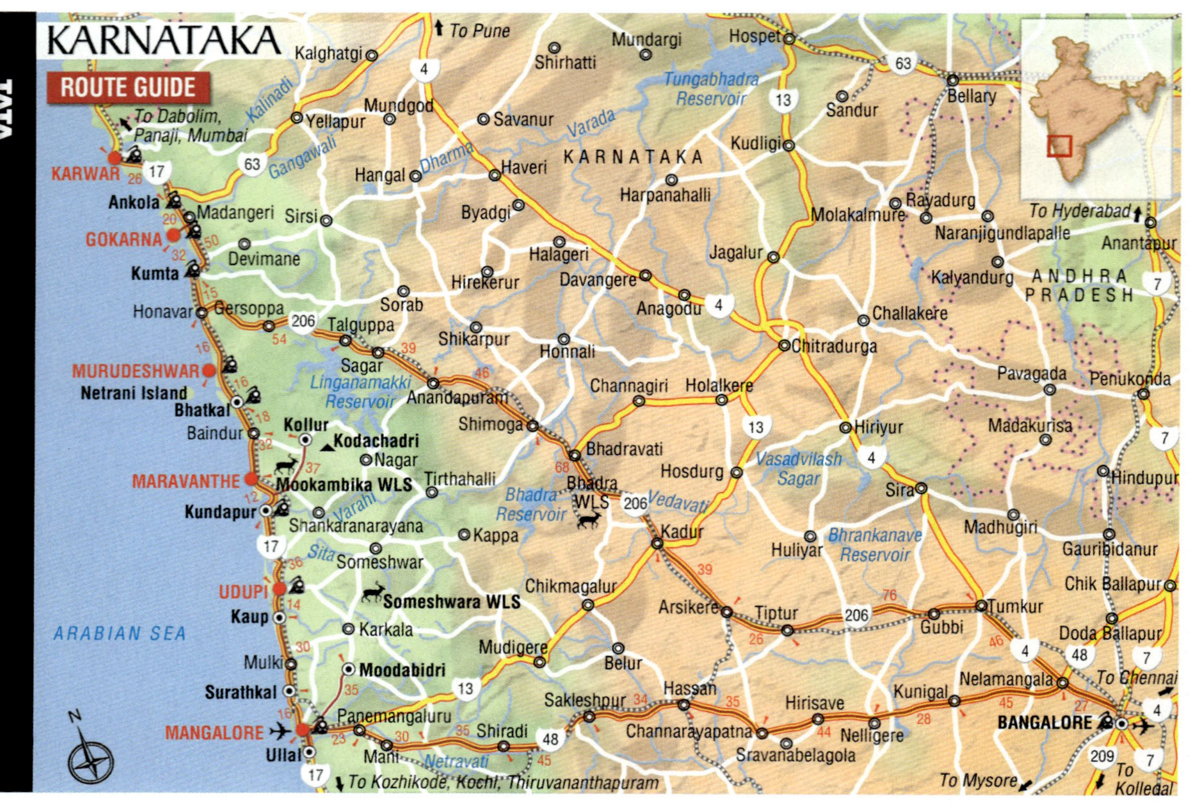

KARNATAKA
ROUTE GUIDE
TATA
SAFARI DiCOR 2.2 VTT
ARABIAN SEA
KARWAR
Ankola
GOKARNA
Kumta
Honavar
MURUDESHWAR
Netrani Island
Bhatkal
Baindur
MARAVANTHE
Kundapur
UDUPI
Kaup
Mulki
Surathkal
MANGALORE
Ullal
To Dabolim, Panaji, Mumbai
To Pune
To Hyderabad
To Chennai
To Kolledal
To Mysore
To Kozhikode, Kochi, Thiruvananthapuram
Kalinadi
Gangawali
Dharma
Varada
Tungabhadra Reservoir
Linganamakki Reservoir
Bhadra Reservoir
Vasadvilash Sagar
Bhrankanave Reservoir
Vedavati
Varahi
Sita
Netravati
Kalghatgi
Yellapur
Mundgod
Madangeri
Sirsi
Devimane
Gersoppa
Talguppa
Sagar
Sorab
Shikarpur
Hirekerur
Byadgi
Hangal
Haveri
Savanur
Shirhatti
Mundargi
Hospet
Bellary
Sandur
Kudligi
KARNATAKA
Harpanahalli
Halageri
Davangere
Honnali
Anagodu
Jagalur
Molakalmure
Rayadurg
Naranjigundlapalle
Kalyandurg
Anantapur
ANDHRA PRADESH
Challakere
Chitradurga
Holalkere
Channagiri
Bhadravati
Shimoga
Anandapuram
Kollur
Kodachadri
Nagar
Mookambika WLS
Tirthahalli
Shankaranarayana
Someshwar
Kappa
Bhadra WLS
Hosdurg
Hiriyur
Pavagada
Penukonda
Madakurisa
Hindupur
Madhugiri
Sira
Huliyar
Kadur
Chikmagalur
Mudigere
Someshwara WLS
Karkala
Moodabidri
Panemangaluru
Mani
Shiradi
Sakleshpur
Belur
Hassan
Channarayapatna
Sravanabelagola
Arsikere
Tiptur
Gubbi
Tumkur
Kunigal
Nelligere
Hirisave
Nelamangala
BANGALORE
Doda Ballapur
Chik Ballapur
Gauribidanur

DINESH SHUKLA

MANGALORE

PORT OF CALL

State Karnataka
Location Mangalore is the last major city at the southern tip of Karnataka's Karavali Coast, 47 km to the north of Kasargode in Kerala
Distance 346 km W of Bangalore
Journey time ***By road*** $7^1/_2$ hrs from Bangalore
Route from Bangalore NH4 to Nelamangala; NH48 to Mangalore via Kunigal, Nelligere, Channarayapatna, Hassan, Sakleshpur and Mani (*see route guide on page 250*)

BY PARIKSHIT RAO

Like many towns in India, Mangalore is an aspirant for the metropolitan tag. It has already acquired the malls and the urban frenzy that befits such a status. Yet, at heart it remains what it was centuries ago — a port town that took its name from a ninth century temple built by King Kundavarma, dedicated to the Goddess Mangaladevi.

Today, Mangalore is more popular for its beaches, which are spread across a fair distance from the city. The stretches of sand and surf are marked by translucent waters shining under a clear blue sky, and white sands pocked with large boulders. All the beaches also share ubiquitous yet grand signboards warning swimmers about the dodgy sea. That doesn't stop Mangaloreans from having fun on the beaches, and it shouldn't stop you either.

Families flock to the beaches for some boisterous picnicking and take home snapshots, in which everyone is smiling, as souvenirs. In the evenings, the coast transforms into a rendezvous point for garrulous locals who share the day's stories and bid each other goodbye over a setting sun. In some ways, it seems then as if Mangalore has gone back to being a small town, having forgotten its intentions of being a snazzy city somewhere in the merrymaking of the evening. It's this heady combination of the old and the new that makes Mangalore such a wonderful destination.

ORIENTATION

Mangalore is a budding conurbation on the far end of the Karnataka Coast. The **railway station** is about a kilometre away from the city centre and the **airport** around 18 km. If you're coming by road, the urban sprawl starts where the lush palm groves end by the NH48, past Kankanady. **Hampankatta** is the city centre, and several commercial establishments are located here. Most hotels are on **KS Rao Road**, while a handful is sited on **PM Rao Road**, a short walk away. The **KSRTC Bus Stand** is at **Bejai**, 3 km north of Hampankatta. A number of local buses start from the State Bank, $1^1/_2$ km south of Hampankatta.

The main beaches in Mangalore are **Tannirubavi** (12 km), **Panambur** (14 km) and **Surathkal** (16 km) to the north, and **Someshwar** (13 km) to the south. Ullal is a small town that boasts of **Someshwar Beach**.

Autos are the most convenient mode of transport. Negotiate beforehand if you want to visit more than two beaches in one trip; expect to pay around Rs 200 to get as far as Panambur. Auto fares for travelling in the city are as per meter and range around Rs 10 per kilometre. It's best to stay in Mangalore and visit these beaches on a day-trip. Only Ullal has a staying and eating option in the Summer Sands Beach Resort.

When to go It's best to visit Mangalore from November to March, when the weather's pleasant. However, the regular tourist season runs from September to June

Tourist office

● Dept of Tourism, Govt of Karnataka
Lighthouse Hill Road
Hampankatta, Mangalore
Tel: 0824-2453926

STD code 0824

BEACH WATCH

Signboards at the entrances of all the beaches warn swimmers against entering the waters. These ominous signboards chronologically detail the number of people who've perished in the seemingly innocuous sea every year. The undulating seashore has deep points, rocky stretches and unpredictable tides. The fact that there are no lifeguards should further detract any daredevils. It's best to dress conservatively on the beaches.

THINGS TO SEE AND DO

Due to the unsafe nature of the beaches, activity on the waterfront is limited. This doesn't mean that you shouldn't get your feet wet in the clean water, or watch the sunset or go for long walks by the sea. The best part about Mangalore's beaches is that they are never crowded.

Tannirubavi Beach

A quiet, splendid beach occupying a long sandbar, Tannirubavi is located adjacent to the New Mangalore Port Trust and is the site of various barge-mounted power projects. This beach is not popular, and hence, you are assured of solitude here. Tannirubavi is ideal for long evening walks, when you can take in the sight of ships docking at the nearby port.

PRASHANT PANJIAR

On the rocks: Tourists enjoy an evening out on Someshwar Beach at Ullal

Panambur Beach

Drive up NH17 and leave behind modern Mangalore's chemical haze to be a part of the congregation on this city's most-visited beach. As entering the water is risky, you'll have to make do with 5-min long camel rides (Rs 20 for adults and Rs 10 for children) here. You may however have to leave the beach after sunset — there's a good chance that the local police will otherwise chase you away. District authorities organise carnivals at Panambur, and the festivities include boat races, air shows and sand sculpture contests. There's no fixed date for the carnivals but details are available in local newspapers. The beach is also a favourite venue with Team Mangalore, which organises kite-flying festivals every summer, usually the week after the International Kite Festival is held in Ahmedabad on January 14. More details are to be found on their website, indiankites.com, or contact Sarvesh Rao on 0824-2495444, 2496333.

Surathkal Beach

This is the best place to enjoy unhindered views of the sea. It boasts of one of the cleanest stretches of the Arabian Sea and an endless expanse of powdery, white sand. The fact that the Regional Engineering College is situated right next door makes it a rendezvous point for the city's hip, young crowd. You can climb up a **lighthouse** here, built in 1972, or lounge on the few benches constructed on the rocks.

◆**Entry fee** Adults Rs 5, children Rs 3 **Timings** 3-5.30 pm

Someshwar Beach

Situated on the other bank of the Netravati River in **Ullal**, Someshwar is popular with Mangaloreans, who head here particularly on weekends. This picturesque beach never seems congested even on the busiest day — thanks to its capacious, golden shore, hemmed in by palm groves. The immaculate beach is dotted with large rocks called 'Rudra Shile'.

The **Summer Sands Beach Resort** (*see Where to Stay on page 258*) located here organises beach volleyball as well as boating trips to **St Mary's Isle**. The boating trips are open to non-guests as well. Trips to St Mary's Isle (Rs 70 per head/ $2^1/_2$ hrs) begin from **Malpe Beach**, which is 2 hrs from Mangalore, and not from the resort.

In the town

Many religious shrines dot Mangalore. Do visit the 19th century **Mangaladevi Temple** (timings 6 am-12 noon and

NAMIT ARORA/ PHOTOINDIA

The stately Milagres Church is designed on the lines of St Peter's Basilica in Rome

4.30-8 pm), on the southern tip of Mangalore, from which the city is said to have derived its name, as well as the **Kadri Manjunatha Temple** (timings 6 am-8 pm) on Kadri Hills, which is among the oldest Shiva temples in the country, dating back to 1068 CE. The 800-year-old **Sharavu Mahaganapathi Temple** (timings 6 am-8 pm) in Hampankatta witnesses major celebrations, especially during Ganesh Chaturthi.

To learn about Mangalore's Portuguese connection, visit **Rosario Cathedral** in Pandeshwara, the city's oldest cathedral, designed on the lines of St Peter's Basilica in Rome. **Milagres Church** (timings 7 am-1 pm), in Hampankatta, is a 1680 monument whose façade is also modelled on St Peter's Basilica.

St Aloysius College Chapel (timings 8.30 am-1 pm and 2-5 pm; visitors not allowed during the divine service), located on Lighthouse Hill Road, is a splendid architectural sight that boasts of a series of paintings by Italian artist Brother Antonio Moscheni covering every inch of its interiors.

You can also rejuvenate yourself with a visit to the **Lighthouse Hill Garden** on Kadri Hills, which has an 18th century lighthouse, believed to have been built by Tipu Sultan's father Haider Ali. The garden offers pretty views of the Arabian Sea and is popular with locals, especially in the evenings.

At Ullal, visit the shrine dedicated to **Syed Mohammad Shareeful Madani**, who's said to have arrived on Mangalore's shores from the holy city of Medina in Saudi Arabia, floating on a piece of cloth, somewhere around 1569. The dargah is open to people of all faiths from 7 am to 7 pm.

SHOPPING

Shopping in Mangalore can be engrossing, and you can spend hours decoding the diversity of items to pick up in this coastal city. Browse through the traditional markets and decade-old cloth and jewellery shops on **Hampankatta** and **KS Rao Road**. You will, incidentally, also find the latest brands of clothes and

accessories at Mangalore's modern malls. **Saibeen Complex** at Lalbagh and **Bharath Mall** at Bejai are popular with the city's hip crowd, who clearly prefer sliding doors to shutters. **Singapore City** on KS Rao Road is a slick mini-mall with shops selling imported appliances.

For souvenirs, check out **Emye**'s seashell crafts on Panambur Beach. They have a whole range of wall hangings, chandeliers and elaborate mirrors made out of shells. The price varies between Rs 100 and 300 depending on the size of the article and the intricacy of the work involved. The rates also depend on your bargaining skills to a large extent. While you are in Mangalore, do make it a point to pick up the city's most famous export: cashews. Drop in at the **Phalguni Cashew Centre** on Balmatta Road or pick them up from any sweet shop or dry fruit centre. Also do not forget to pack home a few bars of Mangalore halwa, a sticky chewy sweet made in pure ghee. Different flavours like guava and banana are available at **Komals**, located in Hampankatta.

→ GETTING THERE

Air Nearest airport: Bajpe (18 km/ 45 mins), connected by flights from Mumbai and Bangalore, by all major airlines. Prepaid taxis are available and cost about Rs 350-400 to Mangalore

Rail Mangalore has a railway junction on the Konkan Railway line, well-connected to cities such as Mumbai and Thiruvananthapuram. However, Kankanadi Station, 16 km from Mangalore, is better connected to southern cities such as Kozhikode and Kochi. Take an auto from the auto stand and pay as per meter (around Rs 10 for a kilometre)

Road NH48 connects Mangalore to Bangalore via Hassan and Sakleshpur. Expect a comfortable drive on this frequently used road. Paulo Travels (Tel: 022-26435762) in Mumbai runs AC, non-AC (Rs 600) and Volvo (Rs 900) buses to Mangalore. In Bangalore, KSRTC (Tel: 080-22872050) operates a number of buses across all classes (Rs 177-400) to Mangalore, starting from 5 am throughout the day and also overnight. For bookings, call KSTDC on 41329222

WHERE TO STAY

Mangalore has ample staying options catering to various pockets, though only a couple offer sea views. Advance bookings are necessary in peak tourist season (September-June), especially if you are travelling in a large group and would like to stay in a particular hotel.

Taj Manjarun (Tel: 0824-6660420; Tariff: Rs 1,800-6,000) on Old Port Road overlooks the confluence of the Arabian Sea with Gurupur and Netravati rivers. Check into one of the 88 centrally air-conditioned rooms in Mangalore's top-end hotel and enjoy the outstanding views. **Hotel Mangalore International** (Tel: 2444857; Tariff: Rs 530-1,390) on KS Rao Road is a luxurious choice with elegantly furnished rooms. **Hotel Poonja International** (Tel: 2440171; Tariff: Rs 700-3,000) is a well-known 104-room extravaganza on KS Rao Road. **Hotel Navratna Palace** (Tel: 2441104; Tariff: Rs 410-891) has 72 luxurious rooms and offers travel assistance, car rentals and laundry services.

Hotel Hindustan (Tel: 2411333; Tariff: Rs 300-1,500) and **Hotel Parkway** (Tel: 2443961; Tariff: Rs 300-999), located on KS Rao Road, are great options for both single travellers and families. The rooms are spanking new and the staff helpful. **Hotel Highland Residency** (Tel: 2433961; Tariff: Rs 300-1,200) is another decent mid-range option close to the city centre.

SAIBAL DAS

A typical spread from the Karavali Coast, including rice, pomfret fry and kokum juice

Hotel Srinivas (Tel: 2440061; Tariff: Rs 425-1,250), situated on GHS Road, is a six-storeyed institution with tidy rooms, helpful staff and also an attached vegetarian restaurant.

Hotel Hindusthan Residency (Tel: 2440743; Tariff: Rs 222-999), opposite the Service Bus Stand, is another good value-for-money staying option in Mangalore. Rooms are equipped with colour TVs and are basic yet clean. The legendary **Woodlands Hotel** (Tel: 2443751; Tariff: Rs 350-950) on Bunts Hostel Road is a hit with government employees and family travellers and one place where you have to book at least 15-20 days in advance during the season. The attached restaurant serves great South Indian fare.

Hotel Vasanth Mahal (Tel: 2441310; Tariff: Rs 140-390) on KS Rao Road has 66 dimly lit rooms that have boldly withstood the onslaught of time. This is the place of choice for foreign budget backpackers. Across the road is **Hotel Venkatesh Lodging** (Tel: 2440793; Tariff: Rs 135-370) with 41 modest rooms. **Hotel New Topaz** (Tel: 2441551; Tariff: Rs 150-250) is another comfortable budget option. The rooms are clean and come with attached bathrooms.

Summer Sands Beach Resort (Tel: 2467690-92; Tariff: Rs 1,600-10,099) at Ullal has 37 AC and 42 non-AC rooms, including some high-end villas. It also has a children's park, a swimming pool and a gym, and organises beach volleyball and trips to St Mary's Isle (*see Udupi on page 261*). The rooms are luxurious and well-appointed and various rejuvenation packages are also offered at an extra price. As it's on the beach, good sea views are on offer here.

For more hotels and details, see Mangalore Accommodation Listings on pages 540-541

WHERE TO EAT

Unsurprisingly, Mangalore is the meeting point of coastal cuisine. The food — a delicious derivative of Konkan, Kerala and Deccan cuisine — is known for its

characteristic tangy and fiery nature and the generous use of coconut in all its forms. Many hotels also dish out lip-smacking South Indian vegetarian fare.

Head down to **Hotel Maharaja** near Jyoti Cinema for their amazing mackerel (*bangda*) fry in tamarind and chilli paste. Another must-try here is the *kane* (lady fish) fry or curry. **Amazon Restaurant** in Empire Mall on MG Road is an overpriced hub for traditional Mangalorean food such as appams, *kori rotti* (a flakey, dry, rice pancake had with tender chicken curry) and *marwai aajadina* (shellfish dry curry).

Head to **Abhimaan Residency** on Kadri Road and dig into the chicken ghee roast here. **Hotel Taj Mahal** in Hampankatta is renowned for its dosas and filter coffee. **Hotel Woodlands** on Bunts Hostel Road is an old-school Udupi joint where you can start your day; the waiters here practically recite the daily menu and a breakfast of steaming idlis is usually an unhurried affair. On an evening out, try out **Froth on Top** on Arya Samaj Road, where you can nurse a beer, chomp on tasty mackerel tawa fry, listen to rock classics and admire the paintings on the walls. Unfortunately, eating options on any of the beaches — barring Someshwar — are few. Several small stalls line the entrance of Panambur Beach, offering diverse snacks such as gobi manchurian, bhel puri and sugarcane juice.

At Someshwar Beach, head to the **Summer Place**, the restaurant at Summer Sands Resort, and dig into their scrumptious squid pepper fry or the spicier chilli version. Head to any of the two outlets of **Ideal Ice Cream Parlour** at Hampankatta for Dakshina Kannada's indigenous dessert, Gadbad ice-cream, which is multiple layers of several flavours of ice-cream in a tall glass. They have more varieties than you can finish in a month! Do try out the extra-sweet Bee-Hive. You can also slurp this layered treat of ice-cream and fresh fruits at **Pabbas** in Lalbagh.

Moodabidri houses many temples

PRASHANT PANJIAR

AROUND MANGALORE

Moodabidri (35 km)

Literally meaning Eastern Bamboo area (*mooda* means east, *bidri* stands for bamboo), this important Jain pilgrimage centre houses a large number of *basadis* (temples) and is known as the Jain Kashi of the South. The most attractive and popular temple here is the **Chandranath Basadi**, also known as the Thousand-Pillared Basadi, which was built by Devaraya Wodeyar in the 14th century. Beautiful carvings grace the roof of this opulent temple, which is supported by a thousand pillars, no two of which are alike. Altogether, there are 18 intricately carved temples in this cultural oasis.

◆**Location** North-east of Mangalore on the Mangalore-Karkala Road, passing through Kaikamba **Chandranath Basadi timings** 9 am to sunset, but avoid going in the afternoon as it gets hot **Connection** Buses for Moodabidri leave from the Service Bus Stand and the fare is about Rs 30. An auto ride costs Rs 350 for a round-trip ■

Photographs by VIVEK M

UDUPI

DIVINE HOLIDAY

State Karnataka
Location The temple town of Udupi is on the Karavali Coast, to the north of Mangalore, on NH17
Distances 60 km N of Mangalore, 406 km W of Bangalore
Journey time ***By road*** $1\frac{1}{2}$ hrs from Mangalore, 9 hrs from Bangalore
Route from Bangalore NH4 to Nelamangala; NH48 to Mangalore via Kunigal and Hassan; NH17 to Udupi via Surathkal and Mulki (*see route guide on page 250*)

BY VIVEK M

Udupi might be famous as a temple town but it has much to offer the tourist seeking sun and sand as well. For, just within a few kilometres of each other are two lovely stretches of beaches, great for a comforting holiday to wash away all your blues, if not — as one would imagine tongue-in-cheek — all your sins.

The beach at Malpe is sure to keep the whole family happy. White sands stretch out unbroken as far as one can walk; the friendly waters of the Arabian Sea look inviting and the sandcastles that you build seem sturdier than ever before. Come evening and there are vendors selling balloons and peanuts, followed by horses and camels. As the skies take on the orange hues of the late evening, the aroma of the catch of the day being fried in beachside shacks rents the air. There couldn't be a better way of watching the sun go down.

The Kaup Beach at Udupi offers a unique and similarly beautiful experience. It has an interesting scatter of

A lighthouse watches over Kaup Beach

rocks; some are small while other formations are huge enough to be a small hill. Climbing onto one such rock, on which a lighthouse is perched, one gets a panoramic view of the beach and, of course, an opportunity to witness a glorious sunset from a height. It's certainly a pretty snapshot of Udupi, one that will remain in your photo albums and memories for long.

ORIENTATION

The **Sri Krishna Temple** on **Car Street** is the epicentre of all activity in the town. The **KSRTC Bus Stand** is half a kilometre from the temple and most hotels are interspersed between the two. The Car Street runs in a rectangle and houses the **Chandramouleeshwara** and **Ananteshwara temples**, as also various mutts. Udupi is a small town and autorickshaws should not charge you more than Rs 20 to take you anywhere within the town.

The **Malpe Beach** is 7 km from the town (auto fare Rs 50), and is approached by a road that passes through **Malpe Village**. The **Paradise Isle Beach Resort** is located on this beach. **Kaup Beach** is 14 km from Udupi (auto fare Rs 150; taxi fare Rs 300), in the southerly direction. **Kaup Village** is on NH17, and a right turn from here just after the **Mariamma Temple** takes you straight to the beach. The best way to get to the beaches and other places of interest is by hiring a taxi. They cost about Rs 1,000 for a day and most hotels can arrange one. Numerous local and express buses also ply on NH17.

BEACH WATCH

Malpe is a safe beach for swimming, although this stretch of sand is not the cleanest due to the weekend crowd that gathers here. Kaup, on the other hand, is unsafe for swimming due to the rocky landscape. There is a huge display on a rock-face warning people not to swim, but it's largely, and unwisely, ignored by visitors. Don't opt for beachwear at either of these places.

THINGS TO SEE AND DO

Udupi's beaches may not be its star attractions but a number of visitors flock to the sands in the evenings. Despite the crowd, the beaches have their own wonderful charm.

Malpe Beach and water sports

The beach has long stretches of sand and although by no means idyllic on weekends, the waters are warm and inviting on other days.

The **Paradise Isle Beach Resort** (*see Where to Stay on page 266*) at Malpe offers water sports, which are open to non-guests as well. They operate speedboats (Rs 1,600 for a maximum of 8 people), water bikes (Rs 400 per person per hour) and banana boats. Two people can cruise on a water bike after a demonstration by the instructor. The long and cylindrical banana boat is ideal for a group of 4 to 6. The speedboats are usually hired for a trip to St Mary's Island (*see facing page*).

Shooting the breeze on Malpe Beach, where crowds flock to on weekends

St Mary's Island

The geography of this island is just as unique as its history. The Portuguese explorer Vasco Da Gama is reported to have docked at this beautiful island in the 1400s before he made his way to Kozhikode (*see page 185*).

The island is dotted with peculiar, hexagonal basalt rock formations along its beach, some huge enough to make it a challenging climb. The island can be reached by taking the boats (20 mins; Rs 70; 9 am-3.30 pm) leaving the **Malpe Port**, on the Malpe Beach, every hour or so. These trips are organised by the **Malpe Development Committee** (Tel: 0820-2538779); the boats aren't operational during the monsoons. The beaches on the island are made of broken shells instead of sand and the waters are crystal-clear. However, swimming is not advisable due to the rocks on the sea floor, which often go unnoticed.

TIP Carry enough food and water since you would be spending more time here than you would imagine. A few vendors sell ice-creams, soft drinks and fish dishes, but these aren't great

Kaup Beach and lighthouse

The rocky beach of Kaup (pronounced Kaa-pu) is an unforgettable sight, especially if you visit it at sunset. Although it's not safe for swimming, there's plenty to do on the beach. You can indulge in a game of volleyball or football here and there is clean sand for children to play and build castles.

The **lighthouse**, which stands on a small hill, was built by the British in 1901. The 130-foot high structure adds more character to the place and is open

When to go October to February
Tourist office
• Dept of Tourism, Govt of Karanataka
Krishna Building, Car Street, Udupi
Tel: 0820-2529718
STD code 0820

Courtesy ADRENO

River adventures

For those looking for some exciting adventure options, river rafting around Udupi is the best bet. About 34 km from Udupi flows the **Sita River**, where a Bangalore-based outfit **Adreno** (Contact Sharat; Tel: 080-23143388; Mobile: 09448166970, 09845407672; Website: adreno.org), in collaboration with the Jungle Lodges and Resorts, offers **river rafting** and **kayaking**. These are also organised at **Varahi River** (50 km from Udupi). While these sports can be enjoyed throughout the year on Varahi, it's conducted on the Sita only between the months of June and October. Rafting on the Sita, with its Grade III rapids (Grade III means moderate irregular waves, and possibly a 3- to 5-foot drop, which may require significant manoeuvring but does not present considerable danger), can be done as either a short run ($1^1/_2$ hrs, Rs 950 per person) or a long run (3 hrs, Rs 1,650 per person). Breakfast and lunch charges are extra.

The group also conducts **treks** in the nearby **Someshwara Wildlife Sanctuary**.

to visitors. The hill itself is a great place to visit; as bonus, it offers great views.
◆**Lighthouse entry fee** Rs 5 **Timings** 5-6 pm
TIP Timings change periodically

Temples and mutts

Udupi is considered to be a temple town because of the many Hindu legends associated with it. It's believed that Lord Vishnu reclaimed Udupi from the Arabian Sea (during his incarnation as Parasurama) after he had donated all his land to Brahmins. The three main temples of Udupi are located on Car Street, within a stone's throw of each other. The Chandramouleeshwara and the Anantheshwara temples are much older than the 800-year-old Sri Krishna Temple and are hence visited first.

The **Chandramouleeshwara Temple** is said to have been built around the sacred spot where the Moon God performed penance and obtained blessings from Lord Shiva to cleanse himself of a certain curse. 'Udupa', another name for moon which means 'lord of the stars' in Sanskrit, could have well been the source for the town's name Udupi.

The **Ananteshwara Temple** is where a pious Brahmin couple once prayed for a child, to be blessed with a boy who later became known as Sri Madhavacharya, the famous 13th century saint. Legend has it that Madhavacharya was sent by Lord Krishna himself in order to correctly interpret the holy scriptures; his teachings subsequently formed the foundation of the Dwaita philosophy.
◆**Timings for both temples** 5.30 am-8.30 pm **Note** Male devotees have to enter bare-chested

The idol at the **Sri Krishna Temple** faces west, which is unusual, and the reason for this is attributed to a story about a so-called lower caste devotee Kanakadasa. The caste-ridden society would not allow him to get a darshan and the idol is said to have turned westwards on its own to enable Kanakadasa

Heeding a trunk call: A tourist gets a jumbo welcome outside a temple

to get a glimpse of the lord through a window on the west side.

At the serene **Madhava Sarovar**, the tank adjacent to the temple, pilgrims wash their feet before darshan. The temple is open from 5.30 am to 9 pm and a number of rituals take place round the clock. The **Car Street** is called thus because of the cars, or the temple chariots, that are drawn along this street during the annual festival that's celebrated in mid-January.

The eight mutts, or monasteries here, established by Madhavacharya to oversee the rituals at the temple on a rotational basis for two years each, are located along the Car Street. Many of these mutts are housed in century-old buildings and exude an old-world charm.

Pajaka and Kunjaru Betta

About 12 km from Udupi is Pajaka, the birthplace of Madhavacharya. The house in which he grew up, with huge wooden rafters and sunlight streaming in through the central courtyard, still exists in a surprisingly good condition. The friendly caretaker takes visitors around. Do look for the tank, the backyard with the banyan tree, and the stone benches; all these have an aura of a lost world.

Kunjaru Betta (*betta* means hill) is a kilometre from Pajaka and has a **Durga Temple** on top. The view from the top is that of the lush green Udupi countryside and the shimmering Arabian Sea. There are no regular buses plying on this route; the best bet therefore would be to take an auto to cover Pajaka and Kunjaru Betta (fare Rs 250).

SHOPPING

Shops on **Car Street** sell a variety of curios such as wooden kitchen paraphernalia and toys; these are available in the shops located close to the **Krishna Temple**. Little elephants made of sandalwood make for a great gift. Tiny conches, used in an Indian game of pegs, can also be picked up here. The departmental stores near the **Mitra Samaj** sell

PRASHANT PANJIAR

Two shop owners on Car Street catch up with news from the rest of the world

GETTING THERE

Air Nearest airport: Bajpe Airport, Mangalore (60 km/ 1½ hrs), well-connected to Bangalore and Mumbai. Taxi to Udupi costs Rs 750

Rail The Udupi Railway Station is 3 km from the bus stand. All major trains traversing the coastal route like the Matsyagandha, Netravati, Madgaon-Mangalore, Jaipur-Ernakulam make a halt here

Road From Bangalore, take NH4 and turn left on NH48 towards Hassan and Sakleshpur. Drive through the ghat road to reach Mangalore and take NH17 to reach Udupi via Surathkal and Mulki. The drive, along the coast, is lovely. There are plenty of overnight luxury bus services (Sugama: Bangalore Tel 080-22250856; Durgamba: 23562383), including KSRTC's Volvo buses, to Udupi from Bangalore

homemade Udupi pickles as well as a variety of condiments.

WHERE TO STAY

With all imaginable creature comforts and more, the **Paradise Isle Beach Resort** (Tel: 0820-2537300, 2537791; Tariff: Rs 3,000-4,500), located bang on the Malpe Beach, is Udupi's most luxurious hotel and offers the best bargain for the facilities available. It has a swimming pool, an Ayurvedic spa and also organises travel around Udupi. The resort offers water sports such as speed boating and water biking, as well as boat rides to St Mary's Isle. The food court complex adjoining the hotel serves good multi-cuisine vegetarian and non-vegetarian dishes, such as fried *kane* (ladyfish) and *bangda* (mackerel), and dosas and uttapams. A coastal speciality restaurant is also being planned. Do inquire about their packages and tariff plans.

The rest of the better hotels are spread out between the Krishna Temple and the main bus stand. **Udupi Residency** (Tel: 2530005; Tariff: Rs 300-850), near the bus stand, is located on a

peaceful street and has neat rooms and spacious baths. The temples are just a few minutes' walk from here.

The older and bigger **Kediyoor Hotel** (Tel: 2522381; Tariff: Rs 375-1,500), at Shiribeedu, has rooms that feel warm, and a good vegetarian restaurant. **Pancharatna Paradise** (Tel: 2520791; Tariff: Rs 300-1,200) on Court Road offers good rooms but the baths are rather small.

The **Karavali Hotel** (Tel: 2522860; Tariff: Rs 530-2,400) on NH17 bypass has somewhat lost its charm, although it's an excellent option if you would like to stay away from the the town. The staff is extremely friendly and will direct you to the right places in case you are interested in the cultural happenings in town. The open field next to the hotel also happens to be a place where tents are pitched for **Yakshagana** performances. This is a form of theatre, enacted through the night in temples and tents, which weds dance, songs and dialogues.

For more hotels and details, see Udupi Accommodation Listings on pages 542-543

Nothing fishy about this delicious dish

WHERE TO EAT

One can never go wrong with food at Udupi, the place that is said to have given birth to the Indian fast-food versions. The best part is that Udupi has a delectable array of dishes for both vegetarians and non-vegetarians.

Mitra Samaj, on Car Street, may not boast of an elaborate menu but is one of the oldest establishments here. It offers authentic Udupi *oota* (meals, or food) for lunch, comprising rice, sambhar, rasam, buttermilk, pappad and pickles, among other things. They have a couple of branches on the same street that serve a long list of dosas and snacks in the evenings. Try their famous masala dosas. There are many vegetarian restaurants spread out around the bus stand; you can safely hop into any one of them, and you won't have a reason to complain.

The **Sagar** and **Sarovar** restaurants of the Karavali Hotel serve excellent coastal cuisine. The local dishes *kori gassi* and *akki roti* (thin, crispy rice bread, usually had with chicken curry) taste excellent. In case you are looking for a late night binge, their 'dhaba' is open till midnight. **Latha Hotel** in Bannanje is a local favourite for fish. This home-cum-restaurant, although quaint and dark, serves fresh fish. The rava fried *kane* is recommended. Go there only for the fish; everything else doesn't quite measure up.

On Malpe Beach, Raju Tonse's **Fish Point** is a must-visit. He picks up the catch of the day at the nearby Malpe Port, marinates them with local masalas and deep fries them right in front of you. *Kane*, kingfish, prawns — everything tastes very good. Girijamma, a sweet old woman, makes the best churmuri, a local version of bhelpuri. Ask for her on Malpe Beach, where she has a stall selling mineral water and wafers.

The **Samudra Bar and Restaurant** on Kaup Beach is crowded in the evenings. Next to it is a vegetarian eatery, **Sandhya**, serving snacks. ■

Photographs by VIVEK M

MARAVANTHE

A BEACH BY A RIVER

State Karnataka
Location The beach at Maravanthe stretches for a little less than 2 km, running parallel to NH17, with the Sowparnika River on the other side of the highway, north of Kundapur Town in Udupi District
Distances 108 km N of Mangalore, 454 km NW of Bangalore
Journey time ***By road*** $2^1/_2$ hrs from Mangalore, 10 hrs from Bangalore
Route from Bangalore NH4 to Nelamangala; NH48 to Mangalore via Kunigal and Hassan; NH17 to Maravanthe via Udupi and Kundapur (*see route guide on page 250*)

BY VIVEK M

It's entirely possible that if you visit Maravanthe on a weekday, you will marvel at how empty the place is. The long stretches of radiant white sand are punctuated by a gathering of lively plovers and terns and the only footprints on the beach are the thin, pointy ones they have left behind. Tiny white crabs scurry in and out of the vents on the sand and suddenly, you wish it would stay this way forever — that no one will ever know about this place, no one will visit, so that there is just this, the beach and you.

For this very reason, Maravanthe may not be everyone's idea of the perfect beach. There are no rainbow-coloured sun umbrellas here, no chairs to stretch out on, and no persuasive vendors selling souvenirs made of shells. But for me, and I am sure for several others too, it's the solitude the place guarantees that makes it such an attractive destination. As you walk along the beach, the waves reach up to caress your feet, as if shyly reminding you of their presence. The sea is warm and inviting, and once you take the plunge, it's difficult to convince yourself to reach for the sands again.

Perhaps the only thing that can lure you out is the Sowparnika River, which flows across a road that stands between the beach and the river. A boat ride on the river will take you past the picture-perfect village of Padukone, and a few small islands. Like a perfect ending for a fairy-tale trip, on the horizon you will see the Kodachadri Hills — yet another destination, beckoning you to start another journey. But the sea remains in your mind, and the waves continue to trade secrets with the wind that ruffles your hair for long.

Fast and furious: Jet-skiing at Baindur

SUSHEELA NAIR

FAST FACTS

When to go Anytime of the year except the monsoons. However, do remember that summers can be quite warm

Tourist Office

- Regional Tourist Office

Department of Tourism
Krishna Building, Car Street
Udupi
Tel: 0820-2529718

STD code 08254

ORIENTATION

For over a kilometre at **Trasi Village**, the NH17 is sandwiched between the **Maravanthe Beach** and the **Sowparnika River**. Even truck drivers plying on the highway, who are usually immune to natural beauty, are seduced by this unique geography and stop to have a cup of tea at the roadside shacks and enjoy the blissful view of the sea and the river coming together — almost, but not quite.

You are most likely to approach the beach from **Kundapur Town**, 12 km from Maravanthe. A taxi to Maravanthe from Kundapur costs Rs 250 and the bus ride Rs 8. Ahead of the **Trasi Bus Stop** on NH17, just before you get a glimpse of the beach, is a small road running to the left. Half a kilometre ahead on this road is the Turtle Bay Resort. **Kanchugodu Village** is located next to it. The **Gangoli fishing port** is 6 km from the Trasi Bus Stand. Back on the highway, ahead on the right, hidden behind casuarinas, is the Sagar Kinara Resort. The Sowparnika River appears on the right a little further on. NH17 continues towards **Baindur** and **Otthinene** (25 km).

Kodi, Koravadi and **Beejady** beaches are to the south of Kundapur (Kodi, the nearest beach, being 5 km away). A round trip to all the three beaches by auto costs about Rs 250, inclusive of waiting charges. A taxi ride costs Rs 400.

BEACH WATCH

Except during the monsoons, the waters at Maravanthe are safe for swimming. However, avoid the rocky part of the beach a little away from the Turtle Bay Resort. Beachwear is best restricted to the stretch right outside the resort. It would be unwise to venture out in such attire near the highway.

Songs of solitude: A villager enjoys a quiet break at the beach

THINGS TO SEE AND DO

At Maravanthe, the best thing to do would be to flop on the sands and let the elements rejuvenate you. Long walks on the beach to find out where the beach and the road decide to part ways are a must-do. The Turtle Bay Resort offers water sports, an option for those interested in something more adventurous. Keep aside two days for enjoying the beautiful beach and the countryside around.

Ride the sea

Most hotels offer boat rides on the Arabian Sea; usually, these rides are to an unnamed island in the sea, roughly 5 km from the shore, which has an abandoned lighthouse and a beach. The charges are about Rs 1,000 for maximum of eight people; the trip lasts $1^1/_2$ hrs. The island is a rocky patch and the lighthouse is small and uninspiring. However, the beach near the lighthouse is clean enough for a dip in the sea.

Water sports

The **Turtle Bay Resort** (*see Where to Stay on page 272*) arranges **snorkelling** and **scuba diving trips** around **Netrani Island** (*also see 'The deep blue sea' in Murudeshwar on page 283*). For the **boat ride**, tourists are first taken on a 45-min drive either to **Bhatkal** (*see page 284*) or **Murudeshwar** (*see page 277*), and from there ferried on boats to the island. A day package costs Rs 1,500 per person, and there has to be a minimum of six people. Charges include transportation costs, lunch and snacks. Abraham Chacko, the instructor, is professionally trained in both snorkelling and scuba diving.

Soans Holiday Pvt Ltd (Tel: 08254-231683; Mobile: 09448120826) at CS Road, Kundapur, also organises **snorkelling trips to Netrani Island**. A package costs Rs 1,500 per head, with a minimum of six people.

Kanchugodu Village

The village, next to the Turtle Bay Resort, provides a lovely glimpse of the lives of fisherfolk. The whole community gathers by the sea in the morning, and on their colourful boats, the fishermen take to the sea. They are usually kind enough to offer to take you on a fishing trip along with them.

Sowparnika River

Locals believe that the river, which flows down from the Kodachadri Hills, carries with it the essence of 64 medicinal herbs that grow on the mountain. Hence, a dip in the river is said to cleanse all ailments away. You must go on a boat ride in the river, which also has a charming little island teeming with coconut palms. The ferry point is just across the road from the beach and a 30-min boat ride will cost you Rs 500, for a maximum of eight people. During the ride, also look out for **Padukone Village**, the **Maharajaswamy Temple** on the left bank and **Kodachadri Hills**.

GETTING THERE

Air Nearest airport: Mangalore (108 km/ $2^1/_2$ hrs). Taxi to Maravanthe costs Rs 1,250 approx

Rail Nearest railhead: Kundapur (12 km/ 30 mins). The Matsyagandha Express (connecting Mangalore and Mumbai) and the Netravati Express (connecting Thiruvananthapuram with Mumbai) stop at Kundapur. Take a local bus or hire a taxi (Rs 450) from here to reach the beach. There are plenty of private local buses; there's one almost every 10 mins or so. These are quite basic but comfortable and fast. There are no direct trains from Bangalore

Road Maravanthe is 454 km from Bangalore, and road is by far the best way to reach the beach from the city. By car, take NH4 till Nelamangala and turn left on NH48. Drive through the ghat roads to reach Mangalore and take the scenic NH17 to reach Maravanthe through Udupi and Kundapur. Plenty of overnight luxury bus services (Sugama: 080-22250856; Durgamba: 23562383) are available from Bangalore to Kundapur, from where you can hire a taxi or board a local bus to get to the beach

Kodi, Koravadi and Beejady beaches

These three beaches can be reached from Kundapur. Kodi is the closest, just 5 km from the town; the other two are 2 and 4 km from Kodi respectively. A round-trip on an autorickshaw will cost you Rs 250 and a taxi Rs 450; the fare is inclusive of waiting charges.

The locally popular **Kinara Restaurant**, with shacks facing the sea, is situated at Kodi. The beach, however, is littered with plastic bottles and other waste and hence not good for a visit unless you have intentions of dining here. Koravadi and Beejady are wonderful stretches of pristine sand with very few visitors. There are no eateries or stalls out here and it's best to carry along plenty of snacks. The two beaches, lined by green palms, are generally considered safe for swimming.

SHOPPING

There is nothing by way of souvenir-shopping in Maravanthe. There are a few small shops that sell shells and conchs. However, these are open only during the weekends.

WHERE TO STAY

Maravanthe has very few stay options but that certainly works in the favour of anyone looking for a quiet getaway. The places that are here have facilities that are adequate enough to make the tourist's experience enjoyable. You can also stay in Kundapur, from where beaches such as Koravadi and Beejady are easily accessed.

In Maravanthe

The **Turtle Bay Resort** (Tel: 08254-265422; Mobile: 09900461609; Tariff: Rs 700-2,600), situated on the southern tip

SAIBAL DAS

As good as it gets: A delicious spread of neer dosa with chicken curry

of the beach, offers the best option for tourists. The resort has cottages and cabanas right next to the beach, and hammocks for afternoon siestas. The beach stretch next to the resort is maintained well and is good for a swim anytime. The hotel arranges sightseeing tours, water sports and treks to Kodachadri. Ayurvedic massages are also on offer here.

Sagar Kinara (Tel: 265401; Mobile: 09448724861; Tariff: Rs 500), on the other side of the highway, to the southern end of the beach, quite proudly announces that it's a resort but it's nothing more than a glorified set of tiled huts. But the rooms are neat though basic and it's best suited for travellers who prefer to spend most of their time outdoors. It helps that the proprietor has lots of information about the area. Sagar Kinara is quite popular as a pit-stop for a day with groups of bikers cruising down the highway.

A similar staying option that is currently coming up is the **Asara Rest House** (Mobile: 09901390129). Located in the same lane as Sagar Kinara, it will have five rooms, and the tariff is expected to begin at Rs 250.

In Kundapur

Hotel Sharon (Tel: 230823-36, 230623; Mobile: 09448120826; Tariff: Rs 385-955) is the best option in Kundapur. The manager is knowledgeable about the Kollur-Maravanthe area and can offer excellent sightseeing tips.

For more hotels and details, see Maravanthe Accommodation Listings on pages 541-542

WHERE TO EAT

The **Turtle Bay Resort** is good but not great as far as seafood is concerned. The mussels, king fish and *bangda* (mackerel) all taste decent but do remember that it's best not to order anything that isn't on the menu. Alcohol is not stocked at the resort but the friendly staff can arrange drinks for you.

Trasi Royal Durbar Dhaba might sound grand but it's just a small restaurant right next to Sagar Kinara. They serve coastal and Punjabi cuisine. The

Many men and a boat: Fishermen from Kanchugodu Village team up at the beach

food is just passable but the ambience on its terrace, especially after the sun goes down, just about makes up for that. Ask the cook for his suggestions before you order anything exotic.

Sagar Kinara serves simple vegetarian food on prior notice and is best frequented only for breakfast. The roadside shacks near the beach offer tender coconuts, soft drinks and some fried snacks in the evenings.

Kundapur has restaurants to please coastal cuisine aficionados. Try the spicy *kane* (ladyfish) masala fry at **Banjara**, Hotel Sharon's non-vegetarian restaurant, or Kundapuri chicken prepared in a smooth gravy with shredded coconut. They also serve succulent prawns.

There are many dhabas along the highway. At no cost should you miss the masala dosa at **Harsha Refreshments** (Hotel Sharon) and the chicken ghee roast at **Shetty Lunch Home**, near the Kundapur main bus stand. People from as far as Mangalore drive in to grab their share at Shetty's. And if you try out the food, it will be easy to understand why.

AROUND MARAVANTHE

Kodachadri Hills (35 km)
A trek up the Kodachadri Hills should feature on the adventure lover's itinerary. The two-day trek, moderately strenuous, takes one through the dense jungles of the **Mookambika Wildlife Sanctuary**, which offers many birdwatching opportunities. Halts are usually at the guest house, $1^1/_2$ km below the summit. Trekkers also camp beside the guest house and make an early morning climb to the peak. You can have simple meals at the **Bhattar Mane** (house of the Bhatt family) near the top. On a clear cloudless day you can even see the Arabian Sea from a certain point along the trek. There is also a jeep track till Bhattar Mane and it costs Rs 1,000 to hire a jeep from Kollur.

In case you don't want to go on a long trek, then you can walk down to the enchanting **Arashinagundi Waterfalls**, 5 km from Kollur. However, you'll need a guide to help you and the treks are best arranged through the hotel you are staying at.

So long and thanks for all the fish!

First the statutory warning: don't visit the Gangoli port and market if you can't stand the smell of fish. But for what it's worth, we shall advise you to be brave and venture out to this fish market in Maravanthe, if only to capture a slice of local culture in its most authentic form. The fishing trawlers and boats dock directly by the market, adding to the chaos and drama, all of which elicit nothing less than a sense of sheer wonder.

The Gangoli fish market comes alive late every morning when the fishing boats return with their catch. The women folk, dressed in colourful saris with woven baskets on their heads, help transfer the fish from the boats, without wasting a minute. There is much confusion but as your eyes get accustomed to the flurry of activity you begin to realise how well-organised everything is. The fish is neatly sorted out, measured and immediately loaded onto trucks packed with ice. These then make their way to towns and cities as far as Bangalore. Auctions also happen as local sellers procure fresh fish here. The market is about 6 km from the beach; it costs Rs 60 by auto.

Soans Holiday Pvt Ltd offers adventure packages that include water sports and trekking in the Kodachadri. They offer easy treks as well, when you can get back by the afternoon or evening.

If you are in a group of 25 people, then you can opt for a moonlight trek at night; be warned that chances of coming face-to-face with wild animals are high while trekking in the night. Soans suggests avoiding weekends for trekking because of the crowd in the hills. They also offer a package wherein you can stay at an island they own in the middle of a river called **Varahi**, about 10 km from Maravanthe. Eight rooms and a dormitory are available here; the tariffs range from Rs 1,500-1,750, and are inclusive of breakfast, lunch and dinner. More details are available at their website soans.com.

Mookambika Temple, Kollur (37 km)
The centuries old Mookambika Temple hosts a deity that many believe is immensely powerful. Don't let the huge queues detract you; the rituals, such as the noon puja, when a necklace with a rare green sapphire is placed on the deity, are worth witnessing. The drive up to the temple (40 km/ 1½ hrs from Kundapur) is beautiful; verdant paddy fields, the **Sowparnika River** and several streams make for wonderful views. Taxis cost Rs 600 for a round-trip.
◆**Temple timings** 5.30 am-9.30 pm

Otthinene (25 km)
Otthinene is a beautiful spot near Baindur where you can spend a memorable evening. The Forest Rest House on a hillock here offers a stupendous view of a river becoming one with the sea. A flight of stairs and a small stretch of road down the hill will lead you to the quaint **Someshwara Temple** overlooking the beach. Don't leave the place until you have seen the setting sun. A round-trip from Maravanthe on an auto costs Rs 250, inclusive of waiting charges. ■

PRASHANT PANJIAR

MURUDESHWAR

SUNNY PARADISE

State Karnataka
Location The sleepy, sun-drenched temple town is close to the halfway mark of the Karavali Coast, between Honavar and Bhatkal
Distances 174 km N of Mangalore, 438 km NW of Bangalore
Journey time ***By road*** 3½ hrs from Mangalore, 10½ hrs from Bangalore
Route from Bangalore NH4 to Tumkur via Nelamangala; NH206 to Honavar via Arsikere, Shimoga and Talguppa; NH17 to Murudeshwar (*see route guide on page 250*)

■ BY PARIKSHIT RAO

At first sight, everything about Murudeshwar appears to be larger than life. A gigantic Shiva idol keeps vigil over this holy town and a long, wide beach dwarfs visitors with its sandy vastness and boundless views of the horizon. It's no surprise then that frolicking tourists arrive every morning to lay siege on this beauty. The nights are far quieter, and the only notes one can hear then are those of the gentle waves lapping against the white, powdery sands, hemmed in by palm trees and arecanut groves.

The weather, in most months of the year, is perfect — for long walks, for watching the sea, or if you walk ahead to the empty stretches of sand, even for some meditation or to indulge in undisturbed musings. It's a bit difficult not to fall in love with Murudeshwar though it's no longer the sleepy, coastal hamlet it once was. In this town that is held sacred by lore, materialistic notions all too often seem to zip past spiritual goals. But the beach is where you can forget this conflict. There are candy sticks to be bought, waves to be chased, and sunsets to be watched. Being in Murudeshwar is a blessing and it's something one knows even if visiting as a tourist and not as a pilgrim.

→ FAST FACTS

When to go The best season to visit Murudeshwar is post-monsoon, between October and March, when the sea is playful and the days not all that sultry

Tourist office
● KSTDC
Central Reservation Office
Badami House, NR Square
Bangalore
Tel: 080-22275869
Website: karnatakatourism.org

STD code 08385

ORIENTATION

The **Murudeshwar Railway Station** is about 4 km from town. If you're travelling by bus from Karwar or Mangalore, you'll be dropped off at **Murudeshwar Cross** on NH17, from where you can take an auto (Rs 15-20) and cover the 2-km distance to the town centre, where the temple is situated. The main road is called the **Temple Road**, and this is where almost all hotels, restaurants, shops and other establishments are located. The **Murudeshwar Beach** stretches around the **Kandukagiri hillock.** The section of the beach that faces the Shiva idol is most popular, while the one behind it is mainly used by fishermen. A road on the way to the temple leads to this serene part of the beach; there are a couple of guest houses here.

You can cover the entire town and the beach by foot, by auto (fares negotiable; the average fare per kilometre ranges around Rs 8) or by renting a bicycle (ask locals for Narasimha Vaidya; Rs 6 per hour). Most hotels are located within a 5-min walk from the beach. Shops selling souvenirs and snacks abound adjacent to the temple complex.

BEACH WATCH

Locals insist the beach at Murudeshwar is safe for swimming. However, authorities beg to differ and a degenerating signboard advises tourists against venturing into the sea. There are no lifeguards here either, so it makes sense to be very careful. Do dress appropriately even while at the beach; as this is a temple town, beachwear is frowned upon.

THINGS TO SEE AND DO

Set aside around three-four days to get around Murudeshwar, Netrani Island,

SONIA JABBAR

Swimming is discouraged at Murudeshwar but locals throw caution to the waves

Bhatkal and other places nearby. It's best to visit the beach either early in the morning or late afternoon. Spend your evenings watching kingfishers and sea gulls diving for crabs and other creatures between the rocks.

Murudeshwar Beach

Although local authorities discourage swimming in the open sea, most people ignore it. Locals come here for an evening of peace, to splash about in the cobalt sea and slurp ice-cream sticks on the beach. The soft, golden sand here looks inviting but is not strong enough to support sandcastle building.

During low tide, **parasailing joyrides**, where the chute is pulled by a jeep, are organised here by locals (Rs 150 for a 1-km ride lasting about 5-8 mins). It's easy to spot the person organising it as he is always on the beach with a colourful parachute. For **boat rides**, which take you around the Kandukagiri hillock to the other section of the beach (Rs 450 per person), ask for Ishwar on the main stretch of the beach. He also rents out boats to visit Netrani Island (Rs 3,000; capacity 12 passengers) and organises **dolphin-spotting trips** to **Kalgudda**, about 15 km away (Rs 2,000). A 2-hr motorboat ride takes you to **Netrani Island** (*see 'The deep blue sea' on page 283*).

En-route Adventurers (Mobile: 09845726790) organises parasailing (Rs 850 for a 30-min ride), **sea kayaking** (Rs 300 for 1 hr), **sea wave rafting** (Rs 300 per person for 1 hr) and **banana boat rides** (Rs 250; 30 mins). Experienced instructors help you with these activities.

Murudeshwar Temple

Lord Shiva is worshipped as 'Aghora', that is, in his ascetic form, in this temple, perched at the base of Kandukagiri. The hillock juts out into the sea and a narrow strip of land connects it to the mainland. ♦**Timings** 6.30 am-1 pm and 3-8 pm

Statue Park

You can't miss the theme park built on Kandukagiri hillock, centred on mythological characters such as Arjuna and Krishna. However, all attention is usually centred on Murudeshwar's tallest claim to fame, the 123-foot high **Shiva statue**. This colossal tribute to the lord, costing well over Rs 1 crore and sculpted over two years, is built in such a way that it catches the sun's rays and appears to be sparkling at dawn. The statue can be seen from almost everywhere in Murudeshwar — even from the railway station, which is a good 4 km away! The park is just 5 mins from the temple. Don't miss this ode to changing times — an exaggerated manifestation of the spirituality that attracts travellers from afar to Murudeshwar.
◆**Entry** Free **Timings** 9 am-6.30 pm

SHOPPING

Shopping in Murudeshwar is a low-key affair. Most visitors, considering they've come only for a holy experience, usually take back a framed picture of the Shiva idol. However, **Lavancha Handicrafts** on Temple Road, opposite Kamat Hotel, offers traditional and surprisingly therapeutic souvenirs. Lavancha (or vetiver) is a medicinal plant widely used in Ayurvedic medicines. Its fragrant roots are used to make wall-hangings, pen holders, jewellery boxes, baskets and Ganapati idols. The rates of these articles depend on their size but usually range around Rs 40-150.

Gadbad ice-cream towers over the rest

PARIKSHIT RAO

WHERE TO STAY

All hotels in Murudeshwar are located close to the temple and beach. Most staying options are mid-range ones, with some budget guest houses that offer pleasant rooms and sea views. Advance bookings are necessary for most hotels in peak tourist season (November-May), especially in mid-January when the town hosts an annual rural fair called **Jatra**, largely supported by the builder RN Shetty, when the room rates soar.

The most prominent hotels in Murudeshwar are the ones owned by the RNS group. **RNS Residency** (Tel: 08385-260060, 268901; Tariff: Rs 1,000-4,000), located near the temple, is the top-end staying option with a health club, swimming pool, gymnasium and a restaurant that serves only vegetarian fare. The wide balconies in some rooms offer splendid sea views.

Naveen Beach Resort (Tel: 260415; Tariff: Rs 1,600-2,600), situated right in front of the beach, has 11 AC sea-facing rooms with plush interiors. The attached open-air restaurant and bar serves excellent seafood. **RNS Guest House** (Tel: 268860; Tariff: Rs 600-3,700) has 97 rooms but not all of them are rented out since it never gets that full. The neat and clean rooms have attached bathrooms with hot water in the mornings.

Kamath Yatri Nivas (Tel: 260871; Tariff: Rs 300-800) on Temple Road is a

PRASHANT PANJIAR

It's time for some food and fun during a boat ride by the Murudeshwar Beach

tidy 25-room staying option that sits atop Kamat Restaurant. Some rooms face the sea, while others face the roofs of the shops below. Hot water is available in the mornings, and room service till 10 pm. Vehicles can be hired here for sightseeing and for trips to nearby pilgrimage spots. **Benzy Intercontinental** (Tel: 260565; Tariff: Rs 400-700) in Mavelli, $1^1/_2$ km from Murudeshwar on NH17, is a decent place that offers AC and non-AC rooms with all essential facilities at an unbeatable price.

Murudeshwar Boarding and Lodging (Tel: 260479; Tariff: Rs 250-500), located on Temple Road, has 17 rooms. The rooms are pretty basic and clean but could do with some additional ventilation and sunlight.

Panchvati Guest House (Tel: 268565; Mobile: 09945104940; Tariff: Rs 200-300) is a quiet, sea-facing family-run guest house situated on the stretch behind the Shiva idol. All seven rooms, spread over two floors, are neat and spacious. Tuck into some homemade food (vegetarian and non-vegetarian) here, but order in advance. The friendly owners can also organise sightseeing tours (Rs 300 for car hire) to nearby places such as Idagunji Mahaganapati Temple and Apsara Konda Waterfalls (*see Around Murudeshwar on page 282*).

Gomes Yatri Niwas (Mobile: 09880286970; Tariff: Rs 400-500), a few houses away from Panchvati, is another family-run guest house situated amid swaying palm trees, right opposite the beach. The six clean and comfortable rooms here are just the right size for a couple and these come with attached showers. Seafood can be prepared upon request. Sightseeing tours and vehicles on rent are available here as well.

For more hotels and details, see Murudeshwar Accommodation Listings on page 542

WHERE TO EAT

The culinary choices in Murudeshwar extend from a simple vegetarian thali worth Rs 10 to a lavish four-course meal with drinks. However, have dinner early. Almost all hotels stop accepting orders or refuse service at 10 pm sharp. Head to **Naveen Seaside Restaurant** (popularly known as the canteen), near the temple, for tasty South Indian vegetarian fare such as aloo bonda and masala dosa.

Living up to traditional values and standing tall amidst a million similarly named clones across the country is the **Kamat Restaurant** on Temple Road, serving hygienic, vegetarian South Indian fare. The pleasant vegetarian thali is excellent value for money. The stringent timings for meals (11 am-4 pm and 7-10 pm) ensure that chairs fill up fast.

For coastal fare, head down to the restaurant at the **Naveen Beach Resort**, where local cooks serve up a tangy array of seafood with the right blend of spices. The assortment of drinks at the attached bar neatly complements their spicy, tender rawa-fried kingfish.

Shamiana Restaurant at Benzy Intercontinental offers South Indian, North Indian and Chinese food right until midnight, with their speciality being the tandoori pomfret fry. Nisarga Residency's two restaurants, **Hotel Nisarga** for non-vegetarian and **Sharavathy** for vegetarian food, are other options. Try mackerel fry at the former and the simple vegetarian thali at the latter.

Visit **Murudeshwar Ice Cream Parlour** for Karavali's most-loved dessert, Gadbad ice-cream, a towering stack of three ice-cream scoops, generously garnished with fresh fruits, honey and dry fruits, served in a tall glass.

→ GETTING THERE

Air Nearest airport: Bajpe, Mangalore (174 km/ 3½ hrs), connected to major metros like Bangalore and Mumbai. Taxi to Murudeshwar costs approx Rs 1,500
Rail Murudeshwar has a railway station but few trains stop here. Trains plying on the Mumbai-Goa-Mangalore Konkan Railway line stop at the more prominent nearest railhead, Bhatkal (16 km/ ½ hr). From Mumbai, the Matsyagandha Express halts at Murudeshwar Station. Autos from Bhatkal (Rs 120) will drop you off at Murudeshwar. Another option is to take a train till Shimoga (6 hrs) from Bangalore and then cover the rest of the journey by road
Road If you're driving from Bangalore, take NH4 to Tumkur via Nelamangala. Switch to NH206 to Honavar via Arsikere, Shimoga and Talguppa and finally turn left towards NH17 to Murudeshwar. Regular state transport and private buses operate between Bangalore and Bhatkal from Majestic Bus Stand. Naik Tours and Travels (Tel: 08385-260335, 09844022915) on Temple Road in Murudeshwar rents out tourist vehicles and also organises bus tickets (ordinary buses or Volvo) to major cities like Mangalore and Bangalore

AROUND MURUDESHWAR

Idagunji Temple (16 km)

This temple houses a Ganesh idol similar to the one at Gokarna (*see page 286*) and goes by the moniker Idakunja. Devotees follow a tradition of offering an idli-like eatable called *mashbhaksha* on all sides of the idol till it reaches its head.

Recently, about 58 ancient palm-leaf manuscripts that describe the cultural inheritance of present-day Uttara Canara, were discovered here. *For how to get here, see Connection on page 284.*

Apsara Konda Waterfalls and Beach (20 km)

Literally meaning 'Pond of the Celestial Nymphs', Apsara Konda Waterfalls, hidden in a small forest, have for long

SONIA JABBAR

NETRANI ISLAND: The deep blue sea

Locals call it Netragudda or Netra Hill. Others call it Pigeon Island. Situated in the middle of the sea between Maravanthe and Murudeshwar, about 10 nautical miles off the coast, this tiny, uninhabited island is an excellent **deep diving site**. You can see schools of angelfish, barracudas, eels, sea turtles and other colourful fish when you go diving here. The visibility is as high as 40m, and the depths range from 6-40m, thereby making it a perfect diving site for beginners and experts alike.

Barracuda Diving India (Website: barracudadiving.com; Tel: 0832-2463333; at the Goa Mariott Resort, available only in season), located in Panaji, Goa, offers diving packages (inclusive of diving gear) here. For info on course fee, packages and custom-made safaris, visit their website. They have provisions for organising diving trips out of Murudeshwar, without the tourist having to go through Goa, but this option is best exercised by someone who has diving experience. Beginners will find the training that the agency provides in its full-fledged facility at Goa useful.

Those who go diving off Netrani Island will not be disappointed by the diverse marine life in the water — diving teams here have even spotted whales.

The names of some of the diving spots accurately reflect what one can expect to see underwater. At Grand Central Station, the many schools of fish are a reminder of the New York terminus at rush hour. The Nursery is ideal for beginners, with its mostly calm waters, which also serve as a breeding ground for stonefish, giant morays and others.

Do note that the Indian Navy sometimes uses the island for shelling practice. There are fixed days for this and the Navy advertises the dates in advance in newspapers, and informs fishermen and the Barracuda Diving agency. The upside is that attempts are on to have the island declared a marine park, a tag that will be invaluable in saving the precious diversity the waters around it hold.

Naik Tours and Travels (*see Getting There on facing page*) organises boat rides to Netrani Island (Rs 1,500-2,000) but not diving excursions. The **Turtle Bay Resort** in Maravanthe and **Soans Holidays Private Ltd** in Kundapur (*for details, see Maravanthe on page 271*) also organise trips to Netrani. ■

ARUN Hc/ INDIAPICTURE

Chasing the waves: Winged visitors to Murudeshwar Beach

bewitched locals. Near the waterfalls is the Apsara Konda Beach, one of the finest to watch sunsets from. There are no staying options here on the beach, and it is practically empty, giving you a perfect perch from which to enjoy the sea.

♦**Location** 2 km after the Sharavathi Bridge near Honavar, off NH17 **Connection** Naik Tours and Travels (*see Getting There on page 282*) rents out taxis (Rs 500) to both Apsara Konda and Idagunji Temple (Rs 300 if you opt for only one of these places). Autos will charge you around Rs 250-300 for each place, including waiting charges for about an hour. Negotiate rates in advance

Bhatkal (16 km)

This ancient port town has numerous temples dating back to the rule of the Vijayanagara Empire and many interesting Jain monuments such as the 15th century **Parshwanatha Basadi**, located on the Bazaar Main Road. Do look out for the monolithic pillar known as **Manasthambha** at the temple entrance, with astonishing, carved marble images. In nearby Haduvalli is the **Padmavati Temple**, which has 24 Tirthankaras engraved in black polished stone.

About 5 km west of Bhatkal Town is the **port**. You can also visit the **lighthouse** (Rs 5 per ticket) close to the port. There's no beach here.

There are a couple of stay options in Bhatkal. **Hotel Kola Paradise** (Tel: 08385-225291; Tariff: Rs 90-650), opposite the KSRTC Bus Stand, is the preferred choice for many tourists in Bhatkal. The rooms are tidy with stray oddities such as heart-shaped dustbins. **Vaibhav Lodge** (Tel: 226357; Tariff: Rs 150-250) is yet another ancient institution on the main road. The rooms are quite basic but clean.

Autorickshaws are the most convenient option for transport in Bhatkal. Negotiate fares well in advance to avoid any inconvenience. Average auto fares from Murudeshwar to Bhatkal are around Rs 100-120. ■

Photographs by VIVEK M

GOKARNA

THE FANTASTIC FOUR

State Karnataka
Location On the Karavali Coast, to the north of Kumta, Gokarna's beaches are nestled between the mouths of the rivers Agnashini and Gangavali
Distances 160 km S of Panaji, 237 km N of Mangalore, 469 km NW of Bangalore
Journey time ***By road*** 4 hrs from Panaji, 5 hrs from Mangalore, 11 hrs from Bangalore
Route from Bangalore NH4 to Tumkur; NH206 to Honavar via Shimoga and Sagar; NH17 to Madangeri via Kumta; district road to Gokarna (*see route guide on page 250*)

BY VIVEK M

There are two kinds of pilgrims in Gokarna. One group comes hoping to discover its secrets, tucked away in temples and ancient dwellings, and looks to the sea for cleansing their souls. The other type of visitors comprises those who worship the sun and the sand, holidaymakers who inevitably find their prayers answered in Gokarna's fabulous four beaches. Whichever group you belong to, you'll certainly find this ancient town's coastal beauty a blessing.

The rocky cliffs and the high promontories interspersed between the picturesque beaches in Gokarna present a geography that's unlike any other. If, like me, the tourist makes full use of this unique offering by trekking from one beach to another, there is much to look forward to — the routes guarantee astonishing views of the Karavali Coast on one side and the lush green countryside of the Uttara Canara District on the other. On the treks, the first glimpse of the coves, especially those of the Om Beach, are exquisite and unforgettable.

The mood at Kudle and Om beaches is usually cheerful and just right for fun lovers who would like to spend their holiday by playing a game of volleyball on the sand or splashing water at each other on a hot afternoon. The numerous cafés on the beaches ensure that great food and chilled beer are just an arm's length away. The secluded beaches of Half Moon and Paradise, guarded by rocky promontories on either side, are the pleasure-seeker's paradise; beach buffs rent out little shacks and linger on for months at these lovely locales, soaking in the good life that's on offer here.

Though touted as a rival to Goa, today's Gokarna presents an interesting study of contrasts. This is where the devout, their foreheads smeared with ash, and the Western tourist, often tattooed and wearing T-shirts with images of Hindu gods, come face to face. Around the narrow lanes of the holy town, a life unfolds that's a world away from the rather hedonistic promises of beach shacks. Signboards outside old, tiled homes announce the lengthy names of their owners and their forefathers, indicators, as it were, of a simpler time. Cows run across the town's alleys, and are fed lovingly by locals. And somewhere on a beach, a wave reaches for the shore, wiping away the footprints of time.

ORIENTATION

Gokarna is a small town and one can easily get around by walking. The bus stand as well as most of the hotels and guest houses are located on **Main Road**, which meets **Car Street** to form an 'L'. A small lane at this junction proceeds straight towards the **Koti Theerta Tank**. Rows of shops line Car Street on either side before the **Maha Ganapathy Temple** appears on the left. **Mahabaleshwara Temple** is a stone's throw from here, to the right. Another lane beginning at the front entrance of this temple takes you to **Gokarna Beach**. Autos charge Rs 20 to take you anywhere within town.

The four main beaches here, **Kudle, Om, Half Moon** and **Paradise**, are located to the south of Gokarna Beach and are best approached through short treks lasting between 20 mins to an hour. It's best for people to travel in groups of four; if less, do not trek from one beach to another when it's dark. Autos from the town also ply to a certain spot (9 km, Rs 100 for a drop, taxi charges Rs 150 for drop) between Kudle and Om beaches, where the road forks. While one leads to a stair of rough steps down to Om, another ends in a shaded foot-track leading to Kudle. No roads lead to Half Moon and Paradise but you can reach these by trekking from Om. Motorboats are also available at the beaches and these take you to the neighbouring ones for a fare of Rs 75-150 per head. A round-trip to all the four beaches, inclusive of

FAST FACTS

When to go From November to March

Tourist offices

- KSTDC

Central Reservation Office
Badami House, NR Square
Bangalore
Tel: 080-22275869
Email: kstdc@vsnl.in

- Department of Tourism

Government of Karnataka
No. 49, Second Floor, Khanija Bhavan
Race Course Road
Bangalore
Tel: 22352828
Website: karnatakatourism.org
Email: info@karnatakatourism.org, discoverkarnataka@vsnl.net

STD code 08386

waiting charges, will set you back by Rs 400 per head. Although the bike culture has not yet taken off, there are a few shops around **Pai Restaurant** on Main Road where bikes are available for hire. Geared bikes cost Rs 250 per day; refrain from taking the gearless ones (Rs 200) as the undulating roads leading to Om and Kudle beaches make it a difficult ride. Bicycles are available for hire from a shop to your right, just before you reach Pai Restaurant on Main Road. It costs Rs 30 per day and Rs 3 per hour. It's also the best option if you want to explore Gokarna's narrow lanes.

GETTING THERE

Air Nearest airport: Dabolim Airport, Goa (140 km/ 3 hrs), well-connected to Bangalore and Mumbai by major airlines. Taxi to Gokarna costs Rs 2,500
Rail The Gokarna Railway Station is situated 6 km from the town. The Matsyagandha Express stops here but most other express trains don't. The nearest major railway stations are Kumta (32 km) and Ankola (20 km). Kumta and Ankola fall on the Konkan Railway route, and are connected to Mumbai, Mangalore and Thiruvananthapuram by trains such as the Matsyagandha and the Netravati Express, among others. There are plenty of local buses from Ankola and Kumta to Gokarna. Taxis charge about Rs 500
Road From Bangalore, take NH4 to Tumkur and then NH206 towards Shimoga. The drive gets pleasant after Bhadravathi as you head towards Honavar via Sagar. From Honavar, one can cruise comfortably on NH17 to Madangeri and thereafter take a left turn towards Gokarna. There are a few overnight luxury bus services (Sugama: 080-22250856; VRL: 080-26992901; KSRTC: 09980915155, 080-22870099); book in advance if travelling on a weekend

BEACH WATCH

Many Western tourists visit Gokarna's beaches and have contributed to making beachwear acceptable. As long as one keeps away from the rocky confines of the beaches, the waters are safe for swimming. However, at Kudle, locals caution that swimming is not advisable. There are no lifeguards at the beaches; swimming is discouraged in the monsoons.

THINGS TO SEE AND DO

Each of the four beaches has its own unique appeal and deserves half a day's time each at the very least. Adventure lovers will be tantalised by the trekking opportunities between the beaches. Although you have to negotiate steep climbs at certain places, the views are well worth the sweat. There are thatched huts on all the beaches, providing basic accommodation, perfect in case you want to experience 'nightlife' near the waters. Gokarna's ancient temples and traditional homes are also must-visits.

Gokarna Beach

This beach is best avoided as it's very crowded; pilgrims take their ritual bath here before heading to the Mahabaleshwara Temple. Besides, it's unclean and at the most worth only a peek.

To reach Kudle Beach from here, head southwards, climb up to the Maneshwara Temple and then take the foot-track towards Kudle. You won't lose your way here if you remember to keep heading south along the coast. Carry plenty of water and something to cover your head with as it can get quite hot during the day.

Kudle Beach

Kudle is a fine stretch of beach that's the closest to the town. It's crescent-shaped,

PRASHANT PANJIAR

Two semi-circular coves join to form an inverted symbol of 'Om'

stretching for nearly a kilometre, hugging a wide cove. There are plenty of thatched huts for overnight halts, especially on the northern side, some perched on the rocky landscape offering excellent views of the sea. Seasonal cafés are spread out along the beach and offer good food and drinks. On the beach, one can find people practising yoga and martial arts or strumming the guitar in the evenings.

Om Beach

Om is another popular beach, reached by a 20-min walk from Kudle. The first sight of the beach from a promontory, before the path descends down, explains why Om Beach was named thus: two semi-circular coves join to form an inverted symbol of 'Om'. The path descends to a sheltered viewpoint with concrete seats, after which a flight of stairs takes you down to the beach. There are many cafés and shacks here, offering food and accommodation for the night. If you want to go **kayaking** in the sea, then head towards the outlet run by the Swaswara Resort (*see Where to Stay on page 291*). They charge Rs 300 per person for a 2-hr ride.

Half Moon and Paradise

It's a wee bit more difficult to reach these two beaches than the others. One has to be prepared for at least a 1-hr walk from the Om Beach. Parts of the trekking route, past casuarinas and palms, are quite enjoyable. The trek, however, can be quite tiring as it involves steep ascents and descents. Half Moon and Paradise can otherwise be reached only via motorboats from the other beaches. All this also means that the beaches are usually empty and perfect if one is looking for complete solitude. The two beaches are much smaller compared to Om or Kudle; very few Indian tourists come this way. There are shacks offering accommodation and cafés that serve excellent food.

Temples and Koti Theerta

The centuries-old **Mahabaleshwara Temple** in Gokarna Town, which hosts

the 6-foot tall *atmalinga*, thought to convey the power of invincibility to the person who possesses it, is worth a visit. The devout take a dip in the sea before heading to the temple to offer prayers.
♦**Temple timings** 6 am-12.30 pm and 5-8 pm **Note** Non-Hindus not allowed

The **Maha Ganapathy Temple** is just around the corner. A narrow lane from the Main Road-Car Street junction takes you to a huge tank called **Koti Theerta**. There are many Brahmin dwellings around the tank. Some of these tiled residences, with teak pillars and spacious verandahs, are over a hundred years old and belong to joint families whose members can number up to 40!
♦**Maha Ganapathy Temple timings** 5 am-1 pm and 4.30-9 pm **Note** Non-Hindus not allowed

SHOPPING

The shops on Car Street have much in store for the tourist. Cotton clothes in interesting styles, such as the airy 'Ali Baba' pants and 'air-conditioned' shirts, are good buys for an outing on the beach. It's amusing to see how enterprising tailors have converted traditional lungis into trendy pants (and anointed these 'Ali Baba'). Other things are on offer too. An Italian tourist who had just visited Goa mentioned that the sarongs, printed T-shirts, lampshades and similar merchandise sold in Goa were available at almost half the price in Gokarna.

Vinod and Indira's **Gujarat-Rajasthan Handlooms** sell good clothes at reasonable rates. The shop run by the young and bubbly Laxmi is also a nice

Moonlighting: Beach trekking at night

REENA CHENGAPPA

One of the most memorable moments to be experienced on the beaches of Gokarna is not when the sun is shining but when the moon is out in its full glory. A trek **from Gokarna Beach to Paradise Beach** on a full moon night, past the silvery sands of Kudle and Om, is an exciting, if romantic, option. The reflection of the moon in the sea, seen from the rocky cliffs along the way, is stunning. Do take a few precautions before the trek: always go in a group of six or more, carry torches and go with someone who has done this trek before. Also carry snacks and plenty of water.

Besides the night trek, you can also go on a longer trek along the coast lasting 3-4 days. One such route starts from the port-village of **Belikeri** near Ankola and goes all the way to Honavar, passing through the beaches of Gokarna. Part of the trek involves crossing the mouth of the **Gangavali River** by boat to continue the trek towards Gokarna. At the village of **Belikan** after the Paradise Beach, one needs to cross the mouth of the **River Aganashini** in a similar fashion. Apart from these rivers, there are numerous streams that open out into the sea along the way. While a few of them are shallow enough to wade across at low tide, for others, trekkers will need to take the help of local fishermen to get across.

The real treat is the expanses of completely deserted and pristine beaches on the way. This kind of adventure requires quite a bit of preparation: tents, sleeping bags and provisions need to be carried. But one is never really far from a friendly home in the villages that are dotted along the way. Hotels at Gokarna should be able to arrange for a guide to lead you on the trek.

Bronze images of elephants and gods for sale in Gokarna's shops

place to pick up clothes. Both the shops are located close to the rickshaw stand on Car Street. A couple of Kashmiri shops sell carpets, miniature paintings, ethnic jewellery and trinkets.

Close to Mahabaleshwara and Maha Ganapathy temples are shops that sell various religious accoutrements. Conches of various sizes are also available, and make for interesting gifts. Makeshift shops next to the Maha Ganapathy Temple sell necklaces and strings made of a variety of beads, some brought in as far as from Agra. Bronze images of gods and elephants are sold in the shops adjacent to the Mahabaleshwara Temple.

WHERE TO STAY

If you are in Gokarna only for the sun and sand, it makes sense to spend the night on the beaches. The accommodation options, which are simple thatched shelters, are cheap (tariffs start from Rs 50) and basic. It's advisable to carry your own sleeping bag although shacks do offer cots with mattresses. Toilets and bathrooms are often shared. The shacks on the isolated beaches of Half Moon and Paradise are usually full during the November-March peak season.

On Kudle Beach

Kudle has plenty of options if one is happy with shack-like accommodation. Most cafés, with exotic names such as Dragon Café, Dancing Waves and Sunset Café, offer accommodation besides food for as little as Rs 80 per head per night. If you don't want to rough it out in the shacks but would still like to spend the night on the beach, head to **Hotel Gokarna International Beach Resort** (Tel: 08386-257843; Tariff: Rs 500-900). They offer clean rooms with spacious balconies facing the sea.

On Om Beach

Ganesh Café and **Om Shree Ganesh** are popular shacks on this beach. The swish and swanky **Swaswara Resort** (Tel: 257132; Tariff: Rs 8,500-16,500), hidden in the lush green countryside just off the Om Beach, is part of the excellent if expensive CGH hotel chain. Swaswara means 'one's inner voice or vibration',

Gokarna's scissor-hands at work, under the watchful eyes of gods

and true to its motto of leading guests on a journey of self-discovery, the resort offers yoga, Ayurveda and sessions of Satsang. The food here is a good mix of organic vegetarian and fresh coastal cuisine. Birdwatching opportunities are also on offer here.

On Half Moon and Paradise

The once temporary shacks on Half Moon and Paradise beaches, usually dismantled after peak season, are now to be found almost the year around (except during the rains). Now, a couple of them even provide Internet access to tourists who find it hard to move out of these beaches. **Om Shanthi Café** and **Paradise Café** on the southernmost stretch of Paradise Beach should keep one happy. The former (tariffs starting from Rs 50) has a relaxed ambience with shady palms and hammocks.

In the town

There are plenty of hotels in Gokarna Town if you prefer to stay close to the temples. **Hotel Shivaprasad** (Tel: 257032; Tariff: Rs 300-900), on Main Road, has spacious and well-kept rooms but is not as close to the centre of the town as the other hotels are. **Hotel Gokarna International** (Tel: 256622; Tariff: Rs 200-700), on Main Road, has neat rooms and a few with balconies overlooking a garden with palms. The baths are a little cramped though. **Hotel Shri Sai Ram** (Tel: 257755; Tariff: Rs 350-800) is a nice option that's close to the main hub. All the hotels arrange autos and taxis to take you around Gokarna. Just outside the town, on Bangle Gudde, is the **Om Beach Resort** (Tel: 257052; Tariff: Rs 1,500-1,800), which has independent, colonial-style rooms spread out in a neatly maintained garden perched on a high ground. It boasts of an Ayurvedic centre and arranges taxis for sightseeing.

For more hotels and details, see Gokarna Accommodation Listings on pages 538-539

WHERE TO EAT

From authentic traditional meals to Italian pastas, a range of dishes can be found in Gokarna. In the town, try the popular **Pai restaurants** (one on Main

Many takers on Kudle Beach for sizzling tuna and seafood pizzas

Road and the other on Car Street) for crispy dosas in the mornings. Hotel Gokarna International's **Purohit Restaurant** also serves great dosas but the service is lax. Their non-vegetarian restaurant **Down Town** is a great place to unwind during hot afternoons with a bottle of chilled beer. The quaint little home opposite Hotel Gokarna International, next to Vinayaka Stores, serves excellent fish and delicious but simple meals for lunch and dinner. Rava fried *kane, bangda* and a bright red fish curry cooked the authentic Kannadiga way are on the menu.

Just off the street leading to the Gokarna Beach from the Mahabaleshwara Temple is the **Brahmana Parishat**, where one can relish simple but tasty Brahmin meals served for free. You can make a small contribution after your meal, but it's not mandatory. **Prema Restaurant**, at the end of the street where Parishat is located, towards the Gokarna Beach, is popular with Westerners. Everything from aloo paranthas to hummus is available here.

Maitreyee Juice Centre on Car Street serves excellent lassi, cold coffee and ice-creams that taste homemade. Try the mango-flavoured ice-creams. **Shree Sakthi Cold Drinks** on the same street serves good stuff for thirsty throats.

The cafés on the beaches serve an interesting array of cuisine: American, Israeli, Italian and Chinese. Many of them have a nice ambience with low tables, sit-outs overlooking the beaches, straw mats to stretch one's legs and Prem Joshua's music in the background. The drinks and food at the cafés, however, seem a little overpriced.

Sunset Café and **Dragon Café** on Kudle Beach offer good breakfast. Fish for lunch is a good bet at any of the cafés on the beach. Service is slow and it's better to be prepared for a delay.

Dolphin Bay Café on Om Beach is a great place to dine. Their prawn preparation with salad and chips is delicious. **Namaste Café** here is another popular joint. On Paradise Beach, both **Om Shanthi** and **Paradise** cafés offer decent meals made from the catch of the day. ■

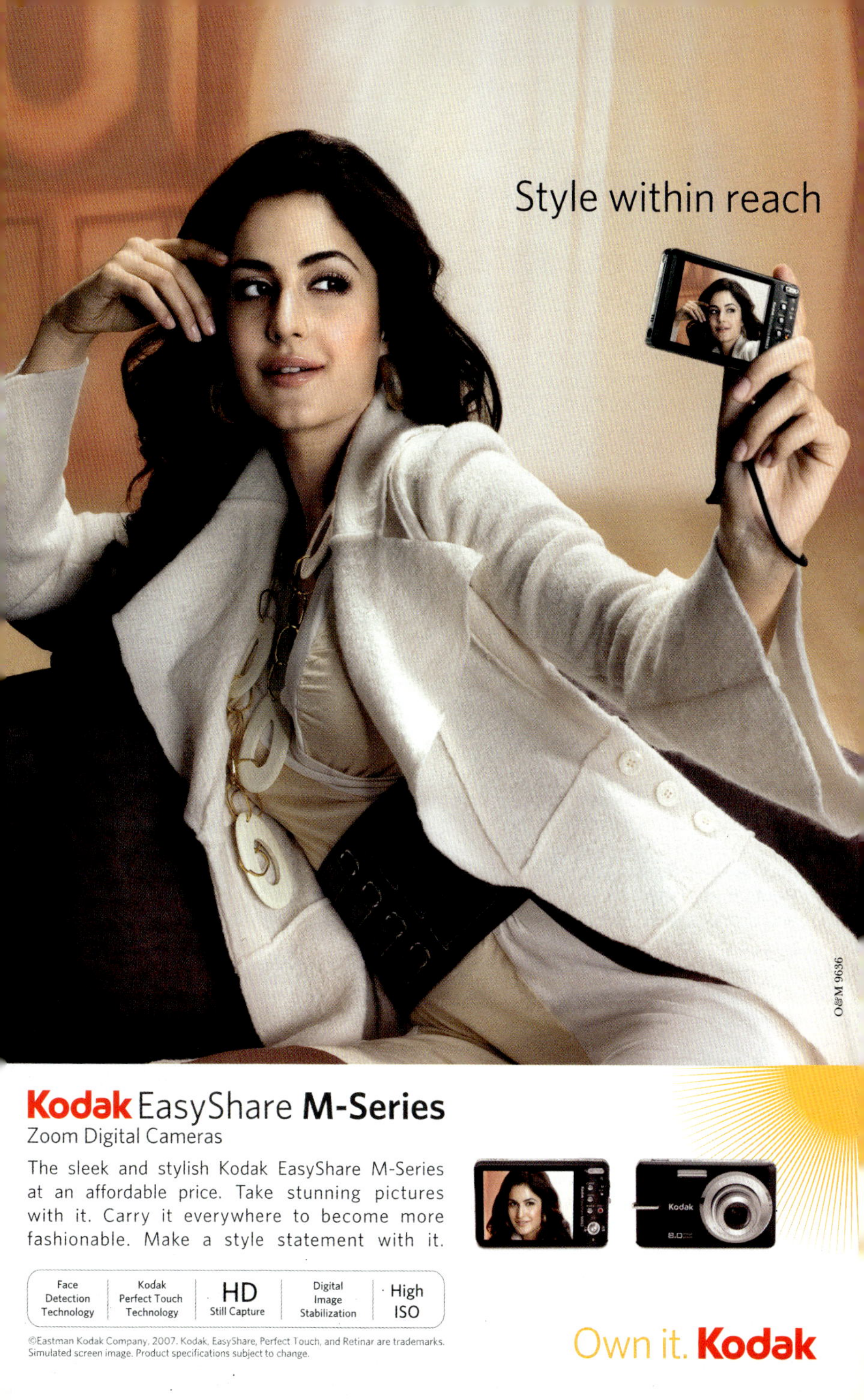
Style within reach
O&M 9636
Kodak EasyShare M-Series
Zoom Digital Cameras
The sleek and stylish Kodak EasyShare M-Series at an affordable price. Take stunning pictures with it. Carry it everywhere to become more fashionable. Make a style statement with it.
Face Detection Technology
Kodak Perfect Touch Technology
HD Still Capture
Digital Image Stabilization
High ISO
©Eastman Kodak Company, 2007. Kodak, EasyShare, Perfect Touch, and Retinar are trademarks. Simulated screen image. Product specifications subject to change.
Kodak
Own it. Kodak

VIVEK M

KARWAR

THE GREAT ESCAPE

State Karnataka
Location The seaside town of Karwar falls in the northernmost part of the Karavali Coast, just 18 km south of Karnataka's border with Goa
Distances 105 km S of Panaji, 298 km N of Mangalore, 513 km NW of Bangalore
Journey time ***By road*** 2 hrs from Panaji, 6 hrs from Mangalore, 12 hrs from Bangalore
Route from Bangalore NH4 to Tumkur via Nelamangala; NH206 to Honavar via Arsikere and Shimoga; NH17 to Karwar via Kumta and Ankola (*see route guide on page 250*)

BY VIVEK M

As the highway swirls and descends towards Karwar, the sudden change in the landscape, from the dull brown and amber hues of the hills to the lush green palm-fringed coast, partly hidden by a mist and punctuated by little rivulets emptying themselves into the sea, is both dramatic and welcoming. The beach appears in sight the very next minute and almost magically, there's nothing between you and the deep blue sea. It's the same stretch of beach that Rabindranath Tagore was referring to when he said, "...the beauty of nature is not a mirage of the imagination but reflects the joy of the infinite...".

This is just a curtain-raiser to what is to follow. The alluring islands off the coast of Karwar, close to the mouth of the mighty Kali River, make this part of the country a sought-after coastal destination. The rustle of the casuarinas at Devbagh is just as soothing as the rhythmic sound of the waves breaking on its secluded beach. Here, after basking in the sun for a while, only the perplexity over the next course of action can somewhat spoil the reverie: should one head back into the woods to feast on freshly caught crabs or slide into a hammock for a quick nap under shady palms or hop on to the next boat to watch friendly dolphins frolicking in the sea?

Robinson Crusoe would have felt at home at Kurumgad, a beautiful private island off Karwar, which has all the ingredients of an adventure similar to the one in Daniel Defoe's celebrated book. There's a 'mystery' creek on the island, occasionally visited by sea otters, and a pristine stretch of beach tucked away from prying eyes, and a dirt track leading to a weird canopy of tree branches. There is also a quaint little temple and the ramparts of a fort.

Back on the beach, with evening come food carts and a refreshing breeze from the sea. As the sun disappears behind the islands, if sitting atop one of the viewpoints at Karwar, you'll be rewarded with a stunning view of the sea and the crimson sky. Many decades after Tagore penned the words on "infinite joy", it remains an apt description of the gift Karwar lavishes on every visitor.

ORIENTATION

After a series of curves, the NH17, just after the **port office**, hits the **BILT Circle**, where one turns right to enter the town; if you head straight, the **Rabindranath Tagore Beach** falls to the left. The **Subhas Circle** is next after the right turn at the BILT Circle, from where continuing straight, through the markets on either side, gets you to the **Main Road**. The **bus stand**, hotels and most commercial establishments are located on this road.

Autos are a convenient mode of transport and charge Rs 10-20 to commute within the town. Taxis can be booked at Rs 1,200 for a day tour. The hotel you are staying at should be able to arrange taxis. To reach **Devbagh** and **Kurumgad islands**, one has to first head to the **jetty at Kodibagh**, which is 3 km from the town (auto fare Rs 50; taxi fare Rs 200), on NH17 towards Goa. Just before you hit the kilometre-long **Kali Bridge**, Hotel Bhadra falls to the right and the office of the **Jungle Lodges** to the left. A few metres after the hotel, a right deviation leads down to the jetty.

Sadashivgad Hill is at the other end of the bridge, split into two by the highway cutting through it. Autos are available in front of Hotel Bhadra and charge Rs 20 to get you across the bridge to Sadashivgad. The Estuary View Resort is perched on top of the eastern half of the hill; the **Durga Temple** and the **Hazrat Shamshuddin Dargah** are located behind this part of the hillock. To reach here, carry on straight after the Kali Bridge till you pass through a toll plaza and take a right to Sadashivgad Village. From here, small roads will take you up (auto fare Rs 40 from Hotel Bhadra).

FAST FACTS

When to go From September to March. Most resorts close during the monsoon

Tourist offices

- KSTDC
Central Reservation Office
Badami House, NR Square
Bangalore
Tel: 080-22275869
Email: kstdc@vsnl.in
- Dept of Tourism, Govt of Karnataka
No. 49, Second Floor
Khanija Bhavan, Race Course Road
Bangalore
Tel: 080-22352828
Email: info@karnatakatourism.org, discoverkarnataka@vsnl.net

STD code 08382

BEACH WATCH

The Rabindranath Tagore Beach at Karwar is a nice and long stretch of sand but is not known for its cleanliness. Swimming is not recommended here. The beach at Devbagh is often prone to strong undercurrents but thankfully the lifeguard keeps an eye on the changing tides and directs visitors to safer swimming spots. The tiny beach at Kurumgad is safe most of the time for a swim. It's perfectly fine to don beachwear at Devbagh and Kurumgad.

→ GETTING THERE

Air Nearest airport: Dabolim Airport, Goa (90 km/ 2 hrs), well-connected to Bangalore and Mumbai by major airlines. Taxi to Karwar costs Rs 1,500

Rail The Karwar Railway Station is situated 2 km from the town. Many of the express trains on the Konkan Railway route, including the Matsyagandha and the Netravati Express, stop here. Autorickshaws are available outside the station, and should not charge over Rs 20 to get you to town

Road From Bangalore, take NH4 to Tumkur and then NH206 towards Shimoga. The drive is quite pleasant after Bhadravathi as you head towards Honavar via Sagar past lush green ghats. From Honavar, one can cruise comfortably on NH17 to reach Karwar. There are quite a few overnight luxury bus services (Sea Bird: 080-22260800; VRL: 26992901; KSRTC: 09980915155, 080-22870099) from Bangalore to Karwar. Buses usually leave the city bus stand from 6 pm onwards. Luxury buses cost approx Rs 400. Buses to Goa also stop at Karwar

THINGS TO SEE AND DO

Make Karwar Town your base if you would like to spend most of your time at the Rabindranath Tagore Beach, avail of water sports facilities and also visit the temples around the town. Otherwise a holiday at Karwar is best enjoyed as a guest at any of the excellent resorts located on the islands and around the estuary.

Rabindranath Tagore Beach

Named after the great poet whose first play was written during his stay at Karwar, the beach is today the nucleus of the town's social life. Locals love to spend a few hours every evening here, chatting with friends and watching children play on the beach. Kids can also enjoy a ride in the **toy train** that runs alongside the beach. You can also take them to the **Naval Museum** or the **aquarium** close by. At the museum, you can watch a short video on naval ships and also see the models and photographs of naval ships that have been displayed.

◆**Museum entry fee** Rs 10 **Aquarium entry fee** Rs 5 **Timings** 10 am-6 pm

The **Karavali Boating and Adventure Centre** (the office is at Aligadde, Baithkol, near the commercial port office; contact Prakash K Harikanth on 09342675079, or Nityananda on 09844847514) organises a variety of water sports on **Aligadde Beach**, which is a continuation of the Rabindranath Tagore Beach on the southern end. **Banana boat rides** (Rs 250 per head per ride, for a minimum of three people), **water surfing** (Rs 350 per head per ride), **beach kayaking**, and rides on rubber dinghies and coracles, are all on offer. The last three sports are best done as a package for Rs 850 per head, which comes with a complimentary meal. They also arrange boat rides to the **Lighthouse Island** (*see page 300*).

Temples in and around Karwar

The **Vithoba-Rakhumai Temple**, built in 1603, is located on Main Road at

LOKESH ABROL

Homeward bound: Fisherfolk line up to carry a long net at Karwar

Kajubagh, just a kilometre away from the bus stand. The temple was recently renovated and the present structure seems a little disappointing. However, the **Dattatreya Temple** at Baad, which is around a century old, still exudes an old-world charm and has a tranquil ambience. The **Muralidhara Mutt** at Kodibagh has an 85-year-old structure, with a tiled roof, carved pillars and airy courtyards. A round-trip to all these places will cost you less than Rs 200 by an auto. ♦**Note** The temples and mutt are open from 6 am onwards till late evening

Bridge across the River Kali

A walk across the Kali River Bridge during the early hours of the day is refreshing. Take occasional breaks on the way to look down: you'll see fisherfolk going out into the estuary in their little canoes and hurling their nets just as the waters begin to glisten in the morning light; and wide-bellied boats leaving the village of Kodibagh to collect sand from the other bank, an activity often seen in these waters.

The **Sadashivgad Hill**, at the northern end of the Kali Bridge, is a popular hangout. At the base of the western half of the hill, there is a play area with stone benches, offering fantastic views of the River Kali merging with the sea. Food carts selling 'Bombay' chaat and ice-cream appear after 4 pm here, as do balloon sellers. Those seeking a bigger panorama of the landscape can climb up the steps to a viewpoint. The more daring can head to the top of the hill, where the ramparts of a fort, built in 1698 by Sonda kings, are to be found.

Devbagh

It's difficult to explain how Devbagh is an island. On the eastern side it's separated from the mainland by the backwaters of the River Kali but the northern end continues with the mainland. Island or not, the 2.5-km stretch of beautiful sand that it flaunts, complete with beach-beds, sun umbrellas and a lifeguard, can only be approached by a 10-min boat ride from the jetty. The **boat rides** are organised by the Jungle Lodges and Resort property, Devbagh Beach Resort; locals do not operate ferry rides to Devbagh.

The now popular **Devbagh Beach Resort** (*also see Where to Stay on page 301*)

is located on this island, offering **water sports** such as **kayaking** (Rs 300 per head) and **banana boat rides** (Rs 300 per head per ride, for a minimum of 4 people). **Parasailing** (Rs 600 per head) is conducted on a beach on the mainland while **snorkelling** (Rs 600 per head) is offered in the clear waters of **Lady Beach**, a secluded beach on the mainland. Parasailing and snorkelling are conducted only if the weather is favourable. Another popular activity is **spotting dolphins**, which appear in the waters early in the morning or late evening. Motorboats are arranged to take tourists out to the sea so that they can catch a glimpse of these creatures; also thrown in are rides around Kurumgad and Sanyasi islands. The dolphin ride is complimentary for guests at the resort. For non-guests, it costs Rs 200.

Devbagh can also be visited without being a guest at the Beach Resort. Jungle Lodges organises boat rides to and fro from the jetty, with a 1-hr jaunt at the island, for Rs 200 per head. However, prior intimation is required to avail of this service, arranged only on demand.

Kurumgad Island

A 25-min boat ride from the jetty takes one to this isolated paradise, owned by a certain Suresh Mathias, whose great-grandfather, Victor Coelho, acquired it during the late 19th century. The **Great Outdoors Resort** (*see Where to Stay on page 302*) is now being run here. The best way to discover the treasures hidden here is to get lost in the maze of foot-tracks that criss-cross this island. One such track passes through thick woods, another leads to a creek, apparently formed during an earthquake that hit the island a few million years ago and often visited by otters now, while a third opens up to stunning 270 degree views of the sea. The small cove at the eastern end of the island is great for **swimming**. Trained professionals conduct **water sports** activities here. As they collaborate with Jungle Lodges for most water activities, the rates are similar to those offered at Devbagh.

Sanyasi and Lighthouse islands

Sanyasi Island is close to Kurumgad but boats cannot dock here due to its ragged

The isolated Kurumgad Island is for the Robinson Crusoe in everyone

SAIBAL DAS

LOKESH ABROL

Fun and frolic: Lazing around at the popular Devbagh Resort

boundaries. The **Lighthouse Island** is the farthest one out in the sea, around 12 km from the mainland, and can be reached either from Kurumgad (Rs 250 per head for a minimum of 4 people) or from the Baithkol Port of Karwar (Rs 1,500 for a **boat trip**, a maximum of 20 people), which can be arranged through the Karavali Boating and Adventure Centre. The trip takes at least half a day. Meals are not included in the charges, so you need to carry enough food and water on this trip. The island is quite empty and only has a lighthouse. But if opting for an early morning ride, you may be able to spot dolphins.

SHOPPING

The markets on the **Main Road** and around the **Subhas Circle** sell a lot of local produce. Karwar is a good place to buy cashews, which are often sold on the streets by women who bring them fresh from the villages. You can also pick up salted cashew nuts and masala-coated ones from the **Kwality Dry Fruits Store** on the Main Road. Whole-mango pickles are also a Karwar speciality. **UK Pickles**, located opposite the Mahadeo Temple at Baad, makes some of the best. To pick up handicrafts, head to the **Arvind Art Centre** on Cutinho Road; they specialise in making wooden mandaps that serve as stands for idols.

WHERE TO STAY

Those who enjoy the luxuries of a resort have a wide range of options to choose from, be it a hotel perched atop the Sadashivgad Hill or an exotic island retreat. Good budget hotels are also available at Karwar in case one decides to make the town the base for the trip.

On Devbagh

The efficiently run **Devbagh Beach Resort** (Tel: 08382-221603, 655077; Tariff: Rs 2,200 per person per night), part of the Jungle Lodges and Resorts group, offers a great holiday on the island. The accommodation is in neatly designed independent cottages, fishermen huts and log huts, all well sheltered by shady casuarinas. The tariff includes

VIVEK M

Speed thrills: Karwar offers a host of water sports for the adventure seeker

all meals, a boat ride, a guided nature walk and a campfire on the beach at night. Since the resort is extremely popular with weekenders from Bangalore, bookings need to be done much in advance. Their 2.5-km stretch of the beach has beach beds, umbrellas and a lifeguard too. All water activities are conducted by in-house trained professionals and are charged extra. The resort also offers **river cruises on houseboats** that come with AC rooms, a kitchen with a cook and staff. For these, the tariff is Rs 3,400 per person per night.

On Kurumgad

On this island, **Great Outdoors Resort** (Mobile: 09448364152, 09243311079; Tariff: Rs 1,500-1,900 per person per night) takes care of the creature comforts of guests who come here to enjoy the complete isolation the place offers. Accommodation is in cottages, log huts and tents spread around the island; some come with great views of the sea. Transfers from the jetty, all meals and a barbecue are included in the tariff. There are extra charges for water sports and boat rides to the Lighthouse Island. The resort is considering re-introducing its day-cruise to Palolem Beach, Goa.

On Sadashivgad Hill

On the mainland, the **Estuary View Resort** (Tel: 08382-265988; Tariff: Rs 1,500-3,000 inclusive of meals) is for those who aren't very keen on getting their feet wet. Perched on the hill and built amidst the ramparts of the fort, the resort offers breathtaking views. They also offer Ayurvedic packages, river cruises and arrange water sports for its guests.

At Hankon

A nice option is the **Riveredge Paradise Resort** (Tel: 266742, 231180; Tariff: Rs 1,250-1,750 per person per night, inclusive of all meals, and a boat ride in the backwaters) at Hankon, located 12 km from the Kali River Bridge on the road to Kaiga. Situated on the banks of the River Kali backwaters, the location is amazingly tranquil and out here one hears nothing but the chirping of birds and the rustle of bamboo leaves. Accommodation is in cottages, log huts and tents. The best part about the resort is the variety of water sports offered: apart from the

regular kayaking, canoeing and tube surfing, wind gliding is also taught to interested guests. Wind glides are fibre-glass floats with sails and one moves forward by manoeuvring the sails in the right direction. The resort has some of the best instructors around for water sports. The calm waters offer the perfect setting for a great swim and angling too.

In the town

In case one wants to stay close to the Kali Bridge, where all the action is centred on, and yet not be a part of any resort, then the only option is **Hotel Bhadra** (Tel: 08382-225212; Tariff: Rs 250-1,250), which is located at the southern end of the bridge. The rooms are decent and basic but some of the baths are dark and unventilated.

Karwar Town has many options for the budget traveller. The newly built **Hotel Premier** (Tel: 229925-26; Tariff: Rs 500-950) on Green Street has clean rooms and efficient service. **Hotel Sai International** (Tel: 229956; Tariff: Rs 350-1,200) on Main Road, with large rooms, is another good option. Right opposite is **Hotel Navarathna** (Tel: 226927; Tariff: Rs 260-750), with decent-sized, clean rooms. All these hotels arrange taxis for sightseeing.

Plump mangoes at a market in Karwar

PRASHANT PANJIAR

For more hotels and details, see Karwar Accommodation Listings on pages 539-540

WHERE TO EAT

All the resorts feature great food on their menu, with a fair mix of South Indian, North Indian and Continental cuisine. Fresh catch from the Baithkol Port and nearby fishing villages are usually part of the day's lunch. The cooks at the **Devbagh Resort** make some great dishes out of mussels and crabs. Alcohol is available at all the resorts except Riveredge, where guests are allowed to bring their own. Hotel Bhadra's **Silver Gate Bar and Restaurant** serves delicious mackerel, seer fish and prawn masala made in the Karwari style. The cuisine is a mix of Maharashtrian and Goan styles and the cooks make use of an unusual chilli. Most dishes are bright red and spicy. Hotel Bhadra's **Udupi Café** offers decent idlis and dosas for breakfast.

Hotel Amrut on Main Road in Karwar is simply the best restaurant in town. The spread of coastal cuisine on offer here, ranging from shell fish to pomfrets, cooked using local spices and masalas, attracts a huge crowd comprising both locals and tourists every night. Try the chilli squid with chilled beer and you'll be left yearning for more. **Hotel Sai International** and **Hotel Premier** also serve a good spread of coastal and North Indian dishes in their restaurants, including *kane*, prawn masala in the Karwari style and fish curry.

Hotel Poornima on Main Road serves good South Indian dishes for breakfast. **Ashirwad Ice Refreshments** on Kaikini Road makes the best ice-creams and milk shakes in town. Do try out their malai ice-cream as well as the 'lighthouse special'. ■

Many waves of pleasure

■ GOA SECTION BY ASHWIN TOMBAT

In Goa, they say, life is a beach. The state certainly has India's most famous and justly popular beaches. It helps that these stretches of sand have everything one can ask for. There's excellent tourist infrastructure, right from a host of stay options to innumerable operators offering a range of water sports. For those looking for quiet alternatives, Goa has beaches that promise relative seclusion. Then there's the rustic beauty of the landscape, the shopping opportunities, the pubs that stay open till late and the shacks that offer superlative food from across the world. To top it all, the water temperatures are just perfect. The only problem — if you can call it that — is, with a 131-km-long coastline, there are far too many options to choose from.

We've ranked each of the 10 beach stretches in this section under different headers (*see table below*) for your convenience. If you like sightseeing, shopping till you drop and living it up till the wee hours, then opt for the beaches that score high on accessibility, food and drink, infrastructure and nightlife, such as Calangute and Dona Paula. If you want to chill out in peace, then look for natural beauty and avoid crowds. Choose Velsao, for instance. If you are adventurous or just a beach aficionado, look for water sports and safety, all of which are to be found in Palolem.

Choose your beach depending on your interests, and of course, you should keep going back so that you can sample everything Goa has to offer.

GOA FACTS

When to go The best time is, of course, winter but it's also the most expensive season **Tourist office** Goa Tourism Development Corporation

BEACHES/ STRETCHES	NATURAL BEAUTY	ACCESSIBILITY (TRANSPORT)	ACCOMMODATION	INFRASTRUCTURE
ANJUNA	6	6	3	6
ARAMBOL	5	9	8	9
BOGMALO	3	4	10	4
CANDOLIM-CALANGUTE-BAGA	9	2	1	1
COLVA, SERNABATIM, BENAULIM, VARCA, MOBOR-CAVELOSSIM	8	3	2	2
MANDREM, ASHWEM, MORJIM	2	8	7	10
MIRAMAR-DONA PAULA	10	1	6	3
PALOLEM, RAJBAGA, AGONDA	1	10	4	7
VAGATOR	4	7	9	8
VELSAO, AROSSIM, UTORDA, MAJORDA, BETALBATIM	7	5	5	5

Limited, Trionora Apartments, Dr Alvares Costa Road, Panaji, Goa **Tel** 0832-2226515/ 728 **Email** gtdcorp@sancharnet.in **Website** goa-tourism.org **STD code** 0832

GETTING TO GOA

Air Dabolim Airport at Vasco da Gama (32 km/ 45 mins from Panaji), connected to most Indian cities. There's a pre-paid taxi counter at the airport and the fare is approximately $1^1/_2$ times the official one-way rate of Rs 8 per km

Rail Goa is served by Konkan and South-Western Railways. The main hub of Konkan Railways is Madgaon Station. Vasco da Gama Station is South-Western Railways' terminus. Karmali Station is 12 km/ 20 mins from Panaji. Taxis charge Rs 500-600 approx

Road Goa is connected by good roads with all the major towns in India via NH4A, NH17 and NH17A. Goa's state-run Kadamba Transport Corporation buses and many private operators connect Mumbai, Pune, Bangalore, Karwar, Mangalore and Hyderabad to Goa ■

→ EASY ACCESS

FOOD AND DRINK	ACTIVITIES	NIGHTLIFE	CROWDS	SAFETY	WATER SPORTS
7	4	3	7	8	7
9	9	7	3	10	3
4	5	6	4	4	4
1	1	1	10	7	1
2	2	2	9	2	2
10	10	10	1	9	10
3	3	8	8	3	5
5	6	5	5	1	6
6	7	4	6	5	9
8	8	9	2	6	8

PRASHANT PANJIAR

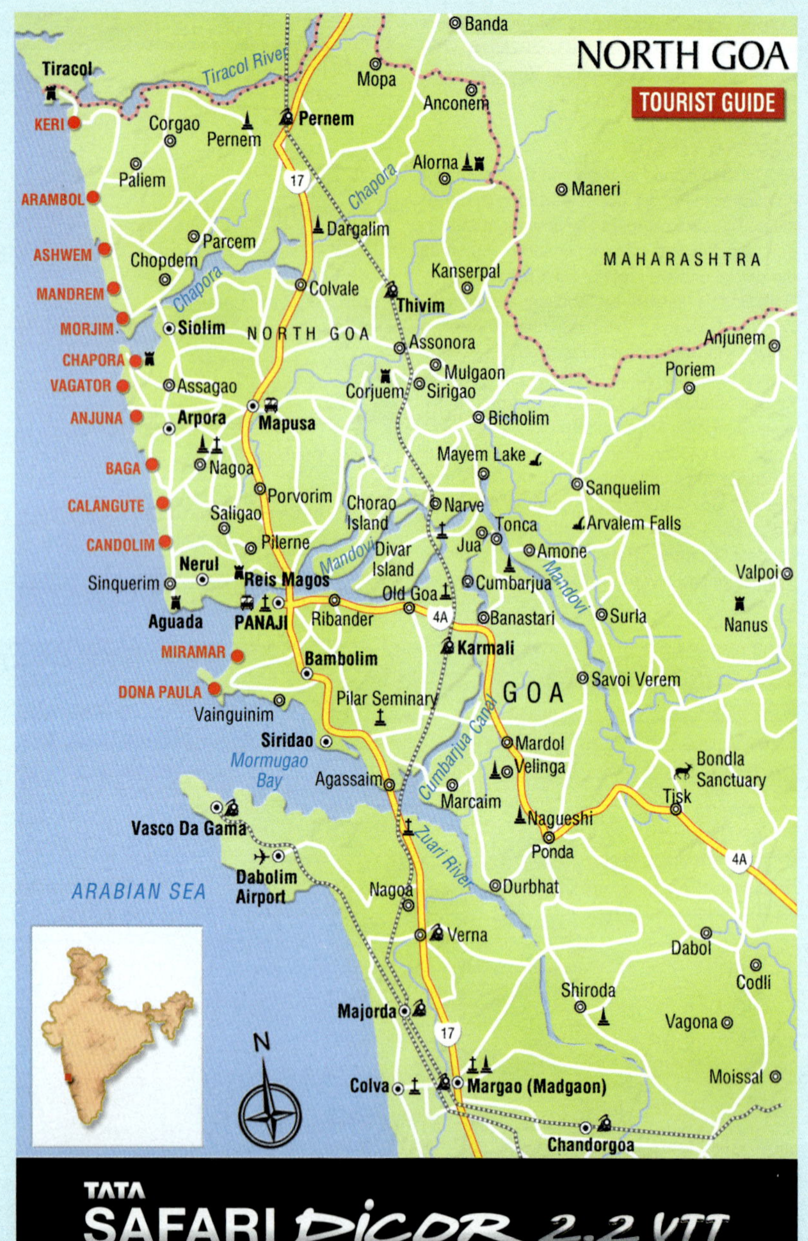
NORTH GOA
TOURIST GUIDE
Banda
Tiracol
Tiracol River
Mopa
Anconem
KERI
Corgao
Pernem
Pernem
Paliem
Alorna
ARAMBOL
17
Chapora
Maneri
Dargalim
Parcem
ASHWEM
Chopdem
MAHARASHTRA
Kanserpal
Colvale
MANDREM
Chapora
MORJIM
Siolim
NORTH GOA
Thivim
CHAPORA
Assonora
Anjunem
Poriem
Mulgaon
VAGATOR
Assagao
Corjuem
Sirigao
ANJUNA
Arpora
Mapusa
Bicholim
Mayem Lake
BAGA
Nagoa
Sanquelim
Porvorim
CALANGUTE
Chorao Island
Narve
Saligao
Tonca
Arvalem Falls
CANDOLIM
Pilerne
Jua
Amone
Mandovi
Divar Island
Nerul
Valpoi
Sinquerim
Reis Magos
Mandovi
Old Goa
Cumbarjua
Aguada
PANAJI
Ribander
4A
Banastari
Surla
Nanus
MIRAMAR
Karmali
Bambolim
Savoi Verem
DONA PAULA
GOA
Pilar Seminary
Vainguinim
Cumbarjua Canal
Siridao
Mardol
Bondla Sanctuary
Mormugao Bay
Velinga
Agassaim
Tisk
Marcaim
Vasco Da Gama
Nagueshi
Ponda
Zuari River
4A
Dabolim Airport
ARABIAN SEA
Nagoa
Durbhat
Verna
Dabol
Codli
Shiroda
Majorda
Vagona
17
N
Moissal
Colva
Margao (Madgaon)
Chandorgoa
TATA
SAFARI DICOR 2.2 VTT

North Goa: Queen of good times

Goa's most developed tourist stretch offers everything a traveller looks for

Two formidable sentries guard Goa's stunning northern beach stretch. At one end of the sun-and-sand bonanza that awaits tourists is the Tiracol Fort, located at the northern tip of the Pernem Taluka, offering a beautiful vista of Keri and Arambol beaches. At the other end is Fort Aguada, in Bardez Taluka, below which spread out the state capital Panaji, the hilltop Cabo Fort, and the Miramar and Dona Paula beaches. If you were to turn around 180 degrees, you will gasp for breath at the view of an unbroken 7-km stretch of sand that forms the Candolim-Calangute-Baga belt. It's only fitting that a fort built to guard the entry point to the erstwhile Old Goa port today guards the state's new big business zone, which is indeed what the stretch has metamorphosed into now. Another fort watches over the riverine border between Pernem and Bardez talukas. Chapora Fort, the charming, sun-kissed and unforgettable locale of such Hindi films as *Dil Chahta Hai* and *Khamoshi*, looks down on Vagator and across the Chapora River to Keri. Dreams even bigger than those hawked by filmmakers come true everyday in North Goa's beach paradise, a stretch that offers everything that a traveller's heart desires and more: adventure on the ocean, lively bars, night markets, quiet beaches and raucous stretches home to lively nightspots. Undoubtedly, this is Goa's most developed tourist stretch. But the northern beaches retain their charm because they manage — despite their glamorous outlook — to remain the seaside villages they originally were. Tradition continues to live alongside modernity, making this part of the world simply magical. ■

ARAMBOL-KERI

HIPPIE DAYS ARE HERE AGAIN

At Arambol Beach, the waves pretty much unravel the story of Goa's hippie connections, which can be traced back to the time when the first tourists came to the state, in the late 1960s. The visitors were mostly conscientious objectors to the Vietnam War, running away from the draft and the greed of the capitalist world in search of a simple land of uncorrupted peoples. Their Shangri La then was the Calangute Beach, which didn't even have electricity at that time. Water had to be drawn from a well, and most of the locals made their living by farming or fishing, or on money orders sent by a family member

ATUL LOKE

working in Mumbai or East Africa. A part of the local economy ran on a barter system. For a runaway from the West, this was paradise. The hippies made the most of it, living as simply as their hosts, communing with nature, and roaming around with little or no clothes on. For years, this idyll continued.

The Goa Government started to seriously 'develop' tourism around the time the Vietnam War ended, in the mid-1970s. Many of the hippies went home and started to lead real lives, but others stayed on — till the crowds began descending on Goa, that is. The hippies then looked for new territory, first heading to Anjuna and then to Vagator, to preserve their freewheeling lifestyle. When these places too became congested, they decided to find an 'inaccessible' beach. That was how, in the early 1980s, Arambol — a Portuguese corruption of the village name, Harmal — became Pernem Taluka's first tourist beach.

A few of the now-ageing hippies still return to Arambol. But the beach is today a favourite with European ravers and backpackers who come here because it's one of those places where you can get by fairly well on very little money. The new face of Arambol fits in with what they are looking for: alternative food, yoga and meditation. It also explains the innumerable Tai Chi, body painting and 'Learn yoga' signs that crowd the lanes leading through Arambol Village to the beach. It certainly isn't the unspoilt paradise that it once was but in Arambol's quieter parts, you'll find the echoes of a secluded beach that the hippie in you seeks out.

ORIENTATION

You can reach Arambol either from **Pernem** in the east, or from the south via **Morjim** and **Mandrem**. Either way, you'll reach **Arambol Junction**, where three roads meet (the third leads north to Tiracol). The post office, petrol pump, bus stop and **Our Lady of Mount Carmel Church** are clustered around the junction. The main **Arambol Road** leads west from here, running the length of the village. It's lined with hotels and restaurants. The main road finally dwindles into a few footpaths. One of these leads to the tiny **Paliem Beach** with its freshwater lake, located in the shadow of **Waghcolomb Hill**.

V MUTHURAMAN

Surfing with the wind and the waves

BEACH WATCH

Arambol is not safe for swimming as the rocks create an unpredictable undertow. There are no lifeguards here, so it's best not to venture in more than waist-deep. At Keri Beach, stay well away from the Tiracol River, as it has a particularly strong undertow.

THINGS TO SEE AND DO

Arambol Beach is lined with shacks and a few stalls selling sarongs and similar assorted stuff, and you can spend your time browsing through the items on sale. Climb up the Waghcolomb Hill for the best possible views of the blue sea and the surf hitting the beach. Incidentally, as is the case across Pernem, it's quite common to see a cow lounging on the sand.

Paliem Beach and lake

Arambol's most wonderful feature is the tiny Paliem Beach at the foot of the **Waghcolomb Hill**. Here, there's a small **freshwater lake** barely 200m from the sea, fed by springs, at the base of the surrounding hillsides. A dip here after bathing in the sea is recommended to wash off the salt. Contrary to the claims of some foreign guidebooks on Goa, there are no 'hot' springs feeding the lake in these parts.

→ ARAMBOL FACTS

- **Location** Arambol Beach is in Goa's northernmost taluka of Pernem, just south of Keri Beach, Goa's northernmost beach
- **Getting There** From Dabolim Airport (60 km/ $1^1/_4$ hrs), a pre-paid non-AC taxi costs Rs 750-850 **From Pernem Station** (22 km/ $^1/_2$ hr), non-AC taxis are available for Rs 300 **From Panaji** (28 km/ 40 mins), a taxi costs Rs 450 **Buses** operate from Panaji, Mapusa (15 km/ 25 mins) and Pernem every hour. Take any bus heading to Tiracol. These will take you right up to Arambol Junction, from where it's just a 10-min walk down to the beach
- **Route from Panaji** Take NH17 across the Mandovi to Mapusa via Porvorim, then turn left to Siolim. Cross the bridge across the Chapora River between Siolim on the Bardez side to Chopdem on the Pernem side. Arambol is a 12-km drive from Chopdem. Ignore the first fork (which goes left to Morjim) and turn left at the second fork. This road leads all the way to Mandrem Village, 5 km short of Arambol. Go through the village and turn left towards Arambol and Tiracol. After you pass Mandrem Beach, look out for the sign saying 'Arambol Beach' on your left

Water sports

Apart from dolphin-spotting trips, which are offered by nearly every outfit here, **Phil's Surf Club** (Mobile: 09822120803) offers windsurfing at Rs 400 a day and boogie boards for Rs 50 per hour. Sand-speed sailing costs Rs 400 per day. This is for true adventure lovers — the board can hit 30 km per hour on water. Kite-buggy rides cost Rs 400.

Paragliding and kite-surfing

Uwe Niesslbeck's **Arambol Paragliding School** offers paragliding from the top of Waghcolomb Hill over the lake. He charges Rs 1,200 for a 20-min flight. You can also take a 4- to 6-day paragliding course for Rs 9,800.

Niesslbeck also runs a kite-surfing school with Stefan. Their 10-hr kite-surfing course costs Rs 8,000.

Keri Beach

If you fancy a walk, then head out beyond the lake. A 10-km long path from Arambol meanders over the hillside, eventually ending at the casuarina-fringed Keri Beach. At low tide, you can even weave your way here between beachside rocks.

There is nothing at Keri except for a few shacks and the **Gangaram Guest House** (Tel: 0832-2249773; Tariff: Rs 250-300), better known as the Sunil Guest House after its *patrao,* near the Ajoba Temple at the southern end of the beach. Sunil has six basic rooms and caters mostly to long-staying backpackers.

This is Goa's northernmost beach, and it's bounded by the Tiracol River on the north. Few people ever come here, save for the occasional Sunday picnicking crowd, so Keri can well be your own private realm.

ATUL LOKE

Motorcycle diaries: Raring to go on Arambol Beach

NIGHTLIFE

Arambol has quite a pulsating nightlife, given the many ravers living here. **Loekie Café**, located on the road to the beach, is a cocktail bar that has jam sessions twice a week, Indian classical music and dance twice a week, a movie once a week and a chess tournament every month.

Mango Tree is a beachside shack next to the road that has jam sessions on the days Loekie's doesn't. It has a better location and better views than Loekie too. **Babylon** is a good place to drink till the wee hours.

WHERE TO STAY

Most of Arambol's seaside hotels are on the north side of the beach, along the path to Paliem. As the road to Arambol nears the beach, it becomes narrow. Bringing a car right up to the beach could be a problem, as there's little or no place to park. Also remember that most places here are seasonal.

Famafa (Tel: 0832-2242516-17; Tariff: Rs 250-400) is located in an ugly concrete three-storeyed building, but the front rooms have sea views and it's just a minute's walk from the beach. The guests are often boisterous Israelis celebrating the end of two years of compulsory military service.

The seaside **Om Ganesh Naik Guest House** (Tel: 2242957; Tariff: Rs 150-300) is one of the nicer hotels in the area. The Naik family owns the hill where their cottages are set up. The hotel has great views and clean rooms.

Piya Guest House (Tel: 2242661; Tariff: Rs 50-200) in Arambol's Modlo Vaddo is just a few minutes' walk from the beach. The road to Modlo Vaddo is to the left of the Arambol Road, not far from Arambol Junction.

Ivon's Guest House (Tel: 2242672; Mobile: 09822127398; Tariff: Rs 300-700), is near Arambol Beach and has 30

Courtesy FORT TIRACOL

The lovely Tiracol Fort, which has been converted into a hotel

spotless rooms. Eleven of these rooms face the sea. There's a restaurant here; the hotel also rents out cars and scooters.

For more Arambol hotels and details, see Goa Accommodation Listings on page 528

WHERE TO EAT

Double Dutch is an excellent bakery run by the Dutch couple Axel and Lucie, who have made Goa their permanent home. Their notice board, cheekily called 'Bullshit Info', is actually the best guide to what's happening in Arambol.

Little Italy has okay food, but it helps that it's located right on the beach. **Eyes of Buddha** has an eclectic menu and a comfortable lounging area. Another nice option is **Oasis**, on the path to the lake. **Relax Inn**, also on the lakeside path, has the best Italian food in Arambol. **21 Coconuts**, right on the beach, has great ambience. **Outrigger** in Modlo Vaddo serves great seafood.

AROUND ARAMBOL

Tiracol Fort

North of Arambol, take the road that ends at the Keri-Tiracol ferry point. On the opposite shore is Goa's northernmost outpost, Tiracol Fort. It was captured by the Portuguese from the Bhonsales of Sawantwadi in 1746, during the Novas Conquistas. Tiracol was and remains a cheeky Goan toehold in Maharashtra.

The chapel of St Anthony, inside the fort, is open only when guided tours arrive. But the ramparts afford a spectacular view of the river and the sea. The fort has been converted into a hotel, **Fort Tiracol** (Tel: 0236-6227631; Tariff: Rs 6,500-8,500). The suite has an entire battlement and a guard turret as its balcony with a truly splendid view. Even if you are just visiting, you can always lunch at their lounge bar.

◆**Keri-Tiracol ferry charges** Passengers free, vehicles Rs 55 **Ferry timings** 6.30 am-9.30 pm, every 1/2 hr ■

TRIBHUVAN TIWARI

MANDREM TO MORJIM

TURTLES LOVE A QUIET BEACH

One imagines it would be futile to go to a Goan beach looking for peace and solitude, for it's most likely that it's overrun with tourists. And doesn't everyone you know go to Goa for a holiday? But just as it's with all things Goan, there's a pleasant surprise tucked away for the skeptical solitude seeker in Mandrem-Morjim in Pernem, Goa's northernmost and least developed taluka. Over here, your cellphone won't work in many of the areas and whatever little tourism exists, it's purely thanks to enterprising locals.

The beach here stretches across three hamlets that are divided by small creeks: Mandrem, Ashwem and Morjim. These are spectacular windswept stretches of sand, made even more beautiful by the fact that there's no one around. There's no trace of the crowd that throngs the beaches south of the Chapora River, which separates Pernem from Bardez Taluka. There are no vendors, and they certainly don't dream of finding potential customers here, or they would have set up shop here eons ago. Come here to enjoy a peaceful holiday far removed from the rave scene that Goa is famous for.

ORIENTATION

Of all the three stretches of sand, Mandrem offers the most accommodation and entertainment. Most of Mandrem's beachside hotels are in an area known as **Junas Vaddo**, so locals often refer to it as **Junas Beach**. Access to the beach can be a bit of a problem as a creek that runs parallel to the waterline is usually neck-deep at high tide. However, most hoteliers get around this by building bamboo bridges across the creek in peak season. For **Morjim**, turn left after the **Chapora Bridge** and then follow the signs. From Mandrem, a road at the end of the market leads straight to **Ashwem**.

BEACH WATCH

Mandrem and Ashwem are considered reasonably safe places to swim, as long as you keep away from the mouth of the creek that separates the two. Morjim is also safe, but keep away from the mouth of the Chapora River. There are no lifeguards on all three beaches, so, unless you are a strong swimmer, don't venture more than waist-deep into the sea.

THINGS TO SEE AND DO

From canoe-rides to dolphin spotting to walking on the beach, there's much to do in this quiet stretch of Goa.

Mandrem Village

The nicest excursion is a walk down to Mandrem Village, to **Suhas Parsekar's Organic Farm**, which is close to the post office. He sells his fresh organic fruit and vegetables right there, and is happy to take visitors for a stroll around his farm.

On the seafront at Junas is a monstrous structure, now abandoned, which was the beach house of the illustrious Deshprabhu family. The Deshprabhus used to be the feudal lords of Pernem, and were conferred a baronetcy by a Portuguese king in the 19th century. The Deshprabhus still own much of the land in Pernem and have so much litigation going on with their tenants that, apparently, one day a week is set aside in the Mapusa courts just for their cases. The present scion of the family is an MLA.

Water sports

Mandrem offers **dolphin-spotting** and **crocodile-spotting** trips. Try and persuade a local fisherman to take you up the creek in his canoe.

Ashwem Beach

Ashwem, just half a kilometre away from Mandrem, is a backpacker's paradise. The beach is great and the accommodation is cheap, but, with very few exceptions, it's all bamboo and mat huts on stilts.

Morjim Beach

Morjim is known as Goa's **turtle nesting beach** because, each year, up to a dozen Olive Ridley turtles nest here, helped by volunteers who guard the nests and help the hatchlings get into the sea.

WHERE TO STAY

There are several options in all three beaches though Ashwem's 'tree houses' are a let-down.

→ MANDREM FACTS

- **Location** Mandrem Beach is south of Arambol and Ashwem, and north of Morjim, in Goa's northernmost taluka of Pernem, 20 km from Panaji
- **Getting There** From Dabolim Airport (63 km/ 1 1/2 hrs), a pre-paid taxi costs Rs 800 approx **From Pernem Station** (20 km/ 1/2 hr), taxis cost Rs 300 approx for a return-trip **From Panaji** (32 km/ 40 mins), a taxi costs around Rs 500 **Buses** operate from Panaji and Mapusa (the nearest big hub) every hour. Buses going to Arambol or Tiracol take you right up to Junas Beach, which is just off the road
- **Route from Panaji** Take NH17 across the Mandovi to Mapusa via Porvorim, then turn left to Siolim. Cross the bridge across the Chapora River between Siolim on the Bardez side to Chopdem on the Pernem side. Drive north, ignore the first fork (which goes left to Morjim), and turn left at the second fork, all the way to Mandrem Village. Go through the village and turn left. After a bend, you will be able to see Mandrem Beach

On Mandrem Beach

Accommodation ranges from rooms built for tourists in existing houses to fairly swank beach resorts. All the options are on Mandrem Beach itself.

Fashion photographer Denzil Sequeira has a picturesque ancestral estate called **Elsewhere** (Website: aseascape.com) on the side of the creek. It consists of four beach houses, each one of which has two or three bedrooms, rented out to a maximum of six adults and three children. The tariff starts at Rs 34,300 per week or Rs 5,000 approx per night during season. Sequeira also runs the **Otter Creek Tents**, each of which is rented out at Rs 26,500 per week (about Rs 3,800 per night). Rates are much, much higher during the Christmas-New Year week.

TRIBHUVAN TIWARI

Ashwem Beach has huts on stilts

> ## → MORJIM FACTS
>
> - **Location** Morjim is the southernmost beach of Pernem, just north of Vagator in Bardez. The Chapora River separates the two
> - **Getting There** From Dabolim Airport (55 km/ 1 hr), a pre-paid taxi costs around Rs 650 **From Pernem Station** (20 km/ $^1/_2$ hr), taxis are available for about Rs 250 **From Panaji** (30 km/ 40 mins), a taxi costs about Rs 500 **Buses** operate from Panaji and Mapusa (the nearest big hub) every hour
> - **Route from Panaji** Take NH17 to Mapusa, then turn left to Siolim. Cross the bridge across the Chapora River to Chopdem. Drive north till the first fork in the road. Decide whether you want to go right to Vithaldas Vaddo, where most of the accommodation is, or straight to Temb Vaddo, where there's the beach, shacks and turtle nests

Mandrem Beach Resort (Tel: 0832-2247115/ 608; Tariff: Rs 1,500-2,800) has a spectacular restaurant set atop a sand dune, affording a grand vista of the sea. Cars can't reach the resort as the last stretch is actually a footpath, but you can step straight onto the beach from the resort.

Vailankanni Guest House (Tel: 2247542; Tariff: Rs 250-500) has two rooms and three huts. The huts offer spectacular sea views. Vailankanni has motorcycles and taxis on hire and organises dolphin-spotting trips. **Dunes Holiday Village** (Tel: 2247071/ 219; Tariff: Rs 500-600) in Junas Vaddo has 25 huts and live entertainment on Sundays, and sometimes on Wednesdays. It has a fabulous sea-facing location and offers good value for money.

Riva Beach Resort (Tel: 2247088; Tariff: Rs 500-2,000) has tents, deluxe and bamboo cottages (most with attached toilets), the Nox Bar and Restaurant, forex services, airport and station transfers and motorcycles and cars for hire. Riva is located next to Dunes.

On Ashwem Beach

Sunset Point (Mobile: 09822175917; Tariff: Rs 400-800) has 6 basic 'tree houses' with shared toilets and showers, and no frills whatsoever. However, the place has a fabulous restaurant with a first floor sit-out that offers an incredible view of the sunset.

Papa Jolly's Goa (Tel: 2244113-14; Tariff: Rs 3,080-8,475) has 12 rooms, no two of which are alike, with huge balconies and bathrooms, a spa, relaxation and regenerative therapies and a nice

FOR BEST DEALS VISIT US AT www.galaxyresortgoa.com

FOR BEST DEALS LOG ON TO WWW.VISTADORIO.COM

ATUL LOKE

Goa rocks to good food at a café on Morjim Beach

restaurant. The hotel is on the road, but there's nothing between it and the beach. It's an Ayurvedic resort, so they only offer all-inclusive packages.

Hotel Nifa (Tel: 2244400; Tariff: Rs 1,000-2,800) has 9 rooms and the Sirushan Garden Restaurant.

TIP Do remember that Nifa accepts only non-smokers as guests. Host Sirus is very particular about this

On Morjim Beach

Montego Bay Beach Village (Tel: 3290997; Tariff: Rs 1,650-8,500) is a 100-year-old beach house, offering tents and log cabins, a beachfront restaurant, Internet access and bikes and taxis on hire. It has lots of hammocks. **Lobo's Paradise** (Tel: 2244394; Tariff: Rs 450-800) has apartments, rooms and 'tree huts', a bar and bikes on hire. This is Morjim's first 'hotel'.

For more hotels and details, see Goa Accommodation Listings on pages 530-531 (Mandrem, Ashwem and Morjim)

WHERE TO EAT

On Mandrem Beach, **Oasis** overlooks the creek, and is located next to Mandrem Beach Resort. They serve tandoori food. Seafood is the speciality at **D'Souza Residency**, one of the nicer restaurants in the area. It's not on the beach, but it's just a 2-min walk away and it's good value for money.

Sand Dune at Mandrem Beach Resort has decent food and a great ambience. On Ashwem Beach, **Nifa's Garden Restaurant** serves Thai and Indian food. The menu changes each day.

Sea View has good Goan food while **Antonio's Paradise** has delicious seafood. **Acacia** is a multi-cuisine restaurant by the sea. Located on Morjim Beach are **Hard Rock Café** and **Planet Hollywood**. Lobo's **Goan Café** specialises in seafood.

Olive Ridley, a British-Belgian-run beachside restaurant at Morjim, specialises in Continental seafood and great desserts. It's very trendy. ■

ATUL LOKE

VAGATOR-CHAPORA

BLOCKBUSTER ON THE BEACH

The magnificent Chapora Fort atop a hill dominates Bardez Taluka's northernmost beach, Vagator. Even first-time visitors to the beach will likely recognise the Chapora Fort from the movies, if Hindi cinema is their staple entertainment, that is. For, the fort looms large across the screen in movies such as Farhan Akhtar's *Dil Chahta Hai* and Sanjay Leela Bhansali's *Khamoshi*.

Standing on the fort's ramparts, you can well imagine why the average film heroine or hero would choose this scenic setting to break into a song. The vistas it offers are stunning: the sea, a river winding its way across the inland, and the sweep of the Morjim Beach in Pernem Taluka. Movie or not, in this part of the world, we can assure you that you'll be humming to yourself before long.

ORIENTATION

Vagator is split into two main beaches by a seaside headland that hosts the **car park** and lots of stalls selling trinkets, clothes, soft drinks and snacks. As you face the sea, on your right is the **North Vagator Beach** and on your left the **Ozrant Beach**, also called **Mini-Vagator Beach**. In between the two, immediately to the left of the car park, is a tiny beach cut off from Ozrant, down the cliff from the famous Disco Valley beach shack. This is **Middle Vagator Beach** aka **Tel Aviv Beach**. All three beaches play host to huge numbers of Israeli and British tourists, a fact reflected in the many shop signs and restaurant menus in Hebrew and English. In mid-May, Goans descend on Baga and Vagator for the sea cure (*see page 324*).

→ VAGATOR FACTS

- **Location** Vagator Beach is the northernmost beach of Bardez Taluka, on the opposite bank of the Chapora River from Morjim in Pernem
- **Getting There** From Dabolim Airport (50 km/ 1 hr), a pre-paid taxi costs around Rs 750-800 **From Thivim Station** (17 km/ 20 mins), taxis and autorickshaws are available for Rs 300 approx **Buses** operate from Panaji (32 km) and Mapusa (10 km), but not too frequently. Take a Siolim bus and get down at Vagator Junction, then take a motorcycle taxi to the beach, about 2 km away. Expect to pay Rs 500-600 for a non-AC taxi from Panaji
- **Route from Panaji** Take NH17 across the Mandovi to Mapusa, then turn left to Anjuna via Assagao. Just before you enter Anjuna, ask for directions to the Anjuna Police Station, go past it and turn left. Follow the signs at every crossroad, and make sure you don't end up in the fishing village of Chapora instead

BEACH WATCH

North Vagator Beach is fairly safe for swimming though Ozrant is not, as the rocks here create an unpredictable undertow. There is a lifeguard at Vagator, but not at Ozrant.

THINGS TO SEE AND DO

From fresh water springs to fort views, there's much on offer here.

Vagator's springs

Of the two freshwater springs here, one is located on North Vagator Beach. The spring is at the foot of a hill, around 100m from the beach. Continue ahead from the little beach here, past the rocks, and the path will wind its way around the base of the hill to the fishing jetty at Chapora Village. The other spring is in Ozrant, at the base of the hill. This is a little more difficult to find, and it's best to ask for directions to the *zor* (spring, in Konkani).

Shiva carving

Further south from Ozrant is an impressive stone face of Lord Shiva, carved into a seaside boulder by an unknown sculptor from the hippie era.

Chapora Fort

This fort, built in 1717 by Goa's viceroy, the Count of Ericia, to protect Bardez from the Marathas and the Bhonsales of Sawantwadi, guards the entrance to the Chapora River. When the Portuguese eventually captured Pernem during the Novas Conquistas in 1788, Chapora Fort lost its importance and was manned by a token garrison. At present, only its ramparts survive and even these are crumbling in places. However, it's a delightful place for the views it offers on all sides. It's possible to climb up the fort from the seaside (recommended only for the very fit) and descend from the roadside (there's a slightly precarious path from

TRIBHUVAN TIWARI

It's all in the location: The Chapora Fort offers delightful views on all sides

the fort to the road), or vice versa. Peacocks, wild hare and jackals can occasionally be spotted on the wooded slopes around the fort.

Chapora Village

Chapora has no beach, but in season, the number of tourists almost equals the number of residents in this little fishing village, set in a charming palm-fringed bend in the river.

What is Chapora's secret? No one can quite define it, but it grows on you. Cheap accommodation could be one reason for this, plus the fact that the sands of Vagator and the nightlife of Anjuna are just a short bike ride away.

Shops in the village sell exotic vegetables, second-hand books and speciality breads. The most famous of these shops is **Kamat's**, located right opposite Chapora's **Holy Cross Chapel**. The village has plenty of pleasant bars and cafés. Walk to the **Chapora fishing jetty** and watch fish being unloaded from trawlers. Like most jetties, this is also a great place for angling. Boat operators take tourists out on river and **dolphin-spotting cruises** from here.

WHERE TO STAY

Accommodation on the beach itself is limited, because the 30 beachfront cottages of the **Diana Buildwell Resorts** (Tel: 0832-2273276; Tariff: Rs 3,000) alone occupy the entire North Vagator beachfront. **Mahalaxmi Guest House** (Tariff: Rs 200-300) is a beachfront restaurant that offers basic rooms. It has existed at Vagator from Portuguese times, which is why it continues to stand right next to the sea.

TIP The location is incredible; try and see if you can persuade the patrao to set up a table outside for you

Siddeshwar Rest House (Tariff: Rs 200-300) is another bar and restaurant that offers rooms, and is located where the road from Mapusa forks, just ahead of the car park and Middle Vagator Beach. Again, this is basic accommodation close to the beach. **Dolrina Guest House** (Tel: 2273382; Tariff: Rs 200-700) is on the right side of the main road as you face the sea, just 25m before it slopes down to the beach.

Vagator also boasts of the three **Jolly hotels** — the **Jolly Jolly Lester Guest House** (Tel: 2273620), **Jolly Jolly Roma Guest House** (Tel: 2273001) and **Julie Jolly Guest House** (Tel: 2273357). They have the same tariffs (Rs 200-1,800) and facilities, such as meals on request, lockers, laundry, attached baths as well as hot water.

Ozrant has a cliff, and so offers nothing that's right on the beach. On both beaches, many places have no names but offer a few rooms on rent, some quite close to the beach. Some restaurants also offer rooms.

You could also opt for a place in Chapora. **Shettor Villa** (Tel: 2274335; Tariff: Rs 100-300) and **Helinda's Guest House** (Tel: 2274345; Tariff: Rs 300-350) are the best options here.

For more Vagator hotels and details, see Goa Accommodation Listings on pages 532-533

The sea cure

Every year in mid-May, thousands of Goans head to the beach, particularly to Baga and Vagator. Here, they camp for a few days and the elderly then 'bathe' in the sea. This is touted as a sure-fire remedy for joint pains and arthritis; the sea cure itself has been practised in Goa for hundreds of years.

At high tide, women sit in the sea at the wave line, letting the waves crash down on their backs for hours until the tide goes down. As there is only one high tide a day, only one 'bath' can be had a day. Village elders prescribe how many baths a person should have, depending on the ailment.

The theory behind this is intrinsically linked to ancient fertility myths. Joint pains are attributed to menopause and the blocking of the flow of blood. The lashing by the waves is believed to remedy this.

Interestingly, high-profile spas in Italy offer a similar treatment, called thallasotherapy (literally, sea therapy); seawater at body temperature is used for this treatment, and waves, swirls and jet pools are artificially created. In the mid-May Goan sun, the seawater near the shore is also warm and the action of the waves is similar to that of thallasotherapy pools. The only difference is that it costs hundreds of dollars there, and here it's free.

WHERE TO EAT

Nine Bar, at the edge of the Ozrant cliff, is encircled by a tall laterite wall and has loud trance music played over a super sound system. **Alcove**, also located on the Ozrant cliffside, offers fabulous views combined with excellent décor and good food. **Le Bluebird**, on the road to Alcove, is an authentic French eatery offering steaks, good seafood and some lovely French wine.

Bean Me Up is a specialist vegetarian tofu restaurant, with a great variety of tofu dishes and other organic health foods. **China Town** is set well back from the beach, at the crossroads where you turn left towards Chapora Fort. It's a popular value-for-money restaurant that serves more than just Chinese food. **Mango Tree** is across the road from China Town. It may seem overpriced, but the food is excellent. **Tin Tin** is a popular British-run eatery, a short walk up from the China Town crossroad.

Ozrant has several shacks, the most well-known of which is the notorious **Disco Valley**, which hosted raves regularly till the police cracked down. Other famous shacks here include **Boom Shankar**, **Kumar's**, which offers a pool table, and **Sharmila**. ■

Villa Anjuna

SANJEEV VALSAN

ANJUNA BEACH

SO MUCH TO RAVE ABOUT

The truth about Anjuna Beach, as any hippie worth his tresses will tell you, is that it's pretty much indescribable. Like some of the best things in life, it has to be experienced to be believed — preferably on a night when the moon is full and the sea silvery, and a lively party has the sands dancing.

The beach's surreal quality makes it even more difficult to pin it down in words. It's the undisputed capital of Goa's rave scene, a beach where anything goes, where people of all kinds congregate. There is the eccentric millionaire, the beach lover perhaps living on the kindness of family and friends, and the double PhD taking a break from her book to stare at the sea.

A sprawl of restaurants is to be found on one side of the beach, stretching all the way to the famous flea market at the extreme south end of the beach. The restaurants sell everything, a bewildering if eclectic mix of global cuisines. The flea market is on Wednesdays but every other day of the week too sees a constant whirl of businesses, with shops and vendors hawking trinkets from all over India.

In spite of all this, Anjuna manages to flaunt some quintessential Goan characteristics. It has a laid-back, 'sussegad' kind of feel, as if to confirm that it's indeed a Goan beach. Anjuna's beauty, and the lovely mix of colours that nature has painted her with, certainly suggests a blissful quality that one associates with the state. A low red laterite cliff borders the beach. To its right are green coconut trees, framing the sea and the sky in the most photogenic of ways. Further down, jagged laterite boulders alternate with little spits of white sand. Azure water swirls

and bubbles between the rocks. Life takes on a different meaning in Anjuna, and before you know it, there you are, dancing away on a moonlit night, free as the wind... just how you had imagined a holiday in Anjuna would be.

ORIENTATION

Anjuna is a long beach, and is divided into **South**, **Middle** and **North Anjuna Beach**. Much of the action, and many of the hotels, bars and restaurants are clustered off North Anjuna Beach in **DeMello, Soronto** and **St Anthony** vaddos. The road from Mapusa goes past Mazil and Temb vaddos and tapers off in DeMello Vaddo, where there's a parking lot to the right. From here, the lanes to the left lead to St Anthony's Church, beyond which lie **Gaunkar Vaddo** and Middle Anjuna Beach. The latter has its own share of beachfront shacks. To the south of Middle Anjuna is the large flea market ground in Dando Vaddo, which leads on to Little, or South, Anjuna Beach.

→ ANJUNA FACTS

- **Location** Anjuna is in North Bardez Taluka, just south of Vagator Beach and north of the Baga-Calangute-Candolim stretch, from which it is cut off by the Baga River
- **Getting There** From Dabolim Airport (50 km / 1$^1/_4$ hrs), a pre-paid, non-AC taxi costs around Rs 750-800 **From Thivim Station** (19 km/ $^1/_2$ hr), a non-AC taxi costs about Rs 300 **From Panaji** (25 km/ 40 mins), a non-AC taxi costs Rs 400 **Motorcycle taxis** (fares negotiable depending on where you get off) get you from Vagator (2$^1/_2$ km) and Calangute (5 km) to Anjuna. A non-AC taxi from Vagator to Anjuna costs Rs 100, and from Calangute Rs 150 **Buses** operate from Panaji and Mapusa about every hour. You can also get autos (Rs 150 for a drop) from Mapusa to Anjuna
- **Route from Panaji** Take NH17 across the Mandovi to Mapusa, then turn left at Khorlim to Anjuna via Assagao

BEACH WATCH

Anjuna is generally unsafe for swimming because of an unpredictable undertow, except at its southern end, off the flea market ground. But if you do not venture more than waist-deep into the sea, you should come to no harm. Swimwear is common, as is the case across Goa.

THINGS TO SEE AND DO

Shop at the flea market, dance to trance music at a bar on the beach or watch the sea's changing colours at Anjuna.

Flea Market

Anjuna's flea market began in the 1970s as a place where hippies hawked their possessions when they were either broke or leaving for home. Banned for several years after the local church ran a campaign against it (they said it was a front for drug dealing), the flea market was revived by the Anjuna Panchayat as the Anjuna Weekly Market about a decade ago, and is now held on Wednesdays over several acres of coconut plantations at the southern edge of the beach.

Most of the vendors are Kashmiris, Tibetans and Lamani women peddling all kinds of trinkets and clothes from across India. The thumb rule here is to bargain hard. Food stalls sell all kinds of goodies, from yak cheese to hummus. The market starts at about noon and people begin to leave after sunset. A nice way of getting to and from the market is by boat. This will help you in avoiding traffic jams; besides, if you set off in the morning you might even spot a dolphin. Boats come from as far away as Palolem, but there are regular services from Baga and Arambol. If the boat is too crowded, get off or, at the very least, demand a life jacket.

MADHU KAPPARATH

Shoppers stop at the colourful and famous flea market on Anjuna Beach

A walk to Baga

From the flea market ground, a path winds its way along the hillside and emerges near the Retreat House in Baga (*see page 336*). Great views and a pleasant time are guaranteed, but don't get caught out after dark, even if you have a torch.

Water sports

With all those rocks in the sea, water sports in Anjuna are limited to its southern end. On calm days, however, you can try some snorkelling.

NIGHTLIFE

Paraiso de Goa (aka Paradisio) is a trance bar that's open till the wee hours. It's set on a hillock next to the beach and offers a fabulous view. Its entry charge is high. **Primrose Café**, located between Anjuna and Vagator, is another option. **Enjoy** on Badem Hill is open till late.

WHERE TO STAY

Anjuna has quite a few options, though not many are right on the beach. **The Tamarind** (Tel: 0832-2274319; Tariff: Rs 990-3,380) is $2^1/_2$ km from the beach, but is among the best options, with a swimming pool and facilities for mini-golf and billiards. **White Negro** (Tel: 2273326; Tariff: Rs 400-1,000), within walking distance of St Anthony's Church, has a politically incorrect name, but it's also one of the nicest places in Anjuna. **Laguna Anjuna** (Tel: 2274131; Tariff: Rs 5,500-12,500), set away from the beach, has 25 individual cottages, no two of which are identical and was designed by the award-winning architect Dean D'Cruz.

Hotel Bougainvilla (formerly Grandpa's Inn; Tel: 2273270-71; Tariff: Rs 650-4,150), though nowhere near the beach, is great value for money. It's set in an old mansion on a wooded estate.

For more Anjuna hotels and details, see Goa Accommodation Listings on pages 527-528

WHERE TO EAT

Anjuna has several restaurants and the beachfront itself is an endless chain of shacks. Most of these are on the edge of

HOTEL SONESTA INN,
CANDOLIM BEACH, GOA, INDIA

A perfect beach side Resort set in a tropical haven of coconut palms and lush gardens having 52 well appointed rooms with a large swimming pool, Gym, Sauna, Jacuzzi and a Beauty Parlour. The In-House restaurants serve Indian, Chinese and Continental food. The Lounge Bar serves Exotic Cocktails and entertains with In-House Retro Music. The business center offers guests the latest in technology and equipment.

Anna Vaddo, Candolim, Goa.
Phone: 0832-6454766/767, 0832- 2489448/449; Fax: 0832-2489551
sonnesta@sancharnet.in | www.sonestainns.com

MADHU KAPPARATH

Tourists take a break from the sands to lounge by the pool at a hotel in Anjuna

the cliffs and the coconut groves that line the beach. **Shore Bar** on the beach is a good location to catch the sunset and to drink beer into the night. It has good food and great atmosphere. **Sea Breeze Café** has good food at moderate prices. **Martha's Breakfast Home** has fabulous pancakes and coffee. **The German Bakery** is justly famous for pastry and a very eclectic menu. It's also a great place to hang around. **The Jam Connection** has great salads, coffee and hearty breakfasts, served in a garden setting. **Tin Tin Tibet**, opposite Jam Connection, serves momos, thukpa and much more.

AROUND ANJUNA

Siolim (10 km)
Goa's largest village is also home to India's biggest pop star, Remo Fernandes (he still lives here). It's just a 20-min drive from Anjuna.

Siolim hosts the **Sangodd Festival** in late June for the feast of St Anthony. Then, each village ward makes 'floats' (two traditional canoes tied together and decorated) and rows them around the village backwaters. Siolim's most unique festival, however, is **Zagor**, held on the first Sunday after Christmas, when a Christian festival is celebrated in a Hindu shrine. A candle-lit procession winds its way around the village, stopping at both Hindu and Catholic houses, before converging at the temple. It culminates in a *tiatr* (Konkani play).

Siolim has a few lovely hotels. **Siolim House** (Tel: 0832-2272138; Tariff: Rs 6,300-9,700), once a crumbling Portuguese mansion, is now a heritage hotel. Staying here gives one a feel of old Goan aristocratic life. **Bay View Apartments** (Tel: 2270808; Mobile: 09823330808; Tariff: Rs 700-3,000) has 15 rooms, two restaurants and a bar. Drop in at the **Papagaya Restaurant** in Sodiem Ward for a meal. Siolim is well known for its *khubé* (large clams), which are gathered from the mud flats of the Chapora River, and sold at the old ferry point. Buy some and ask your hotel to cook them for you. ■

CALANGUTE TO CANDOLIM

ALL HAIL THE QUEEN

With nightlife, flea markets and generous helpings of history, this beach stretch is by far the biggest draw in Goa.

CALANGUTE BEACH

Few beaches can claim to have inspired filmmakers, especially someone of the stature of the late Raj Kapoor. One of the most popular song sequences in that classic Hindi film of his, *Bobby*, wouldn't have been if not for Calangute. It's said that during a visit to the beach, he saw a dance troupe perform the *dekhni*, a local folk dance, and was immediately hooked. He asked music directors Laxmikant-Pyarelal to compose a song with that tune, a request that resulted in the superhit *Ghe re saiba*.

That Calangute's name graces the annals of Hindi film history should come as no surprise. Together with the village of Candolim that flanks it to the south and the hamlet of Baga to its north, Calangute Beach forms the very heartland of tourism in Goa. It's known, somewhat immodestly, as the 'queen' of Goa's

Photographs by MADHU KAPPARATH

Candolim's happening stretch of beach sees many visitors

beaches. After the hippies discovered it in the late 1960s, it went on to become a favourite with Mumbai's biggest film stars in the 1970s. The actor Shashi Kapoor even rented a house here at that time.

In the 21st century, Calangute's visitors are busloads of tourists who tumble out of their vehicles onto the beach and into the restaurants, night-hotspots and night markets. But between the Tai Chi hoardings and the raver's graffiti, you can still catch a glimpse of seaside village vaddos as they used to be before they metamorphosed into Goa's biggest beach destinations. And that, perhaps, is what helps Calangute retain its charm.

ORIENTATION

At Calangute's southern end are **Naika** and **Umta Vaddo**, where Goa Tourism hotels preside over the noisiest part of Calangute Beach. At its northern end is **Khobra Vaddo**, where **Our Lady of Piety Chapel** is located. Within this stretch are hundreds, if not thousands, of shops, from roadside trinket stalls to Oxford Bookstore, Malini Ramani's boutique, a Café Coffee Day, ATMs, travel agencies... everything you would find in a large city like Panaji. Most of these are located on the stretch running from **St Anthony's Chapel** (in the middle of a road), past a market, to Baga.

BEACH WATCH

Calangute is considered a reasonably safe place to swim, though large waves have been known to drag swimmers out into the sea. A river flows to the north of Baga Beach. Keep at least 300m away from the mouth of this river. The best thing to do is to swim in the designated areas.

THINGS TO SEE AND DO

This is tourism country, so there's much to do, from swimming to shopping to water sports.

Calangute Church

If you drive down from Mapusa, this beautiful church with its white dome will

PRASHANT PANJIAR

CALANGUTE FACTS

- **Location** Calangute is at the centre of the Bardez Coast. It's bordered by Candolim Beach to the south and Baga to the north
- **Getting There** From Dabolim Airport (48 km/ 1 hr), a pre-paid non-AC taxi costs around Rs 600-700 **From Thivim Station** (15 km/ 25 mins), taxis cost about Rs 250-300 **From Panaji** (16 km/ 25 mins), a taxi costs Rs 250 approx **Buses** from Panaji and Mapusa arrive every 15 mins
- **Route from Panaji** Cross the Mandovi Bridge and take the CHOGM Road past Porvorim down to Calangute. You can also continue to Mapusa and turn left to Calangute. Both routes are equally convenient

announce your arrival at Calangute. The **Church of St Alex** was first constructed by *gaunkars* (villagers) in 1595, on the site of a Ravalnath Temple. Apparently a certain Venaique set the church on fire in 1602. It was rebuilt but demolished and reconstructed soon after, as it was too small for the growing congregation. The present church — the third — was built by the villagers in 1741, in the Rococo style. It holds a pulpit that originally belonged to the Church of St Francis of Assisi in Old Goa.

Water sports

There are over a dozen water sports operators along the beach who offer **parasailing**, **water-skiing** and **windsurfing**. A number of boat operators also offer dolphin- and crocodile-spotting trips, island trips, fishing expeditions and **river cruises**. (*For contacts of operators, see 'Adventure: The new Goan high' on pages 383-392.*)

WHERE TO STAY

Set in Gaura Vaddo, **Kerkar Retreat** (Tel: 0832-2276017; Tariff: Rs 1,500-4,500) is a good 5-min walk from the beach. Host Subodh Kerkar is an artist and runs a gallery here. Drop in on Tuesday nights for Indian classical music and dance performances held in the auditorium at the back (tickets are for Rs 300).

Hotel Goan Heritage (Tel: 2276761; Tariff: Rs 2,000-3,900), also in Gaura Vaddo, offers good value for money and is right on the beach. **Hotel Golden Eye** (Tel: 2277308-09; Tariff: Rs 500-3,500) is on the beach, near Goan Heritage, offering fairly good rooms. **Dona Cristalina** (Tel: 2279012; Tariff: Rs 250-1,200), further up the beach from Golden Eye, offers comfy rooms.

GTDC's **Calangute Residency** (Tel: 2276024; Tariff: Rs 1,020-4,800) and its **Annexe** (Tel: 2276009; Tariff: Rs 820-1,420) are right on the beach near Souza Lobo Restaurant, but at its most crowded part, in Umta Vaddo.

Johnny's Hotel (Tel: 2277458; Tariff: Rs 350-800), in a lane off the Baga Road, is a lovely place located close to the beach. Patrao Johnny is equally charming. **Colonia Santa Maria** (Tel: 2276107; Tariff: Rs 3,500-5,000), in the 'CSM' lane,

AHTUSHI DESHPANDE

Three cheers: Food, drink and fun all come together for tourists at a pub

is a long line of four-room cottages stretching all the way to the beach.

Villa Goesa Beach Resort (Tel: 2277535; Tariff: Rs 2,300-8,000) has huge tracts of land extending all the way to the beach. **Estrela do Mar** (Tel: 2279085; Tariff: Rs 1,100-6,000), near the crematorium, is about 200m from the beach, but it's all open space in between.

For more Calangute hotels and details, see Goa Accommodation Listings on pages 528-529

WHERE TO EAT

Souza Lobo is Calangute's oldest restaurant and also its best. It offers fantastic Goan food on the beachfront. **Kerkar Retreat** is one of the few places that serves authentic Goan Hindu cuisine. **Emma's Kitchen** nearby offers British food.

A Reverie has eclectic food prepared by Akritee and Virendra Singh. **Utopia**, on the beach, has a pizzeria, an Italian restaurant, juice bar, shack and nightclub. But the most stunning item isn't on the menu — it's the view. **After Eight**, run by two ex-Taj chefs, specialises in seafood and Bengali river fish delicacies.

Lloyd's is on the main road, just a little beyond Gaura Vaddo. Lloyd's mother cooks the most divine Goan Catholic food. Her sorpotel, in particular, comes with great sannas. **Infantaria Bakery**, on the Baga Road next to the chapel, is a delightful combination of a fine dining restaurant and a bakery. Apart from mussels, prawns and pork sorpotel, they offer mousse, apple pie and patties. **Tibetan Kitchen**, located on the main market road, has a mix of Tibetan and Italian cuisine.

BAGA BEACH

Baga is a vaddo of Calangute where Goans flock in mid-May for the sea cure (*see page 324*). It's an endless line of shops, restaurants and hotels. But the beach is still very beautiful, especially when seen against the thickly forested Baga-Anjuna Hill.

Walk up the Baga Hill to the **Baga Retreat House**, established and dedicated to St Francis Xavier in 1953. The path

TRIBHUVAN TIWARI

As pretty as a painting: A girl poses for the camera on Baga Beach

up the hill continues past the retreat house to the other side, and ends at the flea market on South Anjuna Beach. With spectacular views along the way, it's a great walk for the adventurous, but should be done before night falls. Baga is also home to some of the biggest hotspots by night in Goa, including **Tito's** and **Café Mambo**.

High action in Arpora

Arpora Village, spread across a hillock near Baga, is the place to be on Saturday nights in peak season. **Ingo's night market**, which is held here, is far more organised than Anjuna's flea market and can be much more fun. There are stalls offering all kinds of goods and services, including clothes, trinkets, exotic haircuts, body-piercing, tarot-reading, palmistry, sculpture, wood-carvings, and lots of food. Live bands play and the place has a carnival atmosphere.

Mackie's is another Saturday night bazaar on the Arpora-Baga Road, with much smaller crowds. Arpora also has one of Goa's two **go-karting tracks** (Tel: 0832-2497525), next to Ingo's.

WHERE TO STAY

Nani's and Rani's (Tel: 0832-2276313; Tariff: Rs 800-1,200), on the north side of the river, is an old colonial house. **Baia do Sol** (Tel: 2275482; Tariff: Rs 900-6,500), on the south side of the river, has cottages set around a garden. **Cavala** (Tel: 2276090; Tariff: Rs 600-3,950) is a 5-min walk from the beach, and is very charming. On Saturdays, Goa's jet set gathers here for a retro evening. **Sea View Cottages** (Tel: 2276371; Tariff: Rs 2,000), behind Tito's, is within a stone's throw of the beach. **Nilaya Hermitage** (Tel: 2276793-94; Tariff: Rs 6,580-21,150 and above), on Arpora Hill, is Goa's most exclusive boutique hotel.

For more Baga hotels and details, see Goa Accommodation Listings on page 528

WHERE TO EAT

Aquamarine, on a wooden deck overlooking the beach, has a romantic setting with great ambience. **St Anthony's Shack** has fabulous Goan food. You get to

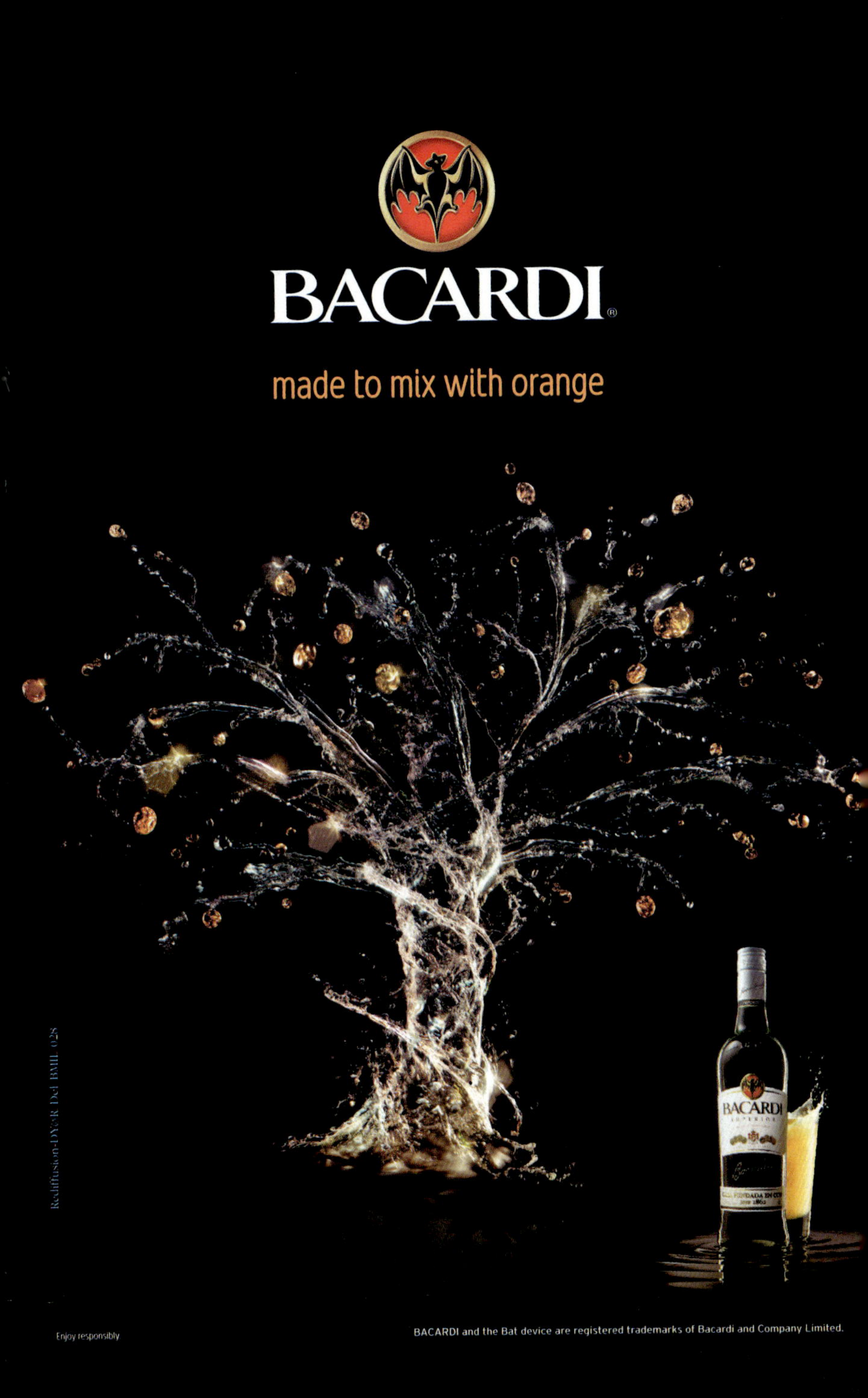
BACARDI®
made to mix with orange
BACARDI
Rediffusion-DY&R Del BMIL 028
Enjoy responsibly.
BACARDI and the Bat device are registered trademarks of Bacardi and Company Limited.

M AMIRTHAM/ DINODIA PHOTO LIBRARY

Riding the waves off Goa, where water sports are hugely popular

sit out on the beach, so the atmosphere is just perfect. **Britto's**, set in an old house on the beach, has incredibly good desserts. **Fiesta** is a good Mediterranean eatery on a sand dune opposite Tito's. **Casa Portuguesa** has a fabulous ambience but okay food. **Starlight**, at Arpora, is the place for hardcore fans of Goan food. The dishes are simple, unpretentious and delicious.

CANDOLIM BEACH

Candolim Beach extends from the Taj hotels near the vaddo of Sinquerim (the Taj likes to call its part of the seafront 'Sinquerim Beach') to Escrivao Vaddo, on the main Candolim-Calangute Road. This road and the lanes off it are packed with shops, hotels and restaurants, but the Candolim beachfront itself is much less crowded.

Candolim is the native village of Fr Abbe Faria, founder of the science of hypnotism. It's also the place where one of the first revolts against Portuguese rule was launched by Goans — that is, the revolt of the Pintos, led by Goan Catholic priests. Abbe Faria apparently suggested to the Pintos that they overthrow the Portuguese and set up a republic in Goa. One Pinto from Candolim offered them the use of his house, and here they met secretly. However, someone betrayed their plot to the Portuguese, who had the house surrounded and the conspirators caught. A few of them were executed, but most were imprisoned in Lisbon. The house where the conspiracy was launched still stands. It now houses the Boscio Hospital, just off the main road in Pinto Vaddo.

BEACH WATCH

Thanks to the grounding of a ship called the River Princess, Candolim is no longer safe for swimming, as there can be an unpredictable undertow at different phases of the tide. To be safe, don't venture in deeper than your waist if you are within 500m of the ship.

The imposing Fort Aguada, built by the Portuguese in the 17th century

THINGS TO SEE AND DO

One of Goa's most beautiful forts is just a short driving distance away from Candolim. Apart from visiting churches, you can go dolphin-spotting and fishing here.

Drive up to Fort Aguada

As you come to the end of Candolim's CHOGM Road, it passes over a deep ditch. This is all that remains of the moat that once surrounded Fort Aguada and cut the fort off from the Bardez mainland. Built by the Portuguese in 1612 to protect Goa from the Dutch, the fort effectively ended a century of Dutch domination of the sea route to India. Climb up to the fort, which lies atop the Sinquerim Plateau. This location affords a stunning panorama of the Mandovi meeting the sea, and of Panaji on the south bank. In the distance, just beyond the cliff-top Cabo Raj Bhavan, huge cargo ships make their way to the Mormugao Port.

Perhaps one of the strongest forts protecting Portuguese territory, Fort Aguada was once the first line of defence for the then trading port of Old Goa. The fort gets its name from the three freshwater springs within it.

Near the arched entrance of the fort are a **citadel** and a **lighthouse**, the first built in Asia in 1846. The fort wall, which circumvents the seashore and goes right to the top of the rocky headland, once boasted of 79 cannons.

Chapel of Saint Lawrence

On the road to the citadel is the beautiful chapel of St Lawrence, dedicated to the patron saint of sailors, arguably boasting of the most advantageous location of all of Goa's chapels. Its feast day is celebrated on August 10, which coincides roughly with Narali Poornima, when fishermen return to the sea after the long monsoon layoff. From the cabana right outside the chapel gates, built by a certain Ramacanta Naique, you can get a good view of **Palacio Aguada**, a huge mansion built by businessman Jimmy Gazdar. This is a favoured spot for taking a photograph against the stunning seascape beyond.

Candolim Church

First built by Fr Pedro de Belem in 1560 and dedicated to Our Lady of Hope, Candolim's church was repaired in 1661, and received its current frosted icing-cake look when the village Communidade remodelled it thanks to contributions from Candolim parishioners. The church has some interesting stained glass panels. The sheer white of this church is enhanced by the rich emerald paddy fields that stretch all the way across the Nerul River to Pilerne in the east, forming the kind of montage that makes Goa's rustic beauty famous.

Dolphins and fishing

A large number of boat operators here offer dolphin- and crocodile-spotting trips, island trips, fishing expeditions and river cruises. Among these is **Day Tripper** (Tel: 0832-2276726; Website: daytrippergoa.com), which organises tours of all kinds. **John's Boat Cruises** (Tel: 2479780; Mobile: 09822182814), located near Marquis Beach Resort in Candolim's Dando Vaddo, offers many tours plus an all-inclusive overnight backwaters cruise in a Kerala-style live-aboard rice boat. Crocodile-spotting and birdwatching are included in the trip. Prices vary from Rs 250-700 approx per person (dolphin spotting guaranteed, otherwise no charge); it's Rs 500-1,000 approx per person for the **half-day crocodile safari cruise** and Rs 3,500 approx per head for the **backwater cruise**. All boats are certified by the Mercantile Marine Department and have safety equipment on board; passengers are also insured.

→ CANDOLIM FACTS

- **Location** Candolim is the southernmost beach of the Bardez Coast. Its border with Calangute is a blur of restaurants and shops
- **Getting There** From Dabolim Airport (45 km/ 1 hr), a pre-paid taxi costs around Rs 600 **From Thivim Station** (19 km/ 25 mins), a taxi costs Rs 300; autos are also available **From Panaji** (13 km/ 15-20 mins), a taxi costs Rs 200, and you can also get a bus **From Mapusa** (10 km/ 15-20 mins), the closest big town, a taxi costs Rs 160-170 approx and buses leave for Candolim about every 15 mins
- **Route from Panaji** Cross the Mandovi Bridge to Porvorim and turn left off the CHOGM Road to Candolim via Pilerne. You can also turn left under the Mandovi Bridge and get to Candolim via Betim, Verem and Nerul

SHOPPING AND NIGHTLIFE

If you are in Candolim, you must visit **Rust**, a lifestyle store. From studio pottery to furniture to conversation pieces, Rust has it all. But not to be missed is Rust's incredible chocolaterie. **10 Downing Street** is a club and pub next to Taj Holiday Village. **Geoffrey's** pub plays music from the eighties at softer volumes.

WHERE TO STAY

Candolim has hundreds of hotels, but few are on the beachfront. **Taj Fort Aguada Beach Resort** (Tel: 0832-6645858; Tariff: Rs 9,000-44,000), India's first 5-star beach resort, also includes the **Taj Hermitage** (Tel: 6645858; Tariff: Rs 10,000-44,000), which was built to accommodate the Commonwealth Heads of Government Meeting (CHOGM) in 1983. The resort also offers a five-hole golf course, squash and the Taj Spa, which boasts of a range of Ayurvedic treatments. The **Taj Holiday Village** (Tel: 6645858; Tariff: Rs 11,000-27,000) has 142 rooms and 9 suites. It's located to the right, towards the end of the CHOGM Road in Sinquerim.

Coqueral Holiday Home (Telefax: 2489070; Tariff: Rs 500-1,500) in Camotim Vaddo is a few minutes walk from the beach, but there's nothing between this

Musicians take a break after a performance at a chapel

hotel and the beach. **Lemon Tree Amarante Beach Resort** (Tel: 3988188; Tariff: Rs 5,600-20,000) has a restaurant, a coffee shop, a bar, a swimming pool and an Ayurveda spa. **Per Avel** (Tel: 2479074; Tariff: Rs 500-1,500) is just 200m from the beach. The hotel has a courtyard and arranges dolphin-spotting trips. **D'Mello's Guest House** (Tel: 2489650; Tariff: Rs 750-1,200) is on the sand dunes in Escrivao Vaddo. **Sonesta Inns** (Tel: 2489448-49; Tariff: Rs 1,500-12,500) nearby is a pleasant hotel. **Dona Florina** (Tel: 2489051; Tariff: Rs 650-1,000) has 21 rooms. As close to the beach as the law allows, **Whispering Palms Beach Resort** (Tel: 2479140-41; Tariff: Rs 6,800-15,000 for 3N/ 4D with breakfast) caters mostly to those on package tours.

For more Candolim hotels, see Goa Accommodation Listings on pages 529-530

WHERE TO EAT

Banyan Tree, at the Taj Holiday Village in Sinquerim, serves outstanding Thai food. **Caravela** at the Taj Aguada Beach Resort has fabulous seafood, especially tiger prawns and lobsters, but obviously at five-star prices. **Oriental Royal Thai Cuisine** is on the way to Coqueral Hotel, a short walk up from the car park in Candolim's Murod Vaddo. As the name suggests, it offers Thai food, at very reasonable prices.

Peacock Pub advertises itself as the 'only English pub' in Candolim. It's a great place with English food, including that country's 'national' dish of chicken tikka masala. **La Fenice** is an Italian restaurant. **Rustler**, above La Fenice, is a great steakhouse. **Bob's Inn**, one of Candolim's oldest restaurants, also serves great steaks.

J-29, a sports bar, has a large screen where F-1 racing as well as premiership and FA cup football matches are aired. It's popular with British football fans. **Moonlight**, run by a couple who formerly worked at the Taj, makes typical British food and has a good selection of wine. **Stone House** specialises in steaks and seafood. **Viva Goa**, on the main road

near the football ground, serves an excellent Goan fish curry.

AROUND CANDOLIM

Coco Beach and Nerul (5 km)
This beach is on a bay off the village of Nerul, but in recent years has acquired its current fashionable name. It can be accessed from Candolim by turning right after the Nerul Bridge. If coming from Panaji, turn left onto the Betim-Verem Road under the Mandovi Bridge; turn left again at the Nerul Market, from where it's about 3 km away. A swish beach shack as well as operators offering water sports had to close shop at Coco Beach after fishermen protested against noisy jet-skis and water scooters which, they said, affected their catch. But there's still Mario Mendes' **St Francis Shack** for a drink and a bite. Ask him to arrange dolphin-spotting trips, or just simple boat rides up the Mandovi River. **Amigo's** is a riverside eatery under the Nerul Bridge serving incomparable Goan seafood. On request, the owner takes guests for a boat ride out on the glassy waters of the Nerul River. The illuminated Our Lady of Hope Church reflected in the shimmering waters is a sight to behold.

At a Candolim restaurant

Reis Magos and Queg de Velim (8 km)
Just ahead of Nerul, the road turns east and runs along the Mandovi all the way to Betim. It's a beautiful stretch, so it's best to drive slowly and soak in the view. The many steps of the **Church of Three Kings** announce your arrival in Reis Magos. The fort that looms atop the cliffs formed the second line of defence of the Mandovi River after Fort Aguada. Every January 6, a **mini mela** is held around these steps for the feast of Three Kings, which commemorates the visit of the three kings Gaspar, Melchior and Balthazar to the newborn Christ. Vendors crowd the base of the steps as Goan bands jam it up on the grounds just beyond, on the riverbank.

If you like what you see, book yourself a room or a riverside cottage in **Bamboo Motel** (Tel: 2401321-23; Tariff: Rs 600-1,500), on the banks of the Mandovi in Reis Magos, and stay a while.

The original Reis Magos Fort was built around 1490 by Adil Shah and was subsequently enlarged on different occasions. It was annexed by the Portuguese and rebuilt in 1760. After liberation from Portuguese rule, the fort was used as a prison and there were plans to convert it into a boutique hotel.

Just beyond Reis Magos is the tiny beach and cove of Queg de Velim. This beach is on the Mandovi River, so it has a pebbled, rocky bed, but it's quite special. You can spend hours here just gazing out on the silver waters of the river. In season, a couple of shacks provide enough liquid refreshments to ensure you stay longer than planned and enjoy a more lovely break than you imagined possible. ■

Photographs by ATUL LOKE

MIRAMAR-DONA PAULA

ALL FOR LOVE

What Chowpatty is to Mumbai and Marina to Chennai, Miramar is to Panaji, Goa's state capital. Goans descend on the beach every evening, especially if it's a Sunday, and the sands metamorphose into the city's unofficial recreational area. In peak season, the beach offers a stunning view of the illuminated Raj Bhavan, which is as good a reason as any to drop by. More excitingly, love and legend merge seamlessly along the length of this beach, more so in the islet-hillock to the south of Miramar known as Dona Paula.

As with all good legends, this one has many versions, all centred around two main characters: Dona Paula and Gaspar Dias. The most romantic one has it that she was the daughter of the Portuguese governor of Goa. She fell in love with a handsome boy from a poor Goan fisherman's family. As with all good love stories, their love was obviously doomed, foreseeing which they jumped off a rocky island hillock so that they could be together in death, if not in life. Her body washed up at what became Dona Paula, his was found at Miramar, and the area subsequently got his name.

The less romantic but perhaps more reliable historic records indicate that Dona Paula was the daughter of a Sri Lankan governor, and was married to the scion of the house of Sotomayor, which owned all of what is now the Miramar-Dona Paula area. Gaspar Dias could have been the son of the Goan commander at the Cabo Fort, which now houses the Raj Bhavan. There are no records about their love, but there is a plaque commemorating Dona Paula at the chapel adjoining Raj Bhavan, which says she is mourned by her husband.

Whatever story you choose to believe, go to Dona Paula, even if it's only for some angling, and you'll find the wind whispering to the waves a love story meant to rival Romeo and Juliet's.

ORIENTATION

Miramar Beach comprises a massive spread of sand to the west of **Panaji**, where the **Mandovi River** joins the sea. From here, the beach continues southwards for over 2 km before it ends at the **National Institute of Watersports**, at the base of the **Cabo Raj Bhavan hillock**. This area has a road running along it, which is sometimes referred to as Goa's Marine Drive. It's very quiet and, except for morning and evening walkers, is mostly deserted.

The **Gaspar Dias Circle** on the main road was once the site of a small fortress of the same name, which, along with **Reis Magos Fort** on the **Queg de Velim hillock** on the other bank, guarded the entrance to the Mandovi River. The fort was demolished after Goa's capital was moved to Panaji, and all that survives is a cannon discovered while the foundations of the nearby Dhempe College were being dug. Just off the circle, on the sand, is the samadhi of Dayanand Bandodkar, Goa's first chief minister, whose mortal remains were cremated at the spot. In mid-May, large numbers of Goan visitors, mostly middle-aged women, come here for the sea cure (*see page 324*).

→ DONA PAULA FACTS

- **Location** Miramar is 3 km and Dona Paula is 7 km from Panaji in West Tiswadi Taluka
- **Getting There** From Panaji, the waterfront Dayanand Bandodkar Road skirts the Mandovi and continues straight to Miramar, and then to Dona Paula. A taxi costs about Rs 200 **Buses** operate at 5-min intervals from the Panaji Bus Stand to the Dona Paula stand **From Dabolim Airport** (32 km), a pre-paid non-AC taxi costs Rs 550-600 **From Margao** (37 km), a non-AC taxi costs Rs 650-700 **From Karmali station** (19 km), non-AC taxis are available for Rs 350-500 approx TIP A Kadamba bus is available for tourists arriving on the Konkan Kanya Express. The fare is Rs 20 to Miramar and Rs 25 to Dona Paula

BEACH WATCH

The Dona Paula beaches are safe for swimming, though the small beach outside Prainha is rocky. There's a lifeguard at Miramar, which is safe except for the area near the Mandovi. Remember to enter the water at least 300m away from the river.

THINGS TO SEE AND DO

From the most elegant of India's Raj Bhavans, a title that Cabo Palace well deserves, to the many charms of the Dona Paula Beach, there's much to discover in this stretch.

Cabo Chapel

This chapel, built in 1541, has a single steeple and is open to the public only for midnight mass on Christmas Eve. What's now the Governor's mansion was originally built as a convent for reformed Franciscans in 1594. In the late 17th century, it became the summer residence of the Archbishop of Goa and, after extensive modifications in 1870, it first became the summer residence and then the palace of the Governor of Goa, after the capital moved from Old Goa to Panaji.

Dona Paula Beach

Dona Paula consists of the 200m-long **Hawaii Beach**, which is located opposite the jetty. Most of Goa's sailing activities take place here. The **Vainguinim Beach**, also part of Dona Paula, is longer, and is entirely enclosed by the five-star resort Cidade de Goa, but there are two public approaches to the beach, from either end.

The backdrop is as stunning as a painting at the lobby of a resort in Goa

The islet-hillock of Dona Paula is landscaped and is topped by a traditional Portuguese pergola, which offers great views of the **Mormugao Harbour** and the Arabian Sea to the south and west, and up to the **Zuari Bridge** to the east. At the base is a sculpture by Baroness Yrsa von Leistner, depicting a man facing west (representing the past) and a woman facing east (representing the future). This is often mistaken to have something to do with the Dona Paula legend.

Water sports

The **Marriott Resort** and **Cidade de Goa** (*for contact details, see Where to Stay alongside*) offer water sports. They also organise **scuba diving** at Grande Island, off Vasco, through Barracuda Diving, run by Venkat and Karen, located at the Marriott.

WHERE TO STAY

Five-star luxury and, in some cases, resorts with private beaches, abound amongst the accommodation options in Miramar and Dona Paula.

In Miramar

Goa Marriott Resort (Tel: 0832-2463333; Tariff: Rs 12,400-23,000) is a 5-star resort on the beach and the best place for combining business with pleasure. It also offers scuba diving. **Swim Sea Beach Resort** (Tel: 2464481; Tariff: Rs 1,400-1,900) is on the beach, with a pool to boot. **Miramar Residency** (Tel: 2464154; Tariff: Rs 950-4,500) is a Goa Tourism property with 60 rooms, a few of which face the beach.

In Dona Paula

Cidade de Goa (Tel: 2454545; Tariff: Rs 11,000-18,500) is a 5-star hotel set in 40 acres. It's the only deluxe hotel in Goa to have an almost private beach and is among Goa's top water sports providers. **Villa Sol** (Tel: 2453052; Tariff: Rs 3,750-7,000), next to Cidade de Goa, is not on the beach but offers great views. **Prainha** (Tel: 2453881-83; Tariff: Rs 600-6,000) shares an almost-private beach with the **O Pescador Dona Paula Beach Resort** (Tel: 2453863-64; Tariff: Rs 900-3,800) next door. Both also have swimming pools.

Courtesy CIDADE DE GOA

Grilled to perfection: Chefs at a five-star resort in Dona Paula lay the dinner table

For more hotels and details, see Goa Accommodation Listings on pages 532 (Miramar and Dona Paula)

WHERE TO EAT

Martin's Beach Corner has an incomparable location on the seaward side of the Miramar-Dona Paula Road, and an impeccable reputation for fabulous seafood. However, regulars say things are not the same after the owner Caetano Martins retired and went to live in his farm near Belgaum. **Sea View**, next to the National Institute of Watersports, has good seafood. The sea-facing **Foodland**, near Miramar Residency, has fast food and seafood.

Sea Pebble is on the seashore next to Dona Paula Beach Resort, with a truly spectacular view of the Dona Paula hillock and the Mormugao Harbour. **Menino's** is conveniently located in the Dona Paula parking lot. Along with its older neighbour, **White Rock Café**, it serves brilliant *choris pao* (spicy sausage in bread). **Goan Delicacies** at Hawaii Beach serves excellent seafood and offers great sea views. **Hawaii Restaurant** can't be beaten for its ambience. Set on the rocks at the edge of the sea, they offer fantastic views and seafood.

AROUND MIRAMAR

Bambolim and Siridao (5 km)
These two beaches are located along the road to Bambolim Hospital. The **Bambolim Beach Resort** (Tel: 0832-245824244; Tariff: Rs 2,000-6,300) is a 3-star resort with a restaurant under a 200-year-old banyan tree.

Just before the road turns uphill to the resort is a crossroad of sorts. A narrow mud road to the right leads to **Coco Inn**, a beach shack specialising in Chinese cuisine. A mud road going straight ahead leads to the part of the beach that's accessible to the public. Next to this is **Sea and Sand**, a restaurant that serves delicious seafood. Ask for the friendly patrao, Cajy. Continue along the road for half a kilometre to a beachside crossroad. This part is known as **Siridao Beach**. Try and get here in the evening to glimpse the beauty of Mormugao Harbour at sunset. ■

SOUTH GOA
TOURIST GUIDE
Karmali Station
Boma
To Panaji, Mumbai
Querim
Siranguli
Bambolim
Mardol
Usgao
Bondla Sanctuary
Toldem
Mormugao Bay
17
Veling
Farmagudi
Vasco Da Gama
17A
Cortalim
Ponda
4A
To Bangalore
Dabolim Airport
Darbandora
Hollant
Verna
Durbhat
BOGMALO
VELSAO
Zuari River
Tatoli
Molem
AROSSIM
GOA
UTORDA
Bhagwan Mahaveer WLS
Nuvem
Vagona
MAJORDA
Shiroda
Rachol
BETALBATIM
Margao (Madgaon)
Collem
COLVA
Oxel
Navelim
BENAULIM
Chandorgoa
Sanvordem
Mulem
Varca
Paroda
Fatrade
Sanguem
Tudou
Quepem
Assolna
Sarzora
Nagvem
Selaulim
Kushavati
MOBOR-CAVELOSSIM
Bati
Rivona Caves
Mobor
Verlim
Balli
Curdi
Betul
Fatorpa
Cavorem
Colomba
Curpem
Canaguinim
Maina
Vadem
N
Molorem
Quedem
Cabo de Rama
Pirla
Barcem Station
Padi
Netravali
Cola
Xelem
Nundem
AGONDA
SOUTH GOA
17
Tudov
PALOLEM
Chaudi
Colomb
Saturli
Patnem
Canacona
Rajbaga
Nadquem
Galjibaga
Poinguinim
Talpona
Galjibaga
Endrem
Tanso
Loliem
KARNATAKA
Polem
To Mangalore

South Goa: Of sand, surf and serenity

The southern beach stretch offers unspoilt sands and relative quietude

When a descending plane circles Goa's airport at Dabolim, one can see from the air a line of sand and surf that stretches unbroken almost as far as the eye can see. And indeed, Goa's southern beach stretch is a 26-km swathe of grainy, soft, flour-like white sand, and is known by as many names as there are hamlets along it — from Velsao in Mormugao Taluka to the sand bar of Mobor at the southernmost tip of Salcete Taluka.

Right at its centre is the village of Colva, just 6 km from the town of Margao, which houses Goa's main railway station (the Konkan Railway spells it the way it's often pronounced, Madgaon). For the purposes of this book, we have divided this beach into the relatively more quiet and secluded northern half (Velsao to Betalbatim) and the developed and more 'happening' southern half (Colva to Mobor). Further down from Mobor stretch the sands of what many hail as Goa's most scenic beach, Palolem. Most of the villages are set well back from the beach (you could call it the traditional coastal zone regulations), which means you will have to cover several kilometres to reach places that are actually nearby if one were to travel straight down the beach.

Most of the resorts are built away from the beach, which means the sands are relatively unspoilt. Only the beach vendors hawking their wares intrude into one's personal space. Most of the beaches can be accessed from the villages via tiny lanes, and it's best to ask for directions at the main market square. Usually, some enterprising soul will have a stall selling snacks and mineral water at a beach's entry points. Once you are on the right path, hit the sand and surf, and let the good times roll! ■

Photographs by DHRITIMAN MUKHERJEE

BOGMALO BEACH

FLIGHT OF FANCY

It's the quintessential, dreamy, beautiful beach, one on which you lavish an astonishing number of adjectives and still find yourself falling short. It's certainly one of Goa's most attractive beaches. It's bounded by green hills on three sides, and its sands are grainy and golden. Out in the sea are just as many charms: the Grande Island, a shipwreck that would send any diving enthusiast into raptures, and yet another lovely little island with a picturesque chapel and many old houses.

As you stand on the beach, to your right, planes will take off and land on the Dabolim Airport plateau. If you are taking an early morning flight out of Goa, Bogmalo makes for an excellent place to stay — it takes less than 10 minutes to reach the airport from the beach. If your flight is in the late afternoon, then this is where you can enjoy a leisurely lunch by the sea. Either way, plan your Goan itinerary to include a detour to Bogmalo, and you won't regret it.

ORIENTATION

Of the places to see around Bogmalo, Issorcim and the San Jacinto Island are must-visits. Just about 1½ km before you reach Bogmalo, there is a fork in the road. Go left and you reach a tiny cove with a little beach, called **Issorcim** or Hollant. **Sao Jacinto Island** is about 5 km from Bogmalo, in the Mormugao Bay, off the Panaji-Vasco Highway, to which it's connected by a causeway.

BEACH WATCH

Bogmalo is mostly safe for swimming though the surf can be a bit dodgy. There's a lifeguard, but only at the designated swimming area. In other parts, it's best to venture no more than waist-deep. At Hollant, there's a stream on one side, so it's best to stay in the waist-deep area when the tide is going out. There's no lifeguard here.

THINGS TO SEE AND DO

Bogmalo offers a comprehensive water sports experience. One of Goa's two PADI diving centres is based here (the other is at Miramar). Besides, Bogmalo has been the venue for two Enterprise Class World Championships in sailing.

Issorcim Beach

This beach is completely bereft of tourists (you'll only see villagers here), and is particularly good for fishing. It has just one restaurant, the **Copacabana Bar and Restaurant**, at the end of the road to Hollant, which is closed most of the time. This is also the only place apart from Grande Island where plate coral grows. Not a particularly attractive species, you'll be able to see it only on days when the water is exceptionally clear, with a visibility of 2m or more. If you're feeling fit, go on a trek from Bogmalo to Hollant for superb views of the Mormugao Coast.

Sao Jacinto Island

This small island has old houses and a picturesque **chapel**. Beyond it, a path goes up the hill to a **lookout point** that may have originally been a Kadamba-period lighthouse.

The island was partly fortified to ward off the possibility of it being used as a staging post for an assault on the Mormugao Fort. In the middle of the village is an **ancient spring** still used by villagers for their drinking water needs.

Chicalim

Further up the road towards Vasco from Sao Jacinto Island is an islet with a crucifix on it, locally called San Antonio. Here, at low tide, hundreds of women and men collect juicy clams or *teesria* from the shallow waters. These go into a delectable coconut milk curry.

Water sports

Goa Diving (Mobile: 09822100380; Tel: 2538204), run by Scotsman Willie Downey, offers casual diving as well as PADI open water courses. Diving is organised at half a dozen sites around Grande Island, including a 20th century wreck. Willie also runs a diving operation in Agatti (*see page 220*) in Lakshadweep.

A single dive costs Rs 1,600 while it's Rs 2,400 for two dives; the fee for the PADI open water course (3-5 days) is Rs 17,000. At the end of the course, you get

A guest house on the beach

→ BOGMALO FACTS

- **Location** Bogmalo Beach is just south of Goa's Dabolim Airport and Vasco da Gama City in Mormugao Taluka
- **Getting There** From Dabolim Airport (4 km), a pre-paid taxi costs Rs 100 **From Vasco** (10 km), buses operate at 30-min intervals from the Vasco Bus Stand, and stop outside the airport on the way to Bogmalo. The four-lane highway past the airport continues straight on towards Verna; a few kilometres ahead, a road to the right leads to Bogmalo. Make sure to take the left fork on the slope, otherwise you will reach Issorcim (Hollant) instead **From Vasco Station** Non-AC taxis (Rs 150-200) and rickshaws are available **From Madgaon Station** (27 km/ $^1/_2$ hr), a pre-paid non-AC taxi costs around Rs 450-500 **From Panaji** (28 km/ $^1/_2$ hr), a non-AC taxi costs Rs 450-500

Testing the waters on Bogmalo Beach

a certificate that entitles you to dive anywhere in the world.

WHERE TO STAY

Towering above the southern end of the beach, the **Bogmalo Beach Resort** (Tel: 0832-2538222-35; Tariff: Rs 6,000-10,000) was lucky to be built before coastal regulation zone restrictions came into force. Its unique construction enables all its 123 rooms to face the sea. **Chances**, the resort's slot machine casino, is open from 10 am to 1.30 am.

Coconut Creek (Tel: 2538090/ 100; Tariff: Rs 4,500-9,500) is a hotel set in green surroundings. The beach is a few minutes away. **Joet's Guest House** (Tel: 2538036; Mobile: 09860765337; Tariff: Rs 2,750), right on the beach, is a fabulous place to stay. Only, it's mostly full, so book in advance. **Sarita Guest House** (Tel: 2538965; Mobile: 09890134533; Tariff: Rs 1,100-2,000) is a charming, family-run guest house on the beach, offering comfortable rooms.

Raj Resorts (Tel: 2538177/ 688; Mobile: 09823233525; Tariff: Rs 1,200-4,400), a little way up the hill, offers sea views from the room balconies.

For more Bogmalo hotels and details, see Goa Accommodation Listings on page 533

WHERE TO EAT

Full Moon Kneipe, outside Bogmalo Beach Resort, specialises in seafood, especially tiger prawns and lobsters. **Joet's** is halfway down the beach. At the end of the main Bogmalo Road, take a right to get to this restaurant, which has excellent food and views. **D'Mello's** at Coconut Creek Resort is owned by Joet's patrao Salvy. It offers Goan, Italian and English food. Take a right turn soon after the St Cosmedamaio Church and carry on till the end of the road where you will find the resort. Raj Resorts has **Jaipur Palace** and **Captain's Cabin Bar**. ■

Courtesy PARK HYATT RESORT AND SPA

VELSAO TO BETALBATIM

WHERE THE FIELDS MEET THE DUNES

Velsao is for the solitude seeker — it's all wooded hills, coconut groves and white sands. The beach sees no crowds, except for the odd picnicking group on a Sunday, and has relatively few resorts. And for this, one has to thank the rice fields bordering the beach, impressively starting where the sand dunes end. Though things are slowly changing now — at least one resort has begun to come up every year — the stretch from Velsao to Betalbatim is still a haven for someone looking for a quiet getaway in Goa.

VELSAO BEACH

This quiet seaside village was short-listed, along with the high-profile Fort Aguada Plateau and the state capital Panaji, as a venue for the International Film Festival of India (IFFI), which moved permanently to Goa from New Delhi in 2004. Panaji finally won, but it should tell you something about how beautiful Velsao is.

Nestled in a valley below the Verna Plateau, Velsao has been blessed with nature's bounty. Even the seas off Velsao are rich, as an event from August 1999 indicates: a school of sardines, obviously swimming close to the shore, got washed ashore by strong monsoon waves. That day, fishermen sold 60 baskets of sardines without using a net!

Velsao's seafront is dotted with fishing huts and canoes. The only blot on the landscape here is the gigantic Zuari Agro Chemicals fertiliser plant, located on the hillside above Velsao. Locals agitated against the plant because of the pollution it created, and as a result, the plant authorities were forced to clean up their act. It has since been winning environmental awards every few years, but it remains an eyesore.

BEACH WATCH

Velsao is a reasonably safe place to swim, as long as you keep away from the tiny creek here. But there's no lifeguard, so unless you are a strong swimmer, be sure not to venture more than waist-deep into the sea.

THINGS TO SEE AND DO

The nicest thing to do is walk down to the end of the beach, towards the Zuari Agro Plant. Sea eagles soar in the sky above, and in the sea you can see canoes and trawlers out fishing.

Velsao Chapel

It's a rather long walk to the chapel, located on the **Hill of Remedies**, or Rameth Dongor, but this is a place you must visit if you would like to see the lush Salcete countryside. Reach there at just about 5.45 pm, and you will be treated to the perfect view of a glorious Goan sunset.

The **chapel of Nossa Senhora dos Remedios** or Our Lady of Cures comes alive every year on January 6, when the villagers of Cansaulim, Velsao and Quelim celebrate the **Feast of Three Kings** (the wise men from the East who followed the star to Bethlehem and adorned the infant Jesus with gold, frankincense and myrrh). This day sees a colourful display of traditional village pageantry.

→ VELSAO FACTS

- **Location** Velsao Beach is a short distance south-east of Bogmalo and Hollant on the Mormugao Coast. It's close to Verna (4 km), and between Panaji and Margao on NH17
- **Getting There** From Dabolim Airport (17 km/ 20 mins), a pre-paid taxi costs around Rs 300. Buses operate from Vasco and Margao (the closest big towns) about every half hour **From Madgaon Station** (25 km/ $^1/_2$ hr), a pre-paid taxi should cost around Rs 450-500 **From Vasco da Gama** (24 km/ $^1/_2$ hr), taxis and autorickshaws will be available for around Rs 450-500 **From Panaji** (30 km/ 45 mins), taxis and autos cost about Rs 600
- **Route from Panaji** Drive down NH17 via Bambolim, Zuari Bridge and Cortalim to Verna. Turn right from the Verna Bypass and look for signs for Cansaulim. Once in Cansaulim Market, ask for the road to Velsao, just a few kilometres away

WHERE TO STAY AND EAT

As the only resort here, known as the Horizon Beach Resort, has been shut down, you'll have to stay at nearby Arossim (*see below*) while visiting Velsao. There are some nice taverns and two restaurants at Velsao, but none of them is really an 'eating-out' place.

AROSSIM BEACH

Located to the south of Velsao, Cansaulim is a large village with a beautiful and accessible stretch of beach in Arossim. The latter is the home of Tristao Braganza Cunha, the father of Goan nationalism. Braganza was the pioneer of the freedom struggle in Goa. He studied in Paris, where he came in touch with other students who went on to become leaders, like China's Zhou en Lai and Vietnam's Ho Chi Minh. He was also a close associate of Romain Rolland, the first Western author to write a biography of Mahatma Gandhi. Cunha's ancestral house is in the vaddo of Quelim.

MADHU KAPPARATH

Goa's favourite sport, football, in progress on Utorda Beach

BEACH WATCH

Arossim is considered a reasonably safe place to swim. There's no lifeguard here, so unless you are a strong swimmer, don't venture in more than waist-deep.

THINGS TO SEE AND DO

Explore the countryside and enjoy the slow rhythms of life in this slice of Goa.

Cansaulim Church

There is some uncertainty about when Cansaulim's Church of Sao Tome (St Thomas the Apostle) was built. Some say it was constructed in 1581 while others claim it was 1588. This church was definitely rebuilt in 1632, and participates in the **Feast of the Magi** celebrations with Velsao and Quelim chapels.

Casa dos Roldao de Souza

The yellow, white and blue Maison Rodesa is not a very old house (it was constructed in the early 20th century), but it's well preserved and built according to a modified Manueline design. Unless somebody is home (the owners live in Margao), you won't be able to go inside.

WHERE TO STAY

Here you have to choose between a 5-star and a 3-star resort. **Park Hyatt Goa Resort** (Tel: 0832-2721234; Tariff: On request) has a large swimming pool with a water slide, several speciality restaurants, an Ayurvedic treatment centre, and an activity centre for children. It offers lots of activities on water.

The only other option here is the **Heritage Village Club** (Tel: 6694444; Tariff: Rs 17,500-26,250 for 3N/ 4D), which has an impressive number of rooms (100 in all) and an Ayurveda spa, offering comprehensive Ayurvedic treatments.

For more Arossim hotels and details, see Goa Accommodation Listings on pages 537-538

TRIBHUVAN TIWARI

Flocking together on Utorda Beach

→ AROSSIM FACTS

- **Location** Arossim Beach is just south of Velsao Beach on the Mormugao Coast, and to the north of Utorda Beach in Salcete
- **Getting There** From Dabolim Airport (20 km/ 1/2 hr), a pre-paid taxi costs Rs 350 approx **From Vasco Station** (25 km/ 1/2 hr), taxis and autorickshaws are available for around Rs 450-500 **From Madgaon Station** (23 km/ 1/2 hr), a pre-paid taxi costs Rs 400-450. There are buses connecting Vasco and Margao with Arossim every 30 mins **From Panaji** (35 km/ 45 mins), a taxi costs around Rs 700-750
- **Route from Panaji** Drive down NH17 via Bambolim, Zuari Bridge and Cortalim to Verna. Turn right from Verna Bypass and look for signs for Cansaulim. Once in Cansaulim's market, it's best to ask locals for the road to Arossim Beach

WHERE TO EAT

Mardol is a speciality Goan restaurant at Verna, and it's worth going out of your way for. **Da Luigi** is the Italian restaurant at Park Hyatt. It serves tasty pasta, authentic trattoria-style specialities and yummy pizzas from its wood-fired ovens. The **Market Grill**, also at the Hyatt, prepares fresh seafood and 'masala' delights, with tandoori and Goan dishes being the highlights.

MAJORDA BEACH

Majorda is actually a large village, where beachside accommodation is limited to three places. This means that the beach is pretty much serene.

BEACH WATCH

Majorda and Betalbatim are generally safe beaches. A few deaths by drowning were reported from Utorda a few years ago. There's no lifeguard at any of the beaches, so unless you are a strong swimmer, do not venture more than waist-deep into the sea.

THINGS TO SEE AND DO

Apart from Majorda, Betalbatim and Utorda are two beaches that promise seclusion and beauty in this stretch.

Mae de Deus Church

Before the villagers of Majorda were converted, they worshipped a devi called 'Mahamaya', meaning Great Mother. After conversion, Mahamaya became Mae de Deus — Mother of God. Founded in 1588, Majorda's Mae de Deus Church was set on fire by the Marathas during their invasion of Goa in April 1738. It was rebuilt in 1739.

Utorda Beach

This is the beach immediately north of Majorda and is the northernmost beach

TRIBHUVAN TIWARI

Sunset beach: On Majorda, a serene stretch of sand in South Goa

on the Salcete Coast. To get here, continue straight up the road from Majorda towards Velsao. Utorda is a few kilometres north of here.

Betalbatim Beach

Betalbatim is further south from Majorda (5 km/ 15 mins), and also borders Colva (3 km south). The village gets its name from the *devchaar* (powerful demon) Betaal, whose temple existed at Fardo Vaddo before the local population converted to Christianity in the 16th century. Its most famous resident — non-resident is more accurate though — is India's cricket maestro Sachin Tendulkar, who comes to his holiday house here a couple of times a year. Walk down to Betalbatim's **Church of Our Lady of Remedios**, built by the Jesuits in 1630. It was reconstructed in 1807.

WHERE TO STAY

There are several options on this stretch, from 5-star hotels to small resorts.

In Majorda

Majorda Beach Resort (Tel: 0832-2754871-80; Tariff: Rs 4,950-10,800) is South Goa's first 5-star hotel. There are a number of reasonably priced Goan restaurants outside the resort.

Palm View Inn (Tel: 2881591; Mobile: 09822798717; Tariff: Rs 1,500-2,000), located on the Majorda Beach Resort Road, is a mid-range option here. It's near the beach and has a restaurant, a bar and a swimming pool. **Shangri La** (Tel: 2881542/ 47; Tariff: Rs 800-1,500) is a lovely family-run place just outside the Majorda Beach Resort. It's just a 5-min walk from the beach.

In Utorda

Utorda has three beachfront resorts. The 5-star **Kenilworth Beach Resort** (Tel: 2754180-04; Tariff: Rs 3,200-10,500) has more than 100 rooms.

The lovely **Casa Ligorio** (Tel: 2755405; Tariff: Rs 1,500-3,000) is much smaller with nine rooms. It's a few minutes walk from the beach.

MADHU KAPPARATH

At a beach shack on Utorda, guests look at dinner options

In Betalbatim

Nanu Resort (Tel: 2880111-19; Tariff: Rs 2,200-5,000) is on the beach and has 100 rooms. **Coconut Grove** (Tel: 2880123; Tariff: Rs 4,500-12,500) is a 4-star hotel with all modern facilities imaginable. An additional factor in favour of both resorts is that they have good restaurants.

→ MAJORDA FACTS

- **Location** Majorda Beach is south of Utorda and north of Betalbatim in Salcete
- **Getting There** From Dabolim Airport (26 km/ 40 mins), a pre-paid taxi costs around Rs 450 **From Madgaon Station** (14 km/ 20 mins), taxis and autos cost about Rs 350. Buses leave from Margao every half hour **From Panaji** (37 km/ 45 mins), a taxi costs around Rs 700-750
- **Route from Panaji** Drive down NH17 and, after Verna Bypass, turn right at the Tata Auto showroom. Look for signs for Majorda Beach Resort **Route from Margao** Drive to Colva, and turn right to Majorda via Betalbatim

For more Majorda, Utorda and Betalbatim hotels and details, see Goa Accommodation Listings on page 538

WHERE TO EAT

Coconut Grove at Adao Vaddo is a multi-cuisine restaurant serving good tandoori food. **Fresh Up**, on the road to Majorda Beach Resort, specialises in seafood. **Five Flowers**, on the road from the highway to the resort, is a popular restaurant.

Zeebop on the Sea at Utorda is Goa's best beach shack. It specialises in superlative seafood. It has showers and toilets, so it can be a day-long hangout.

Betalbatim has **Men Mar**, offering good seafood, on Colva-Majorda Road. But the best is **Martin's Corner**. It's nowhere near the beach, but its outstanding cuisine means it shouldn't be missed. They specialise in seafood, but there is great vegetarian fare as well. It's Sachin Tendulkar's favourite restaurant, and apparently, when the menu was being designed for his signature restaurant in Mumbai, Tendulkar's, the cricketer insisted that some of the items be made the same way as at Martin's. ■

Photographs by ATUL LOKE

COLVA TO MOBOR-CAVELOSSIM

BEACH, UNINTERRUPTED

This stretch easily qualifies as the most versatile in Goa. There's something for everyone: quietude for the holidaymaker looking for solitude, nightspots that stay open till early mornings for those looking to shake a leg, and shops that sell an astonishing array of goods for the compulsive shopper. For the adventure seeker, there's biking, water sports such as windsurfing and jet-skiing, and dolphin-spotting and crocodile-spotting rides. What more could one ask for?

COLVA BEACH

Until tourism came along in the form of a handful of resorts, the peaceful Colva Beach was a place for an evening stroll for Margao's denizens. Crowds would flock to this beach only twice a year: in summer, for the sea cure, and in October, to seek the blessings of Infant Jesus at the Colva Church. From such modest beginnings, Colva has now grown to become South Goa's main beach.

Yet, what makes Colva unique is the fact that it has managed to hold on to its charms despite the crowds that throng it at all times of the year. For one, it's always deserted in the mornings. Two, even after the tourists arrive, if you take the trouble of walking half a kilometre up or down the beach, you'll be able to claim your own space.

Seemingly without any contradiction, Colva also boasts of several shopping opportunities. Goa's main railway station is nearby, as are Margao's shops. The beach's shacks and restaurants remain open till the wee hours of the morning. Colva also has a huge number of hotels, many of which are located close to the beach. If looking for a holiday that presents a judicious blend of tranquility and vivaciousness, then Colva is the best beach for you.

ORIENTATION

The road from Margao goes past a post office and **Our Lady of Mercy Church** before reaching a crossroad, or the **Char Rasta**. The right turn leads to a sprinkling of hotels and cafés in **Colva Village**. The left turn will take you to **Sernabatim**, **Benaulim** and **Mobor Beach**, located at the end of the Salcete Coast. Straight ahead from Char Rasta, the road ends in a broad circle at **Colva Beach**. There's a **car park** to the left. The Tourist Office, hotels and shops are clustered around the circle. Just before the circle is a right turn to Betalbatim and the Velsao-Majorda-Utorda-Betalbatim stretch.

→ COLVA FACTS

- **Location** Colva Beach is 6 km west of Margao, to the south of Betalbatim Beach (3 km) and to the north of Sernabatim (2 km) and Benaulim (2 km) beaches in Salcete Taluka
- **Getting There** From Dabolim Airport (26 km/ 30-40 mins), a pre-paid non-AC taxi costs around Rs 400-450
From Madgaon Station (8 km), a pre-paid taxi costs about Rs 150-200. Buses from Margao's bus stand, opposite Kamat Hotel at the old market, leave every 15 to 30 mins for Colva. An auto from Margao's Municipal Gardens costs around Rs 100. Shared taxis are also available here
From Panaji (36 km/ 45 mins), a taxi costs Rs 700-750
- **Route from Panaji** Drive down NH17 to Margao via Bambolim, Verna and Nuvem. A road goes right to Colva at the roundabout next to the bus stand opposite Kamat Hotel, just before you enter Margao

BEACH WATCH

Colva and Sernabatim are considered safe places to swim. But, unless you are a strong swimmer, don't venture more than waist-deep into the sea.

THINGS TO SEE AND DO

Colva Beach has plenty of shacks and is crowded with revellers in peak season. Grab a table in one of the sea-facing shacks, get your feni and stuffed papad, and enjoy the breeze and the view. If you want a swim, Sernabatim is quieter, but Colva is fine too — if you don't mind the crowds, that is. Walk north along the beach towards the boats lined up on the sand for a glimpse of a fishing village.

Boat trips

Many boatmen on the beach offer dolphin-spotting and crocodile-spotting trips, and island tours. Apart from these and canoe rides, there's little else by way of water sports here. Boatmen charge Rs 100 per person for the boat trips.

Colva Church

The church, dedicated to **Our Lady of Merces** (Mercy), was built in 1581 and then rebuilt in the 18th century. The greatest object of veneration here is not the patron saint of the church but a **statue of Menino (infant) Jesus**. This is said to have been found by a Jesuit priest, Fr Bento Ferreira, on the coast of Mozambique where he was shipwrecked. He managed to survive, a miracle he attributed to the statue. Fr Ferreira brought the statue to Goa and to Colva Church in 1648, when he was posted there. Here, the statue is said to have worked many miracles. Each year, on the second Monday of October, the statue is taken out from the church vault and dressed in finery for **Fama**, a festival that attracts thousands of believers to the church. After being taken around the village in a procession, it's reverently placed in the church.

Fun is on the cards: At a shack on Goa's most versatile beach stretch

Sernabatim Beach

Sernabatim gives you all the peace and quiet of a secluded beach, with inexpensive to mid-range seaside accommodation. There is nothing here save for the beach, which also means that village life is very much alive despite the tourist boom. A little walk around may yield some wonderful sights and pleasant conversations. If you get bored of the quiet, the shops, nightlife and crowds of Colva are just a kilometre away.

NIGHTLIFE

Even the queen of the South enjoys her beauty sleep. Colva has barely enough nightlife to deserve the title of queen. The **Gatsby Pub** has a 24-hr coffee shop. **Outback Bar and Restaurant** is open till the wee hours.

WHERE TO STAY

Colva has a range of budget and mid-range hotels but no 5-star resorts.

On Colva Beach

Colva's first resort, **Longuinhos Beach Resort** (Tel: 0832-2788068-69; Tariff: Rs 2,200-3,000) is also one of its best. It's a sister concern of the famous Longuinhos Restaurant in Margao. You have to take the road to the right, 100m ahead of the beach, to get here. The hotel offers Ayurvedic massage, a dance floor, a swimming pool and a jacuzzi, and also has a handicrafts shop.

Goa Tourism Development Corporation's **Colva Residency** (Tel: 2788047-48; Tariff: Rs 550-1,600) is the first hotel on the right as you reach the beach. Though it's sometimes indifferently maintained, it's still good value. **Hotel Colmar** (Tel: 2788043/ 53; Tariff: Rs 400-2,000) is next to the Colva Residency. The pool can get a little crowded at times, but this is a great place to stay. Ayurvedic treatments are offered here.

Lucky Star (Tel: 2788071; Tariff: Rs 200-600) has 14 very basic rooms, but from the room, you can hear the waves crash against the shore, and look out at the sea. This could quite likely improve the quality of your holiday much more than imagined. **Star Beach Resort** (Tel: 2780092/ 8166; Tariff: Rs 600-3,400) has a restaurant, a swimming pool and offers Ayurvedic massage. It's not really on the beach, but it's very clean and everything works. **Sukhsagar Beach Resort** (Tel: 2788887-88; Tariff: Rs 400-1,450) is closer to the beach than Star, and a little cheaper as well. Overall, it offers better value for money.

On Sernabatim Beach

Some of the hotels here include **Furtado's Beach House** (Tel: 2770396; Tariff: Rs 800-1,500), with 12 basic rooms and a beachfront bar and restaurant. It's popular, so be sure to book ahead. **Quinsan Cottages** (Tel: 2771490; Tariff: Rs 400-1,000) has 11 basic rooms, 5 cottages and a garden restaurant. **Baywatch Resort** (Tel: 6697777; Tariff: Rs 4,500-6,750) has 80 rooms and a nice beachfront bar and restaurant, but it's not as good an option as Furtado's, which is closer to the beach.

A sun worshipper on Colva Beach

For more Colva and Sernabatim hotels and details, see Goa Accommodation Listings on pages 534-535

WHERE TO EAT

Colva has many beach shacks and quite a few cafés. The **Boomerang Beach House** is right on the beach, and serves good pasta and steak. They make an excellent Goan prawn curry. **Kentuckee** is to your left just before you cross the bridge to get onto Colva Beach. It has decent food. **Pasta Hut** at Hotel Colmar has fairly good Continental food. Their speciality, as the name indicates, is pasta and seafood. For more good seafood, head to **Pirate's Cabin**. **Micky's** is run by the same folks as Pirate's Cabin. **Johnny Cool's** is opposite William's Resort. They make pizza and many Goan dishes. The beef dishes are quite good.

BENAULIM BEACH

Parasurama, the sixth avatar of Lord Vishnu, is said to have created the Konkan by shooting an arrow that sent the hills back and pushed up a coastal plain from under the sea. That arrow is supposed to have fallen at Benaulim (pronounced Banavli, *ban* means arrow). Legends aside, Benaulim makes for a lovely holiday spot. In terms of access, it's even closer to Madgaon Station than Colva. Its beach has everything Colva has, minus the crowds. Except for a little section near the road where vendors roam and locals come for their evening constitutional, the beach is uncrowded. The nicest part about Benaulim is that it's just a few kilometres from Colva; if you stay here you can sample the nightlife on Colva Beach and still enjoy a quiet holiday.

RAJEEV SACHDEVA

The sun reaches for the sea as a tourist on Benaulim Beach captures the moment

BEACH WATCH

Benaulim is safe, but be more careful in the water here than at Colva.

ORIENTATION

The road from Colva's Char Rasta takes you past Sernabatim to the main **Maria Hall Square of Benaulim**, 2 km away. Turn right and drive straight down to **Benaulim Beach**.

THINGS TO SEE AND DO

The sight of Benaulim's sloping sands meeting the sea is stunning. Here too, as in Colva, there are beach shacks and boat rides on offer, but on a smaller scale and with a far greater *sussegad* atmosphere.

St John the Baptist Church

This church, located on Colva Road, was built in 1581, and has a Mannerist frontage. Twin balustrade towers in four distinct tiers flank the façade, and the central pedimental gable is topped by finials and spires, showing Hindu influences. The interior makes use of white Italian marble. Inside, you will see a baptismal font carved in basalt stone, where one of Goa's saints, the Blessed Padre Jose Vaz, was baptised in 1651. The church was destroyed by a fire in 1784, but was rebuilt and restored by its parishioners.

Art in crafts

Benaulim is a village of carpenters. Several ornamental altars and artistic images of saints, which adorn not only affluent houses but also churches, endorse their craftsmanship. Carved furniture has been their forte. The legendary Joao Sebastiao Fernandes wrought the main altar of Benaulim's **Patrocinio Chapel**. Domingos Fernandes made the altar of Benaulim's **Holy Trinity Church**.

While here, check out **Manthan**, a boutique located in an old restored Portuguese house on the road from Maria Hall towards the Taj Exotica Hotel. It displays carefully selected articles including beautiful antiques, Christian art, Goan pottery, sculptures, recycled handmade paper and paintings, among several other wonderful things. Goa's claim to fame in

the fashion world, designer Wendell Rodricks, retails from here.
•**Location** House No. 1346, Mazil Vaddo, near Holy Trinity Church **Timings** 9.30 am-8 pm

Water sports

There are many boatmen here organising island tours and dolphin- and crocodile-spotting trips. **Pedro's Restaurant** (Tel: 0832-2770563, 2771308; Mobile: 09822389177), next to the car park located just ahead of the beach, is the place to go for rides and action on water, be it parasailing or jet-skiing. They organise a dolphin dundee boat ride every morning (Rs 250 per person) and a full-day **Paradise Island Trip** (Rs 750, includes food and beverages; underwater snorkelling equipment and fishing rods provided). Another excellent option is a trip by boat all the way up the coast to the **Anjuna flea market** (Rs 500). To get the best of a beautiful Goan sunset over the Arabian Sea, take Pedro's exciting 1½-hr evening **Sunset Trip** (Rs 300, water/ alcoholic beverages included).

If you're lucky, you might spot a dolphin

AMIT PASRICHA

→ BENAULIM FACTS

- **Location** Benaulim Beach is 2 km south of Colva, at the centre of coastal Salcete Taluka
- **Getting There** From Dabolim Airport (28 km/ 40 mins), a pre-paid taxi costs around Rs 400-450 **From Madgaon Station** (8 km), a pre-paid taxi costs about Rs 150-200. Buses from Margao's City Bus Stand near the municipal garden leave every 15 to 30 mins for Benaulim. An auto from here costs around Rs 100
- **Route from Colva** Turn left at Colva's Char Rasta Junction, just before the last stretch to the beach. Benaulim is 2 km down this road

WHERE TO STAY

Benaulim has an interesting mix of accommodation, from shacks that are rented out at rock-bottom rates to expensive 5-star resorts.

Taj Exotica (Tel: 0832-2771234; Tariff: Rs 5,500-18,500), a 5-star Mediterranean-style deluxe hotel in Cal Vaddo in South Benaulim, is the latest addition to Taj's many Goa properties. It has an excellent Ayurvedic spa.

O Palmar (Tel: 2770631; Tariff: Rs 550-750) gets full very quickly. Be sure to book ahead. **Carina Beach Resort** (Tel: 2770413-14; Tariff: Rs 800-1,600) and **Rosario Inn** (Tel: 2770636; Tariff: Rs 250-400) are both good options in Vas Vaddo. The budget **Hotel Failaka** (Tel: 2771270/ 865; Tariff: Rs 650-850) is right near Maria Hall, a 10-min walk from the beach.

For more Benaulim hotels, see Goa Accommodation Listings on pages 533-534

WHERE TO EAT

Pedro's is right on the beach. The service is slow but worth the wait. Goan seafood (particularly the really huge tiger prawns) is fantastic here.

Johncy's serves Indian, Goan and Chinese food, but Goan seafood is their speciality. The patrao, Agnelo Severes, has his own fishing trawlers and boats, so the freshness of the catch is assured. This beach shack is to the right as you

A charming boutique that's run out of an ancient, restored Portuguese house

face the sea. **Hawaii** is a seaside shack near a prawn hatchery that offers great Goan seafood. **Dominics Bar** serves good Continental food. **Joecon's Garden** is near Taj Exotica, towards South Benaulim. It has an excellent range of cocktails and seafood dishes made from the fresh catch of the day. **Goan Hideout** is also near Taj Exotica. Managed by a 5-star chef, it has good food, an unusual ambience and live entertainment.

Taj Exotica seems to have more restaurants than the rest of Benaulim combined. Allegria, Eugenia, Li Bai, Lobster Shack and Miguel Arcanjo are some of the restaurants here; there's also a sandwich counter and fresh fruit bar.

MOBOR-CAVELOSSIM BEACH

There are few places as picturesque as this stretch in Goa. Here the Sal River cuts a broad swathe as it nears the Arabian Sea, forming the beautiful Mobor Peninsula. Till the late 1980s, this was just a barren stretch of sand with one village (Cavelossim), a few fishermen's huts and sands that were used solely to dry fish. Then the Leela and other 5-star hotels moved in, changing the area's character forever.

Yet, along with the palm-shaded Mobor Village that's a burst of green, the beach here has retained its old-world charm. To discover it, all you have to do is to walk or cycle along the beach at sunset. Captured thus against the sky's many hues, the beach's stunning beauty is a reminder that though luxury can be purchased for a bulky wad of notes at the nearest resort, nature's gifts oftentimes come completely free.

BEACH WATCH

The part of Mobor Beach that stretches for about 300m from the mouth of the Sal River is extremely dangerous when the tide is going down; water rushes out then, creating a strong undertow that could drag you half a kilometre out into the sea. Keep clear of this area. Unless

AMIT PASRICHA

River placid: Tourists enjoy a quiet boat ride on the Sal

you are a strong swimmer, don't venture more than waist-deep into the sea. The Varca-Fatrade beaches are generally safe for swimming.

THINGS TO SEE AND DO

This stretch is for fun lovers, with a number of operators offering everything from charming boat rides to adrenaline-laced windsurfing, jet-skiing and several other activities.

Water sports

Water sports in Cavelossim-Mobor is conducted from behind **Betty's Place** (Tel: 0832-2871038), near Dona Sylvia Resort, and from **Jack's** (Tel: 2871132; Mobile: 09822149529), located behind Hotel Haathi Mahal. Both offer a number of **full-day tours on the Sal River** and out at sea. These cost Rs 750 and the fee is inclusive of lunch and refreshments. Both also offer **fishing trips** and **river cruises**.

Goa Coastal Water Sports offers jet-ski and speedboat rides, water-skiing, windsurfing, banana and bump rides and parasailing during peak season, from the pontoon behind Betty's Place. The **Leela Palace** also has a huge water sports set-up, offering plenty of thrills. (*For details of operators and rates, see 'Adventure: The new Goan high' on pages 383-392.*)

Biking

Hiring a bicycle and riding along the firm sand near the water's edge can be great fun. It can also be the fastest way to travel on this stretch. Britishers Peter and Adrian run **Cycle Goa** (Mobile: 09822380031; Website: cyclegoa.com) at the **Mobor Beach Resort** (Tel: 2871167/ 729; Tariff: Rs 1,000-2,500). They rent cycles and organise guided tours in the villages around. Gearless bikes are rented out at Rs 200 per day, and cycles with gears at Rs 350 per day. Their village tour is Rs 550 per head (includes only drinks and lasts

Radisson
WHITE SANDS RESORT GOA

$3^1/_2$ hrs). All day tours to **Cabo de Rama Fort**, south of Mobor in Canacona Taluka, are for Rs 1,850 (includes picnic lunch and drinks). They'll also take you to the **Sri Chandreshwar Bhutnath Temple** near Paroda in Quepem Taluka (Rs 1,850). This is an all-day trip with packed lunch and drinks. All full-day trips have back-up vehicles from Cycle Goa accompanying them.

Varca-Fatrade Beach

Goa's former chief minister and football club owner Churchill Alemao is from Varca. His family-owned Churchill Brothers Football Team has performed very well over the years in the National Football League. He still lives in his ancestral house in this village by the River Sal.

Varca is one of the longest stretches of beaches in Salcete, and is often referred to as two beaches — Varca and Fatrade, or Pedde. Apart from the usual clutch of shacks outside every 5-star resort, there are vast expanses of white sands here where you'll likely be disturbed only by an occasional beach vendor. There's very little non-5-star accommodation along the beach, however.

To get here from Mobor, head towards Benaulim. The early 17th century **Our Lady of Glories Church** is the landmark to look out for in Varca.

→ MOBOR FACTS

- **Location** Mobor-Cavelossim is 16 km south of Colva, at the southern end of the Salcete Coast, where the River Sal empties into the Arabian Sea
- **Getting There** From Dabolim Airport (35 km/ 45 mins), a pre-paid taxi costs around Rs 700-750 **From Madgaon Station** (15 km), a pre-paid taxi costs Rs 250-300. Buses from Margao's City Bus Stand near the Municipal Gardens leave for Mobor every 30 mins or every hour. An auto from here costs around Rs 150. To return to Margao, wave at any bus proceeding in that direction and it will stop to pick you up
- **Ferry service** Cavelossim is connected to Assolna across the River Sal by ferry (there's one every 15 mins). Assolna is a short distance via Chinchinim from NH17, which leads back up to Margao or south to Quepem and Canacona

NIGHTLIFE

A combination of an entertainment lounge, slot machine casino and discotheque, **Aqua** swings in the season. **Hacienda de Oro** is a slot machine casino at the Holiday Inn where punters stay till late sometimes. There are also two nightspots called **Liquid Lounge** on this stretch. One is opposite Dona Sylvia, while the other is at the Mobor Beach Resort. Both stay open till the wee hours, especially on weekends.

WHERE TO STAY

There are only two beachside non-5-star hotels in the Mobor-Cavelossim area (there are several moderately priced hotels away from the beach). The rest are all luxury resorts. Varca and its ward Fatrade have three 5-star hotels and one mid-range hotel between them.

In Mobor-Cavelossim

The **Holiday Inn** (Tel: 0832-2871303-09; Tariff: Rs 4,000-15,000) in Mobor offers all-inclusive 'monsoon madness' packages from June to September at very attractive prices. **Dona Sylvia Beach Resort** (Tel: 2871888; Tariff: Rs 13,500-18,000), also in Mobor, offers only holiday packages, except during the peak season from Xmas to New Year.

Serafino, the genial owner of **Dona Sa Maria** (Tel: 2745290/ 672; Tariff: Rs 500-1,000), is a part-time writer of *tiatr*, or Konkani operettas. The resort is located in the laid-back village of Tamborim, and you get to experience Goan village life if

staying here. **Gato Loco** (Mobile: 09823066709; Tariff: Rs 500-1,200) is the only other beachside non-5-star accommodation that's available in this belt. Originally designed as a lifestyle beach club by owner Garth de Souza, it now functions as a hotel and restaurant.

With six speciality restaurants, a spa and a casino, the **Leela Palace** (Tel: 2871234; Tariff: Rs 19,000-1,00,000) is spread across 45 acres, and is the biggest resort in Goa. **Gaffino's Beach Resort** (Tel: 2871441; Tariff: Rs 1,200-1,500) is away from the beach but it's a lovely family-run hotel with excellent food. Patrao Brian Gaffino is a mine of information on Mobor. **Old Anchor** (Tel: 2871180-82; Tariff: Rs 4,500-14,500), near the beach, has a restaurant and a bar.

In Varca-Fatrade

Club Mahindra Varca Beach Resort (Tel: 0832-2744555; Tariff: Rs 4,000-11,000) is a 5-star time-share resort, which also rents some rooms, studios and apartments to visitors.

Biking on the beach is a fun option

FEDERICK NORONHA

Varca Palms Beach Resort (Tel: 2745411-13; Tariff: Rs 4,000-6,000), formerly Resorte de Goa, is on the beach in Fatrade. **Goa Beach House** (Tel: 2744111-12; Mobile: 09810040042; Tariff: Rs 4,500-5,500) is not on the beach but close enough to hear the waves.

Ramada Caravela Beach Resort (Tel: 2745200-15; Tariff: Rs 4,300-34,625), formerly the Renaissance Goa Resort, is another high-end option. The hotel runs India's only floating casino, the Caravela, in Panaji.

Colonia Jose Menino (Tel: 2745791; Tariff: Rs 600-2,800), originally built as an apartment complex, has been run as a hotel for several years now. There's nothing between it and the beach, but the sea is still a 5-min walk away. All the resorts have their own bars and restaurants.

There are also two excellent beach shacks that come up every year outside the Ramada. **Sunset** relies mostly on customers from the resort and is a great place to chill out. Seafood is the speciality at **Chikita**, which is nearby.

For more Mobor-Cavelossim hotels and details, see Goa Accommodation Listings on pages 534-535

WHERE TO EAT

Mobor-Cavelossim has a plethora of options. **Ocean View Beach Shack** outside the Leela serves divine Goan food and stays open till late. Edwin's **Leisure Place Beach Shack** outside Dona Sylvia has good seafood.

Dominic runs **Fat Willy's Beach Shack** outside Dona Sylvia. He offers good seafood, including lobsters. **Whispers of the Orient** at the Holiday Inn (open only for dinner) serves classic Eastern delicacies. **Panache**, the coffee shop at Mobor Beach Resort, offers excellent coffee and ice-cream. ■

ASHOK NATH/ INDIAPICTURE

PALOLEM-AGONDA

THE SOUND OF SILENCE

Palolem used to be one of the quietest beaches in Goa. It got its first resort only in 1989, but as if to make up for being a late bloomer, hotels and beach shacks have been springing up in every square metre of the beachfront since then.

Today, there is none of the serenity that was found in the Palolem of olden days, but the place still has its charms. Once you visit it, you want to come back again. That's not surprising — Palolem is one of Goa's most beautiful beaches, a shallow bay fringed with white sands and coconut palms. A tiny island stands to its northern side, and snorkelling off its waters, one comes across an array of treasures such as sea urchins and sea cucumbers. Beyond the island lies a hillside that's thickly forested. Explore Palolem and nearby Agonda, and you are bound to come away satisfied.

ORIENTATION

Palolem is located in Goa's southernmost town, **Canacona**, which is locally called Chaudi. At the southern end of the Palolem Beach is a stream; if you turn left here and continue along the path, you'll reach **Pandava's Drum**. At the extreme northern end of the beach is an island, and to reach it, you have to wade across a stream.

BEACH WATCH

Palolem is one of the safest beaches for swimming, as long as you keep away from the stream near the island when the tide is receding. There's a lifeguard, so stick to the designated swimming area if you want to go in more than waist-deep. Patnem is a reasonably safe place to swim, but the little coves of Colomb are best avoided. Besides, the place doesn't have any lifeguards.

THINGS TO SEE AND DO

Set off on a dolphin-spotting trip, throw stones at a rock to hear musical sounds, and go snorkelling off an island that you can actually wade across to.

Pandava's Drum

This is a large cup-shaped rock about which there are several legends. People visit it, however, to throw stones on the rock! This is because if the stone hits a particular spot on the rock, one can hear a resonant sound.

Figueiredo House

Go a little further down the path to Pandava's Drum and you will reach a few small coves. Ahead of these is a house that was built in the early 20th century by the Figueiredo family. It's now part of Neptune Point Hotel.

The island

Cross the stream at the northern end of the beach, and walk past a few funnily shaped rocks here till you see what appears to be a rock bridge. Avoid the bridge — it's tricky. Instead, wade across at low tide just ahead of this bridge.

Apart from frolicking in the shallow water, there's **snorkelling** to be done in the rocks adjoining the island, where you can see mussels, sea urchins, sea cucumbers and the occasional grouper, usually from 6 am to about 8.30 am. At low tide, local fishermen lure crabs and find sea urchins. The island offers a lovely view of the sunset. But rush back immediately after, to avoid wading back in the dark.

Dolphin-spotting trips

There are many dolphins in the area, but one needs to get out early to spot them. If you do take a boat trip (Rs 150-400 per head for an hour) and go north (to the right as you face the sea), don't miss the little **Butterfly Beach** in between Palolem and Agonda. Ask the boatman to take you there for a few minutes. It's less than 100m across and can be reached only by boat. You'll feel like you have the whole beach to yourself, even if only for a few minutes. The water here becomes very deep after about 10m, so be careful.

Patnem-Colomb Beach

Just south of Palolem is the vaddo of Colomb. By itself, Colomb has only a little cove. But the vaddo of Patnem adjoining it has a fine beach about a kilometre long. The nicest thing about staying at Patnem-Colomb is that you can savour the nightlife at Palolem, which is just a 15-min walk away.

Water sports

Apart from canoe rides and dolphin-spotting cruises, there's nothing else by way of water sports here. The fishermen on the beach organise these trips. Typical charges are Rs 1,000 per boat; each boat can carry about six people. The trip takes

An accommodation option at Palolem

TRIBHUVAN TIWARI

about an hour. You can also do a boat trip up the tiny stream for about Rs 100-200 (4 people).

Rajbaga Beach

Just south of Patnem is the isolated, virgin Rajbaga Beach, stretching all the way to the mouth of the Talpona River. This entire beach is dominated by the Intercontinental Grand Resort (*see Where to Stay on facing page for details*).

WHERE TO STAY

Palolem has relatively few hotels. Instead, it has a series of temporary palm-thatch and grass huts and tents all along the shoreline, which come up during the tourist season and come down before the monsoon. Patnem and Colomb have more options.

In Palolem

Palolem Beach Resort (Tel: 0832-2643054/ 4094; Tariff: Rs 400-1,000) has hammocks, rooms and tents. It's Palolem's first resort and falls to the right as the road reaches the beach. **Ciaran's** (Tel: 2643477; Tariff: Rs 900-2,500) has three rooms and 18 huts, bicycles on hire, hammocks and a 'pulp fiction' library. It has the most happening beachfront bar and restaurant.

Hi-Tide Coco Huts (Tel: 2643104, 2644550; Tariff: Rs 350-1,500) has 24 romantic huts on coconut palm stilts. **Cozy Nook** (Tel: 2643550; Tariff: Rs 500-1,500), at the northern end of the beach, has a great location. **Bridge and Tunnel** (Tel: 2643262, 2639311; Tariff: Rs 600-4,000) has cottages and hammocks. Located at the southern extremity of the beach, **Neptune Point** (Tel: 2639547; Tariff: Rs 500-2,500) is a good option set up around the Figueiredo House, between Palolem and Colomb.

In Patnem

Sea View (Tel: 2643110; Tariff: Rs 250-3,000) has 10 rooms and 8 cottages, and is just a few minutes' walk from the beach along a quiet lane. **Namaste Guest House** (Tel: 2643688; Tariff: Rs 300-500) has 6 huts with shared toilets, a bar and a pool table. This is one of the better places with moderate prices. **Solitude** (Tel: 6471530; Mobile: 09422643363; Tariff: Rs 1,500-2,000) has 20 cabanas and a restaurant. **Oceanic** (Tel: 2643059; Tariff: Rs 1,500-3,500) is a boutique hotel, offering great value for money. It's very popular, so book months in advance.

In Colomb

All the 22 cottages in **Bhakti Kutir** (Tel: 2643472; Tariff: Rs 900-3,000) are built from locally available eco-friendly materials. The resort offers an organic food restaurant, yoga and Ayurvedic massage. **Boom Shankar** (Mobile: 09822384634; Tariff: Rs 500-2,000) is one of the older places in Colomb, offering huts with shared toilets, a bar and restaurant. **Tree Shanti** (Tel: 2644460; Tariff: Rs 150-300) practically has a beach to itself.

→ PALOLEM FACTS

- **Location** Palolem Beach is at the centre of coastal Canacona, Goa's southernmost taluka, 43 km from the nearest big hub of Margao
- **Getting There** From Dabolim Airport (67 km/ $1^1/_4$ hrs), a pre-paid (non-AC) taxi costs around Rs 1,200 **From Madgaon Station** (43 km/ 1 hr), a pre-paid taxi costs around Rs 700. Buses operate every hour from Margao to Palolem. You can also take the more frequent buses to Canacona and Karwar until Char Rasta. From here, you can take an auto or a motorcycle taxi to the beach **From Panaji** (76 km/ $1^3/_4$ hrs), a taxi costs around Rs 1,500
- **Route from Panaji** Take NH17 past Margao and Cuncolim to Char Rasta, just before Chaudi. Turn right at Char Rasta and drive straight to Palolem, 2 km away

MADHU KAPPARATH

The splendid interiors of the Figueiredo House in Palolem

On Rajbaga Beach

Intercontinental The Grand Goa Resort (Tel: 0832-2667777; Tariff: Rs 17,000-1,40,000) is a 5-star deluxe hotel with 238 rooms, 14 suites, a nine-hole golf course and a helipad. It's easily Goa's most luxurious hotel. The public access from the road to Rajbaga Beach is from the Talpona riverside.

For more Palolem hotels and details, see Goa Accommodation Listings on pages 536-537

WHERE TO EAT

In Palolem, **Fern's Bar and Restaurant** behind Hi-Tide Coco Huts has excellent seafood and barbecues. The patrao Jack pours a great palm feni. **Draupadi**, located where the road meets the beach, offers excellent barbecues and Italian food.

Italian chefs turn out authentic delicacies using imported ingredients at **Magic Italy**. It's a little pricey, but very, very good. Try their ravioli and pizza. **La Allegro** serves tasty lasagna, besides seafood. **Palolem Beach Resort** has good seafood, especially giant crabs. **Dylan's Bar** on the south side of the beach stays open till late. **Brown Bread**, which was formerly called German Bakery, serves good vegetarian food.

Sun-n-Moon on the main road is always packed, as it serves great food at reasonable prices. **Sea Shore**, one of the older shacks at Patnem, has delicious seafood. **Sea Land** is a good choice for Goan food.

AROUND PALOLEM

Galjibaga Beach (17 km)

To reach Galjibaga, take the highway past Chaudi to Poinguinim, from where a road goes right to Galjibaga. This beach is a turtle nesting site. You could stay at **Brandon Restaurant**, which is 500m from the beach. It has 3 rooms and serves Goan food on order.

AGONDA BEACH

Agonda is for the solitude seeker looking for mid-range stay options.

BEACH WATCH

Agonda is considered to have a dodgy undertow and there's no lifeguard, so don't venture in more than waist-deep.

WHERE TO STAY AND EAT

All 12 rooms at the **Dunhill Beach Resort** (Tel: 0832-2647328; Tariff: Rs 400-450) offer good sea views. **Eldfra** (Tel: 2647378; Tariff: Rs 200-500) is much closer to the beach, with 10 rooms. Situated up on a hillside, **Sunset Beach Guest House** (Tel: 2647381; Tariff: Rs 300-500) has a lovely view, 9 rooms with attached toilets, a bar and restaurant.

Dercy's (Tel: 2647503; Tariff: Rs 250-400) has 9 rooms and 12 huts, all with shared toilets, a bar and a restaurant. The rooms on the first floor have a common balcony.

Each room at the hillside **Palm Beach Lifestyle Resort** (Tel: 2647783; Tariff: Rs 900-1,200) has a sea view with a sit-out. This is Agonda's best hotel. It's also the only year-round resort here. Located on the beach, **Forget Me Not** (Tel: 2647611; Mobile: 09421243541; Tariff: Rs 400-1,500) has 9 rooms and 7 huts. It also has a small restaurant.

For more Agonda hotels and details, see Goa Accommodation Listings on pages 536-537

Agonda is for the solitude-seeker

KHAZANCHI BN/ INDIAPICTURE

→ AGONDA FACTS

- **Location** Agonda is 10 km north of Palolem on the Canacona Coast
- **Getting There** *See Palolem on page 380*
- **Route from Palolem** Take the first turn to the left after Palolem but before Char Rasta. Keep going on until you see the sign for Agonda

AROUND AGONDA

Cola and Canaguinim (5 km)
These rarely visited beaches lie between the Cabo de Rama Fort and Betul in Salcete Taluka. Locals flock here for picnics on holidays, but on all other days of the week, you'll have the beach to yourself. Both have the odd shack, but beaches don't come much more 'virgin' than these South Goa beauties.

Cabo de Rama Fort (10 km)
Cabo de Rama Fort sits high on a headland in South Goa. The Portuguese took over the fort from the Raja of Sonda, only to have it retaken. They finally gained possession of the fort on June 1, 1763. Under the Portuguese, it had military barracks, a chapel and quarters for the use of the commandant and 21 guns for its defence. The fort's ruins give some idea of its size but not of its layout. The views of the sea from the fort are well worth the trek.

◆**Connection** You can drive up from Palolem and Agonda past Cola Beach to Cabo de Rama ■

ASHOK NATH/ INDIAPICTURE

ADVENTURE: THE NEW GOAN HIGH

There's a new kind of rave sweeping across Goa and its thrills are by no means forbidden

■ BY ASHWIN KUMAR

Chasing the clouds from a microlight — a motorised hang-glider for the uninitiated — one can capture the magic of Goa in a sweeping, panoramic view. Down below, the ghats curve as if negotiating a particularly difficult dance step; rich green, palm-fringed paddy fields rustle in a soft breeze; and the coast gleams golden in the sun. Rivers wind their way down the ghats, reaching for the seas. Kites circle above the dense plantations in the foothills. On the seashore, wave upon wave of surf pounds the beaches. Out in the sea, islands hide coral reefs that hold a wealth of marine life.

It's beautiful, certainly, and magical. It's also a paradise for the adventurous. Each vista promises an experience that's different from the other, and as alluring as the next. It's no surprise then that hundreds set out each day on a journey of thrills and discovery. It could involve parasailing, wind-surfing, snorkelling and diving, or for the less adventurously inclined, a dolphin-spotting trip.

Adventure activities and water sports began to make their mark in Goa just a couple of decades ago, but today, they are etched into the Goan landscape. It's now as much a part of the state as — dare we say it — *sussegad*. And rightly so. It makes the Goan beach experience exciting and complete. Initially offered only by a few star hotels, water sports today feature on the boards of almost every private operator in Goa. Here we present a few activities that you can undertake and operators offering these sports.

Parasailing

Parasailing in Goa is an incredible experience. As you soar in the air and feel the wind on your face, the excitement begins to kick in. There are two ways to parasail — winch-boat parasailing, generally done solo, where you take off and land on a winch boat, and beach parasailing, where you're launched from the beach itself. The beach landing can be tricky and requires good coordination and expertise on the part of the ground staff and the powerboat operator. Not every operator can claim high standards when it comes to safety and a case is currently being heard in court, asking for a ban on beach parasailing. Winch-boat parasailing has another advantage over beach parasailing: it lets you go higher.

◆**Where to parasail** Parasailing around Sinquerim-Candolim-Calangute will give you a spectacular view of Fort Aguada and also of the grounded tanker River Princess. The other views to take in are off the Arossim-Cansaulim and Utorda stretches; you can also spot the stunning coastline and the isolated Grande and Bait islands off the Mormugao Coast nearby. Another good place is Mobor Beach, especially the part near The Leela Palace Hotel, where the River Sal meets the Arabian Sea and forms the Mobor Peninsula. From Miramar, you can capture the views of Mandovi River meeting the sea

◆**Rates** Rides last for 3-5 mins and cost between Rs 500 and 1,250; boat ride charges extra

Whichever way the wind blows

The **Board Sailing Association of India** holds a National Windsurfing Championship every year between August and November at different venues in Goa. Various Indian State Association Clubs take turns to host the championship. The Board promotes windsurfing as a competitive sport.

There's no fee for coaching but there's a fee of Rs 100 for entering the championship. Only national-level qualified people can participate; you have to bring your own windsurfing equipment.

◆**For info contact** Fatima, Goa Yachting Association Office, c/o Wallace Pharmaceuticals, Dempo Trade Centre, EDC Complex, Patto Plaza, Panaji. Tel: 0832-2438155

ASHOO SHARMA/ INDIAPICTURE

PRIYA FONSECA MOIZUDDIN

Of skills and skis: Water-skiing is a popular water sport in Goa

◆**Skills required** You should be comfortable with heights and water

SAFETY TIP Double check your harness, cord and other gear before taking off. Apart from the boat operator, ensure there is another observer in the boat, as the boat operator won't be able to keep an eye on you

Jet-skiing

Jet-skiing is for those who love speed. The 100-135 hp-powered jet-skis used in Goa deliver high-adrenalin thrills. With a pretty uncomplicated machine to handle, you could easily get carried away, which is why most operators make it mandatory for an instructor to accompany the rider.

SAFETY TIP The part of the beach used for jet-skiing should always be within the operators' sight, in a pre-defined area

◆**Where to jet-ski** Colva, Candolim, Calangute, Miramar, Arossim, Utorda, Benaulim, Mobor and Rajbaga

◆**Rates** A ride can go on for 2, 10 or 15 mins. Typically, a 2-min round costs Rs 400, a 10-min one costs Rs 1,000 and a 15-min one costs Rs 1,500. The Intercontinental Grand Resort at Rajbaga charges Rs 2,500 for a 30-min jet-ski ride

◆**Skills required** Comfortable with speed and water, riding skills

Water-skiing

Water-skiing requires strength and skill. While learning, be prepared for repeated tumbles and the resulting soreness. To water-ski, you need strong leg and back muscles and a relaxed posture — being stiff doesn't help at all, and you have to practise bending your knees slightly and maintain them parallel to each other. Operators in Goa will train you till you become good enough, or give up (which is also a possibility). Either way this sport is definitely worth a try.

◆**Where to water-ski** Candolim, Calangute, Arossim, Utorda, Mobor and Rajbaga

◆**Rates** Rs 400-1,200, depending on the length of the ride and the operator

◆**Skills required** Comfortable in water, physical stamina

SAFETY TIP Apart from the operator, ensure there is another observer on the boat. If the sea is rough, avoid skiing — choppy waters prevent the boat from maintaining a steady course and speed. Go over the hand signals with the operator to avoid confusion and miscommunication.

One of the more important signals is to let the driver/ observer know you are all right after a fall, by clasping both hands above your head

Knee- and wake-boarding

Knee-boarding is similar to water-skiing. The board has a slot for your knees and that's all there's to it. It requires less focusing on balance than water-skiing and is a far simpler technique. Wake-boarding is a variation of knee-boarding; the skier has one broad board to maintain balance instead of two narrow ones.

◆**Where to knee-board** Candolim, Mobor and Rajbaga

◆**Rates** Rs 700-1,200 for 15 mins

◆**Skills required** Comfortable with water. You should be well-versed in water-skiing to take up this sport

SAFETY TIP Apart from the boat operator there should be an observer

Windsurfing

Windsurfing is a well-known watersport that's by far the toughest, despite being non-mechanised. It's relatively inexpensive, but it can be a very frustrating sport to learn. It requires commitment, good health and a good instructor.

◆**Where and when to windsurf** Bogmalo, Miramar, Calangute, Arossim, Utorda, Benaulim, Vagator and Baga are ideal locations. The Dona Paula Bay is one of the best sites to learn. Mornings have a light and gentle breeze while mid-afternoons have stronger winds, creating a perfect setting

◆**Rates** Rs 300-600 per hour depending on the agent

◆**Skills required** Windsurfing requires a high degree of skill and training

Speedboat rides

Speedboats are the next best thing to jet-skis. They are more powerful and faster too. With a capacity for seating 3 to 6, this is a great group activity. Rides normally last 10 mins to an hour, in which you can explore the Goan coastline. Longer trips may also include leisure fishing, dolphin trips or visits to sheer cliffs.

◆**Where to get rides** Speedboats are available on all major beaches such as Candolim, Calangute, Arossim, Utorda, Colva and Mobor

◆**Rates** Rs 800-1,200 for 3 to 6 people for 10 mins

◆**Skills required** You should be comfortable with water

Goa's most happening beaches

The Goa Coast is dotted with beautiful locations for water sports. The most popular is the stretch from Calangute to Sinquerim. The big hotels on South Goa's serene Arossim and Mobor beaches offer many choices in quieter locales.

The beaches in the north are more crowded, where you can club partying with sports — something that's not recommended as most extreme sports require you not to have a hangover. You'll also find plenty to do off Dona Paula, near Panaji.

AHTUSHI DESHPANDE

◆**Age limit** Unless specified, water sports are open to children aged 10 years and above

◆**Legal disclaimer** All water sports require you to sign a legal disclaimer that states the procedures are being complied with and that you are aware of the risks of the sport and absolve the operator of any responsibility

Courtesy CIDADE DE GOA

Banana rides are a big hit with children but adults give it a try too

Banana, bump and ringo rides

Banana rides are popular with kids and you can see why. You have to sit on a six-seater, banana-shaped contraption, towed by a speedboat. The banana boat will roll and pitch over undulating sea waves, making it even more appealing for kids. Ringo rides, or bump rides, are variations of the same. First-timers should be prepared for the flip at the very end of the ride — it adds that bit of extra excitement, and with everyone in life jackets, it's pretty safe too.

◆**Where to get fun rides** Fun rides are available on all major beaches

◆**Rates** Approx Rs 200 per head for a 15-min ride

◆**Skills required** Comfortable with water

SAFETY TIP Apart from the boat operator, ensure there is an observer in the boat

Catamaran sailing

Catamaran sailing (the craft is also referred to as Hobie cats) is a more relaxed sailing activity. A catamaran is made up of a twin hull with trampoline in between the hulls and a mast for sailing. The usual seating capacity is 4 people. Make sure a trained professional is sailing the catamaran.

◆**Where to sail** Candolim, Calangute, Dona Paula, Arossim, Utorda, Colva, Benaulim and Mobor are ideal locations for sailing

◆**Rates** Rs 600-1,500 per hour

◆**Skills required** Sailing requires a high degree of skill and training

SAFETY TIP Make sure you understand all the emergency procedures and the signals that the professional tells you

Sea fishing

Sea fishing as a sport is a rare activity and has yet to catch on in Goa. A fishing trip could easily take up the better part of the day and you could still end up without a catch. The sport involves going far out into the sea in a specialised motorboat; you can catch tuna, kingfish and jackfish. Operators take groups to Bait and Butterfly islands, close to the shore, for fishing.

◆**Age limit** Adults only

◆**Rates** approx Rs 500 per hour

◆**Skills required** Lots of patience

SAFETY TIP Make sure you understand all the emergency procedures

DIRECTORY OF WATER SPORTS OPERATORS | GOA STD 0832

This is a representative listing of water sports operators in Goa, arranged according to geographical location. These operators could be offering more activities than those listed below, particularly if it's a more common activity like speed boating, so do check with them about any sport that you want to undertake, even if it isn't mentioned against the operator's name. Charges may differ depending on the season and other factors, at the operator's discretion. This listing should not be construed as a recommendation on the part of the publisher or the writer.

NORTH GOA

Arambol

■ **Arambol Paragliding School**
Contact Uwe Niesslbeck **Activities and rates** Paragliding Rs 1,200 for a 20-min tandem flight, 4-6 days paragliding course Rs 9,800

■ **Kite-surfing School**
Contact Uwe Niesslbeck or Stefan **Activities and rates** Their 10-hr kite-surfing course costs about Rs 8,000

■ **Phil's Surf Club**
Mobile 09822120803 **Activities and rates** Windsurfing Rs 400 a day, boogie boards Rs 50 per hour, sand-speed sailing Rs 400 per day, kite-buggy rides (tricycles pulled along by a kite) Rs 400 per day

Candolim

■ **Allison Air Water Sports**
Location Between Fort Aguada and Taj Holiday Village, Candolim **Contact** Elvis Pereira or Dylan **Mobile** 09822181177 **Activities and rates** Parasailing Rs 700 plus boat ride fee of Rs 400 for 2 people, jet-skiing Rs 900 for 2 people, banana rides Rs 150 per head, bump rides Rs 250 per head, water-skiing Rs 400 for 10 mins, sea fishing Rs 500 per head

■ **Thunder Waves Water Sports**
Location Near Taj Holiday Village, Sinquerim Beach, Candolim **Tel** 2479779 **Contact** Peter **Mobile** 09822176985-86 **Activities and rates** Parasailing Rs 800 per head plus boat ride Rs 400 per ride (seats 2-3 people), jet-skiing Rs 900 for 15 mins, banana and bump rides Rs 200 per head each, water-skiing/ knee-boarding Rs 700 for 15 mins, catamaran sailing/ Hobie cat Rs 1,500 for 1 hr, wake-boarding Rs 700, dolphin-spotting trips Rs 250 per head for a 1-hr trip

Calangute

■ **Calangute Beach Water Sports**
Location Calangute, on the main road, opposite Goan Waves Shack **Contact** Pradeep Manjrekar **Mobile** 09822151002 **Activities and rates** Parasailing, boat rides Rs 200 for 3 people, jet-skiing Rs 300 for 2 people, banana rides Rs 200 per head

■ **Sea Wave Water Sports**
Location Khobra Vaddo, Main Baga Road, Calangute **Contact** Felix Fernandes **Tel** 2281145 **Mobile** 09823174669 **Activities and rates** Parasailing Rs 500 per head plus boat rides Rs 500 for 4 people, jet-skiing Rs 300 per head, banana rides Rs 200 per head, bump rides Rs 300 per head, water-skiing Rs 800 for 15 mins on a small boat and Rs 1,200 on a big boat

■ **Goan Bananas Water Sports**
Location Calangute, Near Silver Sand Beach Shack **Contact** Camilo Fernandes or Norman Madgaonkar **Mobile** 09822987806, 09822986544 **Email** meninok@rediffmail. com **Activities and rates** Parasailing Rs 500 plus boat rides Rs 500 for 4 people for 15 mins (40 hp boat) and Rs 1,200 for 4 people for 15 mins (150 hp boat), banana rides Rs 200-400 per head, bump rides Rs 250-500 per head, water-skiing Rs 800 per head for 15 mins (40 hp boat) and Rs 1,200 per head for 15 mins (150 hp boat), water-skiing tuition Rs 1,500 per head for 15 mins

CENTRAL GOA

Dona Paula

■ **Splash at the Goa**
Location Hawai Beach **Contact** Derrick Menzes **Tel** 3292668 **Mobile** 09822124457

Hotel
MENINO
Regency
Panjim, Goa
Centrally located in Panjim, the capital city of Goa. Flanked by swanky shoping arcades, parks, heritage edifices, clubs and entertainment centres.
Whether on business or holiday, check in. Experience the warmth of our services and the comfort of our Luxurious air-conditioned Rooms. Attractive Corporate / Executive and Holiday packages offered.
Dr. Dada Vaidya Road, Panjim, Goa-403001
Ph:+91-832-6641585, 6641586, 2426480. Fax: +91-832-2235180
themeninoregency@yahoo.co.in
www.meninoregency.com
Our other Property "Hotel Menino" is ideally located at the hub of Ponda City, Goa.
Tel: 0832- 2314148
Fax: 0832 – 2314145
The Menino Regency

DIRECTORY OF WATER SPORTS OPERATORS

GOA STD 0832

Activities and rates Splash offers three types of parasailing rides — a long ride with a dip in the water Rs 1,100, regular ride Rs 850, short ride Rs 500, jet-skiing Rs 1,200 for 15 mins, banana rides Rs 350, ski rings Rs 350, dinghy sailing Rs 2,500 for 3 hrs per session, kite-surfing Rs 2,500 for a 3-hr session, wind-surfing Rs 1,000 per hour, windsurfing Rs 2,500 for a 3-hr session, speed boat hire 100 hp Rs 4,500 per hour for 4-5 people, and motorboat rides Rs 3,000 an hr for 4 people

■ **Cidade de Goa**
Location Vainguinim, Dona Paula **Tel** 2454545 **Website** cidadedegoa.com **Activities and rates** Parasailing Rs 1,000 per hour, wind-surfing Rs 800 per hour, water-skiing Rs 950 for 10 mins, jet-skiing Rs 850, fun rides Rs 200 per hour, banana ride Rs 500 per head, ultra high-speed boat ride Rs 3,000 for 10 mins for 5 to 7 persons, power boat high speed Rs 2,000 for 10 mins for 5-7 persons, standard power boat Rs 1,500 for 10 mins for 5-7 persons, sunset trip Rs 1,500 per head, kayak (pedal boat) Rs 500 per head for 1 hr, sitting board (advance booking needed for this) Rs 5,000 for 1 hr for 10-15 persons

■ **SPM National Institute of Water Sports**
Location Aivao, Caranzalem, near Dona Paula Circle Office **Address** Sundial Apartments, AS Road, Altinho, Panaji **Contact** Principal Commander Office **Tel** 2436550, 2436400 **Caranzalem Training Centre Tel** 2453898 **Website** niws.nic.in **Courses and rates** Windsurfing, kayaking and dinghy-sailing are each priced at Rs 2,000 for a 5-day course, water-skiing Rs 3,000 for a 5-day course, scuba diving Rs 15,000 for a 5-day course, and rafting Rs 6,000 for a 19-day course

TIP This Government of India Ministry of Tourism institute offers short courses in water sports at their Caranzalem facility, and sometimes on Mayem Lake in Bicholim

■ **Dominic Cabral** is a private operator who organises deep-sea fishing. A half-day trip costs around Rs 1,500-2,500 per head **Contact** Dominic Cabral, Post Office, NIO, Dona Paula

SOUTH GOA

Arossim-Cansaulim

■ **Park Hyatt Goa Resort and Spa**
Location Arossim Beach, Cansaulim, Salcete Taluka **Contact** Vandhana Kumari, Activity Manager **Tel** 2721234-35 **Activities and rates** Parasailing Rs 1,250 per hour, Hobie cats and windsurfing Rs 600 per hour, water-skiing Rs 900 for 10 mins, 4-hr fishing trips to Bait and Butterfly islands Rs 18,000 for 8-10 people, snorkelling Rs 500 per head (2-3 hrs)

Colva

■ **Chris Water Sports**
Location Colva Beach, Near Hotel Silver Sand **Contact** Christopher Fernandes **Tel** 2780199 **Mobile** 09822142110 **Activities and rates** Parasailing Rs 800, boat rides Rs 300 per head, jet-skiing Rs 800 for 10 mins, banana rides Rs 250 per head, bump rides Rs 600 per head (Rs 800 for 2 people), speed boat rides Rs 150 per head

Utorda

■ **Ocean Blue Water Sports**
Contact Anthony Fernandes **Mobile** 09822165901 **Tel** 2771171 **Activities and rates** Parasailing Rs 800, boat rides Rs 350 per head, jet-skiing Rs 750, banana rides Rs 250 per head, ringo ride Rs 700 for 2 people, speed boat rides Rs 350 per head, water-skiing Rs 750 per head, Hobie cats Rs 500 per hour, windsurfing Rs 400 per hour, one-day fishing trip to Bait Island Rs 1,500 per head including meals, fishing and snorkelling

Mobor-Cavelossim

■ **Leela Beach Resort**
Location Mobor **Tel** 2871076 **Activities and rates** Winch-boat parasailing Rs 1,000 per head, speed boat rides Rs 800 for 2 people, bump rides Rs 1,200 for 2 people, water-skiing Rs 1,000 for 2 people

■ **Ramada Renaissance**
Location Mobor **Tel** 0832-2745200-14 **Activities and rates** Parasailing Rs 1,200 per

DIRECTORY OF WATER SPORTS OPERATORS — GOA STD 0832

head, banana rides Rs 300 for 10 mins, banana rides for kids Rs 250 for 10 mins, jet-skiing Rs 1,000 for 10 mins, water-skiing Rs 800 for 15 mins, catamaran sailing Rs 500 for 10 mins, knee-boarding Rs 500 for 10 mins, windsurfing Rs 300 per hour, fishing Rs 1,800 per head for 2 hrs, ringo ride Rs 500 per head, extreme tube Rs 500 per head, backwater trip Rs 1,500 for 2 hrs, dolphin spotting trip Rs 800 per hour, island trip Rs 1,800 per head for 6 hrs

TIP Ramada Renaissance now has its own boat club, opened in 2004

Rajbaga

■ **Intercontinental The Grand Resort**

Location Rajbaga Beach, south of Palolem, Canacona Taluka **Contact** Activity Manager **Tel** 2667777 **Activities** Parasailing Rs 1,200 per flight, jet-skiing Rs 1,200 for 10 mins and 3,000 for 30 mins, speed boats Rs 1,500 for 10 mins, windsurfing Rs 900 per hour, water-skiing, wake-boarding and knee-boarding Rs 1,200 for 10 mins, dolphin-spotting trip Rs 900 per person for 45 mins, and fishing trip Rs 4,000 for 2 hrs

SCUBA DIVING AND SNORKELLING

Scuba diving can be a magical experience and an amazing way to explore the sea. The thrill of going underwater and being able to swim next to marine animals is an absolute must-do.

Snorkelling, on the other hand, is a simpler activity, perfect for kids, adults and families. Goa's coastline does not have great visibility or a fabulous coral reef, but the beautiful and abundant marine life more than makes up for any other shortfalls. Visibility at dive sites can vary between 2m and 20m depending on the weather and the sea conditions. Underwater life here consists of groupers, damsels, Sergeant-major puffers, goat-fish, lion-fish, scorpion-fish, surgeon-fish, barracuda, tuna, eels, snappers, jacks, batfish, trevally, gobies, blennies, lobsters and sweetlips to name a few.

TIP To get a taste of scuba diving before committing to a full-fledged course, check out the try dives held on Mondays at Sun Village in Arpora, Goa Marriott Resort in Miramar and Cidade de Goa at Vainguinim Beach, Dona Paula

◆**Where to dive** Grande Island off Mormugao Harbour is recommended for scuba diving trips because of good underwater visibility

◆**Rates** The cost of two guided dives including full equipment and snacks is Rs 2,500 per diver for Grande Island

SAFETY TIP The underwater breathing apparatus should be thoroughly checked and its operation understood prior to a dive. Equipment provided on all trips includes a medical kit and portable oxygen kit, carried on board. The diving team consists of three PADI and one CMAS instructors, trained in administering First Aid (*also see 'Sporting Encounters' on page 16*).

DIVING OPERATORS

■ **Barracuda Diving India**

Location C/o Nikkis Travel Services, G3, Donna Rosa, Porba Vaddo, Calangute **Contact** Ashok **Mobile** 09823012025 **Website** barracudadiving.com

Barracuda Diving India, India's only PADI 5-star Gold Palm Centre, arranges scuba diving courses by PADI-qualified instructors. A non-certified course for two mornings costs Rs 3,500, while a two-day PADI Scuba Diver course costs Rs 10,000 and a Certified Open Water Sport Course costs Rs 18,000

■ **Goa Diving Pvt Ltd**

Location Joet's Guest House, Bogmalo Beach **Tel** 2538204

Website goadiving.com

Goa Diving in Vasco imparts certified and introductory courses to beginners and advanced courses for experienced divers. It has PADI-qualified instructors. The introductory course is a half-day course with basic skills taught in a pool, followed by closely supervised shallow water dives. This non-certified introductory dive costs Rs 2,200 ■

MAHARASHTRA

MAHARASHTRA AND DAMAN
ROUTE GUIDE
DAMAN
Vapi
Silvassa
BORDI
Gholvad
Dahanu
Talasari
Kasa Khurd
PALGHAR
Manor
Agashi Bay
Shirsad
Thane
MUMBAI
Panvel
Rewas
Mandwa
Pen
Lonavla
ALIBAUG
Vadkhal Naka
Revdanda
Nagothane
KASHID
Roha
Nandgaon
Mangaon
MURUD-JANJIRA
Goregaon
Lonera Phata
SHRIVARDHAN
Mahad
HARIHARESHWAR
Poladpur
Anjarle
Dapoli
HARNAI-MURUD
Khed
Vashishti
Chiplun
GUHAGAR
Velneshwar
Hedavi
Jaigarh
Sangameshwar
GANAPATIPULE
Nivli
RATNAGIRI
Hathkhamba
Pawas
Lanja
Rajapur
Vijaydurg
Jamsande
Devgad
Nandgaon
KUNKESHWAR
Kankavli
Sindhudurg
Kasal
Malvan
Kudal
TARKARLI
Sawantwadi
VENGURLA
To Dabolim Airport
To Indore
Malegaon
Nandgaon
Nashik
Yeola
Shirdi
Arthur Hill Lake
Sangamner
MAHARASHTRA
Ahmadnagar
Andhra Lake
Rajgurunagar
Mulshi Lake
Pune
To Solapur
Mahabaleshwar
Pandharpur
Koyna Reservoir
Satara
Karad
Vita
Nagaj
Sangli
Kolhapur
Chikodi
To Goa
Belgaum
ARABIAN SEA
N
TATA
SAFARI DICOR 2.2 VTT

DHRITIMAN MUKHERJEE

MUMBAI

MAXIMUM BEACH

■ BY UMA MAHADEVAN-DASGUPTA

At the throbbing heart of the crowded island city of Mumbai is the sea. From Girgaum Chowpatty in the south to Juhu-Versova in the western suburbs and, further up, the fishing beaches of Aksa, Madh Island and Manori, if it were not for the breathing space offered by these oceanfronts, and the vistas of open space and endlessness, Mumbai might have imploded long ago out of sheer claustrophobia. Films and books have for long celebrated the city's shoreline. Who can forget the desperate, crazy closing moments of *Satya*, the Ganpati immersion at Chowpatty, the colour, the drenched sand, the raucous revelry, the rain, the tide coming in; or the bhelpuri outings that are so precious to the police constable's family in Vikram Chandra's sprawling Bombay novel *Sacred Games*?

For residents as well as for visitors to the city, **Chowpatty** is the heart of Mumbai. On one side are the downtown commercial centre and the elegant, crescent-shaped curve of Marine Drive; on the other, the affluent precinct of Malabar Hill. Sandwiched between the two is Mumbai's middle-class paradise, Chowpatty Beach. In the daytime, this sandy stretch is home to those who sit around or doze on the sand under banyan trees. Pigeons flutter around a feeding area at one end of the beach; a few fishing boats bob up and down in the water. For senior citizens, there is a Nana-Nani Park close by; for those who seek some quiet moments, there's a small garden. In the evening, when halogen lamps come on and spill their warm yellow light across the golden stretches, it becomes a glittering open-air party for families, students and, in the quieter margins, self-absorbed lovers.

Further down, nearer the waves, are bhutta stalls, garam chana vendors and paanwallahs. Chai-coffee boys bring their kettles and plastic cups to your mat. Maalish-wallahs offer their services while ear cleaners and astrologers wait hopefully on the sidelines. Vendors sell colourful balloons, clouds of cotton candy, and all manner of plastic goodies — toys, cheery watches, whirring fans and battery-operated planes. Young men offer paid rides for children in small fibreglass cars and jeeps. Over the endless squeaks and yowls of the machines, there's music everywhere, with *Crazy Kiya Re* and the *Dhoom 2* song being the most popular tunes. Other entertainment on offer includes giant wheels, merry-go-rounds, an inflatable Mickey Mouse slide, and a boat-shaped ride that swings from side to side. A group throws rubber rings, mostly without success, at Thums Up bottles.

Families come for their Chowpatty evening armed with plastic packets, footballs, Frisbees and cameras — and then they forget about it all, instead taking off their shoes and settling down on the sand, their legs stretched out, feeling the salty breeze upon their cheeks and grains of sand between their toes. Boys from nearby foodstalls roam around with rolled-up reed mats under their arms and plastic-laminated menus in their hands, urging you to sit on the sand and place your orders. On offer are the variegated delights of Mumbai street food — bhelpuri, sev puri, pani puri, chaats, pao bhaji, as well as heavier snacks like grilled cheese sandwiches, masala dosas, vegetable pulao and that quintessential street item known as *ragda* patties. For thandas after the fiery snacks, there's matka kulfi or Anando milk — unless you prefer to partake of kala khatta, gola sherbets (*sada* Rs 12, Milkmaid Rs 25) or that evocatively named concoction known as slush.

Everyone's a star on Juhu Beach

NITIN KELVALKAR/ DINODIA PHOTO LIBRARY

In the Mumbai suburbs, ensconced amidst the many delights of Juhu — including film star bungalows, notably that of Amitabh Bachchan, the Prithvi Theatre, the ISKCON Temple, and five-star hotels with sea-facing coffee shops — is the **Juhu Beach**. Associated with two icons of Indian history, Gandhiji (who once lived here) and Jamsetji Tata (who owned and developed a part of the beachfront), Juhu is a special part of the city. Apart from the buzzing variety of foodstalls and brilliant neon lights, there are pony rides, mehendi artists, floating soap bubbles, air shooting stalls, wandering photographers, and all sorts of performers that make this beach the complete family experience.

Finally, further up are the weekend beaches of **Aksa**, **Madh Island** and **Maṇori**, where the townies escape when they want a change from the rush of the city. These beaches are nothing like the buzzing stretches of Chowpatty or Juhu. Here are only warm sands, quiet beaches, white-fringed waves, tall swaying palm trees, and an assortment of beach shacks (some of which are the locations of rave parties) — in short, the perfect retreat from the crowded metropolis. ■

THE INFORMATION

It's time for lights and all that jazz for some visitors to Chowpatty Beach

State Maharashtra
Location The island city of Mumbai, which has a natural harbour, is connected to the mainland by bridges, and spreads along the Arabian Sea on the West Coast of India
Distances 154 km NW of Pune, 545 km S of Ahmedabad, 593 km N of Panaji
Journey time *By road* $3\frac{1}{2}$ hrs from Pune, 12 hrs from Ahmedabad, 13 hrs from Panaji
Route from Pune Pune Expressway to Mumbai via Wadgaon, Lonavla and Panvel (*see route guide on page 394*)

ORIENTATION

Though a vast city, Mumbai is easily traversed thanks to its reliable but crowded local train network, divided into three sections or 'lines': Central, Western and Harbour. For **Chowpatty**, the Western line, which runs from Churchgate in South Mumbai to Virar in the north, is the best bet. The closest railway stations are **Marine Lines** and **Charni Road**. **Juhu** too can be accessed from the Western line, and the closest railway station is **Vile Parle**. Taxis and autos are readily available, though they are more expensive (autos are available only in the suburbs, beyond Mahim in the west and Sion in the east). Taxi fares in Mumbai are 14 times the meter reading (fares are 10 times the reading for autos). Minimum fares are: Rs 14 (non-AC taxi), Rs 17 (AC taxi) and Rs 9 (auto). Mumbai's auto and taxiwallahs are usually reliable and always ply to the meter (ask for the fare card; drivers keep them handy). For all the beaches outside Mumbai, such as Aksa and Utan, you can take a train to the closest railway station (all fall on the Western line) and then an auto further ahead; or hire a taxi from Mumbai

BEACH WATCH

Both Chowpatty and Juhu don't have clean waters, so don't consider swimming here. Aksa is not safe for swimming and many people have drowned here. The thumb rule should be to avoid swimming as far as possible as it's unsafe

WHERE TO STAY

It's not easy to find cheap accommodation in Mumbai, especially near the sea. South Mumbai (for Chowpatty) and Juhu also happen to be two places with some of the most expensive hotels in the city.

■ **IN SOUTH MUMBAI** Near Chowpatty, the options include: the landmark **Taj Mahal**

THE INFORMATION

Palace and Tower (Tel: 022-66653366; Tariff: Rs 9,900-1,00,000), which has been offering the best views of the Arabian Sea and the Gateway of India for over a 100 years. It also has some of Mumbai's most famous restaurants (Souk, Zodiac Grill, Shamiana) and wallet willing, even offers a yacht cruise that has AC bedrooms. **Hilton Towers** (Tel: 66324343; Tariff: Rs 8,800-47,700), which faces Marine Drive and was earlier called Oberoi Sheraton, ranks next. Other 5-star properties, each impressive in its own way, include the **Ambassador Hotel** (Tel: 22041131; Tariff: Rs 5,500-25,000), the **Marine Plaza** (Tel: 22851212; Tariff: Rs 7,500-17,500) and the **Intercontinental The Grand** (Tel: 66992222; Tariff: Rs 9,360-60,000). Most hotels come with lovely views of the sea, and the Marine Drive.

Bentley's (Tel: 22882890; Tariff: Rs 1,145-1,680), on Oliver Road in Colaba, is located in a well-maintained, rambling, heritage structure. The service is great. **Sea Green Hotel** (Tel: 22822294; Tariff: Rs 2,100-3,100), on Marine Drive, has an old-world charm, its appeal enhanced by its impressive sea-facing location. The rooms have a cozy feel. A reliable bet is the **YWCA International Guest House** (Tel: 22025053; Tariff: Rs 890-3,124), on Madame Cama Road, which includes breakfast and dinner in the tariff.

■ **NEAR JUHU BEACH** The highly recommended **Royal Garden Hotel** (Tel: 26603516; Tariff: Rs 4,500-7,500), on Juhu Tara Road, has about 36 luxurious rooms and excellent service. The décor is pleasing and aesthetic, the bathrooms are spotless and the linen crisp and clean. **Juhu Residency Hotel** (Tel: 26184546; Tariff: Rs 1,700-3,300), also on the same road, is a standard property with slightly small rooms but clean ones.

Citizen Hotel (Tel: 66932525; Tariff: Rs 5,000-9,000), on the beach in Juhu, is a dream spot to stay while on holiday. The 45 rooms are comfortably big but not intimidatingly so. There are a host of hotels near the domestic airport in Vile Parle East, also close to Juhu. The tariff at **Hotel Avion** (Tel: 26116958; Tariff: Rs 4,100-4,900), on the Western Express Highway and opposite the domestic airport, is inclusive of breakfast and dinner and airport pick-ups and drop-offs. The rooms are clean and spacious. **Hotel Airlink** (Tel: 26183575; Tariff: Rs 1,800-3,600), off Nehru Road, is a 3-star hotel with an airport shuttle service. Their rooms are clean, as are the toilets and linen.

Among the expensive hotels in Juhu are **JW Marriott** (Tel: 66933000; Tariff: Rs 14,400-28,800), **Eastern International Hotel**, formerly **Holiday Inn** (Tel: 66934444; Tariff: Rs 11,000-28,800) and **Sun-N-Sand** (Tel: 66938888; Tariff: Rs 8,500-20,000).

For more details, see Mumbai Accommodation Listings on pages 556-557

The Café Mondegar in Colaba

ATUL LOKE

WHERE TO EAT

Mumbai is famous for its roadside foodstalls, which offer a range of dishes and cuisines varying from Chinese to Chettinad. In South Mumbai, **Brittania** is a lovely Parsi joint in quiet Ballard Estate, legendary for berry pulao, their special raspberry drink and caramel custard. The hot poha and *sabudana* (sago) vadas of the women-run roadside stalls at Nariman Point and Mahapalika Marg must be sampled. **Status Restaurant** at Regent Chambers, Nariman Point, serves vegetarian South Indian, Punjabi and Gujarati food. **Ankur** on Tamarind Lane in the Fort area serves South Indian, Chinese and Mughlai food — the

THE INFORMATION

Courtesy TAJ MAHAL PALACE AND TOWER

ABHIJIT BHATLEKAR

The Taj group's yacht (left) **and outside the Chhatrapati Shivaji Terminus** (right)

South Indian food is most recommended. **Kailas Parbat** on 3rd Pasta Lane, off Colaba Causeway, has Sindhi and Punjabi food. **Café Mondegar** in Colaba is another popular place; the cartoons of Mario Miranda on the walls add to the atmosphere. **Bade Miyan** behind Regal is also popular. **Apoorva** near Horniman Circle, **Trishna** at Kala Ghoda and **Mahesh Lunch Home** at Fort (branch on Juhu-Tara Road) have a following for their Mangalorean seafood. Chowpatty is in itself famous for its bhelpuri, chaat and kulfi stalls. Close by are **Crystal** and **Sukh Sagar**, just off Hughes Road, leading to Chowpatty, which serve excellent vegetarian food.

Juhu has many posh, high-end restaurants but one of the most delicious meals is to be had at the **Govinda Restaurant** in the ISKCON Temple Complex. Their vegetarian thali is sumptuous. The beach itself has innumerable stalls serving all varieties of food, junk and otherwise, fairly clean and cheap. **Hotel Guestline**, on Juhu Tara Road, has good Indian food. There is **Shiv Sagar** on the way to the beach, a good Udupi joint. At **Gajalee**, Vile Parle (E), try the Bombay duck stuffed with prawns. Head to the open-air joint at **Prithvi Theatre**, Juhu, for Irish coffee, their heavenly brownies, and to soak in some theatre.

FAST FACTS

When to go October-March. It's cool in the monsoon, but heavy showers could mean no trains and flooded roads

Tourist offices ■ Govt of India Tourist Office, 123 M Karve Road, Churchgate, Mumbai **Tel** 022-22014155, 22074333-34 **Email** indiatourism@vsnl.com **Website** incredibleindia.org ■ MTDC Mumbai, CDO Hutments, Opposite LIC Building, Madame Cama Road, Mumbai **Tel** 22026713, 22027762 **STD code** 022

GETTING THERE

Air Mumbai is among the best connected cities in India. There is an international airport (popularly called Sahar) and a domestic airport, both named after Chhatrapati Shivaji. Pre-paid taxi stands are there at both airports. They cost slightly more than the regular intra-city cabs but are reliable

Rail Chhatrapati Shivaji Terminus, formerly known as VT or Victoria Terminus (Central Railway), Mumbai Central Station (Western Railway), Lokmanya Tilak Terminus (Konkan Railway) and Dadar Station (Southern and South-Central Railway) connect Mumbai to the length and breadth of the country

Road The Mumbai-Pune Expressway makes for a $2^1/_2$-hr fast drive between the two cities. The Maharashtra State Transport Bus Terminal is located opposite the Mumbai Central Train Station. 'Asiad' buses run between Pune and Dadar Bus Terminal. Numerous private bus operators also offer services to Mumbai. The city is connected to Delhi by NH8 via Jaipur; to Agra by NH3, via Nashik, Indore and Gwalior; NH4 to Pune via Lonavla and NH9 to Hyderabad via Sholapur ■

ABHIJIT BHATLEKAR

A hammock is the best place to put your feet up at a beach resort in Manori

BEACHES OF SUBURBIA

BY PETER GRIFFIN

Mumbai has some pleasant alternatives for short beach holidays. Listed below are a few options.

U-TAN SEA RESORT, UTAN Nestled on the crest of a hill just outside Utan Village, this resort gives you a breathtaking view of the sea. The 'cottages' are two-storeyed cubes, all straight lines, sharp angles, white paint, black metal and glass, softened by the trees they nestle amongst, set in a staggered line, so that each room has its own share of the breeze and sea view through the trees.

The beach, a longish walk downhill, is rocky, and lined with drying fish, and the water rather filthy from the creek and river's effluents. Avoid. The resort has a pool, and a wooded stretch above the main buildings where you can stroll, or sit under a tree with a book while the brats play Veerappan-Police. You can also wander down to the 'tableland' that overlooks the junction of creek and sea; take a boat ride across the creek to see the Bassein Fort; visit the lighthouse or the old churches in Utan. Esselword and Waterworld, if you absolutely insist, are also nearby.

♦**Closest local railway station** Bhayander **Food** Limited menu, but good. No bar **Tel** 022-28451151/ 2345 (resort); 26206063, 26282653 (city booking) **Tariff** Rs 1,650-3,850

DOMONICA'S BEACH RESORT & DOMONICA HOTEL, MANORI Once a single entity, these two resorts are owned by brothers who helped their parents manage the undivided place. They share a common entrance gate, access to the beach, and ambience, and are only separated by a knee-high wall and different staff members. They offer unpretentious accommodation at decent prices. The cottages are strewn in friendly disorder around the tree-lined property. Most have a small balcony or porch. There's a play area for kids, games and indoor sports, and they organise activities on weekends. The main drawback is lack of a sea view. But it's just a minute's walk to the beach.
♦**Closest local railway station** Malad **Resort food** Satisfactory. Indian-Chinese-Mughlai mix, with a few Goan and East Indian dishes thrown in. No alcohol **Tel** 28452163/ 78 (resort); 24462161/ 9735 (city booking) **Tariff** Rs 250-1,000 **Hotel food** Satisfactory **Tel** 28452643/ 280 **Tariff** Rs 250-1,000

MANORIBEL, MANORI Located across the wall from the conjoined Domonica's, the ambience here is more yuppie. It's quieter, with a lot more open space, and it's more expensive. Stone arches predominate, and no groves or other properties block the sea view or the breeze. It has large, airy rooms, with the best ones facing the sea. There's a *machan* to watch the sunset from, and the beach is just over the low wall. The restaurant roof is supported by stone pillars, without any walls, so you eat serenaded by the sea breeze flirting with the coconut palms.
♦**Closest railway station** Malad **Food** Good. No alcohol **Tel** 28452806-09 (resort); 22691301/ 2108 (city booking) **Tariff** Rs 832-4,620

The tempting buffet at a resort

ABHIJIT BHATLEKAR

THE RESORT, AKSA This is 5-star holidaying, and if you're here, it really doesn't matter how inhospitable the beach is, because there's enough to keep you occupied at the hotel itself. It has all that you'd expect — a large pool with great view, gym, sports facilities, kiddie room, massages, steam, business centre, you name it, they have it. The sea-facing rooms have their own balconies.
♦**Closest local railway station** Malad **Food** Two restaurants (one multi-cuisine, one coffee shop). Good food **Tel** 28808888, 28445538 (resort); 26443333 (city booking) **Tariff** Rs 5,800-16,000

THE RETREAT, ERANGAL There's an overall feel of airiness and space here. The curved lines of the pool, with its little island and waterfall, blending into a covered area with a sunken bar where you can swim right up to your drink and sip it sitting on a submerged barstool or clamber out for a snack, all make for a charming and attractive centre-piece. All the standard 5-star amenities are there: gym, health club, lounges, the works.
♦**Closest local railway station** Malad **Food** Three restaurants — Chinese, a coffee shop and a poolside snackbar. Excellent food **Tel** 28816383/ 3500 (resort); 22834441 (city office) **Tariff** Rs 6,600-12,000

For details, see Mumbai Accommodation Listings on pages 557-558 ■

ALIBAUG

BUGGY ON THE BEACH

State Maharashtra
Location On the Konkan Coast, just south of Mumbai, across a narrow stretch of the Arabian Sea
Distance 113 km S of Mumbai
Journey time ***By road*** 3 hrs from Mumbai ***By sea*** 50 mins + 30 mins by road
Route from Mumbai NH17 to Vadkhal Naka via Pen; SH to Alibaug via Poynad and Khandale (*see route guide on page 394*)

BY AMIT MAHAJAN

What a sight it is! I look back and people of all shapes and sizes are walking *splish... splosh... splish... splosh...* into the water, away from the land. The beach and its cluster of buildings are slowly receding into the background. Most people have their dresses hitched up, a meaningless ritual really because below the waist everybody is soaking wet, and by the looks of it, liking it too. I am part of a throng of people, the water is knee deep, then a wave

Photographs by DHRITIMAN MUKHERJEE

comes and the water rises waist high. Every face carries the laughter of disbelief. We are crossing the sea; we are simply and incredibly walking across it!

At Alibaug Beach, this sea crossing is not unusual. Walking across the water is a daily pilgrimage — the walk, or the wade rather, being undertaken to the Kolaba Fort.

All day long people wait for the low tide. The locals knowingly look at the sea and can figure out when the time for the crossing will come. Visitors ask around, looking longingly at the Kolaba Fort, which is tantalisingly close to the beach. However, the water is deep and the fort is inaccessible for most of the day. As the water drains from the narrow divide between the beach and the fort at low tide, people start walking towards the fort. People in hundreds, and with them a few horse-driven buggies for all those who do not want to or are unable to make it on foot.

As you leisurely walk upon the broad walls of the fort, surveying the coast and the sea beyond, the strategic location of the stronghold gives you an insight into the guile of the Marathas, which made them such a formidable force in the late 17th and 18th centuries.

Both the Kolaba Fort and the Alibaug Town owe their existence to the Marathas. Kanhoji Angre, an important admiral of Shivaji, created Alibaug Town and its port. Kolaba Fort was built by Shivaji to counter, mainly the prowess of the Siddis of Murud-Janjira, and also the Portuguese, the Dutch and the English.

Today the popularity of Alibaug lies in its small-town beachside charms, that too just a hop away from Mumbai. The well-heeled from Mumbai zeroed in on the beaches and the green pastures here as the perfect locale for their 'farmhouses', a mere hour-and-a-half away from the Gateway of India. Weekenders followed suit and now they repeatedly grace the vast sprawls of soft sand on offer here.

→ FAST FACTS

When to go September to April is the best time to go; mid-June to August is wet because of the rains. During the monsoon, the region can be gorgeous, even though a tad uncomfortable

Tourist office

- MTDC Main Reservation Office

CDO Hutments, opposite LIC Building
Madame Cama Road, Mumbai-400020
Tel: 022-22026713, 22027762
Email: mahatour@bol.net.in
Website: mtdcindia.com

STD code 02141

ORIENTATION

The name Alibaug refers to two entities in **Raigad District** of Maharashtra: a small town and a bigger administrative region (taluka). Creeks border Alibaug Taluka to the north and the south. On the west is a long shoreline stretching from **Rewas** to **Revdanda**. Alibaug Town is right in the centre of this western shore.

Alibaug Beach is about a kilometre south of the town centre. **Kolaba Fort** is less than a kilometre from the beach. The Alibaug Taluka has many beaches on its shores. **Versoli**, **Kihim**, **Awas**, **Sasavne** and **Mandwa** (from south to north) are to the north of Alibaug Beach. **Akshi** and **Nagaon** lie to the south. The **bus stand** marks the centre of the town. The offices of the boat services (PNP, Ajanta, Maldar) to Mumbai are located here. It's also the place to find autos (unmetered yet never unreasonable; the minimum fare is Rs 15) and shared tempos.

For taxis, contact **Sahara Travels** (Tel: 02141-227711) and **Kavita Travels** (Tel: 228726), or ask your hotel. Alibaug does not have too many taxis; the fare is around Rs 1,200-1,500 per day. Most hotels are located near the Alibaug Beach and the bus stand.

GETTING THERE

Air Nearest airport: Mumbai's Chhatrapati Shivaji Airport (113 km/ 3 hrs), connected by flights from most Indian and international cities. Taxi fare to Alibaug is Rs 2,000 approx

Rail Nearest railhead: Pen (28 km/ 45 mins). Located on the Konkan Railway, Pen is connected to Mumbai, Goa and Mangalore. You can take a taxi (Rs 600) or bus to Alibaug

Road Take NH17 to Vadkhal Naka via Karnala and Pen. Where NH17 turns left to Goa, take the straight road to Alibaug via Poynad and Khandale. There are state transport buses to Alibaug from Mumbai Central and Borivli

Sea Frequent boats and launches for Mandwa Jetty leave from the Gateway of India (50 mins-1 hr) between 6.15 am and 6.30 pm. The ticket fare, which is between Rs 65 and 200, includes a bus drive from Mandwa Jetty to Alibaug (19 km/ 30 mins). The ferry service is discontinued in the monsoon

BEACH WATCH

You need to be careful off the beaches in Alibaug. They are safe for swimming at high tide; be cautious during low tide, and don't go far from the coast in any case. There are no lifeguards on the beaches. Wearing beachwear is okay, but you won't be able to buy it here.

To cross to Kolaba Fort enquire about safe timings from vendors and locals on the beach. It's best to start at least 2 hrs before the time of the lowest tide (that happens twice a day) so that you have enough time to return safely. The time of the lowest ebb shifts by 45 mins daily. Don't try to cross at or near high tide; many people have lost their lives attempting precisely that.

THINGS TO SEE AND DO

Alibaug offers many beaches in and around the town. The beaches are safe and clean enough to enjoy gambolling in the water. None of the beaches have facilities for water sports such as boating, diving or snorkelling. Alibaug Beach is the most popular of the beaches and has a lot of visitors at most times. Other beaches are relatively less frequented. Mornings are ideal for quiet walks and birdwatching. Only those who plan to be continuously in the water should visit the beaches in the afternoons as they are

The sea, the sun and a promenade for tourists on Alibaug Beach

warm and there is not much shade on the beaches to escape the sun. Evenings mean big playful crowds on the beaches — groups, families and lonely souls, all flock here to join the fun. A lot of people come to Alibaug to spend a leisurely weekend, but in fact another day or two won't exhaust its possibilities.

Alibaug Beach

At high tide you might think there is no beach in Alibaug. The water rushes against the concrete embankment that separates the sea and the *thelas* of nariyal pani, bhel puri, *ragda* patties and kulfi. As the water begins to recede, the embankment reveals its stairs looking out to the ocean and the black sand beneath. In the evening, six-seated horse-driven buggies offer rides (Rs 10 per person for 15 mins), and the vendors move across the embankment to sell their stuff on the beach.

Kolaba Fort

The fort is located just across Alibaug Beach on a rock jutting out into the sea and dominates the landscape of the beach and the imagination of its visitors. For most, it's the main reason to visit Alibaug Beach, and rightly so. A couple of hours before low tide, water becomes low enough for people to wade or take horse-rides (Rs 30 per person, 30 mins at the fort) to the fort. The construction of this fort was begun by Chhatrapati Shivaji in the 1680s and it is 900 ft long, 350 ft wide and has 25-foot high walls with 17 bastions! The fort has many shrines, the most important being the 18th-century temple, **Ganesh Panchayatan**. Next to it is a sweet water well that must have been an asset during sieges.

♦**Location** 700m south-west of Alibaug Beach **Entry fee** Indians Rs 5, foreigners Rs 100 **Video cameras** Rs 25

Note Visit only a couple of hours before low tide

Akshi and Nagaon

Akshi Beach is located south of Alibaug, on the road to Revdanda, 3 km from Alibaug. A road through coconut and betel-nut plantations leads to Akshi and the beach itself is lined with *suru* trees.

Travellers and locals who seek quiet are the main visitors to this beach, and are rewarded with nimbu pani and other cool drinks. Nagaon is further south on the same road, 7 km from Alibaug. Keep a lookout for the Shivaji statue and turn right from there, to reach the long, broad and clean beach. Mornings and evenings see a lot of fishing activity here.

Versoli and Kihim

Versoli is situated on the outskirts of Alibaug, about 2 km to the north of Alibaug Beach. It's a lovely walk through green lanes to Versoli. From the beach, you can see the Kolaba Fort and also two other smaller forts — **Khanderi** and **Underi**. Both these forts were built in the late 17th century. You can hire a local boat (Rs 500 or more) from Versoli, Kihim or Thal to visit these forts.

Kihim is situated 11 km from Alibaug to the north; to get here turn left at Chondhi on the Alibaug-Rewas Road. The beach is a stony stretch with white sand. It's a lovely retreat dotted with beautiful farmhouses and thick vegetation. The laid-back village wakes up in the evening to host picnicking crowds, who come to enjoy the clean waters, and the delicious snacks sold here.

Awas and Sasavne

Awas and Sasavne beaches are further north, 18 and 20 km respectively, from Alibaug. They are both huge, playground-like beaches, their waters full of fishing boats whose flags flutter in the breeze. Along the shore are the bungalows of Mumbai's elite, who go to the beaches for their evening constitutional, and gaze at the illuminated Mumbai shoreline across the water.

SHOPPING

Watch out for mangoes, especially the famous Alphonsoes, during the season (April to June). Though Alibaug is north of Ratnagiri and Sindhudurg, the main centres of Alphonso cultivation, it does get a good crop of mangoes (Rs 150 and

Akshi Beach, lined by casuarinas, is for those seeking a quiet stretch of sand

PUNIT PARANJPE

The samadhi to Kanhoji Angre, a much-revered Maratha navy chief, at Alibaug

more per dozen). Cashew, a relatively new crop in the region, is another item worth buying (Rs 200-350 per kilo). The area around the bus stand is where you will find most shops.

WHERE TO STAY

Alibaug has a lot of mid-range and budget accommodation but there are hardly any high-end resorts. The area around Alibaug Beach has the most number of hotels; other places to stay are to be found in Versoli, Kihim and the road to Mandwa. Weekends are busy throughout the year, and it's advisable to book in advance. Most hotels have a stringent checkout time of 9 am.

Sun Glow Resorts (Tel: 02141-221072-73; Tariff: Rs 1,200-1,500) is nice and clean, and is located right on Alibaug Beach, with a superb view of Kolaba Fort. **Hotel Sea View** (Tel: 222605; Tariff: Rs 1,050-1,800) nextdoor is equally well-placed.

Guruji Holiday Resort (Tel: 222266/ 85; Tariff: Rs 600-1,100) is located just a wee bit away from the beach. It's a little run down on the outside but quite clean and comfortable inside. **Hotel Meera Madhav** (Tel: 225279-81; Tariff: Rs 700-1,550), near the ST Bus Stand, is a tidy place located right in the centre of Alibaug Town.

Sun-N-Sea (Tel: 222390/ 697; Tariff: Rs 1,500-3,500) is opposite the district court on the way to Versoli, just 5 mins from the beach. The rooms are well-decorated and there's a swimming pool too for water buffs. **Hotel Big Splash** (Tel: 226801-05; Tariff: Rs 2,000-3,500), a bit flashy as the name suggests, is in Alibaug Village, on the road to Thal. **Sai-Inn Holiday Resort** (Tel: 232801-02; Tariff: Rs 1,900-3,900) is located in Chodhi Village on Alibaug-Rewas Road. The resort is spacious and nicely designed with a swimming pool.

For more hotels and details, see Alibaug Accommodation Listings on pages 551-552

WHERE TO EAT

Alibaug does not offer a great dining experience. In the evening Alibaug

AKSHAY MAHAJAN

One for the sea: The ferry service that connects Mandwa to Mumbai

Beach chokes with foodstalls selling pani puri, bhel puri and similar snacks. There are also Chinese and South Indian dishes on offer.

There is no big restaurant on the beach, and the eating experience has to be of the roadside kind. Restaurants at **Guruji**, **Meera Madhav** and **Big Splash** dish out the usual Mughlai and Chinese fare. For more local flavours, including Konkani fish preparations, crab and thalis, try the smaller places such as **Hotel Sanman**, **Hotel Anirudha** and **Hotel Sarawat**, located between the town centre and the beach. Do not come hoping for cold beer and exotic cocktails on the beaches here. There are some permit rooms offering 'strong beer' and whisky but they lack the ambience for chilling out.

AROUND ALIBAUG

Mandwa Jetty (19 km)
Mandwa is the first port of call in the Raigad District, across the sea from Mumbai, and thus the first choice for Mumbai's well-heeled to have their home away from home. From Alibaug, the road to Mandwa turns left before Rewas and winds its way through small hills on the left and the sea to the right. The jetty is a small but busy structure, with a beautiful curving beach on both sides. Boats to and from Mumbai run morning to evening and are the favoured mode of transport between Mumbai and Alibaug Taluka. A taxi will drop you for Rs 400, while shared tempos will charge about Rs 15.

Rewas Jetty (23 km)
Rewas is the terminus of the Alibaug-Rewas Road; the jetty is located at the edge of the Rewas-Dharamtar creek. There are ferry services to Bhaucha Dhakka in Mumbai ($1^1/_2$ hrs) throughout the day. From the jetty and the nearby isolated beach, you can see the shore of Uran across the sea. A small market selling fruits, vegetables, fish and crabs adds local flavour to this old port. A taxi will get you here for Rs 500; it's Rs 18 by shared tempo. ■

KASHID

THE CATCHER BY THE SEA

State Maharashtra
Location On the Konkan Coast, in Raigad District, amidst the low hills that spread out next to the Arabian Sea
Distance 139 km S of Mumbai
Journey time ***By road*** 4 hrs from Mumbai
Route from Mumbai NH17 to Vadkhal Naka via Pen; SH to Kashid via Alibaug and Revdanda (*see route guide on page 394*)

BY AMIT MAHAJAN

The Frisbee rose again in the air, for a moment it paused mid-flight, savoured the breeze, tilted downwards and began its descent, presenting itself to the other woman at shoulder height. The two women read the wind to perfection, and the disc was a trained bird that did their bidding. The game was a series of flawless movements being performed by two experts in complete sync. However, another couple got bored of splashing in the waves, and joined the Frisbee game. Soon the plastic disc seemed a lifeless thing being hurtled all over the place, in every which manner, and the game became a hilarious pantomime — a source of much fun and laughter.

The Kashid Beach is a day-long playground; most tourists are weekend runaways from Mumbai and Pune, or picnickers from nearby towns. The beach is usually sparsely populated and ideal for a solitary communion with the sea. People do begin trickling in on to the beach right from the morning, but there is never a rush. On weekends, there's an increase in the number of visitors but still not enough to be bothersome. The tall trees close to the beach provide an opportunity to alternate between the

Photographs by CHARUKESI RAMADURAI

sun and the shade through the day. As evening approaches, more and more people are drawn to the water, and they enjoy its swell till it gets dark and home — or as in our case, the hotel — beckons.

Horsing around on Kashid Beach

FAST FACTS

When to go Throughout the year, though May is hot and June-August is recommended for only those who do not mind the rain and choppy seas

Tourist office

- MTDC Main Reservation Office
CDO Hutments, Opp LIC Building
Madame Cama Road, Mumbai-400020
Tel: 022-22026713/ 7762
Email: mahatour@bol.net.in
Website: mtdcindia.com

STD code 02144

ORIENTATION

Kashid is a small village on the **Alibaug-Murud Road** close to the Arabian Sea. The village and the hotels are spread along the highway south of the beach. The beach itself has only a few shacks selling snacks. There are no taxis in Kashid and only a few autos (Rs 10 per km, minimum fare of Rs 20) and shared tempos (Rs 5 or more) pass by.

BEACH WATCH

Notice boards on the beach read: "Treacherous sea. The beach is dangerous; do not go far into the sea. People have lost lives by going far into the sea. The sea is deep." One needs to be especially cautious during low tide. Carry your swimwear; you will not be able to buy it there.

THINGS TO SEE AND DO

Kashid Beach is not a bustling one with lots of activities. Whatever activity you wish to indulge in has to be generated by you. Most people are happy to simply be away from wherever they have come from, and spend the day on the beach watching it change its character with the movement of the sun. The few beach shacks provide snacks and chairs and hammocks. They also rent out volleyballs and footballs and Frisbees. A couple of days are sufficient to have a relaxed holiday in Kashid.

Korlai Fort

Chadai karna, in Hindi literally means, "to climb". It's also used to mean, "conquering or attacking a fort". At Korlai you know why. A narrow strip of a hill juts out into the Arabian Sea at the edge of the Revdanda Creek, and on the ridge-like top of the hill are the remains of a fort. To get to Korlai Fort, turn west on the Alibaug-Murud Road and go through the Korlai Village, past a network of grey lanes made of concrete reaching for the sea. Beyond the village are the sea and the beach where fishing activity goes on in full swing. To the north is a hill, and a bumpy road curves around it to reach a **lighthouse**. Behind the lighthouse, a steep flight of steps rises up the hill to the fort on the top.

The fort was built by the Nizamshah of Ahmednagar towards the end of the 16th century during a power tussle between the Mughals and the Portuguese to control this area and its sea trade. The views from the fort are amazing — the Revdanda creek and fort to the north, and the Korlai Village and beach to the south. The sea spreads on its three sides. ♦**Location** The fort lies 13 km north of Kashid **Entry** Free **Timings** 9 am to 6-7 pm **Connection** An auto from Kashid will cost Rs 500-600 for a return-trip

→ GETTING THERE

Air Nearest airport: Mumbai's Chhatrapati Shivaji Airport (139 km/ 4 hrs), connected by flights from most Indian and international cities. Taxi fare to Kashid is Rs 3,000 approx

Rail Nearest railhead: Roha (43 km/ 1 hr). Located on the Konkan Railway, Roha is connected to Mumbai, Goa and Mangalore. Taxis (Rs 800) and State Transport buses are available from Roha to Kashid

Road Take NH17 to Vadkhal Naka via Karnala and Pen. At the point where NH17 turns left to Goa, take the straight road to Alibaug via Poynad and Khandale. Take the coastal road to Kashid via Revdanda. There are State Transport buses to Kashid from Mumbai Central and Borivli

Sea Frequent boats and launches for Mandwa Jetty leave from the Gateway of India (50 min-1 hr) between 6.15 am and 6.30 pm, except during the monsoon. Tickets, Rs 65 to 200, include a bus drive from Mandwa Jetty to Alibaug (19 km, 30 mins). Kashid is 34 km from Alibaug. One-way taxis cost Rs 800-1,000

TIP You cut an hour's drive if you take the boat. If you plan to drive around, it's best to take your own car as there are only a few autos and no taxis in Kashid

WHERE TO STAY

For a small village Kashid has quite a few staying options. However, none of the hotels are on the beach. **Prakruti Hermitage** (Tel: 02144-278509; Tariff: Rs 5,460-23,940) is a spacious resort on the hillside facing the sea. The higher tariff is for its 4-room villas. **Sai Palace** (Tel: 278629, Tariff: Rs 1,300-2,600) is next-door and has a beautiful garden and decent rooms.

Kashid Beach Resort (Tel: 278501-03; Tariff: Rs 3,500-7,000) is a nicely laid-out resort, green and clean, but not on the beach. **Friends Holiday Home** (Tel: 278611; Tariff: Rs 650-1,000), **Sagar Tourist Home** (Tel: 278525; Tariff: Rs 800-1,000) and **Kashid Beach Villa** (Tel: 022-26408955; Mobile: 09820191822; Tariff: Rs 2,000-10,000) are more homely choices. These are clean places with small gardens right on the main road.

For more hotels and details, see Kashid Accommodation Listings on page 555

WHERE TO EAT

Kashid has no stand-alone restaurants. Mostly, you'll need to have your meals in the hotel you stay in, and don't expect too much from these kitchens. **Kashid Beach Resort** has a multi-cuisine restaurant serving Indian, Continental, Chinese and Konkani dishes. Their menu has everything from veg-au-gratin and mutton stew to dal and noodles. Non-guests can also dine here. The beach has shacks that sell chips, cold drinks, tea, coconut water, Maggi, omelette and such.

AROUND KASHID

Revdanda (17 km)

Driving on the coastal road from Alibaug to Murud you might notice an old

AKSHAY MAHAJAN

Residents of Korlai Village, who speak a Portuguese Creole called Kristi

Mind your language: Korlai's tradition

The few people who visit Korlai usually go there to see the impressively located fort and the amazing views it offers. However, the Korlai Village below the fort has another bit of history hidden among its people.

The less than thousand people who inhabit Korlai speak a language that is unique to them, a Portuguese Creole called Kristi that is spoken nowhere else. They call it No Ling, that is, Our Language.

The Portuguese left Korlai in 1740 after having been there for more than two centuries. Kristi developed during this interaction between the Portuguese and the local population.

Till the 1980s, when the Revdanda creek was bridged by a road, the small peninsula of Korlai was relatively isolated from the surrounding communities, and thus the language survived the last few centuries.

Now the tongue is fast disappearing under the influence of Marathi and Hindi. But if you roam around the concrete streets of Korlai and visit its small church you can still hear snatches of Kristi.

archway that spans the road, and then a small market town and another archway through which you exit. And this will be your experience of Revdanda — if you don't take a right turn between these archways, that is.

If you do, you'll discover, at first, the remains of a huge outer wall, and then many interconnected routes hiding beneath dense greenery, and finally, the ramparts of a **big fort** and a dilapidated **seven-storey tower** right next to the sea. During high tide the waves crash right on to the outer wall of the old fort, but at low tide the water ebbs and reveals a dark blackish beach with magnificent views of the Revdanda creek and the Korlai Fort to the south. The Portuguese built the fort in the 16th century, and its ruins can still evoke the mysteries of a romantic past. An auto from Kashid will cost Rs 700-800 for a return-trip. ■

MURUD-JANJIRA

SUNSET BOULEVARD

State Maharashtra
Location On the Konkan Coast, south of Mumbai in Raigad District
Distance 167 km S of Mumbai
Journey time ***By road*** $4^1/_2$ hrs from Mumbai
Route from Mumbai NH17 to Vadkhal Naka via Pen; SH to Murud via Alibaug, Revdanda and Kashid (*see route guide on page 394*)

BY AMIT MAHAJAN

If you visit Murud as a tourist you might come away believing that life and economy in Murud organise themselves around the daily sunset. And you would not be very much off the mark. Murud Beach waits all day for the sun to turn red over the sea, with the impossibly located Padmadurg Fort, seemingly floating in the water, in the foreground. A long-drawn daily ritual begins about a couple of hours before the sunset. Bhelpuri and panipuri vendors occupy selected spots and get busy, slicing boiled potatoes and mashing chickpeas. Coconut-water sellers pile up the fruit, readying their long, curved knife to chop off the tops. Cold drink vendors arrange ice-slabs and bottles of coloured syrups, and are quick to dole out a *kala khatta* or a *nimbu pani* at the slightest request. Horses, paired and dragging their six-seater carriages, do their warm-up runs; there are some bullock-carts too, all decked up and eager to go. This makes up the supply side of the sunset economy.

From among the representatives of the demand side of the same sunset

economy, the elderly are the first to arrive, taking up prime seats on the benches lining the road next to the beach. The younger lot are happier to be in the nearby restaurants, under the shade of palm trees. As it gets cooler and the sun ever so slowly departs, the crowd gets thicker. Couples and families make their way to the water, and a bold girl gets her ankles wet. It seems as if everyone has been waiting for someone to break the ice. Soon the shallow sea is full of playful people, people splashing water at each other, people riding the waves, and people hysterical with laughter.

The tourists among this crowd can't keep their eyes off the Padmadurg Fort in the distance and compare it with the Janjira Fort they would have visited earlier. The fascinating Janjira is the famous citadel occupying an island close to the Murud Coast.

Equally fascinating is the story of the Siddis, who ruled the Murud region for more than three centuries, and who built this extraordinary fort. The Siddis were trader-warriors from Abyssinia who settled in Murud-Janjira and became part of the population of this region. Some of them ruled the region for about 400 years and became famous along with their fort. Today, apart from the beach, the Janjira Fort and the mystique

FAST FACTS

When to go Throughout the year, though May to August is off-season. Not many visitors come here during the monsoon from mid-June to August, but it's exceedingly green and beautiful. However, the sea will be out of bounds

Tourist office

- MTDC

Main Reservation Office
CDO Hutments, Opp LIC Building
Madame Cama Road
Mumbai-400020
Tel: 022-22026713/ 7762

STD code 02144

ATUL LOKE

enclosed within its moss-covered robust walls are what draw tourists to these beautiful shores.

ORIENTATION

Murud Taluka is part of Raigad District of Maharashtra, spreading along the coast from **Revdanda Creek** to **Aagardanda Creek**. The entire coast is hilly and the coastal highway runs close to the Arabian Sea, through these hills.

→ GETTING THERE

Air Nearest airport: Mumbai's Chhatrapati Shivaji Airport (167 km/ 4½ hrs), connected by flights from most Indian and international cities. Taxi fare to Murud is Rs 3,000 approx

Rail Nearest railhead: Roha (66 km/ 1½ hrs). Located on the Konkan Railway, Roha is connected to Mumbai, Goa and Mangalore. Taxis (Rs 1,000) and State Transport buses are available from Roha to Murud

Road NH17 to Vadkhal Naka via Karnala and Pen. At the point where NH17 turns left to Goa, take the straight road to Alibaug via Poynad and Khandale. Take the coastal road to Murud via Revdanda and Kashid. There are State Transport buses to Murud from Mumbai Central and Borivli

Sea Frequent boats and launches for Mandwa Jetty leave from the Gateway of India (50 mins-1 hr) in Mumbai between 6.15 am and 6.30 pm, except during the monsoon. Tickets, priced from Rs 65 to 200, include a bus drive from Mandwa Jetty to Alibaug (19 km/ 30 mins). Murud is 54 km from Alibaug. One-way taxis cost Rs 1,000-1,200

TIP The boat ride saves you time

Murud Town is small and is located to the south of the taluka. **Janjira**, the prime attraction here, is the famous fort on an island 4 km south of Murud. The town and the fort form a single unit in popular imagination and are collectively referred to as Murud-Janjira.

The **Murud Beach** faces west and fans out from north to south. The **Padmadurg Fort** stands on a rocky outcrop about a mile across the beach into the Arabian Sea. Most hotels and restaurants are located on **Darbar Road** (also called Dr Rajendra Prasad Road), running along **Murud Beach**. **Datta Mandir Road** is the main road going east into town from Darbar Road.

The main modes of transport in Murud are autos and shared tempos. Autos are unmetered; the minimum fare is Rs 15 and Rs 50 will cover most of the town. Murud doesn't have a taxi stand or travel agents. Your hotel will be the best bet to get information and organise trips.

BEACH WATCH

Most of Murud Beach is safe for swimming, provided that you don't venture too far into the sea. At high tide the water comes inland; it's deep enough even right near the coast. At low tide people tend to go far out to reach deep waters, and that increases the danger. Be careful in the southern part of the beach that has a zone which is dangerous because of unexpected dips; the area is marked by two poles with saffron flags. There are no lifeguards here. Murud does not get tourists who are interested in beaches for sunbathing. You will not find many people in swimsuits nor shops selling beachwear.

THINGS TO SEE AND DO

A two- or three-day holiday is ideal to see Murud and its surrounding attractions. While Janjira Fort is the chief reason for visiting Murud, the beautiful

AKSHAY MAHAJAN

Children enjoy an audience with the ocean on Murud Beach

beach is where people spend most of their mornings and evenings. The two island forts — Janjira and Padmadurg — can be seen during the daylight hours. At sunset the best place to be at is the beach or up at Idgah, the highest point in Murud.

Murud Beach

The beach is a sheltered stretch of sand surrounded on three sides by hills. Rocky outcrops flank it to the north and south; to the east lie the Murud Town and the hills beyond.

Early mornings are great for a private audience with the ocean, and a plunge in the rumbling waves. Evenings are more vivacious and playful; crowds converge on the beach to enjoy the breeze, the daily spectacle of the sunset and the sense of belonging to a community. This community indulges in walks, brisk or leisurely, on the wet sand, rides on horse buggies and even bullock carts, and consumes huge amounts of *chatpatta* snacks. Murud does not offer much if you are a water sports enthusiast, but you can enjoy rides on sailboats (Rs 1,000 per hour approx) that can be hired from the fisherfolk at the Rajpuri Jetty.

Padmadurg Fort

The Siddis of Janjira posed a serious challenge to the might of the Marathas, and as a counter strategy, Shivaji's son Sambaji commissioned a fortress, late in the 17th century, on a rock called Kasa, a mile into the sea. The now desolate fort was once guarded by high walls and six bastions, and saw fierce battles between the Siddis and the Marathas. A number of cannons can still be seen within the crumbling walls of the fort, reminders of the fierce rivalry between the various maritime powers of the region. Private boats can be hired to visit the fort (Rs 500 or more, during the daylight hours) with permission from the Superintendent of Customs, whose office is opposite Golden Swan Resort.

Datta Mandir and Idgah

Datta Mandir is located atop a hill to the north of Murud, and is approached by

ATUL LOKE

The invincible Janjira Fort

The boat moved westwards into the sea, dancing noiselessly on gentle waves. The crew of three was sitting on the edges with a nonchalance that was missing in the passengers grouped in the centre of the boat, holding on to various props in an attempt to maintain a semblance of balance and looking open-mouthed at the gigantic structure looming in the distance. Suddenly, the crew moved into action and the three men began a well-orchestrated routine in which they opened the sail and moved it into a different position. The boat changed course and headed northwards towards the fort. The journey to the Janjira Fort, across the Rajpuri creek in a small sail boat, reminds you of the old times when this coast was a busy turf where the sport of sea trade and piracy was played in dead earnest.

The name Janjira is a corrupted form of Zizera, which in Arabic means an island. A wooden fort was initially built in the 15th century by the Koli fishermen of Rajpuri Village on a rock in the sea. It was taken over by the Siddis who are believed to be descendants of East African slaves. The Siddis were first employed in the army of Ahmednagar Sultans and later ran a fiefdom from Janjira. They built a stone citadel, work on which started in 1569 and to which they added over the next 150 years. The fort was spread over 22 acres, and there were 19 towers mounted with cannons and turrets. **Three cannons** — Kala Bangdi, Chavri and Landa Kasam — are particularly huge and can still be seen among the ruins. The largest of these is the **Kala Bangdi**, which is over 18 ft long and of immense weight. Locals like to claim that when it boomed, the fort reverberated for a week.

The fort had two sweet water tanks and earned a reputation for being impregnable — arguably as much an outcome of the diplomatic games the Siddis played with the Marathas, Mughals, Portuguese and the English, as the fort's defences.

The fort was occupied till the 1980s, and has deteriorated fast over the past few decades. It lives a forlorn existence, though the ruins are impressive and worth spending a while. The guides at the fort tell an interesting tale but do not mistake their spicy stories for the truth.

◆**Location** Near Rajpuri Jetty, 4 km from Murud. From Murud to the jetty, auto charges will be around Rs 50 **Entry** Free **Timings** 7 am to 6-7 pm **Guide fee** Rs 250 or more, depending on the number of people in a group

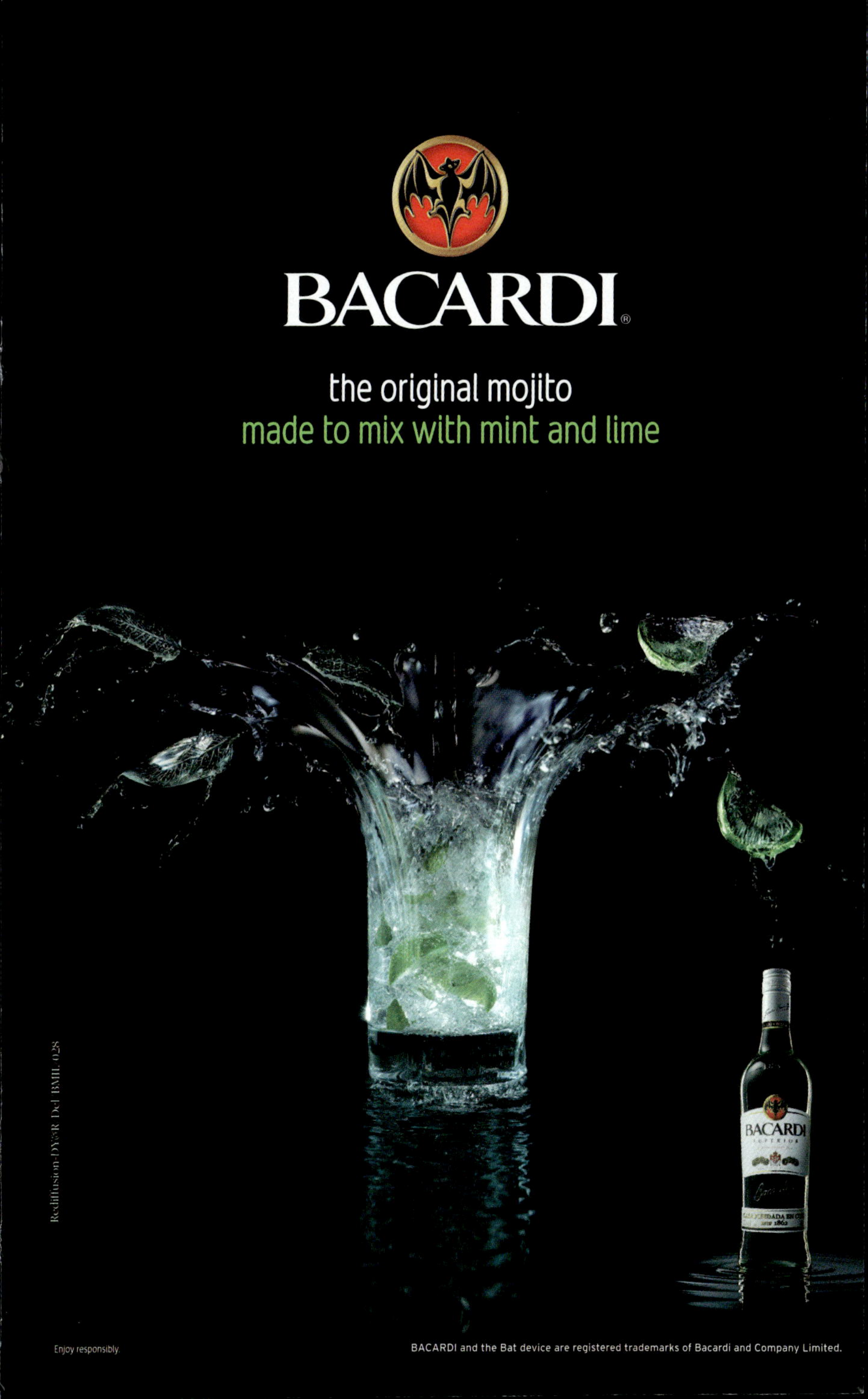
BACARDI®
the original mojito
made to mix with mint and lime
Rediffusion-DY&R Del BMIL 028
BACARDI
Enjoy responsibly.
BACARDI and the Bat device are registered trademarks of Bacardi and Company Limited.

DHRITIMAN MUKHERJEE

The Idgah Mosque lies atop a hill, offering panoramic views of Murud Town

200-odd steps or by a motorable road. The rarely used Idgah mosque is higher up on the same hill. Both these shrines offer panoramic views of Murud Town hiding beneath a green canopy of coconut and areca nut palms. A line of hills rises in the east and there is a lovely blue spread of sea in the west.

Garambi

Eight kilometres to the east of Murud is the scenic spot of Garambi, famous for its **perennial spring** that trickles through laterite rocks. There is a dam here that is over 100 years old, built as part of Victoria Water Works, the water supply system for Murud. Garambi is especially beautiful after the monsoon from October to December with its treasure of deciduous trees and shrubs, which attract a variety of birds and butterflies.

Khokri tombs

There are three tombs at Khokri, a small village 6 km south-east of Murud on the road to Aagardanda Jetty. The tombs, now in a state of ruin and neglect, are nevertheless beautiful specimens of the Indo-Saracenic style of architecture, built in the 18th century by the Siddi dynasty of Janjira.

SHOPPING

Murud is famous for its coconut chikki and barfi. You can buy it from any sweet shop near the ST Bus Stand or in the market near Siddi Bagh. **Hanuman Hotel**, near the bus stand, is also known for its sweets (Rs 100-180 per kilo). Weekend travellers from Mumbai also take home fish — surmai, pomfret and prawns.

WHERE TO STAY

Most hotels in Murud are mid-range and budget, and are concentrated on the road along the beach. Weekends are heavily booked throughout the year, except during the rains, and it's best to book in advance if you plan to come here on a weekend.

Golden Swan Beach Resort (Tel: 02144-274078; Tariff: Rs 1,200-7,500)

Black sands and casuarinas make Kelva the most scenic beach in Palghar

Kelva Beach

About 13 km from the main town, the beach is by far the most scenic in Palghar. Here, the black sands end where the *suru* trees begin. The sea is not as clean as it used to be once but thanks to the fact that it stretches for 7 km, the beach has the most number of tea stalls and cold drink vendors. There is a **fort** towards one end and the **Kelva Dam** 10 km away. Low tide is the best time to visit the fort, though it's now neglected and full of undergrowth. It's a long climb up the walls of the fort, and certainly not for the faint-hearted. Close to the beach is the **Sheetila Devi Mandir**. Make this your base to catch the sunset and sunrise.

WHERE TO STAY

Palghar is not the finest place when it comes to accommodation, but it has adequate options. Do book in advance if visiting over the weekend.

Situated near the beach, the **Kelva Beach Resort** (Tel: 02525-222346; Tariff: Rs 1,250-1,500 per person) has 4 rustic but luxurious bamboo huts, and 7 cement huts. Facilities such as a swimming pool, a badminton court, barbecue arrangements and a pool table are provided, as are meals. They offer a 24-hr checkout. About a 2-min walk from the Kelva Beach Resort is the **Anand Residency** (Tel: 222216; Tariff: Rs 300-500 per person), offering four simple rooms with attached baths for the budget traveller. Food is available; the checkout time is a stringent 9 am. A maximum of six people are allowed in one room. However, this place is not recommended for the solo woman traveller.

Close to the Palghar Railway Station, the **Jungle Resort and Water Park** (Tel: 251300; Tariff: Rs 1,300-1,700) is a tourist favourite, with three swimming pools and a water park. The resort is spread out over a vast area amid greenery, and although the rooms are not luxurious, the tariff is justified by the number of things you can do here.

Sai Residency (Tel: 241309; Tariff: Rs 350-650), near the station, offers a bar, seafood and room service. Rooms are clean and offer good value for money, although there is little difference between the AC and non-AC rooms except for the TV. **Laxmi Guesthouse** (Tel: 253007; Tariff: Rs 75-550), at Kuber Shopping Centre near Paanch Batti, has clean

dormitory beds and deluxe rooms. The spacious deluxe room offers TV and an extra couch. The rooms are clean, but overall the guest house is frequented more by trade owners than families.

For more hotels and details, see Palghar Accommodation Listings on page 559

WHERE TO EAT

Considering Palghar is situated along the Konkan Coast and two of its three beaches offer sights and sounds that are in many ways related to fish, you can't be blamed for expecting good seafood. However, most restaurants in Palghar are 'pure veg', so your options for seafood are limited to **Suruchi Restaurant** at Sai Residency in the main town, and the **Sai Shibir Resort** in Kelva. Suruchi offers Malvani and Chinese, but the seafood is average. **Viva Restaurant** opposite Paanch Batti has Continental, Chinese and South Indian food on its menu. Locals recommend **Rasam**, a restaurant situated opposite the Congress House near Paanch Batti. They also offer basic but good-quality food, snacks and fruit juices.

Situated at Paanch Batti, **Manisha Dairy Farm** is a landmark in its own right, at least as far as the locals are concerned. For less than Rs 20 you can have a tall glass of kesar or mango lassi; don't be surprised by the fact that a spoon is also handed to you along with the glass — the lassi is too thick and laden with sumptuous dry fruits to be sipped. Srikhand is available in lovely, slightly exotic flavours such as black grape, apple and anjeer and has its own cult following. You can drop in here any time between 7 am and 11 pm.

GETTING THERE

Air Nearest airport: Chhatrapati Shivaji Airport, Mumbai (120 km/ $2\frac{1}{2}$ hrs). Taxi to Palghar costs Rs 3,500-4,500

Rail Palghar Station, connected by direct trains from Mumbai. The first train is at 7.25 am from Mumbai Central (Ferozepur Janta Express), and the last one leaves at 10.40 pm (Ahmedabad Passenger). You can also take a fast local train up to Virar, and board one of the many shuttles that ply between Virar and Vapi/ Ahmedabad from there. The trains halt at Kelva Road Station as well. Shared autos from the Palghar Railway Station till Kelva Beach cost Rs 10

Road Take NH8 to Mastan Naka in Manor via Shirsad. Take a left off the highway for Palghar. The bus connections between Palghar and Mumbai are not very good. There are no AC buses running directly to Palghar, but most State Transport buses plying between Mumbai and Ahmedabad halt there

AROUND PALGHAR

Devkop (12 km)

This is a lovely surprise hidden in the hills, frequented by photographers and picnickers during the monsoon. A 10-min trek along a fairly easy path dotted by straw huts on one side and fields on the other takes you to a tiny hill, beyond which lies the **Devkop Lake**. The lake is surrounded by hills on three sides, casting stunning reflections on a clear day. Even in summer — when you might just turn around without even completing the trek, missing the lake — it's a beauty to behold. Look out for a small board to your left on the Palghar-Manor Road, and ask locals for directions. Swimming is not allowed and drowning accidents have happened here in the past. A special autorickshaw from the station charges Rs 80-100. Shared autos are also available for Rs 10, but only up till the main road, from where you will have to walk. ■

Photographs by ABHILASH GAUR

BORDI

SWEET AS A CHIKOO

State Maharashtra
Location On the shores of the Arabian Sea, in Thane District, Bordi is practically Maharashtra's northernmost outpost and lies just 3 km away from the state's border with Gujarat at Zai
Distances 24 km N of Dahanu, 179 km N of Mumbai
Journey time ***By road*** $^1/_2$ hr from Dahanu, 4 hrs from Mumbai
Route from Mumbai NH8 to Kasa Khurd via Manor; SH to Dahanu via Ashagarh; beach road to Bordi via Gholvad (*see route guide on page 394*)

BY ABHILASH GAUR

The waves come in slowly over the gentle slope of Bordi Beach and retreat even more leisurely, raising bubbles from the air trapped in the black sand. Sometimes they leave behind a tiny creature of the sea, or two, and the stray dogs go for it. Apart from their barking, the beach remains quiet for most of the day. You'll be by yourself during those warm hours, immersed in the gossip of the wind and the sea. Late evening is the time when the sea is the farthest out, and you can then easily walk up to the mangroves on the left tip of the beach's crescent. That's also the time when Bordi's adolescents convert the beach into a dozen cricket pitches and fill the air with their shouts. Unless you are visiting on the weekend, you'll be the only one with eyes for the setting sun.

Early in the morning, you'll find that the sea has washed away the evening's

footprints. On the day I visit, Santosh Raut and his four small bullock carts make their way back from the beach to Bordi Village. He's a sand seller who likes to chat up tourists. I ask him why the place is named Bordi. "Because of the boarding schools," he says, laughing.

Nobody knows why Bordi has been named Bordi, but it's an ancient town that was visited by Mahatma Gandhi and his wife Kasturba. The old fire temple here and the many Irani-labelled gateways are proof that this village-town of 8,000 souls has been inhabited for eons. And though it may be only just rising on the tourism circuit, it has already made a name for itself as a centre of learning. Its many Jain- and Parsi-run schools and polytechnics draw thousands of students from neighbouring Gujarat and Thane District of Maharashtra.

Chikoos, Bordi's sweetest offering

→ FAST FACTS

When to go November to February
Tourist office
● MTDC Hotel, Bordi
Tel: 02528-254243
Website: maharashtratourism.gov.in
STD code 02528

ORIENTATION

There are two Bordis: one for tourists and the other for residents. The tourists' Bordi in turn has two components: the **beach** and the **Beach Road**, along which four of the five hotels here are set. If you're coming into Bordi from **Gholvad**, the road will take you past the schools, colleges and polytechnics for which Bordi is famous. After these, the **MTDC Hotel** comes up abruptly on the seaside — it's the only beach hotel in town. Further ahead is the Swatantrya Stambh, which the locals call **Vijay Stambh** (Victory Memorial) and also serves as a traffic island. The main road continues past the **Parsi Fire Temple** and an old Jain dharamshala, where Kasturba Gandhi had stayed. The **bus terminus** and **auto stand** come up next on your left, completely hiding the sea. The road then loops around the middle of the village. Traffic flows one-way thereafter till you exit Bordi and hit the road to **Zai**, Maharashtra's last coastal village. Autos are the only mode of transport here. You can hire one for the day for Rs 600 (the fare is inclusive of waiting charges) for a trip that will cover Zai, Asvali Dam and Gholvad. Autos don't run on meter, so negotiate the fare in advance.

BEACH WATCH

Bordi has a very safe beach with no rocks or undercurrents. The stretch of sand beyond the MTDC Hotel gate is quite clean, but you need to watch your step towards the village, where people still defecate in the open despite admonitions painted all over. There are no water sports, nobody to take you out in a boat, and a swim in the afternoon would mean undertaking a very long walk to get the sea above your knees. Therefore, make the most of the high tide. Beachwear won't cause a riot in Bordi but you'll make a spectacle of yourself among locals and visitors from neighbouring Gujarat.

Fishing boats at Zai, the northernmost village on Maharashtra's coast

THINGS TO SEE AND DO

You can do a lot in Bordi without moving a limb — soak in the sun, take in the sea breeze and give your eardrums a break from the cacophony of the big city. All this is no doubt what makes Bordi such a fine weekend escape for Mumbaikars.

Walking tours

If you enjoy walking, then Bordi Beach is ideal, stretching as it does over 17 km. Depending on the time of day, you can walk under the casuarinas or out in the sun. The water may not be deep enough for swimming but it's alright for splashing around with friends. On weekends, horses do appear somewhat mysteriously for rides. Away from the beach, explore the chikoo orchards or spend time at Anand Resort's (*see Where to Stay on page 433*) water park. You can also go for walks in the village; look for the old houses with tiled roofs and shaded verandahs.

Gholvad

Bordi has its own little railway station called Bordi Road Station but it's so far out that Gholvad Station, just 2 km away, serves as the village-town's chief link with the outside world. On the short ride to the station, you can't miss the line-up of chikoo orchards — Gholvad is the 'Chikoo Bowl' of Maharashtra. There are several old houses of wealthy Iranis here, making for a charming picture.

Zai

Spelt Zai but pronounced Jhai, this is the northernmost village on Maharashtra's coast, and is 3 km from Bordi. You'll find small fishing boats on the sea all the way from Dahanu to Bordi, but never as many as at Zai; there are altogether a few hundred boats here. Glimpses of the fisherfolk's lives are there everywhere: there are vessels lying in a creek to be repaired, and others waiting for the tide to return to the beach.

Asvali Dam

Photography is prohibited at Asvali Dam, which is 6 km east of Bordi, but nobody comes away without clicking a picture or two. For, the green lake formed behind the 1,160-foot long dam is too pretty a sight, and the complete absence of guards too good an opportunity to be missed. There are fields below the dam, and Warli villages. It's altogether a fine picnic spot. Only the road leading up to it from the Bordi Road Railway Station is a disaster. It's best to visit Asvali after hiring an auto for a full-day tour for Rs 600. Auto drivers will charge you return fare even if you don't require the transport back.

→ GETTING THERE

Air Nearest airport: Chhatrapati Shivaji Airport, Mumbai (179 km/ 4 hrs). You can take a taxi to Bordi; fare varies between Rs 1,500 and 1,800

Rail Nearest railhead: Gholvad Station (2 km). A number of shuttle services between Mumbai and Surat halt at the station. However, Dahanu has a bigger station where trains from other places also stop. For instance, the Paschim Express from Delhi stops at Dahanu. Auto fare from Dahanu to Bordi is Rs 150 while from Gholvad it's Rs 30-40. Shared autos (they're a squeeze) charge only Rs 5 from Gholvad. In Dahanu, insist on going by the longer beach road for which the charges are Rs 120

Road From Mumbai, follow NH8 up to Charoti Naka (Kasa Khurd) via Manor. Turn left onto the Dahanu state highway. Dahanu is 28 km away via Ashagarh. At Dahanu, turn right and drive another 24 km along the beach road to Bordi via Gholvad. NH8 is excellent and the beach road is largely smooth

SHOPPING

One shop in Bordi is a must-visit: the tiny **Mahila Grihaudyog** outlet, just a couple of minutes' walk away from the MTDC Hotel towards Bordi Village. As the name suggests, it's a cooperative venture. Around 110 women in the village make various products out of the local chikoo produce, such as chips, pickle, *chikki* and powder. The chips are actually sun-dried pieces of the peeled fruit, without sugar or preservatives, and make for a healthy snack. The sweet pickle has chikoo pieces in a lemon-and-sugar syrup. *Chikki* is the tastiest and most popular, and it's made of chikoo, coconut and sugar. The powder is shipped out of the village to be used in chikoo-shakes through the year. Other interesting products include *khajur* chocolate, which is made of date paste and dry fruits, and gooseberry candy. Most products are sold in tiny packets priced Rs 12-25. The shop opens every morning at 8 am and closes at 7.30 pm.

You can also visit the village market, or *gujari*. Chikoo and chikoo products are available here and if you visit between end-September and December, you can be sure that you will be getting the best of chikoos.

WHERE TO STAY

Bordi is a budget traveller's delight with most rooms available at less than Rs 1,000 a night. Accommodation is at best homely, but the whole point of being here is to spend the maximum time on the beach, so who cares? As Bordi is popular with Mumbaikars as a weekend getaway, hotels have a check-out time of 9 am. It's harsh but makes sense for them as the guests typically leave early in the morning to get back straight to work on Monday. Do remember that none of the places in Bordi are very professionally run as these are homes that have been converted to hotels. The staff is friendly but slow to respond.

has two properties right on Murud Beach. The main resort has AC cottages and AC deluxe rooms, and the other, known as Beach House, has non-AC rooms. The nicely laid-out resort has direct access to the beach and a great view of the Padmadurg Fort.

Sandpiper Resorts (Tel: 274166; Tariff: Rs 1,400-3,200) is located on Idgah Road, on a hillock facing Murud Beach. The resort has non-AC and AC rooms and AC cottages. It has excellent views of the sea, which is just a short distance away.

Shoreline Resort (Tel: 274640-01, 274591; Tariff: Rs 1,200-2,500), **Sea Shell Resort** (Tel: 274306; Tariff: Rs 1,500-2,000) and **Hotel Sea Green** (Tel: 274171; Tariff: Rs 800-1,400) are clean and comfortable places looking out to the sea. These are also the better choices among many hotels on Darbar Road along the beach.

The entrance to the Janjira Fort

CHARUKESI RAMADURAI

For more hotels and details, see Murud-Janjira Accommodation Listings on page 558

WHERE TO EAT

Konkani seafood has to be the grub of choice in Murud, though it's often spicy. The restaurants in **Golden Swan Beach Resort** and **Sandpiper Resort** are good places for Konkani food. They also serve Indian, Tandoori and Chinese cuisines.

Patil Khanaval, Hotel Vinayak and **Hotel Anand Vatika**, all near the beach, have good seafood (jhinga curry and masala fish being two options) and also local vegetarian curries. Of the three, Patil Khanaval is the most popular eating place in Murud. Run by five brothers, the place is said to serve the best fish in Murud, be it rawa, surmai, pomfret or prawns.

The stalls and eateries on the beach also offer mouth-watering batata vada, pakodas, bhel puri and pani puri, and coconut water to wash them down with.

AROUND MURUD

Nandgaon (8 km)
Nandgaon is a small town on Murud-Alibaug Road and it has a **Siddhi Vinayak Temple** that's over three centuries old. The temple attracts all the visitors who come to Nandgaon and the beach lies mostly empty.

The main street of Nandgaon, flanked by beautiful two-storeyed houses, leads to betel nut plantations next to the beach. The 2-km long beach has young boys and men busy with cricket, and older couples enjoying their daily walks. Even so, this blackish beach, protected by hillocks on its two ends, is a solitary experience.

There are no accommodation options in Nandgaon. **RK Restaurant** (you can try the fish curry or chicken masala here) and **McIndia** (serves sandwiches and vada pav) are two eating options here, right on the main road. Autorickshaws (Rs 100) and buses (Rs 5) are available from Murud to Nandgaon. ■

Photographs by PUNIT PARANJPE

PALGHAR

NOT JUST A BEACH

State Maharashtra
Location Situated ahead of Virar in Thane District, Palghar falls on the Mumbai-Ahmedabad rail route. To its east lie the low hills of the Sahyadri Range, and to its west the Arabian Sea
Distance 120 km N of Mumbai
Journey time ***By road*** $2^1/_2$ hrs from Mumbai
Route from Mumbai Western Express Highway to Dahisar Check Naka; NH8 to Manor via Shirsad; SH to Palghar (*see route guide on page 394*)

BY SIMAR PREET KAUR

If you chat up locals in Palghar, they will tell you that the town's visitors largely comprise factory workers or those visiting the court premises here. Nevertheless, as you head towards the industrial town, high-rises gently give way to small rolling hills, making you wonder if there isn't something here for the tourist as well. Those suspicions are thankfully confirmed later in the day when children take out their bicycles for long rides, shared autos — locally called dum-dums — roar as they cart people to and from the station, and the resident fishermen bring in their catch for the day. It's certainly true that there's very little about the main town that would endear itself to travellers, but Palghar's beaches remain a big draw. Here, palm trees and casuarinas serenade the waves, and forts full of history and adventure speak of secrets as old as the land and the sea. Around the beaches are villages where the locals grow bananas and chikoos when not out fishing on the sea. If it's a combination of solitude, sea and history that you are looking for, this relatively unknown slice of North Konkan is just perfect.

ORIENTATION

Palghar is primarily a trade town, and most of the activity happens around the railway station. A little ahead of the station is **Paanch Batti** (Hutatma Chowk). Palghar has three beaches: **Satpati** and **Shirgaon** to the north and **Kelva** to the south. The best options to stay are around **Kelva Beach**, which is a popular weekend getaway for Mumbaikars; the rest of the hotels are located near the station itself. The **bus terminus** is right outside the **railway station**. Although buses ply to all the beaches around, dum-dums (available near the bus stand) are the most popular mode of transport; you can reach most places within a fare of Rs 10. A special auto to any of the three beaches costs Rs 100-120. Make sure you negotiate the rates, and waiting charges, beforehand. The Maharashtra Tourism Development Corporation does not have any office in or around Palghar. For information, contact its Mumbai office (*see below*).

→ FAST FACTS

When to go April to May is the season. Monsoon (June to September) is the best time to go though swimming will take a backseat then

Tourist office

- MTDC

CDO Hutments, Opp LIC Building
Madame Cama Road
Mumbai-400020
Tel: 022-22026713/ 7762

STD code 02525

BEACH WATCH

Swimming is more or less safe off all the beaches but low tide would mean some walking just to reach the water, and then some more to swim. The only activity on offer is at Kelva Beach, where you can go on a camel ride. Carry a sheet to spread out on the black sand, on which you may not want to sprawl otherwise.

THINGS TO SEE AND DO

Palghar is an ideal weekend getaway for Mumbaikars and indeed for anyone who doesn't expect a beach sojourn where parasailing and candle-lit dinners by the sea will be in place.

Shirgaon Beach

About 11 km from town, Shirgaon has a fort to its credit, and one that offers an impressive view of the Arabian Sea as well the Shirgaon Village. A climb up its walls, however, can be precarious. The fort was erected in the 18th century, has underground tunnels, hideouts and a cannon to its credit. All that, however, lies under much neglect and undergrowth. You can relax on the beach, where you will find children playing cricket on weekends. This fairly long beach is mostly frequented by fisherfolk. There are various routes from the main road leading to the beach, and since the fishermen's dwellings are on the way, it's easy to lose your way while heading back. However, people are helpful, and you can even convince one of them to take you for a boat ride. Every February, a fair is held at a dargah that is on the route to Shirgaon Beach.

Satpati Beach

The beach at Satpati, a sleepy hamlet with many palm trees, is close to Shirgaon and 13 km from the town. It's also the least crowded of all the beaches in Palghar. There isn't much to do here except watch the fishermen's boats with their identification flags float by.

The colour of beauty: Red is the dress code for the sea and the sky at Bordi

The **MTDC Tent Resort** (Tel: 02528-254243; Tariff: Rs 750-1,250) is the only hotel on the beach in Bordi. Since it's a little away from the village, it's quiet, and you can hear the sea clearly at night. Their deluxe tent houses in the garden facing the sea are the best rooms in Bordi. Lack of cleanliness is the only downside here but it's nothing that a small tip won't fix.

Anand Resort (Tel: 254102/ 580; Tariff: Rs 600-2,000) is just across the road from the MTDC property and is set amidst a chikoo orchard. The checkout time is 10 am. The dogs at Pervez and Hutokshi Dastur's atmospheric property, **Goolkhush Resort** (Tel: 254182; Mobile: 09822078151; Tariff: Rs 600-1,200), near the Parsi Fire Temple, might scare you for a moment, but the owners are a friendly old couple. They serve Parsi meals on request, and also have a swimming pool.

Although the farthest away from the beach, the **Tapovan Retreat** (Tel: 254649; for bookings, call their Mumbai office at 022-22665322 or 09820191153; Tariff: Rs 750-1,200) is a nice place to stay at. Though their checkout time is 9 am, they extend it to 5 pm if you opt for their packages (1N/ 2D or 2D/ 3N). Room service here is limited to tea/ coffee and packaged snacks and drinks as they outsource meals from a caterer.

Built on a hill at Borigaon, 3 km from Bordi, **Hill Zill** (Tel: 249050, 249119; Tariff: Rs 600-2,500) is far removed from the beach. But it offers other delightful views in a very quiet setting. Stay here if you don't care for the sea or have a car. The checkout time is 10 am.

For more hotels and details, see Bordi Accommodation Listings on page 552

WHERE TO EAT

On a weekday, it's quite possible that you won't find a single place that will serve you food in Bordi. The problem with Bordi is that the last of its tourist groups depart by Monday morning, and then rustling up anything more than a bread-omelette-coffee for a lone guest is too much of a trouble for any of the few hotel restaurants. However, orders will be accepted if you're in a group of four-five

Kings of the castle: Children have fun on Dahanu's Narpad Beach

people. While none of Bordi's hotels will win prizes for culinary excellence, their fare is passable, even palatable. **MTDC's Darya Restaurant** in the hotel's garden (away from the sea) needs to catch up with roadside dhabas on furniture and fixtures. But it serves seafood and beer.

Across the road, the kitchen at **Anand Resort** is recommended for Gujarati thalis (vegetarian), but you need to be there between 12 and 2 pm for lunch and 7 and 9 pm for dinner. Orders need to be placed in advance. The resort also has an orchard restaurant called **Chikooland** (also vegetarian) in homage to the chikoos plopping down from time to time. In the evening, you'll get pani-puri, dahi-puri and bhel-puri and even 'pijha' at the roadside stall just after Anand's. **Goolkhush** serves Parsi delicacies if you inform them at least 3 hrs in advance, while **Tapovan** only has a caterer on call.

AROUND BORDI

Dahanu (24 km)
Just as Bordi is not famous for its chikoos (that honour is reserved for Gholvad), Dahanu is not famous for its beach. But fame apart, its strip of sand deserves the same rating as Bordi's fruit: very good. At least on weekends, the town's **Narpad Beach** is just as alive as the Bordi Beach. Everything from bhel-puri to nariyal pani and horse riding is available.

Dahanu is a complete destination in itself with several hotels. **Pearline Beach Resort** (Tel: 02528-222442; Mobile: 09823037189; Tariff: Rs 650-900) is a sea-facing property with a swimming pool and a garden bar. They serve Parsi food. Their checkout time is 9 am.

Hotel Seawoods (Tel: 213100; Tariff: Rs 900-1,500), located alongside Pearline, is quite popular. The third hotel, **Beachside** (Tel: 223376; Tariff: Rs 500-2,250), lies further down the road. Its restaurant **Kohli-da-Dhaba** serves Konkani, Gujarati, North Indian, Chinese and Continental food.

◆**Connection** Buses connect Bordi to Dahanu; an autorickshaw will get you there for Rs 150

Daman (35 km)
See page 435 ■

AMIT PASRICHA

DAMAN

IN HIGH SPIRITS

Union Territory of Daman and Diu
Location On India's west coast, about 20 km north of Gujarat's border with Maharashtra
Distances 10 km NW of Vapi, 31 km NW of Silvassa, 129 km S of Surat, 192 km N of Mumbai
Journey time ***By road*** 20 mins from Vapi, 40 mins from Silvassa, 2 hrs from Surat, 4 hrs from Mumbai
Route from Surat NH6 to Chalthan; NH8 to Vapi via Palsana, Navsari, Chikhli, Valsad and Pardi; SH to Daman **Route from Mumbai** NH8 to Vapi via Mandvi, Manor, Kasa Khurd and Talasari; rest as above (*see route guide on page 394*)

BY ABHILASH GAUR

People visit Daman for three reasons: its beaches, liquor or history. Of beaches, the town has two, one rocky but touristy, and the other sandy yet silent. If you are at the rocky Devka Beach at sunset, you'll see the wet, black rocks glow red in the sun's dying light, while at the quiet Jampore Beach, the sun slides into the sea's depths modestly, with barely a glance at the shore. In the dark, the waves creep back to the shore, showering you with spray, and keeping you from returning to the television in your hotel room.

Daman is also the child of prohibition in neighbouring Gujarat. Huge signs of the homegrown Jupiter's gin and Royal distilleries are to found everywhere, as are those of Kobra and Kingfisher. But its reputation as a drinking den doesn't do justice to Daman at all. If you were to pause on the bridge across

PUNIT PARANJPE

Lounging around on Jampore Beach

the Damanganga, between Moti and Nani Daman, you'll be able to spot the colourful fishing vessels moored on either side. A walk through the old town will reveal a burst of colonial houses, churches and official buildings. Neither tourism nor the hotel industry has affected the small-town atmosphere of Daman. Its beaches aren't remarkable or exciting, but time flies by on them rather sweetly, with or without a drink.

ORIENTATION

The **Damanganga Creek** bifurcates the 72 sq km across which Daman spreads into **Nani Daman** (Little Daman) and **Moti Daman** (Big Daman). If you arrive from Vapi, the **Dabhel Checkpost** will be your point of entry into Daman. Ahead is the **Nani Daman Market**, from where a right turn leads to **Devka**. The rocky **Devka Beach** lies about 5 km down the road, and is Daman's tourist hub, with many hotels. Beyond Devka is **Kadaiya**, which has the **Mirasol Water Park**. It's located near **Kolak River**, also Daman's northern boundary with Gujarat.

Nani Daman not only has a large market but also the small **St Jerome Fort** overlooking the Damanganga Creek. The **bus terminus** and the Tourism Department's office also lie close to the fort. Most of the sightseeing in Daman is concentrated across the Damanganga, in Moti Daman. Only pedestrians and two-wheelers are allowed over the bridge over the Damanganga, so you'll need to walk across it. The quiet **Jampore Beach** is 3 km south of the fort at Moti Daman. Jampore is Daman's southernmost village, framed by the narrow **Kalai River**, which also forms the Union Territory's southern boundary with Gujarat.

Autos are a convenient mode of transport but you will have to bargain hard as far as the fare is concerned. You can take an auto from Vapi to Devka (fare Rs 100-125). From Devka to the market, they charge Rs 50. From the fort at Moti Daman to Jampore Beach, autos charge Rs 30 one-way. The cheapest (albeit hurried) way to go sightseeing in Daman is to join the $4^1/_2$-hr **Daman Darshan** sightseeing tour (Rs 75 per head), with pick-ups from 18 hotels. It's organised by **Dariya Darshan Hotel** (*for contact details, see Where to Stay on page 440*). The morning trip lasts from 10 am to 2.30 pm and the evening trip from 4 pm to 8.30 pm. Altogether 20 sites are covered, with stoppage time ranging from 5 mins to 1 hr (the latter at Jampore Beach).

BEACH WATCH

Thanks to the sea and three rivers, tiny Daman has a surprisingly long waterfront, of which about $12^1/_2$ km qualifies as seafront or 'beach'. However, the waters are quite unsuitable for water sports, and forget swimming, even taking a dip at Devka is inadvisable as its underwater rocky formations are dangerous. But you can hop about on the rocks at low tide and fill your pockets with shells. Jampore Beach, on the other hand, is all sand without any slope. At

ABHILASH GAUR

Quiet on the water: Tourists enjoy a boat ride in Daman

low tide, which is usually from about 10 am to 6 pm, you will have to walk a mile to get the water up to your knees. But rest assured that the sea here is free of undercurrents.

THINGS TO SEE AND DO

While getting drunk is the easiest thing to do in Daman, it's happily not the only inducement for visiting the town. Why else would so many families come here on the weekends? Why would it be an alternative to Goa on New Year's eve? It may not have the latter's white beaches but nor does it have the crowds. The seafront at Daman may not offer many chances for swimming but nothing stops you from making sand castles and splashing about in the waves. Snacks, seashells and sea breeze are all plentiful.

Devka Beach

While you can't go swimming off Devka Beach, its rocks make for a good perch to catch the sunset. The swimming here happens in hotel pools and 'water parks', but wetting the ankles is not all that difficult even on the gritty beach. The **Mirasol Water Park** at Kadaiya Village, 2 km from Devka Beach, is currently the most popular place for a splash in North Daman. It has a wave pool, party grounds, children's pool, giant water rides, boating, toy train, lakeside restaurant, fast food corner, video games and fountains. The water park charges Rs 200 per head; boating costs Rs 100. Another very popular destination in Devka is the **Devka**

FAST FACTS

When to go November to February

Tourist office

- Assistant Director of Tourism

Paryatan Bhavan, Nani Daman
Tel: 0260-2255104
Website: damantourism.com

STD code 0260

Amusement Park that takes up most of the seafront. It offers joyrides and food, and remains open from 5 am to 10.30 pm. There's another theme park, called **Vaibhav Water World**, which lies on the road to Vapi. Spread over 20 acres, it also offers joyrides and food.

Nani Daman

For tourists at Devka, the town immediately north of the Damanganga is a magnet. It has the regular mithai and chaat shops and also cheaper liquor than what's available in hotel bars. The **Damao Pequeno Jetty** here not only has a popular fast food complex but also the **St Jerome Fort** built by the Portuguese in 1627, to ward off the Mughals. The small fort looks pretty from a distance, with hundreds of boats moored beneath it. Its low south gateway, with a statue of St Jerome set in a niche above the arch, is especially beautiful.

→ GETTING THERE

Air Nearest airport: Chhatrapati Shivaji Airport, Mumbai (192 km/ 4 hrs). Taxi to Daman costs about Rs 3,500

Rail Nearest railhead: Vapi (10 km/ 20 mins). Vapi is an important station with almost all trains halting there for a couple of minutes. The Mumbai-Ahmedabad Shatabdi stops here as does the Mumbai-Delhi August Kranti Rajdhani. But the faster Mumbai-Delhi Mumbai Rajdhani doesn't. Taxi to Daman is available from here as are autos. The fare is about Rs 150 to Devka Beach and Rs 90 to Nani Daman

Road Vapi lies on the four-lane Delhi-Mumbai NH8. On a good day, the drive up from Mumbai takes just around 3 hrs, while the drive down from Surat a little over 2 hrs. Raj National Express' Volvo buses (check rajnationalexpress.in for details on boarding points and contact numbers; their Bandra, Mumbai, office contact number is 022-26423373-75) ply on NH8 between Surat and Mumbai, and you can get off at Vapi. But there are no direct connections to Daman from Mumbai

Moti Daman

The old fort here is packed with ancient buildings, of which the most beautiful are the two churches of Bom Jesus and Our Lady of Rosario. The **Church of Bom Jesus** is larger and older, and decidedly more splendid from the outside, but the other's altar is widely considered the most ornately carved and gilded amongst all Portuguese churches in India. At the time of writing, the Archaeological Survey of India was restoring many of the old buildings here. The fort also houses the **Governor's Palace**, which has a spectacular flight of stairs and ornate chandeliers.

Jampore Beach

Infinitely quieter than Devka, the beach at Jampore has a pastoral air about it. The Tourism Department has thoughtfully placed a few benches under the trees, which locals use for drying fish. On the rare occasion when they don't, you can sit on one and spend a full day just watching boys play cricket or their parents carry fishing nets into the sea. By afternoon, the sea is a long way off and you would have to wade through the squelching black mud in vain to get to it. Unless it's the weekend, few tourists turn up in Jampore and it seems a world removed from bustling Devka.

SHOPPING

By its administration's own admission, Daman was, till a few years ago, notorious as a landing point for contraband. Though they claim smuggling has been

DINESH SHUKLA

The St Jerome Fort, built by the Portuguese, at Nani Daman

checked to a great extent, the **Maharaja Shopping Arcade**, opposite the police station, remains the hub for trade in 'imported' goods, chiefly comprising electronics, toys, cosmetics and toiletries. If you like cheap imported chocolates, imitation jewellery and watches, head to the 60-odd shops at the **200-year-old municipal market** on Char Rasta. At night, the **Beach Road** past the hotels in Devka remains brightly lit, much like the Mall roads of Shimla and Mussoorie. And like them, it offers inexpensive garments, footwear and toys.

WHERE TO STAY

For such a small town, Daman has upwards of 60 hotels and 5,000 beds. Evidently, hospitality is serious business here and most hotels are run professionally. Despite the inflow of a number of tourists every year, room tariffs remain reasonable and a 10 per cent discount can be negotiated on weekdays. Devka Beach has plenty of accommodation but finding rooms on weekends and festive occasions such as Christmas and New Year's can be difficult, so do book in advance.

On Jampore Beach

Hotel China Town (Tel: 0260-2230920; Rs 800-1,600) is the only hotel in Jampore but it lies across the road from the beach. Nevertheless, it has a good view of the casuarinas and the sands. They have a garden restaurant and bar. It's fairly clean but service is lax.

On Devka Beach

Hotel Miramar (Tel: 2250671-73; Tariff: Rs 1,000-5,000) is the swankiest hotel on Devka Beach and also its largest. Their restaurant overlooks the sea and features live music on weekends. As it's a large property, all their rooms are not sea-facing, so check whether you are getting the view you want. The rooms are clean, the corridors are regularly mopped and the service is great. The **Mirasol Resort** (Tel: 2220541-42; Tariff: Rs 3,000-6,000) is

2 km further down the road from Devka, in Kadaiya Village. It is pitched as a party-and-wedding location and its prime attraction is the Mirasol Water Park.

Cidade De Daman (Tel: 2250590; Tariff: Rs 1,700-2,300) is the other swanky hotel on Devka Beach. It has lawns, a sea-view restaurant and a poolside restaurant. Do ask for a sea-facing room. The service is efficient. The **Sandy Resort** (Tel: 2254751; Tariff: Rs 1,150-2,100) is another luxury hotel far down the beach road, but this one is special for its quiet setting far from the town's 'hotel quarter'. The only downside is that it lies across the road from the beach.

Hotel Princess Park (Tel: 2254323/ 997; Tariff: Rs 1,600-4,000) is pitched as 'a complete health club' and this 27-room property has an air-conditioned gym, jacuzzi and sauna. However, it's not in the same league as Hotel Miramar or Cidade de Daman. **High Tide**, their beach garden restaurant-cum-bar, serves Indian and Continental food.

Coconut festival

About three-fourths of Daman is under cultivation, but fishing remains the economy's mainstay, with almost 40 per cent of the population engaged in it. The town ships prawns, Bombay duck, lobsters, silver fish and catfish. During the monsoon, when the sea is dangerous, the town's 500-odd boats remain moored under the Nani Daman and Moti Daman forts, on either side of the Damanganga River. When the sea becomes calmer towards the end of August, it's a time for celebration. The locals observe a festival called **Nariyal Poornima**, as part of which they immerse coconuts in the sea, to please the wind and sea gods. As the name suggests, the festival is held on a full moon day, and, for tourists, its highlights are water sports on the Damanganga Creek and a coconut food festival. Find out the festival's exact dates from the office of the Assistant Director of Tourism (Tel: 0260-2255104).

The fairly decent **Dariya Darshan Hotel** (Tel: 2254476; Tariff: Rs 1,000-2,500) stands across the road from the beach; they also organise a sightseeing tour (*see Orientation on page 436*). **Hotel Jazira** (Tel: 2254330; Tariff: Rs 800-1,600), on the beach, is a clean, dependable property, and it remains popular for the seafood at its restaurant. **Hotel Shilton** (Tel: 2254407/ 558; Tariff: Rs 600-1,200) is quite plain despite its fancy name. They are across the road from the beach, so there are no sea views. **Oliaji's Duke Hotel** (Tel: 2254251; Tariff: Rs 500), on the beach, has unbeatable atmosphere. It's an old Parsi house converted into a hotel, with rooms fronted with verandahs, where you can place chairs and spend a quiet day. The rooms are simply furnished and clean. The property does not have much staff, so you may have to wait awhile before your call is answered. It's said to be the oldest hotel in Daman, set up in 1936.

If you are not interested in staying near the beach, and would like to add a touch of history to your holiday, then opt for **Hotel Marina** (Tel: 2254420; Tariff: Rs 585-675), located behind the police station at Nani Daman, which is a 140-year-old Portuguese homestead. The antique furniture in the room and the lovely courtyard will give you a glimpse of Daman's history.

For more hotels and details, see Daman Accommodation Listings on pages 525-526

WHERE TO EAT

Daman does not have a distinctive cuisine but what it does offer is a variety of food, done well, to cater to its diverse clientele. At any time of the day, you will find in its restaurants a number of tourists from all over the country, none of whom seem distressed by the food. And certainly, most are pleased with their drink, which is cheaper than anywhere else in a few hundred miles' radius

ABHIJIT BHATLEKAR

Pilgrims at the Iranshah Atash Behram, the fire temple at Udvada

(barring Silvassa). In Moti Daman, Jampore Beach has snack shacks, but Bisleri-accustomed guts should stick to nariyal pani here. For anything else, the **Jampore Beach Resort** is your best bet. **Hotel China Town**, across the road, has a garden restaurant and bar. **Gurukripa**, situated between Moti Daman and Devka Beach, offers a rich variety of seafood, from Goan fish curry and rice to Damanese specialities like chicken xacuti, dhara fish fry, butter-garlic tiger prawns and fried squid. **Hotel Sovereign**, a sister concern that's a few buildings down the block, offers vegetarian dishes.

There are many choices across the Damanganga, in Nani Daman. To begin with, there's a fast food complex on Damao Pequeno Jetty, next to the Nani Daman fort. The complex also offers games and rides, and is crowded in the evenings. On Devka Beach, a garden restaurant inside Devka Amusement Park offers everything from pav bhaji to pizza and 'Mexican' fare. Further down the road, the **Oliaji's Duke Hotel** serves Parsi food. The biggest hotel-restaurant in Daman is **Hotel Miramar**, with space for 600. Built on three decks overlooking the sea, it's quite popular with tourists.

AROUND DAMAN

Udvada (7 km)
Once simply *uth vada* or 'grazing ground for camels', Udvada today is the most important spiritual centre for one of the world's oldest religions, Zoroastrianism. A seaside town, it has its beach, but its key attraction is the **Iranshah Atash Behram**, the large fire temple where the sacred fire, originally consecrated in Sanjan in 721 CE, is enshrined. It's believed to be the oldest consecrated fire in the Zoroastrian world. The Atash Behram is out of bounds for non-Parsis. ♦**Location** Just across the Kolak River, which defines Daman's northern boundary **Getting there** Take the Airport Road out of Daman; turn left after crossing the Kolak at Patalia. Udvada lies just down the road. Shared autorickshaws charge Rs 10 up to the border at Patalia, from where you can take an auto registered in Gujarat up to Udvada Village (Rs 15 in a shared auto) ■

SHRIVARDHAN

FOR YOUR EYES ONLY

State Maharashtra
Location Shrivardhan is situated along the Konkan Coast, with the Kushmeshwar Hills as its backdrop
Distance 202 km S of Mumbai
Journey time ***By road*** $4^1/_2$ hrs from Mumbai
Route from Mumbai NH17 to Lonera Phata via Kolad and Mangaon; SH to Shrivardhan via Goregaon, Mhasla and Arathi Road Junction (*see route guide on page 394*)

BY SIMAR PREET KAUR

Shrivardhan is what every devout sea-lover is looking for. It offers such a panoramic view of the sea that you feel as if the rock you are standing on is in fact dancing with the waves. The sea is there, stretching to the horizon, wherever you look. The beaches are for your eyes only — they are empty most of the day and only in the evenings do a few fishermen make a special appearance, arriving, and leaving, just as quickly. The sands are yours again as the sky turns starry.

At one of the beaches, a row of fishing boats lies docked to the rocks. At another,

Photographs by DHRITIMAN MUKHERJEE

Shekhadi Beach offers great views but no swimming opportunities

betel nut orchards and coconut groves, together with a long, empty stretch of sand, transport you to what seems to be paradise. That there are no water sports here, and indeed very few tourists, take away little from Shrivardhan. Instead, it all works like a magical charm, helping you discover and enjoy beauty in the simplest of nature's gifts.

ORIENTATION

The **Shrivardhan Bus Stand** is the main landmark in town. From here, you can board buses to Mangaon as well as Mumbai. Immediately outside is the **auto stand**, from where you can get into a shared auto to commute to nearby places such as **Harihareshwar** (Rs 16). These autos are the most preferred and common mode of transport in the region. Special autos can also be hired, but you'll have to bargain hard to get a decent rate. From the bus stand walk towards the **Peshwa Smarak Temple** and then on to the beach via the **Rest House Road**. This road and the nearby **Dabak Pakhadi** are where most of the guest houses and *gharghuthis* (homes where food can be secured if orders are placed a couple of hours in advance) are located. The town is fairly small and you can get around by walking. However, most of the beaches are on the outskirts. A special auto to cover all the beaches in the north, up till **Diveagar** and **Dighi**, will cost Rs 400-450 (including waiting charges).

BEACH WATCH

Other than the main Shrivardhan Beach, all the surrounding beaches are mostly deserted, so carry your beachwear, sunscreen lotion and food along. The beaches are safe for swimming and the waters calm, but since there is no one around for miles except in the evenings, don't venture too far into the sea.

THINGS TO SEE AND DO

Apart from swimming and taking walks, there isn't much to do here. You'd be lucky to find locals on a beach, so you can safely forget water sport organisers. While two days are enough to explore the temples here and the Shrivardhan Beach, visit with at least four to five days in hand if you would like to travel to nearby beaches. The best bet would be to stay for two nights at Shrivardhan, visit the major attractions and Kondivli Beach, and then head to Diveagar.

Shekhadi Beach

Right on the outskirts of Shrivardhan, around 2 km down SH4, is Shekhadi Beach. Shekhadi is more a place for enjoying beautiful views than adventurous swimming sessions. The blackish sand is only visited by those from the nearby Walvati Village, which has some lovely marble mosques.

Shekhadi, along with Bharadkhol and Dighi, were the sites for the infamous RDX landings over a decade ago. The explosives were used for the bomb blasts in Mumbai in 1993.

Kondivli Beach

This beach, located 5 km away, is Shrivardhan's pride. It's one of the few beaches around that's still secluded. The sands are unmarked by footprints, and the road winds around low-lying cliffs, from where you have to climb down to reach the waters. The currents are a bit unpredictable, but locals claim it's safe for swimming. On a weekday you can be assured that you'll have the beach's brown-black sands all to yourself. On the other side of the road is a two or three centuries' old small **Shankar Temple**, which is dedicated to Lord Shiva and his consort Parvati.

Bharadkhol Beach

A little ahead on the winding SH4 is the Bharadkhol Beach. Another secluded stretch, it's a rocky beach with clusters of colourful boats anchored to the rocks on its black sands. You'll have to climb down a steep but easily negotiable cliff to reach the waters. Watch fishermen from nearby villages bring in their catch for the day every evening.

Temple trail

Shrivardhan's presiding deity, Somaja Devi, is believed to be capable of curing snakebites and reversing even the most vicious cobra's sting. At the **Somaja Devi Temple** in the main town, the victim is made to lie down and burning hot coals are used to cauterise the wound, which is then caressed using peacock feathers by the priest. A short walk away is the **Laxminarayan Temple**, housing age-old idols; also nearby are the temples of **Bhairav**, **Jivaneshwar** and **Kusumdevi**.

Although everyone is welcome into these humble temples throughout the day, it's best to visit before night as most

Kondivli Beach is Shrivardhan's pride

FAST FACTS

When to go November to January

Tourist office

- MTDC
Near Kalbhairav Temple
Harihareshwar
Tel: 02147-226036

STD code 02147

of Shrivardhan shuts shop around 9 pm. There is no prescribed dress code at the temple, but it's best to dress modestly.

Peshwa heritage

Shrivardhan is the hometown and also the birthplace of the founder of the Peshwas, Peshwa Balaji Vishwanath. Peshwas, a powerful ministerial dynasty, took centrestage in Maharashtra during the reign of Chhatrapati Shivaji's grandson, Shahu Maharaj.

Today, the **Peshwa Smarak Temple**, situated in the centre of Shrivardhan town and a landmark in its own right, lies in a state of neglect, and is usually dark due to regular power-cuts, but visitors continue to trickle in. The temple is open through the day.

→ GETTING THERE

Air Nearest airport: Chhatrapati Shivaji Airport, Mumbai (202 km/ 4½ hrs). Taxi to Shrivardhan costs Rs 3,000
Rail Nearest railhead: Mangaon (52 km/ 1¼ hrs). Most trains plying between Mumbai and Goa halt here. Mandovi Express, which leaves Mumbai at 6.55 am, makes for a convenient option as it reaches Mangaon by 10.41 am. From Mangaon there are plenty of direct buses to Shrivardhan. A special autorickshaw charges Rs 900 from Mangaon
Road Drive down NH17 from Panvel to Lonera Phata via Indapur and Mangaon. Turn right off the highway towards Goregaon. Shrivardhan is straight ahead past Mhasla and Arathi Road Junction. Lots of State Transport buses leave from Mumbai Central for Shrivardhan (Rs 132/ 6 hrs). However, it's advisable to book well in advance to avoid a journey wherein you'll have to stand all the way

SHOPPING

Shrivardhan is a small coastal town surviving well on just a couple of grocery stores. However, if beach memories are not enough as souvenirs, pick up one of Shrivardhan's farm products. These tangy treats — pickles such as aamla and ginger-lemon mix, dried papads and kokum sherbets — are available at the shops outside the temples. The sherbets cost Rs 45 each and the aam papad is a mere Rs 15.

WHERE TO STAY

Shrivardhan has mostly humble accommodation options, hygienic but lacking in high-end luxury. Arm yourself with mosquito repellents, leave behind the credit card and order your food 2-3 hrs in advance.

Shiv Shanti Holiday Inn (Tel: 02147-222163; Tariff: Rs 800-1,200), at Dabak Pakadi near the Government Rest House, has 9 well-maintained rooms and cottages, just 5 mins from the Shrivardhan Beach. As far as Shrivardhan is concerned, this is as close as you can get to luxury. They provide 24-hr room service, AC/ non-AC rooms, a swimming pool, TV and a restaurant that also serves seafood. The checkout time is 10 am. Rooms can be booked at their Mumbai office (Tel: 022-24224904) as well.

Right opposite Shiv Shanti is **Niwara** (Tel: 222298; Tariff: Rs 800), approved under MTDC's Bed and Breakfast Scheme. It's one of the best stay options in Shrivardhan, thanks to the homely atmosphere and the couple who run it. They only have 2 rooms, so book in advance. The tariff includes breakfast; the checkout time is noon. There's no AC but there's a TV, an attached bath, and hot water 24 hrs. Lunch and dinner (both vegetarian and non-vegetarian) can be arranged if ordered in advance.

Sagar Darshan (Tel: 222958; Mobile: 09850018213; Tariff: Rs 400-700), also 5 mins from the Shrivardhan Beach along

Homecoming: Boats return to the jetty at Shrivardhan at the end of the day

the Rest House Road, has three basic rooms. The owner likes to boast about their 'Euro-style loos', so that's another facility there! The amenities have remained the same over the years: cable TV; 24-hr water except in summers when you most need it; and a checkout time of 11 am. Good Konkani food is arranged if ordered in advance. Right behind Sagar Darshan is its 'sister concern' **Savali** (Tel: 222958; Tariff: Rs 1,000). They have 2 Konkani huts, with a verandah and two beds each. There is no AC in the rooms but there's cable TV and attached baths (the toilets are Indian-style).

On the road behind the Peshwa Temple is **Kalaprasad Guest Park** (Tel: 222619; Tariff: Rs 400-500), best for those looking for budget accommodation. There are 8 basic, but clean rooms available and a dorm for Rs 60 per bed. The rooms are non-AC with attached baths; there's no television.

Fulora Resort (Mumbai Reservations: 022-24042501; Tariff: Rs 750-2,000) is located midway en route from Shrivardhan Beach to Kondivli, along Dighi Road, and should be your last option. (The resort's phone at Shrivardhan doesn't work.) The rooms have good sea views but that's hardly any compensation for rooms that refuse to cool or the staff's reluctance to switch on the generator. They have 20 rooms (only one is AC), a swimming pool, laundry, room service and cable TV.

For more hotels and details, see Shrivardhan Accommodation Listings on pages 560-561

WHERE TO EAT

Shrivardhan lacks restaurants and therefore you'll have to rely on *gharghuthis*. You need to order at least 2-3 hrs in advance. Konkani food is most readily available, and surmai fish is the most popular dish. **Hotel Prasad** near Rest House Road offers an excellent vegetarian thali for Rs 30, and a fish curry thali for Rs 75. The shrikhand here is a must-try. The hotel is open from 11.30 am to 4 pm, and 8 to 10.30 pm. There is no need to order in advance. **Sagar Darshan** also serves typically Konkani cuisine, including seafood. Popular dishes include surmai rawa fry, *kurkuron bombil* and *modak*, all of which is cooked with generous amounts of coconut seasoning, characteristic of Konkani food. But you will have to place orders in advance.

Shiv Shanti Holiday Inn offers a varied menu serving both vegetarian and non-vegetarian in Konkani, Continental and Gujarati cuisine. The seafood is well cooked and spicy. Most other guest houses can also arrange food; but make sure you place your orders beforehand.

AROUND SHRIVARDHAN

Harihareshwar (11 km)
See page 450

Diveagar (16 km)
While most people are drawn to this paradise because of the **Ganpati idol of pure gold** in the temple here, the long beach in Diveagar is enough to make you want to stay back for days, if not months. *Supari* (betel nut) orchards line one side of the road, and on the other side are coconut groves that part to make way for the isolated beach. Brown sands capture the curiosity of visitors with their endless 'shifting phenomena' — the beach sands shift due to the force of the waves.

The **MTDC Exotica Beach Resort** (Mobile: 09421967767; Tariff: Rs 1,500) is situated 16 km from Shrivardhan, but the resort is right on Diveagar Beach, and has all the luxuries and comforts generally offered by MTDC. There are 10 cosy sea-facing cottages to choose from, with AC, attached bathrooms and TV. A thatched roof restaurant offers delicious non-vegetarian food such as pomfret masala, tender fry rawas and chicken delicacies. Room service is available.

There are also places such as the **Mavli Resort** (Tel: 02147-225225, 225015; Tariff: Rs 600), located near the Ganpati Temple, which offers rooms in a bungalow. All rooms have double-bed accommodation, but there's no AC due to electricity problems. Another option is **Ambiance Cottages** (Tel: 225334; Tariff: Rs 700-900), offering spacious AC as well as non-AC cottages.

It's another golden day in the Konkan

PORPOISE PHOTOSTOCK

Dighi Beach (36 km)
Dighi Beach is around 20 km north of Diveagar. It takes about 25 mins from Dighi Jetty by ferry to reach the Murud-Janjira Fort (*see page 420*). The brown sands on the tranquil beach are enticing and the hills make the landscape look lush and beautiful during the monsoon.

On the same road to Dighi Jetty, 9 km from Shrivardhan, to its north-east, is Devkul Village, which houses the **Pandav Kaling Shiva Temple**. This temple is a must-visit for anyone who cares about exquisite stone carvings that are yet to be affected by vandalism. The temple is open 24/ 7; it has primeval and prehistoric carvings depicting various deities including Lord Shiva. ■

Photographs by BHARAT AGGARWAL

HARIHARESHWAR

SAY A LITTLE PRAYER

State Maharashtra
Location Situated in Raigad District, the temple town of Harihareshwar is surrounded by the four hills of Harihareshwar, Harshinachal, Bramhadri and Pushpadri
Distance 213 km S of Mumbai
Journey time *By road* 5 hrs from Mumbai
Route from Mumbai NH17 to Lonera Phata via Mangaon; SH97 to Shrivardhan via Goregaon and Mhasla; SH98 to Harihareshwar (*see route guide on page 394*)

BY SIMAR PREET KAUR

Most people visit Harihareshwar for its temple. But even if you are travelling there as a bonafide beach buff, a journey from Mumbai can sometimes seem like a pilgrimage in itself. The trip, if undertaken in a rickety state transport bus that was clearly built as a tribute to a tin can, is apparently as endless as it seems to be. But somewhat similar to the spiritual succour that pilgrims find at the end of their arduous journeys, the tourist is rewarded at Harihareshwar with a glorious view that's picture-perfect and worth every hour of a rambling bus trip.

Once the bus deposits me at Harihareshwar, I climb up a small hillock and glimpse an almost 'Om'-shaped beach like the one in Gokarna, but bereft of the hippies one finds there. There are hardly any footprints on the brown sands. Waves lap at the shore, so gently that it seems as if you are standing by a lake. The sea's magnificence is in full view only from atop the rocks dotting the shore. Near the other end of the beach is the residence of the local deity, the Kalbhairav Temple. This side is always abuzz with people, and lies close to a fishing village where an intrinsically rural countryside meets a bracing sea. It's a coming together of sorts and standing on the beach, watching the fishermen bring the day's catch home, you are bound to feel blessed.

ORIENTATION

Harihareshwar is small; almost everything is within 10 mins' walking distance. The **Kalbhairav Temple**, the main tourist attraction in the region, splits the beach into two parts. The north side of the beach is best accessed through steps leading down from the temple. Most hotels, or to be more precise, homes offering rooms to stay, are situated along the narrow road leading to the temple. Just where this road begins is another pathway to the left, winding its way down to the southern beach, which is where the **MTDC Resort** is located. The **ST Bus Stand** is a 2-min walk from the temple. Shared autos are available from here to nearby areas; the fares are fixed (Rs 16 to Shrivardhan). For special autos, negotiate the rates; it costs Rs 200 to Shrivardhan.

BEACH WATCH

Although the clear waters here look inviting, there are strong undercurrents, as locals will obligingly testify based on mishaps in the past. Swim only during high tide, and refrain from venturing too far out. Since it's a religious town, we recommend you stick to the southern side of the beach if opting for beachwear.

THINGS TO SEE AND DO

The Kalbhairav Temple forms the nucleus of this town. The best bet would be to visit the temple in the mornings, retreat for an early noon siesta (life in Harihareshwar is 'slow'), and visit the beach during late afternoon.

On the beach

The northern stretch of Harihareshwar Beach sees few tourists on most weekdays. It has a couple of chaat stalls frequented by pilgrims and fishermen. Apart from munching the snacks on offer there and walking on the beach, there's little else to do here. The sense of isolation is complete on the southern side of the beach, where the black sands and rock formations are usually all yours.

Water world

Harihareshwar Boating Point is the sole reason for even minor excitement here. Their small booth lies just after the MTDC Resort as you climb down to the beach. Operating from morning till twilight, and mostly during peak season, they offer scooter rides (Rs 50/ 5 mins) and 'family' boat rides (Rs 300/ 10 mins). Life jackets are also available. There is no phone at the booth but it's easy to locate. On a water scooter, you can ride into the sunset, and it's quite thrilling even though the controls are handled by an operator.

→ FAST FACTS

When to go Monsoon (June to August) is when Harihareshwar is most green and beautiful, but November to February is best for a beach holiday

Tourist office

● MTDC Resort
Near Kalbhairav Temple
Harihareshwar
Tel: 02147-226036

STD code 02147

Kalbhairav Temple

The Kalbhairav Temple, consisting of idols of the Hindu Trinity as well as the Goddess Parvati, is shrouded in mystery as far as its year of construction is concerned. However, most believe the first Baijirao Peshwa reconstructed it in 1723. The architecture is fairly simple and the one-storeyed structure is located on a large compound facing the sea.
◆**Timings** 6 am-9 pm

GETTING THERE

Air Nearest airport: Chhatrapati Shivaji Airport, Mumbai (213 km/ 5 hrs). Taxi fare to Harihareshwar is approx Rs 3,000. Pune Airport (178 km/ 4½ hrs) is another – albeit not so well-connected – option. Taxi fare is about Rs 2,500. Haggling could help bring down rates
Rail Nearest railhead: Mangaon (63 km/ 1¾ hrs). Although rail connections to Mangaon are poor, most trains plying between Mumbai and Goa halt here. Mandovi Express, which leaves Mumbai at 6.55 am, makes for a convenient option. It reaches Mangaon at 10.40 am. From Mangaon, there are a few direct buses to Harihareshwar. It's best to take a bus to Shrivardhan (Rs 40), and take a shared autorickshaw from there (Rs 16). A special autorickshaw charges Rs 175-200 from Shrivardhan, and Rs 900-1,000 from Mangaon
Road Just two buses (fare Rs 150) leave Mumbai Central ST Stand for Harihareshwar. The one that leaves at 5 am reaches at 12 noon; the second bus leaves at 2.45 pm and reaches at 10 pm. It's best to book at least a week in advance. It's easier catching a bus to Shrivardhan and then travelling to Harihareshwar from there

SHOPPING

At the shops lining the street leading to the temple, you can buy sherbets in flavours such as jambhul, amrit kokum and amla. Also sold here are pendants depicting symbols related to the Hindu religion such as Om.

WHERE TO STAY

The **MTDC Resort** (Tel: 02147-226036; Tariff: Rs 500-1,500), located along the beach, is a reason in itself to visit Harihareshwar. All their cottages/ tents are sea-facing, and the Konkani huts are set in a bamboo grove. Each cottage has an attached balcony, with sliding doors to provide a better view of the sea. The rooms are spacious and well-maintained, with attached bathrooms.

Located on the way to MTDC is **Shiv Sagar Caterers** (Tel: 226038; Mobile: 09271100240; Tariff: Rs 200-700), offering four spacious but modest rooms. They are willing to arrange bonfires and serve Konkani delicacies. The rooms have attached baths but no AC. The staff is eager and hospitable and the food makes it worth staying here.

At the beginning of the temple road is **Ganga Nivas** (Tel: 226243; Tariff: Rs 350), quite a humble stay option. They offer 3 rooms, and vegetarian as well as non-vegetarian food (a vegetarian thali comes for Rs 40), if informed in advance. Rooms have basic furniture but are clean, with attached loos. Ganga Nivas is a good budget option.

Nandanvan (Tel: 226158; Tariff: Rs 350-450) is close to the bus stand, and has six spacious and hygienic rooms (two sea-facing) with attached loos. **Gokul** (Tel: 226439; Tariff: Rs 200-1,200), opposite Kaatal Lake, has 5 basic rooms with attached bathrooms. Food is served only if ordered 2-3 hrs in advance.

For more hotels and details, see Harihareshwar Accommodation Listings on page 554

Stalls selling sherbets and pendants line the narrow temple road in Harihareshwar

WHERE TO EAT

Considering you'll have to walk all around Harihareshwar looking for food if you feel hungry beyond the designated 'supper time' (read 9.30 pm), you would do well to place your order at a *gharghuti* (home serving food) in advance. The ones situated close to the temple, such as **Prachitee, Mohan Kutumbe Restaurant** and **Kiran Wakankar's**, serve only vegetarian food. But there are enough options if you would like to sample typical Konkani seafood. **Shiv Sagar Caterers**, close to MTDC, serves delicious Konkani food, and specialises in prawn masala and crab curry. Kokum is served for a local aftertaste. **Vishranti Bhojanalaya**, a 2-min walk away from the bus stand, is set in a cosy, thatched verandah. A spicy surmai thali, comprising rice, fried surmai fish, fish curry, salad, sol kadi and chappatis, costs Rs 70, and a vegetarian thali Rs 30. A little ahead is the **Guru Geeta** restaurant, popular amongst locals, offering pure vegetarian food. MTDC has stopped serving beer, but their restaurant **Grasshopper Inn**, although more pricey (a vegetarian thali costs Rs 60) than the other humble joints, serves good food in an outdoor setting overlooking the sea.

AROUND HARIHARESHWAR

Bagmandala (4 km)
From the southern beach, across the creek, you can see the **Bankot Fort** perched atop a hill. The fort, which was under the Portuguese and the British, now lies in ruins, and the locals often pass it off as "few walls with nothing to see". Nevertheless, you can convince a local fisherman to take you there in his boat and include a guided tour of the **Peshwa Smarak** (a memorial to the Peshwas). Once ashore, walk past the village of Velas and enjoy the view of the Arabian Sea. If unable to convince a boatman, you'll have to take the much longer road route. Catch a shared auto to Bagmandala (Rs 6) and wait for a fisherman to take you to the fort. You can pay fishermen between Rs 20 and 30.

Shrivardhan (11 km)
See page 443 ■

BHARAT AGGARWAL

HARNAI-MURUD

TWIN TEMPTATION

State Maharashtra
Location Harnai and nearby Murud are situated in Ratnagiri, beyond Dapoli
Distance 262 km S of Mumbai
Journey time ***By road*** 7 hrs from Mumbai
Route from Mumbai NH17 to Khed via Panvel, Pen, Mahad and Poladpur; SH to Harnai via Dapoli (*see route guide on page 394*)

BY SIMAR PREET KAUR

Their proximity to each other has earned them the tag of 'twin beaches' but there's little that Harnai and Murud have in common. If Harnai is chaotic and crowded, Murud (no relation to the one of Janjira fame) acts as its perfect foil. There's solitude here for the asking, and its quiet shoreline is the very antithesis of the beach at Harnai, where even the waves pulsate with the urgent rhythms of fish auctions. Even on days when the overcast sky is the colour of a clamshell, Harnai's fisherfolk will be out in the sea, trawling its waters for fish, and later selling their catch on the shore. The buyers will also turn up in full force, drizzle or otherwise, in autorickshaws, cycles, snazzy cars or on foot. The strong smell of fish will waft through the air, and you will see dried fish hanging everywhere.

The colourful cacophony at Harnai leaves you unprepared for the serenity of Murud Beach. The sky at sunset forms the perfect backdrop for a walk along a winding road that lattices the beach. The moon slowly climbs up and casts its silvery reflection on the waters, and in the solitude, it's easy to imagine that you own this magnificent beach. And fortunately for you, there's usually no one around to dispel such heady notions.

ORIENTATION

Harnai is a small village, but the coastline stretches to **Anjarle** in the north and **Murud** in the south, with jeeps (Rs 10 from Harnai to Anjarle) that are usually filled to the brim connecting all three. **Khed** (28 km) and **Dapoli** are the main towns from where all the ST buses to major cities depart. No shared autos ply between Khed and Harnai, but special autos are available, as are ST buses (Rs 18). Special autos cater to individual tourists, as opposed to shared autos. They charge Rs 350 from Khed to Harnai via Dapoli, and Rs 40-60 from Harnai to Murud. The best places to stay are in Murud and **Karde**, which is a little ahead.

BEACH WATCH

The Harnai Beach, primarily a fishing dock, isn't a good place for swimming; the sand is flecked with ropes and sundry fishermen's items, and the waters aren't clean enough. Murud Beach is safe for swimming, and offers enough privacy to opt for beachwear. Nevertheless, as it's isolated, avoid venturing too far out.

THINGS TO SEE AND DO

There's very little by way of activity on the beaches here. Therefore, it's best to explore Anjarle in the morning, enjoy a swim at Murud, and then head to Harnai for a fish auction in the evening.

Harnai

There are hills on one side of the beach, a mosque in the backdrop and Harnai Bunder (*see below*) on the adjacent side. In the evenings one can see boats anchored near the Bunder, colourful flags fluttering atop them. The fish auctions are what draw people here daily between 5 and 7 pm. The catch of the day is auctioned off to the highest bidder, and the rest is exported to Karnataka, Mumbai and Goa. On weekends the beach comes alive with monkey trainers and balloon sellers.

Harnai Bunder, or **Suvarnadurg Fort** as it's also referred to, is Harnai's forbidden territory. Surrounded by the sea on three sides, the fort is apparently home to wild animals, and locals dissuade visitors from exploring inside. About a kilometre from Harnai, on a hill, are the colourful **Durgadevi Temple** and the **Siddhi Vinayak Ganapati Temple**.

Murud (4 km)

The palm-fringed beach of Murud is just what the doctor ordered. The clear, calm

FAST FACTS

When to go April to June
Tourist office
• MTDC, Collector's Office
Jaystambh, Ratnagiri-415612
Tel: 02352-223847
STD code 02358

waters of the sea meet the black sands dotted with crab holes on a long stretch of beach. Harnai is visible to the right and Karde to the left. You'll have to walk a lot during low tide to reach the waves, but then it's worth it.

Dolphin spotting

If you walk into Kamat's Murud Beach Resort *(see Where to Stay below)* early morning, you can go dolphin spotting aboard a small motorboat. For this, contact Masur (Tel: 02358-234539) beforehand and fix a time for the trip. Masur is an independent organiser who makes use of Kamat's property for his trips; Kamat's itself doesn't organise any. Masur charges Rs 100 per person for a small trip out into the sea.

Karde (7 km)

Walk 3 km south of Murud, past a lovely lagoon and you will reach the isolated beach stretch of Karde. A winding road plays hide and seek with the brown sands, and the only activity to indulge in here is to walk with the sea on one side and the hills on the other.

Anjarle (15 km)

As you move 4 km along the coast from Harnai, passing Paj Pandari Beach en route, you will come across a small jetty. For a fare of Rs 5 per person, you can cross the Jog Creek and reach Anjarle on a precariously balanced boat. On a weekday you might have to shell out the fare for five more people to cross over. If returning late, inform the boatman in advance, or you will have to spend the night at Anjarle. A bridge on the far right can be used if going by road, but that means travelling an additional 10 km.

The black sands of Anjarle Beach are mixed with gravel, dotted with shells and untouched by humans. The beach is a treat for marine life enthusiasts, with a variety of snails, crabs and corals visible near the shore.

GETTING THERE

Air Nearest airport: Chhatrapati Shivaji Airport, Mumbai (262 km/ 7 hrs). Taxi fare till Harnai about Rs 4,000

Rail Nearest railhead: Khed Railway Station (28 km/ 1 hr) is served by the Mandovi Express, also your best option. You can take an auto (fare Rs 25) from Khed Railway Station to Khed Bus Station. There are direct buses (Rs 18/ 1 hr) to Harnai from here. You can also take an auto from LP Auto Stand, opposite the bus stand, till Harnai (fare Rs 250)

Road There are ST buses from Mumbai Central to Harnai (Rs 190). Pritam Travels (Mumbai Tel: 022-65737607; Dapoli Tel: 02358-288083; Mobile: 09820086785) has daily semi-luxury buses (fare Rs 180) from Mumbai Central to Dapoli

WHERE TO STAY

Harnai doesn't have many stay options. The best options, cutting across all budgets, are along Murud and Karde beaches.

On Murud Beach

Kamat's Murud Beach Resort (Tel: 02358-234582/ 709; Tariff: Rs 500-1,100), located on Murud Beach, has 15 cottages. At the time of writing, Kamat's was just beginning to renovate the property. The cottages have clean loos, attached balconies providing privacy, immediate access to the beach, and an in-house restaurant that offers both vegetarian and non-vegetarian food.

A few steps down the road from Kamat's is **Palm Village** (Tel: 234644; Tariff: Rs 600-1,200), with basic but clean rooms that have attached bathrooms and room service facility. There is a common balcony on each of the three floors, and the generator is always on, so you can enjoy the AC (a rare contraption in these areas). Dinner is served between 7.30 and 10 pm in a lovely coconut grove; place your order in advance. The beach is a 5-min walk away.

Silver Sand Beach Resort (Tel: 234501; Tariff: Rs 800-1,100) at Karve Pakhadi in Murud has colourful cottages. Ask for a beach-facing one. It has an open-air restaurant. Hammocks complete the 'beachy' ambience.

Further ahead on Murud Beach is the green and isolated **Kshitij** (Tel: 234603; Tariff: Rs 500), offering 4 non-AC cottages that are clean with no frills. A route here runs past a palm grove and arecanut trees; cross a small bridge on this path and you will be on the beach.

Besides these, the following offer budget stays: **Surbhi Beach Resort** (Tel: 234556; Tariff: Rs 450) on Murud Beach has 8 brick huts furnished only with a bed each. It's a small place with peacocks fluttering around. **Abhiruchi** (Tel: 234651; Tariff: Rs 400-1,200) on Murud Beach has 7 basic cottages with attached bathrooms, all set under casuarinas. **Hotel Kinara** (Tel: 234633; Tariff: Rs 700), also on Murud Beach, has 12 sea-facing cottages, basic but well kept.

On Karde Beach

Sagar Hill Hotel (Tel: 234596, 234740; Tariff: Rs 1,000) is located where Karde Beach begins. There are 19 sea-facing rooms available, providing very little comfort — it should be your last resort, but then there aren't too many hotels on this beach. Hammocks, badminton and table tennis facilities are available. There is no restaurant, but Malvani food can be ordered in advance.

A couple of metres ahead is the **Sea Face Beach Resort** (Tel: 234832; Tariff: Rs 800-1,250), probably the best deal in the area, situated across the road from the sea. This newly opened resort has 18 spacious sea-facing rooms, with a balcony in each, offering an unhindered view of the sea. TV, AC and room service are available. A Konkani food restaurant within provides excellent seafood.

For more hotels and details, see Harnai-Murud Accommodation Listings on pages 554-555

WHERE TO EAT

Although there are plenty of resorts in the vicinity, it's necessary to place your order in advance. There are a few places that do take walk-in orders. **Kamat's Seagull** restaurant serves Indian, Chinese, Konkani, South Indian and Punjabi meals. A vegetarian thali here costs Rs 60. What you must try at Kamat's is the prawn curry, which has a typical Konkani flavour. **Sagar Dhara Restaurant** on Murud Beach, behind the Durgadevi Temple, is the only eating joint open till midnight. The seating arrangement is in a large verandah with a mango tree in the middle, decked up with neon lights. A vegetarian thali costs Rs 38, a non-vegetarian thali Rs 45. But the best deal is pomfret thali, costing Rs 73. **Hotel Laxmi** (open 5 am-10 pm, with a break from 2-5 pm) in Harnai offers seafood and local dishes. **Annapurna**, a small restaurant on Murud Beach, also serves fairly decent Malvani and Konkani food. But they shut by 9 pm.

AROUND HARNAI

Burundi (26 km)

Take a left from the Dapoli checkpost to reach Burundi, a secluded beach frequented mostly by families out on a picnic on weekends. The winding road to Burundi makes for a good drive. The village here offers clean sands as does the nearby **Ladghar Beach**. **Hotel Sagar Sawali** (Tel: 02358-288047) here serves excellent surmai thali (Rs 75) and kolumbi (Rs 40) along with beer. An auto from Murud to Burundi costs Rs 250; the fare is Rs 150 from Dapoli to Burundi. ■

Photographs by ABHILASH GAUR

GUHAGAR

THE SEA OF STORIES

State Maharashtra
Location In Ratnagiri District, halfway between the mouths of Vashishti and Shastri rivers
Distances 43 km W of Chiplun, 313 km S of Mumbai
Journey time ***By road*** 1 hr from Chiplun, 7 hrs from Mumbai
Route from Mumbai NH17 to Chiplun via Pen, Mangaon and Mahad; SH78 to Guhagar via Marg Tamhane (*see route guide on page 394*)

BY ABHILASH GAUR

All day long, the waves crash against the shore, relentlessly pounding the sands. No one's there to listen to its loud rhythms — the beach is mostly empty, and the casuarinas lining its clean stretch shut out the world almost entirely. Sitting on the cool, quiet sand, you find it easy to imagine that Guhagar is a tiny village and not the bustling town-in-the-making that it actually is. In fact, till Enron came, Guhagar was just another village on Maharashtra's coast. As the 'taluka' headquarters and the site of the Wyadeshwar Temple, it was considered more important than most other villages, but it was nowhere close to being a tourist hotspot. The controversial Enron project brought people to the town, and with people came the other trappings: hotels, lodges and eateries. Today, Enron is gone but Guhagar has shaken off its village image. Nearby Velneshwar, with its quiet beach and bobbing boats, now holds that title.

ORIENTATION

The **Wyadeshwar Shiva Temple** lies at the centre of Guhagar. The bus terminus lies to its right. The lane between the temple and the **bus terminus** leads to the sea, hardly 100 yards away. **Chowpatty**, a group of makeshift shops on the beach, is small, and confined to 50 yards at the end of this lane. The buildings behind the temple constitute the **main market**, and house most of the eateries as well as the hotels and lodges. The main **auto stand** is also close to the temple.

BEACH WATCH

The sea here seems violent all through the day, and there's a warning sign telling you not to enter the waters at low tide. It's best to dress conservatively.

THINGS TO SEE AND DO

Guhagar has two attractions: the beach and its temples. Most visitors come here for the beach, and also stop at the Wyadeshwar Temple.

On the beach

The beach's chief attractions are the peace it offers and the clean sands, in that order. It's clean, barring the portion you see first, located between the village and the beach, where there are a few eyesores like a garbage heap. Past this is the Chowpatty, with about a dozen shops that come alive around sunset. Children will enjoy the swings and slides here. Kulfi and camel rides are on offer in the evenings. There are no water sports or boating in Guhagar. The beach is unusual only in one respect: its sand resembles a heap, sloping towards both the village and the sea. The top of this heap and the slope towards the sea are the cleanest.

Other attractions

The **Wyadeshwar Temple** looks newly built, with its cement plaster veneer, but locals claim the underlying structure is made of stone. From Guhagar, you can make an excursion to the **Gopalgarh Fort** (13 km/ Rs 200 by auto), and also visit the **Anjanvel fishing village** while there. The village's rather dirty beach always has a number of fishing boats under construction.

WHERE TO STAY

There are no big hotels in Guhagar, and most are honest enough to describe themselves as lodges. **Kismat Residency** (Tel: 02359-240686; Tariff: Rs 400-650) is a short walk away from the bus terminus, opposite the Marathi School. This is the height of luxury in Guhagar, and the hotel's rear gate opens onto a clean part of the beach. The corner rooms have balconies. Cleanliness can be enforced with sternness before making a deposit. Make sure the AC and the fridge in your room can cool — in my room, these didn't.

Hotel Kautilya (Tel: 240203; Mobile: 09423048234; Tariff: Rs 400-950) is Guhagar's only other 'hotel', a few hundred metres down the road from Kismat Residency. The rooms here are bigger, and its setting is quieter. The beach itself is a minute away across the road. **Manas Lodge** (Mobile: 09423800529; Tariff: Rs 200-500) is the most popular lodge in Guhagar, and it stands opposite the bus terminus. Rooms with TVs cost Rs 250,

→ FAST FACTS

When to go November to February
Tourist office
• MTDC Holiday Resort
Ganapatipule
Tel: 02357-235061, 235248
STD code 02359

GETTING THERE

Air Nearest airport: Chhatrapati Shivaji Airport, Mumbai (313 km/ 7 hrs), well-connected by all airlines to all major towns and cities. Non-AC taxi to Guhagar costs about Rs 4,500

Rail Nearest railhead: Chiplun (43 km/ 1 hr), a major stop on the Konkan Railway, connected by trains from Mumbai such as Konkan Kanya Express and Netravati Express. Autos from Chiplun to Guhagar charge Rs 350 one-way

Road From Mumbai, take the route to Panvel, after which you are on the Panvel-Pen Highway. Continue on NH17 up to Chiplun via Mangaon and Mahad. Guhagar is 43 km away from Chiplun on SH78. A few ST buses run overnight from Mumbai Central, reaching Guhagar in 9 hrs. More buses run from Mumbai to Chiplun, from where you can hire an auto to Guhagar. Ghatge-Patil Roadways (Tel: 022-23421114) in Mumbai has a daily video coach service to Guhagar

while Rs 500 will get you a room with an AC. **Prestige Lodge** (Tel: 240930; Tariff: Rs 200-500) lies behind a row of shops, close to the bus terminus, and is not clean. There's nothing to recommend it, and the Lagoon Bar beside it can get very noisy. **Sagar Lodge** (Tel: 240347; Tariff: Rs 150-350) is close to the Wyadeshwar Temple. The rooms lie above a general store and all have attached bathrooms.

For more hotels and details, see Guhagar Accommodation Listings on pages 553-554

WHERE TO EAT

The best food in Guhagar is available not in hotels but at small roadside eateries. As it's a temple town, most eateries serve only vegetarian meals. And after a hearty repast, you'll be surprised by the meagre amount on the bill. The food here is really cheap.

Two of the best places for vegetarian food in Guhagar are **Suruchi** and **Ruchira**. The local consensus is in favour of Pradip Parchure's Ruchira, but it lies far down the road, close to the high school (not to be confused with the Marathi School). It also does not serve breakfast till 8 am.

Suruchi is more central, just a minute away from the Wyadeshwar Temple, and opens at 7 am. The food is also pretty good. Don't miss the *thalipith* — a kachori-like fried speciality made from a mixture of dal flours. The sol kadi is recommended. Other things worth trying are the idli and medu vada, but the pav accompanying their misal is not soft enough. Non-vegetarians should head straight to Shamkant Khatu's **Annapurna**, which serves chicken masala and mutton masala, apart from regular coastal specialities like pomfret and prawns. The added bonus is that Khatu also books tickets for buses to Mumbai.

AROUND GUHAGAR

Velneshwar (20 km)
This is what Guhagar must have been like 15 years ago: an old temple, a beach, and a couple of lodges. The Western Ghats form the backdrop to Velneshwar, and the road to it is a series of twists and turns. Autos from Guhagar take about half an hour to get here and charge Rs 350 for the 3-hr round-trip, which includes a detour to nearby **Hedavi Village** as well.

The village is named after a Shiva temple, which is largely built of stone. Brightly painted, it's architecturally interesting with its mix of domes and spires. A newly built shrine outside the sanctum has stone idols of local deities worshipped by the fisher folk.

The beach at Velneshwar is quiet, and though the sand isn't so white, it's clean. Navnit Thakur's **Kinara Beach House** (Tel: 243363, 09969195954; Tariff: Rs 300-500) provides basic accommodation away from the temple. The tariffs are negotiable and depend on the tourist rush. He also has an outdoor restaurant on the beach. There's a nicer beach restaurant just behind the temple; stalls on the road offer coconut water and biscuits. **Atithi Hotel** (Tel: 243518; Tariff: Rs 500) is bigger and closer to the temple. It offers 'luxuries' such as TV and hot water, but no AC.

Apart from these two, at the time of writing, MTDC was planning to start a resort at Velneshwar soon, adjacent to the beach. It will be run by a private party; more information can be obtained from the MTDC (*for contact details, see Fast Facts on page 459*).

Hedavi (25 km)
Hedavi is far greener and quieter than either Guhagar or Velneshwar. From Velneshwar, it takes around 10 mins to reach a fork in the road where the routes for Hedavi Village and its beach separate. The hillsides here are completely covered with trees, often clusters of palms, and the best view can be had from the courtyard of the **Dasabhuja Lakshmi Ganesha Temple** in the village. While the temple is just as cheerfully painted as the one at Velneshwar, it's much smaller. It's said that the 10-armed idol of Ganapati inside it was made in Kashmir and gifted to the temple by one of the Peshwas. The idol is beautiful, but while you are there, do pay attention to the wooden chest kept for donations in the outer hall. Its legs are shaped like a lion's feet and the old wood is richly polished.

It takes another 10 mins to reach the beach from the temple. The sand here lies in a narrow strip, with *suru* trees forming a tight border. The rightward curve of the arc is rocky, and has a Shiva temple atop it.

Bamanghai, Hedavi's famous crevice

More interesting than the temple, however, is the crevice called **Bamanghai**, which shoots a jet of seawater (some 25 ft high), every few minutes during high tide. It's said that this occurs due to the air that gets trapped under the water every time the waves force their way into the gap between the rocks.

Accommodation in Hedavi is confined to Abhay Bhatkar's **Suruchi Corner** (Tel: 02359-243209, 243616; Tariff: Rs 500-600), which is a small cluster of self-contained huts amidst the trees by the beach. Bhatkar is known for and proud of his sol kadi, and as a sip will confirm, deservedly so. ■

With inputs from
Outlook Traveller Getaways Desk

Photographs by ABHILASH GAUR

GANAPATIPULE

RHYTHM DIVINE

State Maharashtra
Location By the Arabian Sea on the southern Konkan Coast, to the north of Ratnagiri
Distances 45 km N of Ratnagiri, 153 km NW of Kolhapur, 331 km SW of Pune, 390 km S of Mumbai
Journey time *By road* 1 hr from Ratnagiri, 3½ hrs from Kolhapur, 7 hrs from Pune, 8½ hrs from Mumbai
Route from Mumbai NH17 to Nivli via Kolad, Chiplun and Sangameshwar; district road to Ganapatipule (*see route guide on page 394*)

BY SAYYIDA AMIN AND ABHILASH GAUR

The road to Ganapatipule from Ratnagiri is an indicator — a magical, stunning indicator — of the beauty that lies ahead. On winding roads, a multi-hued landscape rushes past your car windows, bursting with red earth and emerald paddy fields and mango trees laden with fruits.

The beach at Ganapatipule is a revelation. Its sands change colour according to the time of day, and it's best at sunset, when it's all gold, framed by a golden sky. Green coconut trees stand nearby as if to add some more zest to what is an already glorious vista.

The remarkable thing about the beach is that though it's frequented by tourists — many of them devotees who come to visit the temple nearby — it never appears to be crowded. From the hillock behind the temple, the view is glorious: a spectacular blue sea with white-tinged waves spreads out below; a cricket match is in progress on the beach, right next to the water; and like a dream, the coconut trees sway in the breeze. It's the kind of place that makes you want to chuck your job and stay on — forever if possible — with the waves and the sands, the trees and the stars. But even if you're here for just two days, you'll take back something: if nothing else, a snapshot of a mesmerising beach, lurking in your thoughts like the gritty sand sticking to your sandals.

ORIENTATION

Ganapatipule's hub is its **bus terminus**. The road that brings you to Ganapatipule from Ratnagiri continues past the terminus towards **Malgund**, with the town's **market** stretched on both its sides. Across the road from the terminus stands the **MTDC Resort**, and to the left the **Swayambhu Ganapati Temple**, which faces the beach. All the important hotels in Ganapatipule lie along this road. The small town comprises just the beach and the seashore. Autos don't run on meter but drivers are co-operative. Fares are fixed for different distances (Rs 350 for Ratnagiri).

BEACH WATCH

As across the West Coast, swimming is not advised at low tide at Ganapatipule as it's dangerous. There are lifeguards on the beach. Dress conservatively.

THINGS TO SEE AND DO

Strictly speaking, there's only one beach in Ganapatipule. Bhandarpule, located 2 km out of town, also has a beach, but it's not a long one. The unpolluted waters of the sea and the usually clear blue sky (unless you're visiting in the monsoon) contribute their bit too in making Ganapatipule spectacular.

On the beach

In spite of the huge number of people visiting it, the Ganapatipule Beach remains quiet and clean. To the left of the Swayambhu Ganapati Temple, the beach ends in large rocks, while to the right it's cut off by a creek wherein the MTDC offers water sports (*contact the resort office; see Where to Stay on page 465 for details*). They have a motorboat (Rs 30 per head, per round), a water scooter (Rs 40 per round) and a pedal boat (Rs 20 for 15 mins). The rides are on offer from 9 am to noon and again from 3 to 6 pm.

Swayambhu Ganapati Temple

Legend has it that Lord Ganesha manifested himself on a hillock by the beach, which is why a Ganapati Temple was

Swayambhu Ganapati Temple

→ FAST FACTS

When to go Ganapatipule has emerged as a year-round destination, with even summer being a busy time. The sea remains angry throughout the monsoon and this is the official off-season but even the rains draw revellers

Tourist office
- MTDC Holiday Resort ⓘ
Ganapatipule
Tel: 02357-235248/ 235061-62

STD code 02357

built there. The name Ganapatipule, incidentally, means sands (*pule*) blessed by Ganesha. The large temple on the beach does not look very old, but it's pretty and a must-visit. The temple is located at the foot of a verdant hillock facing the beach. A scenic, paved pathway enables devotees to circumambulate the hillock and the temple.

Each year, from February 2 to 8 and between November 2 and 8, the evening sun's rays fall directly on the idol within the temple. Thousands of believers come to Ganapatipule at this time to witness this 'miracle' of the sun 'worshipping' Lord Ganapati.

Malgund

This is an old village on the road to Jaigarh, about 2 km from Ganapatipule. Today, it's known for two things: the open-air museum **Prachin Kokan** (*also see 'A peek into the past' on page 466*), and the **memorial** to the Marathi poet Krishnaji Keshav Damle, who is better known as Keshavsut (Keshav's son). Damle was born in Malgund on October 7, 1866, and made his mark as a reformist poet. His old house is now considered a sacred space.

♦**Entry fee** Rs 5 **Timings** 8.30 am-7 pm daily **Note** Remove your shoes before you enter the house

Malgund also has a beautiful beach called **Gaiwadi**, which you won't find on a tourist map but must not miss for anything in winter. For, between December and March, it's home to large flocks of migratory birds.

Konkan Tourism Development Research Centre, a private agency, offers adventure sports here. You can go parasailing between 8 am and 7 pm (depending upon the wind conditions) for Rs 325 per kilometre. Call Vaibhav Sardesai (Mobile: 09373392733) to book a ride as only 50 rides are offered in a day. He also runs the Prachin Kokan Museum.

GETTING THERE

Air Nearest airport: Dabolim Airport, Goa (286 km/ 6 hrs), connected to all metros by all major airlines. Pre-paid non-AC taxi to Ganapatipule costs Rs 4,300
Rail Nearest railhead: Ratnagiri (45 km/ 1 hr), a major stop on the Konkan Railway. Autos charge Rs 350 one-way. There are also State Transport buses to Ganapatipule from Ratnagiri
Road The Mumbai to Ratnagiri bus fare is approx Rs 340. Ghatge-Patil Roadways (Tel: 022-23421114; 02352-223845) in Mumbai runs an AC bus service; departures are at 9.30 pm. Prashant Tours and Travels (Mobile: 09371903237) runs a service between Ratnagiri and Mumbai

SHOPPING

Ganapatipule is not renowned for any particular handicraft but it has a wealth of horticultural produce that you can take back raw or processed. If you are here in April-May, visit one of the mango orchards in Malgund to buy the famous **Alphonso mangoes**. Otherwise, tinned mango pulp, bottled kokum syrup, amla squash and sun-dried layers of mango, jamun and jackfruit pulp are available at a number of shops. You'll get the best discounts on these at the **Govind V Kelkar Supermarket** on the ground floor of Hotel Durvankur (*see Where to Stay on facing page*). The Kelkars have their own mango orchards and a processing plant, and they sell their products under the brand name Ashok. Be sure to pick up cashewnuts as well.

You can also buy handicrafts from the Konkan districts of Maharashtra at the **Prachin Kokan Museum** in Malgund (*see page 466*).

PRADEEP CHAMARIYA/ AGP PHOTOBANK

The sun, the sand and the trees: The spectacular beach at Ganapatipule

WHERE TO STAY

Ganapatipule has plenty of accommodation to suit all budgets. In fact, every second house in the town is a lodge — as long as there's a tourist to be found, that is.

The **MTDC Holiday Resort** (Tel: 02357-235248; Tariff: Rs 300-2,500) is not one but two properties, with not only separate check-in desks but also a kilometre between them. If you want the best location in town, look no further. Whether you stay in the hotel block upon the hillock or in the cottages and tents on the beach, the sea will be directly before you. More so if you are in one of the **Konkani House cottages** (Tariff: Rs 1,200-1,400) below.

The cottages are clean and well-maintained, and the beach is no further away than the edge of each individual porch. The tents (Rs 300), however, are strictly for backpackers. Approached from the main road, the MTDC property is close to the Ganapati Temple, but if you are walking down the beach, the two are quite far. There's a stringent checkout time of 9 am. If your bus or train will leave only late in the evening, you might want to check out of a more expensive room and leave your bags in a standard room for the rest of the day, while you spend some time at the temple and on the beach. Since the non-AC rooms are well ventilated, they are excellent value for money. Try to get the corner deluxe non-AC room of any cottage for even better cross-ventilation.

Hotel Durvankur (Tel: 235764; Tariff: Rs 800-1,200) would have got our vote for Ganapatipule's best hotel if only it was located on the beach. This is a new property, thoughtfully built and sincerely maintained, and located not far from the beach. The rooms are large and airy and the vegetarian Shivnandan restaurant here serves good food.

Krishnali Beach Resort (Tel: 235351-53; Tariff: Rs 3,330-7,920) is an overpriced paradise that is located 2 km out of town, at Bhandarpule. There's a clean beach that's quite close to its cottages and bungalows but the extra thousands that have to be paid for the view may not be worth it.

A peek into the past

Malgund, just a couple of kilometres out of Ganapatipule on the road to Jaigarh, has the area's newest 'sight': an open-air museum called **Prachin Kokan**, which depicts the region's traditional way of life through life-like models. Spread over 3 acres on a hillside, this beautifully landscaped park is the brainchild of Ganapatipule resident Vaibhav Sardesai. Considering the park's concept, scale and brilliant execution, it's hard to believe that Vaibhav is yet to turn 30. In fact, when he threw open the Prachin Kokan to visitors on December 15, 2004, he was only 27. Today, the park draws nearly 7,000 visitors a month during the tourist season.

The museum depicts everyone from Kolis (fisherfolk) to barbers, potters, sculptors, cobblers and even a village headman. In addition to this, there are displays of ancient implements such as an oil press, kitchen tools like a *modak* (a Maharashtrian sweet with jaggery and coconut filling) cooker, and even a model called Aarmaar, commemorating Shivaji's first naval vessel, the Sangameshwari.

At the top of the hill, there's a *machaan* or watchtower made of bamboo, from where you can see the spread of the village right up to the sea. Nearby is a counter selling handicrafts from Maharashtra's Konkan districts. There are wooden toys from Sawantwadi, puppets from Sindhudurg and food products from Ratnagiri. Their mango shake powder is locally made without additives, and you must definitely buy some.

Prachin Kokan is open from 8.30 am to 6 pm through the week. The entry fee is Rs 15, and the camera fee is Rs 10. Call Vaibhav Sardesai on 09373392733 or email ktdrc@rediffmail.com.

Hotel Landmark (Tel: 235284-85; Tariff: Rs 1,000-2,200) is close to the sea, with an uncharitable checkout time of 9 am. It will take you a few minutes to walk down to the Ganapati Temple and the beach from its gate. It's best to stay here only if MTDC and Durvankur don't have rooms available. **Hotel Shiv Sagar Palace** (Tel: 235070; Tariff: Rs 700-2,000), located on the outskirts of Ganapatipule, offers a view of the sea from every room. The hotel stands on a hillock, so the beach is not easily accessible, and since it's a bit out of town on the highway, you might not find an auto when you need one (say, if you want seafood or a drink; the hotel itself is 'pure veg'). Its worst feature is its outrageous design.

For more hotels and details, see Ganapatipule Accommodation Listings on pages 552-553

WHERE TO EAT

MTDC's properties in Ganapatipule are great to stay at, but the food is disappointing at their two restaurants, **Tarang** and **Surubam**. Their sol kadi is so white that it could pass for garlic-spiced coconut milk.

As it's a temple town, most roadside eateries in Ganapatipule serve only vegetarian fare. And the pick of these lie just a short walk away from the MTDC property. The first of these is **Bhau Joshi's** that serves the best sol kadi in town. Bhau serves lunch from 11 am to 3 pm

Explore a new highway. Search for a forgotten town. Find a new destination. Just hit the road with Speed, the high performance petrol and you will experience greater pick up, smoother drive and superior performance. Speed gives you the confidence to take on the road. Tank up, and head out. The whole of India is waiting for you.
Speed™
High Performance Petrol
INDIA
3.38 million Kms
Road Network
Bharat
Petroleum
Take the first
Road out.
To go places log on to www.speedfuels.com
SAATCHI & SAATCHI-147/2007 M

A boat ride to explore the past at the 17th-century Jaigarh Fort

and dinner from 7.30 to 10 pm, for which you need to order between 9.30 am and 12 noon, and 6.30 and 7.30 pm. His baingan masala is very popular among tourists, and for dessert, his homely shrikhand is recommended.

Further up the road is Hotel Durvankur's sparkling clean **Shivnandan** restaurant. Everything they serve is excellent. Polish off your meal with a bottle of Marco, a locally produced mango drink that puts to shame the much advertised cold drinks available nationwide.

AROUND GANAPATIPULE

North of Ganapatipule, all the way up to Jaigarh, lie some of the finest, whitest, and most unsullied beaches that your travel agent will know nothing about. Hire an autorickshaw for 3 hrs (Rs 300) and check out the amazing countryside. You might be tempted to stay longer at one of these beaches, in which case it's best to negotiate the fare on the way.

Jaigarh (20 km)

Before you drive up to the 17th-century **Jaigarh Fort** overlooking the sea and the **Shastri River** that flows into the sea here, do ask the driver to take you to the **Karhateshwar Temple** nearby. This wooden temple is clearly a few centuries old, but more interesting than it is the palm-fringed view it offers of the sea below. It takes only a few minutes to get to Jaigarh from Karhateshwar, and then you can explore the fort's walls at leisure. The locals ascribe the fort's construction to the sultan of Bijapur. It's not a large fort, but solidly built with 20 bastions. The cannons have been removed but you can take mock shots at the large boats and small ships passing below on their way to the **Jaigarh Jetty**. Next to the jetty is a large fishing village.

◆**Fort entry** Free **Timings** Sunrise to sunset

MTDC has a **backwater cruise** facility at the jetty, which can be booked by calling their tourist office in Ratnagiri (*for contact details, see Fast Facts in Ratnagiri on page 470*). Their catamaran runs from 4 to 6 pm. Each cruise lasts an hour and the rate is Rs 200 per head (free for children aged below 10). The catamaran has a peak capacity of 120 passengers. The ride will take you past the fisherfolk's villages. ■

Photographs by ABHILASH GAUR

RATNAGIRI

THE HOUSE OF GREEN MANGOES

State Maharashtra
Location In South Maharashtra, on the Konkan Coast, to the south of Ganapatipule, more than halfway between Mumbai and Goa
Distances 132 km NW of Kolhapur, 373 km S of Mumbai
Journey time *By road* 3 hrs from Kolhapur, 8 hrs from Mumbai
Route from Mumbai NH17 to Hathkhamba via Chiplun and Sangameshwar; NH204 to Ratnagiri (*see route guide on page 394*)

■ BY ABHILASH GAUR AND ANURADHA KUMAR

For most travellers, Ratnagiri is a pretty stop on the Konkan Railway, where red earth beckons under the rails, and dark green trees laden with mangoes whiz past the train windows. Watching the rolling green hills, somewhere there's a lurking suspicion that there's even greater beauty to be discovered outside the railway station, and fortunately, this is indeed the case. Just 15 mins from the railway station is the sea, part of Ratnagiri's glorious coastline, fringed by bright green hills. The port is what Mumbai must have been like in the 19th century, when the first views that greeted visitors landing at Apollo Bunder would have been strikingly similar to the one served up by Ratnagiri today.

Its relative obscurity means that Ratnagiri has all the charms of a beautiful seaside town: people yawn before giving directions, and the air is suffused with a languor that borders on insolence. But it also means that the beaches are mostly empty, and there's a coconut or mango tree whichever way you turn.

Most beaches are close to the town, and each one is different from the other. Indeed, in Ratnagiri, wherever you go, the sea is never too far away, forever beckoning you to build a sand castle or chase the waves. Like the wind whispering to you to step out of the train, the call of the sea is best heeded. Ratnagiri might have only nature's gifts to offer but some of the most spectacular things in life do come without a price tag.

ORIENTATION

Though not the centre of Ratnagiri, **Thibaw Point** is the highest place close to the sea, about 15 mins from the railway station. Standing here, you can see an old **fishing village** to your right, followed by the **Bhatye Bridge**, which leads to the **Bhatye Beach**. Invisible from the point, but about a kilometre to the left, is the **Thibaw Palace**. The road past it leads to the town's **main market**, from where the **railway station** is about 5 km away. Freedom fighter **Lokmanya Tilak's house** lies in the old residential part of the town, and you can walk to it, but the Ratnadurg or **Bhagwati Fort** and the **Mandavi Beach** below it are best covered by auto. Autos from the railway station charge Rs 400 for a full-day sightseeing trip of the town and its three beaches. Autos don't run on meter.

BEACH WATCH

Of Ratnagiri's three beaches, only the Bhatye Beach is suitable for swimming; the Mandavi Beach is too dirty and rocky, and the Pandre Samudra Beach too smelly. There are no lifeguards around, so swimming is risky. Swimwear would be inappropriate on these beaches.

THINGS TO SEE AND DO

Red earth and green mangoes are Ratnagiri's claim to fame, and its Burmese connection adds to the town's exotic value. There are no water sports on offer on the three beaches.

Bhatye Beach

Ratnagiri has an uneven sea-face, broken by a narrow and deep bay spanned by the

FAST FACTS

When to go November to February
Tourist office
● MTDC, Collector's Office
Jaystambh, Ratnagiri-415612
Tel: 02352-223847
STD code 02352

The watchtower at Thibaw Point, from where one gets a bird's eye-view of Ratnagiri

Bhatye Bridge. At the brown Bhatye Beach, the water rarely comes up above the knees for the first 50 yards. It's still the quietest and nicest of Ratnagiri's three beaches. Its sand isn't white or even golden, but the further away you go from the bridge, the quieter it becomes. The thick barrier of *suru* trees between the beach and the coastal highway prevents sound from travelling either way, and by the time you reach the Regional Coconut Research Station, you practically have the beach to yourself.

Regional Coconut Research Station

Located opposite Bhatye Beach, the research station is a 25-hectare open-air lab where coconut farming is studied in minute detail.

◆**Entry** Free **Timings** 8 am-12 noon and 2-6 pm, Sundays closed

Mandavi

Though this is a lively beach, it's also Ratnagiri's worst one. It lies close to the Ratnadurg Fort (*see alongside*), and has a sizeable crowd of visitors in the evening. But tourists would do well to stay away from the beach itself as it's dirty, and the sand is almost black and littered. Mandavi also has the **Ratnagiri Jetty**, along with the unremarkable **Gateway of Ratnagiri**. It was a mistake to name the structure thus as Mandavi is the least pretty part of Ratnagiri's sea-face.

Pandre Samudra Beach

Located on one side of the Ratnadurg Fort, the beach lives up to its name, which can be literally translated as the White Sea. However, it's the sand and not the sea that's stunningly white. Seen from the ramparts of the fort, it's an inviting sight but closer inspection reveals that it reeks of fish, not necessarily a heady prospect for many.

Ratnadurg Fort

It once sprawled across two hills, looking down at the magnificent blue sea. Maratha Emperor Shivaji's Ratnadurg Fort is known as the **Qila** but all that's left of it today are crumbling walls. Inside the remnants of the fort is the **Sri Devi Bhagwati Mandir**, which gives the fort its other name Bhagwati Qila. The government used the fort's stones to build the **Bhagwati Jetty**, but the jetty itself was never operational. It's still worth visiting the fort for the gorgeous views it offers. The fort is a short 10-min drive up from the main road.

Lokmanya Tilak's birthplace

The freedom fighter's house, located close to the Qila, has been converted into a **museum**. It has many of Tilak's photos; the house is also an example of Konkani architecture. Do remember that you have to remove your shoes at the entrance.
◆**Entry** Free **Timings** 9 am-7 pm, open on all days

GETTING THERE

Air Nearest airport: Dabolim Airport, Goa (241 km/ 5 hrs), connected by flights from most metros. Non-AC taxi to Ratnagiri costs about Rs 3,500 return
Rail Ratnagiri is an important station on the Konkan Railway route, and all major trains, including Rajdhanis, stop here. The station lies a few kilometres out of the town, but plenty of autos are available at its entrance. They charge Rs 50 up to Thibaw Point
Road From Mumbai, it's NH17 all the way to Hathkhamba Junction via Pen, Mahad and Chiplun. From Hathkhamba, Ratnagiri is just 11 km away on NH204, which connects Ratnagiri to Kolhapur. Ordinary and semi-deluxe State Transport buses leave from opposite Mumbai Central, Borivli and Parel bus stations in Mumbai, as well as from Kolhapur and Pune to Ratnagiri. There are several Volvo and luxury buses too from Mumbai, which stop at Hathkhamba or Niwali en route to Goa. Konduskar Travels (Tel: 022-27895205) has one AC bus (fare Rs 300) leaving daily for Ratnagiri from Dadar at 8.30 pm

The Burmese link

Those who have read Amitav Ghosh's *The Glass Palace* will identify Ratnagiri as the setting where an exiled Burmese king's story unfolds. The **Thibaw Palace** is located close to the **Thibaw Point**, which has a new watchtower from where one can get a bird's eye-view of Ratnagiri. It was built for the king of Myanmar (then Burma), who was dethroned and exiled to India by the British. The palace, built under the king's supervision, is modest by royal standards. It was completed in 1910 at a cost of Rs 1.25 lakh. At the time of going to print, restoration work was happening at the palace. The palace also houses a museum of antiquities.
◆**Entry fee** Rs 3 **Museum timings** 10 am-1 pm and 1.30-5.30 pm, closed on Mondays

SHOPPING

Ratnagiri is famous for its Alphonso mangoes, grown over 61,000 hectares. If you are there during April-May, do gift yourself a box of mangoes. March is when the first batch of mangoes ripens, but the fruit is prohibitively expensive at the time (Rs 30-40 apiece in the orchards and Rs 50 apiece at the wholesale market in Mumbai). What you can buy round the year, though, is tinned mango pulp that has a shelf life of two years. The Desais of Pawas (*also see page 475*), who are famous as Ratnagiri's 'First Family of Mangoes', have a shop (Tel: 02352-237270; Mobile: 09422052447) at Jayastambh Chowk, near the district courts, where you get excellent deals on mango products, cashews and kokum sherbet.

WHERE TO STAY

Ratnagiri sees many visitors as it's the district headquarters, and has enough rooms. But most are in the budget range.

Kohinoor Samudra Beach Resort (Tel: 02352-235231-32; Tariff: Rs 4,250-9,750) is Ratnagiri's only luxury resort,

located a few kilometres out of town on the Pawas coastal highway. The resort is located on a hill overlooking the Bhatye Beach. It's clean, although the walls of many rooms show evidence of seepage, and is set amidst sprawling lawns.

Hotel Giri Ratna Railotel (Tel: 231260; Tariff: Rs 900-1,800) is a safe bet. It stands practically inside the Ratnagiri Railway Station compound and has a multi-cuisine restaurant. The rooms here are better than in most other hotels. **Hotel Kaanchan** (Tel: 228250-51; Tariff: Rs 600-900) is also close to the railway station, and has a gym, a multi-cuisine restaurant, and a permit room (bar).

Hotel Landmark (Tel: 220120; Tariff: Rs 795-1,395) is located on Thibaw Palace Road. While it does not come across as luxurious, it does have a fancily named restaurant, Papillon, offering Indian and Chinese, and the essential 'permit room' or bar. **Hotel Prabha** (Tel: 223515; Tariff: Rs 250-600) is the hotel that's most likely going to be recommended by your autorickshaw driver. It's more like a lodge and its location, in the heart of town, not far from the local Congress Bhavan and Tilak Ali, means that the surroundings aren't very quiet.

Boats as seen from the Ratnadurg Fort

Hotel Vihar Deluxe (Tel: 222944-45; Tariff: Rs 400-1,100) was possibly the first hotel to come up in Ratnagiri, in 1980. Located on the main road, close to the ST Stand, with an ATM on its premises, the hotel has 36 rooms. It's fairly large, and its two dining halls, two permit rooms and one terrace restaurant speak volumes for its popularity. A fresh coat of paint would help win more customers. **Hotel Vivek** (Tel: 222162; Tariff: Rs 450-1,500) is close to Vihar Deluxe and equally old, but is better maintained and cheaper. It's not bad for a short stay.

For more hotels and details, see Ratnagiri Accommodation Listings on pages 559-560

WHERE TO EAT

There aren't any major eateries in Ratnagiri, so you will have to eat at the restaurants attached to the hotels. Most of them claim to be multi-cuisine, but don't expect gastronomic excellence here. The local Konkani cuisine is your best bet, followed by Udupi fare: idli, medu vada and dosa. Unless you have a strong scientific temperament, experiments with 'Chinese' and 'Continental' will disappoint. The restaurants at the hotels offer popular Maharashtrian fare such as usal, misal and poha and also rice. **Kohinoor** serves seafood, and its prawns are a speciality, while **Vivek's Downtown** restaurant dishes up a variety of cuisines. At **Hotel Landmark**, uthappams or kanda poha are good bets.

AROUND RATNAGIRI

Pawas (25 km)

Pawas Village is known across Maharashtra as the birthplace and home of the 20th century saint, reformer and activist, Swami Swaroopananda, whose ashram and samadhi are pilgrimage sites

Water world: A boat heads past the beach at Bhatye

today. Swamiji's ancestral home has been preserved, and visitors are allowed up to its door.

A little further into the village lies the Gautami stream, and beyond it is the **Vishveshwara Temple**. This Peshwa-era shrine, made of wood, is remarkable for its richly carved beams and pillars depicting mythological tales. The panels have been brightly painted over but that doesn't lessen their beauty.

Before leaving, do check out **Desai Agro's shop**, across the road from the samadhi. Their mango juice (Rs 25 for a can) is excellent. The Desais got into mango plantations with a few trees in the 1920s, but today they are a legend, with over 12,000 trees spread over 500 hectares. You will find smaller stalls across the road from Desai's, and each of these will have a range of mango products.

A drive down the coastal highway to Pawas, and then a right turn back towards the coast, gets you to the aged **Purnagad Fort**. A coastal village lies below the fort, and it's a peaceful spot from where you can take in sublime views of the sea. Autos from Ratnagiri charge Rs 400 for the 50-km round-trip to Pawas, inclusive of a visit to Ganeshghule Beach (*see below*).

Ganeshghule (29 km)
You will find longer beaches in Ratnagiri, beaches that are no less clean and just as quiet, but there's something magical about the sea and the sand at this tiny settlement of Ganeshghule, located 4 km west of Pawas.

It takes about 15 mins to cover the serpentine route between Pawas and Ganeshghule. It takes another 5 mins to walk from the dusty road to the white sand, cutting across fenced yards and bushes. And then you see it: green waters, an unspoilt beach and not a soul around. Hardly anyone comes to Ganeshghule (apart from the turtles who find it a safe place to lay eggs), so it's free of vendors and the associated litter. Fishing boats are also a rare sight on these waters, and the odd one you might spot would be tiny and without a motor.

Ganapatipule (45 km)
See page 462 ■

Photographs by BHARAT AGGARWAL

KUNKESHWAR

GLOWING IN THE DARK

State Maharashtra
Location On the South Konkan Coast, south of the hapus capital Devgad and the sea fort of Vijaydurg
Distances 160 km N of Dabolim (Goa), 220 km S of Chiplun, 490 km S of Mumbai
Journey time ***By road*** $3^{1}/_{2}$ hrs from Dabolim, $4^{1}/_{2}$ hrs from Chiplun, 10 hrs from Mumbai
Route from Mumbai NH17 to Nandgaon via Chiplun and Tarele; SH116 to Jamsande via Koloshi and Shirgaon; SH4 to Kunkeshwar (*see route guide on page 394*)

■ BY JOAN PINTO

As you drive towards Kunkeshwar, you spy its sloping dunes peeping past palm trees. Close up, it's just what you *don't* expect. It's a stretch of open, beautiful beach that no one seems to visit, not even the pilgrims at the Kunkeshwar Temple. The temple's tower-like, multi-coloured monolith reaches for the blue sky and gives the beach its name — Kunkeshwar, meaning Lord Shiva.

Legend has it that an Arabian trader's dhow got caught in a storm off the Kunkeshwar Coast a few hundred years ago. He prayed for help, and would've drowned if not for the lamp light in the then tiny Shiva temple, which Yadava rulers had built in 1100. The light guided him to the safety of the shore and he built a new temple there as an expression of his gratitude.

There is indeed much to be thankful for at Kunkeshwar. There's the sunset, when the sun appears like a red, shimmering *tikka* on the forehead of the horizon. There are the delicious hapus mangoes, popular across the world, waiting at the orchards at Devgad, just a few kilometres away. There is the white sand and the somewhat hushed whispers of the waves, all of which you can take in by yourself in the magnificent solitude of the beach. But the best gift of all comes your way in the night, when the waters of the sea shimmer because of phosphorescence. Occasionally, a few porpoises leap up with the waves, and the night is suddenly magical, as if a fairy has moved her wand somewhere, leaving behind a trail of twinkling stars.

ORIENTATION

Kunkeshwar is an hour's drive from the nearest big town, **Devgad** (27 km). Like the tiny villages that precede it, Kunkeshwar is an idyllic, pastoral place. Unlike the others though, it lies on the coast. Come down the road from **Jamsande** on SH4, past the village of **Illeye**. The road then winds towards **Kunkeshwar Temple** and the beach. Here, it's lined with matchbox-sized stalls selling food, flowers and temple offerings. Except for a hotel for pilgrims known as **Bhakti Niwas**, located behind the beach, all the hotels are at least 2-3 km away; the nearest is at Jamsande. More hotels are to be found at Devgad. Autos are the most convenient mode of transport here; the minimum fare is Rs 20 (to go around the village). They charge Rs 200 and above to Devgad or **Vijaydurg**. Though State Transport buses stop at a designated place in the village, the drive is long because of the number of halts.

BEACH WATCH

Locals say the water is safe to wade in at Kunkeshwar but it's best to be close to

Fishermen dock outside Vijaydurg Fort

→ FAST FACTS

When to go November to February. If interested in hapus, visit in April. Phosphorescence is seen in winter

Tourist office

● MTDC Tarkarli

(see *Tarkarli Fast Facts on page 486*)

STD code 02364

→ GETTING THERE

Air Nearest airport: Dabolim, Goa (160 km/ 3½ hrs). Taxi to Kunkeshwar costs Rs 1,500

Rail Nearest railhead: Kankavli (47 km/ 1¼ hrs by road). Connected to Mumbai by the Konkan Kanya Express, Shatabdi and Mandovi. Connected to Delhi by the Mangala Express. Autos to Kunkeshwar charge approx Rs 200-250 and private cars Rs 600 approximately. Autos are available outside the railway station or near the bus stand

Road From Mumbai, drive south on NH17 to Nandgaon; here take a right and drive till Devgad Junction near Jamsande. From here you turn left for Kunkeshwar, 17 km away via Shirgaon. En route halts include Mahad and Chiplun. Ordinary and semi-luxury ST buses ply from Mumbai Central, Borivli, Parel and Kurla Nehru Nagar bus stands to Devgad. From here hire an autorickshaw (Rs 300) or take a bus. The roads are tarred and make for a nice drive. Volvo buses and AC buses do not ply directly to Kunkeshwar but the closest stop is Kankavli; these leave from Dadar. Some of the agencies offering services from Mumbai include: Paulo Travels (Tel: 022-26518958, 26433023; fare: Volvo bus Rs 850-950; AC Rs 600-700; non-AC Rs 500-600), which has a daily bus leaving from Dadar at 8.30 pm; and Oswal Travels (Tel: 24092426; fare: Rs 300 for non-AC, Rs 500 for Volvo), whose non-AC buses leave Sion at 6 and 7.30 pm, and Volvo buses leave at 8.30 pm and 9 pm. From Kankavli, one can take an auto to Kunkeshwar (approx Rs 250-300)

TIP Recheck the fares of bus services at the time of travel as they tend to fluctuate a bit

the shore if you plan to swim. There are no lifeguards here. Keep your beachwear conservative as it's a temple town; besides, the place isn't acquainted with tourists. It's also a good idea to keep to the side of the beach that's away from the temple. At high tide, step carefully over the rocks to the right of the beach, as most of them are then partially covered in the water.

THINGS TO SEE AND DO

The temple at Kunkeshwar is a must-visit for the followers of Lord Shiva. But others are blessed too — all they have to do is go down the temple steps and claim the whole 2-km stretch of beach as their own.

The beach

Go past the shops selling offerings in front of the temple, climb down the steps to the back of the temple and feel the sand in your toes. There, in front of you is an empty beach to run wild on. Besides little fishing boats, a stray dog or two and trotting crabs, the beach is all yours. For a panoramic view of the sea, climb up the slope behind the temple, past giant banyans. Sit atop the hillock and watch the sun go down, and it's one memory that's guaranteed to stay with you forever. In the winter months, as the sun goes down and night draws in, the sea comes alive because of phosphorescence. Every rippling wave is crested with a line of a peculiar light that grows in intensity, tingeing the waves here and there with green and white before disappearing. It's a rare phenomenon along the Western Coast; the phosphorescence is created by microscopic sea organisms, especially crustaceans, which, small as they are, collectively look like liquid light when disturbed.

Kunkeshwar Temple

The temple is a monolith with tiers of bright colour on the outside. However,

Devgad's windmills stand like tall, white storks against a blue sky

the serenity inside belies its newly painted, revamped exterior. Lotus flowers, coconut offerings, the temple bell that clangs now and then, and the scent of incense, calm the senses. The original architecture of the temple is visible in a few parts of the structure. During Mahashivaratri, the temple and its surroundings buzz with devotees.

◆**Note** People of all faiths visit the temple; do remember to dress conservatively

Tara Mumbri Beach

Located about 4 km north of Kunkeshwar, Tara Mumbri is a little village with a beach. When the sun sets, take an auto through the village to the beach to see nature's own special show: the surreal-looking **phosphorescence** in the sea. Most tourists visit at this hour to glimpse this phenomenon. On the beach, you'll see fishermen clustering around their little boats, getting ready to go out to the sea for the evening catch. Local women trawl for clams with plate-sized nets in ankle-deep water while their children jump around pretending to help.

Devgad

Reached via winding roads from Kunkeshwar, Devgad is a town dotted with mango groves 27 km away. The trees swoop down to touch the ground, their branches jewelled with pendulous green fruit. The houses here have Mangalore tiles and courtyards; there are hibiscus hedges and golden cashew fruits; and you are sure to run into a scarecrow in the mango groves. Most farmers, however, are a bit skeptical of the idea of people walking around their orchards but you can try and get permission.

But true to its name, Devgad (literally, House of God) is also dotted with temples, the biggest being the **Gajbadevi Temple** at Mithbao (Dagare Wadi), and **Vimleshwar Temple**. The latter is 14 km from Devgad, and is dedicated to Lord Shiva. Stone elephants guard the entrance to this temple. Both temples are open through the day.

Another temple, the **Rameshwar Mandir**, falls on the road to Vijaydurg, at Achara, 23 km from Malvan. The main idol of Lord Shiva here, mounted on a Nandi bull, is believed to be made of solid silver, weighing 50 kilos. The **samadhi of Sambhaji Angre** (son of Kanoji Angre and his first wife Mathurabai) is near the Rameshwar Temple.

Despite its fame as a mango capital, Devgad is also a fishing town, as your nose will tell you as your bus rolls into the bus stand. To see where all that fish comes from, take a leisurely stroll to the jetty in the evening. Also stop to look at Devgad's ultra-modern **windmills** on the way to Vijaydurg, standing like tall white storks against the sky.

The **Devgad Fort** was built by the Angres, who lost it to the marauding British in the early 1800s. What remains of its erstwhile eminence are just ruins. It's located a few kilometres from the Devgad Jetty.

Devgad lies on the stretch north of Kunkeshwar and Tara Mumbri Beach. The easiest way to get here is to take SH4 from Kunkeshwar, and a left onto SH116 at Jamsande for Devgad.

Devgad is famous for its mangoes

SHOPPING

Besides the offerings sold outside the temple, there isn't anything you can shop for at Kunkeshwar. But if you're there in mango season, which falls in April-May, you can always head to **Devgad** and take a crate of Alphonso mangoes home (priced Rs 200 upwards). People pay as much as Rs 2,000 a crate. A large part of the vegetable market in the town is taken over by mango traders at that time.

WHERE TO STAY

There's only one hotel near Kunkeshwar Beach, which is on the temple ground, built for pilgrims. Otherwise, all accommodation is to be found in or near Devgad. Most hotels don't accept credit cards. Rates increase by 10 per cent in April and May when hordes of mango dealers lay siege to the town, so do book in advance.

In and around Kunkeshwar

Savli Resort (Tel: 02364-248614; Tariff: Rs 600-850), located on the coastal road, just over a kilometre from Kunkeshwar Beach, is the best hotel here. It has 5 rooms, but only one of them is air-conditioned. It offers room service, a restaurant and attached bathrooms. The place has a big garden and lawns. Newly renovated, the rooms and baths are spacious and clean.

Bhakti Niwas (Tel: 248650; Tariff: Rs 150-200), just next to the Kunkeshwar Temple, has 120 rooms, but lets out only 14, of which only two have attached baths. Though it has the perfect location, a stone's throw from the beach, the rooms are spartan, with iron cots and mattresses, and are just not clean enough. It doesn't have a restaurant, though meals can be had at the eateries right outside the premises. Be warned that it gets quite crowded during Mahashivaratri and holidays.

The temple to Kunkeshwar, or Lord Shiva, which gave the beach its name

In Devgad
Located opposite the Devgad ST Bus Stand, **Hotel Parijat** (Tel: 262302; Tariff: Rs 150-950) has 12 rooms. We recommend you stick to the air-conditioned rooms as the others are unclean. Parijat has an attached restaurant, a television in every room, and room service. If you're here in April, the hapus bazaar is just a minute away. The hotel is not recommended for single woman travellers.

Hotel Alankar (Tel: 262259; Tariff: Rs 80-250), located near the market and behind the Devgad ST Bus Stand, is a family-run affair. It has 12 rooms and offers room service, a restaurant (with permit room and beer bar) downstairs, cable TV, attached bathrooms in some rooms, and 24 hrs running water. This old and popular hotel is basic, but has clean sheets and baths.

The **Green Villa Guesthouse** (Tel: 262540; Tariff Rs 250-300) at Jamsande has 4 rooms. They provide breakfast, hot water and room service. It's located about 16 km from Kunkeshwar, ahead of Devgad. The higher-end rooms have TV. Other than that, this place has few facilities, but the rooms are airy and clean.

For more hotels and details, see Kunkeshwar Accommodation Listings on pages 555-556

WHERE TO EAT

Around Kunkeshwar Temple, a couple of restaurants offer meals, but don't have a fixed time for lunch or dinner. **Sudha Shanti Uphar Graha Restaurant** is at the entrance to the temple and is open from 7 am to 7 pm. Atul Vidwans, who runs the restaurant, serves what is known as Konkani Brahman food, but you must order at least an hour in advance. Konkani Brahman food makes generous use of coconut, especially in the curries, and has the distinctive sour taste of kokum (the purple berry indigenous to the region).

More well-equipped is the **Abhiruchi Restaurant**, also situated at the foot of the temple. It serves Malvan vegetarian cuisine but again, you have to place your order well in advance. Besides the satisfying vegetarian thali of rice, dal, vegetables, papad, pickle, chutney and sol kadi, the owner Vinayak Bhandari recommends *ukdeele modak* (a fig-shaped sweet made from flour, steamed like a momo, and stuffed with a filling made from sugar and coconut) and *aamras*. Order in advance. Dinner for one costs about Rs 45. The restaurant also offers food products that you can take home such as amla candy and mango pulp.

Annapurna and **Adhar**, just outside the temple, offer good non-vegetarian thalis. Also ask for *vade sagote*, which are puris made from multi-grains, served with thick chicken curry, a speciality of the region. **Savli Resort** serves a vegetarian thali, but the bonus is the unlimited rice that comes along with it. The non-vegetarian thali has a vegetarian dish, fish curry and fish fry. **Sarika Restaurant**, behind Devgad's ST Bus Stand, serves vegetarian and non-vegetarian meals costing between Rs 25 and 40 and is open from 11 am to 3 pm and 7 to 10 pm. The food is typically Konkani.

In Devgad, **Hotel Alankar's** restaurant is a good place to tuck into a big meal of local Konkani food. Dishes include *bharlivangi* or baby brinjals stuffed with coconut, *usal* (yellow peas cooked in a red masala), and *pachadi*, which are tender brinjals cooked with green mangoes and flavoured with coconut and jaggery. Also ask for *bharit* (lightly cooked or raw vegetable in yogurt). As bonus, they have a permit room and a beer bar.

The many flavours of the Konkan coast

ABHIJIT BHATLEKAR

ABHIJIT BHATLEKAR

AROUND KUNKESHWAR

Vijaydurg (37 km)

As you near it, Vijaydurg Fort seems small, leaving you wondering how it could've protected the kingdom from attacks. Only when you are inside do you realise that just walking around its 40-odd sprawling hectares and fortified outer walls could take a few hours.

Once you step past Vijaydurg's ancient wooden doors being held up bravely by posts, you walk back in time to a period when cannons roared and troops shouted "Jai Bhavani" as they went to battle. Though most remembered for the Maratha Emperor Chhatrapati Shivaji, who fortified it during the early 17th century with a triple line of ramparts and numerous towers, Vijaydurg passed through several hands.

The Silaharas, the rulers of the Konkan, built the fort, and it subsequently came under the Adilshahis, the Marathas and the British. Finally, it came under the control of the Dhulup family. (The **Dhulup Mansion** outside the fort houses wall paintings that are worth checking out.)

Today, you see cannon balls laid out in rows under banyan trees. There are dark stairways leading out to the sea, where a boat would've been waiting to help troops escape.

Do note the acoustically designed council hall that amplifies sound inside and cuts it off outside. Some of the landmarks inside include: four freshwater wells (located right by the sea); a banyan that has grown out of one of the wells

Standing tall: The ramparts of Vijaydurg Fort offer spectacular views

and developed thick roots that look like a serpent; and a **temple to Goddess Bhavani**. Also worthy of attention is the **Sahebache Katte** or the Englishman's Platform. It's believed to have been set up by British scientist Sir J Norman Lockyer during the total solar eclipse of 1898. It was here that he discovered the presence of helium on the surface of the sun, it's widely held.

From Vijaydurg's ramparts, there is a spectacular view, extending all the way to Ratnagiri District. Down below, the waves crash against the fort walls. On the left side of the fort, vaulted windows frame the 1-km stretch of **Vijaydurg Beach** dotted by little boats, and the **Vijaydurg Village**. The views alone are worth the long drive from Kunkeshwar.

After a trek through the fort, take your hungry self to the small restaurants just outside or to any of the tiny places serving meals and snacks just outside. **Hotel Suruchi** makes a satisfying brinjal and aloo bhaji with *aamras* for dessert for about Rs 35. Their fish thali usually offers a choice between two fish dishes and consists of the catch of the day. **Hotel Taj** here serves Konkani meals. A regular meal of dal, rice, vegetable, chappati, pickle, papad and onion costs about Rs 25.

Guides can be hired through the newly and locally formed **Paryatan Madati Samiti**. This outfit's office is in a tiny stall right outside the fort. The guide fee is Rs 40; at the time of writing, it was possible for groups of tourists to negotiate rates with the guides. There is no entry fee to the fort; the timings are from 8 am-5 pm (or till sunset).

◆**Connection** It's a long drive from Devgad to Vijaydurg via SH4, Jamsande, Gade and Rameshwar. The road runs parallel to the Vaghotan River, whose mouth is protected by Vijaydurg. It's best to plan a whole-day picnic in the shade of the banyans inside the fort as the trip to and fro takes over 3 hrs ■

Photographs by BHARAT AGGARWAL

TARKARLI

BLISS ON THE BEACH

State Maharashtra
Location On the South Konkan Coast, where the Karli River meets the Arabian Sea, just 7 km from Malvan
Distances 100 km N of Dabolim (Goa), 160 km SW of Kolhapur, 519 km S of Mumbai
Journey time ***By road*** 2½ hrs from Dabolim, 4½ hrs from Kolhapur, 10½ hrs from Mumbai
Route from Mumbai NH17 to Kasal via Chiplun, Rajapur and Kankavli; SH118 to Tarkarli via Malvan (*see route guide on page 394*)

■ BY JOAN PINTO

The *Sunday Times*, London, has called it one of the best beaches in the world. You tend to agree when you drop anchor at the Tarkarli Beach, a long stretch of white sand that seems to run forever. The water is emerald-green, and when the sun's rays fall at the right angle, you can see all the way down to the seabed. A line of casuarinas hides it from the outside world, and when you walk past the trees and out on to the beach's powder sands, you involuntarily let out a long, satisfied sigh.

As I wiggle my toes in the sand in the stillness of the morning, I look out far to the little town of Malvan hugging the sea. From Malvan, it's a beautiful drive down shady, winding paths, past tamarind and coconut trees, to Tarkarli. Further out on Kurte Island, Sindhudurg, the imposing sea fort built by Shivaji, floats like a battleship. Around me children race down the talcum beach and dunk each other into the welcoming, warm, white-capped waves of the sea. At my feet, crabs draw spiral designs in the sand. It's such pure bliss that you understand why an international cruise liner like the Hebridean Spirit fits Tarkarli into its itinerary — this beach is truly world-class.

FAST FACTS

When to go Winter is the best time. Avoid the monsoons. Few, if any, boats will be willing to take you to Sindhudurg Fort in the rains

Tourist offices

- MTDC Holiday Resort
  Tarkarli
  Tel: 02365-252390
- MTDC
  Central Reservations,
  CDO Hutments
  Opposite LIC Building
  Madame Cama Road, Mumbai
  Tel: 022-22026713/ 7762

STD code 02365

ORIENTATION

Tarkarli is an hour's drive down from **Kudal**, and a short drive from **Malvan**; the road leads all the way to **Deobaug Village** to the south. Though you will not want to step away from the Tarkarli Beach, do factor in a visit to nearby shores; Malvan's beach **Chiwla** and Deobaug's stretch of sand are also worth visiting. The hotels are all located close to each other and are a short stroll (not even 100m) from the beach. The closest **bus stand** is at Malvan. State Transport buses stop near the **Maharashtra Tourism Department Corporation (MTDC) Resort** (*see Where to Stay on page 489*). Autos are the quickest way to get anywhere (a minimum of Rs 20 to get to Deobaug; Rs 70 one way to Malvan). Autos don't run by meter, so check rates with hotel officials before you hire one. There's no tourist office at Tarkarli, but the MTDC Resort can help you with information.

Other beaches near Tarkarli are: **Kolamb**, 8 km away and $^1/_2$ hr by auto (fare Rs 80-100), and **Achra Beach**, 28 km away and 1 hr by auto (approx fare Rs 200). Both are clean but don't have restaurants or accommodation nearby.

BEACHWATCH

Tarkarli is safe to wade in but swimming is not recommended because of strong undercurrents. The MTDC has a sign outside that suggests you check with officials before you go swimming. The MTDC Resort is where you can head to before deciding to swim; it's open all day and the manager can tell you if the waters are safe at that time of the year. There are no lifeguards on the beach.

MANOJ NAVALKAR/ DINODIA PHOTO LIBRARY

Net gains: Fishermen on Chiwla Beach, one of Malvan's best-kept secrets

THINGS TO SEE AND DO

At Tarkarli, it's easy to just relax in your hammock, listening to the call of the sea. It's also a place where you can rediscover the child in you — trawl the beach for tiny shells, nature's miniature works of art, or build sand castles.

Tarkarli Beach

Apart from lazing on the beach, which is 8 km long, you can go for walks, play in the sand, or watch the changing colours of the sea. The MTDC is planning to start snorkelling trips here though rates or packages haven't been decided as yet. The sea will be great for snorkelling as its waters are crystal-clear. If you are visiting in November-December, then take a walk on the beach at midnight. Besides being a romantic outing, the walk may also reward you with the rare sight of turtles laying eggs on the beach.

Malvan

This little Konkan town has a bustling jetty, a tangle of boats, a laid-back air and Mangalore-tiled homes, from where the scent of wood-smoke and aromas of fish curry waft into your memories. It is rustic at heart but at the same time striving to be something more than a village, with its restaurants and hotels and an odd Internet café.

You can hire a bicycle from one of the small cycle shops here and drift down its shaded streets. You are most likely to glimpse a cricket match played on a ground in the shade of banyans, a little church, and a peepal tree standing in the middle of the town, a landmark for everyone giving directions. Beyond it lie the jetty and pier. At shouting distance is the **fish market**, most noisy in the evenings when the day's catch is brought in and auctioned. Fishing boats also double as ferries, and leave for **Sindhudurg Fort** (*see page 490*) from a 'tourist pier' here. They charge a nominal round-trip fare (Rs 30 per head) to ferry tourists from the mainland to the fort in 10 mins. (It's not a good idea to take the ferry in the monsoon.) They give you 1 hr to explore the imposing island citadel.

Malvan's waters hold the only marine sanctuary in Maharashtra, spread across 29.25 sq km. Declared a protected area in 1987, it is rich in marine life.

TIP Power-cuts are common in the Sindhudurg region and there is usually a fixed time for load-shedding

Chiwla Beach

Located just 2 km from the bus stand, the Chiwla Beach in Malvan is a well-kept secret. A stretch of soft white sand, just over 1 km long, that makes a small 'C', the beach is a travel writer's dream. The sea is as azure as the sky and lulls you into striking a pose for meditation — well almost. At one end of Chiwla are boats sunning themselves and further down, the **Sarjekot Island**. At the other end is Malvan's **Rock Garden**. In the last days of December, up to New Year, the **Chiwla Festival** is held in Malvan, as part of which songs and dance performances are organised.

GETTING THERE

Air Nearest airport: Dabolim, Goa (100 km/ 2½ hrs). Taxi costs Rs 1,000
Rail Nearest railhead: Kudal (35 km/ 1 hr). Connected to Mumbai by the Konkan Kanya Express, Shatabdi and Mandovi. Connected to Delhi by the Mangala Express. Autos to Tarkarli cost Rs 250-300 and private cars approx Rs 600
Road From Mumbai, turn off NH17 at Kasal, 15 km after Kankavli. Take SH118 to Malvan, 34 km away. Tarkarli is 7 km further down the Malvan Coast. Regular ST buses ply to Malvan Bus Stand from Mumbai Central. Volvo buses and AC buses do not ply directly to Tarkarli. They leave from Dadar and stop at Kudal, the closest stop to Tarkarli, and from there one can take an auto to Malvan, and thereon to Tarkarli (Rs 250-300). The road conditions are good

Deobaug Village

A little fishing village attached by the hip to Tarkarli, Deobaug enjoys the privilege of sitting between the sea and Karli River. Take a leisurely walk through the village, when dappled sunlight filters in through the palms. You'll pass women sorting dried fish outside their homes, boys practising with their cricket bats, and men sitting by the fisheries factory, waiting for it to open. Deobaug is also a bird-lover's paradise, with warblers, white egrets, cuckoos, Indian pond herons, laughing thrush, arrow-tailed swallows and yellow-beaked mynahs having been spotted here.

Backwaters and a beach

You can hire a boat to cruise down the backwaters of the Karli River from Deobaug. As the boat starts, palms sway on both sides, and the river snakes far into the horizon. You see men bobbing in water up to their waists, harvesting mussels with their toes. Fishermen mend their nets on the banks in the little gaps between the mango trees, whose branches brush the water. Schools of little fish slide away as colourful boats, their bellies half in water, wait for their turn to be taken out to the sea. The point where the river meets the sea serves as the exclamation mark at the end of the journey. That's where schools of dolphins glide so close you can hear them breathe. That's also where you can spot striped eels leaping across the water. Next on the itinerary is **Bhogwe Beach**, a huge sandbar at low tide that's a stopover for seagulls. Clap and watch them rise in the air like white tangled kites.

A trip down the river and onto Bhogwe Beach costs Rs 600 for a group of 10 people. Though the boat rides are not official, they're safe and run by locals. Ask your hotel about organising a

A scene from the Deobaug Village, which sits between the sea and the Karli River

trip. Trips leave at about 8 am and take about 1-$1^1/_2$ hrs.

Forts

To the north of Malvan stand a few forts possibly built to serve as support systems for the Sindhudurg Fort. Cross the Kolamb Creek and you reach **Sarjekot Fort**, 2 km north of Rakjot, which was built by Shivaji in 1668. Set on a hillock, at the mouth of the Kalavali creek, its location was once ideal for anchoring ships and shipbuilding. **Padmagad**, set on an island, is said to have been the main shipbuilding base of Shivaji's navy. The once-imposing structure is now in ruins. The auto fare from Tarkarli to Sarjekot is roughly Rs 100 and from Malvan Jetty to Padmagad Rs 70.

SHOPPING

There isn't much by way of shopping in Tarkarli. However, the market at Malvan is a delight. As the slate-boards outside the shops indicate, they sell kokum *aagal*, a sour kokum drink used in curries, amla or gooseberry candy, cashewnuts, cashew laddoos and even kokum wax. The wax is used in Ayurvedic preparations, and is sold as a ball of white that is rubbed on rough, dry cracked skin to heal it.

WHERE TO STAY

There are several options across the various beaches in Sindhudurg, ranging from resorts to homestays. Most stay options tend to be in the mid-range or budget categories.

On Tarkarli Beach

The secluded **MTDC Holiday Resort** (Tel: 02365-252390; Tariff: Rs 950-1,600), on the beachfront, has 20 rooms and is the best hotel located here. It has shaded paths, Konkani-style cottages set amidst casuarinas, hammocks, and the sea outside your window. It also has a beachfront restaurant, and an Ayurvedic centre where you can detox. Do remember to book in advance; an online booking facility (via the website maharashtratourism.gov.in) is also available.

Gajanan (Tel: 251401; Mobile: 09422488055; Tariff: Rs 620), on the

The Iron Fort: A symbol of Maratha glory

From afar, the **Sindhudurg Fort** looks like an intimidating battleship at sea, just as it was meant to. The fishing boat that takes you to the fort rides the waves somewhat crazily, making your heart beat faster, and it is an apt way to begin discovering all that this magnificent structure stands for.

Stepping on the beach on **Kurte Island**, looking up at the fort, you realise why this citadel was the symbol of Maratha dominance. Its walls are 30 ft high and 12 ft thick. Right now though, its 48 acres are home to 18 families, descendants of the Maratha warriors, living in tiled houses all over the island. During the monsoons, they're marooned in the fort. The rest of the year, they depend on country crafts to reach the mainland.

It takes strong legs to climb the big steps to the top of the 2-mile-long ramparts, but the heritage on offer is rewarding. First in line is the fort's most prized relic, the **foot and hand imprints of Chhatrapati Shivaji**, preserved in a slab of dry lime on one of the turrets above the entrance. Inside, much of the fort is in ruins. There are three shrines here, each with a dark cave-like temple of its own. One is dedicated to Mahapurush, a deity worshipped only in South Konkan. The other is the **Sri Shivarajeshwar Temple**, built by Shivaji's son Rajaram in 1695, which houses a statue of the warrior king. It is the only temple where he's worshipped. One of the three shrines hides a secret tunnel, an escape route that led all the way to Kolamb, a few kilometres away. Though now shut, the mouth of the tunnel is still visible.

Over 2,000 *khandis*, or 15,000 tonnes, of iron were used in the castings at Sindhudurg, and the foundation stones were laid firmly in solid lead to protect the 53 bastions against the relentless pounding of the sea. It's said that the warrior king personally lent a hand in building this fort, not to mention, his vision. Standing on battlements that once held cannons, you agree that Sindhudurg deserved to become the naval headquarters of the Marathas. Unfortunately it was denied this honour. Local legend blames this tragedy on the curse of a priest who refused to consecrate the sea fort when it was completed in 1664. He thought that Shivaji's caste was too inferior for him to give the fort his blessings.

Though Sindhudurg is a tribute to man's strategic brilliance, nature makes its own contribution. Right here on this island, surrounded by sea and salt water, are **three fresh water wells**, Sakharbaun, Dudhbaun and Dahibaun. Near the entrance stands a palm with a split trunk. And all are images that you will take back home on the boat ride.

beach, has 6 cottage-style non-AC, spacious rooms with clean bathrooms. There is a shack-like restaurant across the road with good Malvani vegetarian and non-vegetarian cuisine. They organise dolphin-sighting trips with locals.

Chintamani (Tel: 253817, 220313; Tariff: Rs 600-1,200) has 10 rooms, 2 of which are AC, and is located near the beach. Each room has a tiny verandah to the front, and a table and chair facing the garden. Hot water is provided only on request and the access to the beach is through the MTDC property. The rooms are clean and spacious. The **Apoorva Resort** (Tel: 253920; Tariff: Rs 200-600), near the MTDC Resort, has 4 thatched huts, 2 dorm-style huts with 12 beds, and serves meals on order. Hot water is available on request. The rooms are basic but clean as are the bathrooms.

On Chiwla Beach

The **Nath Pai Sevagan** (Tel: 252250; Tariff: Rs 300-350), on the beach, doesn't accept phone reservations but has 8 sea-facing rooms. The rooms are airy and the bathrooms very clean. The hotel provides hot water but the best part about it is the family-run restaurant **Krishnayee** here (*also see Where to Eat on page 492*). As the place is run by a trust, it's usually given out to donors and members, but the management makes exceptions at their own discretion. Absolutely no alcohol allowed here.

Sai Chayya (Tel: 251293; Tariff: Rs 500), near the beach, has 3 non-AC rooms. The rooms are large and the bathrooms clean. The staff is friendly. There's a family-run restaurant behind the hotel. **Om Shraddha** (Tel: 252727, 253135; Tariff: Rs 300-1,000) has 3 non-AC rooms. There's a garden and hot water is provided on request but there is no restaurant. **Sagar Kinara** (Tel: 252137, 252264; Tariff: Rs 750-1,400), near the Malvan Jetty, has television and phones in all rooms, and its USP is the view of the Sindhudurg Fort from the sea-facing rooms. The rooms, though dimly lit, are clean, as are the bathrooms. It has an attached restaurant. Since Sagar Kinara is near the jetty and the market, it gets lonely at night, and isn't recommended for the single woman traveller.

Boats dock outside the Sindhudurg Fort, a symbol of Maratha dominance

For more hotels and details, see Tarkarli Accommodation Listings on page 561

WHERE TO EAT

How to eat Malvani dishes? With absolutely no distractions. And preferably with your hands, just so you get to lick your fingers. As you dig into bangda curry, surmai fry, prawns fried in rava, both succulent and crunchy, you learn to say your prayers before your meals, after your meals, and in-between. Malvani flavours are zesty: a bit sour, thanks to the purple kokum berry indigenous to the region, slightly spicy, and flaming orange with lots of coconut and the freshest fish. When you sit down to a Malvani meal, begin with a large glass of cold kokum sherbet, an appetiser that sparkles like red wine, and with lots of Vitamin C. But honestly, who needs appetisers?

Each of the fish curries leave you asking for more. The slice of surmai, hot from the pan, arrives at your table so fresh, the flesh comes off in white slivers. And then there's *teesrya* or shellfish, cooked in a thick orange masala, made of finely ground coconut, tamarind pulp, coriander and red chillies. Just as delicious are the prawns crusted with rava and deep-fried orange. And then of course there's Malvan's sol kadi, a purple-pink drink made from coconut milk, kokum, and laced with a hint of green chilli and coriander.

Lobsters in good hands?

ABHIJIT BHATLEKAR

Most restaurants specialise in seafood such as Malvani surmai, prawns, *karli* and pomfret. At the top of many people's list is **Chaitanya**, close to the bus stand and the market. Also check out **Arun Bhojnalaya**, near the pipal tree at the centre of town, and the **House of Bamboo** near the main market.

Krishnayee is a small restaurant under the trees attached to the Nayak house, close to Nath Pai Sevangan. They serve excellent *vade sagote* (a puri made from various grains and chicken curry) and fresh *ghavne* (a dosa-like pancake made of rice), with chutney and a syrup made from coconut juice and jaggery, and hot tea. You have to order an hour in advance. **Hotel Ruchira** in the market area is an economical option; a meal costs about Rs 25-30. They serve Malvani fish thali and vegetarian dishes.

At Tarkarli, you could dine under the blue and white canopies of MTDC's **Sagar Darshan**, at **Gajanan's** thatched shack, or at the **Mithbhavkar** residence. The fish thali at MTDC costs about Rs 80 and is your best bet. Add on a plate of fried prawns (Rs 150) and you have a full meal.

AROUND TARKARLI

Dhamapur Lake (20 km)
Sindhudurg's 5-acre lake is famous for its crystal-clear waters. The ancient Bhagwati Temple sits by the water's edge. Boating facilities are available here, and MTDC is developing a lakeside resort. The auto fare to Dhamapur is Rs 150; the drive will take about 45 mins. The boating facilities currently offered are not recognised by the MTDC; there are no fixed rates either. ■

VENGURLA

THE GOOD LIFE

State Maharashtra
Location In South Maharashtra's Konkan Coast, near the border with Goa
Distances 28 km W of Sawantwadi, 519 km S of Mumbai
Journey time ***By road*** 1 hr from Sawantwadi, 10½ hrs from Mumbai
Route from Mumbai NH17 to Kudal via Mahad, Lanja and Kankavli; SH120 to Math; SH121 to Vengurla (*see route guide on page 394*)

BY JOAN PINTO

High atop a lighthouse, in a little balcony circling its rotund, red-striped tower, the wind growls, tugging at me, daring me to fly. In front of me, the sea, a burnished liquid gold, stretches far over a horizon so curved I'm afraid the lonely boat on it will fall off. Holding the metal railing tight, I look down at the sheer drop, and the waves crashing against the hillock on which the lighthouse stands. This is how Christopher Columbus must've felt when he first saw 'undiscovered' land. And if you compare Vengurla to the touristy beaches, it indeed falls into the 'undiscovered' category. Rustic at heart, Vengurla is thankfully modest on touristy trappings, and also oblivious to its simple charms.

As I contemplate the sea, the echo of shouts distracts me. Down below, boats

Photographs by DHRITIMAN MUKHERJEE

slice the waters as they approach a wooden pier, bringing in the day's catch. Walking around the 'deck' to the other side, I spot the countryside, resplendent with rivers snaking past palms and greenery. Bordering it all, like a strip of lace, is the Sagareshwar Beach, one of the many undiscovered beaches in Vengurla.

As I climb down, the sea bids a momentary goodbye to the shore, leaving my poem — scribbled on the sand — untouched. A kingfisher calls from the trees behind me. I head to my cycle, anticipating the pleasures in store. I will leisurely ride past the village, back to my tent-house in the shadow of casuarinas, and to the simple yet exquisite delights of hot, delectable fish curry.

ORIENTATION

Vengurla is just over an hour's drive from the **Sawantwadi Railway Station**. The road goes past **Malgaon**, down SH122, to the main town hugging the sea. Vengurla's beaches — **Vayangani, Sagareshwar, Mochemad, Sagarteerth, Shiroda-Velagar** and **Redi** — lie in a line going south right down the coast of Maharashtra till they rub shoulders with Goa. The roads that lead to Vengurla's main landmarks form a 'T', with the **jetty** and the **lighthouse** at one end, and the **market** at the other. The road to Sagareshwar and the stretch of Vengurla's hidden beaches are all spread out within a 3-km radius.

The **hotels** are located around the jetty, the market and the beaches. The **bus stand** is in the middle of town and ST buses ply daily from here. Autorickshaws are the quickest way to get anywhere (a minimum of Rs 20 to Sagareshwar Beach or the jetty from the main market area). Autos don't run on meter, so check rates with hotel officials before you hire one. You can also hire cycles from **Sagareshwar Corner** near the **MTDC Tent Resort**, or from small cycle stalls opposite **Bamboo Inn**, past the bus stand, or near the crossroads by the market; they come at Rs 4 an hr. The MTDC Tent Resort provides information to tourists.

BEACH WATCH

At all the beaches, there are huge waves at high tide, and therefore, swimming isn't encouraged. Locals warn that there are undercurrents and sudden drops in the

FAST FACTS

When to go November to February
Tourist office
- MTDC Tent Resort
Sagareshwar Beach, Vengurla
Mobile: 09423859750, 09423880986
STD code 02366

seabed, so it's best not to wade too deep. Check with the manager at the MTDC Resort at Sagareshwar if and where it's safe to swim. The office is open all day. There are no lifeguards at any of the beaches. It's best to dress conservatively here.

THINGS TO SEE AND DO

Vengurla's beaches are untouched and it's hard to come by another person here, which is perfect for the beach buff looking for a quiet holiday.

Sagareshwar Beach

Located about 3 km from the bus stand, the beach is hidden away behind rows of tall casuarinas swaying in the wind. Here you can plod up and down soft sand dunes that are white and thick with powdery shell deposits. At night, to the north you can see the lights of the jetty and the **Vengurla lighthouse's** red beam. Up in the clear sky, the flickering constellations have their own light show. On some mornings, dolphins can be seen near the southern end of the beach.

Sagareshwar Beach gets a purple touch

Access to the beach is either through the MTDC Tent Resort or via the path that leads to the ancient **Sagareshwar Temple** of Shiva. The temple, which is on the beach, has a huge *deepastambh*. The structure itself is small; the temple is open only when the priest visits.

Vengurla's lighthouse

About 3 km from the town and near the jetty is the lighthouse, reached via a winding path that passes through shrubs and vegetation. Perched on a hill, it's set on a small plateau. It offers a spectacular view: the sea below you, stretching far into the horizon; the jetty and its boats; the palm-fringed coastline to the left; and a creek far away trailing out to the sea. To the right is a sheer drop down to the sea past jagged cliffs. To the north-west are the **Vengurla Rocks**, also called Burnt Islands, which was an important pointer for seafarers in times long gone (*also see Nivati Beach on page 503*).

It's well worth strolling around the lighthouse. The northern tip overlooks an alluring horseshoe-shaped beach. Small winding pathways lead down to small coves, which are in reality tiny strips of sand with the cliff-face rising on both sides. Only experienced rock-climbers should venture down, and only after checking the timings of the tides.

♦**Entry fee** Rs 5 **Timings** 4-5.30 pm **Note** Strangely and implausibly, single woman travellers aren't allowed up the lighthouse by themselves as the authorities are afraid of suicide attempts! Requests, however, usually work

Vengurla Jetty

From afar, the jetty and the area around looks like a shot from a classic Cary Grant movie: a sea veiled in shifting blue, fishing boats in the foreground, a pier, red-roofed houses clinging to a hillock in the background, and a lighthouse looking over it all.

The jetty at Vengurla was part of a trading settlement set up by the Dutch

Once a bustling port, Vengurla's jetty was part of a trading settlement set up by the Dutch (the ruins of their warehouses are still found in the town). The best time to visit the jetty is in the evening around 5 pm when the boats return with the day's catch. The place comes alive with the sounds of fisherfolk; fisherwomen slip silver fish into their baskets and men anchor their boats with ropes. A little ahead of the slope that leads down to the jetty, look for an inconspicuous set of steps going down to a patch of beach and rocks, hidden by umbrella-like trees.

Vengurla's Fruit Research Centre

If you would like to know how mangoes keep getting bigger and more delicious, head to the **Konkan Farming University and Fruit Research Centre** at Vengurla. You are more likely to find it if you ask for the 'Sanshodhan Kendra' though. At the university, they experiment on mango, cashew and fruits indigenous to the region, and study the effects of pests and fertilisers on fruit. The centre also has a nursery where you can buy all types of saplings. If you want to see the entire process of how cashews are separated, roasted and packed, head to the cashew factory nearby. Do remember that you can't buy cashews here.

◆**Centre location** About 15 mins from the beach, in the Camp area

Vengurla Market

Vengurla's tiny yet bustling market will surprise you with its exotic fruit. Most eye-catching are the plump cashew fruits in all shades of yellow and red, which as the seller will warn you, are to be eaten with salt, first thing in the morning before it ferments. Also sold are pink *jaam*, a slightly sweet fruit the shape and size of a top with a marble-like seed, sour-sweet bulls-heart (*ramphal*, a relative of the sweet custard apple), green betel leaves, and Alphonso mangoes that are as expensive as the ticket back home.

Mochemad and Vayangani

Vayangani and Mochemad lie on either side of Vengurla Town, the first two gems in the string of stunning beaches that trail the coast. Vayangani is a tiny beach, 7 km from Vengurla, and is accessed via shady paths that wind through **Vayangani Gaon**, darting between towering supari and casuarina groves. The way to Mochemad, 9 km from Vengurla, is past a little blue and white church reminiscent of Goa's churches, looking over green fields. The beach is on the road to Shiroda (*see below*), and to access it, you have to get off your vehicle and walk for about a kilometre. With a backdrop of towering hills, the beach is the most scenic on this stretch. There is no accommodation near either of the beaches, so it's best to do a day-trip. Carry some snacks along.

Shiroda and Aravali

Keep your camera ready as you drive past these villages. White egrets dot *paapdi* (a locally grown bean) fields. Small bridges slide over creeks that eventually snake out into the sea. The wind ruffles paddy fields, brushing it with different hues of green. Shiroda, 10 km south of Vengurla, is home to the **Mauli Devi Temple** whose presiding deity is the *kul devi*, or patron goddess, of the region. The **saltpans** in this village are memorable, particularly because Mahatma Gandhi visited the place during the Salt Satyagraha of 1930. The saltpans are located on either side of the road through the village, with fields separating them now and then.

Aravali, Shiroda's twin village, houses the **Sri Vithoba Temple** and the **Sateri Devi Mandir**. The stalls near the temple sell tiny yellow bananas and pink lotuses to offer at the feet of Lord Vithoba.

♦**Temple timings** Open from dawn to dusk **Note** Open to people of all faiths

Both Sagarteerth and Velagar beaches (*see below*) are in Shiroda.

Sagarteerth and Velagar beaches

These beaches are about 14 km south of Vengurla, and are attached to the towns of Shiroda and Aravali. Though both have become popular with tourists from Kolhapur and Belgaum, the beaches are still pristine. The beaches lie in a line, one continuing from where the other leaves off. The white sand glitters silver in the moonlight, thanks to the high content of shell deposits. Dolphin cruises are offered at Velagar Beach by the resorts located there (*see Where to Stay on page 500*). Cruise rates are Rs 700 for 10 people.

Redi

Located about 21 km south of Vengurla, Redi is the southernmost beach in Maharashtra, bordering Terekhol and Goa. Redi is known to many as a small mining town. But it's most famous for its **Ganapati Temple**, close to the beach, and the 6-foot high statue of the elephant god. The signboard outside tells us the story of how the statue was found: Narendra Kambli, a miner, was visited in his dream by Lord Ganesh, who directed him to a mine where he'd find a statue. With the help of a few locals, Kambli dug up the

→ GETTING THERE

Air Nearest airport: Dabolim, Goa (88 km/ 2 hrs). Taxi to Vengurla costs Rs 800-1,000
Rail Nearest railhead: Sawantwadi (28 km/ 1 hr), connected to Mumbai by the Konkan Kanya Express, Shatabdi and Mandovi. Connected to Delhi by the Mangala Express. Autos charge Rs 200 from Sawantwadi Station
Road From Mumbai drive down NH17 till Kudal. Turn right here onto SH120, which ends at Math. From here, SH121 goes straight to Vengurla. Buses for Vengurla leave from the Parel Bus Stand in Mumbai at 6 pm daily, reaching Vengurla at a convenient 8 am. Volvo buses and AC buses do not ply directly to Vengurla. They leave from Dadar and the closest stops are Kudal or Sawantwadi. The road conditions are mostly good

A fisherman casts his net wide in a creek at Aravali Village

site, and found a stone monolith that today attracts pilgrims from all over Maharashtra. Here you can ask to see the photograph of the statue as it looked originally. Stroll down the path behind the temple for a view of a stretch of the beach that goes right down to Mochemad. The access road to the temple is bumpy. Also visit the **Redi Jetty**, 5 mins from the temple, from where you can see barges being loaded with ore from the region, to be taken to Goa to be refined.

SHOPPING

As this is cashew district, you can shop for all kinds of cashew products in the market at Vengurla, ranging from packets of roasted cashews and laddoos to pedas made of cashew. You can also pick up *amla* (gooseberry) candy and mango *poli*, a layered sweet made from ripe mango.

WHERE TO STAY

Vengurla has only a few stay options, one reason why it isn't crowded as yet. Options close to the sea include tented resorts, a few functional lodges and homestays, as permanent structures cannot come up under Coastal Regulation Zone norms. Credit cards are not accepted at most of these places.

Some locals let out rooms to tourists, and shopkeepers in the main market or around the ST Bus Stand should be able to guide you to their houses. Also, do remember that power-cuts are common in the Sindhudurg region. Check with locals for timings and charge your cell phones and digital cameras accordingly.

On Sagareshwar Beach

The secluded **MTDC Tent Resort** (Mobile: 09423859750, 09423880986; Tariff: Rs 500-700), on Sagareshwar Beach, has 10 fibreglass huts with double beds. Though they don't look pretty from the outside, the huts have comfortable interiors. The best feature here is a sliding glass door that opens to give you a framed view of the crashing waves from your bed. It does not have an attached restaurant. Orders for food (both vegetarian and non-vegetarian) can be placed at the Sagareshwar Corner just down the sandy slope ahead of the entrance. The huts that are located right on the beach have spectacular views but tend to get warmer than the others at noon.

Perched on a rocky outcrop, a stone's throw from Vengurla Jetty, is the PWD guest house **Sagar** (Tel: 02366-262411; Tariff: Rs 200) facing the sea, with one VIP and two ordinary rooms. The clean airy rooms have a reception area and an inner room, and food is served in the room if you inform the caretaker at least 2 hrs in advance. The USP of this place is the amazing view of the sea, right up to the horizon. Do note that it is compulsory to make reservations at the **PWD head office** (Tel: 02363-272214) at Moti Talao, Sawantwadi. You have to collect a pass from this office before proceeding to Vengurla. Though the rules dictate that it's only for PWD or government employees, one can make a special request at the Sawantwadi office. For government employees, the rooms cost just Rs 20.

In Vengurla Town

Hotel Laukik (Tel: 263418; Mobile: 09423300972; Tariff: Rs 350-650), near Vengurla Market, has 8 rooms, one of them AC. The rooms and bathrooms are fairly clean. It has an attached restaurant that serves vegetarian and non-vegetarian food. While the prawn biryani has many takers, the Punjabi dosa seems suspect.

The MTDC Tent Resort on Sagareshwar

The sea-facing **Sea View Hotel** (Tel: 262193, 263614; Tariff Rs 200-300), near the jetty, is small and a bit dingy. It has 5 not very clean rooms, and provides hot water on request. **Samir** (Tel: 262112; Tariff: Rs 200), near the Fruit Research Centre in the Camp area, is a PWD property with 2 clean rooms. Reservations have to be made at the PWD head office (Tel: 02363-272214) at Sawantwadi. Don't forget to collect your pass from this office before heading to Vengurla. You can get some good food if you order in advance.

On Sagarteerth Beach

The **Sagarteerth Beach Resort** (Tel: 227456; Mobile: 09822133231; Tariff: Rs 300-400) on the beach is quite basic. It has 16 thatched huts with attached baths and 6 tents, which are a bit tattered, all with common baths. Bathrooms are a bit dingy, but clean. Hot water is available on request and vegetarian and non-vegetarian food is prepared in a small kitchen. Tents are not available in the monsoon.

On Velagar Beach

The best option on the beach is the **Dolphin Bay Beach Resort** (Tel: 227529; Tariff: Rs 350-1,000), which has 5 tents and 2 thatched huts with common baths. Another 2 bamboo huts come with attached baths. They have well-furnished, clean air-conditioned rooms as well. The resort has a pretty, open canopy restaurant that serves Malvani, Goan and other Indian vegetarian and non-vegetarian dishes. Hot water is available on request. They organise dolphin-spotting boat rides (Rs 700 for a group of 10 people), and arrange transportation and campfires on request. Tents are not available in the monsoon.

Many different flavours and colours at the market at Vengurla

Silver Sands-Kothari Beach Resort (Tel: 227987; Tariff: Rs 400-550) has 8 rooms, 6 of which have attached baths. The rooms are basic but clean and airy. It also has an open canopy on a dune acting as a cafeteria area. They serve the regional Malvani cuisine, provide hot water on request, and arrange dolphin-sighting trips (Rs 700 for a group of 10 people). They also make transport arrangements.

Paulo's Green Garden Resorts (Mobile: 09869869470; Tariff: Rs 300-500) is all of 4 thatched huts with cemented floors. Though clean, the huts are tiny and cramped. The attached baths are clean. It has a garden restaurant and hot water is available on request. It's a bit of a walk from the beach and should only be your last option.

For more hotels and details, see Vengurla Accommodation Listings on pages 561-562

WHERE TO EAT

True, the locals cook exotic dishes made from tender green cashewnut, potato-like roots, and *paapdi,* a bean grown locally. They make *kelphoolachi bhaji,* a Konkan dish made of banana flowers. In mango season, their *aamras* is the ambrosial must in any thali. But when it comes to fish, they wield a magic wand. The freshest fish — *bangda* (mackerel), surmai, prawn, *domas, karli,* or whatever the boats just brought in, arrive at your table, ready to be gobbled up with a glass of sol kadi (a drink made from sour kokum berry, coconut milk and coriander, with a hint of green chilli). Every bite of the fish, which is fried golden in rava, or dunked in curry, seems like a blessing. Also ask for *vade sagote,* which are thick puris made with multi-grains, served with pieces of chicken in a thick gravy.

Vengurla has a few small restaurants. **Bamboo Inn** on the road to Sagareshwar Beach, about $1\frac{1}{2}$ km from the ST Bus Stand, serves good seafood, Chinese and vegetarian dishes. It comes with a bar and restaurant, as does **Gajaalee** near the jetty, which, thanks to its location, serves a popular fish thali. You can find several hole-in-the-wall places like **Gomantak** in the market area, which serve both vegetarian and fish dishes.

The best food I ate was at **Sagareshwar Corner**, the shack-like restaurant attached to the MTDC Resort. The fried prawns are out of this world, and the fish gravy is something you can slurp down even after your rice and chappatis are over. You have to place your order at least 2 hrs in advance. For breakfast, ask for *ghavne,* a kind of dosa served with chutney, or *shirwale,* a noodle-like dosa made from rice and served with a syrup made from coconut and jaggery. (Both have to be ordered the previous night.) *Amba poli,* or *amba vadi,* is a layered sweet made from mango pulp and sugar and makes for a nice dessert. *Khaja,* made from gram flour and sweet palm jaggery, is nice to chew on as you stroll around.

Minstrels and their magic

SS GILL

Pause awhile at an inconspicuous grocery shop near the village of Pinguli just off the highway near Kudal, 25 km before Vengurla, to meet Ganpat Sakharam Masge, an amazing artiste. Being the 'police patil' of the area, he will probably be busy working at large formidable ledgers or sorting out life-and-death matters. But he likes to be disturbed by visitors who request to see his art. Even at short notice, he can call his troupe to organise a performance for the same evening. And in the darkness of the night, he will bring out his marionettes, convert the mundane into magic, and the team will hold spectators spellbound with their theatrics, music and words.

Masge is one of the surviving **puppeteers of Pinguli**, whose nomadic forefathers settled in the village in the mid-18th century, where they lived under the patronage of the erstwhile princely state of Sawantwadi. Now their numbers are sadly dwindling and they've been forced to take up agriculture or fishing. Yet, during festivals, Pinguli's puppeteers bring out their treasures. Crafted with care, their lively, endearing puppets throw dramatic shadows on a screen. The string and leather puppets vividly convey war stories from the epics as the puppeteer shows one folio after the other to construct a chain of mythological events.

If you are passing by Pinguli, you could meet with a puppeteer and request him to put up a small show for you. Settle the payment beforehand. You could request him to tell you the narrative that he plans to emote before he begins, so even if it's in Marathi, you'll be able to follow it. According to the rani of Sawantwadi, Parshuram Gangavane is one of the best puppeteers of Pinguli. He migrated south to Maharashtra along with the Sisodia kings of Rajasthan several hundred years ago. These puppeteers once played an important role as spies, burrowing into enemy camps as entertainers and bringing back information.

Today, you can watch Parshuram in action at the **Vishram Puppet Theatre** at Pinguli Village. Along with a troupe of 11 people, he narrates stories through leather and string puppets. The artistes perform the dramatic scenes in an open garden theatre. To watch a show you have to call Gangavane a day ahead. Also stop by at his newly opened **museum** at Pinguli, right opposite his home, covered with murals, and see his collection of puppets, some of which are 500 years old.

♦**Museum entry fee** Rs 10 **Camera fee** Rs 50 **Note** Parshuram Gangavane can be reached on 0236-2222393

Brinda Gill and Joan Pinto

AROUND VENGURLA

Nivati Beach (25 km)
Located to the north of Vengurla, the beach has its own lighthouse on Burnt Islands, thus named because in the old days wood was burned constantly to warn seafaring vessels about the rocks, and to guide them to safety. Also explore Nivati's **sea-fort** built by the Marathas. Here, watching fishermen head out on their boats and turning into tiny silhouettes on the horizon, their nets flying over the water, is like watching a play unfolding. Take an auto from Vengurla to Nivati Beach; the fare is approx Rs 200.

Sawantwadi (28 km)
For the longest time ever, Sawantwadi was just a station on the way to Goa. Today, it has morphed into a place where you can stop over, and one sign of this transformation is the number of hotels sprouting up all over the place. This is a good thing, for the place has much to offer the tourist.

First on the itinerary is a glimpse of the town's royal past. Built in the era of Khem Sawant Bhonsale III (1755-1803), the **palace** here is unlike most others you've seen. A simple, red stone structure covered in ivy, it sits peacefully in the shade of palms, facing **Moti Talao**, the storybook lake at the centre of town. Only the Darbar Hall at the palace is open to the public. Crane your neck to see its striking black and white ceiling. There's a huge silver throne, with the marble bust of Queen Victoria looking a bit out-of-place behind it. Also note the intricately designed wrought-iron balconies from where women could watch the court proceedings. The wooden furniture in the hall has miniature paintings.

Stop to appreciate the artists who painstakingly paint **ganjifa cards**. The artists bring round, coaster-sized cards, or rectangular sets, to life, with colourful and finely detailed miniature depictions of royal life: kings holding court, queens, and warriors in battle, among other things. A queen of the Bhonsale dynasty, Rani Satvashiladevi still lives in a part of the palace complex. The artists are here as part of the rani's attempts to revive the traditional miniature art. The rani can be met by appointment or during her morning open hour, when she sits out in the porch between 10 and 11.30 am.

PUNIT PARANJPE

A craftsperson makes ganjifa cards

The **palace museum** houses statues of Brahma and other deities, dating to the 10th and 11th centuries. You can buy a papier-mâché life-size rooster, ganjifa cards, whizzing tops and chess sets at the showroom. Depending on the item, the costs vary; a papier-mâché pumpkin, for instance, costs Rs 25 while a rooster is priced between Rs 250 and 350. The spinning tops come for Rs 5 each.

◆**Palace entry fee** Rs 25 **Timings** 9.30 am-1 pm and 2-5.30 pm **Museum entry** Free **Timings** 9 am-8 pm

Sawantwadi is also famous for its painted wood toys (*see 'Toy story' on page 504*). There are plans to start boating on

Toy story retold

Stroll down the lanes of Chitarali in Sawantwadi to appreciate the skill that goes into making some of the most exquisite **wooden toys** in the country, ranging from Rolls Royces that are the size of your palm to multi-coloured kitchen sets, jewellery boxes and painted fruit. Most of the families in this village have been making these toys for over 40 years, though the most famous shop here is **PD Kanekar's.** It's also where you can ask to see a 'fruit' changing its avatar from a piece of brown wood to a yellow mango or a melon.

You can visit a little 'factory' shed near **Raghuvanshi Market**, where the magical process of wood turning into high art takes place. Here blocks of wood are run on a lathe, chiselled, and shaped into fruits after several levels of sandpapering and smoothening. At Kanekar's, past the shop counter, a dim corridor opens into a courtyard. Here, artists hand-paint wooden bananas, mangoes and oranges. In another corner of the courtyard, like an upside-down orchard, painted fruit dry in the sun. With most of the youngsters today choosing other professions, this art form seems to be dying a slow death.

Moti Talao, which is circled by heritage buildings — the courts, the Sawantwadi Palace and the colleges. After a day of sightseeing, plonk yourself at **Balkrishna Coldrinks** on College Road, and enjoy their famous fruit-cocktail — a concoction of ice-cream, fruit, cherries, jelly cubes and nuts, topped with a waffle.

You can also buy some amla petha, dahi mirchi, kokum squash, mango jam and cashewnuts. Pick up jamun juice, particularly recommended for diabetics. You will find all this at **Hotel Vrindavan** on College Road and at the **Konkan Dry Fruit Centre** near Gandhi Chowk.

Where to stay and eat

Sawantwadi has a few good hotels in the mid-range and budget categories and one new hotel in the luxury category. **Hotel Mango** (Tel: 02363-271048; Tariff: Rs 800-2,500), with its contemporary décor, does Sawantwadi proud. A new 3-star hotel, it's located in the centre of town on the Main Road, and has 26 beautiful rooms ranging from standard to Presidential suite. It offers a travel desk, room service, a gym and a multi-cuisine restaurant.

With a view of Moti Talao, the **Tourist Reception Centre** (Tel: 271398; Tariff: Rs 800-1,500) is a good value-for-money option run by Hotel Mango's management. **Hotel Tara Central** (Tel: 272923; Tariff: Rs 320-520), in the main town at Gandhi Chowk, has 14 rooms that aren't clean. The hotel has a restaurant and a permit room. **Konkan Crown Fun-O-Tel Central** (Tel: 258555; Tariff: Rs 850-3,000) has a swimming pool, a restaurant, a bar and a children's park. The 24-hr **Food Fiesta** restaurant here serves Konkani food. The rooms just about pass muster but the bathrooms score even less.

Crazy Restaurant and **Ajanta** offer fish and chicken dishes, while **Bharat Mata** and **Visawa** serve a decent vegetarian thali for Rs 30. All these restaurants are located near the intersection of Main Road and College Road.

◆**Sawantwadi Connection** Buses ply between Sawantwadi and Vengurla, via Math and Tulas, from 6 am to 8.30 pm. You can also take an auto (fare Rs 250). Six-seaters ply from Sawantwadi Town to Sawantwadi Station (Rs 15-30 depending on the number of passengers) ■

GUJARAT

Photographs by BHARAT AGGARWAL

THE BEACH AT MANDVI PALACE

THE STAR-SPANGLED SEA

State Gujarat
Location The Beach at Mandvi Palace is located close to Mandvi Town, south of Bhuj, on the southern shore of Kutch, abutting the Gulf of Kutch in the Arabian Sea
Distances 55 km SW of Bhuj, 446 km W of Ahmedabad
Journey time ***By road*** 1 hr 15 mins from Bhuj, 9 hrs from Ahmedabad
Route from Bhuj SH to Mandvi via Dahisara **Route from Ahmedabad** NH8A to Mandvi via Bagodra, Limbdi, Morbi, Samkhiali and Anjar (*see route guide on facing page*)

BY AMIT MAHAJAN

The white cherub-like moon was still hovering above the pale tents when I got up. Having seen the full moon rise the previous evening, I wanted to watch it disappear at dawn. I came out from under the trees into the sweeping expanse of sand, and at the other end of the world, the sun, as if created by some mysterious processes deep beneath the rumbling surface of the ocean, peeked hesitantly, red-faced above the horizon, and then emerged confidently in its white glory. The beach was beautifully proportioned: a wide and even stretch of white sand near the water, sloping gradually into the sea, offering, at high tide, pool-like waters that changed step by step from knee-deep to shoulder-high. The breakfast in the open wood-and-bamboo restaurant was long and lazy, like the beach.

After breakfast I made my way to the edge of the white stretch of the beach and settled there with a book. The palm tree above me had long drooping leaves, reminiscent of the sad neck of a camel in captivity, but it gave ample shade from the sun. I was waiting for the sun and the water to rise higher — the water high enough to be swim-able and frolic-able, and the sun warm enough to make the water nice and inviting.

Also waiting at the edge of the water was a lonely cormorant and a group of seagulls. A few crabs were busy scurrying in the sand, and occasionally a group of small birds flew by, grazing the undulating surface of water — a sport, or a productive activity — who was I to say. For them, the two might not be as divorced as they are in our lives.

ORIENTATION

The Beach at Mandvi Palace, as the resort here is called, is located close to **Mandvi Palace** as well as the beach, which is part of its property (not to be confused with the Mandvi Beach itself, which is in the town). On the road from **Mandvi Town**, turn left at the gate of Mandvi Palace, aka Vijay Vilas Palace, onto 500m of unmetalled road to reach the resort. The palace and the resort are quite isolated. If you don't have your own vehicle, you will need to call for a taxi to venture out. The resort can organise the taxi for you but it will come from Bhuj and you will have to pay extra for the 120-km distance to and from Bhuj (Rs 5 per km/ minimum fare Rs 1,500). The other option is to call **Jai Hind Tours and Travels** (Tel: 02834-231460), located opposite Hotel Sea View, Jain Dharamsala Road, in Mandvi. Indica (non-AC) taxis are available for Rs 1,500 for a day. AC taxis cost Rs 1,800; for shorter trips, the rates are negotiable.

The small town of Mandvi is 8 km to the north. **ST Road**, running along the **Rukmavati River**, is the centre of the town, offering a small hotel or two, a taxi stand and a bus stand, and unmetered autos. For autos, the usual charges are Rs 10 per km, and the minimum fare is at least Rs 20. Shipbuilding, Mandvi's claim to some fame, also happens along this road. On the other side of the town are the **Mandvi Beach** and its tall windmills.

BEACH WATCH

The beach at the resort is safe for swimming. The water is calm, the waves not too high and there are no undercurrents. However, the water here is surprisingly cold and therefore swimming is comfortable only when the sun is bright. Also, the beach is usually secluded and there are no lifeguards, so it's best not to be too adventurous. Beachwear is common at the resort. Hardly anyone swims off the beach at Mandvi Town; dress conservatively here.

THINGS TO SEE AND DO

The resort at Mandvi is the beach-equivalent of a south-facing house — it boasts of uninterrupted views of both sunrise and sunset on its waters, which seem to stretch endlessly. The resort offers an experience of living on the beach with minimal human interference. There's little in terms of construction: unobtrusive tents and wooden buildings that house the kitchen, the restaurant and the staff quarters, all barely visible even in the sparse desert-vegetation.

The beach resort is a place where you are in deep communication with the heavenly bodies — the sun, the moon and the stars. Even on a moonless night, the dark waters occasionally glimmer and, in the distance, the lights of a faraway ship twinkle, making the sea look star-studded.

The resort has exclusive access to a 2-km long stretch of shoreline, the property of the erstwhile royal family of Bhuj. The beach is a wonderful place for walks. The sand is white and clean, and birds are most likely your only company. The management does not encourage water sports, preferring to give the fish a chance to survive, rather than offering loud citizens rides on even louder water scooters. This ensures the beach is calm and quiet. A few days here are ideal for

A crow enjoys a free camel ride on the beach at Mandvi Town

The Vijay Vilas Palace is an elegant structure that blends many architectural styles

rejuvenation and for washing away the sins of hectic urbanisation.

Vijay Vilas Palace

Vijay Vilas Palace is a pleasant and elegant structure, built in the early 20th century by the rulers of Bhuj. The galleries are full of photographs of the family's brush with the rich, the powerful and the mighty — rulers (colonial and democratic), film stars and big cats. From the top of the palace, there are nice views of the grounds around. The land around the palace is a reserve forest. If you spend some time walking around the area, you will come across some nilgai, which will look intently at you till you are too close for comfort and then withdraw a few paces and again wait for you. Wild boars are too furtive to be spotted easily.

♦**Location** 500m west of the beach; 8 km south of Mandvi **Entry fee** Rs 25 per person, Rs 35 on Sundays; Rs 20 per car **Camera** Rs 50 **Timings** 9 am-5 pm

Mandvi Beach

There is an alternative way of visiting Mandvi. Stay in the town, at Hotel Sea View (*see Where to Stay on page 510 for details*), with rooms overlooking hundreds of workmen making ships from wood on the bed of the Rukmavati River. Watch the water rise and fall in the river with the tide, and roam around the town. You can visit the Mandvi Palace Beach (entry Rs 50 if you are not a guest) or the Mandvi Town Beach (entry Rs 10 for cars).

Locals frequent the town beach in the evenings, and they usually congregate here to relish the ragda patties and gol gappas, feed the seagulls, have their evening walks and regrettably leave behind plastic wrappers of potato chips.

→ FAST FACTS

When to go Best from October to March. April to September is warmer but not too hot

STD code 02834

SHOPPING

The obvious souvenirs to pick up here are the famous textiles of the Kutch region. The **bazaar** in Mandvi, off ST Road, is a good area to buy fabrics and garments.

The luxurious tents at the Mandvi resort

GETTING THERE

Air Nearest airport: Bhuj (55 km/ $1^1/_4$ hrs). Connected by flights from Mumbai. Taxi fare to Mandvi Rs 800-1,200

Rail Nearest railhead: Bhuj, which is connected to Delhi, Mumbai and Ahmedabad by Ala Hazrat Express (4 days a week) and Kutch Express (daily). Taxis and buses are available outside the station to Mandvi

Road The road between Bhuj and Mandvi is well-maintained and not crowded. There are frequent buses (Rs 24/ 2 hrs) and the fast but not uncomfortable shared taxis called 'Toofan' (Rs 30/ $1^1/_2$ hrs) that ply between Bhuj and Mandvi bus stands. Several overnight buses run between Ahmedabad and Bhuj; ticket fare varies between Rs 200 (sitting, non-AC bus) to Rs 450 (Volvo buses). For bookings contact Patel Tours (Tel: 079-26577811) or Sahjanand Tours (Tel: 26575988)

Try **Sea View Handicrafts** on Jain Dharamsala Road, and **Bombay Tailors** and **Shah Materials** in **Bandhini Bazaar**. Shawls come for Rs 150-500 while saris range from Rs 230 upwards; salwar-kameez material is priced between Rs 250 and 2,000, and patchwork quilt covers come for anything from Rs 100 to 10,000.

WHERE TO STAY

The staying facility at the **Beach at Mandvi Palace** (Tel: 02834-295725; Mobile: 09879013118; Tariff: Rs 10,999 on weekends for the 2N/ 3D package, Rs 8,999 on weekdays) is a group of tents. If tents convey impressions or memories of a not-too-comfortable stay, then do a rethink. The tents here are spacious, comfortable and neat, standing on cemented squares. The bathrooms are large, with tiled floor and walls. All the tents have air-conditioners and room heaters. The accommodation is spotlessly clean. There are 10 such tents in the resort.

The other staying options include the **Royal Inn Guest House** (Tel: 295725; Tariff: Rs 2,500) in the Vijay Vilas Palace Complex. There are 4 bare and basic units with tiled bedrooms, dressing space and bathrooms. There is no provision for food. In Mandvi, **Hotel Sea View** (Tel: 224481; Mobile: 09825376063; Tariff: Rs 400-1,500) is a nice, clean place on Jain Dharamsala Road.

For more hotels and details, see Mandvi Accommodation Listings on page 538

WHERE TO EAT

The package at Mandvi Palace is inclusive of all meals. These are bed tea, breakfast, lunch, evening tea and dinner. The kitchen is well-equipped to manage decent Indian, Chinese and Continental dishes. The restaurant is open to non-residents with all-you-can eat offers. Breakfast includes fruit, juice, parantha, toast, upma, tea and coffee for

The making of a ship

The Rukmavati River in Mandvi is more a creek than a river, and its water levels follow the ebb and flow of the sea. But whatever be the water level, the river is full of ships; at any given time, 20 to 30 ships can be spotted here. But these are ships with a difference – they don't float on water but are stationed on the riverbed. These are ships in various stages of their birth – some are just bare hulls onto which workmen are adding internal structures, while others are almost complete ships being busily polished. Rukmavati River is indeed a very busy shipbuilding centre.

For many centuries, Mandvi was a famous seaport in Kutch. It was connected with South Africa, Zanzibar, Malaysia, China and Japan. And the building of ships has been going on here since the 16th century.

The ships are relatively small wooden structures, weighing between 800 and 2,000 tonnes. Hundreds of workers specialise in fashioning these fascinating structures out of wood. One can spot Dutch influence in their design, and like many other things in this region, the credit goes to Ram Singh, an 18th century sailor who learned many crafts in Europe and brought them to Bhuj.

Rs 250. Lunch includes soup, salad, dal, vegetables, paneer, chicken, lamb and dessert. Vegetarian food costs Rs 350 and non-vegetarian Rs 400. Dinner is priced at Rs 375 for vegetarian food and Rs 425 for non-vegetarian food. Mandvi Town does not oblige with a restaurant. You will have to make do with dhabas and snacks (pakoras, samosas, patties) at sweet shops or roadside stalls.

AROUND MANDVI

Bhuj (55 km)

Bhuj was the capital of the former state of Kutch for almost 400 years, and is now the headquarters of the Kutch District. Unfortunately, Bhuj is now part of public memory mainly because of the major earthquake in 2001. The scars of the earthquake are even now apparent among the buildings in Bhuj, and in the conversations of its inhabitants and visitors. Among the historical buildings that survived the quake is the **Darbargadh Palace Complex** beside Lake Hamirser. The intricate carvings on the walls and the jali work on the jharokhas are some exquisite reminders of its 16th-century craftsmanship. **Aina Mahal**, the mirror palace, was added to the complex in the 18th century during the reign of Maharao Lakhpatji. It was designed by the mythically famous Ram Singh, who after a shipwreck luckily reached Europe and learned the art of shipbuilding and stone-carving, and introduced them in Kutch (*see above*). The last ruler of Kutch, Maharao Madansinhji, converted it into a museum. This Hall of Mirrors holds a flashy display of the proud possessions of the Kutch royals.

◆**Location** Darbargadh **Entry fee** Adults Rs 10, children Rs 5 **Cameras** Still Rs 30, video Rs 100 **Timings** 9 am-noon, 3-6 pm, Saturdays closed ■

ABHILASH GAUR

DIU

THE LIGHTNESS OF BEING

Union Territory of Daman and Diu
Location A small island that lies off the coast of Gujarat in the Arabian Sea, Diu is separated from the mainland by a long, narrow channel
Distances 423 km SW of Ahmedabad
Journey time ***By road*** 10 hrs from Ahmedabad
Route from Ahmedabad NH8A to Bagodra via Sarkhej; SH to Bhavnagar via Dhandhuka, Barvala, Valabhip and Vartej; NH8E to Una via Talaja and Mahuva; state road to Diu via Delwada (*see route guide on page 507*)

BY ABHILASH GAUR

Two people chat away in Portuguese over mugs of chilled beer, the sea breeze dismantling their coiffure. A church stands tall in the backdrop, a street spreads out almost empty, and a shopkeeper yawns at a nearby store. Time seems to halt in Diu, the idyllic coastal town kissing the Arabian Sea. It's this old-world charm, unbroken by the odd cyber café, which gives Diu its character, so very different from Goa, of which it was once a part.

Diu's white and golden beaches are unspoilt and lovely. As bonus, they are relatively quiet, and devoid of the crowds one sees in Goa, perhaps because of their remote location. This speck of land is far away from any major town, and that should explain why being in Diu is such pure bliss.

ORIENTATION

Diu has two points of entry: the bridge at **Ghoghla**, closer to Una, and another one at **Tad**. If coming from Una, **Ahmedpur**

Mandvi will be the last village in Gujarat, and it shares the beach with Diu's Ghoghla Village. Buses cross the bridge after Ghoghla and drop you off at the **Jethibai Bus Terminus**, close to **Bunder Chowk**. From the chowk, a road leads left into the old town to the fort. Moving west of the town, you pass **Naida Village**, followed by **Fudam, Malala, Nagoa** and **Vanakbara**. Getting around Diu is best done by autorickshaw (Rs 10 minimum fare; Rs 30 for 6-7 km). Tourist taxis charge Rs 150 for 3-4 hrs of sightseeing.

BEACH WATCH

Diu's entire 17-km long coastline is technically a beach, but Nagoa, Ghoghla, Jallandar, Chakratirth and Gomtimata are its main stretches of sand. Ghoghla and Nagoa beaches are the best places for swimming and water sports. The other beaches are not very safe.

THINGS TO SEE AND DO

Diu has a range of attractions, from an old fort to churches and beaches.

Ghoghla Beach

Ghoghla is the best beach in Diu, and yet the least popular — perhaps because it's part of the mainland and has only three hotels. The sea at Ghoghla is safe for swimming, and you also have a choice of water sports here. There's a **water scooter** (Rs 50), **speedboat** (Rs 50), **parasailing** on the beach (by car, Rs 350), parasailing on the sea (by powerboat, Rs 800) and **water skiing** (Rs 250). All rates are per person per kilometre. **Adventure Water Sports** (contact Dharmendra P; Tel: 02875-249483; Mobile: 09879697975), the agency providing the facility, also offers a sea trip to the **Diu Fort** and the island fort of **Panikotha** near it. For a two-seater motorboat they charge Rs 600 while for a 10-seater the tariff is Rs 1,600. A still more enjoyable outing could be the **dolphin trip** (Rs 1,100), offered early in the morning.

FAST FACTS

When to go November to February

Tourist office

● Directorate of Tourism
Marine House, Bander Chowk, Diu
Tel: 02875-252653
Website: diutourism.com

STD code 02875

Old Town

If you enter the old quarter of Diu through the high city wall on the west, you will find quaint houses lining the narrow street. Of these, **Nagar Seth's Haveli** is the finest. Not far from the haveli stands the **Church of St Francis of Assisi**, which was built in 1593. The Gothic **St Thomas' Church** built in 1598 is another imposing sight and serves as a **museum** of Portuguese relics. It's open from 9 am to 9 pm, and there's no entry fee. **St Paul's Church** is counted amongst the finest churches in India. From the church, you can head to the **Diu Fort** (Timings 8 am-6 pm).

Jallandar and Chakratirth beaches

Jallandar is a small beach with golden sands while Chakratirth is quite rocky. You cannot even swim at the latter but what it does offer is the most spectacular sunset in Diu, seen from a hillock, aptly called **Sunset Point**.

Nagoa Beach

This is Diu's only touristy beach and it's beautiful in its own right. The waters are safe for swimming, and **water sports** are also available. The options include **water scooter** (Rs 50), **speedboat** (Rs 50) and **parasailing** on the sea (by powerboat,

ADITYA DOGRA/ PHOTOINDIA

The Diu Fort, which has a lighthouse, is skirted by the sea on three sides

Rs 500). All rates are per person per kilometre. These services are provided by Dr Vijay (Tel: 02875-271456; Mobile: 09426713797, 09824283546). You can also make your bookings through Adventure Water Sports, based in the Magico do Mar Hotel at Ghoghla Beach (*see alongside*). There's also a **Shell Museum** on Nagoa Beach, with over 2,000 types of seashells on display.
◆**Museum entry fee** Adults Rs 10, children Rs 5 **Timings** 10 am-5.30 pm

Gomtimata Beach

For some reason — possibly its isolation — foreigners love this beach on Diu's western extremity, close to the Vanakbara Jetty. However, you cannot swim here and the beach is quite narrow.

SHOPPING

Shopaholics can explore the **Bunder Chowk** area, which has export surplus shirts and shorts at inexpensive rates. One shop here that foreign tourists love is Pradip Bhai's **Sarjan Art Gallery** (Tel: 02875-253993). It stocks shell jewellery and artefacts made by the local Sangheda community and beachwear printed with traditional Saurashtra motifs.

WHERE TO STAY

Diu's hotels are spread across the island. The old town has the maximum hotels, but none in the premium category.

On Ghoghla Beach

The furniture and fittings at **Suzlon Beach Hotel** (Tel: 02875-252212; Tariff: Rs 1,200-2,200) leave a lot to be desired, but the location is excellent, the food is good and the staff courteous. **Magico do Mar** (Tel: 252567; Tariff: Rs 1,100-3,750 per person as part of a package) is not in Diu but stands across the Diu checkpost and so lies in Gujarat's Junagadh District. Built in 1937, it used to be the retreat of the Nawab of Junagadh. **Hotel Sea View** (Tel: 252371; Tariff: Rs 700-1,500) is not as swanky as the other hotels on the beach. It's quite basic with AC thrown in if you pay more.

On Nagoa Beach

Radhika Beach Resort (Tel: 252553-55; Tariff: Rs 1,750-2,950) is not exactly on the beach but it's close enough. The villa-style rooms here are set around a blue swimming pool and are attractive. **Hotel Gangasagar** (Tel: 252249; Tariff: Rs 900-2,400) is the only hotel on the beach in Nagoa, across the road from Radhika.

Rasal Beach Resort (Tel: 255402; Tariff: Rs 1,750-2,550) is a bit away from Nagoa Chowpatty. You can see the sea from your room but the beach here is just the end of the arc stretching on both sides of Chowpatty. **Resort Hoka** (Tel: 253036; Tariff: Rs 1,050-1,550) stands in a quiet, tree-lined lane away from the beach. The rooms are clean and sensibly furnished.

On Chakratirth Beach

Sea Village Resort (Tel: 254345; Tariff: Rs 800-1,000) is the only hotel on this beach, and it doesn't have much to distinguish it. The rooms are simple.

→ GETTING THERE

Air Diu has its own airport (7 km/ 30 mins) near Nagoa Beach, and Jet Airways' Mumbai-Porbandar flights land there everyday barring Saturday. Autos charge Rs 40-50 to town

Rail Nearest railhead: Delwada (8 km/ 30 mins), connected only to Veraval (90 km) by metre gauge. You can get a train to Ahmedabad only at Veraval. The bus service between Una and Veraval is good. Autorickshaws from Diu to Una charge Rs 150

Road Shiva Shakti Travels (Tel: 079-26578777; fare Rs 250), which is located in the Sumeru Complex in Paldi, Ahmedabad, runs sleeper buses (non-AC) daily, between Ahmedabad and Diu. A couple of State Transport buses are also available, but they leave during the day

In Diu Town

Hotel Samrat (Tel: 252354; Tariff: Rs 1,450-2,250), located near the vegetable market, is a popular hotel.

Hotel Cidade de Diu (Tel: 254595; Tariff: Rs 1,100-2,500) is located right behind Samrat, and is a new hotel. The rooms are functional, and the tariffs quite reasonable. At **Hotel Pensao Beira Mar** (Tel: 253031; Tariff: Rs 1,250-1,950), situated near Bunder Chowk, the suites offer sea views.

Government Accommodation

Diu offers a variety of government accommodation with 2 circuit houses and 8 cottages. The tariffs (Rs 600-1,200) for tourists are the same at all three, and they don't fluctuate through the year. **Circuit House-I** (Tel: 252312) is on Jallandar Beach, and has 6 rooms.

To stay at the government-owned **Jallandar Cottages** further down the road, call 255212. The third option, **Circuit House-II** (Tel: 252476), is near Diu Fort. It has 10 rooms, but two of these are always reserved for VIPs.

For more hotels and details, see Diu Accommodation Listings on pages 526-527

WHERE TO EAT

You will find bars or permit rooms everywhere in Diu. But food is a different matter altogether, and you will be better off sticking to the restaurants at the hotel where you are staying.

At Ghoghla Beach, **Magico do Mar** is famous for its seafood platter. Suzlon's **Prato Delicioso** restaurant serves excellent Goan curry and mocktails.

At Nagoa Beach, try tandoori prawns at Radhika's **Riviera** restaurant. While seafood is a common speciality of all the hotels in Diu, their restaurants are multi-cuisine, with Punjabi dishes being the surprise winners. ■

With inputs from
Darshan Desai & OTG Desk

TOURIST OFFICES

INFORMATION 🅘 **INFORMATION & BOOKING** 🅘🅑

ANDAMAN AND NICOBAR ISLANDS

Andaman and Nicobar Tourism
www.tourism.andaman.nic.in

PORT BLAIR
State Tourism Office
Directorate of Information, Publicity and Tourism 🅘🅑
A & N Administration
Director Tourism
Port Blair
Telefax 03192-230933/ 234

METRO OFFICES

CHENNAI
Tourism Dept 🅘
Andaman House, North Main Road Ext, Anna Nagar West Ext, Padi Village, Chennai
Tel 044-26549294

KOLKATA
Tourism Dept 🅘
3-A Auckland Place, Kolkata
Telefax 033-23577628
Mobile 09831175552

NEW DELHI
Tourism Dept 🅘
12, Chanakyapuri (Near Chanakya Cinema), New Delhi
Tel 011-26878120/03

ANDHRA PRADESH

Andhra Pradesh Tourism Development Corporation (APTDC)
www.aptourism.com

HYDERABAD
State Tourism Office
APTDC 🅘🅑
Central Reservation Office
Shankar Bhavan, Fateh Maidan Road, Basheer Bagh Hyderabad
Tel 23298456-57

METRO OFFICES

BANGALORE
APTDC 🅘🅑
Tourist Info Counter
24/1, Race Course Road
Madhavnagar, Bangalore
Tel 080-41136373

CHENNAI
APTDC 🅘
Tourist Info Counter
C/o Tamil Nadu Tourist Complex, 2, Wallajah Road
Chennai
Tel 044-25381213

NEW DELHI
Dept of Tourism 🅘
Tourist Info Centre
Andhra Bhavan, 1 Ashoka Road, New Delhi
Tel 011-23381293

VISAKHAPATNAM
APTDC 🅘🅑
Central Reservation Office
RTC Complex
Visakhapatnam
Tel 0891-2788820
Mobile (Rajesh) 09848813584

DAMAN

Daman Tourism
www.daman.nic.in

DAMAN
State Tourism Office
Tourism Dept 🅘🅑
UT Administration of Daman & Diu
Paryatan Bhavan
Nani Daman, Daman
Telefax 0260-2255104

DIU

Diu Tourism
www.diuindia.com

DIU
State Tourism Office
Tourism Dept 🅘🅑
UT Administration of Daman & Diu
Information Assistant
Diu Jetty, Diu
Tel 02875-252653/ 111

GOA

Goa Tourism Development Corporation Ltd (GTDCL)
www.goa-tourism.com

GOA
State Tourism Office
GTDCL 🅘🅑
Central Reservation Office
Trionora Apt, Dr Alvares Costa Road, Panaji, Goa
Tel 0832-2427972, 2436666

METRO OFFICES

MUMBAI
Dept of Tourism 🅘🅑
Tourist Info Counter
Main Hall
Mumbai Central Rly Stn
Mumbai
Tel 022-23086288

NEW DELHI
GTDCL 🅘🅑
18, Goa Sadan
Amrita Shergil Marg
New Delhi
Tel 011-24629968 Ext 141

GUJARAT

Tourism Corporation of Gujarat Ltd (TCGL)
www.gujarattourism.com

AHMEDABAD
State Tourism Office
TCGL
Tourist Info Bureau, HK House
Ashram Road, Ahmedabad
Tel 079-26587217/ 9172

METRO OFFICES

CHENNAI
TCGL
TTDC Tourist Complex
No. 2 Wallajah Road, Chennai
Telefax 044-25366613

KOLKATA
TCGL
Fifth Floor, 15, Chittaranjan Avenue, Kolkata
Telefax 033-22254317

MUMBAI
TCGL
Khaitan Bhavan
C/o GIIC, Opp Hotel Ritz
JRD Tata Road, Mumbai
Tel 022-22024925

NEW DELHI
TCGL
A/6, State Emporia Complex
Baba Kharak Singh Marg
New Delhi
Tel 011-23744015, 23364724

KARNATAKA

Karnataka State Tourism Development Corporation (KSTDC)
www.kstdc.nic.in

BANGALORE
State Tourism Office
KSTDC
Central Reservation Office
Badami House, NR Square
Bangalore
Tel 080-22275869/ 83

METRO OFFICES

MUMBAI
KSTDC
Mysore Sales International Ltd
World Trade Centre
Cuffe Parade, Mumbai
Tel 022-22181658

NEW DELHI
KSTDC
Mysore Sales International Ltd
C-4, State Emporia Complex
Baba Kharak Singh Marg
New Delhi
Tel 011-23363863/ 66

KERALA

Kerala Tourism Development Corporation (KTDC)
Tourist Information Office
Govt of Kerala
www.ktdc.com

THIRUVANANTHAPURAM
State Tourism Office
KTDC
Central Reservation Office
Mascot Square
Thiruvananthapuram
Tel 0471-2316736

METRO OFFICES

CHENNAI
KTDC
Tourist Info Centre
Tourism Complex
No. 2, Wallajah Road
Chennai
Telefax 044-25382639

KOCHI
KTDC
Tourist Reception Centre
Shanmugham Road
Ernakulam, Kochi
Tel 0484-2353234

MUMBAI
KTDC
Tourist Reception Centre
GF, Kairali Nirmal Bldg
Nariman Point
Mumbai
Telefax 022-22830491

NEW DELHI
KTDC
Tourist Reception Centre
Dilli Haat, Sri Aurobindo Marg
Opp INA Market, New Delhi
Tel 011-24678360

Tourism Dept
Travancore Palace
Bharatiya Vidya Bhavan
KG Marg, New Delhi
Tel 23382067

LAKSHADWEEP ISLANDS

Lakshadweep Tourism
www.lakshadweeptourism.com

KAVARATTI
State Tourism Office
Lakshadweep Tourism
SPORTS
Tourism Bhavan, Kavaratti
Tel 04896-263001-02

METRO OFFICES

KOCHI
Lakshadweep Tourism
SPORTS
Assistant General Manager
Indira Gandhi Road
Willingdon Island
Kochi
Tel 0484-2668387/ 6789

NEW DELHI
Lakshadweep Tourism
F 301, Curzon Road Hostel
KG Marg, New Delhi
Tel 011-23386807

MAHARASHTRA

Maharashtra Tourism Development Corporation (MTDC)
www.maharashtratourism.gov.in, www.mtdcindia.com

MUMBAI
State Tourism Office
MTDC
Central Reservations

CDO Hutments, Opp LIC Bldg
Madame Cama Road
Mumbai
Tel 022-22026713/ 7762

METRO OFFICE

NEW DELHI
MTDC
Room No.10, Hotel Janpath
New Delhi
Tel 011-23366940, 23341413

ORISSA

Orissa Tourism Development Corporation (OTDC)
www.orissatourism.gov.in

BHUBANESWAR
State Tourism Offices
OTDC
Panthanivas, Lewis Road
Bhubaneswar
Tel 0674-2432382/ 762

Dept of Tourism
Paryatan Bhavan
Museum Campus
Bhubaneswar
Tel 0674-2432177

METRO OFFICES

CHENNAI
OTDC
C/o TTDC Tourist Complex
No. 2, Wallajah Road
Chennai
Tel 044-25360891

MUMBAI
OTDC
Hotel New Bengal
Near Crawford Market
DN Road, Mumbai
Tel 022-23401951

NEW DELHI
OTDC
B4, State Emporia Complex
Baba Kharak Singh Marg
New Delhi
Telefax 011-23364580

PONDICHERRY

Pondicherry Tourism Development Corporation (PTDC)
www.tourism.pon.nic.in

PONDICHERRY
State Tourism Office
PTDC
Tourism Info Centre
40, Goubert Avenue
Beach Road, Puducherry
Tel 0413-2339497

METRO OFFICE

CHENNAI
PTDC
Tourism Info Centre
TTDC Tourist Complex
No. 2, Wallajah Road, Chennai
Tel 044-25367853

TAMIL NADU

Tamil Nadu Tourism Development Corporation (TTDC)
www.tamilnadutourism.org

CHENNAI
State Tourism Offices
TTDC
Tourist Complex
No. 2, Wallajah Road, Chennai
Tel 044-25367850-54

Dept of Tourism
Tourist Complex
No. 2, Wallajah Road, Chennai
Tel 25367850-54

METRO OFFICES

BANGALORE
TTDC
Tourist Info Centre
City Rly Stn, Bangalore
Tel 080-22286181

KOLKATA
TTDC
Tourist Info Office
G-26, Dakshinapan Shopping Complex, No. 2, Gariyaghat Road (South), Kolkata
Tel 033-24237432

MUMBAI
TTDC
Tourist Info Office
G-2A, Royal Grace
Lokmanya Tilak Colony
Marg No. 2, Dadar East
Mumbai
Tel 022-24110118

NEW DELHI
TTDC
Tourist Info Office
C-1, State Emporia Complex
Baba Kharak Singh Marg
New Delhi
Tel 011-23745427, 23366327
Mobile 09213142260

WEST BENGAL

West Bengal Tourism Development Corporation (WBTDC)
www.westbengaltourism.com
www.wbtourism.com

KOLKATA
State Tourism Office
WBTDC
3/2, BBD Bagh (East)
Kolkata
Tel 033-22437260, 22485168

METRO OFFICES

CHENNAI
WBTDC
West Bengal Youth Hostel
No. 18, Wallajah Road
Chennai
Tel 044-28532346

NEW DELHI
WBTDC
FF, State Emporia Bldg
Baba Kharak Singh Marg
New Delhi
Tel 011-23742840
Mobile 09899369127

LEGEND

DIST District
FF First Floor
NA Not accepted
NH National Highway
Opp Opposite
PO Post
SF Second Floor
TE Taxes extra

Accommodation type?
Spot these flags
HERITAGE BACKWATERS
TENTS SEA-FACING

Special Hotel needs?
Spot these flags
BIRDWATCHING AYURVEDA
WATER SPORTS SPA

METRO RESERVATIONS

To book any state tourism hotel in your city, see the Tourist Offices listing on page 518-520

HOTELS EASY ACCESS

Disclaimer Only a representative listing of hotels in each area has been given. The facilities listed may not be exhaustive. Tariff indicates the approx range (lowest to highest) of the rates prevailing at the time of going to press. The listings given here should not be construed as recommendations by the publisher

ANDAMAN ISLANDS

DIGLIPUR STD 03192

APWD Guesthouse
Location Marketplace **Address** Subhashgram, Diglipur **Tel** 272204-06 **Rooms** 7 **Tariff** Rs 400-800; Rs 80-160 (for govt employees) **Credit Cards** NA **Facilities** Kitchen, attached bath, hot water

Turtle Resort A&N TOURISM
Location Near the beach **Address** Kalipur, Diglipur **Tel** 220603 **Website** tourism.andaman.nic.in **Rooms** 10, dorms 2 (4 beds) **Tariff** Rs 400-800, dorm bed Rs 150 **Credit Cards** NA **Facilities** Restaurant, laundry, common TV, attached bath, hot water **Metro Reservations** *See page 518*

HAVELOCK ISLAND STD 03192

Barefoot at Havelock WATER SPORTS
Location Beachside **Address** Beach No. 7, Radha Nagar, Havelock **Tel** 282151 **Website** barefootindia.com **Rooms** 18 cottages **Tariff** Rs 2,700-6,000 **Credit Cards** Visa, Master **Facilities** Restaurant, bar, snorkelling, scuba diving, yoga, kayaking **Chennai Reservations** Barefoot Group, B-4, RM Towers, 108 Chamiers Road, Chennai **Tel** 044-24341001 **Port Blair Reservations** Barefoot Group, MB-5, FF, Atlanta Point, Port Blair **Tel** 03192-236008

Café del Mar WATER SPORTS
Location Beach No. 3 **Address** Havelock **Tel** 282151 **Website** barefootindia.com **Rooms** 12 huts **Tariff** Rs 100-2,000 **Credit Cards** Visa, Master **Facilities** Restaurant, bar, snorkelling, scuba diving, nature walks, yoga, kayaking **Chennai and Port Blair Reservations** *See Barefoot At Havelock alongside*

Dolphin Resort A&N TOURISM SEA-FACING
Location Beachside **Address** Havelock Island **Tel** 282411, 282235 **Telefax** 282444 **Website** tourism.andaman.nic.in **Rooms** 34 **Tariff** Rs 1,000-2,000 **Credit Cards** NA **Facilities** Restaurant, travel assistance, laundry, attached bath, TV **Metro Reservations** *See page 518*

Forest Guest House
Location Near beach **Address** Havelock Island **Rooms** 2 **Tariff** Rs 400 **Credit Cards** NA **Facilities** Caretaker, meals on order, attached bath **Reservations** Chief Wildlife Warden, Port Blair **Tel** 03192-233549

Orient Legend SEA-FACING
Location Beachside **Address** Beach No. 5, Vijaynagar Beach, Havelock **Tel** 282389 **Mobile** 09434291008 **Rooms** 20 **Tariff** Rs 200-800 **Credit Cards** NA **Facilities** Restaurant, travel assistance, bike rental, laundry, room service, attached bath, hot water

Silversand Beach Resort
Location Beachside **Address** Beach No. 5, Vijaynagar Beach **Tel** 329499/ 368 **Mobile** 09933239625, 09434280295 **Fax** 233161 **Website** silversandhavelock.com **Rooms** 34 **Tariff** Rs 4,599-7,999 **Credit Cards** Visa, Master **Facilities** Restaurant, bar, boat on charter, snorkelling, scuba diving, Ayurvedic massage, yoga, swimming pool, gym, travel desk, resort transfers, doctor-on-call, room service, TV

Sunrise Hotel
Location Beachfront **Address** Havelock **Tel** 282408 **Mobile** 09474206183 **Rooms** 21 **Tariff** Rs 300-1,000 **Credit Cards** NA **Facilities** Restaurant, bar, resort transfers, bike rental, laundry, room service, attached bath, TV

Wild Orchid Resort WATER SPORTS
Location Near beach **Address** Vijaynagar Beach **Tel** 282472 **Fax** 230109 **Website** wildorchidandaman.com **Rooms** 14 **Tariff** Rs 1,500-3,500 **Credit Cards** Visa, Master **Facilities** Restaurant, bar, Ayurvedic massage, recreation area, fishing, trekking, snorkelling, excursions, laundry, room service **Port Blair Reservations** Travel House, Aberdeen Bazaar, Port Blair **Tel** 03192-233358, 233034

MAYABUNDER STD 03192

Anmol Guesthouse
Location Marketplace **Address** MKS Complex, Main Market, Mayabunder **Tel** 262695 **Mobile** 09474540064 **Rooms** 13 **Tariff** Rs 100-400 **Credit Cards** NA **Facilities** Travel assistance, bike rental, laundry, room service, attached bath, TV

APWD Guesthouse SEA-FACING
Location Clifftop, near sea **Address** Near Jetty, Mayabunder **Tel** 273211 **Rooms** 13 **Tariff** Rs 400-800 **Credit Cards** NA **Facilities** Restaurant, attached bath, hot water **Reservations** **Tel** 273208

IN CUTBERT BAY, RANGAT

Hawksbill Nest A&N TOURISM
Location Beachside **Address** Cutbert Bay, Rangat **Tel** 279159, 232747, 276333 **Website** tourism.andaman.nic.in **Rooms**

8, dorms 2 (4 beds) **Tariff** Rs 400-800, dorm bed Rs 150 **Credit Cards** NA **Facilities** Restaurant, travel assistance, laundry **Metro Reservations** *See page 518*

NEIL ISLAND STD 03192

Hawabill Nest A&N TOURISM

Location Beachfront **Address** Neil Island, South Andamans **Tel** 282630 **Rooms** 4, dorms 2 (4 beds) **Tariff** Rs 600-800, dorm bed Rs 150 **Credit Cards** NA **Facilities** Restaurant, laundry, attached bath, hot water **Metro Reservations** *See page 518*

PORT BLAIR STD 03192

Andaman Teal House

A&N TOURISM

Location 2 km from bus stop **Address** Delanipur, Port Blair **Tel** 232642, 234060-61 **Website** tourism.andaman.nic.in **Rooms** 28 **Tariff** Rs 400-800 **Credit Cards** NA **Facilities** Restaurant, travel assistance, laundry, attached bath **Metro Reservations** *See page 518*

Fortune Resort Bay Island

SEA-FACING

Location Near beach **Address** Marine Hill, Port Blair **Tel** 234101, 232198, 232065 **Website** fortunehotels.in **Rooms** 45 **Tariff** Rs 2,950-8,559 **Credit Cards** Visa, Master **Facilities** Restaurant, bar, swimming pool, private jetty, travel desk, doctor-on-call, laundry, room service, TV

Holiday Resort

Location Central **Address** Prem Nagar, Port Blair **Tel** 235594, 230516 **Telefax** 234231 **Email** holidayresort88@hotmail.com **Rooms** 17 **Tariff** Rs 500-800 **Credit Cards** NA **Facilities** Restaurant, bar, travel assistance, airport transfers, doctor-on-call, laundry, room service, TV

Hornbill Nest Resort

A&N TOURISM

Location Hillside **Address** Corbyn's Cove, Port Blair **Tel** 229130 **Website** tourism.andaman.nic.in **Rooms** 20 **Tariff** Rs 400-800 **Credit Cards** NA **Facilities** Restaurant, travel desk, airport transfers, bike rental, laundry, room service, attached bath, TV **Metro Reservations** *See page 518*

Hotel Dhanalakshmi

Location Near sports complex **Address** Aberdeen Bazaar, Port Blair **Tel** 233952-53 **Fax** 238779, 234964 **Rooms** 38 **Tariff** Rs 400-1,500 **Credit Cards** NA **Facilities** Restaurant, travel assistance, airport transfers, doctor-on-call, lockers, laundry, room service, attached bath, TV

Hotel Shompen

Location Central **Address** Middle Point, Port Blair **Tel** 232644, 232360 **Fax** 232425 **Email** hotelshompen@hotmail.com **Rooms** 38 **Tariff** Rs 800-2,000 **Credit Cards** AmEx, Visa, Master **Facilities** Restaurant, bar, travel agency, airport transfers, doctor-on-call, lockers, laundry, room service, attached bath, hot water, TV

Hotel Sinclairs Bay View

WATER SPORTS

Location Beachfront **Address** South Point, Port Blair **Tel** 227824/ 937 **Website** sinclairshotels.com **Rooms** 24 **Tariff** Rs 2,550-3,900 **Credit Cards** AmEx, Diners, Visa, Master **Facilities** Restaurant, bar, resort transfers, water sports, snorkelling, scuba diving, car rental, laundry, room service, attached bath, hot water, TV **Mumbai Reservations** 156, Maker Chamber VI, Nariman Point, Mumbai **Tel** 022-22818520-22, 22823656

Peerless Beach Resort
Location Beachside **Address** Corbyn's Cove, Port Blair **Tel** 229311/ 13/ 21/ 23 **Website** peerlesshotels.com **Rooms** 47, cottages 4 **Tariff** Rs 3,000-5,500 **Credit Cards** Visa, Master **Facilities** Restaurant, bar, indoor/ outdoor games, sightseeing, scuba diving, travel desk, airport transfers, doctor-on-call, laundry, room service, TV

ANDHRA PRADESH

VISAKHAPATNAM STD 0891

Haritha Hotel APTDC
Location Opp Appu Ghar **Address** MVP Colony, Near Kailasagiri Hill **Tel** 2788824 **Website** aptdc.in **Rooms** 39 **Tariff** Rs 800-1,600; TE **Credit Cards** NA **Facilities** Multi-cuisine restaurant, bar, souvenir shop, laundry, doctor-on-call, travel arranged, room service, attached bath, hot water **Metro Reservations** *See page 518*

Hotel Daspalla
Location Near beach **Address** Suryabagh **Tel** 2564825, 2563141 **Fax** 2562043 **Website** daspallahotels.com **Rooms** 123 **Tariff** Rs 1,350-3,000; TE **Credit Cards** AmEx, Visa, Master **Facilities** Restaurants, health centre, laundry, doctor-on-call, travel desk, room service

Hotel Grand Bay SEA-FACING
Location Beachside **Address** RK Beach, Beach Road **Tel** 2560101-02 **Website** itcwelcomgroup.in **Rooms** 102 **Tariff** Rs 3,800-9,000; TE **Credit Cards** AmEx, Visa, Master **Facilities** Restaurants, coffee shop, swimming pool, health club, travel desk, doctor-on-call, room service

Hotel Supreme
Location Near beach **Address** Beach Road, Collector's Office Down, Near Coastal Battery **Tel** 2782472 **Telefax** 2782475 **Email** hotelsupreme@hotmail.com **Rooms** 54 **Tariff** Rs 700-2,000; TE **Credit Cards** AmEx, Visa, Master **Facilities** Multi-cuisine restaurant, laundry, doctor-on-call, travel desk, room service

Jaabily Beach Inn
Location Near Collector's office **Address** Beach Road, Collector's Office Down **Tel** 2706026/ 468 **Mobile** 09848359977 **Website** jaabilybeachinn.com **Rooms** 25 **Tariff** Rs 400-995; TE **Credit Cards** NA **Facilities** Dining hall, bar, laundry, doctor-on-call, travel desk, lockers, sightseeing, room service, attached bath, TV

Lodge Sagar
Address 16-1-30, Opp Collector's Office **Tel** 2526397, 2569875 **Mobile** 09848535744 **Rooms** 60 **Tariff** Rs 200-600 **Credit Cards** NA **Facilities** Laundry, doctor-on-call, travel and taxi arranged, sightseeing arranged, room service

Palm Beach Hotel AYURVEDA
Location Beachside **Address** RK Beach, Beach Road **Tel** 2754026-27 **Website** hotelpalmbeachvizag.com **Rooms** 38 **Tariff** Rs 2,650-3,550 (with breakfast); TE **Credit Cards** Visa, Master **Facilities** Restaurants, swimming pool, gym, tennis court, private beach, beach volleyball, Ayurvedic massage centre, laundry, doctor-on-call, travel desk, room service

Taj Residency SEA-FACING
Location Near beach **Address** Beach Road **Tel** 2567756, 6667756 **Fax** 2564370 **Website** tajhotels.com **Rooms** 93 **Tariff** Rs 3,800-9,000; TE **Credit Cards** AmEx, Visa, Master **Facilities** Restaurants, bar, lounge, swimming pool, health club, travel desk, laundry, doctor-on-call, room service

The Park SEA-FACING
Location Beachside **Address** Beach Road **Tel** 2754488, 2713600 **Fax** 2754181 **Website** theparkhotels.com **Rooms** 61 **Tariff** Rs 3,800-7,000; TE **Credit Cards** AmEx, Visa, Master **Facilities** Multi-cuisine restaurants, bar, swimming pool, health club, table tennis, lawn tennis, beach volleyball, laundry, doctor-on-call, travel desk, lockers, forex, room service

ON RUSHIKONDA BEACH

Haritha Beach Resort APTDC
Location Beachside **Address** Opp Gitam College, Bhimili Road, Rushikonda **Tel** 2788826 **Website** aptdc.in **Rooms** 58 **Tariff** Rs 1,500-2,500; TE **Credit Cards** NA **Facilities** Multi-cuisine restaurant, bar, souvenir shop, laundry, doctor-on-call, boating, travel and taxi arranged, room service **Metro Reservations** *See page 518*

Sai Priya Beach Resort
Location Beachside **Address** Beach Road, Near Gitam College, Rushikonda **Tel** 2790333/ 583, 2788120 **Website** saipriyabeachresorts.com **Rooms** 33 **Tariff** Rs 605-6,600; TE **Credit Cards** Visa, Master **Facilities** Multi-cuisine restaurant, bar, sliding pool, garden, laundry, doctor-on-call, travel desk, room service

Senora Beach Club

Location Hillside **Address** Sagar Nagar, Beach Road **Tel** 2723666 **Mobile** 09949612266, 09849991274 **Rooms** 5 **Tariff** Rs 1,200-1,500; TE **Credit Cards** Visa, Master **Facilities** Multi-cuisine restaurant, bar, indoor games, laundry, doctor-on-call, travel desk, room service, attached bath

DAMAN

STD 0260

Cidade De Daman SEA-FACING

Location Beachside **Address** Devka Beach, Nani Daman **Tel** 2250590-91/ 467-68 **Website** cidadededaman.com **Rooms** 66 **Tariff** Rs 1,700-2,300 **Credit Cards** AmEx, Visa, Master **Facilities** Restaurant, bar, swimming pool, gym, outdoor games, travel desk, doctor-on-call, laundry, room service **Mumbai Reservations** Citizen Centre, 5, Damodar Bhavan, Vallabhbhai Road, Opp Railway Station, Vile Parle (W), Mumbai **Tel** 022-26175712, 26125945 **Mobile** 09820424153

Hotel China Town

Location Seaside **Address** Jampore Beach, Moti Daman **Tel** 2230920/ 1516 **Rooms** 20 **Tariff** Rs 800-1,600 **Credit Cards** NA **Facilities** Restaurant, bar, travel desk, laundry, room service, TV

Hotel Dariya Darshan

Location Sea-facing **Address** Devka Beach, Nani Daman **Tel** 2254476/ 386, 3090590/ 639 **Website** dariyadarshanhotel.com **Rooms** 30 **Tariff** Rs 1,000-2,500 **Credit Cards** Visa, Master **Facilities** Restaurant, bar, travel desk, car rental, sightseeing, laundry, room service, TV

Hotel Jazira SEA-FACING

Location Beachside **Address** Devka Beach **Tel** 2254330/ 39, 2251986 **Website** hoteljazira.com **Rooms** 25 **Tariff** Rs 800-1,600 **Credit Cards** Visa, Master **Facilities** Restaurant, bar, live entertainment, pool table, video games, travel desk, car rental, sightseeing, doctor-on-call, laundry, room service, TV

Hotel Marina

Location Behind police station **Address** Nani Daman **Tel** 2254420 **Fax** 2255945 **Email** hotelmarina@rediffmail.com **Rooms** 10 **Tariff** Rs 585-675 **Credit Cards** Visa, Master **Facilities** Restaurant, car rental, room service, doctor-on-call, laundry, room service, TV

Hotel Miramar

Location Beachside **Address** Devka Beach, Nani Daman **Tel** 2250671-73, 2254471/ 971 **Website** miramarmirasol.in **Rooms** 80 **Tariff** Rs 1,000-5,000 **Credit Cards** Visa, Master **Facilities** Restaurant, bar, disco, swimming pool, car rental, locker, laundry, room service, TV **Mumbai Reservations** A-2, Datey Bhavan, Opp Van Mali Hall, Near Ideal Book Depot, Dadar (West), Mumbai **Tel** 022-32403798

Hotel Princess Park SEA-FACING

Location Beachside **Address** Devka Beach **Tel** 2250900/ 4323, 2254997 **Fax** 2250800 **Website** hotelprincesspark.in **Rooms** 27 **Tariff** Rs 1,600-4,000 **Credit Cards** Visa, Master **Facilities** Restaurant, bar, cybercafé, pool table, car rental, laundry, room service, TV

Hotel Shilton

Location Beachside **Address** Devka Beach **Tel** 2254407 **Fax** 2263838 **Rooms** 26 **Tariff** Rs 600-1,200 **Credit Cards** AmEx, Visa, Master **Facilities**

Restaurant, bar, car rental, laundry, room service, TV

Mirasol Resort
Location Near Coast Guard Check Post **Address** Kadaiya Village, Nani Daman **Tel** 2220541-42 **Fax** 2254934 **Website** miramarmirasol.in **Rooms** 40 **Tariff** Rs 3,000-6,000 **Credit Cards** Visa, Master **Facilities** Restaurant, bar, boating, water park, swimming pool, car rental, doctor-on-call, lockers, laundry, room service, TV **Mumbai Reservations** *See Hotel Miramar on previous page*

Oliaji's Duke Hotel
Location Beachside **Address** Devka Beach **Tel** 2251292/ 4251 **Rooms** 20 **Tariff** Rs 500 **Credit Cards** NA **Facilities** Restaurant, bar, room service, TV

Sandy Resort AMUSEMENT PARK
Location Near the beach **Address** Devka Beach **Tel** 2254751/ 644/ 744 **Mobile** 09998047177 **Website** sandy resort.com **Rooms** 46 **Tariff** Rs 1,150-2,100 **Credit Cards** AmEx, Visa, Master **Facilities** Restaurant, discotheque, amusement park, swimming pool, travel desk, doctor-on-call, locker, laundry, room service, TV

DIU

STD 02875

Hotel Cidade de Diu
Location Near vegetable market **Address** Behind Hotel Samrat **Tel** 254443/ 595/ 695 **Website** cidadedediu.com **Rooms** 27, suites 4 **Tariff** Rs 1,100-2,500 **Credit Cards** Visa, Master **Facilities** Restaurant, bar, travel desk, airport transfers, doctor-on-call, laundry, room service, TV

Hotel Khushi International SEA-FACING
Location Near beach **Address** Bundar Chowk **Tel** 254199, 255399 **Telefax** 252379 **Website** hotelkhushi.com **Rooms** 36 **Tariff** Rs 600-2,000 **Credit Cards** Visa, Master **Facilities** Restaurant, bar, travel desk, Internet, airport transfers, car rental, forex, doctor-on-call, lockers, laundry, room service, TV

Hotel Samrat
Location Near vegetable market **Address** Old Collectorate Road **Tel** 252354/ 514, 254554 **Website** cidadedediu.com **Rooms** 30 **Tariff** Rs 1,450-2,250 **Credit Cards** Visa, Master **Facilities** Restaurant, bar, travel desk, doctor-on-call, laundry, room service, attached bath, TV

ON CHAKRATIRTH BEACH

Circuit House-I
Location Beachside **Address** Jallandar Beach **Tel** 252312 **Mobile** 09998887193 **Rooms** 6 **Tariff** Rs 600-1,200 **Credit Cards** NA **Facilities** Meals on order, laundry, room service, attached bath, hot water, TV **Reservations Tel** 252444

Circuit House-II
Address Near Diu Fort **Tel** 252476 **Mobile** 09998887193 **Rooms** 10 **Tariff** Rs 600-1,200 **Credit Cards** NA **Facilities** Meals on order, laundry, room service, attached bath, TV **Reservations** *See Circuit House-I above*

Hotel Pensao Beira Mar
Location Opp DMC office **Address** Fort Road **Tel** 253031 **Mobile** 09879564031 **Rooms** 12 **Tariff** Rs 1,250-1,950 **Credit Cards** NA **Facilities** Restaurant, bar, travel assistance, airport transfers, doctor-on-call, laundry, room service, attached bath, TV

Jallandar Cottages
Location Beachside **Address** Jallandar Beach **Tel** 255212 **Mobile** 09998887193 **Rooms** 8 **Tariff** Rs 600-1,200 **Credit Cards** NA **Facilities** Meals on order, laundry, room service, attached bath, TV **Reservations** *See Circuit House-I alongside*

Sea Village Resort
Location Beachfront **Address** Sunset Point, Chakratirth Beach **Tel** 254345 **Mobile** 09879290091 **Rooms** 15 **Tariff** Rs 800-1,000 **Credit Cards** NA **Facilities** Restaurant, travel assistance, doctor-on-call, laundry, room service, attached bath

ON GHOGHLA BEACH

Hotel Sea View
Location Beachside **Address** Ghoghla Beach **Tel** 252371, 253080 **Rooms** 18 **Tariff** Rs 700-1,500 **Credit Cards** NA **Facilities** Restaurant, bar, travel assistance, water sports, parking, doctor-on-call, laundry, room service, TV

Magico Do Mar WATER SPORTS
Location Beachside **Address** Ghoghla Beach, Diu Checkpost, Ahmedpur Mandvi, Dist Junagadh **Tel** 252567 **Website** magicodomar.com **Rooms** 24, cottages 16 **Tariff** Rs 1,100-1,400 **Credit Cards** NA **Facilities** Restaurant, Ayurvedic massage, water sports, boating, camel/ horse rides, travel desk, laundry, room service, TV

Suzlon Beach Hotel
WATER SPORTS
Location Beachside **Address**

Opp Check Post, Ghoghla Beach **Tel** 252212, 253212 **Telefax** 253213 **Website** suzlonbeachhotel.com **Rooms** 20 **Tariff** Rs 1,200-2,200 **Credit Cards** Visa, Master **Facilities** Restaurant, bar, water sports, travel desk, laundry, room service, TV

ON NAGOA BEACH

Hotel Gangasagar
Location Beachside **Address** Nagoa Beach **Tel** 252249 **Mobile** 09824220554 **Fax** 252552 **Rooms** 15 **Tariff** Rs 900-2,400 **Credit Cards** NA **Facilities** Restaurant, bar, travel assistance, laundry, room service, TV

Radhika Beach Resort
SEA-FACING
Location Near beach **Address** Nagoa Beach **Tel** 252553-55 **Website** radhikaresort.com **Rooms** 42 **Tariff** Rs 1,750-2,950 **Credit Cards** Visa, Master **Facilities** Restaurant, bar, health club, swimming pool, travel desk, doctor-on-call, laundry, room service, attached bath, TV

Rasal Beach Resort
Location Near airport **Address** Nagoa Beach **Tel** 255402 **Mobile** 09228591230 **Fax** 252498 **Rooms** 28 **Tariff** Rs 1,750-2,550 **Credit Cards** AmEx, Visa, Master **Facilities** Restaurant, bar, travel assistance, airport transfers, doctor-on-call, laundry, room service, attached bath, TV

NORTH GOA

ANJUNA STD 0832

Hotel Bougainvillea (Granpa's Inn)
Location Near beach **Address** Gaumwaddi, Anjuna Beach, North Goa, Bardez **Tel** 2273270-71 **Fax** 2274370 **Website** granpasinn.com **Rooms** 13 **Tariff** Rs 650-4,150 **Credit Cards** AmEx, Visa, Master **Facilities** Restaurant, bar, swimming pool, billiards, yoga, travel assistance, lockers, forex, Internet, doctor-on-call, room service, attached bath, hot water, TV

Laguna Anjuna SEA-FISHING
Location Near Sacred Heart High School **Address** Sorontto Vaddo, Anjuna **Tel** 2274131/ 305, 2273248 **Website** lagunaanjuna.com **Rooms** 25 cottages **Tariff** Rs 3,200-12,500 **Credit Cards** AmEx Visa, Master **Facilities** Restaurant, bar, swimming pool, massage, yoga, Tai Chi, pool table, travel assistance, birding, sea fishing tours arranged

The Tamarind
Location Opp church **Address** Anjuna, Bardez **Tel** 2274319, 6512399 **Fax** 2273363 **Website** thetamarind.com **Rooms** 22 **Tariff** Rs 990-3,380 **Credit Cards** Visa **Facilities** Restaurant, bar, swimming pool, mini golf, pool table, lockers, forex, library
TIP Kids under 12 years not allowed

White Negro Beach Resort
Location Near beach **Address** Near St Anthony's Chapel, Praise Vaddo, Anjuna Beach, Bardez **Tel** 2273326, 2274226 **Email** dsouzawhitenegro@rediffmail.com **Website** goacom.com/hotels/whitenegro/whitenegro.html **Rooms** 14 **Tariff** Rs 300-1,000 **Credit Cards** NA **Facilities** Restaurant, bar, massage parlour, travel assistance, lockers, forex, doctor-on-call, laundry, attached bath, TV

IN SIOLIM STD 0832

Bay View Apartments
Location Near St Anthony's Church **Address** Vaddi, Siolim, Bardez **Tel** 2270808 **Mobile** 09823330808 **Rooms** 15 **Tariff** Rs 700-3,000 **Credit Cards** NA **Facilities** Restaurants, bar, kitchenette in rooms

Siolim House HERITAGE
Location Opp Wadi Chapel **Address** Vaddi, Siolim, Bardez **Tel** 2272138/ 941 **Mobile** 09822584560 **Website** siolimhouse.com **Rooms** 7 suites **Tariff** Rs 6,300-9,700 **Credit Cards** Visa, Master **Facilities** Restaurant, yoga, swimming pool, Ayurvedic massage on request, Internet, car/ bike rental, room service

ARAMBOL STD 0832

Famafa SEA-FACING
Location Near beach **Address** Khalchwada, Pernem **Tel** 2242516-17 **Fax** 2242471 **Email** fmafa_in@hotmail.com **Rooms** 25 **Tariff** Rs 250-400 **Credit Cards** NA **Facilities** Restaurant, bar, laundry, doctor-on-call, travel assistance, room service

Ivon's Guest House SEA-FACING
Location Near beach **Address** Girkar Vaddo, Arambol **Tel** 2242672 **Mobile** 09822127398 **Rooms** 30 **Tariff** Rs 300-700 **Credit Cards** NA **Facilities** Restaurant, laundry, doctor-on-call, scooter/ car rental, room service, attached bath

Om Ganesh Naik Guest House
Location Beachside **Address** Near Street Lake, Khalchawada Arambol, Pernem **Tel** 2242957 **Rooms** 15 **Tariff** Rs 150-300 **Credit Cards** NA **Facilities** Restaurant, lockers, doctor-on-call, laundry, hot water

Piya Guest House
Location Near beach **Address** Madlo Vaddo, Arambol **Tel** 2242661 **Rooms** 7 **Tariff** Rs 50-200 **Credit Cards** NA **Facilities** Restaurant, bar, travel desk, doctor-on-call, laundry, lockers, attached bath, hot water

IN KERI

Gangaram Guest House
Location Near beach **Address** Talwada, Keri Beach, Pernem **Tel** 2249773 **Rooms** 6, huts 5 **Tariff** Rs 250-300 **Credit Cards** NA **Facilities** Restaurant, room service, attached bath

IN TIRACOL STD 0236

Fort Tiracol HERITAGE
Location Sea-facing **Address** Tiracol Fort, Near Keri Beach, Pernem **Tel** 6227631 **Website** forttiracol.com **Rooms** 7 **Tariff** Rs 6,500-8,500 (with breakfast and dinner); TE **Credit Cards** AmEx, Visa, Master **Facilities** Restaurant, bar, swimming pool, Ayurvedic centre, yoga, gym, forex, travel desk

CALANGUTE-CANDOLIM STD 0832

ON BAGA BEACH

Baia-do-Sol
Location Near river and beach **Address** Baga Beach, Calangute **Tel** 2276084, 2275482 **Website** baiadosol.com **Rooms** 22 **Tariff** Rs 900-6,500;TE **Credit Cards** Visa, Master, AmEx **Facilities** Restaurant, bar, forex, lockers, boutique, piano, room service, TV

Cavala, The Seaside Resort
Location Near beach, opp Banana Republic Café **Address** Calangute-Baga Road, North Baga, Baga-Saunta Vaddo, Calangute **Tel** 2276090, 2277587 **Website** cavala.com **Rooms** 30 **Tariff** Rs 600-3,950; TE **Credit Cards** Visa, Master **Facilities** Restaurants, bar, pool, lockers, laundry, massage, sightseeing, TV

Nani's & Rani's Guest House
Location Beachside **Address** Near Lila Café and Marina Dorado, Baga **Tel** 2276313/ 7014, 6522402 **Email** gizellaferns @yahoo.com **Rooms** 8 **Tariff** Rs 800-1,200 **Credit Cards** NA **Facilities** Restaurant, bar, attached bath, hot water

Nilaya Hermitage
Location Hillside **Address** Arpora, Bhati, Baga **Tel** 2276793-94 **Website** nilaya hermitage.com **Rooms** 12 **Tariff** Rs 6,580-21,150 (with breakfast and dinner) **Facilities** Restaurant, bar, swimming pool, gym, Ayurvedic centre, jogging trail

Sea View Cottages
Location On the beach **Address** Saunta Vaddo, PO Calangute **Tel** 2281924, 2276371 **Fax** 2279773 **Rooms** 61, cottages 10 **Tariff** Rs 2,000 **Credit Cards** NA **Facilities** Restaurant, bar, pool

IN CALANGUTE

Calangute Annexe GTDC
Location Near football ground **Address** Umta Vaddo, Calangute **Tel** 2276009 **Rooms** 19 **Tariff** Rs 820-1,420; TE **Credit Cards** NA **Facilities** Restaurant, bar, room service, TV **Metro Reservations** *See page 518*

Calangute Residency GTDC
Location Sea-facing **Address** Next to DB Bandodkar Statue, Calangute Beach, Calangute, Bardez **Tel** 2276024/ 109 **Website** goa-tourism.com **Rooms** 58 **Tariff** Rs 1,024-4,800; TE **Credit Cards** AmEx, Visa, Master **Facilities** Restaurant, bar, travel desk, sightseeing, room service **Metro Reservations** *See page 518*

Colonia Santa Maria
Location Beachside **Address** Cobra Vaddo, Calangute **Tel** 2276107, 2277299 **Fax**

2415535 **Website** csmgoa.com **Rooms** 100 **Tariff** Rs 3,500-5,000 **Credit Cards** Visa, Master **Facilities** Restaurant, swimming pool, forex, lockers

Dona Cristalina Guest House

Location Near Kerkar Art Gallery **Address** Gaura Vaddo, Calangute, Bardez **Tel** 2279012 **Rooms** 10 **Tariff** Rs 250-1,200 **Facilities** Beach shack, room service, attached bath, TV

Estrela Do Mar Guest House

Location Near beach **Address** Cobra Vaddo, Calangute **Tel** 2279085 **Website** estreladomar goa.net **Rooms** 60 **Tariff** Rs 1,100-6,000 **Credit Cards** Master **Facilities** Restaurant, tailor shop, gym, swimming pool, Ayurvedic massage, sightseeing, car rental, doctor-on-call, laundry, room service

Hotel Goan Heritage SEA-FACING

Location Beachside **Address** Gaura Vaddo, Calangute, Bardez **Tel** 2276761-66 **Fax** 2276120 **Website** goanheritage.com **Rooms** 75 **Tariff** Rs 1,800-2,500 **Credit Cards** Visa, Master **Facilities** Restaurant, swimming pool, gym, children's park, beauty parlour, laundry, Internet, travel desk, indoor games, attached bath, TV

Hotel Golden Eye SEA-FACING

Location Beachside **Address** Gaura Vaddo, Calangute, Bardez **Telefax** 2277308 **Website** hotelgoldeneye.com **Rooms** 26 **Tariff** Rs 500-3,500 **Credit Cards** NA **Facilities** Restaurant, bar, travel desk, gift shop, book shop, forex, lockers, Internet, doctor-on-call, laundry, room service, TV

Johnny's Hotel YOGA

Location Beachside **Address** Cobra Vaddo, Calangute **Tel** 2277458 **Email** johnny_hotel@yahoo.com **Rooms** 12 **Tariff** Rs 350-800 **Credit Cards** NA **Facilities** Restaurant, bar, yoga, massage parlour, car rental, TV

Kerkar Retreat

Location Near beach **Address** Kerkar Art Complex, Holiday St, Gaura Vaddo **Tel** 2276017, 2282691 **Website** subodhkerkar.com **Rooms** 5 **Tariff** Rs 1,500-4,500 **Credit Cards** Visa, Master **Facilities** Restaurant, bar, café, library, open-air auditorium, ceramic studio, art gallery, room service, kitchen facility

Mapple Viva Goa

Location Opp Calangute Panchayat Office **Address** Calangute **Tel** 2275220-24 **Website** mapplehotels.com **Rooms** 56 **Tariff** Rs 10,000-23,000 **Credit Cards** Visa, Master **Facilities** Restaurant, swimming pool, forex, bar, room service

Vila Goesa Beach Resort

Location Seashore **Address** Cobra Vaddo, Calangute **Tel** 2277535, 2281120 **Website** vilagoesa.com **Rooms** 79 **Tariff** Rs 1,520-2,400 **Credit Cards** Visa, Master **Facilities** Restaurant, pool, forex, room service

IN CANDOLIM

Bamboo Motel

Location Riverbank **Address** Verim, Betim, Bardez **Tel** 2401321-23 **Mobile** 09822158410 **Website** bamboo motels.com **Rooms** 50 **Tariff** Rs 600-1,500 **Credit Cards** Visa, Master **Facilities** Restaurant, bar, swimming pool, gym, disco, travel desk, room service, TV

Coqueiral Holiday Home

Location Near the beach **Address** Camotim Vaddo, Candolim Beach **Telefax** 2489070 **Website** coqueiral holiday.com **Rooms** 21 **Tariff** Rs 500-1,500 **Credit Cards** NA **Facilities** Restaurant, travel desk, airport transfers, forex, lockers, laundry, room service, TV

D'Mellos Guest House

Location Opp Labande Supermarket **Address** Escrivao Vaddo, Candolim, Bardez **Tel** 2489650/ 395 **Website** dmellos.com **Rooms** 15 **Tariff** Rs 300-500 **Credit Cards** NA **Facilities** Restaurant, Internet, travel desk, airport transfers, boating, lockers, laundry, room service, TV

Dona Florina SEA-FACING

Location Beachside **Address** Monterio's Road, Candolim **Tel** 2489051 **Website** donaflorina.com **Rooms** 21 **Tariff** Rs 650-1,000 **Credit Cards** NA **Facilities** Meals on order, travel assistance, airport transfers, bike rental, Ayurvedic massage, doctor-on-call, room service

Lemon Tree Amarante Beach Resort SPA

Location Near beach **Address** Vadi, Candolim, Bardez **Tel** 3988188 **Website** lemontreehotels.com **Rooms** 60 **Tariff** Rs 5,600-20,000 **Credit Cards** AmEx, Visa, Master **Facilities** Restaurant, bar, spa, swimming pool, water sports arranged

Marquis Beach Resort

Location Beachside **Address** Dando Vaddo, Candolim, Bardez **Tel** 2479120-22, 2479752 **Fax** 2479889 **Website** marquisgoa.com **Rooms** 30 **Tariff** Rs 7,999 (3N/2D package); TE **Credit Cards** AmEx, Visa, Master **Facilities** Restaurants, swimming pool, gym, Ayurvedic massage, travel desk, forex, locker, garment shop, laundry, TV

Per Avel Beach Holiday Home

Location Near the beach **Address** Opp Chapel and Govt Primary School, Fort Aguada Road, Dando, Candolim, Bardez **Tel** 2479074/ 233 **Website** peravelgoa.com **Rooms** 24 **Tariff** Rs 500-1,500 **Credit Cards** Visa, Master **Facilities** Restaurant, bar, laundry, room service

Sonesta Inns

Location Near beach **Address** Near St Jude's Chapel, Escrivao Vaddo, Candolim **Tel** 2489448-49/ 540 **Website** sonestainns.com **Rooms** 52 **Tariff** Rs 1,500-12,500; TE **Credit Cards** AmEx, Visa, Master, BoB **Facilities** Restaurant, bar, café, gym, swimming pool, travel desk, forex, lockers, room service, TV

Taj Aguada Hermitage GOLF

Location Near beach **Address** Sinquerim, Bardez **Tel** 6645858 **Website** tajhotels.com **Rooms** 15 villas **Tariff** Rs 10,000-44,000; TE **Credit Cards** AmEx, Visa, Master, Diners **Facilities** Restaurants, bar, golf, Ayurvedic treatments, travel desk, sightseeing, swimming pool, spa, health club, water sports, TV

Taj Fort Aguada Beach Resort

WATER SPORTS SPA GOLF

Location Near beach **Address** Sinquerim, Bardez **Tel** 6645858 **Website** tajhotels.com **Rooms** 144, suites 24 **Tariff** Rs 9,000-44,000; TE **Credit Cards** AmEx, Visa, Master, Diners **Facilities** Restaurants, bar, golf, Ayurvedic treatments, swimming pool, spa, health club, water sports, TV

Taj Holiday Village SPA

Location Near the beach **Address** CHOGM Road, Sinquerim, Bardez **Tel** 6645858 **Website** tajhotels.com **Rooms** 142, suites 9 **Tariff** Rs 11,000-27,000 **Credit Cards** AmEx, Visa, Master **Facilities** Restaurant, bar, spa, beauty parlour, forex, travel desk, TV

Whispering Palms Beach Resort

Location Beachside **Address** Sinquerim Beach, Candolim **Tel** 2479140-41/ 428-30 **Website** whisperingpalms.com **Rooms** 106 **Tariff** Rs 6,800-15,000 (3N/4D with breakfast); TE **Credit Cards** AmEx, Visa, Master **Facilities** Restaurants, coffee shop, bar, swimming pool, gym, travel desk, airport transfers, bike rental, forex, lockers, TV

MANDREM STD 0832

Dunes Holiday Village YOGA

Location Near beach **Address** Junas Vaddo, Mandrem Beach **Tel** 2247071/ 219 **Fax** 2247375 **Website** dunesgoa.com **Rooms** 25 huts **Tariff** Rs 500-600 **Credit Cards** NA **Facilities** Restaurant, yoga, laundry, taxi service, attached bath, TV

TIP Beach shack and deck beds in season

Elsewhere – Otter Creek Tents

Address Mandrem Beach **Website** aseascape.com **Rooms** 3 tents **Tariff** Rs 20,800 per week **Credit Cards** Visa, Master **Facilities** Cook, housekeeper, car/ driver on request, laundry **Mumbai Reservations Email** gaze@aseascape.com

TIP Minimum 7 nights' booking

Elsewhere – The Beach Houses

Address Mandrem Beach **Website** aseascape.com **Rooms** 4 beach houses (2-3 rooms each) **Tariff** Rs 40,000 upwards per week **Credit Cards** Visa, Master

Facilities Cook, housekeeper, car/ driver on request, laundry **Mumbai Reservations** *See Otter Creek Tents alongside*
TIP Minimum 7 nights' booking

Mandrem Beach Resort
Location Sea-facing **Address** Junas Vaddo, Mandrem, Pernem **Tel** 2247115/ 608 **Website** prazeresresorts.com/mresort.htm **Rooms** 25 **Tariff** Rs 700-2,200; TE **Credit Cards** Visa, Master **Facilities** Restaurant, bar, laundry, lockers, room service

Riva Beach Resort
Location Beachside **Address** Next to Dunes Resort, Mandrem Beach **Tel** 2247088/ 612 **Website** rivaresorts.com **Rooms** 55, tree houses 5 **Tariff** Rs 500-2,000 **Credit Cards** Visa, Master **Facilities** Restaurant, pub, forex, lockers, massage centre, Internet, airport transfers **Mumbai Reservations Tel** 022-28953709 **Mobile** 09869205113

Vailankanni Guest House SEA-FACING
Location Near beach **Address** Junas Vaddo, Arambol Road, Mandrem Beach **Tel** 2247542 **Mobile** 09422394823 **Rooms** 11 **Tariff** Rs 250-500 **Credit Cards** NA **Facilities** Restaurant, car rental, lockers, boat/ bike renting, dolphin-spotting, room service

ON ASHWEM BEACH

Hotel Nifa YOGA
Location Near beach **Address** H. No. 747, New Vaddo, Morjim **Tel** 2244400, 2264195 **Mobile** 09422442580, 09822133370 **Website** hotelnifa.com **Rooms** 9 **Tariff** Rs 1,000-2,800 **Credit Cards** Visa, Master **Facilities** Restaurant, bar, Ayurvedic massage, yoga, meditation, Internet, travel desk, room service
TIP Non-smoking guests only

Papa Jolly's Goa SEA-FACING
Location Near beach **Address** House No. 741, New Vaddo, Morjim-Ashwem Road, Morjim, Pernem Taluka **Tel** 2244113-14 **Mobile** 09822103780 **Website** papajollysgoa.com **Rooms** 12 **Tariff** Rs 3,080-4,400 **Credit Cards** AmEx, Visa, Master **Facilities** Restaurant, bar, swimming pool, Ayurvedic massage, yoga, meditation, Internet, airport transfers, lockers, laundry, room service, TV **Reservations Mobile** 09822589960

Sunset Point Hotel SEA-FACING
Location Near beach **Address** Ashwem **Tel** 2273447 **Mobile** 09822175917, 09923943151 **Email** albeno27@yahoo.co.in **Rooms** 6 tree houses **Tariff** Rs 400-800 **Credit Cards** NA **Facilities** Restaurant, doctor-on-call, room service, shared toilets

ON MORJIM BEACH

Lobo's Paradise
Location Beachside **Address** Goan Café, Vithaldas Vaddo, Morjim **Tel** 2244394 **Mobile** 09822165100, 09823992442 **Email** anthonyslobo2015@yahoo.co.uk **Rooms** 2, huts 11, villas 4 **Tariff** Rs 450-800 **Credit Cards** AmEx, Visa, Master **Facilities** Restaurant, bike rental, travel desk, laundry, lockers, room service, hot water, attached bath only in some

Montego Bay Beach Village
Location Beachside **Address** Vithaldas Vaddo, Morjim, Pernem **Tel** 3290997 **Mobile** 09822150847 **Website** montegobaygoa.com **Rooms** 5, log cabins 5, tents 12, beach villa 1 **Tariff** Rs 1,650-8,500 **Credit Cards** Visa **Facilities** Restaurant, Internet, indoor games, travel desk, airport transfers, bike rental, room service, attached bath, TV

MIRAMAR-DONA PAULA STD 0832

IN BAMBOLIM STD 0832

Bambolim Beach Resort
Location Beachside **Address** Bambolim **Tel** 2458242-44/ 47-48 **Website** bambolimbeachresort.com **Rooms** 126 **Tariff** Rs 2,000-6,300 **Credit Cards** NA **Facilities** Restaurant, bar, coffee shop, Ayurvedic centre, swimming pool, gym, travel desk, airport transfers, forex, lockers, laundry, room service, TV

IN DONA PAULA

Cidade De Goa SEA-FACING
Location Beachfront **Address** Vainguinim Beach **Tel** 2454545 **Website** cidadedegoa.com **Rooms** 210 **Tariff** Rs 5,000-13,000 **Credit Cards** AmEx, Visa, Master, Diners, BoB **Facilities** Restaurants, bars, café, swimming pools, massage parlour, gym, travel desk, shopping arcade, TV **Mumbai Reservations** 32-33, Mittal Chambers, Mumbai **Tel** 022-22021717, 30617600

O Pescador Dona Paula Beach Resort SEA-FACING
Location Beachfront **Address** Near Dona Paula Jetty **Tel** 2453863-64 **Fax** 2453861 **Website** opescador.com **Rooms** 20 **Tariff** Rs 900-3,800 **Credit Cards** Visa, Master **Facilities** Restaurant, bar, swimming pool, travel desk, forex, room service

Prainha Cottages SEA-FACING
Location Beachside **Address** Near SBI **Tel** 2453881-83 **Fax** 2453884 **Website** prainha.com **Rooms** 45 **Tariff** Rs 600-6,000 **Credit Cards** AmEx, Visa, Master, Diners **Facilities** Restaurant, bar, swimming pool, Internet, travel desk, forex

Villa Sol
Location Near Cidade De Goa **Address** Ashwin Resorts Pvt Ltd, Dona Paula **Tel** 2453052 **Fax** 2453144 **Rooms** 28 **Tariff** Rs 750-3,500 **Credit Cards** Visa, Master **Facilities** Restaurant, bar, pool, travel desk, room service

IN MIRAMAR

Goa Marriott Resort SPA
Location Beachside **Address** Miramar Beach, Panjim **Tel** 2463333 **Website** marriott.com **Rooms** 178 **Tariff** Rs 12,400-23,000; TE **Credit Cards** AmEx, Visa, Master, Diners **Facilities** Restaurants, bars, swimming pool, spa, gym, water sports, lockers, room service, TV

Miramar Residency GTDC
Location Beachside **Address** Miramar Beach, Panjim **Tel** 2464154 **Fax** 2423926 **Website** goa-tourism.com **Rooms** 60 **Tariff** Rs 950-1,750; TE **Credit Cards** Visa, Master **Facilities** Restaurant, bar, tours organised, lockers, room service **Metro Reservations** *See page 518*

Swim Sea Beach Resort
Location Near St Rosary Chapel **Address** Caranzalem Beach, Dona Paula **Tel** 2464481-83 **Fax** 2464480 **Rooms** 29 **Tariff** Rs 1,400-1,904 **Credit Cards** Visa, Master **Facilities** Restaurants, bar, swimming pool, travel desk, forex, lockers, doctor-on-call, laundry, room service, hot water, TV **Mumbai Reservations** Merry Go Round, Bandra, Mumbai **Tel** 022-26435252

VAGATOR STD 0832

Diana Buildwell Resorts
Location Near Chapora Fort **Address** Vagator Beach, Vagator **Tel** 2274470-01, 2273276 **Email** vinaygupta2@indiabulls.com **Website** indiabulls.com **Rooms** 62 **Tariff** Rs 3,000 **Credit Cards** AmEx, Visa, Master **Facilities** Restaurant, bar, swimming pool, laundry, room service, TV

Dolrina Guest House
Location Near beach **Address** House No. 536/1, Vagator **Tel** 2273382, 2274896 **Mobile** 09822980447 **Website** goa-world.com/dolrina **Rooms** 25 **Tariff** Rs 200-700 **Credit Cards** NA **Facilities** Café, car rental, lockers, library, room service

Helinda's Guest House
Location Near Chapora Market **Address** Bondir Vaddo, PO Chapora, Anjuna **Tel** 2274345 **Rooms** 10 **Tariff** Rs 300-350 **Credit Cards** NA **Facilities** Restaurant, bar, car rental, sight-seeing, laundry, attached bath

Jolly Jolly Lester Guest House
Location Near beach **Address** Beach Road, Vagator Beach **Tel** 2273620, 2274897 **Mobile** 09822488536 **Website** hoteljollygoa.com **Rooms** 11 **Tariff** Rs 200-1,800 **Credit Cards** NA **Facilities** Food on order, travel desk, money transfers, lockers, laundry, TV

Jolly Jolly Roma Guest House
Location Near beach **Address** Vagator **Tel** 2273001 **Website** hoteljollygoa.com **Rooms** 8 **Tariff** Rs 200-1,800 **Credit Cards** NA **Facilities** Food on order, travel desk, money transfers, lockers, TV

Julie Jolly Guest House
Location Vagator Village **Address** Vagator **Tel** 2273357 **Website** hoteljollygoa.com

Rooms 19 **Tariff** Rs 200-1,800 **Credit Cards** NA **Facilities** Food on order, travel desk, money transfers, lockers, laundry, TV

Le Bluebird
Location Near beach **Address** Small Vagator, Anjuna, Bardez **Tel** 2273695 **Mobile** 09822587056 **Rooms** 5 **Tariff** Rs 800-3,000 **Facilities** Restaurant, bar, TV

Shettor Villa Guest House
Location Opp Holy Cross **Address** Chapora-Anjuna **Tel** 2274335, 2273766 **Rooms** 15 **Tariff** Rs 100-300 **Facilities** Restaurant, bar, travel assistance, laundry, room service

SOUTH GOA

BOGMALO STD 0832

Bogmalo Beach Resort
SEA-FACING

Location Beachside **Address** PO Bogmalo **Tel** 2538222-35 **Fax** 2538236 **Website** tulipstar.com **Rooms** 123 **Tariff** Rs 6,000-10,000; TE **Credit Cards** AmEx, Visa, Master, BoB, Diners **Facilities** Restaurant, gym, pool, laundry, travel desk, room service

Coconut Creek Hotel
Location Near beach **Address** Bimut Ward, Bogmalo **Tel** 2538090/ 100/ 800 **Fax** 2538880 **Email** coconutcreek@dataone.in **Rooms** 20 **Tariff** Rs 4,500-9,500 **Credit Cards** Visa, Master **Facilities** Restaurant, bar, gym, swimming pool, forex, Internet, room service, TV **Bangalore Reservations** Hammock Leisure Holidays, 314/1, FF, 7th Cross, Domlur Layout, Bangalore **Tel** 080-25351555

Joet's Guest House
Location Beachside **Address** Bogmalo Beach **Tel** 2538036 **Mobile** 09860765337 **Email** joets@sancharnet.in **Rooms** 7 **Tariff** Rs 2,750 **Credit Cards** Visa, Master **Facilities** Restaurant, bar, travel assistance, doctor-on-call, forex, lockers

Raj Resorts
WATER SPORTS

Location Opp Naval Aviation Museum **Address** Bogmalo Beach Road, Dabolim **Tel** 2538177/ 688 **Mobile** 09823233525 **Website** rajresorts-goa.com **Rooms** 18 **Tariff** Rs 1,200-4,400 **Credit Cards** Visa, Master **Facilities** Restaurants, bar, water sports, swimming pool, health club, sightseeing, forex, Internet, room service, TV

Sarita Guest House
Location Beachside **Address** Bogmalo Beach **Tel** 2538965/ 888 **Mobile** 09890134533 **Email** saritasguesthouse@rediffmail.com **Rooms** 13 **Tariff** Rs 1,100-2,000; TE **Facilities** Restaurant, sightseeing, Internet, laundry, room service, TV

COLVA STD 0832

ON BENAULIM BEACH

Carina Beach Resort
Location Near Palm Group **Address** Vas Vaddo, Benaulim **Tel** 2770413-14 **Website** carinabeachresort.com **Rooms** 32 **Tariff** Rs 800-1,600 **Credit Cards** NA **Facilities** Restaurant, bar, swimming pool, forex, lockers

Hotel Failaka
Location Near Maria Hall **Address** Adsulim Nagar **Tel** 2771270/ 865 **Mobile** 09822133048 **Email** hotelfailaka@hotmail.com **Rooms** 16 **Tariff** Rs 600-850; TE **Credit Cards** NA **Facilities** Restaurant, bar, travel desk, room service

O Palmar
Location Beachside **Address** Benaulim Beach **Tel** 2770631, 2771836-37 **Email** opalmar1@dataone.in **Rooms** 22 **Tariff**

Rs 550-700 **Credit Cards** NA **Facilities** Room service, attached bath, hot water

Rosario Inn
Location Opp football ground **Address** 1611 (A), Vas Vaddo, Benaulim **Tel** 2770636 **Mobile** 09822685887 **Email** rosarioinn@sify.com **Rooms** 30 **Tariff** Rs 250-400 **Credit Cards** NA **Facilities** Restaurant, bar, lockers, laundry, room service

Taj Exotica Goa AYURVEDA
Location Beachside **Address** Benaulim Beach, Cal Vaddo, Salcette **Tel** 2771234 **Website** tajhotels.com **Rooms** 140 **Tariff** Rs 5,500-18,500 **Credit Cards** AmEx, Visa, Master, BoB, Diners **Facilities** Restaurants, fresh fruit bar, coffee shop, swimming pool, gym, Ayurvedic spa, yoga, water sports, travel desk, library

ON COLVA BEACH

Colva Residency GTDC
Location Beachside **Address** Colva Beach, Salcette **Tel** 2788047-48 **Website** goa-tourism.com **Rooms** 47 **Tariff** Rs 550-1,600; TE **Credit Cards** AmEx, Visa, Master, BoB, Diners **Facilities** Restaurant, bar, Ayurvedic centre, room service **Metro Reservations** *See page 518*

Hotel Colmar
Location Beachside **Address** Colva Beach, Salcette **Tel** 2788043/ 53 **Fax** 2788134 **Rooms** 131 **Tariff** Rs 400-2,000 **Credit Cards** NA **Facilities** Restaurants, bar, swimming pool, lockers, forex, room service

Longuinhos Beach Resort
Location Sea-facing **Address** Colva Beach, Salcette **Tel** 2788068-69 **Website** longuinhos.net **Rooms** 52 **Tariff** Rs 2,200-3,000; TE **Credit Cards** AmEx, Visa, Master, BoB, Diners **Facilities** Restaurants, swimming pool, Ayurvedic massage, dance floor, forex, lockers, travel desk, TV

Lucky Star SEA-FACING
Location Beachside **Address** Near Longuinhos Beach Resort, Colva Beach **Tel** 2788071 **Email** pradorbaradpopcorn@hotmail.com **Rooms** 14 **Tariff** Rs 200-600 **Credit Cards** NA **Facilities** Restaurant, travel assistance, lockers, forex, attached bath

Star Beach Resort AYURVEDA
Location Beachside **Address** Near Football Ground, 4th Ward, Colva Beach, Salcette **Tel** 2780092/ 8166 **Website** starbeachresortgoa.com **Rooms** 72 **Tariff** Rs 600-3,400 **Credit Cards** Visa, Master **Facilities** Restaurant, swimming pool, Ayurvedic treatment, forex, lockers, travel desk, room service

Sukhsagar Beach Resort
Location Beachside **Address** Colva Beach **Tel** 2788887-88 **Website** sukhsagargoa.com **Rooms** 19 **Tariff** Rs 400-1,450; TE **Credit Cards** Visa, Master **Facilities** Restaurant, bar, travel assistance, doctor-on-call, laundry, room service

IN MOBOR-CAVELOSSIM

Dona Sa Maria
Location Near Ramada Caravela Resort **Address** Tamborim, Cavelossim, Salcette **Tel** 2745290/ 672 **Website** donasamaria.com **Rooms** 27 **Tariff** Rs 500-1,000 **Credit Cards** NA **Facilities** Restaurant, bar, swimming pool, travel desk, forex, laundry, room service

Dona Sylvia Beach Resort
Location Beachside **Address** Cavelossim Beach, Mobor **Tel** 2871888 **Website** donasylvia.com **Rooms** 181 **Tariff** Rs 13,500-18,000 (3N/4D) **Facilities** Restaurants, bars, gym, swimming pool, water sports, Ayurvedic centre, disco, TV

Gaffino's Beach Resort
Location Next to Haathi Mahal Resort **Address** Cavelossim Beach, Salcette **Tel** 2871441 **Email** briangaffino@yahoo.com **Rooms** 16 **Tariff** Rs 1,200-1,500; TE **Credit Cards** NA **Facilities** Restaurant, bar, forex, locker, laundry, room service

Gato Loco Motel Health Resort
Location Near beach **Address** Mad Cat Club, Mobor Beach, Cavelossim **Mobile** 09823066709, 09822489265 **Email** virginia_sinoes2004@yahoo.co.in **Rooms** 6 **Tariff** Rs 500-1,200 **Credit Cards** NA **Facilities** Restaurant, bar, Ayurvedic treatment, meditation, yoga, naturopathy, room service

Holiday Inn Resort YOGA
Location On Mobor Beach **Address** Mobor, Cavelossim, Salcette **Tel** 2871303-09 **Website** holidayinngoa.com **Rooms** 203 **Tariff** Rs 4,000-15,000 **Credit Cards** AmEx, Visa, Master, BoB **Facilities** Restaurants, coffee shop, bar, yoga centre, Ayurvedic massage centre, gym, travel desk, forex, lockers, laundry, room service, TV **Mumbai Reservations** 21 Nimbus Centre, Off Andheri Link Road, Andheri (West), Mumbai **Tel** 022-55026988, 26300466

Mobor Beach Resort
Location Beachside **Address**

Mobor, Cavelossim **Tel** 2871729/ 167 **Mobile** 09823197317, 09823156241 **Website** mobor beachresort.net **Rooms** 25 **Tariff** Rs 1,000-2,500 **Credit Cards** Visa, Master **Facilities** Restaurant, bar, pub, swimming pool, shopping mall, Ayurvedic massage, lockers, forex, TV

Old Anchor

Location Near beach **Address** Cavelossim Beach **Tel** 2871180-82 **Website** dalmiaresorts.com **Rooms** 130 **Tariff** Rs 4,500-14,500 **Credit Cards** Visa, Master **Facilities** Restaurant, bar, café, swimming pool, gym, forex, lockers, room service, TV

The Leela Palace

WATER SPORTS GOLF

Location Beachfront **Address** Mobor Beach, Cavelossim, Salcette **Tel** 2871234 **Website** theleela.com **Rooms** 152 **Tariff** Rs 9,000-28,000 **Credit Cards** AmEx, Visa, Master **Facilities** Restaurants, bar, gaming club, swimming pool, water sports, Ayurvedic massage, golf, lockers

ON SERNABATIM BEACH

Baywatch Resort SPA

Location Beachside **Address** Sernabatim, Salcette **Tel** 6697777 **Website** baywatch resort.in **Rooms** 80 **Tariff** Rs 4,500-6,750 **Credit Cards** Visa, Master **Facilities** Restaurant, bar, swimming pool, gym, spa, room service, TV **Pune Reservations** Baywatch Resort, D-19, Vatsalya Nagari, S. No. 82, Eklavya Polytechnic Road, Kothrud, Pune **Tel** 020-25396723 **Mobile** 09325404947

Furtado's Beach House

Location Beachside **Address** Near Dominic's Travel Agency, Sernabatim Beach, Colva **Tel** 2770396 **Rooms** 12 **Tariff** Rs 800-1,500 **Credit Cards** NA **Facilities** Restaurant, bar, laundry, room service

Quinsan Cottage

Location Beachside **Address** Sernabatim Beach, Colva **Tel** 2771490 **Rooms** 11, cottages 5 **Tariff** Rs 400-1,000 **Credit Cards** NA **Facilities** Cook available, travel assistance, laundry, room service

IN VARCA-FATRADE

Club Mahindra Varca Beach Resort WATER SPORTS

Location Varca Beach **Address** Survey No. 176/1, Varca Village **Tel** 2744555/ 60 **Website** club mahindra.com **Rooms** 168 **Tariff** Rs 4,500-11,000 **Credit Cards** AmEx, Visa, Master, Diners, BoB **Facilities** Restaurants, swimming pools, water sports, gym, Internet, Ayurvedic massage **Mumbai Reservations** Mahindra Holidays & Resorts India Limited, No. 771, 7th Bldg, Solitaire Corporate Park, 167, Guru Hargovindji Marg, Andheri-Ghatkopar Link Road, Chakala, Andheri (East), Mumbai **Tel** 022-40006465 **Fax** 40006464

Colonia Jose Menino Resort

Location Near beach **Address** Fatrade, Varca **Tel** 2745791 **Email** kylesal@sancharnet.in **Website** saldanhaholidays.com **Rooms** 45 **Tariff** Rs 600-2,800 **Credit Cards** Visa **Facilities** Restaurant, bar, swimming pool **Mumbai Reservations** Kylesal Holidays Pvt Ltd, 5/16 Pavan Palace, Station Road, Mahim, Mumbai **Tel** 022-24314301

Goa Beach House

Location Next to Varca Palms **Address** 641-A, Cobia-Pedda, Fatrade, Varca **Tel** 2744111-12 **Mobile** 09810040042 **Website** goabeachhouse.com, goabeach house.co.in **Rooms** 10, cottages 5 **Tariff** Rs 4,500-5,500; TE

Credit Cards Visa, Master **Facilities** Restaurant, bar, pool, travel desk, Ayurvedic massage, forex, room service, TV **Delhi Reservations** 608-B, Madhuban Building, 55 Nehru Place, New Delhi **Tel** 011-26424275-77, Toll Free No. 1800111177

Ramada Caravela Beach Resort

WATER SPORTS YOGA GOLF

Location Beachfront **Address** Varca Beach, Village Fatrade **Tel** 2745200-15 **Website** caravelabeachresort.com **Rooms** 202, suites 4, villas 6 **Tariff** Rs 4,300-34,625; TE **Credit Cards** AmEx, Visa, Master, Diners **Facilities** Restaurants, casino, swimming pool, spa, Ayurvedic centre, yoga, gym, water sports, golf, forex, room service **Mumbai Reservations** Advani Hotels & Resorts (India) Ltd, 1009-10, Dalamal Towers, 211, Nariman Point, Mumbai **Tel** 022-22850101

Varca Palms Beach Resort

Location Near beach **Address** Teen Murti, Fatrade, PO Varca, Salcette **Tel** 2745411-13 **Website** ushalexushotels.com **Rooms** 56 **Tariff** Rs 4,000-6,000; TE **Credit Cards** Visa, Master **Facilities** Restaurant, bar, beach shack, swimming pool, bike rental, forex, room service, TV

PALOLEM STD 0832

Bridge and Tunnel

Location On beach **Address** Palolem Beach, Dr SR Naikgaonkar Road, Canacona **Tel** 2639311, 2643262 **Mobile** 09822584968 **Email** shoumirs@rediffmail.com **Rooms** 16 cottages **Tariff** Rs 600-4,000 **Credit Cards** NA **Facilities** Restaurant, bar, laundry, room service, attached bath, hot water

Ciaran's SEA-FACING

Location Beachside **Address** Palolem Beach, Canacona **Tel** 2643477 **Website** ciarans.com **Rooms** 3, huts 18 **Tariff** Rs 2,000-2,500 **Credit Cards** Visa, Master **Facilities** Restaurant, bar, forex, library, shop

Cozy Nook

Location Beachside **Address** Palolem Beach, Canacona **Tel** 2643550 **Rooms** 24 huts **Tariff** Rs 500-1,500 **Credit Cards** NA **Facilities** Restaurant, bar, room service, attached bath

Hi-Tide Coco Beach Huts

Location Beachside **Address** Palolem Beach, Canacona **Tel** 2643104, 2644550 **Website** goaunplugged.com/hitide.html **Rooms** 19 huts, 5 cottages **Tariff** Rs 350-1,500 **Credit Cards** NA **Facilities** Restaurant, bar, lockers, attached bath, hot water on request

Neptune Point Beach Resort

Location Beachside **Address** Palolem-Colomb Beach, Canacona **Tel** 2639547 **Mobile** 09822584968 **Email** neptunepoint01@rediffmail.com **Rooms** 27 **Tariff** Rs 500-2,500 **Credit Cards** NA **Facilities** Restaurant, bar, travel assistance, lockers, laundry, room service

Palolem Beach Resort

Location Near beach **Address** Palolem Beach, Canacona **Tel** 2643054, 2644094 **Email** sunila@sancharnet.in **Rooms** 13 **Tariff** Rs 400-1,000 **Credit Cards** NA **Facilities** Restaurant, massage centre, lockers, forex

IN AGONDA

Dercy's

Location Near beach **Address** Agonda Beach, Tamdem, Canacona **Tel** 2647503 **Rooms** 9, huts 10 **Tariff** Rs 250-400 **Credit Cards** NA **Facilities** Restaurant, bar, travel desk, room service, attached bath, TV

Dunhill Beach Resort

SEA-FACING

Location Near beach **Address** Agonda Beach **Tel** 2647328 **Email** dunhill_resort@rediffmail.com **Rooms** 12 **Tariff** Rs 400-450 **Credit Cards** NA **Facilities** Restaurant, bar, travel desk, airport transfers, forex, lockers, attached bath, hot water

Eldfra Beach Guest House

Location Beachside **Address** Val Aframento, Agonda, Canacona **Tel** 2647378 **Mobile** 09421251230 **Rooms** 10 **Tariff** Rs 200-500 **Credit Cards** NA **Facilities** Restaurant, bar, travel assistance, airport transfers, forex, lockers, laundry, room service, attached bath

Forget Me Not

Location Beachfront **Address** Agonda Beach **Mobile** 09421243541 **Rooms** 9, huts 7 **Tariff** Rs 400-1,500 **Credit Cards** Visa, Master **Facilities** Restaurant, laundry, attached bath

Palm Beach Lifestyle Resort

Location Near beach **Address** Tamdem, Agonda **Tel** 2647783 **Mobile** 09422450380 **Website** palmbeachgoa.com **Rooms** 9 cottages **Tariff** Rs 900-1,200 **Credit Cards** NA **Facilities** Restaurant, bar, travel desk, airport transfers, forex, lockers, room service, attached bath

Sunset Beach Guest House

Location Near St Anna Church **Address** Val Aframento, Agonda

Tel 2647381 **Rooms** 9 **Tariff** Rs 300-500 **Credit Cards** NA **Facilities** Restaurant, bar, travel desk, lockers, room service, attached bath, hot water

IN COLOMB

Bhakti Kutir YOGA

Location On a hillock **Address** 296 Colomb, Palolem, Canacona **Tel** 2643469/ 72 **Website** bhaktikutir.com **Rooms** 22 cabanas **Tariff** Rs 900-3,000; TE **Credit Cards** NA **Facilities** Restaurant, healing centre, yoga, handicrafts shop, lockers, pool table, airport transfers, laundry, kitchen, mosquito nets

Boom Shankar

Location On a bay **Address** Colomb Beach, Canacona **Mobile** 09822384634 **Rooms** 21 **Tariff** Rs 500-2,000 **Credit Cards** NA **Facilities** Restaurant, bar, attached bath

Tree Shanti Guest House

Location Beach-facing **Address** Colomb Beach **Tel** 2644460 **Mobile** 09822140487 **Email** saritageeta7A@rediffmail. com **Rooms** 7 **Tariff** Rs 150-300 **Credit Cards** NA **Facilities** Restaurant, bar, beauty parlour, common bath, hot water

IN PATNEM

Namaste Guest House

Location Beachside **Address** Patnem Beach, Canacona **Tel** 2643688 **Rooms** 6 huts **Tariff** Rs 150-200 **Credit Cards** NA **Facilities** Restaurant, bar, pool

Oceanic Resort

Location Near beach **Address** Tembi Vaddo, Canacona **Tel** 2643059 **Website** hotel-oceanic. com **Rooms** 6 **Tariff** Rs 1,500-3,500 **Credit Cards** NA **Facilities** Restaurant, bar, swimming pool, lockers, laundry, room service, attached bath, hot water

Sea View Resort

Location Near beach **Address** Patnem Beach, Canacona **Tel** 2643110/ 534 **Email** seaview_1@hotmail.com **Rooms** 32 **Tariff** Rs 250-3,000 **Credit Cards** NA **Facilities** Restaurant, bar, Internet, massage centre, room service, attached bath

Solitude SEA-FACING YOGA

Location Beachside **Address** Near Grand Intercontinental Hotel, Patnem Beach, Canacona **Tel** 2711186, 6471530 **Mobile** 09422643363 **Rooms** 20 cabanas **Tariff** Rs 1,500-2,000 **Credit Cards** NA **Facilities** Restaurant, yoga centre, massage parlour, forex, attached bath

ON RAJBAGA BEACH

InterContinental The Grand Goa Resort SEA-FACING GOLF

Location Beachfront **Address** Raj Baga Beach, Canacona **Tel** 2667777 **Fax** 2667711 **Website** thegrandhotels.net **Rooms** 255 **Tariff** 17,000-1,40,000 **Credit Cards** AmEx, Visa, Master **Facilities** Restaurants, bars, golf course, health club, swimming pool, water sports, Ayurvedic massage, car rental

VELSAO STD 0832

IN AROSSIM

Heritage Village Club SPA

Location Near beach **Address** Arossim Beach, Arossim, Cansaulim **Tel** 2754956-60, 6694444 **Website** selecthotels. co.in **Rooms** 100 **Tariff** Rs 17,500-26,250 (3N/4D) **Credit Cards** Visa, Master **Facilities** Restaurants, bar, swimming pool, boutique, Ayurveda spa

Park Hyatt Goa Resort and Spa

Location Beachside **Address** Arossim Beach, Cansaulim **Tel** 2721234 **Website** goa.park. hyatt.com **Rooms** 249 **Tariff** On request **Credit Cards** AmEx,

Visa, Master **Facilities** Restaurants, bars, juice bar, bakery, cinema, spa, swimming pool, travel desk, forex, taxis/ bicycles rental, room service

IN BETALBATIM

Coconut Grove, The Goan Beach Resort
Location Near beach **Address** Ran Vaddo, Betalbatim Beach, Salcette **Tel** 2880123/ 25 **Website** coconutgrovegoa.com **Rooms** 36, cottages 2 **Tariff** Rs 3,000-5,000 **Credit Cards** Visa, Master **Facilities** Restaurant, bar, pool, massage, travel desk, laundry, lockers, TV

Nanu Resorts AYURVEDA
Location Near beach **Address** Betalbatim Beach, Salcette **Tel** 2880111-19 **Website** nanuindia.com/home.htm **Rooms** 108 **Tariff** Rs 2,200-5,000 **Credit Cards** Visa, Master **Facilities** Restaurant, bar, swimming pool, travel desk, book shop, Ayurvedic clinic, room service **Mumbai Reservations** Shop No. 02, Dhanlaxmi Vihar, Nandapatkar Road, Vile Parle (East), Mumbai **Mobile** 09892766959, 09833124524

IN MAJORDA

Majorda Beach Resort
WATER SPORTS AYURVEDA
Location Sea-facing **Address** Majorda Beach, Salcette **Tel** 2881111-20, 2754871-80 **Website** majordabeachresort.com **Rooms** 120, cottages 10 **Tariff** Rs 4,950-10,800 (with breakfast and air/rail transfers) **Credit Cards** AmEx, Visa, Master, BoB, Diners **Facilities** Restaurant, bar, swimming pools, casino with disco, gym, Ayurvedic massage, water sports **Mumbai Reservations** Majorda Sales Office, c/o Holiday Inn, Balraj Sahani Marg, Juhu, Mumbai **Tel** 022-56934010-13

Shangri La Retreat AYURVEDA
Location Near beach **Address** Majorda Beach, Salcette **Tel** 2881542/ 47 **Mobile** 09370566627 **Website** shangrilagoa.com **Rooms** 10 **Tariff** Rs 800-1,500 **Credit Cards** AmEx, Visa, Master **Facilities** Restaurant, bar, gym, Ayurvedic centre, locker, sightseeing, attached bath

IN UTORDA

Casa Ligorio Holiday Place
Location Near beach **Address** Utorda Beach, Utorda-Majorda, Salcette **Tel** 2755405 **Website** casaligorio.com **Rooms** 9 **Tariff** Rs 1,500-3,000 (with breakfast) **Credit Cards** NA **Facilities** Café, lockers, laundry, room service, TV

Kenilworth Beach Resort
SEA-FACING
Location Beachfront **Address** Utorda Beach, Salcette **Tel** 2755555, 2754180-84 **Fax** 2754183 **Website** kenilworthhotels.com **Rooms** 107 **Tariff** Rs 3,200-10,500; TE **Credit Cards** AmEx, Visa, Master, BoB, Diners **Facilities** Restaurant, bar, swimming pool, Ayurvedic centre, spa, water sports, forex

GUJARAT

MANDVI BEACH STD 02834

Hotel Sea View
Location Near beach **Address** Jain Dharamsala Road **Tel** 224481 **Mobile** 09825376063 **Rooms** 13 **Tariff** Rs 400-1,500 **Credit Cards** NA **Facilities** Breakfast provided, handicrafts showroom, travel desk, lockers, laundry, room service, TV

Mandvi Beach Camp TENTS
Location Beachside **Address** Vijay Vilas Palace Complex **Tel** 295725 **Mobile** 09879013118 **Website** mandvibeach.com **Rooms** 10 tents **Tariff** Rs 11,000 (2N/3D with meals package) **Credit Cards** NA **Facilities** Restaurant, massage, travel desk, camel/ horse rides, private beach, laundry, room service

Royal Inn Guest House
Location Beachside **Address** Vijay Vilas Palace Complex **Tel** 295725 **Rooms** 4 **Tariff** Rs 2,500 **Credit Cards** NA **Facilities** Food arranged at Mandvi Beach Camp, attached bath, hot water

KARNATAKA

GOKARNA STD 08386

ON KUDLE BEACH

Gokarna International Beach Resort
Location Near Uma Maheshwar Temple **Address** Kudle Beach **Tel** 257843, 256622 **Email** hotelgokarna@yahoo.com **Rooms** 10 **Tariff** Rs 500-900 **Credit Cards** NA **Facilities** Restaurant, laundry, taxi arranged, room service, attached bath, hot water

ON OM BEACH

SwaSwara Resort AYURVEDA
Location Beachside **Address** Donibail, Om Beach **Tel** 257131-33, 257845-46 **Website** swaswara.com **Rooms** 24 villas **Tariff** Rs 8,500-16,500 (with meals); TE **Credit Cards** AmEx, Visa, Master **Facilities** Restaurant, Ayurveda centre, yoga, swimming pool, birding, kayaking and archery in season, treks, interactive kitchen, room service **Kochi Reservations** CGH Earth, Casino Building, Willingdon

Island, Kochi **Tel** 0484-2668221, 2666821 **Website** cghearth.com

IN TOWN

Hotel Gokarna International
Location Near bus stand **Address** Main Road **Tel** 256622, 257368 **Fax** 256848 **Email** hotelgokarna@yahoo.com **Rooms** 43 **Tariff** Rs 200-700 **Credit Cards** NA **Facilities** Restaurant, laundry, room service, attached bath, hot water

Hotel Om
Location Near bus stand **Address** Ganjigadde **Tel** 256445/ 244 **Website** hotelom.co.in **Rooms** 23 **Tariff** Rs 150-800 **Credit Cards** NA **Facilities** Restaurant, bar, forex, room service, attached bath

Hotel Shivaprasad
Location Near Checkpost **Address** Melinakeri, Gokarna Main Road **Tel** 257032, 256828 **Mobile** 09448722928 **Rooms** 16 **Tariff** Rs 300-900 **Credit Cards** NA **Facilities** Restaurant, travel/ taxi/ sightseeing arranged, room service, attached bath, hot water

Hotel Shri Sai Ram
Location Near bus stand **Address** Nityananda Nivas, Car Street **Tel** 257755 **Rooms** 12 **Tariff** Rs 350-800 **Credit Cards** NA **Facilities** Restaurant, laundry, travel/ taxi/ sightseeing arranged, room service, attached bath

Om Beach Resort AYURVEDA
Location Near beach **Address** Bungle Gudde, Om Beach Road **Tel** 257052/ 718 **Website** ombeachresort.com **Rooms** 12 **Tariff** Rs 1,800 per person (with meals) **Credit Cards** AmEx, Visa, Master **Facilities** Restaurant, Ayurvedic centre, lockers, forex, Internet, taxi/ sightseeing arranged, room service, TV

Seabird Holiday Resort
Location Near beach **Address** Bungle Gudde, Om Beach Road **Tel** 257689 **Mobile** 09980577488 **Website** greenleaveshospitality.com **Rooms** 21 **Tariff** Rs 1,250-1,500 **Credit Cards** AmEx, Visa, Master **Facilities** Restaurant, laundry, swimming pool, travel desk, taxi/ sightseeing arranged, room service, attached bath, TV

KARWAR STD 08382

Bhadra/Kiran Deluxe Hotel
Address Near Kali Bridge, NH17, Uttara Canara Dist **Tel** 225212-13 **Fax** 227147 **Rooms** 36 **Tariff** Rs 250-1,250 **Credit Cards** AmEx, Visa, Master **Facilities** Restaurant, taxi arranged, parking, room service, TV

Hotel Navrathna
Location Central **Address** Main Road **Tel** 226176/ 927 **Rooms** 80 **Tariff** Rs 260-750; TE **Credit Cards** NA **Facilities** Parking, room service, attached bath, TV

Hotel Premier
Location Near Pikle Hospital **Address** Green Street **Tel** 229925-27 **Mobile** 09480356340 **Email** htlpremier@yahoo.com **Rooms** 20 **Tariff** Rs 500-950; TE **Credit Cards** AmEx, Visa, Master **Facilities** Restaurants, bar, laundry, sightseeing/ travel arranged, room service, TV

Hotel Sai International
Location Opp Hotel Navrathna **Address** Main Road **Tel** 229956 **Telefax** 229957 **Rooms** 21 **Tariff** Rs 350-1,200; TE **Credit Cards** NA **Facilities** Restaurant, laundry, sightseeing/ travel arranged, room service, attached bath, TV

IN DEVBAGH

Devbagh Beach Resort
Location Beachside **Address** Devbagh Beach **Tel** 221603 **Rooms** 4 cottages, 6 fishing

huts, 2 house boats, 8 log huts on stilts **Tariff** Rs 1,900-4,000 per person per night (with lunch, dinner, next day's breakfast and visit to another island) **Credit Cards** NA **Facilities** Buffet meals, snorkelling, parasailing, banana boating, guided trekking **Bangalore Reservations** Jungle Lodges and Resorts Ltd, SF, Shrungar Shopping Complex, MG Road, Bangalore **Tel** 080-25597021/ 24-25 **Website** junglelodges.com

IN HANKON

Riveredge Paradise Resort

TENTS WATER SPORTS

Location Near Kali River **Address** Hankon, Karwar Dist **Tel** 291180, 266742 **Website** paradiseadventureresorts.com **Rooms** 10 cottages, 8 tents **Tariff** Rs 1,250-1,750 per person per day (with meals and water sports) **Credit Cards** Visa, Master **Facilities** Restaurant, rafting, kayaking, canoeing, tubing for children, rock climbing, trekking, room service

ON KURUMGAD ISLAND

Great Outdoors Island Resort

TENTS WATER SPORTS

Address Kurumgad Island, Off the Karwar coast, Karwar **Tel** 655574 **Website** thegreatoutdoorsindia.com **Rooms** 4 cottages, 8 tents **Tariff** Rs 1,500-1,900 per person (with meals, taxes, boat transfers, guided island tours, fishing, trekking, dolphin-spotting) **Credit Cards** Visa, Master **Facilities** Restaurant, aqua/ adventure sports, Ayurvedic massage, boating **Reservations** Adjacent to Marine Engineers Office, NH 17, Bauttakatta, Baithkole, Karwar **Tel** 0824-4279152 **Mobile** 09844042152, 09448364152

ON SADASHIVGAD HILL

Estuary View Resort

WATER SPORTS AYURVEDA

Location Hillside **Address** Sadashivgad Hill, Karwar **Tel** 265988, 655277 **Mobile** 09449191749 **Website** estuaryviewresort.com **Rooms** 12 **Tariff** Rs 1,500-3,000 (with all meals) **Credit Cards** AmEx, Visa, Master **Facilities** Multi-cuisine restaurant, travel assistance, Internet, laundry, sightseeing, Ayurvedic therapies, river cruises, water sports in season, curio shop, private beach, TV **Delhi Reservations** Kairali Corporate Office, C-33 Panchsheel Enclave, New Delhi **Tel** 011-41748064/ 9800

MANGALORE STD 0824

Hotel Highland Residency

Location Opp Highland Hospital **Address** Millennium Towers, Kankanadi **Tel** 2433961-62 **Rooms** 19 **Tariff** Rs 300-1,200; TE **Credit Cards** NA **Facilities** Travel arranged, doctor-on-call, laundry, room service, attached bath, TV

Hotel Hindustan

Location Near old bus stand **Address** KS Rao Road, Hampanakatta **Tel** 2411333 **Mobile** 09845713961 **Rooms** 62 **Tariff** Rs 300-1,500; TE **Credit Cards** AmEx, Visa, Master **Facilities** Travel desk, sightseeing, laundry, sightseeing/ taxi arranged, room service, attached bath, TV

Hotel Hindustan Residency

Location Opp Service Bus Stand **Address** Stone Land Tower, Nehru Maidan, North Road **Tel** 2440743 **Rooms** 32 **Tariff** Rs 222-999; TE **Credit Cards** AmEx, Visa, Master **Facilities** Travel arranged, room service, attached bath, TV

Hotel Mangalore International

Location Near railway station **Address** Ayesha Towers, KS Rao Road, Hampanakatta **Tel** 2444860-64/ 57 **Fax** 2444859 **Rooms** 45 **Tariff** Rs 530-1,390; TE **Credit Cards** Visa, Master **Facilities** Restaurant, travel desk, room service, TV

Hotel Navarathna Palace

Location Near Hotel Poonja International **Address** KS Rao Road, Hampanakatta **Tel** 2441104/ 093 **Rooms** 72 **Tariff** Rs 410-891 **Credit Cards** AmEx, Visa, Master **Facilities** Travel arranged, parking, room service, attached bath, hot water, TV

Hotel New Topaz

Location Central **Address** KS Rao Road, Hampanakatta **Tel** 2441551, 2440463 **Mobile** 09945682603 **Rooms** 31 **Tariff** Rs 150-250; TE **Credit Cards** NA **Facilities** Travel arranged, parking, room service, attached bath, hot water, TV

Hotel Parkway

Location Near Old Bus Stand **Address** KS Rao Road, Hampanakatta **Tel** 2443961-63 **Mobile** 09845713961 **Rooms** 42 **Tariff** Rs 300-999; TE **Credit Cards** AmEx, Visa, Master **Facilities** Travel desk, laundry, sightseeing/ travel arranged, room service, attached bath, TV

Hotel Poonja International

Location Near railway station **Address** KS Rao Road, Hampankatta **Tel** 2440168 **Website** hotelpoonjainternational.com **Rooms** 104 **Tariff** Rs 700-3,000; TE **Credit**

Cards AmEx, Visa, Master **Facilities** Restaurant, bar, locker, travel desk, room service, TV

Hotel Srinivas

Location Near Old Bus Stand **Address** Ganapati High School Road, Hampankatta **Tel** 2440061-65 **Fax** 2423302 **Email** asrao@sancharnet.in **Rooms** 60 **Tariff** Rs 425-1,250; TE **Credit Cards** Visa, Master **Facilities** Restaurant, laundry, travel desk, room service, attached bath, hot water, TV

Hotel Vasanth Mahal

Location Central **Address** KS Rao Road, Hampanakatta **Tel** 2441310-12 **Rooms** 66 **Tariff** Rs 140-390; TE **Credit Cards** AmEx, Visa, Master **Facilities** Travel/ sightseeing arranged, room service, attached bath, TV

Hotel Venkatesh Lodging

Location Central **Address** KS Rao Road, Hampanakatta **Tel** 2440793 **Rooms** 41 **Tariff** Rs 135-370; TE **Credit Cards** NA **Facilities** Travel arranged, room service, attached bath, TV

Hotel Woodlands

Location Near Jyoti Theatre **Address** Bunts Hostel Road **Tel** 2443751-53 **Rooms** 30 **Tariff** Rs 350-950; TE **Credit Cards** Visa, Master **Facilities** Restaurant, laundry, travel arranged, room service, attached bath, TV

Summer Sands Beach Resort

Location Near beach **Address** Ullal, Mangalore **Tel** 2467690-92 **Website** summer-sands.com **Rooms** 79 **Tariff** Rs 1,600-10,099 **Credit Cards** AmEx, Visa, Master **Facilities** Restaurant, swimming pool, beach volleyball, Ayurvedic massage, sports club, sightseeing, laundry, room service, attached bath, hot water

Taj Manjarun Hotel

Location Near State Bank of India Circle **Address** Old Port Road **Tel** 6660420 **Website** tajhotels.com **Rooms** 88 **Tariff** Rs 1,800-6,000; TE **Credit Cards** AmEx, Visa, Master **Facilities** Restaurant, coffee shop, bar, forex, swimming pool **Bangalore Reservations** The Taj West End, Race Course Road, Bangalore **Tel** 080-66605660

MARAVANTHE STD 08254

Aasra Rest House

Location Near beach **Address** Sunlight Beach **Mobile** 09901390129, 09900735994 **Rooms** 6 **Tariff** Rs 400-600 **Credit Cards** NA **Facilities** Restaurant, travel assistance, attached bath, hot water, TV

Hotel Sharon

Location Opp Shastri Park **Address** On NH17, Kundapur, Dist Udupi **Tel** 230823-26/ 623 **Mobile** 09448120826 **Website** soans.com **Rooms** 54 **Tariff** Rs 385-955; TE **Credit Cards** Visa, Master **Facilities** Restaurants, kitchen facility, laundry, travel desk, sightseeing, room service, attached bath, hot water

Sagar Kinara Beach Resort

Location Beachside **Address** Kashi-Maravanthe Beach, Kundapur **Tel** 265401 **Mobile** 09448724861 **Email** sgr_kinara@yahoo.com **Rooms** 7 **Tariff** Rs 500 **Credit Cards** NA **Facilities** Restaurant, boat ride, sightseeing, trekking/ taxi arranged, room service

Turtle Bay Water Sports & Beach Resort YOGA

Location Sea-facing **Address** PO Gujjadi, Trasi, Kanchgodu, Kundapur **Tel** 265422 **Mobile** 09900461609 **Website** turtlebayeco.com **Rooms** 13

cottages, 1 dorm (15 beds) **Tariff** Rs 700-1,500, dorm Rs 2,600 **Credit Cards** NA **Facilities** Restaurant, boating, sightseeing/ taxi arranged, Ayurvedic massage, snorkelling, water sports, attached bath (with cottages)

MURUDESHWAR STD 08385

Benzy Intercontinental

Location Near railway station **Address** NH17, Mavelli **Tel** 260565/ 998-99 **Mobile** 09448818212 **Rooms** 32 **Tariff** Rs 400-700 **Credit Cards** NA **Facilities** Restaurant, laundry, doctor-on-call, travel arranged, room service, attached bath, TV

Gomes Yatri Niwas

Location Opp the beach **Address** Temple Road **Tel** 268693 **Mobile** 09880286970 **Rooms** 6 **Tariff** Rs 200-600 **Credit Cards** NA **Facilities** Laundry, doctor-on-call, travel/ sightseeing arranged, room service, attached bath, hot water

Kamath Yatri Nivas

Location Near beach **Address** Temple Road **Tel** 260871 **Mobile** 09448318471 **Rooms** 25 **Tariff** Rs 300-800 **Credit Cards** NA **Facilities** Restaurant, laundry, travel/ taxi arranged, room service, attached bath, hot water

Murudeshwar Boarding & Lodging

Location Near Murudeshwar Temple **Address** Temple Road **Tel** 260479 **Rooms** 17, dorms 6 (10 beds each) **Tariff** Rs 250-500, dorms Rs 250 each **Credit Cards** NA **Facilities** Doctor-on-call, parking, taxi arranged, hot water

Naveen Beach Resort

Location Sea-facing **Address** PO Murudeshwar, Bhatkal Taluk **Tel** 260415/ 428 **Website** naveenhotels.com **Rooms** 11 **Tariff** Rs 1,600-2,600 **Credit Cards** Visa, Master **Facilities** Restaurant, bar, laundry, room service **Bangalore Reservations** RN Shetty Bhavan, Naveen Complex, 7th Floor, MG Road, Bangalore **Tel** 080-25584181

Panchavati Guest House SEA-FACING

Location Near beach **Address** Temple Road **Tel** 268565 **Mobile** 09945104940 **Rooms** 7 **Tariff** Rs 200-300 **Credit Cards** NA **Facilities** Kitchen, room service, attached bath, hot water

RNS Guest House SEA-FACING

Location Near beach **Address** Bhatkal Taluk, Murudeshwar, Uttara Canara Dist **Tel** 268860, 260425 **Website** naveenhotels.com **Rooms** 50 **Tariff** Rs 600-3,700; TE **Credit Cards** Visa, Master **Facilities** Parking, attached bath, hot water **Bangalore Reservations** *See Naveen Beach Resort alongside*

RNS Residency SEA-FACING

Location Beachside **Address** Murudeshwar **Tel** 268901-03, 260060 **Website** naveenhotels.com **Rooms** 86 **Tariff** Rs 1,000-4,000 **Credit Cards** Visa, Master **Facilities** Restaurant, travel arranged, laundry, swimming pool, health club, room service **Bangalore Reservations** *See Naveen Beach Resort alongside*

IN BHATKAL

Hotel Kola Paradise

Location Opp KSRTC Bus Stand **Address** NH17, Near Circle, Bhatkal **Tel** 225291, 223707 **Mobile** 09902688805 **Rooms** 38, dorms 14 **Tariff** Rs 90-650; TE **Credit Cards** NA **Facilities** Restaurant, laundry, travel/ taxi arranged, room service, attached bath, hot water

Vaibhav Lodge

Location Main road **Address** NH17, Bhatkal **Tel** 226357 **Rooms** 35 **Tariff** Rs 150-250; TE **Credit Cards** NA **Facilities** Restaurant, bar, laundry, travel/ taxi arranged, room service, attached bath, hot water

UDUPI STD 0820

Hotel Pancharatna Paradise

Location Opp Court **Address** Court Road **Tel** 2520791-94 **Mobile** 09986869705 **Rooms** 25 **Tariff** Rs 300-1200; TE **Credit Cards** AmEx, Visa, Master **Facilities** Restaurant, laundry, doctor-on call, travel arranged, sightseeing, room service, attached bath, hot water, TV

Hotel Udupi Residency

Location Central **Address** Opp Service Bus Stand **Tel** 2530005/ 108 **Website** udupiresidency.com **Rooms** 33 **Tariff** Rs 350-850 (with breakfast) **Credit Cards** AmEx, Visa, Master **Facilities** Restaurant, bar, laundry, travel arranged, room service, attached bath, TV

Karaavali Hotel

Location On NH17 Bypass **Address** NH17, Adi Udupi **Tel** 2522860 **Website** karavaligroup.com **Rooms** 38 **Tariff** Rs 530-2,400 **Credit Cards** Visa, Master **Facilities** Restaurant, swimming pool, gym laundry, sightseeing, travel desk, parking, hot water

Kediyoor Hotel

Location Near bus stand **Address** Shiribeedu **Tel** 2522381 **Fax** 2522380 **Email** kediyoor@sancharnet.in **Rooms** 75 **Tariff**

Rs 375-1,500; TE **Credit Cards** AmEx, Visa, Master **Facilities** Restaurants, laundry, travel desk, room service, attached bath, TV

Paradise Isle Beach Resort SPA

Location Beachside **Address** No. 47, Plot No. 2891/1 & 319/3, Malpe Beach **Tel** 2537300/ 7791/ 8666/ 8777 **Website** theparadise isle.com **Rooms** 30 **Tariff** Rs 3,000-4,500; TE **Credit Cards** AmEx, Visa, Master **Facilities** Food court, coffee shop, swimming pool, Ayurvedic spa, snooker, travel desk, water sports, boating, room service

KERALA

ALAPPUZHA CODE 0477

Alleppey Beach Resorts

Location Near railway station **Address** Beach Road **Tel** 2263408, 2260125 **Website** thealleppeybeachresorts.com **Rooms** 8 **Tariff** Rs 1,500-2,990; TE **Credit Cards** AmEx, Visa, Master **Facilities** Restaurant, private beach, houseboat, motor boat, backwater cruises, room service, attached bath, TV

Beach Bungalow HERITAGE

Location Beachside **Address** Beach Road **Tel** 2263347 **Mobile** 09349898088 **Website** beach bungalow.co.in **Rooms** 18 **Tariff** Rs 2,500-5,000 (with breakfast) **Credit Cards** AmEx, Visa, Master **Facilities** Home-cooked meals, self-cooking facility, swimming pool, boat cruises, sightseeing arranged, car rental

Hotel Arcadia

Address Near KSRTC Bus Station **Tel** 2251354/ 735 **Mobile** 09495476708 **Website** arcadiaregency.com **Rooms** 18 **Tariff** Rs 200-1,100 **Credit Cards** NA **Facilities** Restaurant, beer bar, laundry, doctor-on-call, room service, attached bath, TV

Marari Beach Resort

Location Beachside **Address** North SL Puram, PO Mararikulam **Tel** 2863801-09 **Website** cghearth.com **Rooms** 62 **Tariff** Rs 8,500-24,500 (with all meals); TE **Credit Cards** AmEx, Visa, Master **Facilities** Restaurants, bar, Ayurvedic centre, swimming pool, yoga, cycling tours, private beach, forex, boating/ backwater cruises arranged **Kochi Reservations** Casino Hotel, Willingdon Island, Kochi **Tel** 0484-2668221

Padipura Residence

Location Central **Address** Near District Court, Sanathanam Ward **Tel** 2244978, 2245001 **Mobile** 09847744978 **Fax** 2243150 **Rooms** 29, dorms 3 **Tariff** Rs 600-1,100; TE, dorm bed Rs 100 **Credit Cards** NA **Facilities** Food on request, room service, TV

Pagoda Resorts AYURVEDA

Location Near KSRTC Bus Stand **Address** CCNB Road, Near Kallupalam, PO Chungam **Tel** 3091301, 2252549-50, 2251697 **Website** pagoda resorts.com **Rooms** 12 cottages **Tariff** Rs 1,500-3,700; TE **Credit Cards** AmEx, Visa, Master **Facilities** Restaurant, swimming pool, health club, Ayurveda centre, travel desk, Internet, TV

Raheem Residency HERITAGE

Location Near Alleppey Beach **Address** Beach Road **Tel** 2230767, 2239767 **Website** raheemresidency.com **Rooms** 10 **Tariff** Rs 5,178-14,384; TE **Credit Cards** Visa, Master **Facilities** Restaurant, swimming pool, Ayurvedic treatment, travel desk, forex, laundry, library

Yatri Nivas KTDC

Location 4 km from beach **Address** Motel Aram Compound, AS Road, Kalappura **Tel**

2244460/ 760 **Website** ktdc.com **Rooms** 17 **Tariff** Rs 350-1,100; TE **Credit Cards** NA **Facilities** Restaurant, beer parlour, laundry, car rental, boating/ backwater cruises arranged, TV **Metro Reservations** *See page 519*

BEKAL STD 0467

Bekal Boat Stay BACKWATERS
Location On Valiaparamba backwaters **Address** Kottappuram, Nileshwar, Dist Kasargod **Tel** 2282633, 3953311 **Mobile** 09447469747 **Website** bekalboatstay.com **Rooms** 4 houseboats **Tariff** Rs 3,000-18,000; TE **Credit Cards** NA **Facilities** Home-cooked meals, cruise packages, fishing, swimming, canoeing

Chandralayam Homestay
Location 4 km from Bekal **Address** Thiruvakkoli, PO Bekal, Kasargod Dist **Tel** 2236456, 2293712 **Mobile** 09446772414 **Email** krishnan_chandralayam@yahoo.co.in **Rooms** 6 **Tariff** Rs 500-5,000 **Credit Cards** NA **Facilities** Home-cooked meals, sightseeing, library, Internet, houseboat/ backwater cruises, attached bath, hot water

Gitanjali Heritage HOMESTAY BACKWATERS
Location Amidst natural surroundings, 5 km from Bekal Beach **Address** PO Panayal, via Bekal, Dist Kasargod **Tel** 2234159 **Mobile** 09447469747 **Website** gitanjaliheritage.com **Rooms** 6 **Tariff** Rs 2,500-4,000 (with all meals) **Credit Cards** NA **Facilities** Home-cooked meals, laundry, Ayurvedic massage and yoga on request, books, pottery making, sightseeing, organic farm tour, nature walk, swimming, backwater/ houseboat cruises

Hotel Bekal International
Location Near police station **Address** TB Road, Hosdurg, Kanhangad **Tel** 2202017, 2204287 **Website** hotelbekal.com **Rooms** 41 **Tariff** Rs 200-1,300; TE **Credit Cards** AmEx, Visa, Master **Facilities** Restaurant, laundry, travel desk, sightseeing tours, room service, attached bath, TV

K-Tees Residency
Location Near beach **Address** KT Centre, Near Bekal Fort Beach, PO Madathil, Pallikkere, Kasargod **Tel** 2275633 **Mobile** 09447691903 **Website** kteesresidency.com **Rooms** 14, cottages 6 **Tariff** Rs 200-1,500 **Credit Cards** NA **Facilities** Restaurant, laundry, doctor-on-call, taxi arranged, sightseeing, room service, hot water

CHERAI STD 0484

Amaravathy Resorts
Location Sea-facing **Address** Beach Road, Cherai, Vypeen Island, Dist Ernakulam **Tel** 3243521, 2417110 **Mobile** 09349288868, 09447892201 **Website** amaravathyresorts.com **Rooms** 9, dorm 1 **Tariff** Rs 750-3,500; TE **Credit Cards** NA **Facilities** Restaurant, laundry, travel arranged, sightseeing, room service, attached bath

Baywatch Beach Homes SPA
Location Sea-facing **Address** Beach Road, Cherai, Vypeen Island, Dist Ernakulam **Tel** 2480299 **Mobile** 09847150067 **Website** baywatchbeachhomes.com **Rooms** 5 **Tariff** Rs 2,000-2,500 **Credit Cards** NA **Facilities** Restaurant, doctor-on-call, spa, gym, jacuzzi, Internet, forex, locker, travel desk, boating, sightseeing

Cherai Beach Resorts
Location Beachside **Address** Beach Road, Cherai, Vypeen Island, Dist Ernakulam **Tel** 2416949, 2481818 **Mobile** 09847231400 **Website** cheraibeachresorts.com **Rooms** 32 cottages **Tariff** Rs 1,000-4,500 **Credit Cards** AmEx, Visa, Master **Facilities** Restaurant, Ayurvedic spa, boating, beach games, swimming, fishing, canoeing, rafting, backwater cruises, travel assistance, room service

Sealine Beach Resort
Location Beachside **Address** Beach Road, Cherai, Vypeen Island, Dist Ernakulam **Tel** 2418055, 6519593 **Mobile** 09847653653 **Website** sealinebeachresort.com **Rooms** 10 **Tariff** Rs 2,500-4,000; TE **Credit Cards** NA **Facilities** Restaurant, parking, laundry, forex, travel desk, sightseeing, fishing on request (in season only), room service, TV

IN KOCHI STD 0484

ON BOLGATTY ISLAND

Bolghatty Palace KTDC GOLF
Location Lakefront **Address** Mulavukadu **Tel** 2750003/ 500/ 600 **Website** ktdc.com **Rooms** 26 **Tariff** Rs 2,058-8,600 (with breakfast and dinner) **Credit Cards** AmEx, Visa, Master **Facilities** Restaurant, beer parlour, swimming pool, golf course, Ayurveda centre, laundry, doctor-on-call, locker, forex, car rental, room service, TV **Metro Reservations** *See page 519*

IN FORT KOCHI

Ballard Bungalow HERITAGE
Location Near Port Boat Jetty **Address** Ballard Road **Tel** 2215854 **Website**

cochinballard.com **Rooms** 7 **Tariff** Rs 1,200-2,800 (with breakfast); TE **Credit Cards** AmEx, Visa, Master **Facilities** Restaurant, Ayurvedic massage arranged, forex, travel desk, room service, attached bath, TV

Brunton Boatyard AYURVEDA

Location Near Chinese Fishing Nets **Address** Calvetti Road **Tel** 2215461-65 **Fax** 2215562 **Website** cghearth.com **Rooms** 22 **Tariff** Rs 6,600-21,000 (with breakfast); TE **Credit Cards** AmEx, Visa, Master **Facilities** Restaurant, coffee shop-cum-bar, swimming pool, Ayurveda centre, souvenir shop, forex, car rental, sightseeing, room service, TV

Delight Tourist Resort HOMESTAY

Location Near Parade Ground **Address** Post Office Road **Telefax** 2217658 **Mobile** 09846121421 **Website** delightful homestay.com **Rooms** 6 **Tariff** Rs 800-1,400 (with breakfast) **Credit Cards** AmEx, Visa, Master **Facilities** Laundry, travel desk, cookery course, attached bath

Hotel Fort Heritage

Location Near beach **Address** 1/283, Napier Street **Tel** 2215333 **Telefax** 2215455 **Website** fortheritage.com **Rooms** 12 **Tariff** Rs 2,401-2,837 (with breakfast) **Credit Cards** AmEx, Visa, Master **Facilities** Restaurant, lockers, forex, Ayurvedic massage, laundry, car rental, sightseeing, room service

Old Courtyard HERITAGE

Location Near beach **Address** 1/371-372, Princess Street **Tel** 2216302/ 5035 **Website** oldcourtyard.com **Rooms** 8 **Tariff** Rs 2,250-4,600 (with breakfast); TE **Credit Cards** Visa, Master, Diners **Facilities** Restaurant, laundry, travel desk, Internet, lockers, forex, room service, TV

ON WILLINGDON ISLAND

ATS Willingdon AYURVEDA

Location Near Thoppupadi Bridge **Address** Willingdon Island **Tel** 2667643/ 282, 2669223 **Website** atshotels.com **Rooms** 22 **Tariff** Rs 850-1,850; TE **Credit Cards** AmEx, Visa, Master **Facilities** Restaurant, Ayurvedic treatments arranged, forex, laundry, sightseeing, car rentals, room service, TV

Casino Hotel AYURVEDA

Address Willingdon Island **Tel** 2668421/ 221 **Website** cghearth.com **Rooms** 67 **Tariff** Rs 4,100-10,000 (with breakfast); TE **Credit Cards** AmEx, Visa, Master **Facilities** Restaurants, bar, swimming pool, health club, Ayurveda centre, forex, travel desk, room service, TV

Taj Malabar AYURVEDA

Location Near Port Trust Office **Address** Willingdon Island **Tel** 2668292, 2666811 **Website** tajhotels.com **Rooms** 96 **Tariff** Rs 9,000-16,500; TE **Credit Cards** AmEx, Visa, Master **Facilities** Restaurants, bars, swimming pool, Ayurveda spa, travel desk, room service, TV

KANNUR STD 0497

Costa Malabari

Location Near Adikadalayi Temple **Address** Thottada **Tel** 2836174 **Mobile** 09447775691 **Website** costamalabari.com **Rooms** 17 **Tariff** Rs 2,000-2,500 (with all meals) **Credit Cards** NA **Facilities** Home cooked meals, laundry, Ayurvedic massage arranged, car rental

Kannur Beach House HOMESTAY

Location Beachfront **Address** Thottada Beach, Thottada **Tel** 2836530 **Mobile** 09847186330

Website kannurbeachhouse.com **Rooms** 5 **Tariff** Rs 900-1,100 per person per day (with meals) **Credit Cards** NA **Facilities** Home cooked meals, laundry, sightseeing, birding, boating

KK Heritage HOMESTAY

Location Near beach **Address** Adikadalayi, Thottada **Tel** 2835240 **Mobile** 09447486020, 09446677254 **Website** kkheritage.com **Rooms** 5, cottages 2 **Tariff** Rs 1,200-1,500 (with breakfast and dinner) **Credit Cards** NA **Facilities** Home cooked meals, transport arranged, attached bath

Malabar Residency

Location Near railway station **Address** Thavakkara Road **Tel** 2701654-56 **Email** malabar residency2004@yahoo.co.in **Rooms** 36 **Tariff** Rs 600-2,500; TE **Credit Cards** Visa, Master **Facilities** Restaurant, coffee shop, taxi arranged, shopping plaza, Internet, doctor-on-call, Ayurvedic massage, laundry

Mascot Beach Resort AYURVEDA

Location Beachfront **Address** Near Baby Beach, Burnassery **Tel** 2708450/ 55 **Website** mascotresort.com **Rooms** 35 **Tariff** Rs 700-2,500; TE **Credit Cards** Visa, Master **Facilities** Restaurant, Ayurveda school, swimming pool, forex **Bangalore Reservations** Hammock Leisure Holidays, 314/1, Vijay Kiran, 7th Cross, Domlur Layout, Bangalore **Tel** 080-25352877/ 7963

Yatri Nivas KTDC

Location Near KSRTC Bus Stand **Address** Thavakara, Police Club Road **Tel** 2700717, 2705098 **Email** yathriknr@yahoo.com **Website** ktdc.com **Rooms** 17 **Tariff** Rs 250-800; TE **Credit Cards** NA **Facilities** Restaurant, beer parlour, laundry, taxi arranged, parking, travel desk, room service, hot water, TV **Metro Reservations** *See page 519*

KOLLAM STD 0474

Aquaserene WATER SPORTS

Location Facing backwaters **Address** PO South Paravoor, Dist Kollam **Tel** 2512410-17 **Website** aquasereneindia.com **Rooms** 28 **Tariff** Rs 3,200-11,000; TE **Credit Cards** AmEx, Visa, Master **Facilities** Restaurant, Ayurveda centre, swimming pool, Internet, forex, laundry, antique shop, cookery shows, sunset cruise, water sports, sightseeing, car rental, room service

Ashtamudi Resort

Location Lake-facing **Address** Chavara, Malibhagam, Ashtamudi **Tel** 0476-2882310/ 65 **Website** clubmahindra.com **Rooms** 25 **Tariff** Rs 5,000-10,000; TE **Credit Cards** AmEx, Visa, Master **Facilities** Restaurant, swimming pool, Ayurvedic treatments, laundry, doctor-on-call, lockers, forex, travel assistance, sightseeing, boating

Hotel Sea Bee BACKWATERS

Location Near KSRTC Bus Stand **Address** Jetty Road **Tel** 2744696/ 697 **Website** hotel seabee.com **Rooms** 40 **Tariff** Rs 200-2,200; TE **Credit Cards** AmEx, Visa, Master **Facilities** Restaurant, bar, laundry, Internet, lockers, forex, parking, travel desk, taxi arranged, boat cruises, room service, attached bath

Hotel Sudarsan BACKWATERS

Location Central **Address** Parameswar Nagar **Tel** 2744322 **Website** hotelsudarsan.com **Rooms** 28 **Tariff** Rs 450-1,650 **Credit Cards** Visa, Master **Facilities** Restaurant, bar, coffee shop, laundry, doctor-on-call, lockers, forex, Ayurvedic treatments and massage, boat cruise on request, travel arranged, room service, attached bath, TV

Sarovaram Ayurvedic Backwater Resort

Location Near Veerabhadraswami Temple **Address** PO Ashtamudi, Dist Kollam **Tel** 2704686, 2705759 **Website** sarovaramkollam.com **Rooms** 9 cottages **Tariff** Rs 1,200-2,900; TE **Credit Cards** NA **Facilities** Restaurant, Internet, travel assistance, boat cruises arranged, room service, TV

Shantigiri Ayurveda Panchakarma Centre

Location Near Nair Hospital **Address** Uliyakovil Road, Vaidyashala Nagar, Aashramam **Tel** 2763014 **Mobile** 09847461624 **Email** janakanthi kollam@yahoo.co.in **Rooms** 6 **Tariff** Rs 300-750 **Credit Cards** NA **Facilities** Kitchen, Ayurvedic treatment and massage, doctor-on-call, lockers, attached bath

KOVALAM STD 0471

ON CHOWARA BEACH

Manaltheeram Ayurvedic Beach Village BACKWATERS

Location Beachfront **Address** Chowara Beach, South of Kovalam, Thiruvananthapuram **Tel** 2268610, 2266222 **Website** manaltheeram.com **Rooms** 54 **Tariff** Rs 3,000-12,000 **Credit Cards** AmEx, Visa, Master **Facilities** Restaurant, laundry, Ayurveda centre, yoga, meditation, gift shop, forex, swimming pool, beach facilities, fishing, boating, travel desk, backwater cruises, room service

Nikki's Nest Ayurvedic Beach Resort SEA-FACING YOGA

Location On a hilltop **Address** Azhimala Shiva Temple Road, PO Chowara, Pulinkudi, Thiruvananthapuram **Tel** 2268821/22 **Website** nikkisnest.com **Rooms** 37 **Tariff** Rs 3,220-9,500 (with breakfast); TE **Credit Cards** Visa, Master **Facilities** Restaurant, swimming pool, Ayurveda clinic, yoga, beach facilities, laundry, car rental, room service, attached bath

Somatheeram Ayurvedic Beach Resort BACKWATERS

Location Beachfront **Address** Chowara Beach, South of Kovalam, Thiruvananthapuram **Tel** 2268101 **Website** somatheeram.in **Rooms** 44 **Tariff** Rs 3,000-12,000 **Credit Cards** AmEx, Visa, Master **Facilities** Restaurant, doctor-on-call, laundry, Ayurveda centre, yoga, meditation, forex, lockers, beach facilities, fishing, boating, cultural programmes, sightseeing, travel assistance, car rental, backwater cruises, room service, attached bath

ON EVE'S BEACH

Hotel Marine Palace

Location On Eve's (Hawah) Beach **Address** Hawah Beach Road, Kovalam, Thiruvananthapuram **Tel** 2481248 **Telefax** 2485428 **Website** hotelmarinepalace.com **Rooms** 18 **Tariff** Rs 950-3,600; TE **Credit Cards** AmEx, Visa, Master **Facilities** Restaurant, beer parlour, sightseeing, room service

Hotel Seaface BACKWATERS

Location On Eve's (Hawah) Beach **Address** NUP Beach Road, Kovalam, Thiruvananthapuram **Tel** 2481835-36, 2481591, 2486235 **Fax** 2481320 **Website** seaface.com **Rooms** 20 **Tariff** Rs 2,000-7,000; TE **Credit Cards** Visa, Master **Facilities** Restaurant, coffee shop, bar, Ayurvedic massage centre, swimming pool, laundry, travel desk, forex, sightseeing, backwater cruises, water sports, trekking, room service

Swagath Holiday Resort

Location Near beach **Address** Near Upasana Hospital, Kovalam, Thiruvananthapuram **Tel** 2481148-50 **Website** swagathresorts.com **Rooms** 25 **Tariff** Rs 1,000-6,500; TE **Credit Cards** Visa, Master **Facilities** Restaurant, swimming pool, Ayurvedic massage, children's pool, travel desk, room service

ON LIGHTHOUSE BEACH

Hawah Beach Resort SEA-FACING

Location Near beach **Address** Lighthouse Beach, Kovalam, PO Vizhinjam, Thiruvananthapuram **Tel** 2481951, 2482026 **Website** hawahbeach.com **Rooms** 23 **Tariff** Rs 1,400-5,500; TE **Credit Cards** NA **Facilities** Restaurant, lockers, laundry, car rental, sightseeing, room service

Hotel Neelakanta SEA-FACING

Location Beachfront **Address** Lighthouse Beach, Kovalam, Thiruvananthapuram **Tel** 2480321, 2486004 **Website** hotelneelakantakovalam.com **Rooms** 34 **Tariff** Rs 1,800-4,000; TE **Credit Cards** AmEx, Visa, Master **Facilities** Restaurants, travel desk, room service

Hotel Seaweed SEA-FACING

Location Beachfront **Address** Lighthouse Beach, Kovalam, Thiruvananthapuram **Tel** 2480391, 2720806 **Website** hotelseaweed.com **Rooms** 40 **Tariff** Rs 600-1,400; TE **Credit**

Cards Visa, Master **Facilities** Restaurant, laundry, sightseeing, travel desk, room service

Pappukutty Beach Resort
Location Beachfront **Address** Lighthouse Beach, Kovalam, Thiruvananthapuram **Tel** 2480235 **Website** pappukutty.com **Rooms** 31 **Tariff** Rs 500-1,400; TE **Credit Cards** NA **Facilities** Restaurant, Ayurvedic massage centre, yoga, laundry, sightseeing, car rental, room service, attached bath, TV

IN POOVAR

Estuary Island Resort BACKWATERS
Location 2-3 km from Poovar Island **Address** PO Poovar, Thiruvananthapuram **Tel** 2214355/ 66 **Website** estuaryisland.com **Rooms** 72 **Tariff** Rs 3,000-8,000 (with breakfast); TE **Credit Cards** AmEx, Visa, Master **Facilities** Restaurants, swimming pool, kid's pool, gift shop, gym, Ayurvedic massage centre, country boat rides, backwater cruises, room service

Isola di Cocco BACKWATERS
Location 2-3 km from Poovar Island **Address** PO Poovar, Thiruvananthapuram **Tel** 2210008/ 800 **Website** isoladicocco.com **Rooms** 67 cottages **Tariff** Rs 2,500-9,000 (with breakfast); TE **Credit Cards** AmEx, Visa, Master **Facilities** Restaurants, swimming pool, Ayurveda centre, yoga, laundry, car rental, cultural programmes, backwater cruises, room service

Poovar Island Resort SEA-FACING
Location Near beach **Address** KP7/911, Pozhiyoor, PO Poovar, Thiruvananthapuram **Tel** 2212068-69/ 73 **Website** poovarislandresort.com **Rooms** 68 cottages **Tariff** Rs 4,000-12,000; TE **Credit Cards** AmEx, Visa, Master **Facilities** Restaurant, Ayurvedic restaurant, swimming pool, Ayurveda centre, car rental, bird watching, backwater cruises, room service, TV

ON SAMUDRA BEACH

Hotel Samudra KTDC
Location On beach **Address** KTDC Beach Resort, GV Raja Road, Kovalam, Thiruvananthapuram **Tel** 2480089 **Fax** 2480242 **Website** ktdc.com **Rooms** 64 **Tariff** Rs 3,369-9,218 **Credit Cards** AmEx, Visa, Master **Facilities** Restaurant, bar, Ayurveda centre, swimming pool, sea-front barbecue, laundry, forex, travel assistance, sightseeing, room service **Metro Reservations** *See page 519*

Puja Mahal Ayurvedic Beach Resort
Location Near beach **Address** GV Raja Road, Vellar, Kovalam, Thiruvananthapuram **Tel** 2481245 **Mobile** 09895710938 **Website** hotelpujamahal.com **Rooms** 45 **Tariff** Rs 1,500-3,500; TE **Credit Cards** NA **Facilities** Restaurants, swimming pool, Ayurvedic centre, doctor-on-call, travel desk, library, room service, attached bath

Taj Green Cove Resort SPA
Location On beach **Address** GV Raja Vattapara Road, Kovalam, Thiruvananthapuram **Tel** 2487733 **Website** tajhotels.com **Rooms** 60 **Tariff** Rs 7,500-23,600; TE **Credit Cards** AmEx, Visa, Master **Facilities** Restaurant, coffee shop, swimming pool, health club, spa, lockers, forex, travel desk, room service

The Leela Kempinski SPA
Location Near beach **Address** Kovalam, Thiruvananthapuram **Tel** 2480101 **Website** theleela.com **Rooms** 180 **Tariff** Rs 7,500-55,000; TE **Credit Cards** AmEx, Visa, Master **Facilities** Restaurants, bar, private beach, swimming pool, Ayurvedic wellness spa, fitness centre, travel desk, room service

KOZHIKODE STD 0495

Fortune Hotel
Location Central **Address** Kannur Road, Chakkorathukulam **Tel** 2768888 **Fax** 2768111 **Website** fortunehotels.in **Rooms** 63 **Tariff** Rs 1,980-2,970; TE **Credit Cards** AmEx, Visa, Master **Facilities** Restaurant, coffee shop, swimming pool, health club, laundry, lockers, car rental, room service

Harivihar HOMESTAY
Location Near Bilathikulam temple **Address** Bilathikulam, Kozhikode **Tel** 2765865 **Mobile** 09847072203 **Website** harivihar.com **Rooms** 7 **Tariff** Rs 4,000-5,000 (with meals) **Credit Cards** NA **Facilities** Home cooked meals, yoga, Ayurvedic treatments, laundry, sightseeing

Kadavu Resorts AYURVEDA
Location Riverside **Address** NH Bypass Road, Azhinjilam, Malapuram Dist **Tel** 0483-2830023/ 027/ 570 **Website** kadavuresorts.com **Rooms** 84 **Tariff** Rs 2,500-8,500; TE **Credit Cards** AmEx, Visa, Master **Facilities** Restaurants, bar, Ayurveda centre, swimming pool, forex **Bangalore Reservations** RS Hospitality Services Ltd, St Patrick's Business Complex, 21 Museum Road, Bangalore **Tel** 080-25325302

Malabar Mansion KTDC

Location Near LIC office **Address** Mananchira Square, SM Street **Tel** 2722391 **Website** ktdc.com **Rooms** 16 **Tariff** Rs 250-650; TE **Credit Cards** NA **Facilities** Restaurant, beer parlour, laundry, room service **Bangalore Reservations** *See page 519*

Taj Residency AYURVEDA

Location Central **Address** PT Usha Road **Tel** 2765354 **Website** tajhotels.com **Rooms** 74 **Tariff** Rs 3,100-6,500; TE **Credit Cards** AmEx, Visa, Master **Facilities** Restaurant, coffee shop, laundry, swimming pool, gym, health centre, Ayurveda centre, forex, room service

Tasara – Centre for Creative Weaving

Location 3 km from Beypore Beach **Address** North Beypore **Tel** 2414832/ 233 **Website** tasaraindia.com **Rooms** 8 **Tariff** Rs 1,500-2,500 **Credit Cards** NA **Facilities** Dining hall, training in weaving, dyeing and printing, raw material provided

The Renaissance Cochin Kappad Beach Resort

Location Near beach **Address** PO Chemanchery, Thoovapara **Tel** 0496-2688777, 2689191-93 **Mobile** 09961445546 **Telefax** 2689194 **Website** renaissance kappadbeach.com **Rooms** 16 **Tariff** Rs 2,000-3,000; TE **Credit Cards** AmEx, Visa, Master **Facilities** Restaurant, laundry, swimming pool, gym, Ayurveda centre, travel desk, room service

THALASSERY STD 0490

Hotel Paris Presidency

Location Central **Address** PO No. 33, New Paris Complex, Logans Road **Tel** 2342666-68 **Website** parispresidency.com **Rooms** 24 **Tariff** Rs 360-780; TE **Credit Cards** Visa, Master **Facilities** Restaurant, forex, laundry, car rental, room service, attached bath, hot water, TV

Hotel Sharara Plaza

Location Near bus stand **Address** AVK Nair Road **Tel** 2341101-03 **Rooms** 35 **Tariff** Rs 500-1,800; TE **Credit Cards** AmEx, Visa, Master **Facilities** Restaurant, laundry, travel desk, room service, attached bath

Pearlview Regency AYURVEDA

Location Central **Address** Pearlview Junction **Tel** 2326702-03/ 08 **Fax** 2325741 **Website** pearlview regency.com **Rooms** 48 **Tariff** Rs 800-1,550; TE **Credit Cards** AmEx, Visa, Master **Facilities** Restaurant, bar, Ayurveda centre, swimming pool, Internet, forex, car rental, room service, TV

Razena Beach Resort HOMESTAY

Location Sea-facing **Address** Near District Court, Holloway Road **Tel** 2320672, 2323993 **Mobile** 09847352910 **Email** razenanazer@hotmail.com **Rooms** 4 **Tariff** US$150 (with all meals) **Credit Cards** NA **Facilities** Home-cooked meals, laundry, sightseeing/ car rental

Saravanapriya Tourist Home

Location Opp Peralassery Sri Subramanya Temple **Address** PO Peralassery, Mundalur, Kannur Dist **Tel** 0497-2827333 **Fax** 2826533 **Rooms** 62 **Tariff** Rs 90-495; TE **Credit Cards** NA **Facilities** Restaurant, attached bath, hot water

VARKALA STD 0470

AT NORTH CLIFF

Deshadan Cliff & Beach Resort

Location Near beach **Address** Kurakkanni Cliff, Varkala **Tel** 3204242, 3202057 **Mobile**

09846031005 **Website** deshadan.com **Rooms** 12 **Tariff** Rs 3,000; TE **Credit Cards** AmEx, Visa, Master **Facilities** Restaurant, swimming pool, Ayurvedic treatment/ yoga on request, elephant ride, travel desk, sightseeing, room service

Krishnatheeram Ayur Holy Beach Resort AYURVEDA

Location Beachfront **Address** Thiruvambadi Beach, Varkala **Tel** 2601305, 2156444 **Website** krishnatheeram.com **Rooms** 28 **Tariff** Rs 1,000-3,800; TE **Credit Cards** Visa, Master **Facilities** Restaurants, Ayurveda centre, laundry, travel desk, sightseeing, room service, attached bath

Raja Park Beach Resort

Location Near beach **Address** Near Papanasam North Cliff, Varkala **Tel** 2607060 **Fax** 2608060 **Website** rajapark.com **Rooms** 25 **Tariff** Rs 700-3,200; TE **Credit Cards** AmEx, Visa, Master **Facilities** Restaurants, swimming pool, Internet, laundry, travel desk, sightseeing, room service, attached bath

AT SOUTH CLIFF

Green Palace Seaside Hotel

Location Near beach **Address** Cliff Top, Varkala, Dist Thiruvananthapuram **Tel** 2601962/ 055 **Email** greenpalace@eth.net **Rooms** 15 **Tariff** Rs 1,500-3,000; TE **Credit Cards** AmEx, Visa, Master **Facilities** Restaurant, laundry, travel desk, sightseeing tours, room service, attached bath

Hindustan Beach Retreat

Location Near beach, sea-facing **Address** Papanasam Beach, PO Janardhanapuram, Varkala **Tel** 2604254-55 **Mobile** 09249770326 **Website** hindustanbeachretreat.com **Rooms** 27 **Tariff** Rs 3,000-5,000; TE **Credit Cards** AmEx, Visa, Master **Facilities** Restaurant, coffee shop, laundry, swimming pool, backwater cruises and water sports (seasonal), room service

Preeth Beach Resort

AYURVEDA

Location Near beach **Address** Near Papanasam Cliff **Tel** 2602341 **Website** preethbeachresort.com **Rooms** 27 **Tariff** Rs 560-2,800; TE **Credit Cards** AmEx, Visa, Master **Facilities** Restaurant, beer parlour, Ayurveda centre, swimming pool, travel desk, room service

Sea Pearl Chalets

Location Beachfront **Address** Papanasam Beach, Varkala **Tel** 2660105 **Mobile** 09447719465 **Website** seapearlchalets.com **Rooms** 10 **Tariff** Rs 850-1,500 **Credit Cards** AmEx, Visa, Master **Facilities** Breakfast provided, laundry, forex, travel/ sightseeing arranged, houseboats available

Taj Garden Retreat

Location Near beach **Address** Janardhanapuram, Varkala **Tel** 2603000 **Website** tajhotels.com **Rooms** 30 **Tariff** Rs 4,000-6,000; TE **Credit Cards** AmEx, Visa, Master **Facilities** Restaurant, sunken bar, sunset bar, swimming pool, Ayurvedic massage parlour, laundry, forex, lockers, travel desk, backwater cruises on Kappil beach, room service

ON THIRUVAMBADI BEACH

Seabreeze

Location Beachside, sea-facing **Address** Thiruvambadi Beach, Varkala **Tel** 2603257 **Mobile** 09846004243 **Website** seabreezevarkala.com **Rooms** 12 **Tariff** Rs 500-2,800; TE **Credit Cards** AmEx, Visa, Master **Facilities** Restaurant, laundry, sightseeing, travel desk, room service, attached bath

Thiruvambadi Beach Retreat

Location Near beach **Address** North End Down Cliff, Thiruvambadi Road, Varkala, Dist Thiruvananthapuram **Tel** 2601028 **Fax** 2604345 **Website** thiruvambadihotel.com **Rooms** 10 **Tariff** Rs 800-2,500; TE **Credit Cards** AmEx, Visa, Master **Facilities** Restaurant, Ayurvedic treatments, yoga, meditation, lockers, forex, library, garden with hammocks, travel desk, sightseeing, room service

ON KAPPIL BEACH

Lake Sagar Beach Resort & Water Safari Park

WATER SPORTS

Location Off the beach **Address** Kappil, Paravur, Dist Kollam **Tel** 0474-2514300, 3201485 **Email** lakesagar@puthooram.com **Rooms** 7 **Tariff** Rs 400-1,350 **Credit Cards** NA **Facilities** Restaurant, boating, elephant ride, water sports, room service

LAKSHADWEEP ISLANDS

Agatti Island Beach Resort

Location Near airport **Address** Agatti **Website** agattiislandresorts.com **Rooms** 19 cottages, dorm **Tariff** Rs 3,250-10,175; TE **Credit Cards** Master, Visa **Facilities** Restaurant, water sports, boating, kayaking, travel desk, airport transfers, attached bath, TV **Kochi Reservations** Behind HPO, Market Road, Kochi **Tel** 0484-2362232 **Fax** 2362234

Bangaram Island Resort

Location 8 km from Agatti **Address** Bangaram **Website** cghearth.com **Rooms** 30 beach huts, 4 bungalows **Tariff** Rs 14,500-28,000; TE **Credit Cards** Master, Visa **Facilities** Restaurant, bar, library, water sports, boating, kayaking, travel desk, airport transfers, Ayurvedic massage, room service **Kochi Reservations** CGH Earth, Casino Building, Willingdon Island, Kochi **Tel** 0484-2668221/ 6821

Kadmat Beach Resort

LAKSHADWEEP TOURISM

Location Beachside **Address** Kadmat **Tel** 04897-274203 **Website** lakshadweeptourism.com **Rooms** 30 **Tariff** Rs 3,000-4,000; TE **Facilities** Restaurant, scuba diving, boating, travel assistance, airport transfers, laundry, room service, TV **Metro Reservations** *See page 519*

Kavaratti Tourism Huts

LAKSHADWEEP TOURISM

Location Near jetty **Address** Kavaratti **Tel** 04896-262289 **Website** lakshadweeptourism.com **Rooms** 5 cottages **Tariff** Rs 3,000; TE **Facilities** Restaurant, scuba diving, water sports, swimming, snorkelling, travel assistance, airport transfers, laundry, room service, attached bath, hot water, TV **Metro Reservations** *See page 519*

Minicoy Resort

LAKSHADWEEP TOURISM

Location Near lighthouse **Address** Minicoy **Tel** 04892-222425 **Website** lakshadweeptourism.com **Rooms** 15 cottages **Tariff** Rs 3,000-4,000; TE **Facilities** Restaurant, scuba diving, travel assistance, airport transfers, laundry, room service, attached bath, TV **Metro Reservations** *See page 519*

MAHARASHTRA

ALIBAUG STD 02141

Guruji Holiday Resort

Location Beachside **Address** Alibaug Beach **Tel** 222266/ 85 **Rooms** 18 **Tariff** Rs 650-1,100; TE **Credit Cards** NA **Facilities** Restaurant, bar, travel desk, room service, TV **Mumbai Reservations** Anand Travels, Opp Shiv Sena Bhavan, FF Vavda Building, Dadar (W), Mumbai **Tel** 022-24443486-87 **Fax** 24443489

Hotel Big Splash

Location Near bus depot **Address** Chandra, Rewas Road **Tel** 226801-05 **Website** bigsplashalibagh.com **Rooms** 54 **Tariff** Rs 2,000-3,500; TE **Credit Cards** Visa, Master **Facilities** Restaurant, bar, mini golf, swimming pool, room service, TV

Hotel Meera Madhav

Address Opp bus stand **Tel** 225279-81 **Telefax** 2257982 **Email** hotelmeeramadhav@rediffmail.com **Rooms** 32 **Tariff** Rs 700-1,550; TE **Credit Cards** Visa, Master **Facilities** Restaurant, bar, indoor games, travel desk, laundry, room service, TV

Hotel Sea View SEA-FACING

Location Sea-facing **Address** Near Ceda Bhavan, Alibaug Beach **Tel** 222605 **Telefax** 224062 **Website** seaviewalibag.com **Rooms** 24 **Tariff** Rs 1,050-1,800; TE **Credit Cards** Master **Facilities** Dining hall, swimming pool, sightseeing, laundry, room service, TV **Mumbai Reservations** Zaramica, 7 Ketki Apartments, GV Scheme Road, Mulund (E), Mumbai **Tel** 022-55991901, 25680195

Sai Inn Holiday Resort

Location Near Kihim Beach **Address** Alibaug-Rewas Road, Village Chondi, Kihim

Tel 232801-02 **Website** sai-inn.com **Rooms** 39 **Tariff** Rs 1,900-3,900; TE **Credit Cards** AmEx, Visa, Master, BoB, Diners **Facilities** Restaurant, travel desk, room service, TV **Mumbai Reservations** MN Narvekar & Co, 2, Ajanta Apartments, 75, Sai Bhagat Singh Road, Colaba, Mumbai **Tel** 022-22181678, 22161666/ 39

Sun Glow Resort

Location Beachside **Address** Zilla Parishad Road **Tel** 221072-73 **Telefax** 221074 **Website** sunglowresort.com **Rooms** 10 **Tariff** Rs 1,200-1,500; TE **Credit Cards** Visa, Master **Facilities** Restaurant, bar, swimming pool, kitchenette, travel desk, room service, TV

Sun-N-Sea Beach Resort

Location Near beach **Address** Opp District Court, LT Road **Telefax** 222697/ 390 **Mobile** 09881670465 **Website** sunnsea beachresort.com **Rooms** 37 **Tariff** Rs 1,500-3,500 **Credit Cards** NA **Facilities** Restaurant, swimming pool, indoor games, travel desk, locker, laundry, room service, attached bath, TV **Mumbai Reservations** Ask House, 106, Marol Co-op Industrial Estate, Off MV Road, Andheri (East), Mumbai **Tel** 022-65164632, 65961518

Tushar Govt Rest House

SEA-FACING

Location Near beach **Address** PWD Office, Alibaug Fort **Tel** 222132 **Rooms** 8 **Tariff** Rs 200 **Credit Cards** NA **Facilities** Cook, laundry, hot water

BORDI STD 02528

Goolkhush Resort

Location Off the beach **Address** Opp Parsi Fire Temple, Next to Stambh, At Bordi **Tel** 254182/ 336 **Mobile** 09822078151 **Rooms** 10 **Tariff** Rs 600-1,200; TE **Credit Cards** NA **Facilities** Restaurant, swimming pool, travel assistance, room service, attached bath, hot water, TV **Mumbai Reservations** 275 J, New Cama Building, Zoroastrian Colony, Opp Matru Mandir, Tardeo Road **Tel** 022-23821494

Hill Zill

Location Hillside **Address** Bordi Road, Borigaon **Tel** 249050/ 119 **Mobile** 09824121460 **Website** hillzill.com **Rooms** 35, bungalows 2 **Tariff** Rs 600-2,500 **Credit Cards** NA **Facilities** Restaurant, bar, swimming pool, kids' pool, travel desk, lockers, room service, attached bath, TV **Mumbai Reservations** Milky Way Resorts Pvt Ltd, FF, 13 Gajanan Krupa, Ganesh Peth Lane, Behind Shivaji Mandir, Dadar (West), Mumbai **Tel** 022-24382134

Tapovan Retreat

Location Opp Vijay Stambh **Address** Bordi **Tel** 254649 **Website** tapovanretreat.com **Rooms** 11 **Tariff** Rs 750-1,200 **Credit Cards** NA **Facilities** Meals on order, trekking on request, doctor-on-call, room service, attached bath, hot water, TV **Mumbai Reservations** Kiritco, SF, PNB House, Sir PM Road, Fort, Mumbai **Tel** 022-22665322 **Mobile** 09820191153

Tent Resort MTDC

Location Beachside **Address** Bordi, Taluka Dahanu, Dist Thane **Tel** 254243 **Website** maharashtra tourism.gov.in **Rooms** 8, tents 6 **Tariff** Rs 750-1,250 **Credit Cards** NA **Facilities** Restaurant, travel desk, lockers, room service, TV **Metro Reservations** *See pages 519-520*

IN DAHANU

Hotel Beachside

Location Beachside **Address** Narpad Beach, Dahanu (West) **Tel** 223376, 225971 **Telefax** 224476 **Website** hotelbeach side.com **Rooms** 20 **Tariff** Rs 500-2,250 **Credit Cards** Visa, Master **Facilities** Restaurant, bar, swimming pool, travel desk, laundry, room service, TV **Mumbai Reservations** 3, Dwarka, Shastri Hall, Tardeo Road, Mumbai **Tel** 022-23870880 **Fax** 23879388

Pearline Beach Resort

Location Sea-facing **Address** Agar Road, Dahanu Beach, Dahanu (West), Dist Thane **Tel** 222442, 225655/ 791 **Mobile** 09823037189, 09422577253 **Fax** 223768 **Website** pearline beachresort.com **Rooms** 14 **Tariff** Rs 650-900 **Credit Cards** Visa, Master **Facilities** Restaurant, bar, swimming pool, gym, travel desk, camping, sightseeing, room service, TV

Seawoods Beach Hotel

SEA-FACING

Location Near Pearline Beach Resort **Address** Opp Dahanu Beach, Agar Road, Dahanu (West), Dist Thane **Tel** 213100, 225669 **Website** seawoods beachhotel.com **Rooms** 9 **Tariff** Rs 900-1,500 **Credit Cards** NA **Facilities** Restaurant, coffee shop, swimming pool, gym, travel desk, airport transfers, bike rental, forex, laundry, room service, attached bath, TV

GANAPATIPULE STD 02357

Holiday Resort MTDC

Location Beachside **Address** AT

& PO Ganapatipule **Tel** 235061-62, 235248 **Fax** 235328 **Rooms** 90, tents 16, Konkani houses 12 **Tariff** Rs 1,200-2,500 TE **Credit Cards** Visa, Master **Facilities** Restaurant, water sports, room service **Metro Reservations** *See pages 519-520*

Hotel Durvankur

Location Near the temple **Address** C/o Kelkar Udyog Society **Tel** 235764/ 91 **Fax** 235782 **Rooms** 20 **Tariff** Rs 800-1,200 **Credit Cards** Visa, Master **Facilities** Restaurant, super-market, travel assistance, laundry, room service, attached bath, TV

Hotel Landmark

Location Seashore **Address** Bhandarpuli Road **Tel** 235212/ 84-85 **Rooms** 32 **Tariff** Rs 1,000-2,200; TE **Credit Cards** NA **Facilities** Restaurant, travel desk, swimming pool, laundry, doctor-on-call, TV **Mumbai Reservations** Landmark Resort Pvt Ltd, A-1 Bhavishya Darshan, Ratannagar, Char Bungalow, Andheri (West), Mumbai **Tel** 022-26354124/ 4229

Hotel Shiv Sagar Palace

Location Hillside **Address** AT & PO Ganapatipule **Tel** 235726 **Rooms** 31 **Tariff** Rs 700-2,000; TE **Credit Cards** NA **Facilities** Restaurant, attached bath, TV

Krishnali Beach Resort

Location Seashore **Address** Bhandarpule Road **Tel** 235351-53 **Fax** 235330 **Website** krishnaliresorts.com **Rooms** 32 cottages, 3 bungalows **Tariff** Rs 3,330-7920 **Credit Cards** Visa, Master **Facilities** Restaurant, travel desk, swimming pool, health club, puja arranged, laundry **Mumbai Reservations** Krishnali Resorts Pvt Ltd, 1, Ram Building, Dr Balram Marg **Tel** 022-23860918, 23822999

GUHAGAR STD 02359

Hotel Kautilya

Location Near beach **Address** Khalchapaat **Tel** 240203/ 575 **Mobile** 09423048234 **Rooms** 15 **Tariff** Rs 400-950 **Credit Cards** NA **Facilities** Room service, attached bath, hot water, TV

Kismat Residency

Location Opp Marathi School No. 1 **Address** Khalchapaat **Tel** 240686, 240156-58 **Mobile** 09820513358, 09869480384 **Rooms** 18 **Tariff** Rs 400-650 **Credit Cards** NA **Facilities** Restaurant, permit room, kids' pool, travel assistance, laundry, room service, TV **Mumbai Reservations** 220/222, B-15/16, Sagar Mahim CHS, Veer Savarkar Marg, Mahim, Mumbai **Tel** 022-24467015

Manas Lodge

Location Central **Address** Opp Guhagar Bus Terminus **Tel** 240684 **Mobile** 09423800529 **Rooms** 17 **Tariff** Rs 200-500 **Credit Cards** NA **Facilities** Room service, attached bath, hot water, TV (some rooms)

Prestige Lodge

Location Central **Address** Near Guhagar bus terminus **Tel** 240930 **Rooms** 24 **Tariff** Rs 200-500 **Credit Cards** NA **Facilities** Room service, attached bath, hot water, TV (some rooms)

Sagar Lodge

Location Near Wyadeshwar Temple **Address** Bazaarpet **Tel** 240347 **Rooms** 22 **Tariff** Rs 150-350; a single bed Rs 50 **Credit Cards** NA **Facilities** Room service, attached bath, hot water, TV (some rooms)

IN HEDAVI

Suruchi Corner

Location Near beach **Address**

PO Hedavi, Taluka Guhagar **Tel** 243209/ 616 **Mobile** 09421934344 **Rooms** 5, huts 6 **Tariff** Rs 500-600 **Credit Cards** NA **Facilities** Restaurant, room service, attached bath, hot water

IN VELNESHWAR

Atithi Hotel

Address Near Shankar Temple **Tel** 243518 **Rooms** 10 **Tariff** Rs 500 **Credit Cards** NA **Facilities** Meals on order, room service, attached bath, TV

Kinara Beach House

Location Beachside **Address** Thakur Stop **Tel** 243363 **Mobile** 09969195954 **Rooms** 7 **Tariff** Rs 300-500 **Credit Cards** NA **Facilities** Meals on order, room service, attached bath (some rooms), hot water

HARIHARESHWAR STD 02147

Beach Resort MTDC

Location Beachside **Address** Near Harihareshwar Temple, Taluka Shrivardhan, Dist Raigad **Tel** 226036 **Website** maharashtratourism.gov.in **Rooms** 27 **Tariff** Rs 500-1,500 **Credit Cards** NA **Facilities** Restaurant, travel assistance, room service, attached bath, TV **Mumbai Reservations** *See pages 519-520*

Ganga Nivas

Location Start of Temple Road **Address** Shivajinagar, Taluka Shrivardhan, Dist Raigad **Tel** 226243 **Rooms** 3 **Tariff** Rs 350 **Credit Cards** NA **Facilities** Meals on order, room service, attached bath, hot water

Gokul Hotel

Location Opp Kaatal Lake **Address** Near Harihareshwar Temple, Taluka Shrivardhan, Dist Raigad **Tel** 226439 **Rooms** 5 **Tariff** Rs 200-1,200 **Credit Cards** NA **Facilities** Meals on order, room service, attached bath, hot water, TV

Nandanvan

Location Near bus stand **Address** Near Bank of India, Taluka Shrivardhan **Tel** 226158 **Rooms** 6, dorm 1 (10 beds) **Tariff** Rs 350-450, dorm bed Rs 80 **Credit Cards** NA **Facilities** Meals on order, room service, attached bath, hot water

Shiv Sagar Caterers

Address Near MTDC Resort, Taluka Shrivardhan, Dist Raigad **Tel** 226038 **Mobile** 09271100240, 09213268486 **Rooms** 4, dorm 1 **Tariff** Rs 200-700 **Credit Cards** NA **Facilities** Food on order, doctor-on-call, laundry, room service, attached bath, hot water

HARNAI-MURUD STD 02358

Abhiruchi

Location Beachside **Address** Near Durga Temple, Murud **Tel** 234651, 693049 **Mobile** 09420050957 **Rooms** 7 cottages **Tariff** Rs 400-1,200 **Credit Cards** NA **Facilities** Restaurant, travel desk, boating, doctor-on-call, lockers, laundry, room service, attached bath, hot water

Hotel Kinara

Location Near beach **Address** Karde Pakhadi **Tel** 234633 **Mobile** 09420376661, 09869185343 **Rooms** 12 **Tariff** Rs 700; TE **Credit Cards** NA **Facilities** Restaurant, travel assistance, boating (in season), doctor-on-call, laundry, attached bath, hot water

Kamat's Murud Beach Resort

Location Beachside **Address** AT & PO Murud, Dapoli **Tel** 234709/ 582/ 828 **Rooms** 15 cottages **Tariff** Rs 500-1,100; TE **Credit Cards** NA **Facilities** Restaurant, travel assistance, room service, attached bath, hot water, TV **Mumbai Reservations** Kamat's Holidays, Lotus Suites, Andheri-Kurla Road, International Airport Zone, Andheri (East), Mumbai **Tel** 022-28271155, 32411074

Kshitij Beach Resort

Location Near beach **Address** AT & PO Murud, Dapoli **Tel** 234603 **Rooms** 4 **Tariff** Rs 500 **Credit Cards** NA **Facilities** Restaurant, doctor-on-call, room service, attached bath, hot water

Palm Village

Location Near beach **Address** Plot No. 379, Varchi Pakhadi, AT & PO Murud, Dapoli, Dist Ratnagiri **Tel** 234644 **Rooms** 17 **Tariff** Rs 600-1,200 **Credit Cards** NA **Facilities** Restaurant, travel desk, power back-up, room service, attached bath, hot water **Pune Reservations** 725, Sadashiv Peth, Chitrashala Chowk, Kumtekar Road, Pune **Tel** 020-24476263

Sagar Hill Hotel

Location Beachside **Address** Karde Beach **Tel** 234596/ 740 **Rooms** 19 **Tariff** Rs 1,000 **Credit Cards** NA **Facilities** Restaurant, hammocks, laundry, room service, attached bath, hot water

Sea Face Beach Resort

Location Near beach **Address** Near Dhabol Enron and Keshavraj Temple, Village Karde, Taluka Dapoli **Tel** 234832/ 656 **Rooms** 18 **Tariff** Rs 800-1,250; TE **Credit Cards** NA **Facilities** Restaurant, travel assistance, doctor-on-call, laundry, room service, attached bath, TV

Silver Sand Beach Resort

Location Beachside **Address** Karde Pakhadi, Murud **Tel** 234501, 234872-73 **Rooms** 17 **Tariff** Rs 800-1,100 **Credit Cards** NA **Facilities** Restaurant, hammocks, laundry, attached bath, TV **Mumbai Reservations** Ram Kunj Smriti, 5th Floor, Ram Maruti Road, Near Sindhudurg Hotel, Dadar, Mumbai **Tel** 022-24300066

Surbhi Beach Resort

Location Beachside **Address** Khalchi Pakhadi, Murud, Taluka Dapoli **Tel** 234556 **Mobile** 09423832343 **Rooms** 8 **Tariff** Rs 450 **Credit Cards** NA **Facilities** Restaurant, doctor-on-call, laundry, attached bath

KASHID STD 02144

Friends Holiday Home

Location Near beach **Address** Kashid **Tel** 278636/ 11 **Mobile** 09270371274 **Rooms** 7 **Tariff** Rs 650-1,000 **Credit Cards** NA **Facilities** Meals on order, travel assistance, room service, attached bath, hot water **Pune Reservations** Mihir Tourism, Pune **Tel** 020-5428752

Kashid Beach Resort

Location Hillside **Address** PO Kashid **Tel** 278501-03 **Fax** 278504 **Rooms** 24 **Tariff** Rs 3,500-7,000 **Credit Cards** NA **Facilities** Restaurant, disco, kids play area, doctor-on-call, lockers, laundry, room service **Mumbai Reservations** DS & Sons, 85/46, Waroda Road, Bandra (West), Mumbai **Tel** 022-26439602/ 8312

Kashid Beach Villa

Location Adjacent to Prakruti Resorts **Address** Village & PO Kashid, Murud-Janjira Road **Mobile** 09820191822, 09270151606 **Email** faraaz_911 @hotmail.com **Rooms** 5 **Tariff** Rs 2,000-10,000 **Credit Cards** NA **Facilities** Meals on order, power back-up, pool, travel assistance, laundry, room service, TV **Mumbai Reservations** Rubina Khan, Jawaharabad, SF, Flat No. 9, 9th Road, TPS 1V, Bandra, Mumbai **Tel** 022-26408955

Prakruti Resorts AYURVEDA

Location Hillside **Address** Village & PO Kashid, Murud-Janjira Road **Tel** 278509 **Website** prakrutiresorts.net **Rooms** 99 **Tariff** Rs 5,460-23,940 (with food) **Credit Cards** AmEx, Visa, Master **Facilities** Restaurant, swimming pool, travel desk, Ayurvedic massage, pool table, mini golf club, forest safari, power back-up, room service, TV **Mumbai Reservations** 205, Vaishali Garden, Chembur, Mumbai **Tel** 022-67973156-58

Sagar Tourist Resort

Location Near beach **Address** PO Kashid, Taluka Murud **Tel** 278525/ 640 **Mobile** 09226042729, 09422692463 **Rooms** 5 **Tariff** Rs 800-1,000 **Credit Cards** NA **Facilities** Food on order, room service, TV in some rooms

Sai Palace

Location Hillside **Address** Alibaug-Murud Road **Tel** 278629 **Rooms** 10 **Tariff** Rs 1,300-2,600 **Credit Cards** NA **Facilities** Restaurant, garden, attached bath, hot water

KUNKESHWAR STD 02364

Bhakti Niwas

Location Near beach **Address** PO Kunkeshwar **Tel** 248650 **Rooms** 120 **Tariff** Rs 150-200 **Credit Cards** NA **Facilities** Basic accommodation only, attached bath with some rooms

Savli Resort

Location On coastal road

Address PO Kunkeshwar **Tel** 248614/ 44 **Rooms** 5, dorm 1 **Tariff** Rs 600-850 **Credit Cards** NA **Facilities** Restaurant, room service, attached bath, hot water

IN DEVGAD

Greenvilla Guesthouse
Location Opp petrol pump **Address** 873, Sri Krishna Nagar, Jamsande, Devgad Taluka **Tel Mobile** 09422381141 **Rooms** 4 **Tariff** Rs 250-300 **Credit Cards** NA **Facilities** Breakfast provided, laundry, room service, attached bath, hot water, TV

Hotel Alankar
Location Near market **Address** Behind Devgad ST Bus Stand **Tel** 262259 **Rooms** 12 **Tariff** Rs 80-250 **Credit Cards** NA **Facilities** Restaurant, room service, attached bath in some rooms, running water, TV

Hotel Parijat
Location Near market **Address** Opp Devgad ST Bus Stand **Tel** 262302, 262630 **Rooms** 12 **Tariff** Rs 150-950 **Credit Cards** NA **Facilities** Restaurant, room service, attached bath in some rooms, hot water, TV in some rooms

MUMBAI STD 022

Ambassador Hotel
Location South Mumbai **Address** Veer Nariman Road, Churchgate **Tel** 22041131 **Website** ambassadorindia.com **Rooms** 126 **Tariff** Rs 5,500-25,000 (with breakfast) **Credit Cards** AmEx, Visa, Master **Facilities** Restaurants, bar, coffee shop, health centre, laundry, room service, TV

Bentley's Hotel
Location Opp Phalke Restaurant **Address** 17, Oliver Road, Colaba **Tel** 22841474/ 1733, 22882890 **Fax** 22871846 **Website** bentleys hotel.com **Rooms** 36 **Tariff** Rs 1,145-1,680 **Credit Cards** Visa, Master **Facilities** Room service, attached bath, hot water

Citizen Hotel
Location On Juhu Beach **Address** 960, Juhu Tara Road **Tel** 66932525, 26607273 **Website** citizenhotelmumbai. com **Rooms** 45 **Tariff** Rs 5,000-9,000 **Credit Cards** Visa, Master **Facilities** Restaurants, bar, laundry, doctor-on-call, room service, attached bath, TV

Eastern International Hotel
Location Near Juhu Beach **Address** Balraj Sahani Marg **Tel** 66934444 **Fax** 66934455/ 66 **Website** eihlimited.com **Rooms** 191 **Tariff** Rs 11,000-28,800 **Credit Cards** Visa, Master **Facilities** Restaurants, bar, coffee shop, travel desk, parking, swimming pool, yoga, health club, shopping arcade, beauty salon, baby sitting, laundry, Internet, room service, TV

Hilton Towers YOGA
Location Near beach **Address** Nariman Point **Tel** 66324343 **Fax** 66324142 **Website** hilton.com **Rooms** 547 **Tariff** Rs 8,800-47,700 **Credit Cards** AmEx, Visa, Master **Facilities** Restaurants, bar, travel desk, parking, swimming pool, yoga, health club, laundry, doctor-on-call, room service, TV

Hotel Airlink
Location Opp domestic airport **Address** 75, Off Nehru Road, Vile Parle (East) **Tel** 26183575 **Website** hotelairlink.com **Rooms** 30 **Tariff** Rs 1,800-3,600; TE **Credit Cards** Visa, Master **Facilities** Restaurant, bar, laundry, doctor-on-call, room service, attached bath, TV

Hotel Avion
Location Opp domestic airport **Address** Nehru Road, Vile Parle (East) **Tel** 26109576, 26116958 **Website** avionhotel.com **Rooms** 43 **Tariff** Rs 4,100-4,900; TE **Credit Cards** Visa, Master **Facilities** Restaurant, airport transfers, laundry, doctor-on-call, room service, TV

Hotel Marine Plaza SEA-FACING
Location Sea-facing **Address** 29, Marine Drive **Tel** 22851212 **Fax** 22828585 **Website** hotel marineplaza.com, sarovar hotels.com **Rooms** 68, suites 4 **Tariff** Rs 7,500-17,500; TE **Credit Cards** Visa, Master **Facilities** Multi-cuisine restaurant, bar, coffee shop, travel desk, health club, laundry, doctor-on-call, room service, attached bath, hot water, TV

Intercontinental the Grand
Location Near airport **Address** Sahar Airport Road, Andheri (East) **Tel** 66992222 **Website** thegrand hotels.net, ichotelsgroup.com **Rooms** 369 **Tariff** Rs 9,360-60,000 **Credit Cards** AmEx, Visa, Master, Diners **Facilities** Restaurants, bar, travel desk, swimming pool, health centre, shopping arcade, parking, laundry, doctor-on-call, room service, TV

ISKCON Temple Guest House
Location Near Juhu Beach **Address** ISKCON Ashram, Hare Krishna Land, Juhu **Tel** 26206860/ 5214/ 0870/ 2226 **Website** iskconmumbai.com **Rooms** 46 **Tariff** Rs 1,600-2,000

Credit Cards Visa **Facilities** Restaurant, room service, attached bath, hot water

Juhu Residency Hotel

Location Opp JW Marriot **Address** 148-B, Juhu Tara Road **Tel** 26184546 **Rooms** 20 **Tariff** Rs 1,700-3,300; TE **Credit Cards** AmEx, Visa, Master **Facilities** Kitchen, laundry, room service, attached bath, TV

JW Marriot Hotel SPA

Location Near Juhu Bus Stand **Address** Juhu Tara Road, Juhu Beach **Tel** 66933000 **Website** marriot.com **Rooms** 358 **Tariff** Rs 14,400-28,800 **Credit Cards** AmEx, Visa, Master **Facilities** Restaurants, bar, coffee shop, travel desk, beauty saloon, spa and health club, swimming pool, laundry, room service, TV

Royal Garden Hotel

Location Opp Juhu Beach **Address** Juhu Tara Road, Santa Cruz (West) **Tel** 26603516, 66919800 **Website** royalgarden hotelmumbai.com **Rooms** 34, suites 2 **Tariff** Rs 4,500-7,500; TE **Credit Cards** AmEx, Visa, Master **Facilities** Restaurant, bar, airport transfers, laundry, room service, attached bath, TV

Sea Green Hotel

Location Near Brabourne Stadium **Address** 145, Marine Drive **Tel** 66336525, 22822294 **Fax** 66336530 **Website** seagreen hotel.com **Rooms** 34 **Tariff** Rs 2,100-3,100; TE **Credit Cards** AmEx, Visa, Master, Diners **Facilities** Laundry, doctor-on-call, room service, attached bath, hot water, TV

Sun-N-Sand

Location Beachside **Address** 39, Juhu Beach **Tel** 66938888 **Website** sunnsandhotel.com **Rooms** 120 **Tariff** Rs 8,500-20,000; TE **Credit Cards** AmEx, Visa, Master **Facilities** Restaurants, bar, travel desk, beauty saloon, health club, swimming pool, laundry, doctor-on-call, room service, TV

The Oberoi SEA-FACING GOLF

Location Sea-facing **Address** Nariman Point **Tel** 56325757 **Fax** 66325757 **Website** oberoi-mumbai.com **Rooms** 333, suites 22 **Tariff** Rs 13,000-75,000; TE **Credit Cards** AmEx, Visa, Master, Diners **Facilities** Restaurants, bar, travel desk, swimming pool, fitness centre, golf, beauty saloon, laundry, doctor-on-call, room service, TV

The Taj Mahal Palace & Tower

Address Apollo Bunder **Tel** 66653366 **Fax** 66650323-24 **Website** tajhotels.com **Rooms** 565, suites 46 **Tariff** Rs 9,900-1,00,000 **Credit Cards** AmEx, Visa, Master, Diners, BoB **Facilities** Restaurants, bar, travel desk, parking, swimming pool, health club, golf, baby sitting, beauty saloon, laundry, doctor-on-call, room service, TV

YWCA International Guest House

Location Near Regal Cinema **Address** 18, Madame Cama Road, Fort **Tel** 22025053 **Rooms** 20 **Tariff** Rs 890-3,124 (with breakfast and dinner) **Credit Cards** Visa, Master, Diners **Facilities** Restaurant, travel desk, car rental, laundry, doctor-on-call, room service, attached bath, hot water, TV

AROUND MUMBAI STD 022

ON AKSA BEACH

The Resort SPA

Location Across the creek from Essel World and Water Kingdom **Address** 11, Madh-Marve Road, Aksa Beach, Malad (West) **Tel** 28808888, 28445538/ 260/ 318 **Fax** 28804444 **Website** theresortmumbai.com **Rooms**

88, suites 3, cottages 2 **Tariff** Rs 5,800-16,000; TE **Credit Cards** AmEx, Visa, Master **Facilities** Restaurant, coffee shop, bar, discotheque, swimming pool, gym, spa, baby sitting, travel desk, Internet, outdoor games, forex, beauty salon, doctor-on-call, laundry, room service, TV **Mumbai Reservations Tel** 022-26443333

ON ERANGAL BEACH

The Retreat

Location On Madh Marve Road **Address** Erangal Beach, Madh Island, Marve Road, Malad (West) **Tel** 28813500, 28816383 **Fax** 28811919 **Website** kraheja hospitality.com **Rooms** 145 **Tariff** Rs 6,600-12,000 **Credit Cards** AmEx, Visa, Diners **Facilities** Restaurant, coffee shop, bar, swimming pool, book shop, gym, travel desk, airport transfers, bike rental, forex, beauty parlour, doctor-on-call, lockers, laundry, room service, TV **Mumbai Reservations** Rampart House, SF, K Dubhash Marg, Fort, Mumbai **Tel** 022-22834441/ 4426

IN MANORI

Domonica's Beach Resort

Location Near Domonica Bus Stop **Address** Manori **Tel** 28452163/ 78 **Rooms** 32 **Tariff** Rs 700-1,000; dorm Rs 250-350 **Credit Cards** NA **Facilities** Restaurant, room service, attached bath, TV in some rooms **Mumbai Reservations Tel** 022-24462161/ 9735

Domonica Hotel

Location Near Domonica Bus Stop **Address** Manori **Tel** 28452643/ 280 **Rooms** 8 **Tariff** Rs 700-1,000; dorm Rs 250-350 **Credit Cards** NA **Facilities** Restaurant, room service, attached bath, hot water, TV in some rooms **Mumbai Reservations** *See Domonica's Beach Resort alongside*

Manoribel YOGA

Location 3 km from Gorai **Address** Near Manori Village, via Marve Road, Malad (West) **Tel** 28452806-09 **Website** manoribel.com **Rooms** 22 **Tariff** Rs 832-3,740 **Credit Cards** Visa, Master **Facilities** Restaurant, utility shop, massage, yoga and meditation, gym, travel desk, doctor-on-call, laundry, room service, TV **Mumbai Reservations** No. 9, FF, Ashoka Shopping Centre, LT Marg (Metro-Crawford Market), Mumbai **Tel** 022-22691301 **Fax** 22692108

IN UTAN

U-Tan Sea Resort SEA-FACING

Location Near beach **Address** Chowk Dongri, via Utan, Bhayander (West), Dist Thane **Tel** 28451151/ 2345 **Website** u-tan.com **Rooms** 26 **Tariff** Rs 1,650-3,850 **Credit Cards** Visa, Master **Facilities** Restaurant, outdoor games, swimming pool, travel assistance, doctor-on-call, laundry, room service, attached bath, hot water, TV **Mumbai Reservations Tel** 022-26206063, 26282653

MURUD-JANJIRA STD 02144

Golden Swan Beach Resort

Location Sea-facing **Address** Opp Customs Office, Darbar Road **Tel** 274078, 276580 **Website** goldenswan.com **Rooms** 29 **Tariff** Rs 1,200-7,500; TE **Credit Cards** AmEx, Visa, Master **Facilities** Multi-cuisine café, indoor/ outdoor games, travel desk, laundry, room service, TV **Mumbai Reservations** 76 Regency Park, Near Khar Subway, Santacruz, Mumbai **Tel** 022-26174517-19

Hotel Sea Green

Location Near beach **Address** Dutt Mandir, Police Station **Tel** 274171 **Rooms** 8 **Tariff** Rs 800-1,400; TE **Credit Cards** NA **Facilities** Meals on order, room service, attached bath, TV **Mumbai Reservations** A-16, Manekji Street, Colaba, Mumbai **Tel** 022-22830326/ 4710

Sand Piper Resorts

Location Sea-facing hillock **Address** Idgah Road, Behind Police Station **Tel** 274166 **Website** sandpiperresorts.com **Rooms** 22 **Tariff** Rs 1,400-3,200; TE **Credit Cards** Visa, Diners **Facilities** Restaurant, swimming pool, room service, TV **Mumbai Reservations** Sand Piper Resorts, FF, Iqbal Bungalow, 33 Rebello Road, Bandra, Mumbai **Mobile** 09820198337 **Fax** 022-26408502

Sea Shell Resort

Location Sea-facing **Address** Near Police Station **Tel** 274306 **Rooms** 12 **Tariff** Rs 1,500-2,000; TE **Credit Cards** Visa, Master **Facilities** Meals on order, garden, room service

Shoreline Resort

Location Opp the beach **Address** Darbar Road **Tel** 274640-41 **Telefax** 274591 **Rooms** 20 **Tariff** Rs 1,200-2,500 **Credit Cards** NA **Facilities** Restaurant, travel assistance, doctor-on-call, laundry, room service, TV **Mumbai Reservations** A/1, Garibdas CHS, 5th Road, JBTD Scheme, Juhu, Mumbai **Tel** 022-26203286 **Mobile** 09869691273

PALGHAR STD 02525

Anand Residency (MTDC approved)

Location Near the beach **Address** Kelva Beach **Tel** 222216 **Mobile** 09823137216, 09823341862 **Rooms** 6, dorm 1 (25 beds) **Tariff** Rs 300-500 per person **Credit Cards** NA **Facilities** Restaurant, laundry, room service, attached bath, hot water, TV **Metro Reservations** *See pages 519-520*

Jungle Resort and Water Park

Location Near railway station **Address** Veoor Village **Tel** 251300 **Email** jungleresort@mtnl.net.in **Rooms** 9, dorms 4 **Tariff** Rs 1,300-1,700 (with meals) **Credit Cards** NA **Facilities** Restaurant, gym, swimming pool, water park, room service, TV **Mumbai Reservations** 14A, Dr MC Jhavle Road, Dadar (West), Mumbai **Tel** 66661300 **Mobile** 09323131300

Kelva Beach Resort

Location Near beach **Address** Behind Shitla Devi Temple, Kelva **Tel** 222346 **Mobile** 09960121875 **Website** kelvabeachresort.com **Rooms** 11 huts **Tariff** Rs 1,250-1,500 per person (with meals) **Credit Cards** NA **Facilities** Restaurant, swimming pool, badminton, pool table, doctor-on-call, laundry, room service, attached bath, hot water **Mumbai Reservations** Rampart Business Centre, 16/24, Bake House, MCC Lane, Kala Ghoda, Mumbai **Tel** 022-66310581

Laxmi Guesthouse

Location Near Paanch Batti **Address** Kuber Shopping Centre **Tel** 253007 **Rooms** 24 **Tariff** Rs 75-550 **Credit Cards** NA **Facilities** Doctor-on-call, laundry, room service, attached bath, hot water, TV

Sai Residency

Address Mahim Road **Tel** 241309/ 18 **Rooms** 16 **Tariff** Rs 350-650 **Credit Cards** Visa, Master **Facilities** Restaurant, bar, swimming pool, travel desk, laundry, room service, attached bath, hot water, TV **Mumbai Reservations** Sai Travels, Sheetal Chhaya Building, Dagriwadi, SK Bhole Cross Road, Near Kabutar Khana, Dadar (West), Mumbai **Tel** 022-24313012

IN MANOR

Silent Hills Resort

Location Near petrol pump **Address** NH-8, Vaitarna River Bridge, Manor, Palghar **Tel** 237170/ 243-47 **Mobile** 09890747997 **Website** silenthillsresort.com **Rooms** 24 **Tariff** Rs 2,100-4,100 **Credit Cards** Visa, Master **Facilities** Restaurant, bar, swimming pool, water slides, kids' pool, boating, gym, travel desk, mini amusement park, doctor-on-call, lockers, laundry, room service, attached bath, hot water, TV **Mumbai Reservations** Plot No. 14, Jawahar Nagar, SV Road, Goregaon (West), Mumbai **Tel** 022-28720532/ 2463 **Mobile** 09967362161

RATNAGIRI STD 02352

Hotel Giri Ratna

Address Opp railway station **Tel** 231260, 230888 **Rooms** 20 **Tariff** Rs 900-1,800 **Credit Cards** Visa, Master **Facilities** Restaurant, travel assistance, lockers, laundry, room service, attached bath, TV **Mumbai Reservations** Ek Ram building, Dr Bhalerao Marg, Girgaum, Mumbai **Tel** 022-23860918

Hotel Kaanchan

Location Near railway station **Address** MIDC, Mirjoli **Tel** 228250-51 **Rooms** 24 **Tariff** Rs 600-900 **Credit Cards** NA

Facilities Restaurant, bar, swimming pool, gym, travel desk, doctor-on-call, laundry, room service, attached bath, TV

Hotel Landmark
Location Near Thibaw Palace **Address** Thibaw Palace Road **Tel** 220120 **Fax** 220124 **Rooms** 32 **Tariff** Rs 595-1,395 **Credit Cards** Visa, Master **Facilities** Restaurant, bar, swimming pool, gym, kids' park, travel desk, doctor-on-call, laundry, room service, attached bath, hot water, TV **Mumbai Reservations** A-1, Bhavishya Darshan, Ratan Nagar, Four Bungalows, Opp Sai Temple, Andheri (West), Mumbai **Tel** 022-26354124/ 229

Hotel Prabha
Location Near local Congress Bhavan **Address** Tilak Ali **Tel** 223515, 221947 **Rooms** 17 **Tariff** Rs 250-600 **Credit Cards** Visa, Master **Facilities** Restaurant, travel desk, doctor-on-call, laundry, room service, attached bath, hot water, TV

Hotel Vihar Deluxe
Location Opp ST Office **Address** S-70, Junamal Naka, Shivaji Nagar **Tel** 222944-45 **Rooms** 28 **Tariff** Rs 400-1,100 **Credit Cards** Visa, Master **Facilities** Restaurant, kids' park, travel desk, doctor-on-call, laundry, room service, attached bath, hot water, TV

Hotel Vivek
Location Central **Address** 540-B/1, Main Road **Tel** 222162, 220689 **Fax** 220390 **Rooms** 30 **Tariff** Rs 450-1,500 **Credit Cards** Visa, Master **Facilities** Restaurant, bar, travel desk, doctor-on-call, laundry, room service, attached bath, TV

Kohinoor Samudra Resort
Location Hilltop **Address** Bhatye, Ratnagiri-Pawas Coastal Highway **Tel** 235231-32 **Fax** 235013 **Website** kohinoorhotels.com **Rooms** 24 **Tariff** Rs 4,250-9,750 (with meals) **Credit Cards** Visa, Master **Facilities** Restaurant, bar, water sports, boating, swimming pool, gym, indoor games, travel desk, doctor-on-call, laundry, room service, attached bath, hot water, TV **Mumbai Reservations** Hotel Kohinoor Park, Opp Siddhi Vinayak Temple, Prabhadevi, Mumbai **Tel** 022-24385555

SHRIVARDHAN STD 02147

Fulora Resort
Location On a hill **Address** Jivna Kond Hill, Dighi Road **Tel** 223300 **Rooms** 20 **Tariff** Rs 750-2,000 **Credit Cards** NA **Facilities** Restaurant, swimming pool, travel assistance, doctor-on-call, attached bath, hot water

Kalaprasad Guest Park
Location Near Narayan Temple **Address** Narayan Pakadhi **Tel** 222619 **Mobile** 09850182065 **Rooms** 8, dorm 1 **Tariff** Rs 400-500; dorm bed Rs 60 **Credit Cards** NA **Facilities** Meals on order, power back-up, travel assistance, doctor-on-call, laundry, attached bath, hot water

Niwara
Location Near beach **Address** Dabak Pakhadi **Tel** 222298 **Rooms** 2 **Tariff** Rs 800 **Credit Cards** NA **Facilities** Meals on order, travel assistance, doctor-on-call, laundry, attached bath, hot water, TV

Sagar Darshan
Location Near beach **Address** Rest House Road **Tel** 222958 **Mobile** 09850018213, 09326754079 **Rooms** 3 **Tariff** Rs 400-700 **Credit Cards** NA **Facilities** Meals on order, travel assistance, power back-up, laundry, room service, attached bath, hot water, TV

Savali
Location Behind Sagar Darshan **Address** Bhairavnath Pakhadi **Tel** 222958 **Mobile** 09850018213, 09326754079 **Rooms** 2 suites **Tariff** Rs 1,000 **Credit Cards** NA **Facilities** Meals on order, power back-up, travel assistance, doctor-on-call, laundry, room service, attached bath, hot water, TV

Shiv Shanti Holiday Inn
Location Govt Rest House **Address** Dabak Pakadi **Tel** 222163 **Rooms** 24 **Tariff** Rs 800-1,200 **Credit Cards** NA **Facilities** Restaurant, swimming pool, travel assistance, doctor-on-call, laundry, room service, attached bath, hot water, TV **Mumbai Reservations** **Tel** 022-24224904

IN DIVEAGAR

Ambiance Cottages
Location Near beach **Address** Near Suvarna Ganapati Temple, Diveagar, Taluka Shrivardhan **Tel** 225334 **Rooms** 8 cottages **Tariff** Rs 700-900 **Credit Cards** NA **Facilities** Restaurant, generator, doctor-on-call, laundry, room service, attached bath, TV

Mavli Resort
Location Near Ganapati Temple **Address** PO Diveagar, Taluka Shrivardhan **Tel** 225225/ 015 **Mobile** 09324485569 **Rooms** 10 **Tariff** Rs 600 **Credit Cards** NA **Facilities** Meals on order, inverter, travel assistance,

doctor-on-call, room service, attached bath, hot water, TV

MTDC Exotica Beach Resort

Location Beachside **Address** Diveagar, Taluka Shrivardhan **Tel** 202012 **Mobile** 09421967767, 09869068676 **Rooms** 10 cottages **Tariff** Rs 1,500 **Credit Cards** NA **Facilities** Restaurant, travel assistance, laundry, room service, attached bath, hot water, TV **Metro Reservations** *See pages 519-520*

TARKARLI STD 02365

Apoorva Resort

Location Near MTDC Resort **Address** Tarkali **Tel** 253920 **Rooms** 4, dorms 2 **Tariff** Rs 400-600 **Credit Cards** NA **Facilities** Meals on order, attached bath

Hotel Chintamani

Location Near beach **Address** Opp MTDC Resort **Tel** 253817, 220313 **Rooms** 10 **Tariff** Rs 600-1,200 **Credit Cards** NA **Facilities** Restaurant, room service, attached bath, hot water

Hotel Gajanan

Location Beachside **Address** Near MTDC Resort **Tel** 251401 **Mobile** 09422488055 **Rooms** 6 **Tariff** Rs 620 **Credit Cards** NA **Facilities** Restaurant, room service, attached bath, hot water on request

MTDC Holiday Resort

Location Beachfront **Address** Tarkarli, Dist Sindhudurg **Tel** 252390 **Website** maharashtra tourism.gov.in **Rooms** 20 **Tariff** Rs 950-1,600 **Credit Cards** NA **Facilities** Restaurant, beer bar, travel desk, laundry, room service, attached bath, TV **Metro Reservations** *See page xxx*

ON CHIWLA BEACH

Nath Pai Sevagan

Location Beachside **Address** Chiwla Beach, Dhuriwada, Malvan **Tel** 252250 **Rooms** 8 **Tariff** Rs 300-350 **Credit Cards** NA **Facilities** Restaurant, room service, attached bath

Om Shraddha

Location Near beach **Address** Chiwla Beach, Dhuriwada, Malvan **Tel** 252727, 253135, 539555 **Rooms** 7 **Tariff** Rs 300-1,000 **Credit Cards** NA **Facilities** Room service, attached bath

Sagar Kinara

Location Near Malvan Jetty **Address** Opp Port, Dhuriwada, Malvan **Tel** 252264/ 137 **Rooms** 16 **Tariff** Rs 750-1,400 **Credit Cards** NA **Facilities** Restaurant, bar, parking, room service, attached bath, hot water, TV

Sai Chayya

Location Near beach **Address** Dhuriwada, Malvan **Tel** 251293 **Rooms** 6 **Tariff** Rs 500 **Credit Cards** NA **Facilities** Restaurant, room service, attached bath

VENGURLA STD 02366

Hotel Laukik

Location Marketplace **Address** Sarla Sadan, Ram Maruti Road **Tel** 263418 **Rooms** 7 **Tariff** Rs 350-650 **Credit Cards** NA **Facilities** Meals on order, room service, attached bath, TV

Sagar Guest House PWD

Location Sea-facing **Address** Near Vengurla Jetty **Tel** 262411 **Rooms** 2 **Tariff** Rs 200 **Credit Cards** NA **Facilities** Room service, attached bath **Reservations** PWD Head Office, Moti Talao, Sawantwadi **Tel** 02363-272214

Samir Guest House PWD

Location Near Fruit Research Centre **Address** Camp Area

Tel 262112 **Rooms** 2 **Tariff** Rs 200 **Credit Cards** NA **Facilities** Meals on order, room service, attached bath **Reservations** *See Sagar Guest House on previous page*

Sea View Hotel SEA-FACING
Location Sea-facing **Address** Vengurla Port, Barrister Kardikar Road **Tel** 262192-93 **Rooms** 5 **Tariff** Rs 200-300 **Credit Cards** NA **Facilities** Meals on order, room service, attached bath

ON SAGARESHWAR BEACH

MTDC Tent Resort MTDC
Location Beachside **Address** Sagareshwar Beach, PO Ubhadanda, Taluka Vengurla **Mobile** 09423859750, 09423880986 **Rooms** 10 huts **Tariff** Rs 500-700 **Credit Cards** NA **Facilities** Room service, attached bath, TV **Metro Reservations** *See pages 519-520*

ON SAGARTEERTH BEACH

Sagarteerth Beach Resort
Location Beachside **Address** Aravali, PO Sagarteerth, Vengurla Shiroda Road **Tel** 227456 **Mobile** 09822133231 **Rooms** 16 huts, 6 tents, 1 dorm **Tariff** Rs 300-400, dorm bed Rs 100 **Credit Cards** NA **Facilities** Kitchen, room service, laundry arrangements, attached bath (some rooms)
TIP Tents not available in the monsoon

ON VELAGAR BEACH

Dolphin Bay Beach Resort
Location Beachside **Address** Aravali, Velagar **Tel** 227529 **Rooms** 3, tents 5, huts 7 **Tariff** Rs 350-1,000 **Credit Cards** NA **Facilities** Restaurant, dolphin spotting, boat rides, travel assistance, camp fires, room service, attached bath (some rooms), hot water on request
TIP Tents not available in the monsoon

Paulo's Green Garden Resorts
Address Shiroda-Velagar Road **Mobile** 09869869470 **Rooms** 4 huts **Tariff** Rs 300-500 **Credit Cards** NA **Facilities** Restaurant, room service, laundry, attached bath, hot water on request

Silver Sands-Kothari Beach Resort
Location Near the beach **Address** Aravali, Velagar **Tel** 227987 **Rooms** 8 **Tariff** Rs 400-550 **Credit Cards** NA **Facilities** Restaurant, dolphin spotting, boat rides, travel assistance, campfires, room service, attached bath, hot water

IN SAWANTWADI STD 02363

Hotel Mango
Location Near bus stand and fish market **Address** G-90, Main Road, Kumthekar Complex **Tel** 271041/ 48 **Fax** 274132 **Rooms** 26 **Tariff** Rs 800-2,500 **Credit Cards** NA **Facilities** Restaurant, laundry, room service, TV

Hotel Tara Central
Location Near bus station **Address** Gandhi Chowk **Tel** 272923/ 644 **Mobile** 09822135451 **Rooms** 14 **Tariff** Rs 312-520 **Credit Cards** NA **Facilities** Restaurant, bar, swimming pool, travel assistance, doctor-on-call, laundry, room service, attached bath, TV

Konkan Crown Fun-O-Tel Central
Location Near Sawantwadi Railway Station **Address** Nirwade, Sindhudurg **Tel** 258555 **Website** konkancrown.net **Rooms** 25 **Tariff** Rs 850-3,000; TE **Credit Cards** Visa, Master **Facilities** Restaurant, bar, swimming pool, travel desk, laundry, room service, TV **Mumbai Reservations** 1108, Samarth Vaibhav, New Link Road, Oshiwara, Andheri (W), Mumbai **Tel** 022-26301705/ 06

Tourist Reception Centre
Location Opp Moti Talao **Address** Mumbai-Goa Highway **Tel** 271398/ 461 **Rooms** 18 **Tariff** Rs 800-1,500; TE **Credit Cards** NA **Facilities** Restaurant, travel assistance, laundry, room service, attached bath, TV

ORISSA

CHANDIPUR STD 06782

Hotel Anandamayee
Location Beachfront **Address** Chandipur **Tel** 270012 **Rooms** 57 **Tariff** Rs 475-1,150; TE **Credit Cards** NA **Facilities** Restaurant, attached bath , TV

Hotel Chandipur
Location Beachfront **Address** Chandipur **Tel** 270030 **Rooms** 22 **Tariff** Rs 225-650 **Credit Cards** NA **Facilities** Restaurant, attached bath, TV

Hotel Subham
Location On the beach **Address** Chandipur **Tel** 270025/ 225/ 381 **Rooms** 50 **Tariff** Rs 400-1,000; TE **Credit Cards** NA **Facilities** Restaurant, children's park, power back-up, attached bath, TV

Panthaniwas OTDC
Location Beachfront **Address** Chandipur **Tel** 270051 **Rooms** 34 **Tariff** Rs 400-1,200; TE **Credit Cards** NA **Facilities** Restaurant, basic amenities, attached bath **Metro Reservations** *See page 520*

GOPALPUR-ON-SEA STD 0680

Hotel Green Park
Location Near beach **Address** Gopalpur-on-Sea **Tel** 2242016 **Rooms** 17 **Tariff** Rs 350-600 **Credit Cards** NA **Facilities** Restaurant, attached bath, TV

Hotel Kalinga
Location Beachside **Address** Gopalpur-on-Sea **Tel** 2242067/69 **Rooms** 20 **Tariff** Rs 500-800 **Credit Cards** Visa, Master **Facilities** Restaurant, laundry, doctor-on-call, attached bath, TV

Hotel Sea Pearl
Location Near lighthouse **Address** Gopalpur-on-Sea **Tel** 2242556 **Rooms** 15 **Tariff** Rs 660-1,200 **Credit Cards** Visa, Master **Facilities** Restaurant, laundry, doctor-on-call, attached bath, TV

Hotel Seaside Breeze
Location Near beach **Address** Beach Road, Gopalpur-on-Sea **Tel** 2242075 **Rooms** 13 **Tariff** Rs 400-500 **Credit Cards** NA **Facilities** Restaurant, attached bath, TV

Panthaniwas OTDC
Location Behind Oberoi Hotel **Address** Arya Marg, Gopalpur-on-Sea **Tel** 2243931 **Rooms** 9 **Tariff** Rs 400-650 **Credit Cards** NA **Facilities** Restaurant, attached bath, TV **Metro Reservations** *See page 520*

Song of the Sea
Location Near lighthouse **Address** Gopalpur-on-Sea **Tel** 2242347 **Rooms** 10 **Tariff** Rs 750-1,200; TE **Credit Cards** NA **Facilities** Restaurant, garden, attached bath, TV

Swosti Palm Resort
Location On beach **Address** Gopalpur-on-Sea **Tel** 2242455 **Email** palmresort@swosti.com **Website** swosti.com **Rooms** 26 **Tariff** Rs 1,980-4,950; TE **Credit Cards** Visa, Master **Facilities** Restaurant, attached bath

KONARK STD 06758

Panthanivas OTDC
Location Near Sun Temple **Address** PO Konark, Dist Puri **Tel** 236831 **Rooms** 11 **Tariff** Rs 250-450 **Credit Cards** NA **Facilities** Restaurant, snack bar, garden, attached bath, TV **Metro Reservations** *See page 520*

Yatri Nivas OTDC
Location Near Sun Temple **Address** PO Konark, Dist Puri **Tel** 236820 **Rooms** 44 **Tariff** Rs 350-1,500 **Credit Cards** NA **Facilities** Restaurant, attached bath, TV **Metro Reservations** *See page 520*

PURI STD 06752

BNR Heritage Hotel
Location Near beach **Address** Chakratirtha Road **Tel** 222063 **Rooms** 34 **Website** irctc.co.in **Tariff** Rs 650-1,700 (with all meals) **Credit Cards** Visa, Master **Facilities** Restaurant, laundry, hot water, TV

Hans Coco Palms
Location Beachside **Address** Swargadwar **Tel** 230038, 230951-52 **Website** hanshotels.com **Rooms** 36 **Tariff** Rs 3,600-6,000 **Credit Cards** Visa, Master **Facilities** Restaurant, bar, swimming pool, indoor games, laundry, room service, hot water, TV

Hotel Holiday Resort SPA
Location Near railway station **Address** Chakratirtha Road **Tel** 222440 **Rooms** 92 **Tariff** Rs 1,350-4,800; TE **Credit Cards** NA **Facilities** Restaurant, gym, spa, swimming pool, room service

Hotel Lee Garden
Location Near beach **Address** VIP Road **Tel** 229986, 223647 **Mobile** 09937158989 **Rooms** 32 **Tariff** Rs 500-1,700 **Credit Cards** NA **Facilities** Restaurant, travel assistance, room service

Hotel Sapphire International
Location Near the sea **Address** Chakratirtha Road, Near Sonar Gauranga Temple **Tel** 226488 **Mobile** 09861105179 **Rooms** 35 **Tariff** Rs 1,800-2,000; TE **Credit Cards** NA **Facilities** Restaurant, spa, room service

Hotel Shreehari
Location Beachside **Address** Sagardwar, Near Lighthouse, Valaipanda **Tel** 231644/ 55 **Website** hotelshreehari.com **Rooms** 22 **Tariff** Rs 1,800-2,200 **Credit Cards** NA **Facilities** Restaurant, swimming pool, Ayurvedic massage, travel assistance, forex, room service

Mayfair SPA
Location Beachside **Address** Chakratirtha Road **Tel** 227800, 224242 **Website** mayfairhotels.com **Rooms** 34 **Tariff** Rs 5,000-7,500 **Credit Cards** Visa, Master **Facilities** Restaurant, swimming pool, health club, spa, massage centre, laundry, room service, TV

Panthanivas OTDC
Location On the beach **Address** Chakratirtha Road **Tel** 222562, 222740 **Rooms** 49 **Tariff** Rs 690-1,500; TE **Credit Cards** NA **Facilities** Restaurant, laundry, hot water, TV **Metro Reservations** *See page 520*

Puri Beach Resort
Location Near lighthouse **Address** Marine Drive **Tel** 231788 **Rooms** 24 **Tariff** Rs 950-2,200 **Credit Cards** NA **Facilities** Restaurant, laundry, attached bath, TV

Puri Hotel
Location On the beach **Address** Sea Beach **Tel** 222114 **Rooms** 150 **Tariff** Rs 330-1,200 **Credit Cards** NA **Facilities** Restaurant, library, laundry, hot water, on request, TV

Rangers
Location On the beach **Address** Konark-Puri Marine Drive **Tel** 211057 **Rooms** 2, tent 1 **Tariff** Rs 300-2,000 **Credit Cards** NA **Facilities** Restaurant, caretaker for tent

Toshali Sands ETHNIC
Location Beachside **Address** Marine Drive **Tel** 250571 **Website** toshalisands.com **Rooms** 102 **Tariff** Rs 3,200-7,700; TE **Credit Cards** Visa, Master **Facilities** Restaurant, bar, gym, spa, Ayurveda centre, private beach, swimming pool, travel desk, forex, room service

Vijoya International Hotel
Location Near Mayfair Hotel **Address** Chakratirtha Road **Tel** 223705 **Rooms** 44 **Tariff** Rs 800-2,450; TE **Credit Cards** NA **Facilities** Restaurant, room service, TV

PONDICHERRY

STD 0413

Ashok Beach Resort
SEA-FACING
Location Near the beach on ECR **Address** Chinnakalapet **Tel** 2655160-63 **Fax** 2655140 **Website** ashokresort.com **Rooms** 22 **Tariff** Rs 2,500-3,500 **Credit Cards** AmEx, Visa, Master **Facilities** Restaurant, bar, laundry, forex, travel/ taxi arranged, room service, TV

Continental Guest House
Location Near beach **Address** 48, Rue Labourdonnais **Tel** 2225828, 4210821 **Rooms** 12 **Tariff** Rs 300-550 **Credit Cards** NA **Facilities** Restaurant, laundry, room service, attached bath, hot water, TV

Dumas Guest House
Location Near beach **Address** No. 31, Rue Dumas **Tel** 2225726 **Mobile** 09894172255 **Fax** 4210518 **Email** pierre_blancetcie2003@yahoo.co.in **Rooms** 8 **Tariff** Rs 600-1,500 **Credit Cards** AmEx, Visa, Master **Facilities** Laundry, Ayurvedic massage on request, travel/ taxi arranged, room service

Hotel De L'Orient
Location Central **Address** 17, Rue Romain Rolland **Tel** 2343067-68, 2343074 **Website** neemranahotels.com **Rooms** 16 **Tariff** Rs 2,000-5,000 **Credit Cards** AmEx, Visa, Master **Facilities** Restaurant, bar, gift shop, sightseeing, taxi arranged, room service

Hotel de Pondichery
Location Near beach **Address** 38, Rue Dumas **Tel** 2227409 **Fax** 2277410 **Email** hoteldepondichery@yahoo.co.in **Rooms** 10 **Tariff** Rs 1,500-2,800 **Credit Cards** Visa, Master **Facilities** Restaurant, bar, Ayurveda centre, sightseeing, room service

Hotel Mass
Location Adjacent to new bus stand **Address** Maraimalai Adigal Salai **Tel** 2204001-11, 4207001 **Website** hotelmass.com **Rooms** 111 **Tariff** Rs 1,500-

5,000 (with breakfast) **Credit Cards** AmEx, Visa, Master **Facilities** Restaurants, bar, laundry, Internet, room service,

Hotel Surguru

Location Near railway station **Address** 104, SV Patel Road **Tel** 2227290, 2339022 **Website** hotelsurguru.com **Rooms** 57 **Tariff** Rs 860-1,350 **Credit Cards** Visa, Master **Facilities** Restaurant, Internet, travel desk, laundry, parking, room service

Kailash Beach Resort

Location Beachside **Address** Sudalai Street, Poornankuppam Village, Ariyankuppam **Tel** 2619700-03 **Website** kailash beachhotel.com **Rooms** 36 **Tariff** Rs 2,300-4,500 **Credit Cards** AmEx, Visa, Master **Facilities** Restaurants, bar, swimming pool, massage, book shop, laundry, travel arranged, room service

Le Dupleix

Location French Colony **Address** No. 5, Rue de la Caserne **Tel** 2226999 **Website** ledupleix.com, sarovarhotels.com **Rooms** 14 **Tariff** Rs 2,850-6,500 **Credit Cards** AmEx, Visa, Master **Facilities** Restaurants, bar, laundry, room service

The Dune

Location Beachside, 15 km north of Pondicherry **Address** Pudhukuppam, Keelputhupet, via Pondicherry University **Tel** 2655751-54 **Website** thedune hotel.com **Rooms** 36 **Tariff** Rs 3,300-14,500 (with breakfast) **Credit Cards** AmEx, Visa, Master **Facilities** Restaurants, private beach, swimming pool, organic farm, bicycles/ battery car to tour the premises, pottery, kite flying, boat rides, fishing

The Promenade

Location Next to Old Light House **Address** 23, Goubert Avenue **Tel** 2227750 **Website** sarovarhotels.com **Rooms** 30 **Tariff** Rs 5,000-9,000 **Credit Cards** Visa, Master **Facilities** Restaurants, bar, swimming pool, reflexology and spa massages

IN TRANQUEBAR STD 04364

Tamil Nadu Hotel

Location Behind The Bungalow on the Beach **Address** 24, King Street, Tharangambadi, Dist Nagapattinam **Tel** 288065, 289034-36 **Mobile** 09884456380 **Website** neemranahotels.com **Rooms** 5, dorms 2 (10 beds each) **Tariff** Rs 600, dorm bed Rs 150 **Credit Cards** AmEx, Visa, Master **Facilities** Restaurant, sightseeing, boating, room service, attached bath, TV **Reservations** Neemrana Hotels, No. 13, Nizamuddin East Market, New Delhi **Tel** 011-41825001-02

The Bungalow On The Beach

Location Beachside **Address** 24, King Street, Tharangambadi, Dist Nagapattinam **Tel** 288065, 289034-36 **Mobile** 09884456380 **Website** neemranahotels.com **Rooms** 8 **Tariff** Rs 4,000-5,000; TE **Credit Cards** AmEx, Visa, Master **Facilities** Restaurant, boating facilities, laundry, sightseeing, travel/ taxi arranged, room service **Reservations** *See Tamil Nadu Hotel alongside*

TAMIL NADU

CHENNAI STD 044

Hotel Nilgiri's Nest

Location Opp Woodlands Hotel **Address** 105, Dr Radhakrishnan Road, Mylapore **Tel** 28115111/ 5222/ 1772-73 **Website** nilgiris1905.com **Rooms** 35 **Tariff** Rs 1,700-2,950 (with breakfast); TE **Credit Cards** Visa, Master **Facilities** Restaurant, departmental store, bakery, wi-fi connectivity, lockers, forex, travel desk, room service

ACCOMMODATION LISTINGS

Hotel Palmgrove

Location Near Anna flyover **Address** No. 13, Kodambakkam High Road **Tel** 28271881/ 7650 **Website** ballalgrouphotels.com **Rooms** 89 **Tariff** Rs 900-2,600 (with breakfast); TE **Credit Cards** Visa, Master **Facilities** Restaurant, bar, travel desk, TV

Hotel President

Location 1 km from Marina Beach **Address** 25, Dr Radhakrishnan Road, Mylapore **Tel** 28472211/ 3683 **Website** presidenn.com **Rooms** 144 **Tariff** Rs 1,200-3,500; TE **Credit Cards** AmEx, Visa, Master **Facilities** Restaurant, bar, swimming pool, travel desk, room service

Le Royal Meridien

Location Central **Address** No. 1, GST Road, St Thomas Mount **Tel** 22314343 **Website** leroyal meridien-chennai.com **Rooms** 240 **Tariff** Rs 12,500-40,000 (with breakfast); TE **Credit Cards** AmEx, Visa, Master **Facilities** Restaurants, bar, swimming pool, health club, forex, room service

New Woodlands Hotel

Location Central **Address** No. 72, Dr Radhakrishnan Road, Mylapore **Tel** 28113111 **Website** newwoodlands.com **Rooms** 175 **Tariff** Rs 750-5,760 **Credit Cards** Visa, Master **Facilities** Restaurants, laundry, travel desk, room service, attached bath

Park Sheraton & Towers SPA

Location 4 km from Marina and Elliot beaches **Address** No. 132, TTK Road, Alwarpet **Tel** 24994101 **Website** welcom group.com **Rooms** 283 **Tariff** Rs 11,000-35,000 (with breakfast); TE **Credit Cards** AmEx, Visa, Master **Facilities** Restaurant, bar, swimming pool, spa, Ayurvedic massage, travel desk

Quality Inn Sabari

Location Opp Kamaraj Memorial House **Address** No. 29, Tirumalai Pillai Road, T Nagar **Tel** 28343030 **Website** qualityinnsabari.com **Rooms** 72 **Tariff** Rs 3,200-4,500 **Credit Cards** AmEx, Visa, Master **Facilities** Restaurants, forex, travel desk, room service

Sheraton Chola

Location Opp Music Academy **Address** No. 13, Cathedral Road, Gopalapuram **Tel** 28110101 **Website** itcwelcom group.in **Rooms** 92 **Tariff** Rs 9,000-12,000 (with breakfast); TE **Credit Cards** AmEx, Visa, Master **Facilities** Restaurants, bar, swimming pool, health club, forex, travel desk, room service

Taj Connemara

Location Next to Spencer Plaza **Address** No. 2, Binny Road **Tel** 66000000 **Website** tajhotels.com **Rooms** 150 **Tariff** Rs 8,500-30,000 (with breakfast); TE **Credit Cards** AmEx, Visa, Master **Facilities** Restaurants, coffee shop, bar, health club, swimming pool, Ayurvedic massage, room service

Taj Coromandel

Location Opp Income Tax Office, next to Gemini flyover **Address** 37, MG Road, Nungambakkam **Tel** 66002827 **Website** tajhotels.com **Rooms** 207 **Tariff** Rs 9,500-40,000 (with breakfast); TE **Credit Cards** AmEx, Visa, Master **Facilities** Restaurants, bar, swimming pool, fitness centre, room service

The Chariot

Location Central **Address** No. 4, Tirumalai Pillai Road, T Nagar **Tel** 28341212 **Website** thechariot chennai.com **Rooms** 40 **Tariff** Rs 1,800-3,200 (with breakfast); TE **Credit Cards** AmEx, Visa, Master **Facilities** Restaurant, travel desk, room service, TV

The Raintree Ecotel Hotel

Location Opp Old HM Hospital **Address** No. 120, St Mary's Road, Alwarpet **Tel** 42252525, 24304050 **Website** raintree hotels.com **Rooms** 105 **Tariff** Rs 6,000-13,000 (with breakfast); TE **Credit Cards** AmEx, Visa, Master **Facilities** Restaurants, coffee shop, bar lounge, swimming pool, wi-fi connectivity, forex, travel desk, room service

The Residency

Location Opp Vani Mahal **Address** No. 49, GN Chetty Road, T Nagar **Tel** 28253434, 42121122 **Website** theresidency.com **Rooms** 86 **Tariff** Rs 2,700-5,000 (with breakfast); TE **Credit Cards** AmEx, Visa, Master **Facilities** Restaurants, coffee shop, lockers, forex, laundry, travel desk, room service

KANYAKUMARI STD 04652

Hotel Maadhini

Location Near beach **Address** East Car Street **Tel** 246787/ 757/ 887 **Fax** 246657 **Email** hotel_maadhini@sancharnet.in **Rooms** 75 **Tariff** Rs 500-1,500; TE **Credit Cards** Visa, Master **Facilities** Restaurant, bar, travel arranged, room service

Hotel Melody Park

Location Near beach **Address** East Car Street **Tel** 246667, 247667/ 557/ 527/ 577 **Fax** 247587 **Email** melodypark@sancharnet.in **Rooms** 42 **Tariff** Rs 650-3,000 **Credit Cards** NA

Facilities Restaurant, laundry, travel arranged, room service

Hotel Samudra
Location Near the Kumari Temple **Address** Sannathi Street **Tel** 246162-63/ 65 **Fax** 247967 **Rooms** 40 **Tariff** Rs 370-1,350; TE **Credit Cards** AmEx, Visa, Master **Facilities** Restaurant, laundry, travel arranged, room service, attached bath

Hotel Sea View
Location Near beach **Address** East Car Street **Tel** 247841-45 **Website** hotelseaview.in **Rooms** 56 **Tariff** Rs 1,400-3,800; TE **Credit Cards** Visa, Master **Facilities** Restaurant, bar, travel arranged, forex, room service, TV

Hotel Singaar International
Location Opp railway station **Address** 5/22, Main Road **Tel** 247992-98 **Website** hotelsingaarinternational.in **Rooms** 102 **Tariff** Rs 950-4,000 **Credit Cards** AmEx, Visa, Master **Facilities** Restaurant, bar, swimming pool, travel desk, room service, TV

Hotel Tamil Nadu TTDC
Location Near lighthouse **Address** Kovalam Road, Beach Road **Tel** 246257-58/ 426 **Website** tamilnadutourism.org **Rooms** 45 **Tariff** Rs 475-1,200; TE **Credit Cards** AmEx, Visa, Master **Facilities** Restaurant, laundry, room service **Metro Reservations** *See page 520*

MAMMALLAPURAM STD 044

GRT Temple Bay & Beach Resort
Location Beachside **Address** Kovalam Road **Tel** 27443636 **Website** grttemplebay.com, grthotels.com **Rooms** 72 **Tariff** Rs 7,000-14,000; TE **Credit Cards** AmEx, Visa, Master **Facilities** Restaurants, bar, Ayurvedic health centre, private beach, travel desk, room service

Hotel Golden Sun and Beach Resort
Location Near beach **Address** 59, Covelong Road **Tel** 27442245-46/ 946 **Website** hotelgoldensun.com **Rooms** 58 **Tariff** Rs 1,300-2,800; TE **Credit Cards** Visa, Master **Facilities** Restaurant, bar, pool, laundry, travel desk, Ayurvedic massage, forex, room service

Hotel Mamalla Heritage
Location Central **Address** No. 104, East Raja Street **Tel** 27442060/ 260/ 360 **Website** hotelmamallaheritage.com **Rooms** 43 **Tariff** Rs 1,050-2,000; TE **Credit Cards** AmEx, Visa, Master **Facilities** Restaurants, swimming pool, kids' pool, forex, travel desk, room service, TV

Hotel Tamil Nadu TTDC
Location Sea-facing **Address** Beach Resort Complex **Tel** 27442361-63 **Rooms** 34 **Tariff** Rs 500-2,500; TE **Credit Cards** Master, Visa **Facilities** Restaurant, bar, laundry, pool, travel arrangements, room service, attached bath, hot water **Metro Reservations** *See page 520*

Ideal Beach Resort
Location Beachside **Address** East Coast Road, Devaneri Village **Tel** 27442240/ 443 **Website** resortsindia.com **Rooms** 45 **Tariff** Rs 1,850-12,000; TE **Credit Cards** Visa, Master **Facilities** Restaurant, bar, swimming pool, gift shop, Ayurvedic massage, travel desk, forex, Internet, lockers, room service **Chennai Reservations** #3, 2nd Street, Dr Thirumurthy Nagar, Nungambakkam, Chennai **Tel** 044-28237583, 28215232

Mahabs Inn
Location Near Shore Temple,

behind SBI ATM **Address** No. 68, East Raja Street **Tel** 27442643-45 **Mobile** 09444283695, 09283134671 **Website** mahabsinn.com **Rooms** 48 **Tariff** Rs 1,200-1,500; TE **Credit Cards** NA **Facilities** Restaurant, travel desk, Internet, laundry, room service, TV

Mamalla Beach Resort

Location Near beach, on the ECR **Address** 108, Kovalam Road **Tel** 27442375/ 475 **Website** mamallaresort.com **Rooms** 35 **Tariff** Rs 1,300-1,750; TE **Credit Cards** AmEx, Visa, Master **Facilities** Restaurant, laundry, travel desk, swimming pool, room service

Sterling Mahabalipuram Beach Resort

Location Next to Shore Temple **Address** Shore Temple Road **Tel** 27442287/ 3914-15 **Website** sterlingmahabalipuram.net **Rooms** 30 **Tariff** Rs 2,200-5,000; TE **Credit Cards** AmEx, Visa, Master **Facilities** Restaurant, bar, swimming pool, Ayurvedic centre **Chennai Reservations** 56, 4th Street, Abhiramapuram, Alwarpet, Chennai **Tel** 044-24998121 **Mobile** 09444410394

Taj Fisherman's Cove Resort

Location Beachside **Address** Covelong Beach, Kanchipuram Dist **Tel** 67413333 **Website** tajhotels.com **Rooms** 88 **Tariff** Rs 10,000-16,000; TE **Credit Cards** AmEx, Visa, Master **Facilities** Restaurant, coffee shop, bar, spa, travel desk

Tina Blue View Lodge and Restaurant

Location Near beach **Address** 34, Ottovadai Street **Tel** 27442319 **Rooms** 15 **Tariff** Rs 200-500 **Credit Cards** NA **Facilities** Restaurant, Ayurvedic massage centre, camping site, room service, attached bath

Uma Guest House

Location Near beach **Address** Ottovadai Street **Tel** 27442697 **Rooms** 19 **Tariff** Rs 200-900 **Credit Cards** NA **Facilities** Sightseeing and taxi arranged, room service, attached bath

WEST BENGAL

BAKKHALI 03210

Bakkhali Tourist Lodge WBTDC

Location Near beach **Address** Bakkhali **Tel** 225260 **Rooms** 12, dorms 3 (8 beds) **Tariff** Rs 400-800, dorm bed Rs 80 **Credit Cards** NA **Facilities** Restaurant, bar, room service **Metro Reservations** *See page 520*

Balaka Lodge

Location Near bus stand **Address** Bakkhali **Tel** 225207 **Rooms** 32 **Tariff** Rs 250-550 **Credit Cards** NA **Facilities** Kitchen, canteen, basic accommodation, room service

Hotel Ambrabati

Location Near beach **Address** Bakkhali **Tel** 225248-49 **Mobile** 09732619340, 09732614070 **Rooms** 20 **Tariff** Rs 200-500 **Credit Cards** NA **Facilities** Room service, attached bath, TV

Hotel Deepak

Location Near beach **Address** Frazergunj **Tel** 225277 **Rooms** 53 **Tariff** Rs 450-850 **Credit Cards** NA **Facilities** Restaurant, bar, attached bath, TV

Hotel Dolphin

Location Near beach **Address** Bakkhali-Frazergunj Road, Chowrasta **Tel** 225296 **Mobile** 09836543585 **Rooms** 26 **Tariff** Rs 500-1,200 **Credit Cards** Visa, Master **Facilities** Restaurant, garden, attached bath Kolkata **Reservations** Dolphin Group of Hotels, 47, Bhupen Bose Avenue, Kolkata **Tel** 033-25550702/ 4652

Hotel Sea View

Location Near bus stand **Address** Bakkhali-Frazerganj Road **Tel** 225282 **Mobile** 09732828266 **Rooms** 31 **Tariff** Rs 350 **Credit Cards** NA **Facilities** Room service, attached bath, TV

ON HENRY'S ISLAND

Mangrove Tourist Complex

Address Henry's Island Fisheries Project **Tel** 225511 **Rooms** 10 **Tariff** Rs 300-1,000 **Credit Cards** NA **Facilities** Restaurant, attached bath, TV **Kolkata Reservations** **Tel** 033-23376470, 23586832, 23572979

Sundari Tourist Complex

Address Henry's Island Fisheries Project **Tel** 225511 **Rooms** 8 **Tariff** Rs 500 **Credit Cards** NA **Facilities** Restaurant, attached bath, TV **Kolkata Reservations** **Tel** 033-23376470, 23586832

DIGHA STD 03220

Hotel Sea Hawk

Location Near the beach **Address** East Medinipur, Digha **Tel** 266235 **Rooms** 100 **Tariff** Rs 200-1,900 **Credit Cards** NA **Facilities** Restaurant, bar, room service, TV

Saikatabas

Location Near beach **Address** Digha **Tel** 266234/ 254 **Rooms** 37 **Tariff** Rs 170-340 **Credit Cards** NA **Facilities** Canteen

The Palm Resort
Location Near Reliance Petrol Pump **Address** Shibalaya Road, Old Digha **Tel** 266489 **Mobile** 09239234407 **Website** thepalmresortdigha.com **Rooms** 28 **Tariff** Rs 1,500-3,000; TE **Credit Cards** NA **Facilities** Restaurant, bar, swimming pool, garden, TV **Reservations** 47, Deshapran Shanshmal Road, Kolkata **Tel** 033-65343254, 24245966 **Mobile** 09830052736

SHANKARPUR STD 03220

Hotel Ashoka Lodge
Location 2 km before Digha **Address** Shankarpur **Tel** 264275 **Rooms** 17 **Tariff** Rs 250-700 **Credit Cards** NA **Facilities** Restaurant, basic accommodation

Hotel Nest
Address PO Bodhra, East Medinipur **Tel** 264074/ 164 **Rooms** 15 **Tariff** Rs 750-1,800 **Credit Cards** NA **Facilities** Restaurant, bar, private beach, paddle boat

Hotel Sandy Bay
Location Near harbour **Address** Post Bodhra, East Medinipur **Tel** 264693 **Rooms** 16 **Tariff** Rs 700-1,100 **Credit Cards** NA **Facilities** Restaurant, bar, laundry, room service, TV **Kolkata Reservations** 033-24425453

Jowar Guesthouse
Location Near Fisheries Harbour **Address** PO Bodhra, East Medinipur **Tel** 265059 **Rooms** 32, dorms 2 **Tariff** Rs 350-825, dorm bed Rs 60 **Credit Cards** NA **Facilities** Restaurant, room service, attached bath, TV **Reservations** Global Tour and Travels, 1, Netaji Subhash Road, Kolkata **Tel** 033-22133759

Kinara Guesthouse
Location Near Fisheries Harbour **Address** PO Bodhra, East Medinipur **Tel** 264577 **Rooms** 6 **Tariff** Rs 300-700 **Credit Cards** NA **Facilities** Restaurant, laundry, attached bath, TV **Kolkata Reservations** Benfish Tourism, Kolkata **Tel** 033-23554931 **Mobile** 09831033181

Matsyagandha Guesthouse
Location Near Fisheries Harbour **Address** PO Bodhra, East Medinipur **Tel** 265059 **Rooms** 7 **Tariff** Rs 350-825 **Credit Cards** NA **Facilities** Restaurant, room service, attached bath, TV **Reservations** Global Tour and Travels, 1 Netaji Subhash Road, Kolkata **Tel** 033-22133759

Sweet Home Inn
Location Near beach **Address** East Medinipur **Tel** 265088 **Mobile** 09831003490 **Rooms** 8 **Tariff** Rs 500-1,000 **Credit Cards** NA **Facilities** Restaurant, room service, parking, attached bath **Reservations Tel** 033-22415258

IN MANDARMANI

Hotel Garden Retreat
Location 15 km from Digha **Address** Chaulkhola **Mobile** 09732995188, 09332355586, 09831167537 **Rooms** 8, dorm 1 (15 beds) **Tariff** Rs 450, dorm Rs 800 **Facilities** Kitchen, room service

Rose Valley Hotel
Location 22 km before Digha **Address** East Medinipur, Chaulkhola **Rooms** 34 **Tariff** Rs 1,500-3,000; TE **Facilities** Restaurant **Kolkata Reservations Tel** 033-25006470

Samudra Sakshi
Location Near beach **Address** East Medinipur **Mobile** 09332024328, 09830381880 **Rooms** 20 **Tariff** Rs 400-600 **Credit Cards** NA **Facilities** Restaurant, attached bath, TV **Reservations Tel** 033-28442053

ABOUT THE AUTHORS

abhijit gupta teaches English at Jadavpur University in Kolkata. He is the co-editor of the *Book History in India* series, and is currently compiling a seemingly unending bibliographical database of all Bengali books ever printed till Independence. He is the reluctant owner of several cats and has been writing for *Outlook Traveller* since 2003

Most people who know him believe that **abhilash gaur** travels too much, though he seldom spends more than a week each month out of Delhi. All he has managed to see in the past six years are 10 districts of Himachal and less of Punjab. At this pace, he has at least 30 years of domestic travel figured out

amit mahajan started his career as a journeyman engineer, making journeys on engineering pretexts. These days, he practises reflexology. Travelling has persisted as a primary urge

ashwin kumar is a web designer by profession and thoroughly enjoys his work. He loves travelling, writing and photography, and freelances for various publications when time permits. He is passionate about adventure sports

ashwin tombat was a journalist (editor of *Gomantak Times* and *Goa Today*, assistant editor of *Gentleman*), a researcher (MacArthur Foundation Population Fellow) and a street theatre activist (with Aavhaan Natya Manch). He is now a writer and media consultant. When he is not sailing or swimming, he's coaching children in these sports

A journalist for the past 15 years, **charu soni** has worked previously with *The Statesman*, *The Hindustan Times* and *Tehelka*. Besides these publications, she has written extensively for *Outlook Traveller*, *Outlook Traveller Getaways* and *Outlook Delhi City Limits*

joan pinto is a Mumbai-based freelance writer who likes to blow bubbles, study the colours in people, sip chai, hum off-key, wander through graveyards, and travel. She also likes to write, everything from essays to haiku to to-do lists. Her non-fiction writing credits include *The Times of India, Femina, Design Today, India Today Travel, The Christian Science Monitor* and *Gulf News*. Her story 'How Rifka Made Things Right' appears in *Favourite Stories For Girls* (Puffin). Another short story, 'The Saint of Lost Things', will appear in *First Proof 3*, an anthology of new writing (Penguin)

latha anantharaman is a writer, editor, translator and amateur pepper farmer based in Palakkad

nilanjana biswas is a Bangalore-based freelance journalist with a passion for travel. She also writes on development and gender issues

ornella d'souza graduated from St Xavier's College, Mumbai, with a Bachelor's degree in Mass Media in 2007. Currently a trainee features writer with *Outlook Mumbai City Limits*, she is also a mezzo-soprano in The Stop Gaps Choral Ensemble and is pursuing her Masters in Politics from the University of Mumbai through correspondence

parikshit rao is a travel writer and photographer. He lived in Mumbai for a decade before setting off to the Himalaya, where he hopes to spend a year. He is unimpressed by airplanes and people who opt for package tours. He prefers travelling atop local buses, hiking to silent monasteries, and marvelling at riverside towns. He is currently working on a couple of his own projects apart from freelancing for national magazines and guide books

peter griffin is a former copy editor. He is now a communications consultant, travel writer, columnist, web producer, editor and entrepreneur. He is also a poet, Internet addict and ne'er-do-well. He lives in Navi Mumbai and plans to grow up some day

pn venugopal is the editor of the Quest Features and Footage, Kochi. He contributes regularly to national and Malayalam newspapers and periodicals, writing mainly on issues such as environment, development with a human face, and public administration. He has translated nine books from English and other languages into Malayalam, and this list includes Albert Camus' *The Fall*, Italo Calvino's *Mr Palomar* and Satyajit Ray's *My Years with Apu*

Apart from Lacadives, **prahlad kakar** can also be associated with terms such as tea connoisseur, cigar manufacturer and restaurant owner. But he is mostly recognised as the man behind Genesis, his ad agency that was voted the top production house by *Brand Equity* in a nationwide survey of agencies in 2003. In 2005, he received the Distinctive Recognition Award from the Advertising Club at the 38th ABBY Awards in Mumbai. Kakar is also known as the man who made cricketing stalwarts like Sachin and Dravid act. He is co-founder and member of the NGO Reefwatch Marine Conservation, which is involved in marine conservation

rajashri dasgupta, formerly of the *Business Standard* and *The Telegraph*, is now working as a freelance journalist. She has a special interest in issues relating to gender, health, social movements and politics. She is a contributing editor with *Himal Southasian* and is active in movements centred on women and peace

Writing and its related aspects have always fascinated Bhubaneswar-based **sarojini nayak**. An independent journalist, she dabbles in editing, research and documentation. Her writing focuses on women, children, culture and the environment. Besides co-authoring a book on woman's empowerment, she has been a columnist on social and civic affairs, a campaigner for mural paintings and a media consultant

sheetal vyas is a freelance journalist, writer and editor based in Hyderabad. Self-confessed serial hobbyist, she includes among her interests reading, writing, blogging, music and birding along with her hobby *du jour*. She loves travel of all sorts — luxury to slumming, adventure sport to laidback doses of culture, dusty buses to armchair travelling. She has big plans for a book or a script, whichever comes first

simar preet kaur is a young writer from Delhi who's a self-proclaimed 'last hippie standing'. Her life's passion loosely translates into wandering across India on ramshackle buses and trains, making friends and finding character in the peeling walls of guest houses. Despite having travel on her mind 24/ 7, she also manages to find time to read up on the Beat Generation, to listen to psychedelic rock and to paint abstract designs on backpacks. She has written for various in-flight magazines, international travel websites and guide books

tishani doshi is a writer based in Chennai. Her collection of poems *Countries of the Body* won the Forward Prize for Poetry in 2006. Her first novel *The Pleasure Seekers* is forthcoming from Bloomsbury. She has also worked for the last six years with the Chandralekha dance group

uma mahadevan-dasgupta is a civil servant currently based in Mumbai

vaishna roy lives in Chennai, the city of temples, idlis and filter *kaapi*. She writes, travels, cooks occasionally, reads greedily, salsas bravely, and consumes vast quantities of desserts regularly. And when not thus occupied, she likes to play guide to first-time visitors to her beloved city

venkatesh charloo is the owner and operator of Barracuda Diving India, based at the Marriott Resort in Goa. An ex-banker, he has been diving for the past 20 years in Hong Kong, Philippines, New Zealand, Malaysia, Indonesia, Lakshadweep and the Andaman Islands, besides Goa. Barracuda is the first and only Gold Palm Resort of the California-based international diving accreditation agency, Professional Association of Diving Instructors. More details on Barracuda, which was set up 14 years ago, are available at the website barracudadiving.com

vivek m is a freelance photographer based in Bangalore. He specialises in documentary, editorial and travel photography. He studied art at the Ken School of Art, Bangalore, and completed his studies in medicine in Kolar, Karnataka. He worked briefly as a surgical resident at a corporate hospital in Bangalore before he quit his practice to devote time for photography. In his personal work, Vivek seeks ideas that serve humanitarian purposes

OTHER TITLES FROM OUTLOOK TRAVELLER GETAWAYS

52 Weekend Breaks from Delhi
ISBN 81-901724-4-1
512 pages

52 Weekend Breaks from Mumbai
ISBN 81-901724-3-3
480 pages

52 Weekend Breaks from Bangalore
ISBN 81-901724-2-5
512 pages

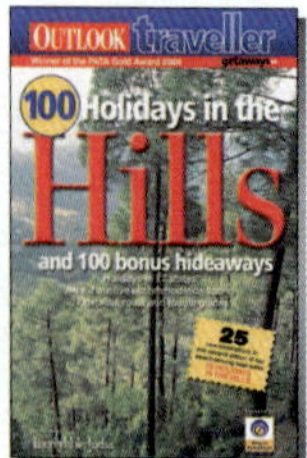

100 Holidays in the Hills
ISBN 81-901724-6-8
544 pages

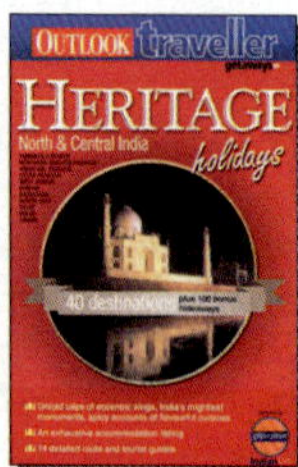

Heritage Holidays in North & Central India
ISBN 81-901724-5-X
544 pages

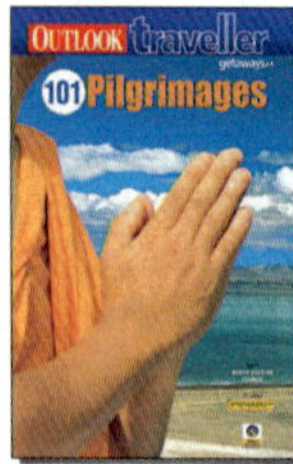

101 Pilgrimages
ISBN 81-89449-03-6
1,088 pages

Rajasthan State Guide
ISBN 81-89449-05-2
512 pages

Uttarakhand State Guide
ISBN 81-89449-06-0
528 pages

52 Weekend Breaks from Chennai
ISBN 81-89449-07-9
544 pages

Himachal State Guide
ISBN 81-89449-09-5
544 pages

INTERNATIONAL TITLES FROM OUTLOOK TRAVELLER

In association with Insight Guides
Fourth Edition
368 pages

In association with Insight Guides
Seventh Edition
400 pages

In association with Insight Guides
Fifth Edition
304 pages

In association with Insight Guides
Fifth Edition
356 pages

Heritage Holidays in South, West & East India
ISBN 81-901724-8-4
576 pages

Goa State Guide
ISBN 81-901724-9-2
544 pages

Trekking Holidays in India
ISBN 81-89449-00-1
576 pages

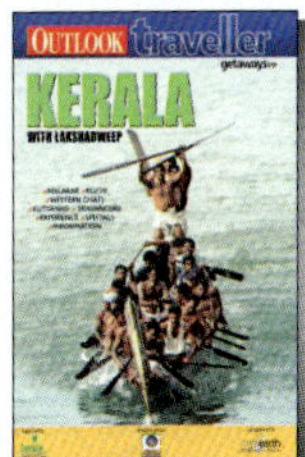

Kerala with Lakshadweep State Guide
ISBN 81-89449-01-X
720 pages

64 Wildlife Holidays in India
ISBN 81-89449-02-8
720 pages

OUTLOOK traveller getaways» WELNESS Holidays in India

Wellness Holidays in India
ISBN 81-89449-10-9
512 pages

ROMANTIC HOLIDAYS IN INDIA

Coming Soon!

HYDERABAD WEEKEND BREAKS

Coming Soon!

CITY GUIDES

Delhi and NCR City Guide
ISBN 81-89449-04-4
528 pages

MUMBAI CITY GUIDE

Coming Soon!

In association with Insight Guides
Third Edition
328 pages

In association with Insight Guides
Fifth Edition
376 pages

In association with Insight Guides
Tenth Edition
424 pages

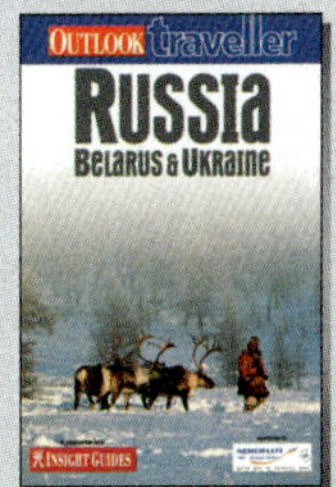

In association with Insight Guides
Third Edition
386 pages

PHOTO CREDITS

Back Cover

Above: Water scooter at Baga Beach ASHOO SHARMA/ INDIAPICTURE
Below: Sea trout under leather coral

Inside the book

AGATTI BEACH RESORT
SECTION OPENER *Page 211* Couple walk on a fallen tree

AGUADA BEACH RESORT
Page 309 (bottom middle) Aerial view of Aguada Beach Resort, Goa

AHTUSHI DESHPANDE
Page 309 (top right) View from Vagator Beach, Goa

AKSHAY MAHAJAN
SECTION OPENER *Page 393* View from Janjira Fort

AMIT PASRICHA
CONTENTS *Page 8* Paragliding in Goa

ATUL LOKE
CONTENTS *Page 7* Janjira Fort SECTION OPENER *Page 305* Sunbathing on Baga Beach, Goa *Page 355* (top middle) Sweet bolinas

BANGARAM BEACH RESORT
CONTENTS *Page 9* The ferry arrives at the resort *Page 124* A scuba diver spots a sea turtle

BHARAT AGGARWAL
SECTION OPENER *Page 505* On the beach at Mandvi, Gujarat

B HARIDAS
CONTENTS *Page 5* At Vijayanagar Beach, Andamans

DHRITIMAN MUKHERJEE
CONTENTS *Page 5* Playing volleyball on Digha Beach *Page 9* Enjoying pani puri on Juhu Beach SECTION OPENER *Page 59* Little girls flaunt their catch at Vodarevo Beach

H SATISH
CONTENTS *Page 4* Camel ride on Puri Beach

KUMAR ROY
CONTENTS *Page 7* and SECTION OPENER *Page 21* View from Bakkhali Beach, West Bengal *Page 41* Sand sculpture on Puri Beach

MADHU KAPPARATH
Page 309 (bottom right) Goan food

MAHESH BHATT
Page 355 (top left) View from Arossim Beach

MANU BAHUGUNA/ PHOTOINDIA
CONTENTS *Page 7* Water sports, Goa

NAMIT ARORA/ PHOTOINDIA
CONTENTS *Page 6* Celeb cut-outs on Marina Beach, Chennai

PARIKSHIT RAO
Page 309 (bottom left) At Anjuna's Flea Market in Goa

PARK HYATT RESORT AND SPA
Page 355 (bottom middle) Swimming pool at Park Hyatt Resort and Spa, Goa

PARVIN SINGH
CONTENTS *Page 6* and SECTION OPENER *Page 71* Vivekananda Rock, Kanyakumari

PRASHANT PANJIAR
CONTENTS *Page 4* Lounging around on the sands of Cherai Beach

RAJEEV SACHDEVA
Page 355 (top right) Water sports in Goa

SANJOY GHOSH
SECTION OPENER *Page 103* A snorkeller off the Andaman Coast

SONIA JABBAR
CONTENTS *Page 8* Scuba diving off Netrani Island

SWAPAN NAYAK
CONTENTS *Page 8* View from BNR Hotel, Puri

TEAM MANGALORE
CONTENTS *Page 5* The famous kite festival, Mangalore SECTION OPENER *Page 249* A participant flies a huge Kathakali kite on a Mangalore beach

TIRACOL FORT
Page 309 (top middle) Interiors of Tiracol Fort, Goa

TRIBHUVAN TIWARI
Page 309 (top left) Tourists on Baga Beach, Goa *Page 355* (bottom left) A shack on Agonda Beach, Goa

VIVEK R NAIR
SECTION OPENER *Page 143* View of the beach in Varkala

Route & Tourist Guide Credits

Graphics: Rajesh KG
Editorial Research: Prerna Singh

BEACH HOLIDAYS IN INDIA

FEEDBACK FORM

We need your valuable suggestions to help us improve our guide and make it more user friendly. Mail this form to enable us to send you free updates on special packages, events and new destinations

PERSONAL INFORMATION

(BLOCK LETTERS PLEASE)

Name (Mr/ Ms) ....

Address..

....

....

PIN Code ....

Tel. ....

Email..

Age .... Gender: Male ☐ Female ☐

Occupation ....

Organisation ....

Single/ Married ....

No. of Children/ Ages ....

TRAVEL HISTORY

1. How often do you take a vacation?

Every 1-2 months ☐

Every 3-6 months ☐

Every 6-12 months ☐

Others (please specify) ☐

....

2. How long was your last vacation?

Weekend ☐

1-2 weeks ☐

2-4 weeks ☐

Others (please specify) ☐

....

3. Where did you stay?

Hotels/ Resorts ☐

Govt accommodation ☐

Friends/ Relatives ☐

4. How much did you spend on your vacation?

Less than Rs 5,000 ☐

Rs 5,000-Rs 10,000 ☐

Rs 10,000-Rs 20,000 ☐

Rs 20,000 and above ☐

5. Your idea of a holiday?

Adventure ☐

Leisure ☐

Pilgrimage ☐

Wildlife ☐

Others (please specify) ☐

....

6. Do you refer to a guide during your travels?

Yes ☐ No ☐

If yes, please specify ....

ABOUT US

1. Where did you hear about this book?

Advertising in the Outlook Group magazines ☐

Bookshop/ newsagent ☐

www.outlooktraveller.com ☐

Others (please specify) ☐

....

2. Rate us

Excellent (E) Good (G) Fair (F) Average (A)

Content ☐ Design ☐

Destinations ☐ Facts ☐

Route guides ☐ Photographs ☐

YOUR RECOMMENDATIONS

I recommend for inclusion/ exclusion

Name of accommodation/ restaurant/ sights/ place

....

....

Address..

....

Tel. ....

Reason ....

....

....

....

Make as many recommendations as you like. Attach with this form and drop it in the mail.

Mail to

The Editor
Outlook Traveller Getaways
AB-10, Safdarjung Enclave
New Delhi-110029